SECOND EDITION

BUSINESS MATHEMATICS

MARVIN L. BITTINGER
Indiana University—Purdue University at Indianapolis

WILLIAM B. RUDOLPH
Iowa State University

ADDISON-WESLEY PUBLISHING COMPANY
Reading, Massachusetts ▪ Menlo Park, California ▪ London
Amsterdam ▪ Don Mills, Ontario ▪ Sydney

Sponsoring Editor:	*Jeffrey Pepper*
Production Manager:	*Herbert Nolan*
Production Editor:	*Herbert Merritt*
Text Designer:	*Vanessa Piñeiro*
Illustrator:	*Jay's Publishers Services, Inc.*
Cover Designer:	*Maria Szmauz*
Cover Photograph:	*Four by Five, Inc.*
Art Coordinator:	*Susanah H. Michener*
Manufacturing Supervisor:	*Ann DeLacey*

Photographs for the Chapter titles are by Rick Harton, Latent Images, Carmel, Ind.

To Lowell and Chris Bittinger, my two little exponents
M.L.B.

To my mother, Mildred B. Rudolph, and the memory of my father, Herman L. Rudolph
W.B.R.

Library of Congress Cataloging in Publication Data

Bittinger, Marvin L.
   Business mathematics.

   Includes index.
   1. Business mathematics.   I. Rudolph, William B., 1938– . II. Title.
HF5691.B58 1984   513'.93   83-15885
ISBN 0-201-11221-3

Reprinted with corrections August 1985

Copyright © 1984, 1980 by Addison-Wesley Publishing Company, Inc. All rights reserved. No part of this publication may be reproduced, stored in a retrieval system, or transmitted, in any form or by any means, electronic, mechanical, photocopying, recording, or otherwise, without the prior written permission of the publisher. Printed in the United States of America. Published simultaneously in Canada.

EFGHIJ-MU-89876

PREFACE

This textbook provides students with the mathematical skills necessary for day-to-day business operations, including banking, credit transactions, record keeping, purchasing, pricing, and payroll. Also included are chapters on taxes, depreciation, insurance, investments, and statistics. The material is useful not only to the student in business or business technology but also to the student as a consumer.

WHAT'S NEW IN THE SECOND EDITION?

This second edition of *Business Mathematics* incorporates up-to-date information needed in business and consumer matters. For example, since publication of the first edition, banking has been deregulated, interest rates have changed, tax matters are vastly different, and new depreciation methods exist. These changes and others make the materials quite timely. Other significant changes have been made. Among them are the following:

TOPIC EXPANSION AND REORGANIZATION

- **Expansion.** Topic coverage has been greatly expanded. For example, Individual Retirement Accounts (IRAs), Keogh Plans, and other annuities are presented. Financial statements are clearly and concisely explained as are the underlying ratios.

- **Reorganization.** The chapters have been rearranged more logically into four parts. Part 1, *Basics*, covers Whole Numbers, Fractions, Decimals, Equations, Ratio, Percent, and Interest. Part 2, *Personal Finance*, covers Checking, Loans, Annuities, Credit, Stocks, Bonds, Insurance, and Taxes. Part 3, *Retailing/Accounting*, covers Financial Statements, Purchasing, Inventory, Depreciation, Pricing, and Payroll. Part 4, *Statistics*, covers Statistics and Graphs. The Appendix on the Metric System has been retained.

Each chapter and section now starts with an overview which sets the stage for and motivates the material which follows. Suggestions and tips show the reader how to apply certain ideas to his or her situation.

NEW SUPPLEMENTS

Several new supplements are now available for the book:

- **Career Chapter Openers.** A significant addition to this edition is the inclusion of career chapter opening photographs and discourse. An extensive survey was conducted to determine the anticipated careers of students taking this type of course. People actually in such careers were then photographed and are featured together with various kinds of information such as preparation needed, aspects of the work, and possible salaries.

- **Annotated Teacher's Edition.** New to this edition is an annotated teacher's edition which uses an alternate color to provide information such as all the answers written where the exercises occur, commentary and teaching suggestions, and references to other sources of study.

- **Instructor's Manual.** The Instructor's Manual has been enhanced to include transparencies for class lectures, extra sample forms, student projects, and three alternate forms of each test.

PREFACE

- **Software Tables.** Because interest rates have varied so erratically in recent years, it is difficult to prepare tables which remain adequate. To alleviate this problem, we have programmed software on a diskette for use with Apple computers. One simply enters the interest rate, the total number of compounding periods, and the kind of compounding, and an appropriate table can be printed. The kinds of tables which can be produced are simple interest; interest compounded annually, semiannually, quarterly, monthly, and daily; interest compounded continuously; Present Value of Compound Interest; and Present Value of Annuities.

FEATURES

There are many other salient features of the book, most of which are new to this edition.

- **Objectives.** Domino symbols like ⚀ are used to key objectives to their development in the text. Problems in the exercise sets and chapter tests are keyed to the objectives and are matched with similar worked-out examples by the corresponding domino symbol. This allows the student to locate readily sources of immediate help when solving problems.

- **Readiness Checks.** Review of skills which will be used in the chapter is provided by the readiness checks. These skills are keyed to their previous development in the text for those needing review.

- **Development.** Each concept and skill has been thoroughly developed using motivational materials, examples, and margin exercises. The margin exercises allow the user to become actively involved in the development and are much like the examples and homework exercises. This greatly enhances the students' ability to read and study the mathematics on their own. Answers for all the margin exercises are at the back of the book.

- **Realisitic Problems.** Problems taken from everyday situations are extensively used. Ads, charts, diagrams, business and banking forms, and tables help to provide motivation and a realistic setting as materials are developed.

- **Exercises.** Exercise sets, which appear at the ends of sections on tear-out sheets, have been greatly expanded. The tear-out sheets allow easy removal and subsequent checking. Each item is carefully indexed to an objective and identified with a domino symbol. Answers for the odd-numbered exercises may be found at the back of the book. All other answers are in the Teacher's Edition. Optional calculator problems are included at the end of certain exercise sets.

- **Color.** The development is more readily learned by the effective use of color. For example, color is used to highlight important ideas and helps to clarify the development, thus improving readability.

- **Chapter Tests or Reviews.** Chapter tests or reviews contain items which are carefully indexed to the objectives by the domino symbols. These tests or reviews are on tear-out sheets which may be easily removed for checking. Answers for all the items are found at the back of the book. Additional tests are provided in the Instructor's Manual.

WAYS TO USE THIS BOOK

This book may be used in many ways. A few are listed:

- **As an Ordinary Textbook.** The instructor may lecture on the material and assign problems to be done outside of class. The margin exercise format, as mentioned, greatly enhances the student's ability to read and study alone.
- **For a Modified Lecture.** The instructor presents material and has students do marginal exercises at the appropriate time in class.
- **As a Self-study Textbook.** The user progresses at his or her own pace. Materials are very readable and the format encourages a user to immediately check progress toward the study objective.
- **For a Nonlecture Class.** The students study on their own, marking trouble spots and exercises they cannot do. The use of class time is then maximized by just spending it to work on student difficulties, eliminating the need to lecture on anything the students can learn on their own.

ACKNOWLEDGMENTS

Business Mathematics, Second Edition, has many people to thank for their help, advice, and cooperation.

We especially want to thank those who consented to having their photographs appear as chapter openers. Their names will not be listed here since they appear with the photographs, but we are deeply grateful. Our photographer, Rick Haston of *Latent Images* in Carmel, Indiana, performed as the true artist he is in the preparation of the photographs. He merits great appreciation.

To ensure the relevance of the applied material, the authors have consulted with many persons in the business world. We wish to thank them for giving so generously of their time and advice. They are as follows: Paul W. Poppe, Toshiba America, Inc.; Lois Poppe, Cytronics, Inc.; Robert J. Ertle, Iowa-Des Moines National Bank; Bill Strickler, State Farm Insurance Co.; Andrew Engel, Certified Public Accountant; Clarence W. Schnicke, Stock Broker; and Barton L. Kaufman, CLU, General Agent, Indianapolis Life Insurance Co.

We also wish to thank Sue Haberhern, Judy Penna, and Virginia McCarthy for their meticulous proofreading of the manuscript and checking of the answers. Special thanks also are given to William P. Rudolph, who developed the computer programs which accompany this text.

The textual presentation has been improved considerably by the valuable comments and suggestions from users of the first edition. We thank these individuals and the following reviewers: Bill Heckman, Arapahoe Community College; Julian Bernard, Bronx Community College; Jeanne McKinnon, Central Piedmont Community College; John Drury and Donald Williams, Columbus Technical Institute; Robert Rizzo, Indian River Community College; John H. Carpenter, Polk Community College; and John Snyder and Judy K. Stimpson, Sinclair Community College.

Indianapolis, Indiana M.L.B.
Ames, Iowa W.B.R.
October 1983

CONTENTS IN BRIEF

BASICS

CHAPTER 1 Whole Numbers and Fractions 1
CHAPTER 2 Decimal Notation and Equations 61
CHAPTER 3 Ratio and Percent 113
CHAPTER 4 Interest 161

PERSONAL FINANCE

CHAPTER 5 Checking, Savings, and Money Market Accounts 213
CHAPTER 6 Loans and Annuities 245
CHAPTER 7 Installment and Consumer Credit 285
CHAPTER 8 Stocks and Bonds 327
CHAPTER 9 Insurance 347
CHAPTER 10 Taxes 379

RETAILING/ACCOUNTING

CHAPTER 11 Financial Statements 405
CHAPTER 12 Purchasing and Inventory 431
CHAPTER 13 Depreciation 459
CHAPTER 14 Pricing 483
CHAPTER 15 Payroll 505

STATISTICS

CHAPTER 16 Statistics and Graphs 545

APPENDIX The Metric System 565
TABLES T–1
ANSWERS A–1
INDEX I–1

CONTENTS

BASICS

1 WHOLE NUMBERS AND FRACTIONS

- 1.1 Addition of whole numbers 2
- 1.2 Subtraction of whole numbers 7
- 1.3 Multiplication 13
- 1.4 Division 19
- 1.5 Fractions and mixed numerals 25
- 1.6 Multiplying and simplifying using fractional notation 31
- 1.7 Division using fractional notation 37
- 1.8 Least common multiples and denominators 43
- 1.9 Addition using fractional notation 47
- 1.10 Subtraction using fractional notation 53
- Test or review 59

2 DECIMAL NOTATION AND EQUATIONS

- 2.1 Decimal notation 62
- 2.2 Addition and subtraction with decimals 69
- 2.3 Multiplication and division using decimals 75
- 2.4 Estimating and more conversion 83
- 2.5 Exponents 89
- 2.6 Order of operations 93
- 2.7 Equation solving 97
- 2.8 Formulas 103
- 2.9 Solving problems 107
- Test or review 111

3 RATIO AND PERCENT

- 3.1 Ratio and proportion 114
- 3.2 Proportion problems 121
- 3.3 Percent notation 125
- 3.4 Percent problems 133
- 3.5 Application of percent 145
- 3.6 Percent increase and decrease 151
- Test or review 159

4 INTEREST

- 4.1 Simple interest 162
- 4.2 Banker's 360-day method 169
- 4.3 Exact interest method 175
- 4.4 Other methods of computing interest 179
- 4.5 Simple-interest tables 183
- 4.6 Compound interest 191
- 4.7 Compound-interest tables 195
- 4.8 Daily and continuous compound interest 199
- 4.9 Nominal and effective interest rates 203
- 4.10 Present value 207
- Test or review 211

PERSONAL FINANCE

5 CHECKING, SAVINGS, AND MONEY MARKET ACCOUNTS

5.1 Paying by check 214
5.2 Reconciling a bank statement with a check record 229
5.3 Other financial transactions 235
Test or review 241

6 LOANS AND ANNUITIES

6.1 Notes and discounts 246
6.2 The United States Rule 253
6.3 The Merchant's Rule 259
6.4 Annuities 265
6.5 Individual Retirement Accounts and Keogh Plans 271
6.6 Present value of an annuity 277
Test or review 283

7 INSTALLMENT AND CONSUMER CREDIT

7.1 The annual percentage rate (APR) 286
7.2 Finding the payment amount 295
7.3 Interest on other loans 303
7.4 Early payment of a loan 309
7.5 Charge cards 315
Test or review 325

8 STOCKS AND BONDS

8.1 Stocks and commissions 328
8.2 Stocks: yield and price-earnings ratio 335
8.3 Bonds and commissions 339
Test or review 345

9 INSURANCE

9.1 Business and homeowner's insurance 348
9.2 Automobile insurance 359
9.3 Life insurance 367
Test or review 377

10 TAXES

10.1 Sales tax 380
10.2 Property tax 385
10.3 Federal income tax 389
Test or review 401

RETAILING/ACCOUNTING

11 FINANCIAL STATEMENTS

11.1 Profit and loss 406
11.2 Income statements 411
11.3 Balance sheets 417
Test or review 427

12 PURCHASING AND INVENTORY

12.1 Discount and price 432
12.2 Several trade discounts 437
12.3 Changing several discount rates to a single rate 441
12.4 Cash discounts 445
12.5 Inventory 449
12.6 Special inventory methods 453
Test or review 457

13 DEPRECIATION

13.1 Depreciation: the straight-line method 460
13.2 Depreciation: the declining-balance method 467
13.3 Depreciation: the sum-of-the-years'-digits method 471
13.4 Depreciation: ACRS and federal taxes 475
Test or review 481

14 PRICING

14.1 Pricing goods: cost price basis 484
14.2 Pricing goods: selling price basis 491
14.3 Markdown 497
Test or review 503

15 PAYROLL

15.1 Employee wages 506
15.2 Piecework plans 511
15.3 Salaried employees 515
15.4 Commissions 519
15.5 Withholding of federal income tax 525
15.6 Social security 531
15.7 Payroll 535
Test or review 543

CONTENTS

STATISTICS
16 STATISTICS AND GRAPHS

16.1 Averages, medians, and modes **546**
16.2 Bar graphs and frequency distributions **551**
16.3 Line graphs and circle graphs **555**
Test or review **563**

APPENDIX: THE METRIC SYSTEM 565

TABLES T–1

ANSWERS A–1

INDEX I–1

PART I
BASICS

1
WHOLE NUMBERS AND FRACTIONS

Career: Legal Secretary This is Roxanne Borczon. Roxanne took a course just like this one at a business college, where she received an Associate Degree in Secretarial Science.

Roxanne is a highly regarded Legal Secretary for a law firm. As a Legal Secretary, one of Roxanne's main responsibilities is the operation of a word processor, a computer-operated machine for the preparation and typing of legal documents. The four basic mathematical operations of addition, subtraction, multiplication, and division are vital to the successful programming of the word processor. People, such as Roxanne, who are successful as legal secretaries can expect to make salaries from $15,000 to $20,000 per year.

Roxanne works for three attorneys, each of whom has a different area of specialty. In this capacity those qualities which make for success, beyond the ability to operate a word processor, are patience and perseverance. Workdays can be quite hectic, but the work is exciting and always interesting.

Legal secretaries may also be responsible for issuing checks, reconciling bank statements, preparation and payment of income taxes, purchasing supplies, and the preparation of payroll. These topics are covered in this text.

Roxanne's hobbies include reading, rug hooking, raising parakeets, and sailing.

2

OBJECTIVES

After finishing Section 1.1, you should be able to:

■ Write word names for whole numbers.

■■ Add whole numbers.

■■■ Solve problems involving addition of whole numbers.

Write a word name.

1. 24

2. 37

3. 88

Write a short word name.

4. 5,674,316,997

5. 220,456,203

Write a word name.

6. 5,674,316,997

7. 220,456,203

ANSWERS ON PAGE A–1

WHOLE NUMBERS AND FRACTIONS

1.1 ADDITION OF WHOLE NUMBERS

In this chapter we review the basic operations of addition, subtraction, multiplication, and division of whole numbers together with related problem solving. We begin with addition.

■ PLACE VALUE AND WORD NAMES

"Four hundred seventy-eight" is a *word name*. Word names for most two-digit numbers contain hyphens.

Example 1 Write word names for 58, 72, and 97.

Solution

58	Fifty-eight
72	Seventy-two
97	Ninety-seven

DO EXERCISES 1–3 (IN THE MARGIN).

Recently the United States government owned

$11,718,123,786

worth of gold. To find a word name for such a number we use a place value chart.

Billions	Millions	Thousands	Ones	← Period
Hundreds Tens Ones	Hundreds Tens Ones	Hundreds Tens Ones	Hundreds Tens Ones	← Place
1 1 ,	7 1 8 ,	1 2 3 ,	7 8 6	← Digit

Example 2 Write a short word name for 11,718,123,786.

Solution 11 billion, 718 million, 123 thousand, 786

Each comma represents a *period*. To write the full word name we write out the word names in each period.

Example 3 Write a full word name for 11,718,123,786.

Solution Eleven billion, seven hundred eighteen million, one hundred twenty-three thousand, seven hundred eighty-six.

DO EXERCISES 4–7.

■■ ADDITION

The whole numbers are 0, 1, 2, 3, 4, 5, 6, 7, 8, 9, 10, 11, and so on. To add whole numbers we add the ones first, then tens, then hundreds, and so on.

Example 4 Add: 6433 + 4345.

1.1 ADDITION OF WHOLE NUMBERS

Solution

a)
```
  6 4 3 3     Add ones.
+ 4 3 4 5
        8
```

b)
```
  6 4 3 3     Add tens.
+ 4 3 4 5
      7 8
```

c)
```
  6 4 3 3     Add hundreds.
+ 4 3 4 5
    7 7 8
```

d)
```
    6 4 3 3   Add thousands.
+   4 3 4 5
  1 0 7 7 8
```

Write only this:
```
   6 4 3 3
+  4 3 4 5
  1 0,7 7 8
```

DO EXERCISES 8–10.

We use the following terminology with addition:

$$6433 + 4345 = 10{,}778.$$

Addend   Addend   Sum

Sometimes we need to carry numbers to another column. For example, if we are adding ones and we get 14 ones, we leave 4 in the ones column and carry 1 ten to the tens column.

Example 5 Add: 8765 + 6495.

Solution

a)
```
      1
    8 7 6 5     Add ones. Write a 0 in the ones column. Carry a 1
  + 6 4 9 5     above the tens column. Why? Because 5 + 5 =
          0     10 = 1 ten + 0 ones.
```

b)
```
    1 1
    8 7 6 5     Add tens. Write a 6 in the tens column. Carry a 1
  + 6 4 9 5     above the hundreds column. Why? Because 1 ten +
        6 0     6 tens + 9 tens = 16 tens or 1 hundred + 6 tens.
```

c)
```
  1 1 1
    8 7 6 5     Add hundreds. Write a 2 in the hundreds column.
  + 6 4 9 5     Carry a 1 above the thousands column.
      2 6 0
```

d)
```
  1 1 1
    8 7 6 5     Add thousands.
  + 6 4 9 5
  1 5 2 6 0
```

DO EXERCISES 11 AND 12.

Add.

8.
```
  4 6
+ 2 3
```

9.
```
  4 5 7
+ 7 0 2
```

10. 8436 + 2351

Add.

11.
```
  9 9 5 6
+ 4 9 8 8
```

12. 7377 + 881

ANSWERS ON PAGE A–1

13. It takes an average of 993 kWh of electricity to operate a clothes dryer for a year. It takes 103 kWh for a washing machine and 4219 kWh for a water heater. How much electricity does it take to run all three?

5315

14. Below are the annual cost of driving a compact car to work when the daily round trip is 20 miles. Find the total annual cost.

Gasoline and oil	$176
Maintenance	109
Parking	145
Insurance	176
Depreciation	143

$749

ANSWERS ON PAGE A–1

WHOLE NUMBERS AND FRACTIONS

PROBLEMS INVOLVING ADDITION

Certain problems can be solved using 6 addition.

Example 6 It takes an average of 1761 kilowatt-hours (kWh) of electricity to operate a frostfree freezer for one year. It takes 1217 kWh for a forstfree refrigerator and 455 kWh for a range. How much electricity does it take to run all three?

Solution

Electricity for all three = Electricity for freezer + Electricity for refrigerator + Electricity for range

= 1761 + 1217 + 455

We add as follows:

```
  ¹ ¹ ¹
  1 7 6 1
  1 2 1 7
+     4 5 5
  ─────────
  3 4 3 3
```

It takes 3433 kWh to operate all three appliances for one year.

DO EXERCISE 13.

Example 7 Below are the annual costs of driving a standard-size car to work for a year when the daily round trip is 20 miles. Find the total annual cost.

Gasoline and oil	$234
Maintenance	130
Driving	145
Insurance	189
Depreciation	250

Solution We find the total annual cost by adding.

```
    ² ¹
  $2 3 4
   1 3 0
   1 4 5
   1 8 9
+  2 5 0
  ──────
  $9 4 8
```

The total amount is $948.

DO EXERCISE 14.

EXERCISE SET 1.1

NAME _____ CLASS _____

EXERCISE SET 1.1

■ Write a word name.

1. 38   2. 21

3. 76   4. 92

Write a short word name.

5. 56,789   6. 78,204

7. 7,894,556,745   8. 18,235,872,234

Write a word name.

9. 56,789   10. 78,204

11. 7,894,556,745   12. 18,235,872,234

■■ Add.

13. 1 7
    + 6

14. 2 4
    + 8

15. 7 6
    +3 2

16. 9 5
    +1 4

17. 802 + 74

18. 754 + 42

19. $54,963 + $29,248

20. $129,345 + $6279

21. 7 4 8
    +2 8 6

22. 8 8 8
    +2 2 2

23. 7 6 9
    +4 8 8

24. 9 0 9
    +1 0 1

25. 7 8 1 9
    +1 4 9 0

26. 9 1 1 8
    +1 9 9 6

27. 8 8 6 6
    +6 6 4 5

28. 9 9 9 9
    +7 6 4 8

29. 5 4,8 7 9
    +2 3,7 8 7

30. 6 7,4 4 3
    +1 0,8 9 8

31. 9 8,7 8 6
    +6 7,7 8 6

32. 8 8,5 4 3
    +3 4,6 8 6

33. 8 6 3
     5 9 6
     4 1 2
    +3 3 3

34. 9 9 2
     2 0 3
     8 4 7
    +2 1 4

35. 9 2 3
     2 0 3 7
        7 7
    +3 3 4 8

36. 7 8 1 9
        1 9
     6 2 3 0
    + 3 7 6

ANSWERS
1. _____
2. _____
3. _____
4. _____
5. _____
6. _____
7. _____
8. _____
9. _____
10. _____
11. _____
12. _____
13. _____
14. _____
15. _____
16. _____
17. _____
18. _____
19. _____
20. _____
21. _____
22. _____
23. _____
24. _____
25. _____
26. _____
27. _____
28. _____
29. _____
30. _____
31. _____
32. _____
33. _____
34. _____
35. _____
36. _____

6 WHOLE NUMBERS AND FRACTIONS

ANSWERS	

Solve.

37. It takes an average of 363 kWh of electricity to operate a dishwasher for a year. It takes 83 kWh to run a deep-fat fryer. How much electricity does it take for both?

37. _446 kWh_

38. It takes an average of 860 kWh of electricity to operate a room air conditioner for a year. It takes 163 kWh to run a humidifier. How much electricity does it take for both?

38. _1023 kWh_

39. A business pays monthly salaries of $1432, $2031, $1800, and $1625 to its four salespeople. How much is paid in all?

39. _$6888_

40. A business pays monthly salaries of $2100, $1948, $1200, and $1667 to its four salespeople. How much is paid in all?

40. _$6915_

41. One year a car dealer sells 48 wagons, 72 sedans, 10 trucks, and 52 compact cars. How many vehicles were sold?

41. _182_

42. One month a salesperson sells 23 color TVs, 16 transistor radios, 9 stereos, and 4 CBs. How many appliances were sold?

42. _52_

43. At the end of one year $187 in interest is added to $2340 in a savings account. How much is then in the account?

43. _$2527_

44. At the end of one year $365 in interest is added to $3950 in a savings account. How much is then in the account?

44. _$4315_

45. A consumer has assets of $9876 in real estate, $2190 in a savings account, and $4200 in stock. What are the total assets?

45. _$16266_

46. A consumer has assets of $10,780 in real estate, $3745 in a checking account, and $4898 in municipal bonds. What are the total assets?

46. _$19,423_

47. The following salaries were paid by a business one year. Find the total salaries paid.

$65,700
48,795
23,890
22,566
18,444
12,295

47. _$191,690_

48. One month a real estate agent made these sales. Find the total sales.

$114,990
64,700
89,999
76,500
84,300
49,990

48. _$480,479_

1.2 SUBTRACTION OF WHOLE NUMBERS

In this section we review subtraction of whole numbers and related problem solving.

◘ SUBTRACTION

We define $a - b$ to be that number which when added to b gives a. Thus, $7 - 5 = 2$ because $7 = 5 + 2$. *Think:* 7 is 5 plus what number? $7 - 5 = 2$ and $7 = 5 + 2$ are called *related sentences*.

DO EXERCISES 1–3.

To subtract whole numbers we can subtract ones first, then tens, then hundreds, and so on.

Example 1 Subtract: $6849 - 2831$.

Solution

a) $\begin{array}{r} 684\boxed{9} \\ -283\boxed{1} \\ \hline 8 \end{array}$ Subtract ones.

b) $\begin{array}{r} 68\boxed{4}9 \\ -28\boxed{3}1 \\ \hline 18 \end{array}$ Subtract tens.

c) $\begin{array}{r} 6\boxed{8}49 \\ -2\boxed{8}31 \\ \hline 018 \end{array}$ Subtract hundreds.

d) $\begin{array}{r} \boxed{6}849 \\ -\boxed{2}831 \\ \hline 4018 \end{array}$ Subtract thousands.

Write only this:
$\begin{array}{r} 6849 \\ -2831 \\ \hline 4018 \end{array}$

DO EXERCISES 4–6.

We use the following terminology with subtraction:

$$\underset{\text{Minuend}}{6849} - \underset{\text{Subtrahend}}{2831} = \underset{\text{Difference}}{4018}$$

Sometimes we need to borrow one unit from the column to the left.

OBJECTIVES

After finishing Section 1.2, you should be able to:

◘ Subtract whole numbers.

◘◘ Solve problems involving subtraction of whole numbers.

Subtract.

1. $10 - 4$

2. $\begin{array}{r} 12 \\ -5 \\ \hline \end{array}$

3. $\begin{array}{r} 17 \\ -9 \\ \hline \end{array}$

Subtract.

4. $\begin{array}{r} 278 \\ -104 \\ \hline \end{array}$

5. $\begin{array}{r} 78 \\ -35 \\ \hline \end{array}$

6. $7849 - 2038$

ANSWERS ON PAGE A–1

8

WHOLE NUMBERS AND FRACTIONS

Subtract.

7. 718
   −240

Example 2 Subtract: 647 − 395.

Solution

a)   6 4 **7**
    −3 9 **5**
    ─────
         2   Subtract ones.

b)   6 **4** 7
    −3 **9** 5
    ─────
       ? 2   Subtract tens, if possible.
                   Think: 40 − 90 is not a whole number.

c)   ⁵ ¹⁴
     6 4̷ 7
    −3 9 5
    ─────
         2   Borrow 1 hundred. Write 5 above the hundreds column
                  and 14 above the tens because 4 tens + 10 tens =
                  14 tens.

d)   ⁵ ¹⁴
     6̷ 4̷ 7
    −3 9 5
    ─────
       5 2   Subtract tens.

8. 529 − 439

e)   ⁵ ¹⁴
     6̷ 4̷ 7
    −3 9 5
    ─────
     2 5 2   Subtract hundreds.

   Write only this:
        ⁵ ¹⁴
        6̷ 4̷ 7
       −3 9 5
       ──────
        2 5 2

Subtract.

9. 8429
   −3687

DO EXERCISES 7 AND 8.

Subtraction can always be checked by addition.

Example 3 Subtract: 8325 − 1978. Check by addition.

Solution

a)   ¹ ¹⁵
      8 3 2̷ 5̷
     −1 9 7 8
     ────────
             7   Borrow 1 ten. Then subtract ones.

b)   ¹¹
         ² ¹̷ ¹⁵
      8 3̷ 2̷ 5̷
     −1 9 7 8
     ────────
           4 7   Borrow 1 hundred. Then subtract tens.

10. 6164
    −5783

ANSWERS ON PAGE A–1

1.2 SUBTRACTION OF WHOLE NUMBERS

c)
```
        12 11
    7   2  1 15
    8   3  2  5     Borrow 1 thousand. Then subtract hundreds. Then
  − 1   9  7  8     subtract thousands.
  ─────────────
    6   3  4  7
```

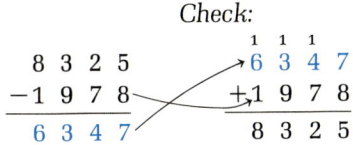

d)
```
                            1  1  1
    8  3  2  5          →   6  3  4  7
  − 1  9  7  8         +    1  9  7  8
  ─────────────       ──────────────────
    6  3  4  7              8  3  2  5
```
Check:

DO EXERCISES 9 AND 10 (ON THE PRECEDING PAGE).

Example 4 Subtract: 704 − 158.

Solution

```
    6  9 14
    7  0  4      704 is 7 hundreds + 4 ones, or 70 tens + 4 ones. We borrow
  − 1  5  8      1 ten, leaving 69 tens. Then we subtract ones, tens, and
  ──────────     hundreds.
    5  4  6
```

Example 5 Subtract: 8001 − 3654.

Solution

```
    7  9  9 11
    8  0  0  1     8001 is 8 thousands + 1 one, or 800 tens + 1 one. We
  − 3  6  5  4     borrow 1 ten, leaving 799 tens. Then we subtract ones,
  ─────────────    tens, hundreds, and thousands.
    4  3  4  7
```

Examples Subtract.

Solution

6.
```
    5  9  9 10
    6  0  0  0
  − 2  7  1  9
  ─────────────
    3  2  8  1
```

7.
```
            11
    5  9  1 14
    6  0  2  4
  − 3  5  6  8
  ─────────────
    2  4  5  6
```

DO EXERCISES 11–14.

●● PROBLEMS INVOLVING SUBTRACTION

Certain problems can be solved using subtraction.

Example 8 Alaska has the highest per capita income (the highest income per person) in the country. It is about $14,415 per year. Per capita income in New Jersey is $12,067. How much more do people in Alaska make?

Solution

$$\begin{matrix}\text{Extra in}\\\text{Alaska}\end{matrix} = \begin{matrix}\text{Income in}\\\text{Alaska}\end{matrix} - \begin{matrix}\text{Income in}\\\text{New Jersey}\end{matrix}$$

$$= \$14{,}415 - \$12{,}067$$

Subtract.

11.
```
    9 0 7
  − 1 2 8
```

12.
```
    5 0 0 4
  − 3 7 6 8
```

13.
```
    9 0 0 0
  − 5 6 1 3
```

14. 7052 − 2467

ANSWERS ON PAGE A–1

15. Per capita income in Michigan is $10,754. In Kentucky it is $9379. How much more is the per capita income in Michigan?

1375

16. A consumer has $902 in a checking account and writes checks for $84 and $77. How much is left in the account?

ANSWERS ON PAGE A–1

WHOLE NUMBERS AND FRACTIONS

We subtract as follows:

$$\begin{array}{r} 3\cancel{8}\overset{10}{\cancel{1}}15 \\ 14{,}4\cancel{1}\cancel{5} \\ -12{,}067 \\ \hline 2{,}348 \end{array}$$

A person in Alaska makes $2348 more than a person in New Jersey (but the cost of living is higher in Alaska).

DO EXERCISE 15.

Example 9 A consumer has $876 in a checking account and writes checks for $89 and $46. How much is left in the account?

CHECK NO.	DATE	CHECKS ISSUED TO OR DESCRIPTION OF DEPOSIT	AMOUNT OF CHECK	T	CHECK FEE (IF ANY)	AMOUNT OF DEPOSIT	BALANCE
							876 00
279	4/16/85	Sally's Sport Shop	89 00				
280	4/16/85	Joe's Snaks Heaven	46 00				?

Solution

$$\begin{array}{l} \text{Amount} \\ \text{left} \end{array} = \begin{array}{l} \text{Original} \\ \text{amount} \end{array} - \begin{array}{l} \text{Amount of} \\ \text{first check} \end{array} - \begin{array}{l} \text{Amount of} \\ \text{second check} \end{array}$$

$$= \$876 - \$89 - \$46$$

We subtract 89 from 876, and then 46 from that answer.

$$\begin{array}{r} \overset{7}{\cancel{8}}\overset{16}{\cancel{7}}\overset{16}{\cancel{6}} \\ -89 \\ \hline 787 \end{array} \qquad \begin{array}{r} 787 \\ -46 \\ \hline 741 \end{array}$$

There is $741 left in the account. (This problem could also have been done by adding 89 and 46 and subtracting that answer from 876.)

DO EXERCISE 16.

EXERCISE SET 1.2

Subtract.

1. 16 − 5
2. 28 − 7
3. 25 − 9
4. 76 − 8

5. 74 − 51
6. 79 − 68
7. 83 − 67
8. 62 − 19

9. 678 − 106
10. 798 − 403
11. 734 − 708
12. 947 − 509

13. 725 − 317
14. 953 − 246
15. 932 − 747
16. 825 − 598

17. 8431 − 4420
18. 9887 − 9456
19. 6345 − 2859
20. 7428 − 2679

21. 8641 − 909
22. 7843 − 799
23. 90 − 54
24. 130 − 46

25. 580 − 279
26. 690 − 325
27. 7002 − 1328
28. 6100 − 2758

29. 68,070 − 29,691
30. 50,680 − 17,387
31. 79,411 − 56,856
32. 90,000 − 14,567

Solve.

33. Per capita income in New Jersey in $8067. In Ohio it is $6412. How much more is the per capita income in New Jersey?

34. Per capita income in Illinois is $7347. The national average is $6399. How much more is the per capita income in Illinois?

35. A consumer has $1042 in a checking account and writes checks for $98 and $87. How much is left in the account?

36. A consumer has $2105 in a checking account and writes checks for $179 and $48. How much is left in the account?

ANSWERS

1.
2.
3.
4.
5.
6.
7.
8.
9.
10.
11.
12.
13.
14.
15.
16.
17.
18.
19.
20.
21.
22.
23.
24.
25.
26.
27.
28.
29.
30.
31.
32.
33. $1655
34. $948
35. $857
36. $1878

12

WHOLE NUMBERS AND FRACTIONS

ANSWERS

37. A bookstore owner has an inventory of 6704 books. During one week 1985 books are sold and 789 new books are received from suppliers. How many books were in the inventory at the end of the week?

37. 5508

38. A clothing store had 2590 suits in stock. One week 879 suits are sold and 1240 new suits are received from suppliers. How many suits were in stock at the end of the week?

38. 2951

39. A business has $23,678 in its corporate checking account. One week it writes checks for $1250, $1485, $2899, and $7050. How much is left in the account?

39. $10994

40. A business has $19,990 in its corporate checking account. One week it writes checks for $2800, $4678, $8905, and $1004. How much is left in the account?

40. $2603

41. The price of a used car is $3400. It is reduced $785 for quick sale. What is the new selling price?

41. $2615

42. The price of a used truck is $5300. It is reduced $1994 for quick sale. What is the new selling price?

42. $3306

43. A financial institution has a cash balance of $34,567,980. It pays out $18,567,876 and receives $12,788,984. What is the new cash balance?

44. A Lockheed L-1011 TriStar has 1,285,000 rivets and fasteners. Of these, 580,000 are titanium fasteners and 5000 are stainless-steel fasteners. The rest are aluminum rivets. How many aluminum rivets are there?

43.

45. *A magic square.* The sum along any row, column, or diagonal of the table below should be the same number. But one number is incorrect. Use your calculator to find it. What number should it be?

44.

27	69	10	65
60	15	77	19
75	20	58	17
9	67	25	70

45.

1.3 MULTIPLICATION

In this section we review multiplication of whole numbers and related problem solving.

◼ MULTIPLICATION

Multiplication can be thought of as repeated addition.

$3 \times 5 = \underbrace{5 + 5 + 5}_{3 \text{ fives}} = 15$

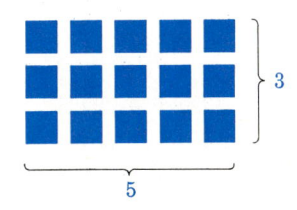

We can also use a dot "·" for multiplication rather than "×." That is,

$3 \times 5 = 3 \cdot 5.$

We use the following terminology with multiplication:

$\underset{\text{Factor}}{3} \times \underset{\text{Factor}}{5} = \underset{\text{Product}}{15}.$

DO EXERCISES 1–3.

The product 27 × 86 can be thought of as

(7 × 86) plus (20 × 86).

Example 1 Multiply: 27 × 86.

Solution

a)
```
      4
      8 6
  ×   2 7
  ─────────
      6 0 2    Multiply 7 times 86 and get 602.
```

b)
```
      1
      4
      8 6
  ×   2 7
  ─────────
      6 0 2
    1 7 2 0    Multiply 20 times 86 and get 1720.
  ─────────    Add.
    2 3 2 2
```

DO EXERCISES 4 AND 5.

OBJECTIVES

After finishing Section 1.3, you should be able to:

◼ Multiply whole numbers.

◼◼ Solve problems involving multiplication of whole numbers.

Multiply. Think of repeated addition.

1. 4 × 7   2. 5 · 8

3.   9
  ×7

Multiply.

4.   6 5
  ×4 7

5.   9 1
  ×6 8

ANSWERS ON PAGE A–1

14

WHOLE NUMBERS AND FRACTIONS

Multiply.

6.   8 5 7
    ×   3 9

Example 2 Multiply: 396 × 824.

Solution

a)
```
      1 2
      8 2 4
    ×   3 9 6
    ─────────
      4 9 4 4     Multiply 6 times 824 and get 4944.
```

b)
```
        2 3
      1 2
      8 2 4
    ×   3 9 6
    ─────────
      4,9 4 4
     7 4,1 6 0    Multiply 90 times 824 and get 74,160.
```

7.   9 1 8
    × 4 6 3

c)
```
          1
        2 3
      1 2
      8 2 4
    ×   3 9 6
    ─────────
      4,9 4 4
     7 4,1 6 0
    2 4 7,2 0 0   Multiply 300 times 824 and get 247,200.
    ─────────
    3 2 6,3 0 4   Add.
```

Multiply.

8.   8 7 4
    × 3 0 2

DO EXERCISES 6 AND 7.

Example 3 Multiply: 408 × 139.

Solution

```
        1 3 9
    ×   4 0 8       408 = 4 hundreds + 8 ones.
    ─────────
        1,1 1 2     Multiply 8 times 139 and get 1112.
      5 5,6 0 0     Multiply 400 times 139 and get 55,600.
    ─────────       (Write 00 and then multiply 4 times 139.)
      5 6,7 1 2     Add.
```

9.   8 3 4 4
    × 6 0 0 7

DO EXERCISES 8 AND 9.

Example 4 Multiply: 480 × 613.

Solution

Multiply.

10.   9 1 8
    ×   7 6 0

```
        6 1 3
    ×   4 8 0       480 = 4 hundreds + 8 tens.
    ─────────
      4 9,0 4 0     Multiply 80 times 613 and get 49,040.
    2 4 5,2 0 0     (Write 0 and then multiply 8 times 613.)
    ─────────       Multiply 400 times 613, and get 245,200.
    2 9 4,2 4 0     (Write 00 and then multiply 4 times 613.)
                    Add.
```

11.   1 5 6 8
    × 2 3 0 0

DO EXERCISES 10 AND 11.

ANSWERS ON PAGE A–1

1.3 MULTIPLICATION

●● PROBLEMS INVOLVING MULTIPLICATION

Now we consider problems that can be solved using multiplication.

Example 5 A Chevrolet Camaro with a 250-cubic-inch, 6-cylinder engine gets 25 miles per gallon for highway driving. How far can it go on 23 gallons?

Solution

$$\text{Distance car can travel} = \frac{\text{Miles per}}{\text{gallon}} \times \frac{\text{Number of}}{\text{gallons}}$$
$$= 25 \times 23$$

We multiply as follows:

```
     2 3
  ×  2 5
  ─────
     1 1 5
     4 6 0
  ─────
     5 7 5
```

The car can go 575 miles.

DO EXERCISE 12.

Example 6 What is the total cost of three tickets from Indianapolis to Boston and seven tickets from Indianapolis to San Francisco?

SuperSaver Everywhere

FROM INDIANAPOLIS TO:	MON-THURS SUPERSAVER
Albany	$284
Boston	$215
San Francisco	$410
Tucson	$409
Tulsa	$283
Washington	$245

Solution

Cost = Cost of Boston tickets + Cost of San Francisco tickets
= (Number of tickets) × (Cost per Boston ticket)
+ (Number of tickets) × (Cost per San Francisco ticket)
= 3 × $215 + 7 × $410   *See the advertisement.*

When multiplications and additions occur in the same sentence, the multiplications are to be done first, followed by the additions.

---

12. A Dodge Colt with a 98-cubic-inch, 4-cylinder engine gets 45 miles per gallon for highway driving. How far can it go on 23 gallons?

ANSWER ON PAGE A–1

13. What is the total cost of eight tickets from Indianapolis to Tucson and six tickets from Indianapolis to Washington? (See the advertisement.)

We multiply as follows:

$$\begin{array}{r} \overset{1}{2}\,1\,5 \\ \times 3 \\ \hline 6\,4\,5 \end{array} \qquad \begin{array}{r} 4\,1\,0 \\ \times 7 \\ \hline 2\,8\,7\,0 \end{array}$$

We then add as follows:

$$\begin{array}{r} \overset{1}{}\overset{1}{} \\ 6\,4\,5 \\ +2\,8\,7\,0 \\ \hline 3\,5\,1\,5 \end{array}$$

The total cost of the tickets is $3515.

DO EXERCISE 13.

EXERCISE SET 1.3

NAME   **CLASS**   ANSWERS

● Multiply.

1.   3 0
     ×   8

2.   4 0
     ×   7

3.   3 2 1
     ×   4 0

4.   8 3 4
     ×   6 0

5.   9 0 0
     × 6 0 0

6.   8 0 0
     × 7 0 0

7.   6 8
     ×   3

8.   7 6
     ×   4

9.   9 3 2
     ×   8

10.   7 4 8
      ×   7

11.   4 7
      × 2 8

12.   7 4
      × 5 8

13.   8 5 6
      ×   7 2

14.   9 7 4
      ×   3 9

15.   8 8 8
      ×   8 8

16.   3 3 4
      ×   3 4

17.   6 0 8
      × 3 0 4

18.   4 0 2
      × 7 5 0

19.   4 5 9
      × 2 0 6

20.   3 8 4
      × 5 0 2

21.   6 4 3 2
      ×   1 0 5

22.   7 4 0 8
      ×   1 0 7

23.   2 0 0 9
      × 4 0 0 3

24.   6 7 0 0
      × 5 0 0 6

25.   9 9 9 9
      ×   1 1

26.   3 3 3 5
      ×   2 2

27.   9 8 7 6
      × 2 3 3 4

28.   7 8 8 4
      × 1 9 8 4

WHOLE NUMBERS AND FRACTIONS

ANSWERS

Solve.

29. A Ford LTD with a 400-cubic-inch, 8-cylinder engine gets 18 miles per gallon for highway driving. How far can it go on 56 gallons of gasoline?

29. 1008 mi

30. An American Motors Hornet with a 232-cubic-inch, 6-cylinder engine gets 23 miles per gallon for highway driving. How far can it go on 56 gallons of gasoline?

30. 1288 mi

31. What is the cost of 18 color TVs at $576 each?

32. What is the cost of 24 stereos at $498 each?

31. $10,368

33. A student pays $78 a month for each of 9 months for a dorm room. How much is paid in all?

32. $11,952

34. What is the cost of 9 portable TVs at $95 each?

33. $702

35. An employee makes $6 per hour for 40 hours and $9 per hour for 16 hours of overtime. How much does the employee make?

34. $855

36. A car wash makes $3 for washing an ordinary-size car and $5 for washing a station wagon. How much do they make washing 16 cars and 12 wagons?

37. Referring to the advertisement in Example 6, determine the total cost of 14 tickets from Indianapolis to Albany and 28 tickets from Indianapolis to Tulsa.

35. $384

38. Referring to the advertisement in Example 6, determine the cost of 29 tickets from Indianapolis to Boston and 34 tickets from Indianapolis to Washington.

36. $108

39. A corporation pays each of its 2116 employees a salary of $13,458 one year. What was the total amount paid?

37. $11,900

40. If the national debt were paid off, each of the 220 million people in this country would owe $4327. What is the national debt?

38. $14,565

41. Replace each frame □ by one of the digits 1, 2, 3, 4, 5, 6, 7, or 8 to get the given number. Use your calculator.

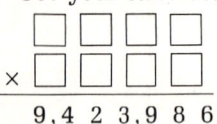

□□□□
× □□□□
9,4 2 3,9 8 6

39. $28,477,128

42. Use your calculator to do the first four calculations. Look for a pattern and use it to find the last calculation without the aid of the calculator.

40. 951,940 million

49 × 49
499 × 499
4,999 × 4,999
49,999 × 49,999

41.

499,999 × 499,999

42.

1.4 DIVISION

In this section we review division of whole numbers and related problem solving.

● DIVISION

We define $a \div b$ to be that number which when multiplied by b gives a. Thus, $12 \div 3 = 4$ because $12 = 3 \cdot 4$. *Think:* 12 is 3 times what number? We can think of this as an array of 12 objects, 3 in a row.

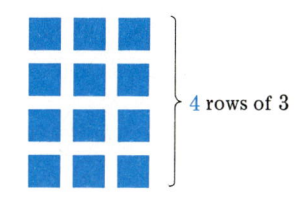

4 rows of 3

Since there are 4 rows of 3 objects, it follows that

$12 \div 3 = 4.$

The following terminology is used with division:

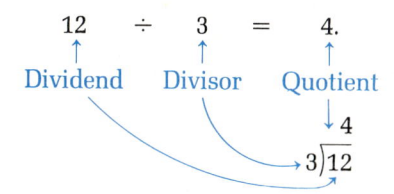

$12 \div 3 = 4.$

Dividend   Divisor   Quotient

$3\overline{)12}$ with quotient 4

DO EXERCISES 1–3.

Example 1 Divide: $8322 \div 38$.

Solution

a)
```
      2
38 ) 8 3 2 2
     7 6
     ───
       7 2
```
Consider $83 \div 38$; 38 is about 40 and 83 is about 80. Then $80 \div 40$ is 2. You could also do this by checking multiples.

b)
```
       2 1
38 ) 8 3 2 2
     7 6
     ───
       7 2
       3 8
       ───
       3 4
```
Think of this as $70 \div 40$, which is 1.

OBJECTIVES

After finishing Section 1.4, you should be able to:

● Divide whole numbers.

●● Solve problems involving division of whole numbers.

Divide.

1. $15 \div 3$

2. $12 \div 2$

3. $54 \div 6$

ANSWERS ON PAGE A–1

Divide.

4. $1\overline{)29468}$

5. $2\overline{)7847}$

Divide.

6. $5\overline{)3542}$

ANSWERS ON PAGE A–1

WHOLE NUMBERS AND FRACTIONS

c)
$$\begin{array}{r} 21\,9 \\ 38\overline{)832} \\ 76 \\ \hline 72 \\ 38 \\ \hline 342 \\ 342 \\ \hline 0 \end{array}$$

Think of this as 340 ÷ 40, which would be 8, but 8 × 38 = 304, and

$$\begin{array}{r} 342 \\ -304 \\ \hline 38 \end{array}$$

We see that this estimate is too small, so we increase the 8 to 9.

The answer is 219. The number 0 is the remainder. We do not write 0 remainders in answers.

DO EXERCISES 4 AND 5.

Zeros can occur in quotients.

Example 2 Divide: 1661 ÷ 8.

Solution

a)
$$\begin{array}{r} 2 \\ 8\overline{)1661} \\ 16 \\ \hline 61 \end{array}$$
16 ÷ 8 = 2

b)
$$\begin{array}{r} 20 \\ 8\overline{)1661} \\ 16 \\ \hline 61 \end{array}$$
We divide 6 by 8. There are no 8's in 6. We write a 0 to indicate this.

c)
$$\begin{array}{r} 207 \\ 8\overline{)1661} \\ 16 \\ \hline 61 \\ 56 \\ \hline 5 \end{array}$$
61 ÷ 8 is 7 remainder 5.

The answer is 207 R 5.

DO EXERCISE 6.

Example 3 Divide: 20,733 ÷ 28.

Solution

a)
$$\begin{array}{r} 7 \\ 28\overline{)20{,}733} \\ 196 \\ \hline 113 \end{array}$$
Estimate 210 ÷ 30, which is 7.

1.4 DIVISION

b)
```
        7 4
   28 ) 20,733
        19 6
         1 13
         1 12
             13
```
Estimate this as 110 ÷ 30, which is 3, but 3 × 28 = 84, and

```
  113
−  84
   29
```

We see that this estimate is too small so we increase the 3 to 4.

c)
```
        7 4 0
   28 ) 20,733
        19 6
         1 13
         1 12
             13
```
There are no 28's in 13. We write a 0.

The answer is 740 R 13.

DO EXERCISE 7.

●● PROBLEMS INVOLVING DIVISION

Now we consider problems that can be solved using division.

Example 4 How many 12-ounce bottles of soda can be filled by 3475 ounces of soda? How many ounces of soda will be left over?

Solution

$$\text{Number of bottles} = \text{Number of ounces} \div \text{Amount in each bottle}$$
$$= 3475 \div 12$$

We divide as follows:
```
         2 8 9
   12 ) 3 4 7 5
         2 4
         1 0 7
           9 6
           1 1 5
           1 0 8
                7
```

Thus 289 bottles can be filled. There will be 7 ounces left over.

DO EXERCISE 8.

Example 5 An Oldsmobile Omega gets 19 miles to the gallon in city driving. How many gallons will it take to travel 4940 miles of city driving?

Divide.

7. 14) 7840

8. How many 16-ounce bottles can be filled by 3475 ounces of soda? How many ounces will be left over?

ANSWERS ON PAGE A–1

9. An Oldsmobile Omega gets 26 miles to the gallon for highway driving. How many gallons would it take to go 1170 miles?

10. There are 167 employees in a corporation. One month $181,696 in salaries is paid. What is the average salary of each employee?

ANSWERS ON PAGE A–1

WHOLE NUMBERS AND FRACTIONS

Solution We first draw a picture. This is often helpful in problem solving.

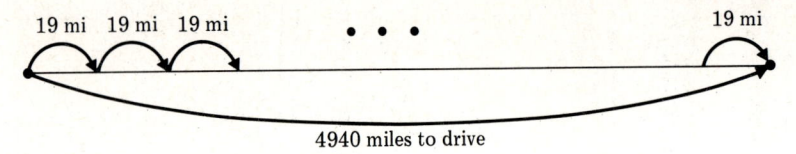

19 mi 19 mi 19 mi . . . 19 mi

4940 miles to drive

Repeated addition applies here. Thus the following multiplication corresponds to the situation:

$$\begin{pmatrix} \text{Miles per} \\ \text{gallon} \end{pmatrix} \text{ times } \begin{pmatrix} \text{Number of} \\ \text{gallons} \\ \text{needed} \end{pmatrix} \text{ is } \begin{pmatrix} \text{Number of} \\ \text{miles to} \\ \text{drive} \end{pmatrix}$$

$$19 \cdot n = 4940$$

To find n, we move 19 to the other side and write a division.

$$n = 4940 \div 19.$$

This sentence tells us what to do. We divide.

```
       2 6 0
 1 9)4 9 4 0
     3 8 0 0
     ───────
     1 1 4 0
     1 1 4 0
     ───────
           0
```

Thus 260 gallons will be needed.

DO EXERCISE 9.

Example 6 There are 248 employees in a corporation. One month $314,216 in salaries is paid. What is the average salary of each employee?

Solution

$$\text{Average salary} = \frac{\text{Total amount paid in salaries}}{\text{Number of employees}}$$

$$= \frac{\$314{,}216}{248}$$

We divide as follows:

```
           1 2 6 7
  2 4 8)3 1 4,2 1 6
        2 4 8
        ─────
          6 6 2
          4 9 6
          ─────
          1 6 6 1
          1 4 8 8
          ───────
            1 7 3 6
            1 7 3 6
            ───────
                  0
```

The average salary is $1267.

DO EXERCISE 10.

| NAME | CLASS | ANSWERS |

EXERCISE SET 1.4

● Divide.

1. 4)399   2. 6)709   3. 8)928   4. 5)865

5. 9)5487   6. 7)6885   7. 3)9651   8. 2)1746

9. 40)975   10. 50)887   11. 21)688   12. 53)847

13. 55)2530   14. 98)2352   15. 78)9057   16. 64)8444

17. 9)4536   18. 5)3515   19. 6)3302   20. 9)3247

21. 38)34,200   22. 61)18,300

23. 112)2807   24. 109)2620

25. 325)2275   26. 468)4212

27. 218)40,459   28. 326)50,764

Answers:
1. __
2. __
3. __
4. __
5. __
6. __
7. __
8. __
9. __
10. __
11. __
12. __
13. __
14. __
15. __
16. __
17. __
18. __
19. __
20. __
21. __
22. __
23. __
24. __
25. __
26. __
27. __
28. __

24

WHOLE NUMBERS AND FRACTIONS

ANSWERS

:: Solve.

29. How many 24-bottle cases can be filled by 2077 bottles? How many bottles will be left over?

29. 86, 13

30. How many 12-jar cases can be filled by 581 jars? How many jars will be left over?

30. 48, 5

31. There are 4 servings in a pound of pork chops. How many pounds of pork chops would a catering service need for 3452 servings?

31. 863

32. There are 3 servings in a pound of rump roast. How many pounds of rump roast would a hotel need for 2874 servings?

32. 958

33. A Volkswagon Beetle can be expected to travel 792 miles of highway driving on 24 gallons of gasoline. What is the average number of miles per gallon?

33. 33

34. A Renault can be expected to travel 504 miles of city driving on 24 gallons of gasoline. What is the average number of miles per gallon?

34. 21

35. A consumer is to pay off a $3744 loan in 24 equal payments. How much is each payment?

35. 156

36. A consumer is to pay off a $7668 loan in 36 equal payments. How much is each payment?

36. 213

37. A real estate agent sells 38 homes one year. Their total value is $1,805,000. What is the average selling price of each home?

37. $47,500

38. An insurance agent sells $705,600 worth of ordinary life insurance one year. There were 56 policies in all. What was the average value of each policy?

38. $12,600

39. There are 220,522,442 people in the United States. The area of the United States is 3,615,122 square miles. How many people are there per square mile?

39. 61

40. A brokerage firm sells 298 shares of a stock for $79,566. What is the value of each share?

40. 267

Divide.

41. $4516\overline{)35{,}658{,}336}$

42. Use your calculator to do the first four calculations. Look for a pattern and use it to find the last calculation without the calculator.

$10{,}101 \div 3$
$20{,}202 \div 6$
$30{,}303 \div 9$
$40{,}404 \div 12$
$50{,}505 \div 15$

41.

42.

1.5 FRACTIONS AND MIXED NUMERALS

● FRACTIONS

The study of arithmetic begins with the whole numbers

0, 1, 2, 3, 4, 5, 6, 7, 8, 9, 10, 11,   and so on.

The need soon arises for halves, thirds, fourths, and so on. These numbers are called *fractions*. The following numbers are fractions:

$$\frac{1}{2}, \frac{3}{4}, \frac{8}{5}, \frac{11}{23}.$$

This way of writing numbers names is called *fractional notation*. The top number is called the *numerator* and the bottom number is called the *denominator*.

Example 1 Identify the numerator and denominator.

Solution

$\frac{7}{8}$ ⟵ Numerator
⟵ Denominator

DO EXERCISES 1–3.

Example 2 What part is shaded?

Solution

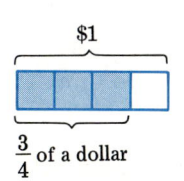

$\frac{3}{4}$ of a dollar

The object is divided into 4 parts of the same size, and 3 of them are shaded. This is $3 \cdot \frac{1}{4}$, or $\frac{3}{4}$. Thus, $\frac{3}{4}$ (*three-fourths*) of the object is shaded.

DO EXERCISES 4–8.

We also use fractions to indicate parts of a set in which the individual parts are not equal.

Example 3 In a company four out of every seven people are secretaries. What fraction are secretaries?

Solution

$\frac{4}{7}$ are secretaries.

DO EXERCISE 9.

OBJECTIVES

After finishing Section 1.5, you should be able to:

● Identify the numerator and denominator of a fraction, and write fractional notation for part of an object or part of a set of objects.

●● Simplify fractional notation for whole numbers.

●●● Convert between fractional notation and mixed numerals.

Identify the numerator and denominator.

1. $\frac{1}{6}$ 2. $\frac{5}{7}$ 3. $\frac{22}{3}$

What part is shaded?

4.

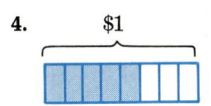

5.

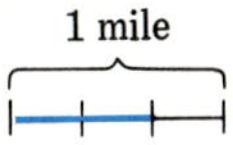

6.

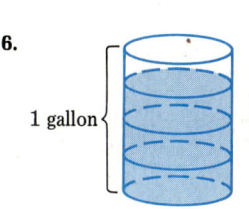

7.

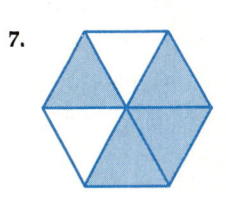

8.

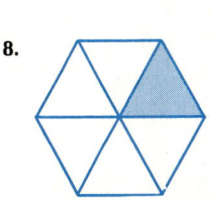

9. You have three pennies, four dimes, seven quarters, and five nickels. What fraction of the total number of coins is pennies? What fraction is dimes?

ANSWERS ON PAGE A–1

Simplify.

10. $\dfrac{6}{6}, \dfrac{3}{3}, \dfrac{100}{100}$

Simplify.

11. $\dfrac{0}{8}, \dfrac{0}{9}, \dfrac{0}{217}$

ANSWERS ON PAGE A–1, A–2

WHOLE NUMBERS AND FRACTIONS

◼◼ FRACTIONAL NOTATION FOR WHOLE NUMBERS

Fractions equal to 1 are shown below.

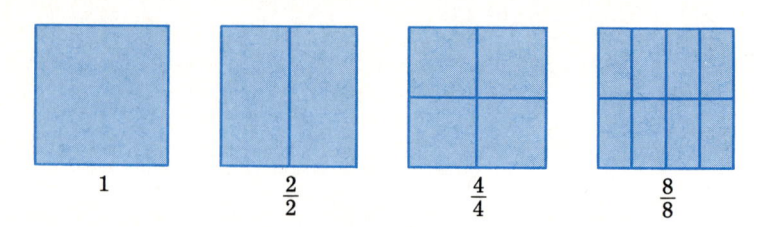

$1 \qquad \dfrac{2}{2} \qquad \dfrac{4}{4} \qquad \dfrac{8}{8}$

For any nonzero number n,

$$\dfrac{n}{n} = 1.$$

Example 4 Simplify: $\dfrac{7}{7}, \dfrac{8}{8},$ and $\dfrac{36}{36}.$

Solution

$\dfrac{7}{7} = 1, \qquad \dfrac{8}{8} = 1, \qquad \dfrac{36}{36} = 1$

A fraction $\dfrac{a}{b}$ also means division $a \div b.$ Thus, $\dfrac{n}{n} = 1$ because $n \div n = 1.$

DO EXERCISE 10.

Consider $\dfrac{0}{3}.$ This is 0 since $0 \div 3 = 0.$

For any nonzero number n,

$$\dfrac{0}{n} = 0.$$

Example 5 Simplify: $\dfrac{0}{4}, \dfrac{0}{7},$ and $\dfrac{0}{58}.$

Solution

$\dfrac{0}{4} = 0, \qquad \dfrac{0}{7} = 0, \qquad \dfrac{0}{58} = 0$

DO EXERCISE 11.

Consider $\dfrac{4}{1}.$ This is 4 since $4 \div 1 = 4.$

1.5 FRACTIONS AND MIXED NUMBERS

> For any number n,
> $$\frac{n}{1} = n.$$

Example 6 Simplify: $\frac{5}{1}$, $\frac{9}{1}$, and $\frac{48}{1}$.

Solution

$$\frac{5}{1} = 5, \quad \frac{9}{1} = 9, \quad \frac{48}{1} = 48$$

DO EXERCISE 12.

▪▪▪ MIXED NUMERALS

Below we see a drawing representing the fraction $\frac{11}{4}$.

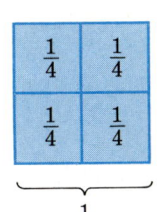

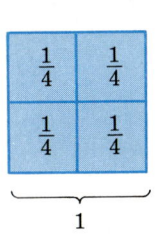

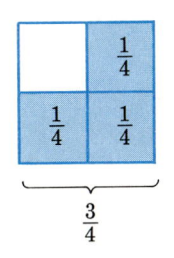

This is also $2 + \frac{3}{4}$. We can write this as a *mixed numeral*.

$$2\frac{3}{4} = 2 + \frac{3}{4}$$

Mixed numeral ↑
Whole number ↗   Fraction between 0 and 1 ↖

Example 7 Write a mixed numeral: $3 + \frac{4}{5}$.

Solution

$$3 + \frac{4}{5} = 3\frac{4}{5}$$

DO EXERCISES 13 AND 14.

Suppose we wanted to convert $\frac{11}{4}$ to a mixed numeral. We see above that $\frac{11}{4} = 2\frac{3}{4}$. Since $\frac{11}{4}$ means $11 \div 4$, we consider the division:

```
    2    ─── Quotient
  ┌────
4 │ 1 1              11      3
    8                ── = 2 ──
    ─                 4      4
    3    ─── Remainder      Keep the denominator.
```

Simplify.

12. $\frac{6}{1}$, $\frac{10}{1}$, $\frac{277}{1}$

Write a mixed numeral.

13. $6 + \frac{7}{8}$

14. $15 + \frac{9}{10}$

ANSWERS ON PAGE A-2

Convert to a mixed numeral.

15. $\dfrac{65}{8}$

16. $\dfrac{19}{4}$

17. $\dfrac{89}{16}$

Convert to fractional notation.

18. $2\dfrac{1}{3}$

19. $3\dfrac{7}{8}$

20. $10\dfrac{14}{15}$

Divide, if possible. If not possible, write "impossible."

21. $\dfrac{8}{4}$ 22. $\dfrac{5}{0}$

23. $12 \div 0$

24. $100 \div 10$

25. $\dfrac{5}{3-3}$

26. $\dfrac{8-8}{4}$

ANSWERS ON PAGE A-2

Example 8 Convert to a mixed numeral: $\dfrac{77}{8}$.

Solution

$$8 \overline{)77} \quad \dfrac{77}{8} = 9\dfrac{5}{8}$$
$$\underline{72}$$
$$5$$

DO EXERCISES 15–17.

Example 9 Convert to fractional notation: $3\dfrac{4}{5}$.

Solution

$$3\dfrac{4}{5} = \dfrac{(3 \times 5) + 4}{5}$$

a) Multiply the whole number and the denominator of the fraction.
b) Add the numerator.
c) Keep the denominator.

$$= \dfrac{15 + 4}{5}$$

$$= \dfrac{19}{5}$$

DO EXERCISES 18–20.

DIVISION BY ZERO

Why can't we divide by 0 or have 0 for a denominator in fractional notation? Suppose the number 4 could be divided by 0. Then if ☐ were the answer,

$4 \div 0 = $ ☐   and this would mean $4 = $ ☐ $\cdot \, 0 = 0.$ False!

Suppose 12 could be divided by 0. If ☐ were the answer,

$12 \div 0 = $ ☐   and this would mean $12 = $ ☐ $\cdot \, 0 = 0.$ False!

Thus $a \div 0$ would be some number ☐ such that $a = 0 \cdot$ ☐ $= 0$. So the only possible number that could be divided by 0 would be 0 itself. But such a division would give us any number we wish, for

$0 \div 0 = 8$ because $0 = 8 \cdot 0$
$0 \div 0 = 3$ because $0 = 3 \cdot 0$ All true!
$0 \div 0 = 7$ because $0 = 7 \cdot 0$

We avoid the preceding difficulties by agreeing to exclude division by 0.

Division by 0 is not defined. (We agree not to divide by 0.)

DO EXERCISES 21–26.

EXERCISE SET 1.5   **29**

NAME _____ CLASS _____

EXERCISE SET 1.5

● Identify the numerator and denominator.

1. $\dfrac{5}{6}$ 2. $\dfrac{2}{9}$ 3. $\dfrac{51}{13}$ 4. $\dfrac{1}{100}$

5. By weight, 2 parts out of 3 of the human body are water. What fraction is water? What fraction is not water?

6. At present, 1 out of 3 food dollars is spent in a restaurant. What fraction is this? By 1987, 1 out of 2 food dollars will be spent in a restaurant. What fraction is this?

7. There are 8760 hours in a year. The average TV set is in operation 2200 of these hours. What fraction of the hours in a year is this?

8. By area, 3 out of every 4 square miles of the earth's surface are water. What fraction is this?

●● Simplify.

9. $\dfrac{10}{10}$ 10. $\dfrac{34}{34}$ 11. $\dfrac{0}{45}$ 12. $\dfrac{0}{97}$

13. $\dfrac{19}{1}$ 14. $\dfrac{24}{1}$ 15. $\dfrac{24}{24}$ 16. $\dfrac{0}{1}$

●●● Write a mixed numeral.

17. $18 + \dfrac{8}{9}$ 18. $24 + \dfrac{2}{3}$ 19. $59 + \dfrac{11}{12}$ 20. $67 + \dfrac{14}{25}$

ANSWERS

1. $\dfrac{5}{6}$ N/D
2. $\dfrac{2}{9}$ N/D
3. $\dfrac{51}{13}$ N/D
4. $\dfrac{1}{100}$ N/D
5. $\dfrac{2}{3}$, $\dfrac{1}{3}$
6. $\dfrac{1}{3}$, $\dfrac{1}{2}$
7. $\dfrac{2200}{8760}$
8. $3/4$
9. 1
10. 1
11. 0
12. 0
13. 19
14. 24
15. 1
16. 0
17. $18\,8/9$
18. $24\,2/3$
19. $59\,11/12$
20. $67\,14/25$

Copyright © 1984, by Addison-Wesley Publishing Company Inc. All rights reserved.

WHOLE NUMBERS AND FRACTIONS

Convert to a mixed numeral.

21. $\dfrac{9}{5}$ 22. $\dfrac{9}{7}$ 23. $\dfrac{19}{8}$ 24. $\dfrac{5}{4}$

25. $\dfrac{47}{10}$ 26. $\dfrac{63}{10}$ 27. $\dfrac{55}{6}$ 28. $\dfrac{62}{9}$

29. $\dfrac{347}{6}$ 30. $\dfrac{225}{8}$ 31. $\dfrac{879}{100}$ 32. $\dfrac{5677}{1000}$

Convert to fractional notation.

33. $1\dfrac{1}{3}$ 34. $2\dfrac{1}{8}$ 35. $7\dfrac{2}{5}$ 36. $5\dfrac{4}{6}$

37. $9\dfrac{3}{10}$ 38. $14\dfrac{7}{10}$ 39. $99\dfrac{44}{100}$ 40. $78\dfrac{999}{1000}$

41. $14\dfrac{8}{9}$ 42. $15\dfrac{6}{7}$ 43. $24\dfrac{13}{15}$ 44. $57\dfrac{11}{16}$

Convert to fractional notation.

45. 🧮 $4567\dfrac{1267}{8910}$ 46. 🧮 $9898\dfrac{2121}{8877}$

Divide, if possible. If not possible, write "impossible."

47. $\dfrac{6}{0}$ 48. $\dfrac{14}{7}$ 49. $\dfrac{0}{7}$ 50. $\dfrac{8}{16-16}$

1.6 MULTIPLYING AND SIMPLIFYING USING FRACTIONAL NOTATION

MULTIPLYING USING FRACTIONAL NOTATION

To multiply using fractional notation.
a) Multiply numerators.
b) Multiply denominators.

Example 1 Multiply: $\dfrac{2}{3} \cdot \dfrac{5}{7}$.

Solution

a) Multiply numerators:

$$\dfrac{2}{3} \cdot \dfrac{5}{7} = \dfrac{2 \cdot 5}{3 \cdot 7} = \dfrac{10}{21}.$$

b) Multiply denominators:

DO EXERCISES 1–3.

● SIMPLIFYING USING FRACTIONAL NOTATION

Note the following:

$$1 = \dfrac{1}{1}, \quad 1 = \dfrac{2}{2}, \quad 1 = \dfrac{5}{5}, \quad 1 = \dfrac{18}{18}, \quad 1 = \dfrac{200}{200}, \quad 1 = \boxed{\dfrac{n}{n}}.$$

When a fraction is multiplied by 1, we get an equal fraction. For example,

$$\dfrac{2}{3} = \dfrac{2}{3} \cdot 1 = \dfrac{2}{3} \cdot \boxed{\dfrac{5}{5}} = \dfrac{2 \cdot 5}{3 \cdot 5} = \dfrac{10}{15}.$$

DO EXERCISE 4.

All of the following are equal, or *equivalent*, to $\dfrac{2}{3}$:

$$\dfrac{2}{3}, \quad \dfrac{4}{6}, \quad \dfrac{6}{9}, \quad \dfrac{10}{15}, \quad \dfrac{12}{18}, \quad \dfrac{16}{24}.$$

We say that $\tfrac{2}{3}$ is *simplest* because the numerator and denominator have no common factor greater than 1. To *simplify*, we remove common factors greater than 1. We accomplish this by doing the reverse of multiplying by 1.

Example 2 Simplify: $\dfrac{12}{18}$.

OBJECTIVES

After finishing Section 1.6, you should be able to:

● Simplify using fractional notation.

●● Multiply using fractional notation or mixed numerals, and simplify.

●●● Solve problems involving multiplication of fractions.

Multiply:

1. $\dfrac{1}{3} \cdot \dfrac{1}{4}$ $\dfrac{1}{12}$

2. $\dfrac{3}{5} \cdot \dfrac{1}{8}$ $\dfrac{3}{40}$

3. $\dfrac{5}{6} \cdot \dfrac{11}{12}$ $\dfrac{55}{72}$

Complete this multiplication.

4. $\dfrac{2}{3} = \dfrac{2}{3} \cdot 1 = \dfrac{2}{3} \cdot \dfrac{6}{6} =$

ANSWERS ON PAGE A–2

Simplify.

5. $\dfrac{10}{15}$ $\dfrac{2}{3}$

Simplify.

6. $\dfrac{15}{24}$ $\dfrac{5}{8}$

7. $\dfrac{18}{24}$ $\dfrac{3}{4}$

Simplify.

8. $\dfrac{4}{8}$ $\dfrac{1}{2}$

9. $\dfrac{6}{24}$ $\dfrac{1}{4}$

Simplify.

10. $\dfrac{63}{7}$ 9

11. $\dfrac{48}{6}$ 8

ANSWERS ON PAGE A–2

WHOLE NUMBERS AND FRACTIONS

Solution

$$\dfrac{12}{18} = \dfrac{2 \cdot 6}{3 \cdot 6}$$ We factor the numerator and denominator. The largest common factor is 6.

$$= \dfrac{2}{3} \cdot \dfrac{6}{6}$$

$$= \dfrac{2}{3} \cdot 1 \qquad \dfrac{6}{6} = 1$$

$$= \dfrac{2}{3}$$

DO EXERCISE 5.

Example 3 Simplify: $\dfrac{16}{20}$.

Solution

$$\dfrac{16}{20} = \dfrac{4 \cdot 4}{5 \cdot 4} = \dfrac{4}{5} \cdot \dfrac{4}{4} = \dfrac{4}{5}$$

DO EXERCISES 6 AND 7.

Example 4 Simplify: $\dfrac{3}{6}$.

Solution

$$\dfrac{3}{6} = \dfrac{1 \cdot 3}{2 \cdot 3}$$ The 3 is written as 1 · 3 to allow us to have the same number of factors in the numerator as in the denominator.

$$= \dfrac{1}{2} \cdot \dfrac{3}{3}$$

$$= \dfrac{1}{2}$$

DO EXERCISES 8 AND 9.

Example 5 Simplify: $\dfrac{54}{6}$.

Solution

$$\dfrac{54}{6} = \dfrac{9 \cdot 6}{1 \cdot 6} = \dfrac{9}{1} \cdot \dfrac{6}{6} = \dfrac{9}{1} = 9$$

You can also think of this as 54 ÷ 6, which is 9.

DO EXERCISES 10 AND 11.

1.6 MULTIPLYING AND SIMPLIFYING USING FRACTIONAL NOTATION

■■ MULTIPLYING AND SIMPLIFYING USING FRACTIONAL NOTATION

After multiplying you can often simplify. This should be done whenever possible.

> **To multiply:**
> a) Convert to fractional notation, if necessary.
> b) Multiply numerators.
> c) Multiply denominators.
> d) Simplify, if possible. When the numerator is larger than the denominator, convert to a mixed number.

Example 6 Multiply and simplify: $\dfrac{2}{3} \cdot \dfrac{5}{8}$.

Solution

$$\dfrac{2}{3} \cdot \dfrac{5}{8} = \dfrac{2 \cdot 5}{3 \cdot 8} = \dfrac{10}{24} = \dfrac{5 \cdot 2}{12 \cdot 2} = \dfrac{5}{12} \cdot \boxed{\dfrac{2}{2}} = \dfrac{5}{12}$$

DO EXERCISE 12.

Example 7 Multiply and simplify: $12 \cdot \dfrac{2}{3}$.

Solution

$$12 \cdot \dfrac{2}{3} = \dfrac{12}{1} \cdot \dfrac{2}{3} = \dfrac{12 \cdot 2}{1 \cdot 3} = \dfrac{24}{3} = 8$$

DO EXERCISE 13.

Example 8 Multiply and simplify: $4\dfrac{1}{5} \cdot 6\dfrac{2}{3}$.

Solution

$$4\dfrac{1}{5} \cdot 6\dfrac{2}{3} = \dfrac{21}{5} \cdot \dfrac{20}{3} = \dfrac{21 \cdot 20}{5 \cdot 3} = \boxed{\dfrac{5 \cdot 3}{5 \cdot 3}} \cdot \dfrac{7 \cdot 4}{1} = 28$$

DO EXERCISE 14.

Example 9 Multiply and simplify: $4\dfrac{1}{3} \cdot 5\dfrac{6}{7}$.

Solution

$$4\dfrac{1}{3} \cdot 5\dfrac{6}{7} = \dfrac{13}{3} \cdot \dfrac{41}{7} = \dfrac{13 \cdot 41}{3 \cdot 7} = \dfrac{533}{21} = 25\dfrac{8}{21}$$

DO EXERCISE 15.

Multiply and simplify.

12. $\dfrac{3}{4} \cdot \dfrac{8}{9}$ $\dfrac{2}{3}$

Multiply and simplify.

13. $15 \cdot \dfrac{4}{5}$ $= 12$

Multiply and simplify.

14. $5\dfrac{1}{3} \cdot 1\dfrac{1}{8}$ $= 6$

Multiply and simplify.

15. $4\dfrac{1}{2} \cdot 5\dfrac{2}{3}$ $\dfrac{17}{3} = \dfrac{51}{2} = 25\dfrac{1}{2}$

ANSWERS ON PAGE A–2

16. How much steak would it take to serve 50 people if each gets $\frac{2}{3}$ lb of steak?

[handwritten: $50 \times \frac{2}{3} = \frac{100}{3} = 33\frac{1}{3}$]

17. A car travels on an interstate highway at 55 mph for $3\frac{1}{2}$ hours. How far does it travel?

[handwritten: $55 \times \frac{7}{2} = \frac{385}{2} = 192\frac{1}{2}$ mi]

ANSWERS ON PAGE A-2

WHOLE NUMBERS AND FRACTIONS

▰▰▰ PROBLEM SOLVING

Example 10 An employee earns $55 for a full work day. How much would the employee earn working $\frac{1}{4}$ of the work day?

Solution

$$\begin{pmatrix} \text{Amount earned} \\ \text{in } \frac{1}{4} \text{ of the day} \end{pmatrix} = \begin{pmatrix} \text{Amount earned} \\ \text{in full day} \end{pmatrix} \text{ times } \begin{pmatrix} \text{Fraction of} \\ \text{a work day} \end{pmatrix}$$

$$= \$55 \quad \cdot \quad \frac{1}{4}$$

Think of the word "of" translating to "times."

We multiply as follows:

$$55 \cdot \frac{1}{4} = \frac{55}{1} \cdot \frac{1}{4} = \frac{55 \cdot 1}{1 \cdot 4} = \frac{55}{4} = 13\frac{3}{4}.$$

The employee would earn $13\frac{3}{4}$ working $\frac{1}{4}$ of the work day.

DO EXERCISE 16.

Example 11 A long-playing record makes $33\frac{1}{3}$ revolutions per minute. It plays 12 minutes. How many revolutions does it make?

Solution

We first draw a picture. It is often helpful in problem solving to draw a picture or at least visualize the situation.

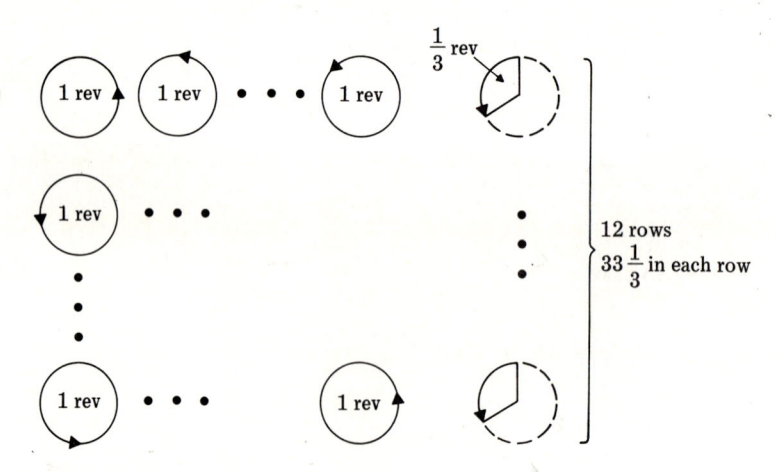

[diagram of circles representing revolutions, arranged in 12 rows with $33\frac{1}{3}$ in each row]

Then we translate and solve as follows:

$$\begin{pmatrix} \text{Revolutions} \\ \text{per minute} \end{pmatrix} \cdot \begin{pmatrix} \text{Number of} \\ \text{minutes played} \end{pmatrix} = \begin{pmatrix} \text{Total number} \\ \text{of revolutions} \end{pmatrix}$$

$$33\frac{1}{3} \quad \cdot \quad 12 \quad = \quad n$$

This tells us what to do. We multiply:

$$33\frac{1}{3} \cdot 12 = \frac{100}{3} \cdot \frac{12}{1} = \frac{1200}{3} = 400.$$

It makes 400 revolutions in 12 minutes.

DO EXERCISE 17.

EXERCISE SET 1.6

● Simplify.

1. $\frac{2}{10}$
2. $\frac{4}{12}$
3. $\frac{9}{12}$
4. $\frac{6}{10}$

5. $\frac{24}{8}$
6. $\frac{25}{5}$
7. $\frac{14}{24}$
8. $\frac{42}{48}$

9. $\frac{6}{16}$
10. $\frac{15}{24}$
11. $\frac{56}{7}$
12. $\frac{125}{25}$

13. $\frac{300}{50}$
14. $\frac{400}{80}$
15. $\frac{125}{425}$
16. $\frac{17}{51}$

●● Multiply and simplify.

17. $\frac{2}{3} \cdot \frac{1}{2}$
18. $\frac{1}{4} \cdot \frac{2}{3}$
19. $\frac{8}{9} \cdot \frac{5}{12}$
20. $\frac{15}{16} \cdot \frac{4}{5}$

21. $18 \cdot \frac{5}{6}$
22. $12 \cdot \frac{3}{4}$
23. $360 \cdot \frac{1}{4}$
24. $120 \cdot \frac{1}{3}$

25. $\frac{3}{5} \cdot 10$
26. $\frac{2}{3} \cdot 24$
27. $3\frac{1}{5} \cdot 3\frac{3}{4}$
28. $4\frac{1}{2} \cdot 2\frac{2}{3}$

29. $3\frac{2}{5} \cdot 1\frac{1}{4}$
30. $1\frac{3}{5} \cdot 3\frac{1}{3}$
31. $6\frac{3}{10} \cdot 5\frac{7}{10}$
32. $8\frac{1}{10} \cdot 2\frac{9}{10}$

33. $28 \cdot 5\frac{1}{4}$
34. $40 \cdot 3\frac{5}{8}$
35. $1\frac{5}{8} \cdot \frac{2}{3}$
36. $6\frac{2}{3} \cdot \frac{1}{4}$

ANSWERS

1. 1/5
2. 1/3
3. 3/4
4. 3/5
5. 3
6. 5
7. 7/12
8. 7/8
9. 3/8
10. 5/8
11. 8
12. 5
13. 6
14. 5
15. 5/17
16. 1/3
17. 1/3
18. 1/6
19. 10/27
20. 3/4
21. 15
22. 9
23. 90
24. 40
25. 6
26. 16
27. 12
28. 12
29. 4 1/4
30. 5 1/3
31. 35 91/100
32. 23 49/100
33. 147
34. 145
35. 1 1/12
36. 1 2/3

36 WHOLE NUMBERS AND FRACTIONS

ANSWERS

Solve.

37. An employee earns $68 for a full work day. How much would the employee earn working $\frac{1}{5}$ of the work day?

37. $\$13^{3}/_{5}$

38. An employee earns $563 one week and donates $\frac{1}{10}$ to charity. How much was donated?

38. $\$56^{3}/_{10}$

39. An investor purchases 100 shares of Chrysler stock at $19\frac{5}{8}$ per share. What was the total amount invested?

39. $\$1962\frac{1}{2}$

40. An investor purchases 100 shares of IBM stock at $240\frac{3}{8}$ per share. What was the total amount invested?

40. $\$24,037\frac{1}{2}$

41. On a map 1 inch represents 240 miles. How much does $\frac{2}{5}$ inch represent?

42. On a map 1 inch represents 180 miles. How much does $\frac{3}{4}$ inch represent?

43. A car travels at a speed of 55 mph for $4\frac{1}{2}$ hours. How far does it go?

41. 96 mi

44. In shankless ham there are about $4\frac{1}{2}$ servings per pound. How many servings are there in 20 pounds?

Below is a recipe for rattlesnake steaks.

42. 135

Rattlesnake Steaks

Ingredients:
- 5 lb rattlesnake meat
- $1\frac{1}{4}$ cups flour
- $\frac{2}{3}$ teaspoon pepper
- $2\frac{1}{2}$ cups vinegar
- 6 cups cooking oil

43. $247\frac{1}{2}$ mi

Decapitate the snake with an axe about six inches behind the head. Remove the skin. Cut the meat into one-inch thick steaks. Soak for ten minutes in vinegar. Remove and sprinkle with salt and pepper, and flour. Fry in deep fat. Delicious!

44. 90

45. $2\frac{1}{2}$ $1\frac{1}{4}$
    $5/8$
45. $1/3$ 3

46. 15
    $3\frac{3}{4}$ $7\frac{1}{2}$
46. 2   18

45. What are the ingredients for $\frac{1}{2}$ the recipe?

46. What are the ingredients for 3 recipes?

1.7 DIVISION USING FRACTIONAL NOTATION

◼ RECIPROCALS

Consider the following products:

$$\frac{4}{5} \cdot \frac{5}{4} = \frac{4 \cdot 5}{5 \cdot 4} = \frac{20}{20} = 1; \qquad 6 \cdot \frac{1}{6} = \frac{6}{1} \cdot \frac{1}{6} = \frac{6 \cdot 1}{1 \cdot 6} = \frac{6}{6} = 1.$$

Two numbers whose product is 1 are called *reciprocals*. Thus, $\frac{4}{5}$ and $\frac{5}{4}$ are reciprocals, and 6 and $\frac{1}{6}$ are reciprocals.

> To find the reciprocal of a number in fractional notation, interchange the numerator and denominator.

Example 1 Find the reciprocal of $\frac{7}{8}$.

Solution

$$\frac{7}{8} \rightleftarrows \frac{8}{7}$$

The reciprocal of $\frac{7}{8}$ is $\frac{8}{7}$.

DO EXERCISES 1 AND 2.

Example 2 Find the reciprocal of $\frac{1}{3}$.

Solution

The reciprocal of $\frac{1}{3}$ is $\frac{3}{1}$, or 3.

DO EXERCISES 3 AND 4.

Example 3 Find the reciprocal of 12.

Solution We first express 12 as $\frac{12}{1}$.

$$\frac{12}{1} \rightleftarrows \frac{1}{12}$$

The reciprocal of 12 is $\frac{1}{12}$.

DO EXERCISES 5 AND 6.

OBJECTIVES

After finishing Section 1.7, you should be able to:

◼ Find the reciprocal of a number.

◼◼ Divide using fractional notation or mixed numerals, and simplify.

◼◼◼ Solve problems involving division of fractions.

Find the reciprocal.

1. $\frac{3}{4}$ $\frac{4}{3}$

2. $\frac{6}{5}$ $\frac{5}{6}$

Find the reciprocal.

3. $\frac{1}{6}$ 6

4. $\frac{1}{24}$ 24

Find the reciprocal.

5. 18 $\frac{1}{18}$

6. 54 $\frac{1}{54}$

ANSWERS ON PAGE A–2

37

WHOLE NUMBERS AND FRACTIONS

■ ■ DIVISION

To divide:
a) Convert to fractional notation, if necessary.
b) Multiply the dividend by the reciprocal of the divisor.
c) Simplify, if possible. When the numerator is larger than the denominator, convert to a mixed numeral.

Example 4 Divide: $\dfrac{2}{3} \div \dfrac{4}{5}$.

Solution

$$\dfrac{2}{3} \div \dfrac{4}{5} = \dfrac{2}{3} \cdot \dfrac{5}{4} \qquad \text{The reciprocal of } \dfrac{4}{5} \text{ is } \dfrac{5}{4}.$$

$$= \dfrac{2 \cdot 5}{3 \cdot 4}$$

$$= \dfrac{10}{12} = \dfrac{5 \cdot 2}{6 \cdot 2} = \dfrac{5}{6} \cdot \boxed{\dfrac{2}{2}} = \dfrac{5}{6} \qquad \text{Check: } \dfrac{5}{6} \cdot \dfrac{4}{5} = \dfrac{5 \cdot 4}{6 \cdot 5} = \dfrac{4}{6} = \dfrac{2}{3}$$

DO EXERCISE 7.

Example 5 Divide: $\dfrac{3}{5} \div \dfrac{1}{8}$.

Solution

$$\dfrac{3}{5} \div \dfrac{1}{8} = \dfrac{3}{5} \cdot 8 \qquad \text{The reciprocal of } \dfrac{1}{8} \text{ is } 8.$$

$$= \dfrac{3}{5} \cdot \dfrac{8}{1}$$

$$= \dfrac{3 \cdot 8}{5 \cdot 1} = \dfrac{24}{5} = 4\dfrac{4}{5}$$

DO EXERCISE 8.

Example 6 Divide: $\dfrac{4}{5} \div 16$.

Solution

$$\dfrac{4}{5} \div 16 = \dfrac{4}{5} \cdot \dfrac{1}{16} \qquad \text{The reciprocal of 16 is } \dfrac{1}{16}.$$

$$= \dfrac{4 \cdot 1}{5 \cdot 16} = \dfrac{4}{80} = \dfrac{1 \cdot 4}{20 \cdot 4} = \dfrac{1}{20} \cdot \boxed{\dfrac{4}{4}} = \dfrac{1}{20}$$

DO EXERCISE 9.

1.7 DIVISION USING FRACTIONAL NOTATION

Example 7 Divide: $84 \div 5\frac{1}{4}$.

Solution

$$84 \div 5\frac{1}{4} = 84 \div \frac{21}{4} = 84 \cdot \frac{4}{21} = \frac{84}{1} \cdot \frac{4}{21} = \frac{84 \cdot 4}{21} = \frac{336}{21} = 16$$

DO EXERCISE 10.

Example 8 Divide: $8\frac{2}{3} \div 5\frac{7}{9}$.

Solution

$$8\frac{2}{3} \div 5\frac{7}{9} = \frac{26}{3} \div \frac{52}{9}$$

$$= \frac{26}{3} \cdot \frac{9}{52}$$

$$= \frac{26 \cdot 9}{3 \cdot 52}$$

$$= \frac{13 \cdot 3 \cdot 2}{13 \cdot 3 \cdot 2} \cdot \frac{3}{2}$$

$$= \frac{3}{2}$$

$$= 1\frac{1}{2}$$

DO EXERCISE 11.

▰▰▰ PROBLEM SOLVING

Example 9 A car travels 406 miles on $20\frac{3}{10}$ gallons of gasoline. How many miles per gallon does it get?

Solution

$$\text{Miles per gallon} = \text{Total miles driven} \div \text{Gallons of gasoline used} \quad \text{"per" means "for each"}$$

$$= 406 \div 20\frac{3}{10}$$

We divide as follows:

$$406 \div 20\frac{3}{10} = 406 \div \frac{203}{10} = 406 \cdot \frac{10}{203} = \frac{406}{1} \cdot \frac{10}{203} = \frac{4060}{203} = 20.$$

The car gets 20 miles per gallon.

DO EXERCISE 12.

Divide.

10. $56 \div 4\frac{2}{3}$

Divide.

11. $2\frac{1}{3} \div 1\frac{3}{4}$

12. How many jars, each containing $\frac{3}{4}$ lb, can be filled with 600 lb of peanuts?

ANSWERS ON PAGE A-2

13. A car travels 302 miles on $15\frac{1}{10}$ gallons of gas. How many miles per gallon did it get?

$302 \times \frac{10}{151} = 20$

Example 10 A long-playing record makes $33\frac{1}{3}$ revolutions per minute. It makes 500 revolutions. How long does it play?

Solution We first draw a picture.

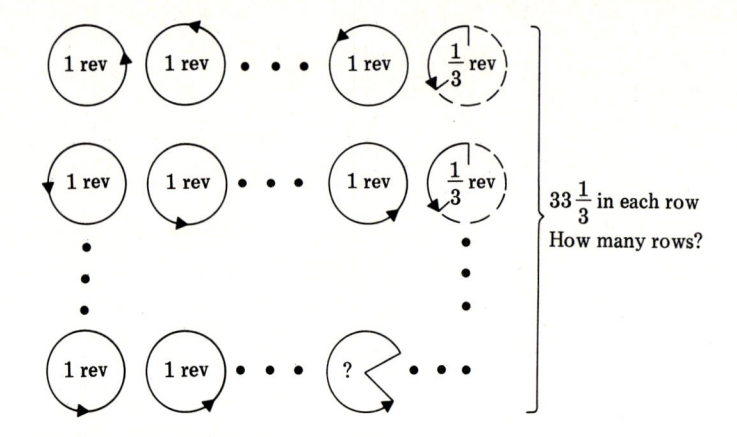

$33\frac{1}{3}$ in each row
How many rows?

The last row may be incomplete.

The division that corresponds to the situation is

$$500 \div 33\frac{1}{3} = t.$$

This tells us what to do. We divide:

$$500 \div 33\frac{1}{3} = \frac{500}{1} \div \frac{100}{3} = \frac{500}{1} \cdot \frac{3}{100} = \frac{1500}{100} = 15.$$

It plays 15 minutes.

DO EXERCISE 13.

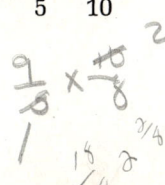

EXERCISE SET 1.7

Find the reciprocal.

1. $\dfrac{5}{6}$
2. $\dfrac{9}{10}$
3. 6
4. 5

5. $\dfrac{1}{18}$
6. $\dfrac{1}{20}$
7. $\dfrac{13}{12}$
8. $\dfrac{22}{17}$

Divide. Simplify, if possible.

9. $\dfrac{3}{5} \div \dfrac{3}{4}$
10. $\dfrac{6}{7} \div \dfrac{3}{5}$
11. $\dfrac{9}{8} \div \dfrac{1}{3}$
12. $\dfrac{10}{9} \div \dfrac{1}{2}$

13. $\dfrac{12}{7} \div 4$
14. $\dfrac{8}{7} \div 2$
15. $7 \div \dfrac{1}{5}$
16. $10 \div \dfrac{1}{4}$

17. $\dfrac{7}{8} \div \dfrac{7}{8}$
18. $\dfrac{5}{3} \div \dfrac{5}{3}$
19. $\dfrac{8}{15} \div \dfrac{4}{5}$
20. $\dfrac{6}{13} \div \dfrac{3}{26}$

21. $\dfrac{9}{5} \div \dfrac{8}{10}$
22. $\dfrac{5}{12} \div \dfrac{25}{36}$
23. $32 \div 3\dfrac{1}{5}$
24. $45 \div 2\dfrac{1}{4}$

ANSWERS

1. 6/5
2. 10/9
3. 1/6
4. 1/5
5. 18
6. 20
7. 12/13
8. 17/22
9. 4/5
10. 1 3/7
11. 3 3/8
12. 2 2/9
13. 3/7
14. 4/7
15. 35
16. 40
17. 1
18. 1
19. 2/3
20. 4
21. 2 1/4
22. 3/5
23. 10
24. 20

42   WHOLE NUMBERS AND FRACTIONS

ANSWERS				
25. $\frac{1}{6}$	25. $4\frac{1}{3} \div 26$	26. $5\frac{1}{2} \div 22$	27. $2\frac{1}{2} \div 1\frac{1}{4}$	28. $3\frac{1}{2} \div 2\frac{2}{3}$
26. $\frac{1}{4}$				
27. 2	29. $4\frac{3}{8} \div 2\frac{5}{6}$	30. $6\frac{7}{8} \div 1\frac{2}{3}$	31. $7\frac{3}{10} \div 5\frac{9}{10}$	32. $6\frac{1}{10} \div 2\frac{1}{10}$
28. $1\,5/16$				
29. $1\,37/68$	33. $16\frac{1}{3} \div 70$	34. $20\frac{1}{5} \div 10$	35. $11\frac{1}{4} \div 2\frac{1}{2}$	36. $10\frac{1}{3} \div 3\frac{2}{5}$
30. $4\frac{1}{8}$				
31. $1\,14/59$	●●● Solve.			
32. $2\,19/21$	37. A car travels 561 miles on $18\frac{7}{10}$ gallons of gasoline. How many miles per gallon does it get?			
33. $7/30$				
34. $2\,1/50$	38. How many boxes of powder, each containing $\frac{2}{3}$ oz, can be filled with 150 oz of powder?			
35. $4\frac{1}{2}$				
36. $3\,2/51$	39. Sirloin steak contains $2\frac{1}{2}$ servings per pound. How many pounds does a catering service need for 1000 servings?			
37. 30				
38. 225	40. Round steak contains $3\frac{1}{2}$ servings per pound. How many pounds does a hotel need for 1050 servings?			
39. 400				
40. 300	41. How many pieces of wire, each $2\frac{3}{5}$ ft, can be cut from 65 ft of wire?			
41. 25				
42. 18	42. How many pieces of rope, each $8\frac{1}{3}$ ft, can be cut from 150 ft of rope?			
43. $85\frac{1}{3}$	43. How many 12-oz soda cans can be filled with 1024 oz of soda?			
44. $95\frac{1}{8}$	44. How many 16-oz soda cans can be filled with 1522 oz of soda?			
45. 27 hrs	45. After working 18 hours an employee had completed $\frac{2}{3}$ of a job. How many hours would it take to do the entire job?			
46. 16 hrs	46. After working 12 hours an employee had completed $\frac{3}{4}$ of a job. How many hours would it take to do the entire job?			

1.8 LEAST COMMON MULTIPLES AND DENOMINATORS

■ LEAST COMMON MULTIPLES

The number 12 is a *multiple* of 4 because it can be written as a product of 4 and another nonzero *number*:

$$12 = 4 \cdot 3.$$

The number 72 is a *common multiple* of 12 and 18 because it is a multiple of both 12 and 18. The number 36 is the *least common multiple*, or LCM, of 12 and 18 because it is the smallest nonzero number that is a multiple of both.

> The *least common multiple*, or LCM, of two nonzero whole numbers is the smallest number that is a multiple of both.

DO EXERCISE 1.

The following is an efficient method for finding LCMs.

> To find the LCM of a set of numbers:
> a) Check to see if the largest number is a multiple of the other numbers. If so, it is the LCM.
> b) If (a) is not so, compute multiples of the larger number until a number is obtained that is a multiple of the others. That number will be the LCM.

Example 1 Find the LCM: 8 and 10.

Solution

a) Is 10 a multiple of 8? No, so 10 is not the LCM.

b) Compute multiples of 10 until a multiple of 8 is obtained:

$2 \cdot 10 = 20,$ not a multiple of 8;
$3 \cdot 10 = 30,$ not a multiple of 8;
$4 \cdot 10 = 40,$ 40 is a multiple of 8.

The LCM is 40.

DO EXERCISE 2.

■■ LEAST COMMON DENOMINATORS

> The *least common denominator*, LCD, is the LCM of the denominators.

Example 2 Find the LCD: $\frac{3}{5}$ and $\frac{1}{8}$.

OBJECTIVES

After finishing Section 1.8, you should be able to:

■ Find the least common multiple of a set of numbers.

■■ Find the least common denominator of a set of fractions.

1. Consider 12 and 18.

   a) Make a list of multiples of 12 by multiplying by 1, 2, 3, and so on.

   $1 \times 12 = 12 \qquad 6 \times 12 = 72$
   $2 \times 12 = 24$
   $3 \times 12 = 36$
   $4 \times 12 = 48$
   $5 \times 12 = 60$

   b) Make a list of multiples of 18 by multiplying by 1, 2, 3, and so on.

   $1 \times 18 = 18$
   $2 \times 18 = 36$
   $3 \times 18 = 54$
   $4 \times 18 = 72$
   $5 \times 18 = 90$

   c) Make a list of those numbers common to both lists.

   36

   d) What is the smallest number in (c)? It is the LCM.

   36

2. Find the LCM: 12 and 15. Use the method of Example 1.

   $2 \cdot 2 \cdot 3$
   $3 \cdot 5$
   $\overline{2 \cdot 2 \cdot 3 \cdot 5} = 60$

ANSWERS ON PAGE A–2

44

Find the LCD.

3. $\dfrac{5}{6}$ and $\dfrac{4}{7}$

WHOLE NUMBERS AND FRACTIONS

Solution The denominators are 5 and 8.

a) Is 8 a multiple of 5? No, so 8 is not the LCM.

b) Compute multiples of 8 until a multiple of 5 is obtained:

$2 \cdot 8 = 16$, not a multiple of 5;
$3 \cdot 8 = 24$, not a multiple of 5;
$4 \cdot 8 = 32$, not a multiple of 5;
$5 \cdot 8 = 40$, 40 is a multiple of 5.

The LCD is 40.

> When two numbers have no common factor greater than 1, their LCM is the product of the numbers.

This is the case in Example 2.

DO EXERCISE 3.

Example 3 Find the LCD: $\dfrac{1}{10}, \dfrac{3}{100}$, and $\dfrac{77}{1000}$.

Solution The denominators are 10, 100, and 1000.

a) Is 1000 a multiple of 10 and a multiple of 100? Yes, so it is the LCD. The LCD is 1000.

DO EXERCISE 4.

Find the LCD.

4. $\dfrac{1}{3}, \dfrac{4}{5}$, and $\dfrac{11}{15}$

ANSWERS ON PAGE A–2

EXERCISE SET 1.8

• Find the LCM.

1. 10 and 15
2. 6 and 8
3. 5 and 10
4. 20 and 40

5. 7 and 9
6. 4 and 11
7. 3 and 15
8. 6 and 18

9. 18 and 24
10. 12 and 16
11. 35 and 45
12. 24 and 36

•• Find the LCD.

13. $\dfrac{2}{3}$ and $\dfrac{5}{12}$
14. $\dfrac{4}{5}$ and $\dfrac{7}{10}$
15. $\dfrac{3}{4}$ and $\dfrac{5}{6}$
16. $\dfrac{5}{6}$ and $\dfrac{7}{9}$

17. $\dfrac{9}{10}$ and $\dfrac{34}{100}$
18. $\dfrac{23}{10}$ and $\dfrac{71}{100}$
19. $\dfrac{3}{10}$ and $\dfrac{11}{20}$
20. $\dfrac{1}{10}$ and $\dfrac{7}{50}$

ANSWERS

1. 30
2. 24
3. 10
4. 40
5. 63
6. 44
7. 15
8. 18
9. 72
10. 48
11. 315
12. 72
13. 12
14. 10
15. 12
16. 18
17. 100
18. 100
19. 20
20. 50

46 WHOLE NUMBERS AND FRACTIONS

ANSWERS

21. 48
22. 60
23. 24
24. 30
25. 16
26. 20
27. 24
28. 36
29. 8
30. 20
31. 40
32. 30
33. ~~33.~~
34. ~~34.~~
35. ~~35.~~
36. ~~36.~~

21. $\dfrac{3}{16}$ and $\dfrac{1}{12}$
22. $\dfrac{5}{12}$ and $\dfrac{2}{15}$
23. $\dfrac{1}{8}$ and $\dfrac{2}{3}$
24. $\dfrac{1}{5}$ and $\dfrac{1}{6}$

25. $\dfrac{3}{8}$ and $\dfrac{7}{16}$
26. $\dfrac{3}{4}$ and $\dfrac{1}{20}$
27. $\dfrac{1}{8}$ and $\dfrac{7}{12}$
28. $\dfrac{5}{12}$ and $\dfrac{7}{9}$

29. $\dfrac{1}{2}, \dfrac{3}{4},$ and $\dfrac{7}{8}$
30. $\dfrac{3}{4}, \dfrac{2}{5},$ and $\dfrac{1}{20}$
31. $\dfrac{3}{8}, \dfrac{1}{4},$ and $\dfrac{7}{10}$
32. $\dfrac{2}{5}, \dfrac{3}{10},$ and $\dfrac{1}{15}$

Find the LCM. Use your calculator to find successive multiples.

33. 1260 and 216
34. 150 and 625
35. 64 and 240
36. 96 and 840

1.9 ADDITION USING FRACTIONAL NOTATION

● ADDING

To add, using fractional notation, when there is a common denominator (the same denominator):

a) Add the numerators.
b) Put the sum over the common denominator.

Example 1 Add: $\frac{3}{5} + \frac{1}{5}$.

Solution

a) Add the numerators:

$$\frac{3}{5} + \frac{1}{5} = \frac{3+1}{5} = \frac{4}{5}.$$

b) Put the sum over the common denominator.

DO EXERCISE 1.

Example 2 Add and simplify: $\frac{3}{16} + \frac{5}{16}$.

Solution

$$\frac{3}{16} + \frac{5}{16} = \frac{3+5}{16} = \frac{8}{16} = \frac{1}{2}$$

DO EXERCISE 2.

With mixed numerals, we add the fractions first and then the whole numbers.

Example 3 Add and simplify: $9\frac{5}{8} + 14\frac{7}{8}$.

Solution

$$\begin{array}{r} 9\ \frac{5}{8} \\ +\ 14\ \frac{7}{8} \\ \hline 23\ \frac{12}{8} \end{array} = 23\frac{3}{2} = 23 + \frac{3}{2} = 23 + 1\frac{1}{2} = 24\frac{1}{2}$$

— Add the fractions.
— Add the whole numbers.

DO EXERCISE 3.

OBJECTIVES

After finishing Section 1.9, you should be able to:

● Add using fractional notation or mixed numerals, and simplify.

●● Solve problems involving addition of fractions.

Add.

1. $\frac{2}{8} + \frac{3}{8}$ = $\frac{5}{8}$

Add and simplify.

2. $\frac{3}{12} + \frac{5}{12}$ $\frac{8}{12} = \frac{2}{3}$

Add and simplify.

3. $18\frac{3}{6} + 7\frac{5}{6}$

$25\frac{8}{6} = 26\frac{2}{6} = 26\frac{1}{3}$

ANSWERS ON PAGE A–2

48

WHOLE NUMBERS AND FRACTIONS

Add and simplify.

4. $\dfrac{5}{9} + \dfrac{11}{18}$

[handwritten: $\dfrac{10}{18} + \dfrac{11}{18} = \dfrac{21}{18} = 1\dfrac{3}{18} = 1\dfrac{1}{6}$]

[handwritten: $\dfrac{5}{9} \times \dfrac{2}{2} = \dfrac{10}{18}$]

To add, using fractional notation when denominators are different:

a) Determine the LCD.
b) Multiply by 1 so that each fraction has the LCD.
c) Add as with common denominators.

Example 4 Add and simplify: $\dfrac{1}{3} + \dfrac{5}{6}.$

Solution The LCD is 6, since 6 is a multiple of 3.

$$\dfrac{1}{3} + \dfrac{5}{6} = \dfrac{1}{3} \cdot \dfrac{2}{2} + \dfrac{5}{6}$$

Think: 3 × ? = 6. The answer is 2 so we multiply by $\dfrac{2}{2}$ to get a denominator of 6.

$$= \dfrac{2}{6} + \dfrac{5}{6}$$

$$= \dfrac{7}{6} = 1\dfrac{1}{6}$$

DO EXERCISE 4.

Example 5 Add and simplify: $\dfrac{2}{5} + \dfrac{3}{8}.$

Solution The LCD is 40.

$$\dfrac{2}{5} + \dfrac{3}{8} = \dfrac{2}{5} \cdot \dfrac{8}{8} + \dfrac{3}{8} \cdot \dfrac{5}{5}$$

Think: 5 × ? = 40. The answer is 8, so we multiply by $\dfrac{8}{8}$.

Think: 8 × ? = 40. The answer is 5, so we multiply by $\dfrac{5}{5}$.

$$= \dfrac{16}{40} + \dfrac{15}{40} = \dfrac{31}{40}$$

DO EXERCISE 5.

Add and simplify.

5. $\dfrac{1}{7} + \dfrac{2}{3}$

[handwritten: $\dfrac{3}{21} + \dfrac{14}{21} = \dfrac{17}{21}$]

ANSWERS ON PAGE A–2

1.9 ADDITION USING FRACTIONAL NOTATION

Example 6 Add and simplify: $\frac{3}{4} + \frac{5}{6}$.

(handwritten: $\frac{9}{12} + \frac{10}{12} = \frac{19}{12} = 1\frac{7}{12}$)

Solution The LCD is 12.

$\frac{3}{4} + \frac{5}{6} = \frac{3}{4} \cdot \boxed{\frac{3}{3}} + \frac{5}{6} \cdot \boxed{\frac{2}{2}}$

Think: $4 \times ? = 12$. The answer is 3, so we multiply by $\frac{3}{3}$.

Think: $6 \times ? = 12$. The answer is 2, so we multiply by $\frac{2}{2}$.

$= \frac{9}{12} + \frac{10}{12} = \frac{19}{12} = 1\frac{7}{12}$

DO EXERCISE 6.

Example 7 Add and simplify: $9\frac{3}{5} + 2\frac{7}{10}$.

(handwritten: $\frac{6}{10} + \frac{7}{10} = 1\frac{3}{10}$)

Solution The LCD is 10.

$9\frac{3}{5} = 9 + \frac{3}{5} = 9 + \boxed{\frac{3}{5} \cdot \frac{2}{2}} = 9 + \frac{6}{10}$

$+2\frac{7}{10} = 2 + \frac{7}{10} = 2 + \frac{7}{10} \qquad = 2 + \frac{7}{10}$

$\qquad\qquad\qquad\qquad\qquad\qquad\qquad\qquad 11 + \frac{13}{10} = 11 + 1\frac{3}{10} = 12\frac{3}{10}$

DO EXERCISE 7.

Example 8 Add and simplify: $11\frac{5}{6} + 4\frac{7}{8}$.

Solution The LCD is 24.

$11\frac{5}{6} = 11 + \frac{5}{6} = 11 + \boxed{\frac{5}{6} \cdot \frac{4}{4}} = 11 + \frac{20}{24}$

$+ 4\frac{7}{8} = 4 + \frac{7}{8} = 4 + \boxed{\frac{7}{8} \cdot \frac{3}{3}} = 4 + \frac{21}{24}$

$\qquad\qquad\qquad\qquad\qquad\qquad\qquad\qquad 15 + \frac{41}{24} = 15 + 1\frac{17}{24} = 16\frac{17}{24}$

DO EXERCISE 8.

Add and simplify.

6. $\frac{5}{6} + \frac{1}{8}$

(handwritten: $\frac{20}{24} + \frac{3}{24} = \frac{23}{24}$)

Add and simplify.

7. $15\frac{3}{4} + 6\frac{7}{8}$

*(handwritten: $\frac{3}{4} + \frac{7}{8} = \frac{6}{8} + \frac{7}{8} = \frac{13}{8} = 1\frac{5}{8}$
$+ 21 = 22\frac{5}{8}$)*

Add and simplify.

8. $10\frac{1}{8} + 10\frac{7}{12}$

*(handwritten: $\frac{3}{24} + \frac{14}{24} = \frac{17}{24}$
$20\frac{17}{24}$)*

ANSWERS ON PAGE A–2

WHOLE NUMBERS AND FRACTIONS

9. On a recent day the stock of Delta Airlines opened at 45\frac{1}{4}$ and gained 2\frac{7}{8}$. What was the closing price?

10. A fabric store sold two pieces of material $6\frac{1}{4}$ yd and $10\frac{5}{6}$ yd long. What was the total length of the material?

SOLVING PROBLEMS

Example 9 On a recent day the stock of IBM opened at 69\frac{7}{8}$ per share and gained 1\frac{3}{4}$. What was the closing price?

Solution

$$\text{Closing price} = \text{Value at opening} + \text{Amount of gain}$$

$$= \$69\frac{7}{8} + \$1\frac{3}{4}$$

The LCD is 8. We add as follows:

$$69\frac{7}{8} = 69 + \frac{7}{8} \qquad = 69 + \frac{7}{8}$$

$$+\ 1\frac{3}{4} = 1 + \frac{3}{4} \cdot \frac{2}{2} = 1 + \frac{6}{8}$$

$$70 + \frac{13}{8} = 70 + 1\frac{5}{8} = 71\frac{5}{8}$$

The closing price was $71\frac{5}{8}$.

DO EXERCISE 9.

Example 10 On two business days a salesperson drove $144\frac{9}{10}$ miles and $87\frac{1}{4}$ miles. What was the total distance driven?

Solution We translate.

$$\begin{pmatrix}\text{Distance driven}\\\text{first day}\end{pmatrix} + \begin{pmatrix}\text{Distance driven}\\\text{second day}\end{pmatrix} = \begin{pmatrix}\text{Total distance}\\\text{driven}\end{pmatrix}$$

$$144\frac{9}{10} \qquad + \qquad 87\frac{1}{4} \qquad = \qquad d$$

The sentence tells us what to do. We add.

The LCM is 20.

$$144\frac{9}{10} = 144\ \frac{9}{10} \cdot \frac{2}{2} = 144\frac{18}{20}$$

$$+\ 87\frac{1}{4} = +\ 87\ \frac{1}{4} \cdot \frac{5}{5} = +\ 87\frac{5}{20}$$

$$231\frac{23}{20} = 232\frac{3}{20}$$

The total distance driven was $232\frac{3}{20}$ miles.

DO EXERCISE 10.

EXERCISE SET 1.9

● Add and simplify.

1. $\dfrac{3}{12} + \dfrac{7}{12}$

2. $\dfrac{5}{10} + \dfrac{7}{10}$

3. $\dfrac{2}{3} + \dfrac{1}{9}$

4. $\dfrac{1}{2} + \dfrac{5}{6}$

5. $\dfrac{1}{6} + \dfrac{1}{9}$

6. $\dfrac{1}{12} + \dfrac{1}{8}$

7. $\dfrac{4}{5} + \dfrac{7}{10}$

8. $\dfrac{1}{18} + \dfrac{2}{3}$

9. $\dfrac{3}{8} + \dfrac{5}{6}$

10. $\dfrac{2}{9} + \dfrac{7}{12}$

11. $\dfrac{3}{10} + \dfrac{5}{12}$

12. $\dfrac{11}{16} + \dfrac{9}{10}$

13. $\dfrac{3}{4} + \dfrac{2}{5}$

14. $\dfrac{1}{8} + \dfrac{2}{3}$

15. $\dfrac{7}{10} + \dfrac{31}{100}$

16. $\dfrac{9}{10} + \dfrac{7}{100}$

17. $4\dfrac{1}{6} + 3\dfrac{5}{6}$

18. $6\dfrac{1}{8} + 2\dfrac{7}{8}$

19. $8\dfrac{2}{3} + 5\dfrac{2}{3}$

20. $6\dfrac{3}{10} + 8\dfrac{9}{10}$

21. $2\dfrac{3}{4} + 2\dfrac{2}{5}$

22. $1\dfrac{2}{3} + 5\dfrac{3}{4}$

23. $3\dfrac{1}{2} + 5\dfrac{1}{6}$

24. $4\dfrac{1}{3} + 5\dfrac{2}{9}$

ANSWERS

1. 5/6
2. 1 1/5
3. 7/9
4. 1 1/3
5. 5/18
6. 5/24
7. 1 1/2
8. 13/18
9. 1 5/24
10. 29/36
11. 43/60
12. 1 47/80
13. 1 3/20
14. 19/24
15. 1 1/100
16. 97/100
17. 8
18. 9
19. 14 1/3
20. 15 1/5
21. 5 3/20
22. 7 5/12
23. 8 2/3
24. 9 5/9

52 WHOLE NUMBERS AND FRACTIONS

ANSWERS

25. $10\ 19/24$
26. $8\ 7/18$
27. $14\ 9/10$
28. $18\ 4/5$
29. $29\ 9/16$
30. $45\ 11/12$
31. $14\ 7/8$
32. $3\ 3/16$
33. $17\ 7/8$
34. $29\ 5/6$
35. $51\ 11/20$
36. $40\ 3/5$
37. $51\ 3/8$
38. $67\ 1/8$
39. $84\ 4/5$; $44\ 43/100$
40. $99\ 3/5$; $612\ 16/25$
41. $21\ 1/12$
42. $25\ 1/24$
43. $23\ 7/15$
44. $37\ 3/8$
    438
    $641\ 2/5$

25. $4\frac{3}{8} + 6\frac{5}{12}$ 26. $5\frac{1}{6} + 3\frac{2}{9}$ 27. $8\frac{4}{5} + 6\frac{1}{10}$ 28. $7\frac{1}{2} + 11\frac{3}{10}$

29. $13\frac{5}{16} + 16\frac{1}{4}$ 30. $23\frac{5}{6} + 22\frac{1}{12}$ 31. $14\frac{5}{8} + \frac{1}{4}$ 32. $\frac{1}{2} + 2\frac{11}{16}$

33. $5\frac{7}{8} + 12$ 34. $25 + 4\frac{5}{6}$ 35. $16\frac{1}{4} + 35\frac{3}{10}$ 36. $24\frac{3}{5} + 16\frac{1}{10}$

:: Solve.

37. On a recent day the stock of Nabisco opened at $\$49\frac{7}{8}$ per share and gained $\$1\frac{1}{2}$. What was the closing price?

38. On a recent day the stock of RCA opened at $\$65\frac{1}{2}$ and gained $\$1\frac{5}{8}$. What was the closing price?

39. A standard size for a book is $18\frac{3}{10}$ centimeters by $24\frac{1}{10}$ centimeters. What is the distance around the book, the perimeter? What is the area? (*Hint:* Area is length times width.)

40. A standard sheet of paper is $27\frac{9}{10}$ centimeters by $21\frac{3}{5}$ centimeters. What is the distance around such a sheet of paper? What is the area?

41. A consumer bought $8\frac{3}{4}$ yd of cotton fabric and $12\frac{5}{6}$ yd of silk. How much fabric in all was purchased?

42. A consumer bought two pieces of plastic sheeting. One was $10\frac{3}{8}$ yd and the other was $14\frac{2}{3}$ yd. How much plastic sheeting was purchased?

43. A glazier used $4\frac{2}{3}$ lb, $8\frac{4}{5}$ lb, and 10 lb of glazing compound. How much compound was used?

44. A painter used $10\frac{3}{4}$, $12\frac{5}{8}$, and 14 gallons of paint. How much paint was used?

45. A salesperson drove $150\frac{3}{10}$, $200\frac{4}{5}$, and $86\frac{9}{10}$ miles. How many miles were driven?

46. A salesperson drove $184\frac{7}{10}$, $216\frac{3}{5}$, and $240\frac{1}{10}$ miles. How many miles were driven?

1.10 SUBTRACTION USING FRACTIONAL NOTATION

◉ SUBTRACTING

To subtract using fractional notation when there is a common denominator:

a) Subtract the numerators.
b) Put the difference over the common denominator.

Example 1 Subtract: $\frac{3}{5} - \frac{1}{5}$.

Solution

a) Subtract the numerators:

$$\frac{3}{5} - \frac{1}{5} = \frac{3-1}{5} = \frac{2}{5}.$$

b) Put the difference over the common denominator.

DO EXERCISES 1 AND 2.

Example 2 Subtract and simplify: $13\frac{7}{8} - 9\frac{3}{8}$.

Solution

$$\begin{array}{r} 13\frac{7}{8} \\ -\ 9\frac{3}{8} \\ \hline 4\frac{4}{8} \end{array} = 4\frac{1}{2}$$

← Subtract the fractions.
← Subtract the whole numbers.

DO EXERCISE 3.

To subtract, using fractional notation when denominators are different:

a) Determine the LCD.
b) Multiply by 1 so each fraction has the LCD.
c) Subtract as with common denominators.

Example 3 Subtract and simplify: $\frac{1}{2} - \frac{3}{10}$.

Solution The LCD is 10.

$$\frac{1}{2} - \frac{3}{10} = \frac{1}{2} \cdot \frac{5}{5} - \frac{3}{10} = \frac{5}{10} - \frac{3}{10} = \frac{2}{10} = \frac{1}{5}$$

DO EXERCISE 4.

OBJECTIVES

After finishing Section 1.10, you should be able to:

◉ Subtract using fractional notation or mixed numerals, and simplify.
◉◉ Solve problems involving subtraction of fractions.

Subtract and simplify.

1. $\frac{10}{12} - \frac{2}{12}$ $= \frac{8}{12} = \frac{2}{3}$

2. $\frac{11}{6} - \frac{7}{6}$ $= \frac{4}{6} = \frac{2}{3}$

Subtract and simplify.

3. $19\frac{5}{6} - 11\frac{1}{6}$

$8\frac{4}{6} = 8\frac{2}{3}$

Subtract and simplify.

4. $\frac{5}{6} - \frac{7}{12}$

$\frac{10}{12} - \frac{7}{12} = \frac{3}{12} = \frac{1}{4}$

ANSWERS ON PAGE A–3

54

WHOLE NUMBERS AND FRACTIONS

Subtract and simplify.

5. $\dfrac{1}{5} - \dfrac{1}{6}$

$\dfrac{6}{30} - \dfrac{5}{30} = \dfrac{1}{30}$

Example 4 Subtract and simplify: $\dfrac{3}{5} - \dfrac{4}{9}$.

Solution The LCD is 45.

$$\dfrac{3}{5} - \dfrac{4}{9} = \dfrac{3}{5} \cdot \dfrac{9}{9} - \dfrac{4}{9} \cdot \dfrac{5}{5} = \dfrac{27}{45} - \dfrac{20}{45} = \dfrac{7}{45}$$

DO EXERCISE 5.

Example 5 Subtract and simplify: $\dfrac{5}{6} - \dfrac{5}{8}$.

Solution The LCD is 24.

$$\dfrac{5}{6} - \dfrac{5}{8} = \dfrac{5}{6} \cdot \dfrac{4}{4} - \dfrac{5}{8} \cdot \dfrac{3}{3} = \dfrac{20}{24} - \dfrac{15}{24} = \dfrac{5}{24}$$

DO EXERCISE 6.

Subtract and simplify.

6. $\dfrac{8}{9} - \dfrac{5}{7}$

$\dfrac{56}{63} - \dfrac{45}{63} = \dfrac{11}{63}$

Example 6 Subtract and simplify: $8\dfrac{1}{3} - 2\dfrac{4}{5}$.

Solution The LCD is 15.

$$8\dfrac{1}{3} = 8 + \dfrac{1}{3} = 8 + \dfrac{1}{3} \cdot \dfrac{5}{5} = 8 + \dfrac{5}{15} = 7 + \dfrac{20}{15}$$

$$-2\dfrac{4}{5} = 2 + \dfrac{4}{5} = 2 + \dfrac{4}{5} \cdot \dfrac{3}{3} = 2 + \dfrac{12}{15} = 2 + \dfrac{12}{15}$$

$$5 + \dfrac{8}{15} = 5\dfrac{8}{15}$$

In this problem we could not subtract until we borrowed:

$$8 + \dfrac{5}{15} = 7 + 1 + \dfrac{5}{15} = 7 + \dfrac{15}{15} + \dfrac{5}{15} = 7 + \dfrac{20}{15}.$$

DO EXERCISE 7.

Subtract and simplify.

7. $11\dfrac{1}{8} - 4\dfrac{5}{12}$

$11\dfrac{1}{8} = \dfrac{3}{24} = 10\dfrac{27}{24}$

$4\dfrac{5}{12} = -4\dfrac{10}{24}$

$\overline{7\dfrac{}{24}}$ $6\dfrac{17}{24}$

ANSWERS ON PAGE A-3

1.10 SUBTRACTION USING FRACTIONAL NOTATION

Example 7 Subtract and simplify: $13 - 1\frac{3}{4}$.

Solution

$$13 = 12\frac{4}{4} \qquad 13 = 12 + 1 = 12 + \frac{4}{4} = 12\frac{4}{4}$$

$$-1\frac{3}{4} = 1\frac{3}{4}$$

$$\overline{\phantom{-1\frac{3}{4}}\,11\frac{1}{4}}$$

DO EXERCISE 8.

◨ SOLVING PROBLEMS

Example 8 On a recent day the stock of IBM opened at $\$68\frac{1}{4}$ per share and dropped $\$1\frac{5}{8}$. What was the closing price?

Solution

$$\text{Closing price} = \text{Value at opening} - \text{Amount of drop}$$

$$= \$68\frac{1}{4} - \$1\frac{5}{8}$$

The LCD is 8. We subtract as follows:

$$68\frac{1}{4} = 68 + \boxed{\frac{1}{4} \cdot \frac{2}{2}} = 68 + \frac{2}{8} = 67 + \frac{10}{8}$$

$$-1\frac{5}{8} = 1 + \frac{5}{8} = 1 + \frac{5}{8} = 1 + \frac{5}{8}$$

$$\overline{66 + \frac{5}{8} = 66\frac{5}{8}}$$

The closing price was $\$66\frac{5}{8}$.

DO EXERCISE 9.

Subtract and simplify.

8. $10 - 7\frac{5}{8}$

$$10 = 9\frac{8}{8}$$
$$-7\frac{5}{8} \quad -7\frac{5}{8}$$
$$\overline{2\frac{3}{8}}$$

9. On a recent day the stock of TWA opened at $\$20$ per share and dropped $\$1\frac{1}{8}$. What was the closing price?

$$20 = 19\frac{8}{8}$$
$$-1\frac{1}{8} \quad -1\frac{1}{8}$$
$$\overline{18\frac{7}{8}}$$

ANSWERS ON PAGE A–3

10. There are $20\frac{1}{3}$ gallons of water in a barrel. $5\frac{3}{4}$ gallons are poured out and $8\frac{2}{3}$ gallons are poured back in. How many gallons of water are then in the barrel?

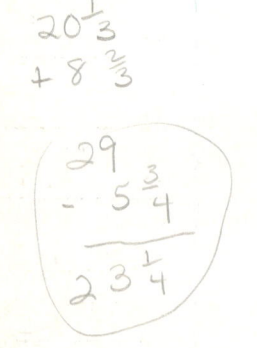

Example 9 One morning the stock of XYZ Corporation opened at a price of $\$100\frac{3}{8}$ per share. By noon the price had risen $\$4\frac{7}{8}$. At the end of the day it had fallen $\$10\frac{3}{4}$ from the price at noon. What was the closing price?

Solution We first draw a picture or at least visualize the situation.

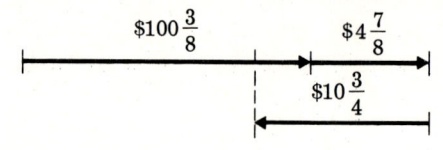

This is a two-step problem.

a) We first add $\$4\frac{7}{8}$ to $\$100\frac{3}{8}$ to find the price of the stock at noon.

$$100\frac{3}{8}$$
$$+ 4\frac{7}{8}$$
$$\overline{104\frac{10}{8} = 105\frac{1}{4}}$$

b) Next we subtract $\$10\frac{3}{4}$ from $\$105\frac{1}{4}$ to find the price of the stock at closing.

$$105\frac{1}{4} = 104\frac{5}{4}$$
$$- 10\frac{3}{4} = 10\frac{3}{4}$$
$$\overline{94\frac{2}{4} = 94\frac{1}{2}}$$

The stock closed at $\$94\frac{1}{2}$.

DO EXERCISE 10.

ANSWER ON PAGE A–3

EXERCISE SET 1.10

Subtract and simplify.

1. $\dfrac{7}{10} - \dfrac{3}{10}$

2. $\dfrac{9}{12} - \dfrac{7}{12}$

3. $\dfrac{3}{4} - \dfrac{1}{8}$

4. $\dfrac{2}{3} - \dfrac{1}{9}$

5. $\dfrac{5}{6} - \dfrac{1}{2}$

6. $\dfrac{4}{5} - \dfrac{1}{10}$

7. $\dfrac{1}{6} - \dfrac{1}{9}$

8. $\dfrac{1}{8} - \dfrac{1}{10}$

9. $\dfrac{5}{12} - \dfrac{3}{8}$

10. $\dfrac{7}{12} - \dfrac{2}{9}$

11. $\dfrac{3}{4} - \dfrac{3}{20}$

12. $\dfrac{2}{3} - \dfrac{1}{18}$

13. $\dfrac{9}{10} - \dfrac{7}{100}$

14. $\dfrac{1}{10} - \dfrac{1}{100}$

15. $\dfrac{5}{12} - \dfrac{2}{15}$

16. $\dfrac{9}{10} - \dfrac{11}{16}$

17. $8\dfrac{7}{9} - 2\dfrac{1}{9}$

18. $7\dfrac{5}{6} - 1\dfrac{1}{6}$

19. $8\dfrac{2}{5} - 4\dfrac{1}{3}$

20. $9\dfrac{2}{3} - 6\dfrac{1}{2}$

21. $7\dfrac{1}{4} - 2\dfrac{3}{4}$

22. $10\dfrac{1}{3} - 8\dfrac{2}{3}$

23. $18\dfrac{3}{4} - 5\dfrac{1}{6}$

24. $12\dfrac{5}{6} - 7\dfrac{3}{8}$

ANSWERS

1. 2/5
2. 1/6
3. 5/8
4. 5/9
5. 1/3
6. 7/10
7. 1/18
8. 1/40
9. 1/24
10. 13/34
11. 3/5
12. 11/18
13. 83/100
14. 9/100
15. 17/60
16. 17/80
17. 6 2/3
18. 6 2/3
19. 4 1/15
20. 3 1/6
21. 4 1/2
22. 1 2/3
23. 13 7/12
24. 5 1/3

58 WHOLE NUMBERS AND FRACTIONS

ANSWERS

25. $8\frac{4}{5}$
26. $10\frac{3}{10}$
27. $31\frac{17}{24}$
28. $24\frac{1}{2}$
29. $5\frac{3}{4}$
30. $4\frac{7}{8}$
31. $14\frac{1}{2}$
32. $19\frac{7}{12}$
33. $17\frac{1}{8}$
34. $10\frac{1}{5}$
35. $16\frac{15}{16}$
36. $6\frac{1}{2}$
37. $27\frac{5}{8}$
38. $59\frac{5}{8}$
39. $14\frac{9}{10}$
40. $16\frac{9}{10}$
41. $13/24$
42. $9\frac{1}{2}$
43. $114\frac{1}{3}$
44. $3\frac{7}{12}$
45. $2\frac{5}{12}$
46.

25. $20\frac{3}{10} - 11\frac{1}{2}$
26. $18\frac{1}{10} - 7\frac{4}{5}$
27. $34\frac{1}{3} - 2\frac{5}{8}$
28. $28\frac{1}{6} - 3\frac{2}{3}$

29. $7 - 1\frac{1}{4}$
30. $8 - 3\frac{1}{8}$
31. $15\frac{1}{8} - \frac{3}{4}$
32. $20\frac{1}{4} - \frac{5}{6}$

33. $22 - 4\frac{7}{8}$
34. $18 - 7\frac{4}{5}$
35. $23\frac{3}{16} - 6\frac{1}{4}$
36. $18\frac{1}{6} - 11\frac{2}{3}$

● ● **Solve.**

37. On a recent day the stock of General Mills opened at $29\frac{1}{8}$ and dropped $1\frac{1}{2}$. What was the closing price?

38. On a recent day the stock of General Motors opened at $61 and dropped $1\frac{3}{8}$. What was the closing price?

39. A $20\frac{1}{2}$-ft flagpole was set $5\frac{3}{5}$ ft in the ground. How much of the flagpole was above the ground?

40. The standard pencil is $18\frac{4}{5}$ centimeters long. The eraser is $1\frac{9}{10}$ centimeters. How much of the pencil is wood?

41. A corporation is owned by three people. One owns $\frac{1}{2}$ and the second owns $\frac{3}{8}$. What fraction does the third own?

42. A business is owned by three people. One owns $\frac{1}{3}$ and the second owns $\frac{1}{8}$. What fraction does the third own?

43. A driver knows it is $185\frac{1}{4}$ miles from City A to City B. After driving $90\frac{3}{4}$ miles, how much of the trip remains?

44. A driver knows it is 290 miles from City A to City B. After driving $175\frac{2}{3}$ miles, how much of the trip remains?

45. A worker knows it will take $12\frac{1}{2}$ hr to complete a job. The first day $3\frac{1}{4}$ hr are spent on the job and the second day $5\frac{2}{3}$ hr are spent. How much time will it take to finish the job?

46. A worker knows it will take $16\frac{2}{3}$ hr to complete a job. The first day $8\frac{1}{2}$ hr are spent on the job and the second day $5\frac{3}{4}$ hr are spent. How much time will it take to finish the job?

TEST OR REVIEW—CHAPTER 1

NAME _____   SCORE _____   ANSWERS

TEST OR REVIEW—CHAPTER 1

If you miss an item, review the indicated section and objective.

[1.1, ••]   Add.

    1.   9 8 7 6
       +3 0 9 8
       12974

    2.   6 7 4 5
         3 3 4 8
         2 4 6 8
       +9 0 5 4
       21615

1. *12974*

2. *2145*

[1.1, •••]   3. A business pays salaries of $1188, $2345, $2287, and $789. How much is paid in all?

1188   3533   5820
2345   2287   789
3533   5820   6609

3. *6609*

[1.2, •]   Subtract.

    4.   8 4 7 2
       −4 3 6 1
       4111

    5.   9 0 1 8
       −4 7 5 9
       4259

4. *4111*

5. *4259*

[1.2, ••]   6. The average annual fuel costs for a Chevrolet Corvette with automatic transmission are $650. Costs for a Corvette with manual transmission are $574. How much more does fuel cost for a car with an automatic transmission?

650
−574
76

6. *76*

[1.3, •]   Multiply.

    7.   4 5 6
       ×   8
      3648

    8.   9 0 8
      ×1 6 7

7. *3648*

8. *151,636*

[1.3, ••]   9. What is the cost of 125 TVs at $109 each?

9. *13,625*

[1.4, •]   Divide.

10. 8)3 7 5   *46 r7*

11. 5 6)1 1,7 0 4   *209*

10. *46 7/8*

11. *209*

[1.4, ••]   12. A consumer pays off a $5820 loan in 12 equal payments. How much is each payment?

485
12)5820

12. *485*

Copyright © 1984, by Addison-Wesley Publishing Company Inc. All rights reserved.

60 WHOLE NUMBERS AND FRACTIONS

ANSWERS

13. $3/17$

14. $17/3$

15. $4\ 5/12$

16. $1/8$

17. $22\ 3/4$

18. $5512\ 1/2$

19. $6\ 2/3$

20. 4

21. 1000

22. 48

23. $1\frac{1}{2}$

24. $14\ 7/12$

25. $39\ 1/1$

26. $1/12$

27. $3\ 3/8$

28. $2\frac{1}{2}$ "

[1.5, ●●●] 13. Simplify: $\dfrac{12}{68}$.

[1.5, ●●●] 14. Convert to fractional notation: $5\dfrac{2}{3}$.

[1.6, ●] 15. Convert to a mixed numeral: $\dfrac{53}{12}$.

[1.6, ●●] Multiply and simplify.

16. $\dfrac{5}{12} \cdot \dfrac{3}{10}$ 17. $4\dfrac{1}{3} \cdot 5\dfrac{1}{4}$

[1.6, ●●●] 18. An investor purchases 100 shares of CBS stock at $55\dfrac{1}{8}$ per share. What is the total amount invested?

[1.7, ●●] Divide and simplify.

19. $\dfrac{5}{2} \div \dfrac{3}{8}$ 20. $20\dfrac{2}{3} \div 5\dfrac{1}{6}$

[1.7, ●●●] 21. Rib roast contains $2\dfrac{1}{2}$ servings per pound. How many pounds does a hotel need for 400 servings?

[1.8, ●] 22. Find the LCM: 12 and 16.

[1.9, ●] Add and simplify.

23. $\dfrac{2}{3} + \dfrac{5}{6}$ 24. $6\dfrac{3}{4} + 7\dfrac{5}{6}$

[1.9, ●●] 25. A standard sheet of paper is $8\dfrac{1}{2}$ in. by 11 in. What is the distance around such a sheet of paper?

[1.10, ●] Subtract and simplify.

26. $\dfrac{5}{6} - \dfrac{3}{4}$ 27. $10\dfrac{1}{8} - 6\dfrac{3}{4}$

[1.10, ●●] 28. In item 25, how much longer is the length than the width?

Career: Restaurant Management This is Ho Ming Hsia. He is the manager of Ho Ming Restaurant, which specializes in the sale of carryout Chinese food and Chinese cookware.

Anytime Ho makes a sale he must add decimals. He adds the cost of each food item, then the tax. He then rings up the charges on the cash register and uses subtraction of decimals to make change. Actually, most of the mathematics in this book is relevant to the operation of a restaurant. In particular, there are interest charges which are made on business loans. Other kinds of business mathematics topics of relevance are checking accounts, insurance charges, taxes, financial statements, purchasing, inventory, depreciation, pricing, and payroll.

There are many attributes which make for success in the restaurant business. One is the point of view of looking at the work as a long-term career, rather than a job. This may seem like an intangible quality, but one needs an attitude of caring and service towards customers. A restaurant manager should enjoy working with people. Of utmost importance is integrity in all phases of the business operation.

Salaries are quite variable. Managers of fast food restaurants can make $23,000 per year plus bonuses. Other salaries can range from $15,000 to $60,000.

Ho immigrated to the United States from Taiwan. Before leaving, he earned a BS degree in Public Administration from Cheng Chi University as well as an MS degree in Anthropology. His hobbies include Chinese herb medicine and food medicine. In particular, he likes to show how to use such medicines to cure canker sores and lower back pains.

2
DECIMAL NOTATION AND EQUATIONS

READINESS CHECK — SKILLS FOR CHAPTER 2

Add.

1. $\begin{array}{r} 2\ 3 \\ +1\ 5 \\ \hline \end{array}$
2. $\begin{array}{r} 6\ 8\ 1 \\ +1\ 4\ 9 \\ \hline \end{array}$

3. $\dfrac{15}{100} + \dfrac{23}{100}$
4. $\dfrac{681}{1000} + \dfrac{149}{1000}$

Subtract.

5. $\begin{array}{r} 2\ 6\ 7 \\ -\ \ 8\ 5 \\ \hline \end{array}$
6. $\dfrac{267}{100} - \dfrac{85}{100}$

Multiply and simplify.

7. $25 \cdot 7$
8. $\dfrac{1}{10} \cdot \dfrac{1}{10}$

9. $\dfrac{1}{10} \cdot \dfrac{1}{100}$
10. $\dfrac{1}{10} \times 38$

11. $\dfrac{5}{10} \times \dfrac{9}{10}$
12. $\dfrac{7}{20} \cdot \dfrac{5}{5}$

Divide.

13. $4\overline{)3\ 6}$
14. $2\ 4\overline{)8\ 2\ 0\ 8}$

15. $2\ 5\overline{)4\ 0\ 0}$
16. $4\overline{)3\ 4\ 8}$

OBJECTIVES

After finishing Section 2.1, you should be able to:

▪ Write a word name, given decimal notation; and write a word name for an amount of money.

▪▪ Convert from decimal to fractional notation or to a mixed numeral.

▪▪▪ Convert from certain fractional notation to decimal notation and from a mixed numeral to decimal notation.

▪▪▪▪ Convert from dollars to cents and from cents to dollars.

2.1 DECIMAL NOTATION

The set of *arithmetic numbers*, or *nonnegative rational numbers*, consists of the whole numbers

    0, 1, 2, 3, 4, 5, 6, 7, 8, 9, 10,   and so on,

and fractions such as

    $\dfrac{1}{2}, \dfrac{2}{3}, \dfrac{7}{8}, \dfrac{17}{10},$ and so on.

We studied the use of fractional notation for arithmetic numbers in Chapter 1. In this chapter we will study the use of decimal notation. We are still considering the same set of numbers, but we are using different notation. For example, instead of using fractional notation for $\tfrac{7}{8}$ we use decimal notation 0.875.

2.1 DECIMAL NOTATION

■ DECIMAL NOTATION AND WORD NAMES

The cost of a stereo system is

$1768.95.

This is *decimal notation*. The place-value chart below gives the meaning of decimals.

Thousands	Hundreds	Tens	Ones	Tenths	Hundredths	Thousandths
1000	100	10	1	$\frac{1}{10}$	$\frac{1}{100}$	$\frac{1}{1000}$
1	7	6	8 .	9	5	

Example 1 Write a word name for 1768.95.

Solution One thousand, seven hundred sixty-eight and ninety-five hundredths

DO EXERCISES 1–3.

Example 2 Write a word name for $1768.95, as on a check.

Solution One thousand, seven hundred sixty-eight and $\frac{95}{100}$ dollars

DO EXERCISES 4 AND 5.

■■ CONVERTING FROM DECIMAL TO FRACTIONAL NOTATION

Decimals are defined in terms of fractions—for example,

$$0.1 = \frac{1}{10}, \quad 0.6875 = \frac{6875}{10,000}, \quad 53.47 = \frac{5347}{100}.$$

From these examples we obtain the following procedure.

Write a word name.

1. 18.49

2. 0.645

3. 12.0005

Write a word name as on a check.

4. $18.49

5. $2346.76

ANSWERS ON PAGE A–3

64

DECIMAL NOTATION AND EQUATIONS

Convert to fractional notation. Do not simplify.

6. 0.568 $\dfrac{568}{1000}$

7. 2.3 $\dfrac{23}{10}$

8. 89.04 $\dfrac{8904}{100}$

Convert to a mixed numeral.

9. 18.3 $18\dfrac{3}{10}$

10. 7.3019 $7\dfrac{3019}{10,000}$

To convert from decimal to fractional notation:

a) Count the number of decimal places.   4.98   2 places

b) Move the decimal point that many places to the right.   4.98.   Move 2 places

c) Write the answer over a denominator with the same number of zeros. $\dfrac{498}{100}$ 2 zeros

Example 3 Convert to fractional notation: 0.876. Do not simplify.

Solution

$$0.876 \qquad 0.876. \qquad 0.876 = \dfrac{876}{1000}$$
3 places

Example 4 Convert to fractional notation: 1.5018. Do not simplify.

Solution

$$1.5018 \qquad 1.5018. \qquad 1.5018 = \dfrac{15{,}018}{10{,}000}$$

DO EXERCISES 6–8.

Example 5 Convert to a mixed numeral: 9.73.

Solution

$$9.73 = \dfrac{973}{100} = 9\dfrac{73}{100}$$

DO EXERCISES 9 AND 10.

▪▪▪ FROM FRACTIONAL TO DECIMAL NOTATION

We reverse the procedure we used before.

To convert from fractional to decimal notation:

a) Count the number of zeros. $\dfrac{8679}{1000}$ 3 zeros

b) Move the decimal point that number of places to the left. Leave off the denominator.   8.679   Move 3 places

ANSWERS ON PAGE A–3

2.1 DECIMAL NOTATION

Example 6 Convert to decimal notation: $\frac{47}{10}$.

Solution

$\frac{47}{10}$ 4.7. $\frac{47}{10} = 4.7$

1 zero

Example 7 Convert to decimal notation: $\frac{123,067}{10,000}$.

Solution

$\frac{123,067}{10,000}$ 12.3067. $\frac{123,067}{10,000} = 12.3067$

4 zeros

DO EXERCISES 11–13.

Example 8 Convert to decimal notation: $14\frac{3}{10}$.

Solution We first convert to fractional notation, and then proceed as before.

$14\frac{3}{10} = \frac{143}{10} = 14.3$

DO EXERCISES 14–17.

■■ APPLICATIONS

Let us use the previous methods to convert from dollars to cents and cents to dollars.

> $1 = 100¢;
>
> 1¢ = $\frac{1}{100}$ = $0.01

Example 9 Convert to cents: $17.98.

Solution

$17.98 = $17\frac{98}{100} = $\frac{1798}{100} = 1798¢$

We can convert to cents by moving the decimal point two places to the right.

DO EXERCISES 18 AND 19.

Convert to decimal notation.

11. $\frac{4131}{1000}$ 4.131

12. $\frac{4131}{10,000}$ .4131

13. $\frac{573}{100}$ 5.73

Convert to decimal notation.

14. $14\frac{57}{100}$ 14.57

15. $22\frac{7}{100}$ 22.07

16. $3\frac{19}{1000}$ 3.019

17. $7\frac{6783}{10,000}$ 7.6783

Convert to cents.

18. $76.95   7695

19. $0.14   14

ANSWERS ON PAGE A–3

Convert to dollars.

20. 95¢

21. 795¢

DECIMAL NOTATION AND EQUATIONS

Example 10 Convert to dollars: 32¢

Solution

$$32¢ = \$\frac{32}{100} = \$0.32$$

We can convert to dollars by moving the decimal point two places to the left.

DO EXERCISES 20 AND 21.

EXERCISE SET 2.1

▪ Write a word name.

1. 34.891 2. 12.345 3. 0.0903 4. 0.4013

Write a word name, as on a check.

5. $326.48 6. $125.99 7. $0.67 8. $3.25

▪▪ Convert to fractional notation. Do not simplify.

9. 0.001 10. 0.1 11. 0.01 12. 0.0001

13. 4.9 14. 1.3 15. 0.59 16. 0.81

17. 3.09 18. 7.02 19. 907.5 20. 101.3

21. 9.999 22. 1.111 23. 78.43 24. 19.95

25. 2.0007 26. 4.0008 27. 7889.8 28. 1122.3

29. 12.1456 30. 23.3131 31. 617.499 32. 813.798

Convert to a mixed numeral. Do not simplify.

33. 18.46 34. 89.95 35. 4.013 36. 1.058

37. 234.5 38. 456.8 39. 5.4111 40. 12.6788

▪▪▪ Convert to decimal notation.

41. $\frac{1}{10}$ 42. $\frac{1}{100}$ 43. $\frac{1}{10{,}000}$ 44. $\frac{1}{1000}$

45. $\frac{7}{10}$ 46. $\frac{4}{10}$ 47. $\frac{7}{100}$ 48. $\frac{33}{100}$

ANSWERS

1.
2.
3.
4.
5.
6.
7.
8.
9. 1/1000
10. 1/10
11. 1/100
12. 1/10,000
13. 49/10
14. 13/10
15. 59/100
16. 81/100
17. 309/100
18. 702/100
19. 9075/10
20. 1013/10
21. 9999/1000
22. 1111/1000
23. 7843/100
24. 1995/100
25. 2.0007/10000
26. 40008/10000
27. 78898/10
28. 11223/10
29. 121456/10000
30. 23531/10000
31. 617499/1000
32. 813798/1000
33. 18 46/10
34. 89 95/100
35. 4 13/1000
36. 1 58/1000
37. 234 5/10
38. 456 8/10
39. 5 4111/10000
40. 12 6788/10000
41. .10
42. .01
43. .0001
44. .001
45. .7
46. .4
47. .07
48. .33

68 DECIMAL NOTATION AND EQUATIONS

ANSWERS

49. .89
50. .75
51. 7.74
52. 6.95
53. 307.9
54. 179.6
55. 999.9
56. .017
57. .0039
58. .4578
59. .0001
60. .0094
61. 9.3
62. 8.9
63. 17.95
64. 27.75
65. 6.014
66. 9.342
67. 126.8
68. 2345.1
69. 8995
70. 7834
71. 45
72. 13
73. 109
74. 208
75. 12895
76. 578902
77. .95
78. .11
79. 1.79
80. 2.84
81. 12.95
82. 67.89
83. .42
84. .19

49. $\dfrac{89}{10}$
50. $\dfrac{75}{10}$
51. $\dfrac{774}{100}$
52. $\dfrac{695}{100}$

53. $\dfrac{3079}{10}$
54. $\dfrac{1796}{10}$
55. $\dfrac{9999}{1000}$
56. $\dfrac{17}{1000}$

57. $\dfrac{39}{10,000}$
58. $\dfrac{4578}{10,000}$
59. $\dfrac{1}{100,000}$
60. $\dfrac{94}{100,000}$

61. $9\dfrac{3}{10}$
62. $8\dfrac{9}{10}$
63. $17\dfrac{95}{100}$
64. $27\dfrac{75}{100}$

65. $6\dfrac{14}{1000}$
66. $9\dfrac{342}{1000}$
67. $126\dfrac{8}{10}$
68. $2345\dfrac{1}{10}$

Convert to cents.

69. $89.95
70. $78.34
71. $0.45
72. $0.13

73. $1.09
74. $2.08
75. $128.95
76. $5789.02

Convert to dollars.

77. 95¢
78. 11¢
79. 179¢
80. 284¢

81. 1295¢
82. 6789¢
83. 42¢
84. 19¢

2.2 ADDITION AND SUBTRACTION WITH DECIMALS

■ ADDITION

Adding with decimal notation is similar to adding whole numbers. We add the thousandths, and then the hundredths, carrying if necessary. Then we go on to the tenths, then the ones, and so on. To keep place values straight, line up the decimal points in a vertical column.

Example 1 Add: $74 + 26.46 + 0.998$.

Solution

a)
```
   7 4.
   2 6.4 6
+  0.9 9 8
```
Line up the decimal points in a vertical column. If there is a whole number such as 74, write in the decimal point.

b)
```
   7 4.
   2 6.4 6
+  0.9 9 8
           8
```
Add thousandths.

c)
```
        1
   7 4.
   2 6.4 6
+  0.9 9 8
         5 8
```
Add hundredths. Write 5 in the hundredths place and carry 1 above the tenths column.

d)
```
       1 1
   7 4.
   2 6.4 6
+  0.9 9 8
      .4 5 8
```
Add tenths. Write 4 in the tenths place and carry 1 above the ones column. Write a decimal point in the answer below the others.

e)
```
     1 1 1
   7 4.
   2 6.4 6
+  0.9 9 8
     1.4 5 8
```
Add ones. Write 1 in the ones place and carry 1 above the tens column.

f)
```
    1 1 1
   7 4.
   2 6.4 6
+  0.9 9 8
  1 0 1.4 5 8
```
Add tens.

You may put extra zeros to the right of any decimal point so there are the same number of decimal places, but this is not necessary. The preceding problem would look like this:

```
   7 4.0 0 0
   2 6.4 6 0
+   0.9 9 8
  1 0 1.4 5 8
```

DO EXERCISES 1 AND 2.

OBJECTIVES

After finishing Section 2.2, you should be able to:

■ Add using decimal notation.

■■ Subtract using decimal notation.

■■■ Solve problems involving addition and subtraction using decimal notation.

Add.

1. $69 + 1.785 + 213.67$

   1.785
   69
   284.455

2. $17.95 + 14.68 + 236$

   17.95
   14.68
   63

ANSWERS ON PAGE A-3

Subtract.

3. 29.35 − 1.674

27.676

4. 92.375 − 27.692

Subtract.

5. 100 − 0.41

99.59

6. 240 − 0.117

ANSWERS ON PAGE A–3

DECIMAL NOTATION AND EQUATIONS

SUBTRACTION

Subtracting with decimal notation is similar to subtracting whole numbers. We subtract the thousandths, borrowing if necessary. Then we go on to the hundredths, the tenths, and so on. To keep place values straight, we line up the decimal points.

Example 2 Subtract: 76.14 − 18.953.

Solution

a)
```
  7 6 . 1 4 0
− 1 8 . 9 5 3
```
Line up the decimal places. We put an extra zero to the right of the decimal point in 76.14 to get the same number of decimal places.

b)
```
           3  10
  7 6 . 1  4̸  0̸
− 1 8 . 9  5  3
                7
```
Borrow 1 hundredth. Then subtract thousandths.

c)
```
          13
       0  3̸  10
  7 6 . 1̸  4̸  0̸
− 1 8 . 9  5  3
             8  7
```
Borrow 1 tenth. Then subtract hundredths.

d)
```
       10 13
     5  0̸  3̸  10
  7 6̸ . 1̸  4̸  0̸
+ 1 8 .  9  5  3
        . 1  8  7
```
Borrow 1 one. Then subtract tenths. Write a decimal point in the answer below the others.

e)
```
     15 10 13
   6  5̸  0̸  3̸  10
  7̸ 6̸ . 1̸  4̸  0̸
− 1 8 .  9  5  3
     7 . 1  8  7
```
Borrow 1 ten. Then subtract ones.

f)
```
     15 10 13
   6  5̸  0̸  3̸  10
  7̸ 6̸ . 1̸  4̸  0̸
− 1 8 .  9  5  3
 5 7 . 1  8  7
```
Subtract tens.

DO EXERCISES 3 AND 4.

Example 3 Subtract: 200 − 0.68.

Solution
```
  1  9  9  9  10
  2  0̸  0̸ . 0̸  0̸
−          0 . 6  8
  1  9  9 . 3  2
```

DO EXERCISES 5 AND 6.

2.2 ADDITION AND SUBTRACTION WITH DECIMALS

▶▶▶ PROBLEM SOLVING

Example 4 When making a deposit in a savings account one might have some currency, some coins, and some checks. Find the net deposit in the following figure.

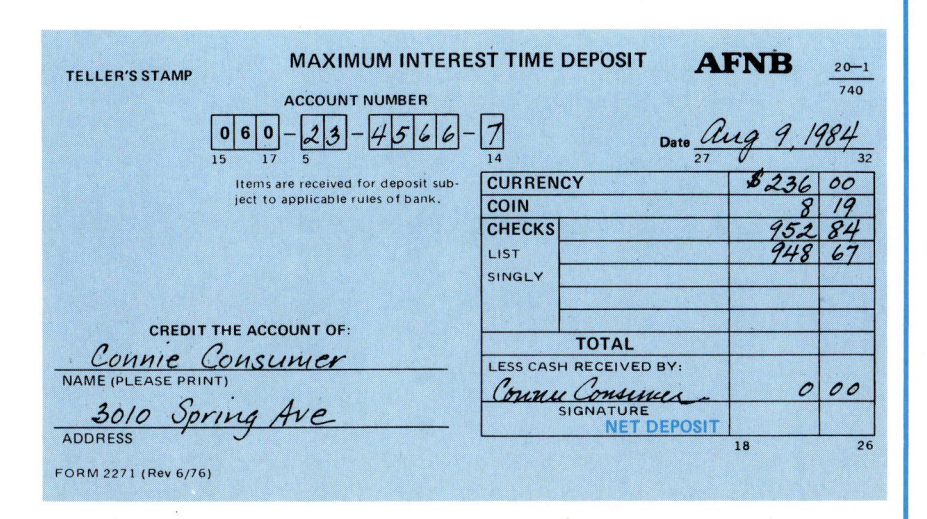

Solution We add the currency, the coins, and the checks as follows:

```
  1 2 1 2
    2 3 6.0 0
          8.1 9
    9 5 2.8 4
+   9 4 8.6 7
  ─────────────
    2 1 4 5.7 0
```

The net deposit is $2145.70.

DO EXERCISE 7.

Example 5 It can happen that one deposits several checks, gets some cash, and leaves the rest in a checking account. Find the net deposit below.

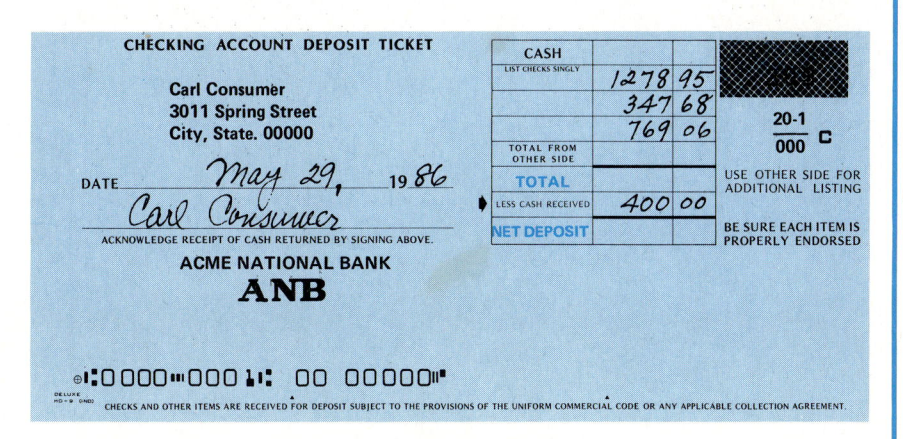

7. Find the net deposit below.

CURRENCY	785	00
COIN	2	49
CHECKS	679	43
	98	29
	822	97
TOTAL		
LESS CASH	0	00
NET DEPOSIT		

$2388.18

ANSWER ON PAGE A-3

8. Find the net deposit below.

CASH LIST CHECKS SINGLY	805	97
	766	66
	438	89
TOTAL FROM OTHER SIDE	220	03
TOTAL		
LESS CASH RECEIVED	300	00
NET DEPOSIT		

1931.55

Solution

We first add the amounts on the checks:

$$\begin{array}{r} 1278.95 \\ 347.68 \\ +769.06 \\ \hline 2395.69 \end{array}$$ This is TOTAL above.

Then we subtract the amount of cash received.

$$\begin{array}{r} 2395.69 \\ -400.00 \\ \hline 1995.69 \end{array}$$

The net deposit is $1995.69.

DO EXERCISE 8.

EXERCISE SET 2.2

● **Add.**

1. $4\ 1\ 5.7\ 8$
    $+\ 2\ 9.1\ 6$

2. $7\ 0\ 8.9\ 9$
    $+\ 7\ 5.4\ 8$

3. $2\ 3\ 4.0\ 0\ 0$
    $+1\ 5\ 6.6\ 1\ 7$

4. $1\ 3\ 4\ 5.1\ 2$
    $+\ 5\ 6\ 6.9\ 8$

5. $85 + 67.95 + 2.774$

6. $119 + 43.74 + 18.876$

7. $0.785 + 0.8 + 0.56$

8. $0.4 + 0.48 + 0.478$

9. $9.9 + 99 + 999$

10. $0.88 + 8.8 + 0.088$

11. $17.95 + 16.99 + 28.85$

12. $14.59 + 16.79 + 19.95$

13. $28 + 4.35 + 0.367 + 0.4791$

14. $347 + 10.08 + 3.5 + 0.238$

●● **Subtract.**

15. $7\ 8.1\ 1$
    $-4\ 5.8\ 7\ 6$

16. $1\ 4.0\ 8$
    $-\ 9.1\ 9\ 9$

17. $3\ 8.7\ 0\ 0$
    $-1\ 1.8\ 6\ 5$

18. $3\ 0\ 0.0\ 0\ 0$
    $-\ 2\ 4.6\ 7\ 7$

19. $5.4 - 4.8$

20. $48.31 - 4.25$

21. $57.86 - 9.95$

22. $2.6 - 1.08$

23. $1 - 0.004$

24. $2 - 0.007$

25. $3 - 1.0807$

26. $5 - 3.4051$

27. $100 - 0.79$

28. $200 - 0.67$

29. $2.508 - 1.527$

30. $374.8 - 104.07$

31. $79.342 - 4.341$

32. $11.892 - 7.889$

33. $1 - 0.8888$

34. $20 - 19.0101$

●●● In Exercises 35–38, find the net deposit.

35.
CURRENCY	875	00
COIN	4	68
CHECKS	345	95
LIST	24	87
SINGLY	98	69
	45	39
TOTAL		
LESS CASH RECEIVED BY:	0	00
NET DEPOSIT		

36.
CURRENCY	1240	00
COIN	23	42
CHECKS	945	78
LIST	673	73
SINGLY	888	99
	67	04
	93	12
TOTAL		
LESS CASH RECEIVED BY:	0	00
NET DEPOSIT		

ANSWERS

35. 1394.58
36. 5105.04

74 DECIMAL NOTATION AND EQUATIONS

ANSWERS

37. 4493.22

38. 4627.27

39. 3.21

40. 6.05

41. 6.34

42. 6.64

43. 39,595.3

44. 19,034.7

45. 1022.6

46. 3088.4

47. 6.4

48. 1.37

49. _____

50. _____

37.

CASH	1348	95
LIST CHECKS SINGLY	943	68
	1204	95
	995	64
TOTAL FROM OTHER SIDE		
TOTAL		
LESS CASH RECEIVED	650	00
NET DEPOSIT		

38.

CASH	2048	95
LIST CHECKS SINGLY	1134	02
	668	94
	775	36
TOTAL FROM OTHER SIDE		
TOTAL		
LESS CASH RECEIVED	250	00
NET DEPOSIT		

39. A sweatshirt is bought for $16.79 and paid for with a $20 bill. How much change is there?

40. A quart of paint is bought for $3.95 and paid for with a $10 bill. How much change is returned?

41. An inexpensive cereal is the kind to be cooked, such as oatmeal. The cost-per-month for a family of five for cereal to be cooked is $6.74. One-serving packages of the ready-to-eat cereal would cost $13.08. How much cheaper is the cereal to be cooked?

42. Protein is a very important dietary concern. Bologna costs $9.73 per pound of protein. Peanut butter costs $3.09 per pound of protein. How much cheaper is the protein in peanut butter than the protein in bologna?

43. The odometer on a car read 39,105.7 before a 489.6-mile trip. What did it read at the end of the trip?

44. The odometer on a car read 18,458.9 before a 575.8-mile trip. What did it read at the end of the trip?

45. The odometer on a car read 22,389.4 before a trip and 23,412.0 at the end. How many miles were driven?

46. The odometer on a car read 58,412.3 before a trip and 61,500.7 at the end. How many miles were driven?

47. Normal body temperature is 37°C. Butter melts at 30.6°C. How much lower is this than normal body temperature?

48. In May in Indianapolis normal precipitation is 3.9 in. In February it is 2.53 in. How much more precipitation is there in May?

49. One year a business paid the following salaries. What was the total of the salaries paid?

$62,459.78
57,577.98
23,400.00
22,999.99
19,680.44
19,742.66

50. Find the net deposit.

	Dollars	Cents
CURRENCY		
COIN		
CHECKS List singly Be sure each item is endorsed	125,678	95
	86,435	34
	78,881	24
	34,685	93
	46,784	66
TOTAL		
LESS CASH RETURNED	28,060	88
NET DEPOSIT		

2.3 MULTIPLICATION AND DIVISION USING DECIMALS

◧ MULTIPLICATION

Look at this product.

$$5.14 \times 0.8 = \frac{514}{100} \times \frac{8}{10} = \frac{514 \times 8}{100 \times 10} = \frac{4112}{1000} = 4.112$$

2 places   1 place   3 places

We can also do this by multiplying the whole numbers 8 and 514 and determining the position of the decimal point.

> **To multiply using decimal notation:**
> a) Ignore the decimal points and multiply as whole numbers.
> b) Place the decimal point in the result of (a) by adding the number of decimal places in the numbers.

Example 1 Multiply: 5.14 × 0.8.

Solution

a) Ignore the decimal points and multiply as whole numbers.

```
   1 3
   5.1 4
 ×   0.8
 ───────
   4 1 1 2
```

b) Place the decimal point in the result of (a) by adding the number of places in the numbers.

```
    5 1 4    ┌─ 2 decimal places
 ×    0.8  + └─ 1 decimal place
 ─────────
    4.1 1 2
           └── 3 decimal places
```

DO EXERCISES 1 AND 2.

Example 2 Multiply: 8127 × 0.0056.

Solution

a) Ignore the decimal points and multiply as whole numbers.

```
      8 1 2 7   ┌─ 0 decimal places
 ×  0.0 0 5 6 + └─ 4 decimal places
 ─────────────
      4 8 7 6 2
    4 0 6 3 5 0
 ─────────────
    4 5.5 1 1 2
           └── 4 decimal places
```

b) Place the decimal point in the result of (a) by adding the number of places in the numbers.

DO EXERCISE 3.

OBJECTIVES

After finishing Section 2.3, you should be able to:

◧ Multiply using decimal notation.
◧◧ Divide using decimal notation.
◧◧◧ Solve problems involving multiplication and division using decimal notation.

Multiply.

1.   6.5 2
     ×   0.9
   ─────────
      5.8 6 8

2.   6.5 2
     ×0.0 9
   ─────────
      .5 8 6 8

Multiply.

3.   6 7 4 2
     ×   0.9 5
   ─────────
      3 3 7 1 0
     5 9 7 7 8
   ─────────
     6 3 1 4.9 0

ANSWERS ON PAGE A–4

DECIMAL NOTATION AND EQUATIONS

Multiply.

4. $\quad\begin{array}{r} 56.76 \\ \times 0.908 \\ \hline \end{array}$

Multiply.

5. $\quad\begin{array}{r} 268.1 \\ \times \quad\;\; 10 \\ \hline \end{array}$

6. $\quad\begin{array}{r} 268.1 \\ \times \quad 100 \\ \hline \end{array}$

7. $\quad\begin{array}{r} 268.1 \\ \times 1000 \\ \hline \end{array}$

Multiply.

8. $\quad\begin{array}{r} 268.1 \\ \times \quad\;\; 0.1 \\ \hline \end{array}$

9. $\quad\begin{array}{r} 268.1 \\ \times \quad 0.01 \\ \hline \end{array}$

10. $\quad\begin{array}{r} 268.1 \\ \times 0.001 \\ \hline \end{array}$

ANSWERS ON PAGE A-4

Example 3 Multiply: 0.927×0.18.

Solution

a) $\quad\begin{array}{r} 0.927 \\ \times \quad 0.18 \\ \hline 7416 \\ 9270 \\ \hline 0.16686 \end{array}$

b) 3 decimal places
+ 2 decimal places
⎯⎯⎯⎯⎯⎯
5 decimal places

DO EXERCISE 4.

Example 4 Multiply: 17.95×100.

Solution

$\quad\begin{array}{r} 17.95 \\ \times \quad\;\; 100 \\ \hline 1795.00 \end{array}$

2 decimal places
+ 0 decimal places
⎯⎯⎯⎯⎯⎯
2 decimal places

To multiply by 10, 100, 1000, and so on, count the number of zeros and move the decimal point that many places to the right.

DO EXERCISES 5–7.

Example 5 Multiply: 19.78×0.001.

Solution

$\quad\begin{array}{r} 19.78 \\ \times \quad 0.001 \\ \hline 0.01978 \end{array}$

2 decimal places
+ 3 decimal places
⎯⎯⎯⎯⎯⎯
5 decimal places

To multiply by 0.1, 0.01, 0.001, and so on, count the number of decimal places and move the decimal point that many places to the left.

DO EXERCISES 8–10.

▪▪ DIVISION

Division of Decimals by Whole Numbers

Note that $37.6 \div 8 = 4.7$ because $37.6 = 8 \times 4.7$. If we write this as

$$\begin{array}{r} 4.7 \\ 8\overline{)37.6} \\ \underline{32} \\ 56 \\ \underline{56} \\ 0 \end{array}$$

2.3 MULTIPLICATION AND DIVISION USING DECIMALS

we see how the following method can be used to divide by a whole number.

> **To divide by a whole number:**
> a) Place the decimal point in the quotient directly above the decimal point in the dividend.
> b) Divide as though whole numbers.

Example 6 Divide: $216.75 \div 25$.

Solution

a)
```
      .
25)216.75
```

b)
```
    8.67
25)216.75
   200
    167
    150
     175
     175
       0
```

DO EXERCISES 11 AND 12.

It is sometimes helpful to write extra zeros to the right of the decimal point. The answer is not changed. Remember that the decimal point for a whole number, though not normally written, is to the right of the number.

Example 7 Divide: $54 \div 8$.

Solution

a)
```
    .
8)54.
```

b)
```
   6.75
8)54.00    Extra zeros are written to the right of the decimal point
  48       as needed.
   60
   56
    40
    40
     0
```

DO EXERCISES 13 AND 14.

Divisors That Are Not Whole Numbers

Suppose we wanted to do the division

$$0.46\overline{)24.748}$$

Divide.

11. $7\overline{)342.3}$

12. $16\overline{)253.12}$

Divide.

13. $25\overline{)320}$
```
   12.8
25)320
   25
    70
    50
    200
    200
```

14. $38\overline{)682.1}$
```
    17.9...
38)682.1
   38
   302
   ...
```

ANSWERS ON PAGE A-4

DECIMAL NOTATION AND EQUATIONS

Divide

15. 0.0 2 4) 2 0.5 4 4

Let's first write this using fractional notation and multiply by 1 using $\frac{100}{100}$:

$$\frac{24.748}{0.46} = \frac{24.748}{0.46} \times \frac{100}{100} = \frac{24.748 \times 100}{0.46 \times 100} = \frac{2474.8}{46}.$$

We see that we have changed the original division

0.4 6) 2 4.7 4 8

to one in which the divisor is a whole number:

4 6) 2 4 7 4.8

The decimal points in the numerator (dividend) and denominator (divisor) have been moved two places to the right.

> **To divide when the divisor is not a whole number:**
> a) Move the decimal point in the divisor as many places to the right as it takes to make it a whole number. Move the decimal point in the dividend the same number of places to the right.
> b) Divide as though whole numbers, adding zeros if necessary.

Example 8 Divide: $83.79 \div 0.098$.

Solution

a)

0.0 9 8.) 8 3.7 9 0.

b)

```
               8 5 5.
0.0 9 8. ) 8 3.7 9 0.
           7 8 4
           ─────
             5 3 9
             4 9 0
             ─────
               4 9 0
               4 9 0
               ─────
                   0
```

DO EXERCISE 15.

Example 9 Divide: $1.081 \div 2.3$.

Solution

Divide.

16. 4.6) 3.9 1   .85

a)

2.3.) 1.0. 8 1

b)

```
            0.4 7
2.3. ) 1.0. 8 1
         9 2
         ───
         1 6 1
         1 6 1
         ─────
             0
```

DO EXERCISE 16.

2.3 MULTIPLICATION AND DIVISION USING DECIMALS

Example 10 Divide: $18 \div 0.32$.

Solution

a)
```
0.32.)1 8.0 0.
```

b)
```
           5 6.2 5
0.3 2.)1 8.0 0.0 0
       1 6 0
         2 0 0
         1 9 2
             8 0
             6 4
             1 6 0
             1 6 0
                 0
```

DO EXERCISE 17.

▰▰▰ PROBLEM SOLVING

Example 11 At Peso Rent-a-Car the daily cost of an intermediate-size car is $29.95 plus 28¢ a mile. What is the cost, in dollars, of driving 240 miles in one day?

Solution

Cost = Basic charge + Cost per mile × Number of miles
    = $29.95   + $0.28   ×   240

We do the multiplication first. We multiply as follows:

```
      2 4 0
   ×  0.2 8
      1 9 2 0
      4 8 0 0
      6 7.2 0
```

We then add on the basic charge, $29.95:

```
      6 7.2 0
   + 2 9.9 5
      9 7.1 5
```

The cost is $97.15.

DO EXERCISE 18.

Divide.

17. $35 \div 0.16$

16.75

18. At Davis Rent-a-Car the cost of an intermediate-size car is $24.95 plus 29¢ a mile. What is the cost, in dollars, of driving 320 miles?

117.75

ANSWERS ON PAGE A–4

19. Find the gas mileage.

First odometer reading:
 22,587.2

Second odometer reading:
 23,000.0

Number of gallons at the last fill:
 12.9

32

DECIMAL NOTATION AND EQUATIONS

Example 12 *Computing gas mileage.* Get the gas tank filled and write down the mileage on the odometer, say 19,560.7. The next time the tank is filled write down the mileage, say 19,938.1. From the gasoline pump find the number of gallons it takes to fill the tank, say 18.5. Then subtract the odometer readings and divide by the number of gallons on the second fill. Find the gasoline mileage.

Solution

$$\text{Gasoline mileage} = \frac{\text{Difference in the odometer readings}}{\text{Number of gallons at the last fill}}$$

$$= \frac{19{,}938.1 - 19{,}560.7}{18.5}$$

We subtract:

```
   8 13 7 11
 1 9,9 3 8.1
−1 9,5 6 0.7
─────────────
     3 7 7.4
```

We then divide the answer by 18.5:

```
              2 0.4
      ┌─────────────
1 8.5.)3 7 7.4.0
       3 7 0
       ─────
           7 4 0
           7 4 0
           ─────
               0
```

The mileage is 20.4 miles per gallon.

DO EXERCISE 19.

EXERCISE SET 2.3

● Multiply.

1. 6.2 3
    × 1.6

2. 5.4 4
    × 3.2

3. 5 6 7 8
    ×0.0 6 8

4. 1 2 4 5
    ×0.1 0 7

5. 1 7.9 5
    × 1 0

6. 1 7.9 5
    × 1 0 0

7. 1 8.9 4
    × 0.0 1

8. 1 8.9 4
    × 0.1

9. 1 4.7
    ×1.0 4

10. 0.3 4 2
    × 1 0.6

11. 2 1.9 7
    × 2 4

12. 3 6.6 7
    × 5 3

13. 0.4 5 7
    × 3.0 8

14. 0.0 0 2 4
    × 0.0 1 5

15. 3.6 4 2
    × 0.9 9

16. 2 8 7.4
    × 1.0 8

●● Divide.

17. 1 2)1 5

18. 1 5)9

19. 4 8)1 9.6 8

20. 7 2)1 6 5.6

21. 5.2)4 4.2

22. 8.5)4 4.2

23. 7.8)7 2.5 4

24. 9.9)0.2 2 7 7

25. 1 0 0)9 5

82 DECIMAL NOTATION AND EQUATIONS

ANSWERS

26. 1 0 0) 5 7.8
27. 1 0 0 0) 5 6 8 9
28. 1 0 0 0) 7 8 4.9

26. _____

29. 0.6 4) 1 2
30. 1.6) 7 5
31. 1.0 5) 6 9 3

27. _____

32. 1.0 7) 8 5 6

28. _____

••• Solve.

33. At Murtz Rent-a-Car the daily cost of an intermediate-size car is $34.95 plus 38¢ a mile. What is the cost, in dollars, of driving 290 miles in one day?

29. _____

34. At Nudgit Rent-a-Car the daily cost of a compact car is $33.95 plus 30¢ a mile. What is the cost, in dollars, of driving 345 miles?

30. _____

35. A tax deduction of 17¢ per mile is allowed for mileage driven while on business. What deduction, in dollars, is allowed for 478 miles?

31. _____

32. _____

36. A print shop charges 6¢ per page for copies. What is the cost of 750 copies?

33. 145.15

Find the gas mileage.

37. First odometer reading: 34,095.6
Second odometer reading: 34,836.6
Number of gallons at the last fill: 28.5

34. 137.45

35. 81.26

38. First odometer reading: 18,456.2
Second odometer reading: 19,317.5
Number of gallons at the last fill: 29.7

36. 45

37. 25.97

39. A business paid $72,495.12 to 4 employees. What was the average amount paid?

38. 29

40. A business paid $99,678.96 to 8 employees. What was the average amount paid?

39. 18123.78

41. What is the total cost of 16 record albums at $7.99 each and 7 tapes at $8.95 each?

40. 12459.87

42. What is the total cost of 12 cartons of cola at $1.89 each and 9 packages of buns at $0.69 each?

41. 190.49

43. An investor bought 2448 shares of IBM stock at $265.75 per share. How much did it cost?

42. 28.89

44. A business pays $639,309.64 to 29 employees. What is the average amount paid?

43. 650556

45. The average video game costs 25¢ and runs for 90 seconds. Assuming the player does not win any free games and plays continuously, how much money, in dollars, will be spent in one hour?

44. 22045.16

45. _____

2.4 ESTIMATING AND MORE CONVERSION

● ROUNDING

Estimating has many uses. It can be done before a problem is attempted to get an idea of the answer. It can be done afterward as a check. In many situations an estimate is all we need. We usually estimate by rounding the numbers so that there are 1 or 2 nonzero digits.

> To round to a certain place:
> a) Locate the digit in that place.
> b) Then consider the digit to its right.
> c) If the digit to the right is 5 or higher, round up;
>   If the digit to the right is less than 5, round down.

Example 1 Round 3872.2459 to the nearest tenth.

Solution

a) Locate the digit in the tenths place.

  3 8 7 2 . 2 4 5 9
          ↑

b) Then consider the next digit to the right.

  3 8 7 2 . 2 4 5 9
              ↑

c) Since that digit is less than 5, round down.

  3 8 7 2 . 2 ← This is the answer.

Note that 3872.3 is *not* a correct answer to Example 1. It is incorrect to round from the ten-thousandths place over as follows:

  3872.246,   3872.25,   3872.3

Example 2 Round 3872.2459 to the nearest hundredth.

Solution

a) Locate the digit in the hundredths place.

  3 8 7 2 . 2 4 5 9
            ↑

b) Then consider the next digit to the right.

  3 8 7 2 . 2 4 5 9
              ↑

c) Since that digit is 5 or higher, round up.

  3 8 7 2 . 2 5 ← This is the answer.

DO EXERCISES 1–6.

Example 3 Round 13,465 to the nearest ten, and hundred.

Solution

  Ten: 13,470
  Hundred: 13,500

DO EXERCISES 7 AND 8.

OBJECTIVES

After finishing Section 2.4, you should be able to:
● Round numbers to a specified place.
●● Convert from fractional to decimal notation.
●●● Solve problems involving rounding and estimating.

Round to the nearest tenth.

1. 2.76   2. 13.85

   2.8   13.9

3. 7.009

   7.0

Round to the nearest hundredth.

4. 7.834   5. 34.675

   7.83   34.68

6. 0.025

   .03

Round to the nearest ten.

7. 7894

   7890

Round to the nearest hundred.

8. 7894

   7900

ANSWERS ON PAGE A–4

84

Round to the nearest thousandth.

9. 0.9434

.943

10. 8.0038

8.004

11. 43.1119

43.112

12. 37.4005

37.401

Round 7459.3549 to the nearest

13. thousandth

7459.355

14. hundredth

7459.34

15. tenth

7459.4

16. one

7459

17. ten
(*Caution:* "Tens" are not "tenths.")

7460

18. hundred

7500

19. thousand

7000

Round to the nearest cent.

20. $0.018

2

21. $17.965

17.97

22. $1267.89347

12.6789

ANSWERS ON PAGE A–4

DECIMAL NOTATION AND EQUATIONS

Example 4 Round 3872.2459 to the nearest thousandth, hundredth, tenth, one, ten, hundred, and thousand.

Solution

Thousandth:	3872.246
Hundredth:	3872.25
Tenth:	3872.2
One:	3872
Ten:	3870
Hundred:	3900
Thousand:	4000

Example 5 Round 0.007 to the nearest tenth.

Solution

a) Locate the digit in the tenths place.

0.0 0 7
  ↑

b) Then consider the next digit to the right.

0.0 0 7
   ↑

c) Since that digit is less than 5, round down.

0.0, or simply 0, is the answer.

DO EXERCISES 9–19.

We sometimes use the symbol ≈, meaning "is approximately equal to." Thus,

46.124 ≈ 46.1

Example 6 Round to the nearest cent: $1639.495.

Solution "Cents" are "hundredths."

$1639.4 9 5 $1639.49 5
       ↑   ↑
Digit to be rounded to.   Digit to the right is 5 so we round up.

When we add 1 to 9 we have to carry.

Thus, $1639.495 rounded to the nearest cent is $1639.50.

DO EXERCISES 20–22.

∷ MORE CONVERSION FROM FRACTIONS TO DECIMALS

Since $\frac{7}{8}$ means $7 \div 8$, we can find a decimal for $\frac{7}{8}$ by division.

Example 7 Convert to decimal notation: $\frac{7}{8}$.

TABLES **T-1**

TABLE 1
DAY OF THE YEAR

DAY THIS YEAR

DAYS IN EACH MONTH
	31	28	31	30	31	30	31	31	30	31	30	31
	JAN	FEB	MAR	APR	MAY	JUN	JUL	AUG	SEP	OCT	NOV	DEC
DAY 1	1	32	60	91	121	152	182	213	244	274	305	335
DAY 2	2	33	61	92	122	153	183	214	245	275	306	336
DAY 3	3	34	62	93	123	154	184	215	246	276	307	337
DAY 4	4	35	63	94	124	155	185	216	247	277	308	338
DAY 5	5	36	64	95	125	156	186	217	248	278	309	339
DAY 6	6	37	65	96	126	157	187	218	249	279	310	340
DAY 7	7	38	66	97	127	158	188	219	250	280	311	341
DAY 8	8	39	67	98	128	159	189	220	251	281	312	342
DAY 9	9	40	68	99	129	160	190	221	252	282	313	343
DAY 10	10	41	69	100	130	161	191	222	253	283	314	344
DAY 11	11	42	70	101	131	162	192	223	254	284	315	345
DAY 12	12	43	71	102	132	163	193	224	255	285	316	346
DAY 13	13	44	72	103	133	164	194	225	256	286	317	347
DAY 14	14	45	73	104	134	165	195	226	257	287	318	348
DAY 15	15	46	74	105	135	166	196	227	258	288	319	349
DAY 16	16	47	75	106	136	167	197	228	259	289	320	350
DAY 17	17	48	76	107	137	168	198	229	260	290	321	351
DAY 18	18	49	77	108	138	169	199	230	261	291	322	352
DAY 19	19	50	78	109	139	170	200	231	262	292	323	353
DAY 20	20	51	79	110	140	171	201	232	263	293	324	354
DAY 21	21	52	80	111	141	172	202	233	264	294	325	355
DAY 22	22	53	81	112	142	173	203	234	265	295	326	356
DAY 23	23	54	82	113	143	174	204	235	266	296	327	357
DAY 24	24	55	83	114	144	175	205	236	267	297	328	358
DAY 25	25	56	84	115	145	176	206	237	268	298	329	359
DAY 26	26	57	85	116	146	177	207	238	269	299	330	360
DAY 27	27	58	86	117	147	178	208	239	270	300	331	361
DAY 28	28	59	87	118	148	179	209	240	271	301	332	362
DAY 29	29	0	88	119	149	180	210	241	272	302	333	363
DAY 30	30	0	89	120	150	181	211	242	273	303	334	364
DAY 31	31	0	90	0	151	0	212	243	0	304	0	365

ADD 1 DAY FOR LEAP YEAR IF FEBRUARY 29 FALLS BETWEEN THE TWO DATES

principle × table # ÷ 100 = int

TABLE 2
SIMPLE INTEREST ON $100 (360-day Basis)

DAY	16.00 % INTEREST	DAY	16.25 % INTEREST	DAY	16.50 % INTEREST	DAY	16.75 % INTEREST	DAY	17.00 % INTEREST	DAY	17.25 % INTEREST
1	0.044444	1	0.045139	1	0.045833	1	0.046528	1	0.047222	1	0.047917
2	0.088889	2	0.090278	2	0.091667	2	0.093056	2	0.094444	2	0.095833
3	0.133333	3	0.135417	3	0.137500	3	0.139583	3	0.141667	3	0.143750
4	0.177778	4	0.180556	4	0.183333	4	0.186111	4	0.188889	4	0.191667
5	0.222222	5	0.225694	5	0.229167	5	0.232639	5	0.236111	5	0.239583
6	0.266667	6	0.270833	6	0.275000	6	0.279167	6	0.283333	6	0.287500
7	0.311111	7	0.315972	7	0.320833	7	0.325694	7	0.330556	7	0.335417
8	0.355556	8	0.361111	8	0.366667	8	0.372222	8	0.377778	8	0.383333
9	0.400000	9	0.406250	9	0.412500	9	0.418750	9	0.425000	9	0.431250
10	0.444444	10	0.451389	10	0.458333	10	0.465278	10	0.472222	10	0.479167
11	0.488889	11	0.496528	11	0.504167	11	0.511806	11	0.519444	11	0.527083
12	0.533333	12	0.541667	12	0.550000	12	0.558333	12	0.566667	12	0.575000
13	0.577778	13	0.586806	13	0.595833	13	0.604861	13	0.613889	13	0.622917
14	0.622222	14	0.631944	14	0.641667	14	0.651389	14	0.661111	14	0.670833
15	0.666667	15	0.677083	15	0.687500	15	0.697917	15	0.708333	15	0.718750
16	0.711111	16	0.722222	16	0.733333	16	0.744444	16	0.755556	16	0.766667
17	0.755556	17	0.767361	17	0.779167	17	0.790972	17	0.802778	17	0.814583
18	0.800000	18	0.812500	18	0.825000	18	0.837500	18	0.850000	18	0.862500
19	0.844444	19	0.857639	19	0.870833	19	0.884028	19	0.897222	19	0.910417
20	0.888889	20	0.902778	20	0.916667	20	0.930556	20	0.944444	20	0.958333
21	0.933333	21	0.947917	21	0.962500	21	0.977083	21	0.991667	21	1.006250
22	0.977778	22	0.993056	22	1.008333	22	1.023611	22	1.038889	22	1.054167
23	1.022222	23	1.038194	23	1.054167	23	1.070139	23	1.086111	23	1.102083
24	1.066667	24	1.083333	24	1.100000	24	1.116667	24	1.133333	24	1.150000
25	1.111111	25	1.128472	25	1.145833	25	1.163194	25	1.180556	25	1.197917
26	1.155556	26	1.173611	26	1.191667	26	1.209722	26	1.227778	26	1.245833
27	1.200000	27	1.218750	27	1.237500	27	1.256250	27	1.275000	27	1.293750
28	1.244444	28	1.263889	28	1.283333	28	1.302778	28	1.322222	28	1.341667
29	1.288889	29	1.309028	29	1.329167	29	1.349306	29	1.369444	29	1.389583
30	1.333333	30	1.354167	30	1.375000	30	1.395833	30	1.416667	30	1.437500
31	1.377778	31	1.399306	31	1.420833	31	1.442361	31	1.463889	31	1.485417
32	1.422222	32	1.444444	32	1.466667	32	1.488889	32	1.511111	32	1.533333
33	1.466667	33	1.489583	33	1.512500	33	1.535417	33	1.558333	33	1.581250
34	1.511111	34	1.534722	34	1.558333	34	1.581944	34	1.605556	34	1.629167
35	1.555556	35	1.579861	35	1.604167	35	1.628472	35	1.652778	35	1.677083
36	1.600000	36	1.625000	36	1.650000	36	1.675000	36	1.700000	36	1.725000
37	1.644444	37	1.670139	37	1.695833	37	1.721528	37	1.747222	37	1.772917
38	1.688889	38	1.715278	38	1.741667	38	1.768056	38	1.794444	38	1.820833
39	1.733333	39	1.760417	39	1.787500	39	1.814583	39	1.841667	39	1.868750
40	1.777778	40	1.805556	40	1.833333	40	1.861111	40	1.888889	40	1.916667
41	1.822222	41	1.850694	41	1.879167	41	1.907639	41	1.936111	41	1.964583
42	1.866667	42	1.895833	42	1.925000	42	1.954167	42	1.983333	42	2.012500
43	1.911111	43	1.940972	43	1.970833	43	2.000694	43	2.030556	43	2.060417
44	1.955556	44	1.986111	44	2.016667	44	2.047222	44	2.077778	44	2.108333
45	2.000000	45	2.031250	45	2.062500	45	2.093750	45	2.125000	45	2.156250
46	2.044444	46	2.076389	46	2.108333	46	2.140278	46	2.172222	46	2.204167
47	2.088889	47	2.121528	47	2.154167	47	2.186806	47	2.219444	47	2.252083
48	2.133333	48	2.166667	48	2.200000	48	2.233333	48	2.266667	48	2.300000
49	2.177778	49	2.211806	49	2.245833	49	2.279861	49	2.313889	49	2.347917
50	2.222222	50	2.256944	50	2.291667	50	2.326389	50	2.361111	50	2.395833
30	1.333333	30	1.354167	30	1.375000	30	1.395833	30	1.416667	30	1.437500
60	2.666667	60	2.708333	60	2.750000	60	2.791667	60	2.833333	60	2.875000
90	4.000000	90	4.062500	90	4.125000	90	4.187500	90	4.250000	90	4.312500
120	5.333333	120	5.416667	120	5.500000	120	5.583333	120	5.666667	120	5.750000
150	6.666667	150	6.770833	150	6.875000	150	6.979167	150	7.083333	150	7.187500
180	8.000000	180	8.125000	180	8.250000	180	8.375000	180	8.500000	180	8.625000
210	9.333333	210	9.479167	210	9.625000	210	9.770833	210	9.916667	210	10.062500
240	10.666667	240	10.833333	240	11.000000	240	11.166667	240	11.333333	240	11.500000
270	12.000000	270	12.187500	270	12.375000	270	12.562500	270	12.750000	270	12.937500
300	13.333333	300	13.541667	300	13.750000	300	13.958333	300	14.166667	300	14.375000
330	14.666667	330	14.895833	330	15.125000	330	15.354167	330	15.583333	330	15.812500
360	16.000000	360	16.250000	360	16.500000	360	16.750000	360	17.000000	360	17.250000
365	16.222222	365	16.475694	365	16.729167	365	16.982639	365	17.236111	365	17.489583
366	16.266667	366	16.520833	366	16.775000	366	17.029167	366	17.283333	366	17.537500

Reprinted by permission from the *Thorndyke Encyclopedia of Banking and Financial Tables*, 1982 edition. Copyright © 1982 by Warren, Gorham, and Lamont, Inc., 210 South St., Boston MA 02111. All rights reserved.

TABLE 3
SIMPLE INTEREST ON $100 (365-day Basis)

DAY	16.00 % INTEREST	DAY	16.25 % INTEREST	DAY	16.50 % INTEREST	DAY	16.75 % INTEREST	DAY	17.00 % INTEREST	DAY	17.25 % INTEREST
1	0.043836	1	0.044521	1	0.045205	1	0.045890	1	0.046575	1	0.047260
2	0.087671	2	0.089041	2	0.090411	2	0.091781	2	0.093151	2	0.094521
3	0.131507	3	0.133562	3	0.135616	3	0.137671	3	0.139726	3	0.141781
4	0.175342	4	0.178082	4	0.180822	4	0.183562	4	0.186301	4	0.189041
5	0.219178	5	0.222603	5	0.226027	5	0.229452	5	0.232877	5	0.236301
6	0.263014	6	0.267123	6	0.271233	6	0.275342	6	0.279452	6	0.283562
7	0.306849	7	0.311644	7	0.316438	7	0.321233	7	0.326027	7	0.330822
8	0.350685	8	0.356164	8	0.361644	8	0.367123	8	0.372603	8	0.378082
9	0.394521	9	0.400685	9	0.406849	9	0.413014	9	0.419178	9	0.425342
10	0.438356	10	0.445205	10	0.452055	10	0.458904	10	0.465753	10	0.472603
11	0.482192	11	0.489726	11	0.497260	11	0.504795	11	0.512329	11	0.519863
12	0.526027	12	0.534247	12	0.542466	12	0.550685	12	0.558904	12	0.567123
13	0.569863	13	0.578767	13	0.587671	13	0.596575	13	0.605479	13	0.614384
14	0.613699	14	0.623288	14	0.632877	14	0.642466	14	0.652055	14	0.661644
15	0.657534	15	0.667808	15	0.678082	15	0.688356	15	0.698630	15	0.708904
16	0.701370	16	0.712329	16	0.723288	16	0.734247	16	0.745205	16	0.756164
17	0.745205	17	0.756849	17	0.768493	17	0.780137	17	0.791781	17	0.803425
18	0.789041	18	0.801370	18	0.813699	18	0.826027	18	0.838356	18	0.850685
19	0.832877	19	0.845890	19	0.858904	19	0.871918	19	0.884932	19	0.897945
20	0.876712	20	0.890411	20	0.904110	20	0.917808	20	0.931507	20	0.945205
21	0.920548	21	0.934932	21	0.949315	21	0.963699	21	0.978082	21	0.992466
22	0.964384	22	0.979452	22	0.994521	22	1.009589	22	1.024658	22	1.039726
23	1.008219	23	1.023973	23	1.039726	23	1.055479	23	1.071233	23	1.086986
24	1.052055	24	1.068493	24	1.084932	24	1.101370	24	1.117808	24	1.134247
25	1.095890	25	1.113014	25	1.130137	25	1.147260	25	1.164384	25	1.181507
26	1.139726	26	1.157534	26	1.175342	26	1.193151	26	1.210959	26	1.228767
27	1.183562	27	1.202055	27	1.220548	27	1.239041	27	1.257534	27	1.276027
28	1.227397	28	1.246575	28	1.265753	28	1.284932	28	1.304110	28	1.323288
29	1.271233	29	1.291096	29	1.310959	29	1.330822	29	1.350685	29	1.370548
30	1.315068	30	1.335616	30	1.356164	30	1.376712	30	1.397260	30	1.417808
31	1.358904	31	1.380137	31	1.401370	31	1.422603	31	1.443836	31	1.465068
32	1.402740	32	1.424658	32	1.446575	32	1.468493	32	1.490411	32	1.512329
33	1.446575	33	1.469178	33	1.491781	33	1.514384	33	1.536986	33	1.559589
34	1.490411	34	1.513699	34	1.536986	34	1.560274	34	1.583562	34	1.606849
35	1.534247	35	1.558219	35	1.582192	35	1.606164	35	1.630137	35	1.654110
36	1.578082	36	1.602740	36	1.627397	36	1.652055	36	1.676712	36	1.701370
37	1.621918	37	1.647260	37	1.672603	37	1.697945	37	1.723288	37	1.748630
38	1.665753	38	1.691781	38	1.717808	38	1.743836	38	1.769863	38	1.795890
39	1.709589	39	1.736301	39	1.763014	39	1.789726	39	1.816438	39	1.843151
40	1.753425	40	1.780822	40	1.808219	40	1.835616	40	1.863014	40	1.890411
41	1.797260	41	1.825342	41	1.853425	41	1.881507	41	1.909589	41	1.937671
42	1.841096	42	1.869863	42	1.898630	42	1.927397	42	1.956164	42	1.984932
43	1.884932	43	1.914384	43	1.943836	43	1.973288	43	2.002740	43	2.032192
44	1.928767	44	1.958904	44	1.989041	44	2.019178	44	2.049315	44	2.079452
45	1.972603	45	2.003425	45	2.034247	45	2.065068	45	2.095890	45	2.126712
46	2.016438	46	2.047945	46	2.079452	46	2.110959	46	2.142466	46	2.173973
47	2.060274	47	2.092466	47	2.124658	47	2.156849	47	2.189041	47	2.221233
48	2.104110	48	2.136986	48	2.169863	48	2.202740	48	2.235616	48	2.268493
49	2.147945	49	2.181507	49	2.215068	49	2.248630	49	2.282192	49	2.315753
50	2.191781	50	2.226027	50	2.260274	50	2.294521	50	2.328767	50	2.363014
30	1.315068	30	1.335616	30	1.356164	30	1.376712	30	1.397260	30	1.417808
60	2.630137	60	2.671233	60	2.712329	60	2.753425	60	2.794521	60	2.835616
90	3.945205	90	4.006849	90	4.068493	90	4.130137	90	4.191781	90	4.253425
120	5.260274	120	5.342466	120	5.424658	120	5.506849	120	5.589041	120	5.671233
150	6.575342	150	6.678082	150	6.780822	150	6.883562	150	6.986301	150	7.089041
180	7.890411	180	8.013699	180	8.136986	180	8.260274	180	8.383562	180	8.506849
210	9.205479	210	9.349315	210	9.493151	210	9.636986	210	9.780822	210	9.924658
240	10.520548	240	10.684932	240	10.849315	240	11.013699	240	11.178082	240	11.342466
270	11.835616	270	12.020548	270	12.205479	270	12.390411	270	12.575342	270	12.760274
300	13.150685	300	13.356164	300	13.561644	300	13.767123	300	13.972603	300	14.178082
330	14.465753	330	14.691781	330	14.917808	330	15.143836	330	15.369863	330	15.595890
360	15.780822	360	16.027397	360	16.273973	360	16.520548	360	16.767123	360	17.013699
365	16.000000	365	16.250000	365	16.500000	365	16.750000	365	17.000000	365	17.250000
366	16.043836	366	16.294521	366	16.545205	366	16.795890	366	17.046575	366	17.297260

Reprinted by permission from the *Thorndyke Encyclopedia of Banking and Financial Tables*, 1982 edition. Copyright © 1982 by Warren, Gorham, and Lamont, Inc., 210 South St., Boston MA 02111. All rights reserved.

TABLE 4
COMPOUND INTEREST
(Amount When $1.00 is Compounded)

Period	1¼%	1½%	1¾%	2%	2½%	3%
1	1.012500	1.015000	1.017500	1.020000	1.025000	1.030000
2	1.025156	1.030225	1.035306	1.040400	1.050625	1.060900
3	1.037970	1.045678	1.053424	1.061208	1.076891	1.092727
4	1.050945	1.061363	1.071859	1.082432	1.103813	1.125509
5	1.064082	1.077283	1.090617	1.104081	1.131408	1.159274
6	1.077383	1.093442	1.109703	1.126163	1.159693	1.194052
7	1.090850	1.109844	1.129123	1.148686	1.188685	1.229874
8	1.104486	1.126492	1.148883	1.171660	1.218402	1.266770
9	1.118292	1.143389	1.168988	1.195093	1.248862	1.304773
10	1.132271	1.160540	1.189445	1.218995	1.280084	1.343916
11	1.146424	1.177948	1.210260	1.243375	1.312086	1.384233
12	1.160754	1.195617	1.231440	1.268243	1.344888	1.425760
13	1.175263	1.213551	1.252990	1.293608	1.378510	1.468533
14	1.189954	1.231754	1.274917	1.319480	1.412973	1.512589
15	1.204828	1.250230	1.297228	1.345870	1.448297	1.557967
16	1.219888	1.268983	1.319929	1.372787	1.484504	1.604706
17	1.235137	1.288018	1.343028	1.400243	1.521617	1.652847
18	1.250576	1.307338	1.366531	1.428248	1.559657	1.702432
19	1.266208	1.326948	1.390445	1.456813	1.598648	1.753505
20	1.282036	1.346852	1.414778	1.485949	1.638614	1.806110
21	1.298061	1.367055	1.439537	1.515668	1.679579	1.860293
22	1.314287	1.387561	1.464729	1.545981	1.721568	1.916102
23	1.330716	1.408374	1.490362	1.576901	1.764607	1.973585
24	1.347350	1.429500	1.516443	1.608439	1.808722	2.032793
25	1.364192	1.450943	1.542981	1.640608	1.853940	2.093777
26	1.381244	1.472707	1.569983	1.673420	1.900289	2.156590
27	1.398510	1.494798	1.597458	1.706888	1.947796	2.221288
28	1.415991	1.517220	1.625414	1.741026	1.996491	2.287927
29	1.433691	1.539978	1.653859	1.775847	2.046403	2.356565
30	1.451612	1.563078	1.682802	1.811364	2.097563	2.427262
31	1.469757	1.586524	1.712251	1.847591	2.150002	2.500080
32	1.488129	1.610322	1.742215	1.884543	2.203752	2.575082
33	1.506731	1.634477	1.772704	1.922234	2.258846	2.652334
34	1.525565	1.658994	1.803726	1.960679	2.315317	2.731904
35	1.544635	1.683879	1.835291	1.999893	2.373200	2.813861
36	1.563943	1.709137	1.867409	2.039891	2.432530	2.898277
37	1.583492	1.734774	1.900089	2.080689	2.493343	2.985225
38	1.603286	1.760796	1.933341	2.122303	2.555677	3.074782
39	1.623327	1.787208	1.967174	2.164749	2.619569	3.167025
40	1.643619	1.814016	2.001600	2.208044	2.685058	3.262036
41	1.664164	1.841226	2.036628	2.252205	2.752184	3.359897
42	1.684966	1.868844	2.072269	2.297249	2.820989	3.460694
43	1.706028	1.896877	2.108534	2.343194	2.891514	3.564515
44	1.727353	1.925330	2.145433	2.390058	2.963802	3.671450
45	1.748945	1.954210	2.182978	2.437859	3.037897	3.781594
46	1.770807	1.983523	2.221180	2.486616	3.113844	3.895042
47	1.792942	2.013276	2.260051	2.536348	3.191690	4.011893
48	1.815354	2.043475	2.299602	2.587075	3.271482	4.132250
49	1.838046	2.074127	2.339845	2.638817	3.353269	4.256218
50	1.861022	2.105239	2.380792	2.691593	3.437101	4.383905

TABLE 4 (cont.)

Period	3½%	4%	5%	6%	7%	8%
1	1.035000	1.040000	1.050000	1.060000	1.070000	1.080000
2	1.071225	1.081600	1.102500	1.123600	1.144900	1.166400
3	1.108718	1.124864	1.157625	1.191016	1.225043	1.259712
4	1.147523	1.169859	1.215506	1.262477	1.310796	1.360489
5	1.187686	1.216653	1.276281	1.338226	1.402552	1.469328
6	1.229255	1.265319	1.340095	1.418520	1.500731	1.586874
7	1.272279	1.315932	1.407100	1.503631	1.605782	1.713824
8	1.316809	1.368569	1.477455	1.593849	1.718187	1.850930
9	1.362897	1.423312	1.551328	1.689480	1.838460	1.999004
10	1.410598	1.480244	1.628894	1.790849	1.967152	2.158924
11	1.459969	1.539454	1.710339	1.898300	2.104853	2.331638
12	1.511068	1.601032	1.795856	2.012198	2.252193	2.518169
13	1.563955	1.665073	1.885649	2.132930	2.409847	2.719623
14	1.618693	1.731676	1.979931	2.260906	2.578536	2.937193
15	1.675347	1.800943	2.078928	2.396560	2.759034	3.172168
16	1.733984	1.872981	2.182874	2.540354	2.952166	3.425941
17	1.794673	1.947900	2.292018	2.692775	3.158818	3.700016
18	1.857487	2.025816	2.406619	2.854342	3.379935	3.996017
19	1.922499	2.106849	2.526950	3.025603	3.616530	4.315698
20	1.989786	2.191123	2.653298	3.207139	3.869687	4.660954
21	2.059429	2.278768	2.785963	3.399567	4.140565	5.033830
22	2.131509	2.369919	2.925261	3.603541	4.430405	5.436536
23	2.206112	2.464716	3.071524	3.819753	4.740533	5.871459
24	2.283326	2.563305	3.225100	4.048938	5.072370	6.341176
25	2.363242	2.665837	3.386355	4.291874	5.427436	6.848470
26	2.445955	2.772470	3.555673	4.549386	5.807357	7.396348
27	2.531563	2.883369	3.733457	4.822349	6.213872	7.988056
28	2.620168	2.998704	3.920130	5.111690	6.648843	8.627100
29	2.711874	3.118652	4.116137	5.418391	7.114262	9.317268
30	2.806790	3.243395	4.321944	5.743494	7.612260	10.062649
31	2.905028	3.373134	4.538041	6.088104	8.145118	10.867661
32	3.006704	3.508059	4.764943	6.453390	8.715276	11.737074
33	3.111939	3.648381	5.003190	6.840593	9.325345	12.676040
34	3.220857	3.794316	5.253350	7.251029	9.978119	13.690123
35	3.333587	3.946089	5.516018	7.686091	10.676587	14.785333
36	3.450263	4.103933	5.791819	8.147256	11.423948	15.968160
37	3.571022	4.268090	6.081410	8.636091	12.223624	17.245613
38	3.696008	4.438814	6.385481	9.154256	13.079278	18.625262
39	3.825368	4.616367	6.704755	9.703511	13.994827	20.115283
40	3.959256	4.801022	7.039993	10.285722	14.974465	21.724506
41	4.097830	4.993063	7.391993	10.902865	16.022678	23.462466
42	4.241254	5.192786	7.761593	11.557037	17.144265	25.339463
43	4.389628	5.400497	8.149673	12.250459	18.344364	27.366620
44	4.543337	5.616517	8.557157	12.985487	19.628469	29.555950
45	4.702354	5.841178	8.985015	13.764616	21.002462	31.920426
46	4.866936	6.074825	9.434266	14.590493	22.472634	34.474060
47	5.037279	6.317818	9.905979	15.465923	24.045718	37.231985
48	5.213584	6.570531	10.401278	16.393878	25.728918	40.210544
49	5.396059	6.833352	10.921342	17.377511	27.529942	43.427388
50	5.584921	7.106686	11.467409	18.420162	29.457038	46.901579

TABLE 5
DAILY COMPOUND INTEREST ON $100
(365-day Basis)

5.25 %
Effective Rate is 5.39%

Description: This table shows the interest on $100 for each day from 1 day to 366 days. Interest is computed on the basis of a 365-day year. Interest is compounded daily.

Example: Interest on $100 at 5.25% for 270 days is $ 3.96. On $10,000 the interest is $ 395.97.

DAY	INTEREST	DAY	INTEREST	DAY	INTEREST	DAY	INTEREST	DAY	INTEREST	DAY	INTEREST
1	0.014384	66	0.953766	131	1.901972	196	2.859084	261	3.825186	326	4.800362
2	0.028769	67	0.968287	132	1.916630	197	2.873879	262	3.840120	327	4.815436
3	0.043157	68	0.982810	133	1.931289	198	2.888676	263	3.855056	328	4.830512
4	0.057547	69	0.997335	134	1.945950	199	2.903475	264	3.869994	329	4.845590
5	0.071938	70	1.011862	135	1.960614	200	2.918276	265	3.884934	330	4.860671
6	0.086332	71	1.026391	136	1.975279	201	2.933080	266	3.899876	331	4.875754
7	0.100728	72	1.040922	137	1.989947	202	2.947885	267	3.914821	332	4.890839
8	0.115126	73	1.055456	138	2.004617	203	2.962693	268	3.929768	333	4.905926
9	0.129527	74	1.069991	139	2.019289	204	2.977502	269	3.944716	334	4.921015
10	0.143929	75	1.084528	140	2.033963	205	2.992314	270	3.959667	335	4.936106
11	0.158333	76	1.099068	141	2.048639	206	3.007128	271	3.974620	336	4.951200
12	0.172739	77	1.113610	142	2.063317	207	3.021944	272	3.989576	337	4.966295
13	0.187148	78	1.128153	143	2.077997	208	3.036763	273	4.004533	338	4.981393
14	0.201558	79	1.142699	144	2.092680	209	3.051583	274	4.019493	339	4.996493
15	0.215971	80	1.157247	145	2.107364	210	3.066405	275	4.034454	340	5.011596
16	0.230385	81	1.171797	146	2.122051	211	3.081230	276	4.049418	341	5.026700
17	0.244802	82	1.186349	147	2.136740	212	3.096057	277	4.064384	342	5.041807
18	0.259221	83	1.200903	148	2.151431	213	3.110886	278	4.079352	343	5.056915
19	0.273642	84	1.215460	149	2.166124	214	3.125717	279	4.094323	344	5.072026
20	0.288065	85	1.230018	150	2.180819	215	3.140550	280	4.109295	345	5.087139
21	0.302490	86	1.244579	151	2.195516	216	3.155385	281	4.124270	346	5.102255
22	0.316917	87	1.259141	152	2.210215	217	3.170223	282	4.139247	347	5.117372
23	0.331346	88	1.273706	153	2.224917	218	3.185062	283	4.154226	348	5.132492
24	0.345777	89	1.288273	154	2.239620	219	3.199904	284	4.169207	349	5.147614
25	0.360210	90	1.302841	155	2.254326	220	3.214748	285	4.184190	350	5.162738
26	0.374646	91	1.317412	156	2.269034	221	3.229594	286	4.199175	351	5.177864
27	0.389083	92	1.331985	157	2.283744	222	3.244442	287	4.214163	352	5.192992
28	0.403523	93	1.346561	158	2.298456	223	3.259292	288	4.229152	353	5.208122
29	0.417964	94	1.361138	159	2.313170	224	3.274144	289	4.244144	354	5.223255
30	0.432408	95	1.375717	160	2.327886	225	3.288999	290	4.259138	355	5.238390
31	0.446854	96	1.390299	161	2.342605	226	3.303855	291	4.274135	356	5.253527
32	0.461302	97	1.404882	162	2.357325	227	3.318714	292	4.289133	357	5.268666
33	0.475752	98	1.419468	163	2.372048	228	3.333575	293	4.304133	358	5.283808
34	0.490204	99	1.434056	164	2.386773	229	3.348438	294	4.319136	359	5.298951
35	0.504658	100	1.448645	165	2.401499	230	3.363303	295	4.334141	360	5.314097
36	0.519114	101	1.463237	166	2.416228	231	3.378171	296	4.349148	361	5.329245
37	0.533572	102	1.477831	167	2.430960	232	3.393040	297	4.364157	362	5.344395
38	0.548032	103	1.492427	168	2.445693	233	3.407912	298	4.379168	363	5.359547
39	0.562495	104	1.507026	169	2.460428	234	3.422785	299	4.394182	364	5.374702
40	0.576959	105	1.521626	170	2.475166	235	3.437661	300	4.409197	365	5.389858
41	0.591426	106	1.536228	171	2.489905	236	3.452539	301	4.424215	366	5.405017
42	0.605894	107	1.550833	172	2.504647	237	3.467420	302	4.439235		
43	0.620365	108	1.565440	173	2.519391	238	3.482302	303	4.454257		
44	0.634838	109	1.580048	174	2.534137	239	3.497186	304	4.469281		
45	0.649313	110	1.594659	175	2.548885	240	3.512073	305	4.484308		
46	0.663790	111	1.609272	176	2.563635	241	3.526962	306	4.499336		
47	0.678269	112	1.623887	177	2.578387	242	3.541852	307	4.514367		
48	0.692750	113	1.638504	178	2.593142	243	3.556745	308	4.529400		
49	0.707233	114	1.653123	179	2.607898	244	3.571641	309	4.544435		
50	0.721718	115	1.667745	180	2.622657	245	3.586538	310	4.559472		
51	0.736206	116	1.682368	181	2.637418	246	3.601437	311	4.574511		
52	0.750695	117	1.696994	182	2.652181	247	3.616339	312	4.589553		
53	0.765187	118	1.711621	183	2.666946	248	3.631243	313	4.604597		
54	0.779680	119	1.726251	184	2.681713	249	3.646148	314	4.619643		
55	0.794176	120	1.740883	185	2.696482	250	3.661056	315	4.634691		
56	0.808674	121	1.755517	186	2.711253	251	3.675967	316	4.649741		
57	0.823174	122	1.770153	187	2.726027	252	3.690879	317	4.664793		
58	0.837676	123	1.784791	188	2.740803	253	3.705793	318	4.679848		
59	0.852180	124	1.799432	189	2.755580	254	3.720710	319	4.694904		
60	0.866686	125	1.814074	190	2.770360	255	3.735629	320	4.709963		
61	0.881194	126	1.828718	191	2.785142	256	3.750550	321	4.725024		
62	0.895704	127	1.843365	192	2.799927	257	3.765473	322	4.740087		
63	0.910217	128	1.858014	193	2.814713	258	3.780398	323	4.755153		
64	0.924731	129	1.872665	194	2.829501	259	3.795325	324	4.770220		
65	0.939248	130	1.887317	195	2.844292	260	3.810255	325	4.785290		

TABLES T-7

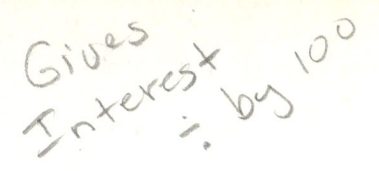

TABLE 6
DAILY COMPOUND INTEREST ON $100
(360-day Basis)

5.25 %
Effective Rate is 5.47%

Description: This table shows the interest on $100 for each day from 1 day to 366 days. Interest is computed on the basis of a 360-day year. Interest is compounded daily.

Example: Interest on $100 at 5.25% for 270 days is $ 4.02. On $10,000 the interest is $ 401.57.

DAY	INTEREST	DAY	INTEREST	DAY	INTEREST	DAY	INTEREST	DAY	INTEREST	DAY	INTEREST
1	0.014583	66	0.967076	131	1.928640	196	2.899361	261	3.879327	326	4.868626
2	0.029169	67	0.981800	132	1.943505	197	2.914367	262	3.894476	327	4.883919
3	0.043756	68	0.996527	133	1.958371	198	2.929376	263	3.909628	328	4.899215
4	0.058346	69	1.011256	134	1.973240	199	2.944386	264	3.924781	329	4.914513
5	0.072938	70	1.025986	135	1.988111	200	2.959399	265	3.939937	330	4.929813
6	0.087532	71	1.040719	136	2.002985	201	2.974414	266	3.955095	331	4.945115
7	0.102128	72	1.055454	137	2.017860	202	2.989431	267	3.970255	332	4.960420
8	0.116726	73	1.070192	138	2.032738	203	3.004450	268	3.985417	333	4.975726
9	0.131327	74	1.084931	139	2.047617	204	3.019472	269	4.000582	334	4.991035
10	0.145929	75	1.099673	140	2.062499	205	3.034495	270	4.015748	335	5.006346
11	0.160534	76	1.114416	141	2.077383	206	3.049521	271	4.030917	336	5.021660
12	0.175140	77	1.129162	142	2.092270	207	3.064549	272	4.046089	337	5.036976
13	0.189749	78	1.143910	143	2.107158	208	3.079580	273	4.061262	338	5.052293
14	0.204360	79	1.158660	144	2.122049	209	3.094612	274	4.076438	339	5.067614
15	0.218973	80	1.173413	145	2.136942	210	3.109647	275	4.091615	340	5.082936
16	0.233589	81	1.188167	146	2.151837	211	3.124684	276	4.106795	341	5.098261
17	0.248206	82	1.202924	147	2.166734	212	3.139723	277	4.121978	342	5.113587
18	0.262826	83	1.217683	148	2.181633	213	3.154764	278	4.137162	343	5.128916
19	0.277447	84	1.232443	149	2.196535	214	3.169807	279	4.152349	344	5.144248
20	0.292071	85	1.247207	150	2.211438	215	3.184853	280	4.167538	345	5.159581
21	0.306697	86	1.261972	151	2.226344	216	3.199901	281	4.182729	346	5.174917
22	0.321325	87	1.276739	152	2.241252	217	3.214951	282	4.197922	347	5.190255
23	0.335955	88	1.291509	153	2.256162	218	3.230003	283	4.213118	348	5.205595
24	0.350588	89	1.306280	154	2.271075	219	3.245057	284	4.228315	349	5.220938
25	0.365222	90	1.321054	155	2.285989	220	3.260114	285	4.243515	350	5.236282
26	0.379859	91	1.335830	156	2.300906	221	3.275172	286	4.258718	351	5.251629
27	0.394497	92	1.350608	157	2.315825	222	3.290233	287	4.273922	352	5.266979
28	0.409138	93	1.365389	158	2.330746	223	3.305297	288	4.289129	353	5.282330
29	0.423781	94	1.380171	159	2.345669	224	3.320362	289	4.304337	354	5.297684
30	0.438426	95	1.394956	160	2.360594	225	3.335429	290	4.319548	355	5.313040
31	0.453074	96	1.409742	161	2.375522	226	3.350499	291	4.334762	356	5.328398
32	0.467723	97	1.424531	162	2.390452	227	3.365571	292	4.349977	357	5.343758
33	0.482375	98	1.439322	163	2.405384	228	3.380645	293	4.365195	358	5.359121
34	0.497028	99	1.454116	164	2.420318	229	3.395722	294	4.380415	359	5.374486
35	0.511684	100	1.468911	165	2.435254	230	3.410800	295	4.395637	360	5.389853
36	0.526342	101	1.483709	166	2.450193	231	3.425881	296	4.410861	361	5.405222
37	0.541002	102	1.498508	167	2.465133	232	3.440964	297	4.426088	362	5.420594
38	0.555664	103	1.513310	168	2.480076	233	3.456049	298	4.441317	363	5.435968
39	0.570329	104	1.528114	169	2.495021	234	3.471136	299	4.456548	364	5.451344
40	0.584995	105	1.542920	170	2.509968	235	3.486226	300	4.471781	365	5.466722
41	0.599664	106	1.557729	171	2.524918	236	3.501318	301	4.487016	366	5.482103
42	0.614335	107	1.572539	172	2.539869	237	3.516412	302	4.502254		
43	0.629008	108	1.587352	173	2.554823	238	3.531508	303	4.517494		
44	0.643683	109	1.602167	174	2.569779	239	3.546606	304	4.532736		
45	0.658360	110	1.616984	175	2.584737	240	3.561707	305	4.547981		
46	0.673039	111	1.631803	176	2.599697	241	3.576809	306	4.563227		
47	0.687721	112	1.646624	177	2.614660	242	3.591914	307	4.578476		
48	0.702404	113	1.661448	178	2.629624	243	3.607021	308	4.593727		
49	0.717090	114	1.676273	179	2.644591	244	3.622131	309	4.608980		
50	0.731778	115	1.691101	180	2.659560	245	3.637242	310	4.624236		
51	0.746468	116	1.705931	181	2.674531	246	3.652356	311	4.639493		
52	0.761160	117	1.720763	182	2.689505	247	3.667472	312	4.654753		
53	0.775855	118	1.735597	183	2.704480	248	3.682590	313	4.670015		
54	0.790551	119	1.750434	184	2.719458	249	3.697711	314	4.685280		
55	0.805250	120	1.765272	185	2.734438	250	3.712833	315	4.700546		
56	0.819950	121	1.780113	186	2.749420	251	3.727958	316	4.715815		
57	0.834653	122	1.794956	187	2.764404	252	3.743085	317	4.731086		
58	0.849358	123	1.809801	188	2.779391	253	3.758214	318	4.746360		
59	0.864066	124	1.824648	189	2.794379	254	3.773346	319	4.761635		
60	0.878775	125	1.839498	190	2.809370	255	3.788479	320	4.776913		
61	0.893486	126	1.854349	191	2.824363	256	3.803615	321	4.792193		
62	0.908200	127	1.869203	192	2.839358	257	3.818753	322	4.807475		
63	0.922916	128	1.884059	193	2.854356	258	3.833893	323	4.822759		
64	0.937634	129	1.898917	194	2.869355	259	3.849036	324	4.838046		
65	0.952354	130	1.913777	195	2.884357	260	3.864180	325	4.853335		

T-8 TABLES

Gives Amount per $100 investment

Gives Amount

TABLE 7
5% COMPOUNDED DAILY
(360-day Basis)*

Period	Amount of 1	Period	Amount of 1	Period	Amount of 1
1	1.000 138	61	1.008 507	121	1.016 946
2	1.000 277	62	1.008 647	122	1.017 087
3	1.000 416	63	1.008 787	123	1.017 228
4	1.000 555	64	1.008 927	124	1.017 370
5	1.000 694	65	1.009 068	125	1.017 511
6	1.000 833	66	1.009 208	126	1.017 652
7	1.000 972	67	1.009 348	127	1.017 794
8	1.001 111	68	1.009 488	128	1.017 935
9	1.001 250	69	1.009 628	129	1.018 076
10	1.001 389	70	1.009 768	130	1.018 218
11	1.001 528	71	1.009 909	131	1.018 359
12	1.001 667	72	1.010 049	132	1.018 501
13	1.001 807	73	1.010 189	133	1.018 642
14	1.001 946	74	1.010 330	134	1.018 784
15	1.002 085	75	1.010 470	135	1.018 925
16	1.002 224	76	1.010 610	136	1.019 067
17	1.002 363	77	1.010 751	137	1.019 208
18	1.002 502	78	1.010 891	138	1.019 350
19	1.002 642	79	1.011 031	139	1.019 491
20	1.002 781	80	1.011 172	140	1.019 633
21	1.002 920	81	1.011 312	141	1.019 774
22	1.003 060	82	1.011 453	142	1.019 916
23	1.003 199	83	1.011 593	143	1.020 058
24	1.003 338	84	1.011 734	144	1.020 190
25	1.003 478	85	1.011 874	145	1.020 341
26	1.003 617	86	1.012 015	146	1.020 483
27	1.003 756	87	1.012 155	147	1.020 625
28	1.003 896	88	1.012 296	148	1.020 766
29	1.004 035	89	1.012 436	149	1.020 908
30	1.004 175	90	1.012 577	150	1.021 050
31	1.004 314	91	1.012 718	151	1.021 192
32	1.004 454	92	1.012 858	152	1.021 334
33	1.004 593	93	1.012 999	153	1.021 475
34	1.004 733	94	1.013 140	154	1.021 617
35	1.004 872	95	1.013 280	155	1.021 759
36	1.005 012	96	1.013 421	156	1.021 901
37	1.005 151	97	1.013 562	157	1.022 043
38	1.005 291	98	1.013 703	158	1.022 185
39	1.005 430	99	1.013 843	159	1.022 327
40	1.005 570	100	1.013 984	160	1.022 469
41	1.005 710	101	1.014 125	161	1.022 611
42	1.005 849	102	1.014 266	162	1.022 753
43	1.005 989	103	1.014 407	163	1.022 895
44	1.006 129	104	1.014 548	164	1.023 037
45	1.006 269	105	1.014 689	165	1.023 179
46	1.006 408	106	1.014 830	166	1.023 321
47	1.006 548	107	1.014 971	167	1.023 463
48	1.006 688	108	1.015 112	168	1.023 606
49	1.006 828	109	1.015 252	169	1.023 748
50	1.006 968	110	1.015 394	170	1.023 890
51	1.007 107	111	1.015 535	171	1.024 032
52	1.007 247	112	1.015 676	172	1.024 174
53	1.007 387	113	1.015 817	173	1.024 317
54	1.007 527	114	1.015 958	174	1.024 459
55	1.007 667	115	1.016 099	175	1.024 601
56	1.007 807	116	1.016 240	176	1.024 743
57	1.007 947	117	1.016 381	177	1.024 886
58	1.008 087	118	1.016 522	178	1.025 028
59	1.008 227	119	1.016 663	179	1.025 170
60	1.008 367	120	1.016 805	180	1.025 313

TABLE 8
5% COMPOUNDED CONTINUOUSLY
(360-day Basis)*

Period	Amount of 1	Period	Amount of 1	Period	Amount of 1
1	1.000 138	61	1.008 508	121	1.016 947
2	1.000 277	62	1.008 648	122	1.017 088
3	1.000 416	63	1.008 788	123	1.017 230
4	1.000 555	64	1.008 928	124	1.017 371
5	1.000 694	65	1.009 068	125	1.017 512
6	1.000 833	66	1.009 208	126	1.017 654
7	1.000 972	67	1.009 348	127	1.017 795
8	1.001 111	68	1.009 489	128	1.017 936
9	1.001 250	69	1.009 629	129	1.018 078
10	1.001 389	70	1.009 769	130	1.018 219
11	1.001 528	71	1.009 909	131	1.018 360
12	1.001 668	72	1.010 050	132	1.018 502
13	1.001 807	73	1.010 190	133	1.018 643
14	1.001 946	74	1.010 330	134	1.018 785
15	1.002 085	75	1.010 471	135	1.018 926
16	1.002 224	76	1.010 611	136	1.019 068
17	1.002 363	77	1.010 751	137	1.019 209
18	1.002 503	78	1.010 892	138	1.019 351
19	1.002 642	79	1.011 032	139	1.019 493
20	1.002 781	80	1.011 173	140	1.019 634
21	1.002 920	81	1.011 313	141	1.019 776
22	1.003 060	82	1.011 453	142	1.019 917
23	1.003 199	83	1.011 594	143	1.020 059
24	1.003 338	84	1.011 734	144	1.020 201
25	1.003 478	85	1.011 875	145	1.020 343
26	1.003 617	86	1.012 016	146	1.020 484
27	1.003 757	87	1.012 156	147	1.020 626
28	1.003 896	88	1.012 297	148	1.020 768
29	1.004 035	89	1.012 437	149	1.020 910
30	1.004 175	90	1.012 578	150	1.021 051
31	1.004 314	91	1.012 719	151	1.021 193
32	1.004 454	92	1.012 859	152	1.021 335
33	1.004 593	93	1.013 000	153	1.021 477
34	1.004 733	94	1.013 141	154	1.021 619
35	1.004 872	95	1.013 281	155	1.021 761
36	1.005 012	96	1.013 422	156	1.021 903
37	1.005 152	97	1.013 563	157	1.022 045
38	1.005 291	98	1.013 704	158	1.022 186
39	1.005 431	99	1.013 844	159	1.022 328
40	1.005 571	100	1.013 985	160	1.022 470
41	1.005 710	101	1.014 126	161	1.022 612
42	1.005 850	102	1.014 267	162	1.022 755
43	1.005 990	103	1.014 408	163	1.022 897
44	1.006 129	104	1.014 549	164	1.023 039
45	1.006 269	105	1.014 690	165	1.023 181
46	1.006 409	106	1.014 831	166	1.023 323
47	1.006 549	107	1.014 972	167	1.023 465
48	1.006 688	108	1.015 113	168	1.023 607
49	1.006 828	109	1.015 254	169	1.023 749
50	1.006 968	110	1.015 395	170	1.023 892
51	1.007 108	111	1.015 536	171	1.024 034
52	1.007 248	112	1.015 677	172	1.024 176
53	1.007 388	113	1.015 818	173	1.024 318
54	1.007 528	114	1.015 959	174	1.024 461
55	1.007 668	115	1.016 100	175	1.024 603
56	1.007 808	116	1.016 241	176	1.024 745
57	1.007 948	117	1.016 382	177	1.024 887
58	1.008 088	118	1.016 523	178	1.025 030
59	1.008 228	119	1.016 665	179	1.025 172
60	1.008 368	120	1.016 806	180	1.025 315

*Courtesy of the Financial Publishing Company of Boston.

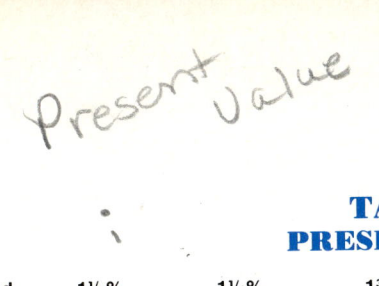

TABLE 9
PRESENT VALUE

Period	1¼%	1½%	1¾%	2%	2½%	3%
1	.987654	.985221	.982801	.980392	.975609	.970873
2	.975461	.970661	.965898	.961168	.951814	.942595
3	.963419	.956316	.949285	.942322	.928599	.915141
4	.951525	.942184	.932959	.923845	.905950	.888487
5	.939777	.928260	.916912	.905730	.883854	.862608
6	.928175	.914542	.901142	.887971	.862296	.837484
7	.916716	.901026	.885643	.870560	.841265	.813091
8	.905399	.887711	.870411	.853490	.820746	.789409
9	.894221	.874592	.855441	.836755	.800728	.766416
10	.883181	.861667	.840728	.820348	.781198	.744093
11	.872278	.848933	.826269	.804263	.762144	.722421
12	.861509	.836387	.812057	.788493	.743555	.701379
13	.850873	.824027	.798091	.773032	.725420	.680951
14	.840369	.811849	.784365	.757875	.707727	.661117
15	.829994	.799851	.770875	.743014	.690465	.641861
16	.819747	.788031	.757617	.728445	.673624	.623166
17	.809627	.776385	.744586	.714162	.657195	.605016
18	.799632	.764911	.731780	.700159	.641165	.587394
19	.789760	.753607	.719194	.686430	.625527	.570286
20	.780009	.742470	.706825	.672971	.610270	.553675
21	.770380	.731497	.694668	.659775	.595386	.537549
22	.760869	.720687	.682720	.646839	.580864	.521892
23	.751475	.710037	.670978	.634155	.566697	.506691
24	.742198	.699543	.659438	.621721	.552875	.491933
25	.733035	.689205	.648096	.609530	.539390	.477605
26	.723985	.679020	.636950	.597579	.526234	.463694
27	.715047	.668985	.625995	.585862	.513399	.450189
28	.706219	.659099	.615228	.574374	.500877	.437076
29	.697500	.649358	.604646	.563112	.488661	.424346
30	.688889	.639762	.594247	.552070	.476742	.411986
31	.680385	.630307	.584027	.541245	.465114	.399987
32	.671985	.620992	.573982	.530633	.453770	.388337
33	.663688	.611815	.564110	.520228	.442702	.377026
34	.655495	.602774	.554408	.510028	.431905	.366044
35	.647402	.593866	.544873	.500027	.421371	.355383
36	.639409	.585089	.535501	.490223	.411093	.345032
37	.631516	.576443	.526291	.480610	.401067	.334982
38	.623719	.567924	.517239	.471187	.391284	.325226
39	.616019	.559531	.508343	.461948	.381741	.315753
40	.608414	.551262	.499600	.452890	.372430	.306556
41	.600902	.543115	.491008	.444010	.363346	.297628
42	.593484	.535089	.482563	.435304	.354484	.288959
43	.586157	.527181	.474263	.426768	.345838	.280542
44	.578920	.519390	.466106	.418400	.337403	.272371
45	.571773	.511714	.458090	.410196	.329174	.264438
46	.564714	.504152	.450211	.402153	.321145	.256736
47	.557743	.496702	.442468	.394268	.313312	.249258
48	.550857	.489361	.434858	.386537	.305671	.241998
49	.544056	.482129	.427379	.378958	.298215	.234950
50	.537339	.475004	.420028	.371527	.290942	.228107

TABLE 9 (cont.)

Period	3½%	4%	5%	6%	7%	8%
1	.966183	.961538	.952380	.943396	.934579	.925925
2	.933510	.924556	.907029	.889996	.873438	.857338
3	.901942	.888996	.863837	.839619	.816297	.793832
4	.871442	.854804	.822702	.792093	.762895	.735029
5	.841973	.821927	.783526	.747258	.712986	.680583
6	.813500	.790314	.746215	.704960	.666342	.630169
7	.785990	.759917	.710681	.665057	.622749	.583490
8	.759411	.730690	.676839	.627412	.582009	.540268
9	.733731	.702586	.644608	.591898	.543933	.500248
10	.708918	.675564	.613913	.558394	.508349	.463193
11	.684945	.649580	.584679	.526787	.475092	.428882
12	.661783	.624597	.556837	.496969	.444011	.397113
13	.639404	.600574	.530321	.468839	.414964	.367697
14	.617781	.577475	.505067	.442300	.387817	.340461
15	.596890	.555264	.481017	.417265	.362446	.315241
16	.576705	.533908	.458111	.393646	.338734	.291890
17	.557203	.513373	.436296	.371364	.316574	.270268
18	.538361	.493628	.415520	.350343	.295863	.250249
19	.520155	.474642	.395733	.330512	.276508	.231712
20	.502565	.456386	.376889	.311804	.258418	.214548
21	.485570	.438833	.358942	.294155	.241513	.198655
22	.469150	.421955	.341849	.277505	.225713	.183940
23	.453285	.405726	.325571	.261797	.210946	.170315
24	.437957	.390121	.310067	.246978	.197146	.157699
25	.423147	.375116	.295302	.232998	.184249	.146017
26	.408837	.360689	.281240	.219810	.172195	.135201
27	.395012	.346816	.267848	.207367	.160930	.125186
28	.381654	.333477	.255093	.195630	.150402	.115913
29	.368748	.320651	.242946	.184556	.140562	.107327
30	.356278	.308318	.231377	.174110	.131367	.099377
31	.344230	.296460	.220359	.164254	.122773	.092016
32	.332589	.285057	.209866	.154957	.114741	.085200
33	.321342	.274094	.199872	.146186	.107234	.078888
34	.310476	.263552	.190354	.137911	.100219	.073045
35	.299976	.253415	.181290	.130105	.093662	.067634
36	.289832	.243668	.172657	.122740	.087535	.062624
37	.280031	.234296	.164435	.115793	.081808	.057985
38	.270561	.225285	.156605	.109238	.076456	.053690
39	.261412	.216620	.149147	.103055	.071455	.049713
40	.252572	.208289	.142045	.097222	.066780	.046030
41	.244031	.200277	.135281	.091719	.062411	.042621
42	.235779	.192574	.128839	.086527	.058328	.039464
43	.227805	.185168	.122704	.081629	.054512	.036540
44	.220102	.178046	.116861	.077009	.050946	.033834
45	.212659	.171198	.111296	.072650	.047613	.031327
46	.205467	.164613	.105996	.068537	.044498	.029007
47	.198519	.158282	.100949	.064658	.041587	.026858
48	.191806	.152194	.096142	.060998	.038866	.024869
49	.185320	.146341	.091563	.057545	.036324	.023026
50	.179053	.140712	.087203	.054288	.033947	.021321

2.4 ESTIMATING AND MORE CONVERSION

Solution

```
     0.8 7 5
8)7.0 0 0      7/8 = 0.875
  6 4
    6 0
    5 6
      4 0
      4 0
        0
```

DO EXERCISES 23 AND 24.

Some decimals repeat.

Example 8 Convert to decimal notation: $\frac{7}{12}$.

Solution

```
        0.5 8 3 3
   12)7.0 0 0 0
      6 0
      1 0 0
        9 6
          4 0
          3 6
            4 0
            3 6
              4
```

We have 4 repeating as a remainder, so the digits will repeat in the quotient. Therefore,

$\frac{7}{12} = 0.583333\ldots$

Instead of the dots, we often put a bar over the repeating part. Thus,

$\frac{7}{12} = 0.583\overline{3}$ or $0.58\overline{3}$.

DO EXERCISES 25 AND 26.

Example 9 Convert to decimal notation: $\frac{41}{11}$.

Solution

```
         3.7 2 7 2
    11)4 1.0 0 0 0
       3 3
         8 0
         7 7
           3 0
           2 2
             8 0
             7 7
               3 0
               2 2
                 8
```

Convert to decimal notation.

23. $\frac{5}{8}$ .625

24. $\frac{7}{4}$ 1.75

Convert to decimal notation.

25. $\frac{1}{6}$ .1$\overline{6}$

26. $\frac{2}{3}$.$\overline{6}$

ANSWERS ON PAGE A–4

Convert to decimal notation.

27. $\dfrac{84}{11}$

28. $\dfrac{1}{11}$

29. Find the gas mileage. Round to the nearest tenth of a mile per gallon.

First odometer reading: 39,401.2

Second odometer reading: 39,622.0

Number of gallons at the last fill: 12.6

DECIMAL NOTATION AND EQUATIONS

The 8 and 3 keep repeating as remainders, so 72 keeps repeating in the quotient. Therefore,

$$\dfrac{41}{11} = 3.727272\ldots \quad \text{or} \quad \dfrac{41}{11} = 3.\overline{72}.$$

DO EXERCISES 27 AND 28.

••• SOLVING PROBLEMS

When decimals repeat in problems, we usually round. To do that we carry the division out one place beyond the place to which we are to round, and then round back.

Example 10 Find the gas mileage. Round to the nearest tenth of a mile per gallon.

First odometer reading: 42,689.3

Second odometer reading: 42,886.7

Number of gallons at the last fill: 15.6

Solution

$$\text{Gasoline mileage} = \dfrac{\text{Difference in the odometer readings}}{\text{Number of gallons at the last fill}}$$

$$= \dfrac{42{,}886.7 - 42{,}689.3}{15.6}$$

$$= \dfrac{197.4}{15.6}$$

We divide and round as follows:

```
              1 2. 6 5
    1 5.6.)1 9 7.4.0 0
           1 5 6
           ─────
             4 1 4
             3 1 2
             ─────
             1 0 2 0
               9 3 6
               ─────
                 8 4 0
                 7 8 0
                 ─────
                   6 0
```

We stop the division at the hundredths place and round. The gas mileage is about 12.7 miles per gallon.

DO EXERCISE 29.

EXERCISE SET 2.4   **87**

NAME _____   CLASS _____   ANSWERS

EXERCISE SET 2.4

● Round to the nearest hundredth, tenth, one, ten, and hundred.

1. 745.06534 **2.** 317.18565 **3.** 6780.50568 **4.** 840.15493

745.07   317.19   6780.51   840.15
745.1   317.2   6780.5   840.2
745   317   6781   840
750   320   6780   840
700   300   6800   800

Round to the nearest cent and to the nearest dollar (nearest one).

5. $17.988 **6.** $20.492 **7.** $346.075 **8.** $4.718

17.99   20.49   346.08   4.72
18.00   20.00   346   5.00

Round to the nearest dollar.

9. $16.95 **10.** $17.50 **11.** $189.50 **12.** $567.24

●● Convert to decimal notation.

13. $\frac{3}{8}$ **14.** $\frac{1}{8}$ **15.** $\frac{3}{5}$ **16.** $\frac{4}{5}$

17. $\frac{13}{16}$ **18.** $\frac{1}{16}$ **19.** $\frac{29}{40}$ **20.** $\frac{42}{125}$

21. $\frac{5}{3}$ **22.** $\frac{1}{3}$ **23.** $\frac{5}{6}$ **24.** $\frac{11}{6}$

1. _____
2. _____
3. _____
4. _____
5. _____
6. _____
7. _____
8. _____
9. 17.00
10. 18.00
11. 190.00
12. 567.00
13. .375
14. .125
15. .6
16. .8
17. .8125
18. .0625
19. .725
20. .336
21. 1.$\overline{6}$
22. .$\overline{3}$
23. 8.$\overline{3}$
24. 1.8$\overline{3}$

88 DECIMAL NOTATION AND EQUATIONS

ANSWERS

25. $\dfrac{4}{9}$ 26. $\dfrac{7}{9}$ 27. $\dfrac{13}{11}$ 28. $\dfrac{4}{11}$

25. .$\overline{4}$

26. .$\overline{7}$

29. $\dfrac{49}{12}$ 30. $\dfrac{65}{12}$ 31. $\dfrac{17}{20}$ 32. $\dfrac{17}{25}$

27. 1.1$\overline{8}$

■■■ Solve. Find the gas mileage. Round to the nearest tenth of a mile per gallon.

33. First odometer reading: 16,322.9
    Second odometer reading: 16,606.7
    Number of gallons at the last fill: 8.9

28. .3$\overline{6}$

29. 4.08$\overline{3}$

34. First odometer reading: 54,113.5
    Second odometer reading: 54,432.1
    Number of gallons at the last fill: 11.6

30. 5.41$\overline{6}$

31. .85

35. A consumer earned $22 working 9 hours. What was the hourly wage? Round to the nearest cent.

32. .68

36. One week a worker earned $197.32 working 40 hours. What was the hourly wage? Round to the nearest cent.

33. 31.9

37. A dozen softballs cost $72.95. What was the cost per ball? Round to the nearest cent.

34. 27.5

38. A dozen sweatshirts cost $89.98. What was the cost per shirt? Round to the nearest cent.

35. 2.44

39. A builder paid $33,000 for a 2.8-acre lot. What was the cost per acre? Round to the nearest dollar.

36. 4.93

37. 6.10

40. A builder paid $44,000 for a 3.7-acre lot. What was the cost per acre? Round to the nearest dollar.

38. 7.50

41. ▦ Convert each to decimal notation.

$\dfrac{1}{9}, \dfrac{1}{99}, \dfrac{1}{999}$

Look for a pattern in the above and convert the following to decimal notation without using the calculator.

39. 11,786

$\dfrac{1}{9999}$ .0001

40. 11,892

41. .$\overline{1}$, .$\overline{01}$, .$\overline{001}$

42. ▦ Divide and round to the nearest ten-thousandth, thousandth, hundredth, tenth, and one.

$\dfrac{1000}{81}$ 12.3457   12.3

42.   12.346   12

                   12.35

2.5 EXPONENTS

■ EXPONENTIAL NOTATION

Exponents provide a shorter way of writing products. For example,

$\underbrace{5 \times 5 \times 5 \times 5}_{4}$ is shortened to 5^4 ← Exponent
Base

We read 5^4 as "five to the fourth power," 4^2 as "four squared," and 7^3 as "seven cubed." 5^4 is an example of *exponential notation*.

Example 1 Write exponential notation: $10 \cdot 10 \cdot 10 \cdot 10 \cdot 10 \cdot 10$.

Solution

$10 \cdot 10 \cdot 10 \cdot 10 \cdot 10 \cdot 10 = 10^6$

DO EXERCISES 1–4.

■■ EVALUATING EXPONENTIAL EXPRESSIONS

Example 2 Evaluate: 10^3.

Solution

$10^3 = 10 \cdot 10 \cdot 10 = 1000$ ($10 \cdot 10 = 100$, and $100 \cdot 10 = 1000$)

Example 3 Evaluate: 3^4.

Solution

$3^4 = 3 \times 3 \times 3 \times 3 = 81$

Example 4 Evaluate: $(1.08)^2$.

Solution

$(1.08)^2 = 1.08 \times 1.08 = 1.1664$

DO EXERCISES 5–8.

One as an Exponent

Note the following. We divide by 8 each time.

$8 \cdot 8 \cdot 8 \cdot 8 = 8^4 = 4096$
$8 \cdot 8 \cdot 8 = 8^3 = 512$
$8 \cdot 8 = 8^2 = 64$
$8 = 8^? = 8$

If the pattern were to continue, we would have

$8 = 8^1$

We define 8^1 to be 8. In general,

We define $a^1 = a$.

OBJECTIVES

After finishing Section 2.5, you should be able to:

■ Write exponential notation for a product.

■■ Evaluate exponential expressions.

Write exponential notation.

1. $5 \cdot 5 \cdot 5$

    5^3

2. $5 \cdot 5 \cdot 5 \cdot 5 \cdot 5$

    5^5

3. 1.08×1.08

    1.08^2

4. $10 \cdot 10 \cdot 10 \cdot 10$

    10^4

Evaluate.

5. 10^4

    10000

6. 8^3 512

7. $(1.1)^3$ 1.331

8. $(1.0125)^2$ 1.0251

ANSWERS ON PAGE A–4

Evaluate.

9. 5^1

10. 43^1

11. $(5.8)^1$

Evaluate.

12. 8^0

13. 52^0

14. $(1.07)^0$

ANSWERS ON PAGE A–4

DECIMAL NOTATION AND EQUATIONS

Example 5 Evaluate: 37^1.

Solution

$37^1 = 37$

DO EXERCISES 9–11.

Zero as an Exponent

Note the following. We divide by 5 each time.

$5 \cdot 5 \cdot 5 = 5^3 = 125$
$5 \cdot 5 = 5^2 = 25$
$5 = 5^1 = 5$
$1 = 5^? = 1$

If the pattern were to continue, we would have

$1 = 5^0$

We define 5^0 to be 1. In general,

> We define $a^0 = 1$, for any nonzero number a.

Example 6 Evaluate: 42^0.

Solution

$42^0 = 1$

DO EXERCISES 12–14.

EXERCISE SET 2.5

● Write exponential notation.

1. $3 \times 3 \times 3 \times 3$

2. $2 \times 2 \times 2 \times 2 \times 2$

3. 5×5

4. $13 \cdot 13 \cdot 13 \cdot 13 \cdot 13 \cdot 13$

5. $7 \cdot 7 \cdot 7 \cdot 7 \cdot 7$

6. $10 \cdot 10 \cdot 10$

7. $10 \cdot 10 \cdot 10 \cdot 10 \cdot 10$

8. $10 \times 10 \times 10 \times 10$

9. $1 \cdot 1 \cdot 1 \cdot 1 \cdot 1 \cdot 1 \cdot 1 \cdot 1$

10. $16 \cdot 16$

●● Evaluate.

11. 5^2 12. 7^3 13. 9^5 14. 12^4 15. 10^2

16. 11^2 17. 9^4 18. 2^4 19. 8^3 20. 10^3

21. 1^5 22. 1^4 23. $(1.8)^2$ 24. $(2.3)^2$ 25. $(0.1)^3$

ANSWERS

1. 3^4
2. 2^5
3. 5^2
4. 13^6
5. 7^5
6. 10^3
7. 10^5
8. 10^4
9. 1^8
10. 16^2
11. 25
12. 343
13. 59,049
14. 20,736
15. 100
16. 121
17. 6561
18. 16
19. 512
20. 1000
21. 1
22. 1
23. 3.24
24. 5.29
25. .001

92 DECIMAL NOTATION AND EQUATIONS

ANSWERS

26. .04
27. 219.04
28. 416.16
29. 16/25
30. 9/64
31. 1
32. 6
33. 28.3
34. 1
35. 5
36. 4
37. 27
38. 15
39. 1
40. 1
41. 1
42. 1
43. 1
44. 1
45. 1
46. 1
47. 677.12
48. .002
49. 1259.712
50. 1310.796

26. $(0.2)^3$
27. $(14.8)^2$
28. $(20.4)^2$
29. $\left(\dfrac{4}{5}\right)^2$ = $\dfrac{16}{25}$
30. $\left(\dfrac{3}{8}\right)^2$ = $\dfrac{9}{64}$

31. 8^0
32. 6^1
33. $(28.3)^1$
34. $(33.4)^0$

35. 5^1
36. 4^1
37. 27^1
38. 15^1

39. 5^0
40. 6^0
41. 10^0
42. 14^0

43. 54^0
44. 43^0
45. $(22.7)^0$
46. $\left(\dfrac{11}{12}\right)^0$

Compute.

47. $8 \times (9.2)^2$
48. $20 \times (0.01)^2$
49. 🖩 $1000 \times (1.08)^3$
50. 🖩 $1000 \times (1.07)^4$

2.6 ORDER OF OPERATIONS

■ SIMPLIFYING EXPRESSIONS

Suppose we have a calculation like the following:

34 · 56 − 17.

How do we find an answer? Do we subtract 17 from 56 and then multiply by 34, or do we multiply 34 by 56 and then subtract? In the first case the answer is 1326. In the second case the answer is 1887. Consider the calculation

7 · 14 − (12 + 18).

What do the parentheses mean? To deal with these questions we have to make some agreement regarding the order in which we perform operations. These rules are as follows:

> **To carry out a calculation:**
> a) First, carry out operations inside parentheses.
> b) Second, evaluate exponential expressions.
> c) Third, do all multiplications and divisions in order, from left to right.
> d) Fourth, do all additions and subtractions in order, from left to right.

Example 1 Simplify: 34 · 56 − 17.

Solution There are no parentheses or exponential expressions, so we start with the third step.

34 · 56 − 17 = 1904 − 17   Do all multiplications in order, from left to right.

= 1887   Do all additions and subtractions in order, from left to right.

Example 2 Simplify: 7 · 14 − (12 + 18).

Solution

7 · 14 − (12 + 18) = 7 · 14 − 30   First, carry out operations inside parentheses.

= 98 − 30   There are no exponential expressions. Third, do all multiplications and divisions in order, from left to right.

= 68   Fourth, do all additions and subtractions in order, from left to right.

DO EXERCISES 1–4.

OBJECTIVE

After finishing Section 2.6, you should be able to:

■ Simplify expressions using the rules for order of operations.

Simplify.

1. 23 · 82 − 43

    1843

2. 104 ÷ 4 + 57

    83

3. 25 · 26 − (56 + 10)

    584

4. 75 ÷ 5 + (83 − 14)

    84

ANSWERS ON PAGE A-4

Simplify.

5. $28 \cdot (103 - 47)$

728

Simplify.

6. $5^3 + 26 \cdot 71 - (16 + 25 \cdot 3)$

125 + 1846 − 91
= 1880

7. $4^3 + 10 \cdot 20 + 8^2 - 23$

64 + 200 + 64 − 23
= 305

Simplify.

8. $2000 \times (3 + 1.14)^2$

342,192

DECIMAL NOTATION AND EQUATIONS

Example 3 Simplify: $14 \times (82.6 + 67.9)$.

Solution

$14 \times (82.6 + 67.9) = 14 \times 150.5$ First, carry out operations inside parentheses.

$= 2107$ Then multiply.

DO EXERCISE 5.

Example 4 Simplify: $2^4 + 51 \cdot 4 - (37 + 23 \cdot 2)$.

Solution

64 + 204 − (83)

$2^4 + 51 \cdot 4 - (37 + 23 \cdot 2)$

$= 2^4 + 51 \cdot 4 - (37 + 46)$ Carry out operations inside parentheses. To do this we first multiply 23 by 2.

$= 2^4 + 51 \cdot 4 - 83$ Complete the addition inside parentheses.

$= 16 + 51 \cdot 4 - 83$ Evaluate exponential expressions.

$= 16 + 204 - 83$ Do all multiplications.

$= 220 - 83$ Do all additions and subtractions in order, from left to right.

$= 137$

DO EXERCISES 6 AND 7.

Example 5 Simplify: $3000 \times (1 + 0.16)^3$.

Solution

$3000 \times (1 + 0.16)^3 = 3000 \times (1.16)^3$ Carry out the operation inside the parentheses.

$= 3000 \times 1.560896$ Evaluate exponential expressions.

$= 4682.688$ Multiply.

DO EXERCISE 8.

EXERCISE SET 2.6

● Simplify. Use a calculator whenever you wish.

1. $16 \cdot 24 + 50$

2. $23 + 18 \cdot 20$

3. $15 \cdot 24 - 10 \cdot 20$

4. $23 \cdot 17 + 14 \cdot 50$

391

5. $28 \cdot (15 + 35)$

6. $28 \cdot 15 + 28 \cdot 35$

420

7. $125 \cdot 3 - 125 \cdot 2$

375

8. $125 \times (3 - 2)$

9. $2^4 + 2^3 - 10$

16 + 8

10. $40 - 3^2 - 2^3$

40 - 27 - 8

22222

11. $275 \div 25 + 256 \div 16$

11 + 16

12. $324 \div 20 - 225 \div 25$

16.2 - 9

13. $2^5 \cdot (16 + 42)$

32 · 58

ANSWERS

1. 434
2. 383
3. 175
4. 1091
5. 1400
6. 1400
7. 125
8. 125
9. 14
10. 5
11. 27
12. 7.2
13. 1856

96   DECIMAL NOTATION AND EQUATIONS

ANSWERS

14. $23 \times 51 + 4 \times 16.3 - (3 \times 14 + 2 \times 15)$

1173 + 65.2 − 72

14. 1166.2

15. $2^3 + 2^4 + 2^5 - 3^2$

8 + 16 + 32 − 9

15. 3136

16. $4 \times 16.8 + 5 \times 23.2 + 36 \times 41.9 + 72 \times 9.8 - 32 \times 50$

16. 2136

17. $200 \cdot 5 - 15 \cdot 4 - 20 \cdot 3 + 500 \cdot 2 + 16 \cdot 16$

(1000) − (60) − (60) + (1000) + 256

17. 364

18. $4 \cdot (18 + 32 + 16 + 23 + 14 + 78 - 90)$

18.

19. $10{,}000 \times (1 + 0.12)^2$

19. 12544

20. $5500 \times (1 + 0.13)^2$

20. 7022.95

2.7 EQUATION SOLVING

In this section we introduce the notions of *equations*, *solutions of equations*, and methods of solving equations using arithmetic.

● EQUATIONS AND SOLUTIONS

Let's find a number that we can put in the box to make this sentence true:

$9 = 3 + \Box$.

We are asking "9 is 3 plus what number?" The answer is 6.

$9 = 3 + \boxed{6}$

DO EXERCISES 1 AND 2.

A sentence with = is called an *equation*. A *solution* of an equation is a number that makes the sentence true. Thus, 6 is a solution of

$9 = 3 + \Box$ because $9 = 3 + \boxed{6}$ is true.

But 7 is not a solution of

$9 = 3 + \Box$ because $9 = 3 + \boxed{7}$ is false.

DO EXERCISES 3 AND 4.

We can use a letter (also called a *variable*) instead of a box. For example,

$x + 8 = 11$.

> A *solution* is a replacement for the letter or variable that makes the equation true. When we find all the solutions, we say we have *solved* the equation.

Example 1 Solve $x + 12 = 27$ by trial.

Solution We replace x by several numbers.

If we replace x by 13 we get a false equation: $13 + 12 = 27$.
If we replace x by 14 we get a false equation: $14 + 12 = 27$.
If we replace x by 15 we get a true equation: $15 + 12 = 27$.

No other replacement makes the equation true, so the solution is 15.

Example 2 Solve: $7 + n = 22$.

Solution

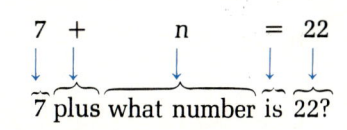

$7 + n = 22$

7 plus what number is 22?

The solution is 15.

OBJECTIVES

After finishing Section 2.7, you should be able to:

● Solve equations by trial.

●● Solve equations like $t + 37 = 54$ and $4x = 36$ by writing related sentences.

Find a number that makes each sentence true.

1. $8 = 72 \div \Box$

2. $\Box - 2 = 7$

3. Determine whether 7 is a solution of $\Box \cdot 5 = 20$.

4. Determine whether 4 is a solution of $\Box \cdot 5 = 20$.

ANSWERS ON PAGE A–4

Solve by trial.

5. $n + 3 = 8$

6. $x - 2 = 8$

7. $45 - 13 = y$

8. $10 \cdot t = 320$

Solve.

9. $m + 32 = 77$

10. $78.9 + t = 155.4$

11. $7877 = x + 4566$

ANSWERS ON PAGE A-4

DECIMAL NOTATION AND EQUATIONS

Example 3 Solve: $104 \div 4 = y$.

Solution

$$104 \div 4 = y$$

104 divided by 4 is what number?

The solution is 26.

Notice, as in Example 3, that when the letter is alone on one side of the equation, the other side shows us what calculations to do to find the solution.

DO EXERCISES 5–8.

◼◼ SOLVING EQUATIONS

We need more efficient ways to solve equations. We can use any of the following principles to solve an equation.

> If an equation is true, then we can do any of the following and still get a true equation:
>
> a) add any number on both sides of the equation;
> b) subtract any number on both sides of the equation;
> c) multiply by any number on both sides of the equation;
> d) divide by any nonzero number on both sides of the equation.
>
> The goal is to get the letter, or variable, alone on one side of the equation.

Example 4 Solve: $t + 28 = 54$.

Solution

$t + 28 - 28 = 54 - 28$ Subtracting 28 on both sides to get the variable alone on one side.

$t + 0 = 26$

$t = 26$

The solution is 26.

Example 5 Solve: $182.3 = 65.8 + n$.

Solution

$182.3 - 65.8 = 65.8 + n - 65.8$ Subtracting 65.8 on both sides.

$116.5 = n + 0$

$116.5 = n$

The solution is 116.5.

DO EXERCISES 9–11.

2.7 EQUATION SOLVING

Many kinds of notation for multiplication are used in mathematics. For example, $5 \times y$, $5 \cdot y$, and $5y$, all mean the same thing: "5 times y." You need to be familiar with them all. Keep in mind, though, that when a multiplication symbol is missing, there must be a variable. That is, $5y$ means "5 times y," but 53 means "fifty-three," not $5 \cdot 3$.

Example 6 Solve: $10 \cdot x = 240$.

Solution

$\dfrac{10 \cdot x}{10} = \dfrac{240}{10}$ Dividing on both sides by 10.

$x = 24$

The solution is 24.

Example 7 Solve: $61.393 = 8.41b$.

Solution

$\dfrac{61.393}{8.41} = \dfrac{8.41b}{8.41}$ Dividing on both sides by 8.41.

$7.3 = b$

The solution is 7.3.

DO EXERCISES 12–14.

Example 8 Solve: $t - 7 = 24$.

Solution

$t - 7 + 7 = 24 + 7$ Adding 7 on both sides.

$t = 31$ Think of $t - 7 + 7$ as $t + 7 - 7$.

The solution is 31.

Example 9 Solve: $127.3 = x - 89.8$.

Solution

$127.3 + 89.8 = x - 89.8 + 89.8$ Adding 89.8 on both sides.

$217.1 = x$ Think of $x - 89.8 + 89.8$ as $x + 89.8 - 89.8$.

The solution is 217.1.

DO EXERCISES 15–17.

Example 10 Solve: $\dfrac{x}{225} = 47$.

Solution

$225 \cdot \dfrac{x}{225} = 225 \cdot 47$ Multiplying on both sides by 225.

$x = 10{,}575$

The solution is 10,575.

Solve.

12. $9 \cdot n = 144$

13. $5152 = 8t$

14. $9.2y = 79.12$

Solve.

15. $x - 67 = 89$

16. $56.78 = m - 13.4$

17. $134{,}000 = t - 278{,}896$

ANSWERS ON PAGE A–4

Solve.

18. $\dfrac{t}{840} = 14.29$

12003.6

19. $1600 = m \div 1.25$

2000

20. $79.95 = \dfrac{y}{0.08}$ *6.396*

DECIMAL NOTATION AND EQUATIONS

Example 11 Solve: $4480 = t \div 1.12$.

Solution

$4480 \cdot 1.12 = t$ Multiplying on both sides by 1.12

$5017.6 = t$

DO EXERCISES 18–20.

ANSWERS ON PAGE A-4

EXERCISE SET 2.7

• Solve by trial.

1. $5 + x = 12$
2. $3 + t = 9$
3. $n + 9 = 17$
4. $x + 0 = 14$

5. $17 - 12 = t$
6. $19 - 11 = y$
7. $13 + 5 = n$
8. $18 + 3 = p$

9. $x = 23 - 8$
10. $y = 25 - 9$
11. $45 \div x = 5$
12. $840 \div 2 = q$

•• Solve.

13. $13 + x = 20$
14. $15 + t = 22$
15. $12 + m = 12$
16. $16 + t = 16$

17. $x + 10 = 89$
18. $x + 20 = 57$
19. $y + 16 = 61$
20. $w + 17 = 53$

21. $n - 47 = 84$
22. $p - 92 = 56$
23. $x - 78 = 144$
24. $z - 67 = 133$

25. $389 = x - 214$
26. $333 = x - 221$
27. $x - 567.3 = 902.8$

28. $x + 438.7 = 807.2$
29. $2344 + y = 6400$
30. $83.22 + t = 92.81$

ANSWERS

1. 7
2. 6
3. 8
4. 14
5. 5
6. 8
7. 18
8. 21
9. 15
10. 16
11. 9
12. 420
13. 7
14. 7
15. 0
16. 0
17. 79
18. 37
19. 45
20. 36
21. 131
22. 148
23. 222
24. 200
25. 603
26. 554
27. 1470.1
28. 368.5
29. 4056
30. 9.59

102 DECIMAL NOTATION AND EQUATIONS

ANSWERS

#	Answer
31.	8
32.	7
33.	14
34.	18
35.	32
36.	24
37.	143
38.	247
39.	1166.4
40.	136.16
41.	1857.5
42.	114.21
43.	15
44.	55
45.	480
46.	4.9
47.	124
48.	320.31578 (circled)
49.	45
50.	75
51.	155 (circled)
52.	125 (circled)
53.	159,744
54.	154350
55.	205
56.	280
57.	95
58.	55
59.	impossible
60.	any number

31. $3 \cdot x = 24$

32. $6 \cdot x = 42$

33. $8 \cdot n = 112$

34. $9 \cdot n = 162$

35. $96 = 3 \cdot m$

36. $96 = 4 \cdot y$

37. $715 = 5 \cdot z$

38. $741 = 3 \cdot t$

39. $\dfrac{p}{0.6} = 1944$

40. $\dfrac{w}{3404} = 0.04$

41. $371.5 = \dfrac{x}{5}$

42. $12.69 = \dfrac{t}{9}$

43. $11 \cdot n = 165$

44. $12 \cdot n = 660$

45. $1.3 \cdot t = 624$

46. $160 \cdot y = 784$

47. $18x = 2232$

48. $19x = 6080$

49. $40x = 1800$

50. $20x = 1500$

51. $y \div 24 = 3720$

52. $y \div 28 = 3500$

53. $\dfrac{h}{32} = 4992$

54. $4410 = \dfrac{t}{35}$

55. $58 \cdot m = 11{,}890$

56. $75y = 21{,}000$

57. $233x = 22{,}135$

58. $198 \cdot x = 10{,}890$

Solve.

59. $0 \cdot x = 5$

60. $x + 3 = 3 + x$

2.8 FORMULAS

◉ SUBSTITUTION IN FORMULAS

Suppose the owner of a store sells a video game cartridge for $26.95 and that in the course of a month the store sells 30 such cartridges. Then total sales of that kind of cartridge are given by

Total Sales = (Number of cartridges) × (Price per cartridge)
= 30 × $26.95
= $808.50.

If next month the price is lowered to $25.95 and the store sells 35 cartridges, the total sales are given by

Total Sales = (Number of cartridges) × (Price per cartridge)
= 35 × $25.95
= $908.25.

We can generalize the situation as follows:

$S = np$,   *np* means $n \cdot p$, or $n \times p$.

where S = total sales, n = number of cartridges sold, and p = price per cartridge. The equation is called a *formula*. It is a recipe for doing a certain kind of calculation. You are probably familiar with certain formulas such as

$I = P \times R \times T$, $A = L \times W$,   and $P = 2L + 2W$.

You need to be able to make substitutions into formulas.

Example 1 Evaluate $I = P \times R \times T$ if $P = 389$, $R = 0.13$, and $T = \frac{3}{4}$.

Solution Substituting 389 for P, 0.13 for R, and $\frac{3}{4}$ for t, we get

$I = 389 \times 0.13 \times \frac{3}{4}$ Multiplying 389 by 0.13.

$= 50.57 \times \frac{3}{4}$ Multiplying 50.57 by $\frac{3}{4}$ is the same as multiplying 50.57 by 3 and then dividing by 4.

$= 37.9275$.

DO EXERCISES 1 AND 2.

OBJECTIVES

After finishing Section 2.8, you should be able to:

◉ Evaluate formulas by substituting numbers for letters.

◉◉ Solve a formula for a specified letter.

1. Evaluate $I = P \times R \times T$ if $P = 2000$, $R = 0.16$, and $T = \frac{3}{4}$.

$I = 2000 \cdot .16 \cdot \frac{3}{4}$

240

2. Evaluate $S = np$ if $n = 40$ and $p = \$17.79$.

711.6

ANSWERS ON PAGE A–5

104

DECIMAL NOTATION AND EQUATIONS

3. 🖩 Evaluate $A = P(1 + i)^n$ when $P = \$2000$, $i = 0.14$, and $n = 2$.

$A = 2000(1+.14)^2$

2599.2

Example 2 🖩 Evaluate $A = P(1 + i)^n$ when $P = \$3000$, $i = 0.16$, and $n = 3$.

Solution Substituting 3000 for P, 0.16 for i, and 3 for n we get

$$A = 3000 \times (1 + 0.16)^3$$
$$= 3000 \times (1.16)^3$$
$$= 3000 \times 1.560896$$
$$= \$4682.69.$$

DO EXERCISES 3 AND 4.

◐◐ SOLVING FORMULAS FOR LETTERS

Suppose with the formula $S = np$ we know that total sales S are \$808.50 and that the price per cartridge p is \$26.95, and we want to find out how many cartridges n were sold. Substituting 808.50 for S and 26.95 for p we get

$$S = np$$
$$808.50 = n \times 26.95.$$

We then find n by dividing on both sides by 26.95.

$$\frac{808.50}{26.95} = n$$
$$30 = n$$

If we were to do this several times, it might be easier to create a formula for n in terms of S and p. We do this by dividing on both sides by p.

$$S = np$$
$$\frac{S}{p} = n$$

We have solved the formula $S = np$ for n.

4. Evaluate $A = I + P$ when $P = \$2000$ and $I = \$320$.

2320

5. Solve $I = P \cdot R \cdot T$ for T.

6. Solve $Q = a - b$ for a.

Example 3 Solve $I = P \times R \times T$ for R.

Solution To get R alone on one side we divide on both sides by $P \times T$.

$$\frac{I}{P \times T} = R$$

Example 4 Solve $A = I + P$ for P.

Solution We subtract I on both sides.

$$A - I = P$$

DO EXERCISES 5 AND 6.

ANSWERS ON PAGE A–5

EXERCISE SET 2.8

• Evaluate each formula for the given values of the letters.

1. $S = np$ when $n = 50$ and $p = \$249.95$

2. $A = L \cdot W$ when $L = 16$ ft and $W = 12$ ft

3. $I = P \cdot R \cdot T$ when $P = \$4000$, $R = 0.14$, and $T = \frac{3}{5}$

4. $I = P \cdot R \cdot T$ when $P = \$10,000$, $R = 0.11$ and $T = \frac{5}{6}$

5. $C = 3.14D$ when $D = 16$ yd

6. $A = 3.14\, r^2$ when $r = 8$ miles

7. $A = P(1 + i)^n$ when $P = \$10,000$, $i = 0.12$, and $n = 2$

8. $A = P(1 + i)^n$ when $P = \$5500$, $i = 0.13$, and $n = 2$

•• Solve each formula for the indicated letter.

9. $A = L \cdot W$ for L

10. $A = L \cdot W$ for W

ANSWERS

1. 12497.5

2. 192

3. 336

4. $1916.66

5. 50.24

6. 200.96

7. 12544

8. 7022.95

9. $L = \dfrac{A}{W}$

10. $W = \dfrac{A}{L}$

106   DECIMAL NOTATION AND EQUATIONS

ANSWERS

11. $P = \dfrac{I}{R \cdot T}$

12. $D = \dfrac{C}{\pi}$

13. $P = A - I$

14. $N = M + t$

15. $y = A - 2x$

16. $H = \dfrac{V}{L \cdot W}$

17. $\dfrac{A - y}{3} = x$

18. $\dfrac{C}{3n} = T$

19. $P = \dfrac{A}{(1+i)^n}$

20. $N = \dfrac{3M - Q}{2}$

---

11. $I = P \cdot R \cdot T$ for P

12. $C = \pi D$ for D

13. $A = I + P$ for P

14. $M = N - t$ for N

15. $A = 2x + y$ for y

16. $V = L \cdot W \cdot H$ for H

17. $A = 3x + y$ for x

18. $C = 3nT$ for T

19. $A = P(1 + i)^n$ for P

20. $Q = 3M - 2N$ for N

$2N + Q = 3M \qquad \dfrac{3M - Q}{2}$

2.9 SOLVING PROBLEMS

● PROBLEMS

Why learn to solve equations? Because problems can be solved using equations. To do this, we first translate the problem situation to an equation and then solve the equation. The problem situation may be explained in words (as in a textbook) or may come from an actual situation in the real world.

Example 1 Translate to an equation. Then solve and check. What number plus 478.6 is 3019.2?

Solution We translate the problem to an equation as follows:

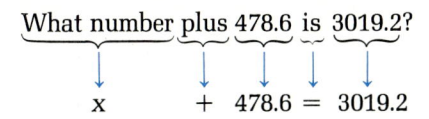

$$\underbrace{\text{What number}}_{x} \underbrace{\text{plus}}_{+} \underbrace{478.6}_{478.6} \underbrace{\text{is}}_{=} \underbrace{3019.2?}_{3019.2}$$

The translation gives us the equation

$x + 478.6 = 3019.2.$

We solve it:

$x = 3019.2 - 478.6$ Subtracting 478.6 on both sides
$x = 2540.6$

To check, we find out if 2540.6 plus 478.6 is 3019.2:

$2540.6 + 478.6 = 3019.2.$

Therefore, 2540.6 checks and is the answer.

DO EXERCISES 1 AND 2.

Example 2 Translate to an equation. Then solve and check. Sixteen hundredths of what number is thirty-five?

Solution

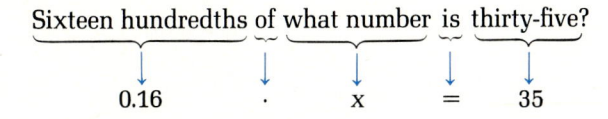

$$\underbrace{\text{Sixteen hundredths}}_{0.16} \underbrace{\text{of}}_{\cdot} \underbrace{\text{what number}}_{x} \underbrace{\text{is}}_{=} \underbrace{\text{thirty-five?}}_{35}$$

The translation gives us the equation

$0.16 \cdot x = 35.$

We solve it:

$x = \dfrac{35}{0.16}$ Dividing by 0.16 on both sides

$x = 218.75.$

To check, we find out if sixteen hundredths of this number is 35:

$0.16 \cdot 218.75 = 35$

The number 218.75 is the answer.

OBJECTIVE

After finishing Section 2.9, you should be able to:

● Solve applied problems by translating to equations and solving.

Translate to an equation. Then solve and check.

1. What number plus thirty-seven is seventy-three?

2. What number minus 256.4 is 377.9?

ANSWERS ON PAGE A–5

108

DECIMAL NOTATION AND EQUATIONS

Translate to an equation. Then solve and check.

3. Seven tenths of what number is forty-nine?

$\frac{7}{10}x = 49$

$\cancel{x}\frac{7}{\cancel{7}} \times \frac{10}{1} = 70$

Translate to an equation. Then solve and check

4. In Australia there are 145 million sheep. This is 132 million more than the number of people. How many people are in Australia?

$x + 132 = 145$

$x = \underline{}\begin{array}{c}-132\\\hline 13\end{array}$ million

Translate to an equation. Then solve and check.

5. An investment was made that grew to $14,500 after one year. This was 1.16 times what was originally invested. How much was originally invested?

$1.16x = 14500$

$\frac{14500}{1.16} = \boxed{12{,}500}$

ANSWERS ON PAGE A–5

> Note that in translating, *is* translates to =. The word *of* translates to ×, and the unknown number translates to a variable.

DO EXERCISE 3.

Sometimes it helps to reword a problem before translating.

Example 3 One year Carla Consumer earned a salary of $23,400. This was $1700 more than she earned last year. What was her last year's salary?

Solution

Last year's salary plus $1700 is this year's salary.

Translating: x   +   1700   =   23,400

The translation gives us the equation

   x + 1700 = 23,400.

We solve it:

   x = 23,400 − 1700   Subtracting 1700

   x = 21,700.

To check, we add $1700 to $21,700:

   $1700 + $21,700 = $23,400.

The answer is $21,700.

DO EXERCISE 4.

Example 4 A solid-state color television set uses about 420 kilowatt hours (kWh) of electricity in a year. This is 3.5 times that used by a solid-state black and white set. How many kWh does the black and white set use each year?

Solution

Rewording: 3.5 times the black and white set is 420

          3.5   ×   y   = 420

The translation gives us the equation

   3.5y = 420

We solve it:

   $y = \frac{420}{3.5}$.   Dividing by 3.5

   y = 120

To check, we multiply 120 by 3.5: 3.5 · 120 = 420.

The answer is 120 kWh.

DO EXERCISE 5.

EXERCISE SET 2.9

● Translate to equations. Then solve and check.

1. Sixty-four hundredths of what number is forty-eight?

$.64x = 48$

1. 75

2. Eight hundredths of what number is fifty-six?

$.08x = 56$

2. 700

3. What number plus five is twenty-two?

$x + 5 = 22$

3. 17

4. What number plus eight is sixty-three?

$x + 8 = 63$

4. 55

5. What number is 4 more than 5?

$4 + 5 = 9$

5. 9

6. What number is 7 less than 10?

$10 - 7$

6. 3

110
DECIMAL NOTATION AND EQUATIONS

ANSWERS

7. The area of Lake Superior is four times the area of Lake Ontario. The area of Lake Superior is 78,114 km². What is the area of Lake Ontario?

7. 19,528.5

8. The area of Alaska is about 483 times the area of Rhode Island. The area of Alaska is 1,519,202 km². What is the area of Rhode Island?

8. 3145.3457 km²

9. Izzi Zlow's typing speed is 35 words per minute. This is two fifths of Ty Preitter's speed. What is Preitter's speed?

   2/5 × 35   x · 2/5 = 35 ÷ x2/5   2/5 x = 35 × 5/2

9. 87.5

10. Walter Logged's body contains 57 kg of water. This is two thirds of his weight. What is Logged's weight?

    2/3 · x = 57

10. 85.5

11. The boiling point of ethyl alcohol is 78.3°C. This is 13.5°C more than the boiling point of methyl alcohol. What is boiling point of methyl alcohol?

11. 64.8

12. The height of the Eiffel Tower is 295 m. This is about 203 m more than the height of the Statue of Liberty. What is the height of the Statue of Liberty?

12. 92

13. A color television set with tubes uses about 640 kilowatt hours of electricity in a year. This is 1.6 times that used by a solid-state color set. How many kilowatt hours does the solid-state color model use each year?

    640 = 1.6 x
    ───────
       1.6

13. 400

14. The distance from the earth to the sun is about 150,000,000 km. This is about 391 times the distance from the earth to the moon. What is the distance from the earth to the moon?

    150 000 000
    ─────────── =
        391

14. 383631.7

15. Recently, the average cost of having a baby in one Ohio hospital was $1175. This was about 1.8 times the average cost for a certain California hospital. What was the cost of having a baby in the California hospital?

    1175 ÷ 1.8 = x

15. 652.77

16. It takes a 60-watt bulb about 16.6 hours to use one kilowatt hour of electricity. This is about 2.5 times as long as it takes a 150-watt bulb to use one kilowatt hour. How long does it take a 150-watt bulb to use one kilowatt hour?

    2.5x = 16.6

16. 6.64

TEST OR REVIEW—CHAPTER 2

NAME _____ CLASS _____ ANSWERS

If you miss an item, review the indicated section and objective.

[2.1, ▪▪]   1. Convert to fractional notation: 6.78.

1. $678/100$

[2.1, ▪▪▪]   2. Convert to decimal notation: $\frac{1895}{100}$.

2. 18.95

[2.1, ▪▪]   3. Convert to dollars: 1399¢.   4. Convert to cents: $1.39.

3. $13.99

4. 139¢

[2.2, ▪]   5. Add: 6.04 + 78 + 1.9898.

5. 86.0298

[2.2, ▪▪]   6. Subtract: 20.4 − 11.058

6. 9.342

[2.2, ▪▪▪]   7. Find the net deposit.

CASH	1274	39
LIST CHECKS SINGLY	865	79
	403	52
	816	95
TOTAL FROM OTHER SIDE		
TOTAL		
LESS CASH RECEIVED	350	00
NET DEPOSIT		

7. 2983.65

[2.3, ▪]   8. Multiply: 1 7 . 9 5
                       ×   2 4

8. 430.8

[2.3, ▪▪]   9. Divide: 2.8) 1 5 5.6 8

9. 55.6

[2.3, ▪▪▪]   10. What is the cost of eight record albums at $6.99 each?

10. 55.92

Copyright © 1984, by Addison-Wesley Publishing Company Inc. All rights reserved.

112   DECIMAL NOTATION AND EQUATIONS

ANSWERS

11. __34.1__

12. __124__

13. __1.1875__

14. __2.916̄__

15. __15.2̄__

16. __1.1236__

17. __909__

18. __358.22__

19. __4000__

20. __B/R__

21. __20,000__

[2.4, •] **11.** Round to the nearest tenth: 34.067

12. Round to the nearest dollar: $123.69.

[2.4, • •] Convert to decimal notation.

13. $\dfrac{19}{16}$ **14.** $\dfrac{35}{12}$

[2.4, • • •] **15.** Find the gas mileage. Round to the nearest tenth of a mile per gallon.

First odometer reading: 8095.4
Second odometer reading: 8259.8
Number of gallons at the last fill: 10.8

[2.5, • •] **16.** Evaluate: $(1.06)^2$.

[2.6, •] **17.** Simplify: $42 \cdot 18 + 3^4 - 24 \div 3 + 10^2$.

756 + 81 − 8 + 100

[2.7, • •] Solve.

18. $x + 141.78 = 500$ **19.** $1.18 \cdot x = 4720$

[2.8, • •] **20.** Solve $B = P \cdot R$ for P.

[2.9, •] Solve.

21. An investment was made that grew to $22,400 after one year. This was 1.12 times what was originally invested. How much was originally invested?

Career: Advertising/Marketing This is Mary Anne Butters. Formerly a race car driver (as seen in the pictures on the wall to the right), she is now President of an advertising firm, The Meridian Marketing Group, Inc. To Mary Anne, the advertising business is truly a three-way marriage of mathematics, language, and art.

The notion of percent permeates Mary Anne's work. For example, her firm recently conducted an advertising campaign to increase the ratings of a radio station. Before the campaign, the station held a 1.8% share of the audience. This meant that 1.8% of those listening to the radio were listening to the station. After the campaign, the station held an 11.8% share.

There are many other applications of percent that relate to Mary Anne's work. Suppose there are three pizza restaurants, A, B, and C, in an area. The average person, wanting to buy a pizza, has a percentage "mind set" about where to buy a pizza. Perhaps there is a 60% chance of going to A, a 10% chance of going to B, and a 30% chance of going to C. Restaurant B might be willing to spend $20,000 in advertising dollars to change their "mind set" percentage to 40%. When they go to a firm such as Mary Anne's, the usual fee they pay the firm for the advertising campaign is 15% of the $20,000, or $3000.

Mary Anne was actually a political science major in college, but also took lots of mathematics and English. She worked as a newspaper reporter for 10 years. It is a fairly normal progression to move from journalism to advertising. People who are successful in her work can make anywhere from $35,000 to $150,000 per year.

As you read these photograph captions throughout the book, you will notice that, on a day-to-day basis, no other chapter in the book is as important as this one on ratio and percent.

3
RATIO AND PERCENT

OBJECTIVES

After finishing Section 3.1, you should be able to:

■ Write fractional notation for ratios.

■■ Determine whether two pairs of numbers are proportional.

■■■ Solve proportions.

■■■■ Give the ratio of two different kinds of measures as a rate.

1. Find three other pairs of numbers whose ratio is $\frac{2}{1}$. Answers may vary.

2. Find three pairs of numbers whose ratio is $\frac{3}{2}$. Answers may vary.

ANSWERS ON PAGE A-5

RATIO AND PERCENT

READINESS CHECK—SKILLS FOR CHAPTER 3

Test for equality.

1. $\frac{12}{8} \quad \frac{6}{4}$

2. $\frac{4}{7} \quad \frac{5}{9}$

Divide. Write decimal notation for the answer.

3. $9 \div 100$

4. $95 \div 10$

5. $47 \div 100$

6. $342 \div 2.25$

Multiply.

7. 0.43×100

8. 8×0.01

9. 86.7×0.01

10. 0.07×100

Convert to a mixed numeral

11. $\frac{100}{3}$

12. $\frac{75}{2}$

Convert to decimal notation.

13. $\frac{2}{3}$

14. $\frac{7}{8}$

3.1 RATIO AND PROPORTION

In this chapter we consider two concepts, *ratio* and *percent*. These concepts are basic to most of the rest of the book.

■ RATIO

When we say that one number is twice as large as another, the *ratio* of the first number to the second is 2 to 1. We can show this by fractional notation

$$\frac{2}{1},$$ or by the notation 2:1.

Some pairs of numbers whose ratio is $\frac{2}{1}$ are: 20 and 10, 32 and 16, and 8 and 4.

DO EXERCISE 1.

Since

$$\frac{30}{20} = \frac{6}{4},$$

we say that the pair of numbers 30 and 20 have the same ratio as the pair of numbers 6 and 4.

DO EXERCISE 2.

3.1 RATIO AND PROPORTION

Example 1 Write fractional notation for the ratio 0.4 to 54.

Solution

$$\frac{0.4}{54}$$

Example 2 Write fractional notation for the ratio 5 to 6.

Solution

$$\frac{5}{6}$$

DO EXERCISES 3–6.

Example 3 In the triangle at the right,

a) What is the ratio of the length of the longest side to the length of the shortest?

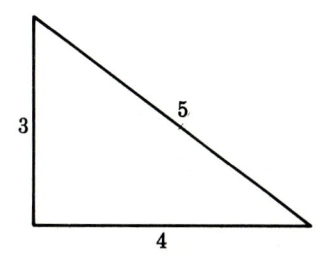

Solution

$$\frac{5}{3}$$

b) What is the ratio of the length of the shortest to the longest?

Solution

$$\frac{3}{5}$$

DO EXERCISES 7 AND 8.

Example 4 A family earning $21,400 per year will spend about $3210 for car expenses. What is the ratio of car expenses to yearly income?

Solution

$$\frac{3210}{21{,}400}$$

DO EXERCISES 9 AND 10.

●● PROPORTION

When two pairs of numbers—say 3, 2 and 6, 4—have the same ratio, we say they are *proportional*. The equation

$$\frac{3}{2} = \frac{6}{4}$$

states that 3, 2 and 6, 4 are proportional. Such an equation is called a *proportion*. A *proportion* states that two ratios are the same. We sometimes read

$$\frac{3}{2} = \frac{6}{4}$$

as "3 is to 2 as 6 is to 4."

Write fractional notation for each ratio.

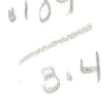

3. 3 to 2 $3/2$

4. 7 to 11 $7/11$

5. 0.189 to 3.4 $\frac{.189}{3.4}$

6. 9 to 3 $9/3$

In this rectangle,

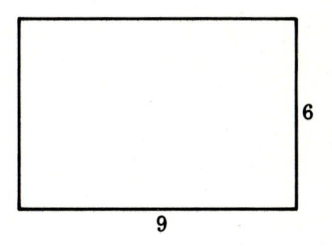

7. What is the ratio of the length of the longest side to the length of the shortest? $9:6$ $9/6$

8. What is the ratio of the length of the shortest side to the length of the longest? $6:9$ $6/9$

9. A family earning $22,800 per year will spend about $5928 for food. What is the ratio of food expenses to yearly income?

$$\frac{5928}{22800}$$

10. A pitcher gives up 4 earned runs in $7\frac{2}{3}$ innings of pitching. What is the ratio of earned runs to the number of innings pitched? $4/7\frac{2}{3}$

ANSWERS ON PAGE A–5

116

RATIO AND PERCENT

Determine whether proportional.

11. 3, 4 and 6, 8

12. 1, 4, and 10, 39

13. 1, 2 and 20, 39

Solve.

14. $\dfrac{x}{63} = \dfrac{2}{9}$

ANSWERS ON PAGE A–5

Example 5 Determine whether 1, 2 and 3, 6 are proportional.

Solution We can use cross products:

$$1 \cdot 6 = 6 \quad \dfrac{1}{2} \:\:\: \dfrac{3}{6} \quad 2 \cdot 3 = 6.$$

Since the cross products are the same, we know that the numbers are proportional.

Example 6 Determine whether 2, 5 and 4, 7 are proportional.

Solution We can use cross products:

$$2 \cdot 7 = 14 \quad \dfrac{2}{5} \:\:\: \dfrac{4}{7} \quad 5 \cdot 4 = 20.$$

Since the cross products are not the same, we know that the numbers are not proportional.

DO EXERCISES 11–13.

••• SOLVING PROPORTIONS

Let's solve some proportions.

Example Solve: $\dfrac{x}{8} = \dfrac{6}{4}$.

Solution To solve, we think of x/8 as x ÷ 8 and multiply on both sides by 8.

$$8 \cdot \dfrac{x}{8} = 8 \cdot \dfrac{6}{4} \quad \text{Multiply on both sides by 8.}$$

$$x = \dfrac{48}{4}, \text{ or } 12 \quad \text{Simplifying. Multiply by 8 and divide by 4.}$$

The solution is 12.

Note that x = 12 is easier to solve than x/8 = 6/4. The solution of x = 12 is 12, and 12 is also the solution of

$$\dfrac{x}{8} = \dfrac{6}{4}.$$

We can check that 12 is the solution by replacing x by 12 and using cross products:

$$12 \cdot 4 = 48 \quad \dfrac{12}{8} \:\:\: \dfrac{6}{4} \quad 8 \cdot 6 = 48.$$

Since the cross products are the same, the numbers 12, 8 and 6, 4 are proportional, and 12 is the solution of the equation.

DO EXERCISE 14.

Example 8 Solve: $\dfrac{x}{7} = \dfrac{5}{3}$. Write a mixed numeral for the answer.

3.1 RATIO AND PROPORTION

Solution

$$7 \cdot \frac{x}{7} = 7 \cdot \frac{5}{3} \qquad \text{We multiply on both sides by 7.}$$

$$x = \frac{35}{3}, \text{ or } 11\frac{2}{3} \qquad \text{Simplifying. Multiply 5 by 7 and convert to a mixed numeral by division.}$$

The solution is $11\frac{2}{3}$.

DO EXERCISE 15.

Example 9 Solve: $\frac{7.7}{15.4} = \frac{x}{2.2}$. Write decimal notation for the answer.

Solution

$$2.2 \cdot \frac{7.7}{15.4} = 2.2 \cdot \frac{x}{2.2} \qquad \text{We multiply on both sides by 2.2.}$$

$$\frac{16.94}{15.4} = x \qquad \text{Multiply 7.7 by 2.2.}$$

$$1.1 = x \qquad \text{Dividing}$$

The solution is 1.1.

DO EXERCISE 16.

Note that

$$\frac{2}{4} = \frac{3}{6} \quad \text{and} \quad \frac{4}{2} = \frac{6}{3}.$$

If two numbers are the same, so are their reciprocals.

When a variable is in a denominator, take the reciprocal of both sides. Then proceed as before.

Example 10 Solve: $\frac{3}{x} = \frac{6}{4}$.

Solution

$$\frac{x}{3} = \frac{4}{6} \qquad \text{Taking the reciprocal of both sides}$$

$$3 \cdot \frac{x}{3} = 3 \cdot \frac{4}{6} \qquad \text{We multiply on both sides by 3.}$$

$$x = \frac{12}{6}, \text{ or } 2 \qquad \text{Simplifying}$$

The solution is 2.

DO EXERCISE 17.

Example 11 Solve: $\frac{3.4}{4.93} = \frac{10}{x}$. Write decimal notation for the answer.

Solve.

15. $\frac{x}{9} = \frac{5}{4}$

Solve.

16. $\frac{21}{5} = \frac{n}{2.5}$

Solve.

17. $\frac{2}{3} = \frac{6}{x}$

ANSWERS ON PAGE A–5

118

RATIO AND PERCENT

Solve.

18. $\dfrac{0.4}{0.9} = \dfrac{4.8}{t}$

Solution

$\dfrac{4.93}{3.4} = \dfrac{x}{10}$ Taking the reciprocal of both sides

$10 \times \dfrac{4.93}{3.4} = 10 \cdot \dfrac{x}{10}$ Multiply on both sides by 10.

$\dfrac{49.3}{3.4} = x$ Simplifying

$14.5 = x$ Dividing

The solution is 14.5.

DO EXERCISE 18.

What is the rate, or speed, in kilometers per hour?

19. 45 km, 9 hr   20. 120 km, 10 hr

5 Km hr   *12 Km hr*

■■ RATES

When a ratio is used to compare two different kinds of measures, we call it a *rate*. Suppose a car is driven 200 kilometers in 4 hours. The ratio

$\dfrac{200 \text{ km}}{4 \text{ hr}}$, or $50 \dfrac{\text{km}}{\text{hr}}$, or 50 kilometers per hour   (Recall that "per" means "for each.")

is the rate traveled in kilometers per hour. A ratio of distance traveled to time is also called *speed*.

Example 12 A student drives 145 kilometers on 2.5 liters of gas. What is the rate in kilometers per liter?

Solution

$\dfrac{145 \text{ km}}{2.5 \text{ L}}$, or $58 \dfrac{\text{km}}{\text{L}}$,

21. 3 km, 10 hr

.3 Km hr

Example 13 It takes 60 ounces of grass seed to seed 3000 square feet of lawn. What is the rate in ounces per square foot?

Solution

$\dfrac{60 \text{ oz}}{3000 \text{ square feet}}$, or $0.02 \dfrac{\text{oz}}{\text{sq ft}}$.

What is the rate, or speed, in meters per second?

22. 2200 m, 2 sec   23. 52 m, 13 sec

1100   *4*

Example 14 A cook buys 10 pounds of potatoes for 95¢. What is the rate in cents per pound?

Solution

$\dfrac{95¢}{10 \text{ lb}}$, or $9.5 \dfrac{¢}{\text{lb}}$.

Example 15 A student earned $3690 for working 3 months one summer. What was the rate of pay?

Solution The rate of pay is the ratio of money earned per time worked, or

$\dfrac{\$3690}{3 \text{ mo}} = \$1230$ per month.

24. 232 m, 16 sec

14.5

ANSWERS ON PAGE A–5

DO EXERCISES 19–24.

EXERCISE SET 3.1

• Write fractional notation for each of the following ratios.

1. 4 to 5
2. 178 to 572
3. 0.4 to 12
4. 0.078 to 3.456

5. In a bread recipe, there are 2 cups of milk to 12 cups of flour. What is the ratio of cups of milk to cups of flour?

6. There are 2 women to 1 man enrolled in Coed College. What is the ratio of the number of women enrolled to the number of men?

•• Determine whether proportional.

7. 5, 6 and 7, 9
8. 7, 5 and 6, 4
9. 1, 2 and 10, 20
10. 7, 3 and 21, 9

••• Solve.

11. $\dfrac{18}{4} = \dfrac{x}{10}$
12. $\dfrac{x}{45} = \dfrac{20}{25}$
13. $\dfrac{x}{8} = \dfrac{9}{6}$
14. $\dfrac{8}{10} = \dfrac{n}{5}$

15. $\dfrac{t}{12} = \dfrac{5}{6}$
16. $\dfrac{12}{4} = \dfrac{x}{3}$
17. $\dfrac{2}{5} = \dfrac{8}{n}$
18. $\dfrac{10}{6} = \dfrac{5}{x}$

19. $\dfrac{n}{15} = \dfrac{10}{30}$
20. $\dfrac{2}{24} = \dfrac{x}{36}$
21. $\dfrac{16}{12} = \dfrac{24}{x}$
22. $\dfrac{7}{11} = \dfrac{2}{x}$

23. $\dfrac{6}{11} = \dfrac{12}{x}$
24. $\dfrac{8}{9} = \dfrac{32}{n}$
25. $\dfrac{20}{7} = \dfrac{80}{x}$
26. $\dfrac{5}{x} = \dfrac{4}{10}$

27. $\dfrac{12}{9} = \dfrac{x}{7}$
28. $\dfrac{x}{20} = \dfrac{16}{15}$
29. $\dfrac{x}{13} = \dfrac{2}{9}$
30. $\dfrac{1.2}{4} = \dfrac{x}{9}$

ANSWERS

1. 4/5
2. 178/572
3. .4/12
4. .078/3.456
5. 2/12
6. 2/1
7. no
8. no
9. yes
10. yes
11. 45
12. 36
13. 12
14. 4
15. 10
16. 9
17. 20
18. 3
19. 5
20. 3
21. 18
22. 3.142857
23. 22
24. 36
25. 28
26. 12.5
27. 9.3
28. 21.3
29. 2.8
30. 2.7

120

RATIO AND PERCENT

ANSWERS

31. .66
32. 39.05
33. 5
34. 25
35. 1
36. 1
37. 1
38. .6428571
39. 14
40. 0
41. 40
42. 2
43. 11
44. 8
45. 152
46. 8.2
47. 25
48. .2, 5
49. .623
50. 4.5
51. 2.5
52. 5

31. $\dfrac{t}{0.16} = \dfrac{0.15}{0.40}$

32. $\dfrac{x}{11} = \dfrac{7.1}{2}$

33. $\dfrac{25}{100} = \dfrac{n}{20}$

34. $\dfrac{35}{125} = \dfrac{7}{m}$

35. $\dfrac{7}{\frac{1}{4}} = \dfrac{28}{x}$

36. $\dfrac{x}{6} = \dfrac{1}{6}$

37. $\dfrac{\frac{1}{4}}{\frac{1}{2}} = \dfrac{\frac{1}{2}}{x}$

38. $\dfrac{1}{7} = \dfrac{x}{4\frac{1}{2}}$

39. $\dfrac{1}{2} = \dfrac{7}{x}$

40. $\dfrac{x}{3} = \dfrac{0}{9}$

In Exercises 41–46, find the rates as ratios of distance to time.

41. 120 kilometers, 3 hours

42. 18 kilometers, 9 hours

43. 440 meters, 40 seconds

44. 200 miles, 25 seconds

45. 342 yards, 2.25 days

46. 492 meters, 60 seconds

47. A car is driven 500 kilometers in 20 hours. What is the rate in kilometers per hour? in hours per kilometer?

48. A student eats 3 hamburgers in 15 minutes. What is the rate in hamburgers per minute? in minutes per hamburger?

49. To water a lawn adequately it takes 623 gallons of water for every 1000 square feet. What is the rate in gallons per square foot?

50. An 8-lb shankless ham contains 36 servings of meat. What is the rate in servings per pound?

51. A 12-lb boneless rib roast contains 30 servings of meat. What is the rate in servings per pound?

52. A car is driven 200 kilometers on 40 liters of gasoline. What is the rate in kilometers per liter?

3.2 PROPORTION PROBLEMS

◼ PROBLEM SOLVING

Proportions have applications in many fields such as business, chemistry, biology, health sciences, and home economics; as well as to areas of daily life.

Example 1 A car travels 800 kilometers in 3 days. At this rate, how far would it travel in 15 days?

Solution Let x represent the distance traveled in 15 days. Then translate to a proportion.

$$\text{Distance} \longrightarrow \frac{x}{15} = \frac{800}{3} \longleftarrow \text{Distance} \atop \longleftarrow \text{Time}$$

Both sides of the equation represent the same ratio. That is the meaning of the sentence. It may be helpful in setting up a proportion to read the above, as "the unknown distance x is to 15 days, as the known distance 800 kilometers is to 3 days."

Solve: $15 \cdot \dfrac{x}{15} = 15 \cdot \dfrac{800}{3}$ Multiplying by 15 on both sides

$$x = \frac{12{,}000}{3}$$

$$x = 4000$$

Thus the car travels 4000 kilometers in 15 days.

DO EXERCISE 1.

Example 2 If 7 tickets cost $45.50, what is the cost of 17 tickets?

Solution Let x represent the cost of 17 tickets. Then translate to a proportion.

Think: 7 is to $45.50 as 17 is to x.

$$\text{Tickets} \longrightarrow \frac{7}{45.50} = \frac{17}{x} \longleftarrow \text{Tickets} \atop \longleftarrow \text{Cost}$$

Solve: $\dfrac{45.50}{7} = \dfrac{x}{17}$ Taking the reciprocal on both sides

$17 \cdot \dfrac{45.50}{7} = 17 \cdot \dfrac{x}{17}$ Multiplying on both sides by 17

$\dfrac{773.50}{7} = x$ Multiplying 45.50 by 17

$110.50 = x$

The cost of 17 tickets is $110.50.

DO EXERCISE 2.

OBJECTIVE

After finishing Section 3.2, you should be able to:

◼ Solve problems involving proportions.

1. A car travels 700 kilometers in 5 days. At this rate, how far would it travel in 24 days?

$\dfrac{700}{5} = \dfrac{x}{24}$ 3360

2. If 4 shirts cost $54, what is the cost of 11 shirts?

$\dfrac{4}{54} = \dfrac{11}{x}$

$148.50

ANSWERS ON PAGE A–6

RATIO AND PERCENT

3. A car is driven 800 miles in 3 days. At this rate, how many miles will it be driven in 15 days?

$$\frac{800}{3} = \frac{x}{15}$$

4000

Example 3 A consumer buys a car. It is driven 10,000 miles in the first eight months. At this rate, how far will the car be driven in one year?

Solution Let x = the number of miles driven in one year. We use 12 months for 1 year. *Think:* 10,000 is to 8 as x is to 12. Write a proportion.

Miles ⟶ $\dfrac{10{,}000}{8} = \dfrac{x}{12}$ ⟵ Miles
Months ⟶ ⟵ Months

Solve: $12 \cdot \dfrac{10{,}000}{8} = 12 \cdot \dfrac{x}{12}$ Multiplying on both sides by 12

$\dfrac{120{,}000}{8} = x$ Multiplying 10,000 by 12

$15{,}000 = x$

The car will be driven 15,000 miles.

DO EXERCISE 3.

Example 4 It takes 60 ounces of grass seed to seed 3000 square feet of lawn. At this rate, how much would be needed for 5000 square feet of lawn?

Solution Let g = number of ounces of grass seed. Then translate to a proportion.

Grass seed needed ⟶ $\dfrac{g}{5000} = \dfrac{60}{3000}$ ⟵ Grass seed needed
Amount of lawn ⟶ ⟵ Amount of lawn

Solve: $5000 \cdot \dfrac{g}{5000} = 5000 \cdot \dfrac{60}{3000}$

$g = \dfrac{5000 \cdot 60}{3000}$

$g = 100$

Thus 100 ounces are needed for 5000 square feet of lawn.

DO EXERCISE 4.

4. In Example 4 how much seed would be needed for 7000 square feet of lawn?

$$\frac{60}{3000} = \frac{x}{7000}$$

140

ANSWERS ON PAGE A-6

EXERCISE SET 3.2 123

NAME _____ CLASS _____ ANSWERS

EXERCISE SET 3.2

● Solve.

1. If 3 cans of beans cost $0.79, what is the cost of 5 cans?

   $$\frac{3}{79} = \frac{5}{x}$$

   1. $1.31

2. If 5 sweatshirts cost $22, what is the cost of 3 sweatshirts?

   $$\frac{5}{22} = \frac{3}{x}$$

   2. $13.20

3. A car travels 320 miles on 24 gallons of gasoline. How far does it travel on 10 gallons?

   $$\frac{320}{24} = \frac{x}{10}$$

   3. 133.3

4. A car travels 168 miles on 13 gallons of gasoline. How much gasoline would it take to travel 252 miles?

   $$\frac{13}{168} = \frac{x}{252}$$

   4. 19.5

5. A quality-control inspector checks 100 transistor radios and finds 7 defective. At this rate, how many would be defective in a daily production of 360 radios?

   $$\frac{7}{100} = \frac{x}{360}$$

   5. 25.2

6. A quality-control inspector checks 100 blouses and finds defects in 8 of them. At this rate, how many blouses would be defective out of the 3000 the company makes in a week?

   $$\frac{100}{8} = \frac{3000}{x}$$

   6. 240

7. A family earning $15,400 per year will spend $4004 for food. How much will a family earning $18,000 spend for food?

   $$\frac{15400}{4004} = \frac{18000}{x}$$

   7. 4680

8. A family earning $15,400 per year will spend $2310 for car expenses. How much will a family earning $11,000 spend for car expenses?

   $$\frac{15400}{2310} = \frac{11000}{x}$$

   8. 1650

9. A 12-lb turkey contains 9 servings of meat. How many servings are there in a 15-lb turkey?

   $$\frac{12}{9} = \frac{15}{x}$$

   9. 11.25

10. If 2 pounds of round steak contain 7 servings, how many pounds of round steak would be needed for 16 servings?

    $$\frac{2}{7} = \frac{x}{16}$$

    10. 4.57

124

RATIO AND PERCENT

ANSWERS

11. Coffee beans from 14 trees are required to produce 17 pounds of coffee, which each person in the United States drinks each year. How many trees are required to produce 391 pounds of coffee?

$$\frac{14}{17} = \frac{x}{391}$$

11. _322_

12. A baseball team won 11 of its first 18 games. At this rate, how many games will it win in the 162-game season?

$$\frac{11}{18} = \frac{x}{162}$$

12. _99_

13. A student bought a car. In the first 16 months it was driven 10,000 kilometers. At this rate, how many kilometers was the car driven in 1 year? Use 12 months for 1 year.

$$\frac{16}{10,000} = \frac{12}{x}$$

13. _7500_

14. In a metal alloy, the ratio of zinc to copper is 3 to 13. If there are 520 pounds of copper, how much zinc is there?

$$\frac{3}{13} = \frac{x}{520}$$

14. _120_

15. When a tree 8 meters tall casts a shadow 5 meters long, how long a shadow is cast by a person 2 meters tall?

$$\frac{8}{5} \quad \frac{2}{x}$$

15. _1.25 m._

16. A quality-control inspector examined 200 light bulbs and found 18 defective. At this rate, how many defective bulbs would there be in a lot of 22,000?

$$\frac{18}{200} = \frac{x}{22000}$$

16. _1980_

17. On a map $\frac{1}{4}$ inch represents 50 actual miles. If two cities are $3\frac{1}{4}$ inches apart on the map, how far are they actually apart?

$$\frac{1/4}{50} \quad \frac{3\frac{1}{4}}{x}$$

17. _650_

18. In a bread recipe, the ratio of flour to milk is $\frac{4}{3}$. If 5 milliliters of flour are used, how many milliliters of milk are used?

$$\frac{4}{3} = \frac{5}{x}$$

18. _3.75_

19. It is known that 5 people produce 13 kilograms of garbage in one day. Birmingham, Alabama, has 300,000 people. How many kilograms of garbage are produced in Birmingham in one day?

$$\frac{5}{13} \quad \frac{300,000}{x}$$

19. _780,000_

20. It is known that 5 people produce 13 kilograms of garbage in one day. San Diego, California, has 700,000 people. How many kilograms of garbage are produced in San Diego in one day?

$$\frac{5}{13} \quad \frac{700,000}{x}$$

20. _1,820,000_

3.3 PERCENT NOTATION

On the average, a family will spend 26% of its income for food. What does this mean? It means that out of every $100 earned, $26 will be spent for food. Thus, 26% is a ratio of 26 to 100.

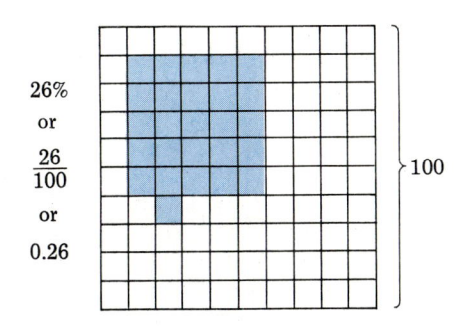

26% or $\frac{26}{100}$ or 0.26

◼ PERCENT

The following is the definition of percent.

> $n\%$ means $\frac{n}{100}$ or $n \times \frac{1}{100}$ or $n \times 0.01$.

Example 1 Write three kinds of notation for 78%.

Solution

a) $78\% = \frac{78}{100}$ A ratio of 78 to 100

b) $78\% = 78 \times \frac{1}{100}$ Replacing % by $\times \frac{1}{100}$

c) $78\% = 78 \times 0.01$ Replacing % by $\times 0.01$

Convert % to decimal

Example 2 Write three kinds of notation for 67.8%.

Solution

a) $67.8\% = \frac{67.8}{100}$ A ratio of 67.8 to 100

b) $67.8\% = 67.8 \times \frac{1}{100}$ Replacing % by $\times \frac{1}{100}$

c) $67.8\% = 67.8 \times 0.01$ Replacing % by $\times 0.01$

DO EXERCISES 1–3.

OBJECTIVES

After finishing Section 3.3, you should be able to:

◼ Write three kinds of notation for a percent.

◼◼ Convert from percent to decimal notation.

◼◼◼ Convert from decimal to percent notation.

▦ Convert from fractional to percent notation.

▦ Convert from percent to fractional notation.

▦ Memorize the table of decimal, fractional, and percent equivalents, and be able to use them for conversions.

Write three kinds of notation.

1. 90%

2. 3.4%

3. 100%

ANSWERS ON PAGE A–6

Find decimal notation.

4. 34%

.34

5. 78.9%

.789

6. One year the rate of inflation was 12.08%. Find decimal notation for 12.08%.

.1208

7. The present world population growth rate is 2.1% per year. Find decimal notation for 2.1%.

.021

ANSWERS ON PAGE A–6

RATIO AND PERCENT

CONVERTING FROM PERCENT TO DECIMAL NOTATION

Consider 78%.

$78\% = 78 \times 0.01$ Replacing % by × 0.01 since we are converting to decimal notation

$= 0.78$

We can convert from percent to decimal notation by moving the decimal point two places to the left.

To convert from percent to decimal notation,	36.5%
a) drop the percent symbol, and	36.5
b) move the decimal point two places to the left.	0.36.5 Move 2 places

Example 3 Find decimal notation for 99.44%.

Solution

a) Drop the percent symbol. 99.44

b) Move the decimal point two places to the left. 0.99.44

$99.44\% = 0.9944$

Example 4 The population growth rate of Europe is 1.1%. Find decimal notation for 1.1%.

Solution

a) Drop the percent symbol. 1.1

b) Move the decimal point two places to the left. 0.01.1

$1.1\% = 0.011$

DO EXERCISES 4–7.

CONVERTING FROM DECIMAL TO PERCENT NOTATION

Consider 0.38.

$0.38 = 38 \times 0.01$ We factor out 0.01.

$= 38\%$ Using the definition of percent, replacing × 0.01 by %.

We can convert from decimal to percent notation by moving the decimal point two places to the right.

To convert from decimal to percent notation,	0.675
a) move the decimal point two places to the right and	0.67.5 Move 2 places
b) write a % symbol.	67.5%

3.3 PERCENT NOTATION

Example 5 Find percent notation for 1.27.

Solution

a) Move the decimal point two places to the right.   1.27

b) Write a % symbol.   127%

1.27 = 127%

Example 6 Television sets are on 0.25 of the time. Find percent notation for 0.25.

Solution

a) Move the decimal point two places to the right.   0.25

b) Write a % symbol.   25%

0.25 = 25%

DO EXERCISES 8–11.

3.8 CONVERTING FROM FRACTIONAL TO PERCENT NOTATION

To convert from fractional to percent notation,

a) find decimal notation by division, and

$$\frac{3}{5}$$

0.6
5)3.0
  3 0
  ───
    0

b) convert the answer to percent notation.   0.6 = 0.60 = 60%

Example 7 Find percent notation for $\frac{3}{8}$.

Solution

a) Find decimal notation by division.

```
   0.3 7 5
8)3.0 0 0
  2 4
  ───
    6 0
    5 6
    ───
      4 0
      4 0
      ───
        0
```

b) Convert the answer to percent notation.

0.37.5

$\frac{3}{8} = 37.5\%$ or $37\frac{1}{2}\%$

DO EXERCISES 12 AND 13.

Find percent notation.

8. 0.24

    24%

9. 3.47

    347%

10. 1

    100%

11. Muscles make up 0.4 of a person's body. Find percent notation for 0.4.

    40%

Find percent notation.

12. $\frac{1}{4}$ 25%

13. $\frac{7}{8}$ 87.5%

ANSWERS ON PAGE A–6

128

RATIO AND PERCENT

14. The human body is $\frac{2}{3}$ water. Find percent notation for $\frac{2}{3}$.

Example 8 $\frac{1}{3}$ of all meals are eaten outside the home. Find percent notation for $\frac{1}{3}$.

Solution

a) Find decimal notation by division.

$$\begin{array}{r} 0.3\ 3\ 3 \\ 3\overline{)1.0\ 0\ 0} \\ \underline{9} \\ 1\ 0 \\ \underline{9} \\ 1\ 0 \\ \underline{9} \\ 1 \end{array}$$

b) Convert the answer to percent notation.

$0.33.\overline{3}$

$\frac{1}{3} = 33.\overline{3}\%$ or $33\frac{1}{3}\%$

We get a repeating decimal:

$0.33\overline{3}$

DO EXERCISES 14 AND 15.

In some cases division is not the easiest way to convert. The following are some optional ways this might be done.

Find percent notation.

15. $\frac{5}{6}$

Example 9 Find percent notation for $\frac{69}{100}$.

Solution We use the definition of percent.

$\frac{69}{100} = 69\%$

Example 10 Find percent notation for $\frac{17}{20}$.

Solution We multiply by 1 to get 100 in the denominator.

$\frac{17}{20} \cdot \frac{5}{5} = \frac{85}{100} = 85\%$

Find percent notation.

16. $\frac{57}{100}$

DO EXERCISES 16 AND 17.

17. $\frac{19}{25}$

CONVERTING FROM PERCENT TO FRACTIONAL NOTATION

To convert from percent to fractional notation,	30%
a) use the definition of percent, and	$\frac{30}{100}$
b) simplify, if possible.	$\frac{3}{10}$

ANSWERS ON PAGE A–6

3.3 PERCENT NOTATION

Example 11 Find fractional notation for 75%.

Solution

$$75\% = \frac{75}{100} \quad \text{Definition of percent}$$

$$= \frac{3}{4} \cdot \frac{25}{25} \Bigg\} \text{Simplifying}$$
$$= \frac{3}{4}$$

Example 12 Find fractional notation for 62.5%.

Solution

$$62.5\% = \frac{62.5}{100} \quad \text{Definition of percent}$$

$$= \frac{62.5}{100} \times \frac{10}{10} \quad \begin{array}{l}\text{Multiplying by 1 to get rid of the}\\ \text{decimal point in the numerator}\end{array}$$

$$= \frac{625}{1000}$$

$$= \frac{5}{8} \cdot \frac{125}{125} \Bigg\} \text{Simplifying}$$
$$= \frac{5}{8}$$

Example 13 Find fractional notation for $16\frac{2}{3}\%$.

Solution

$$16\frac{2}{3}\% = \frac{50}{3}\% \quad \begin{array}{l}\text{Converting from the mixed numeral to}\\ \text{fractional notation}\end{array}$$

$$= \frac{50}{3} \times \frac{1}{100} \quad \text{Definition of percent}$$

$$= \frac{50}{300} \quad \text{Multiplying}$$

$$= \frac{1}{6} \cdot \frac{50}{50} \Bigg\} \text{Simplifying}$$
$$= \frac{1}{6}$$

DO EXERCISES 18–20.

⁝⁝⁝ DECIMAL, FRACTIONAL, AND PERCENT EQUIVALENTS

The table on the inside front cover contains decimal, fractional, and percent equivalents that are used so often you should memorize them. For example, $\frac{1}{3} = 0.3\overline{3}$, so we say that the *decimal equivalent* of $\frac{1}{3}$ is $0.3\overline{3}$, or that $0.3\overline{3}$ has the *fractional equivalent* $\frac{1}{3}$. Memorize the table.

DO EXERCISE 21.

Find fractional notation.

18. 60%

$.60 = \frac{60}{100} = \frac{6}{10} = 3/5$

19. 3.25%

$.0325 = \frac{325}{10,000} = \frac{13}{400}$

20. $66\frac{2}{3}\%$

$= \frac{200}{3} \times \frac{1}{100} = \frac{200}{300}$
$= 2/3$

Complete this table.

21.

Fractional notation	$\frac{1}{5}$	.2	20%
Decimal notation	$\frac{833}{1000}$	$0.8\overline{3}$	83⅓%
Percent notation	$\frac{375}{1000}$	.375	$37\frac{1}{2}\%$

ANSWERS ON PAGE A–6

EXERCISE SET 3.3

:. Write three kinds of notation.

1. 80%   2. 43.8%   3. 12.5%   4. 120%

:: Find decimal notation.

5. 18%   6. 0.7%   7. 78.9%   8. 56.2%

9. 1%   10. 100%   11. 425%   12. 163%

13. 1.18%   14. 2.01%   15. 67.11%   16. 88.99%

⋮ Convert to percent notation.

17. 0.78   18. 0.93   19. 0.08   20. 0.07

21. 0.562   22. 0.995   23. 0.8   24. 0.9

25. 1.00   26. 2.00   27. 1.015   28. 2.003

:: Convert to percent notation.

29. $\frac{79}{100}$ 30. $\frac{19}{100}$ 31. $\frac{6}{100}$ 32. $\frac{1}{100}$

33. $\frac{9}{10}$ 34. $\frac{1}{10}$ 35. $\frac{3}{2}$ 36. $\frac{3}{4}$

37. $\frac{1}{8}$ 38. $\frac{3}{8}$ 39. $\frac{3}{5}$ 40. $\frac{4}{5}$

41. $\frac{1}{6}$ 42. $\frac{7}{6}$ 43. $\frac{5}{3}$ 44. $\frac{10}{3}$

45. $\frac{21}{20}$ 46. $\frac{27}{25}$ 47. $\frac{23}{40}$ 48. $\frac{37}{50}$

132 RATIO AND PERCENT

ANSWERS

49. 3/5
50. 7/10
51. 1/8
52. 3/8
53. 2/3
54. 1/3
55. 5/6
56. 59/100
57. 7/80
58. 13/400
58. 19/25 (?)
59. 1 12/25
60. 7/20
61. 3/50
62.
64. 22.2%
65. 6.3063%
66. 4.56045%
67. 6.78906%
68. 104.49897%
69. 116.12591%

Convert to fractional notation.

49. 60%   50. 70%   51. 12.5%   52. 37.5%

53. $66\frac{2}{3}\%$ 54. $33\frac{1}{3}\%$ 55. $83\frac{1}{3}\%$ 56. $58\frac{1}{3}\%$

57. 8.75%   58. 3.25%   59. 136%   60. 148%

61. The United States uses 35% of the world's energy. Find fractional notation for 35%.

62. The United States has 6% of the world's population. Find fractional notation for 6%.

Complete the table.

63.

Fractional notation	$\frac{1}{8}$	$\frac{1}{6}$	$\frac{1}{5}$	$\frac{1}{4}$	$\frac{1}{3}$	$\frac{3}{8}$	$\frac{2}{5}$	$\frac{1}{2}$	$\frac{3}{5}$	$\frac{5}{8}$	$\frac{2}{3}$	$\frac{3}{4}$	$\frac{4}{5}$	$\frac{5}{6}$	$\frac{7}{8}$	1
Decimal notation	.125	.16	.20	0.25	.3	.375	.40	0.5	.6	0.625	.6	0.75	.80	.83	.875	1.00
Percent notation	$12\frac{1}{2}\%$ or 12.5%	16.6%	20%	25%	$33\frac{1}{3}\%$ or 33.3%	$37\frac{1}{2}\%$ or 37.5%	40%	50%	60%	62.5%	66.6%	75%	80%	$83\frac{1}{3}\%$ or 83.3%	$87\frac{1}{2}\%$ or 87.5%	100%

Convert to percent notation. Round to the nearest tenth of a percent.

64. $\frac{82}{369}$ 65. $\frac{63}{999}$ 66. $\frac{456}{9999}$ 67. $\frac{6789}{99,999}$

68. $\frac{511}{489}$ 69. $\frac{6013}{5178}$

3.4A PERCENT PROBLEMS

■ TRANSLATING PERCENT PROBLEMS

To solve problems involving percents, it is helpful to first translate to equations. Then solve the equation.

Example 1 Translate: 23% of 5 is what?

Solution $23\% \times 5 = a$

> "Of" translates to "×."
> "What" translates to some letter.
> "Is" translates to "=."

Example 2 Translate: 3 is 10% of what?

Solution $3 = 10\% \times b$ Any letter can be used.

Example 3 Translate: What percent of 50 is 7

Solution $n \quad \% \quad \times 50 = 7$

DO EXERCISES 1–6.

■■ SOLVING PERCENT PROBLEMS

Finding a Percentage

Example 4 What is 11% of 49?

Solution *Translate:* $a = 11\% \times 49.$

This tells us what to do. We convert 11% to decimal notation and multiply.

$$\begin{array}{r} 4\,9 \\ \times 0.1\,1 \\ \hline 4\,9 \\ 4\,9\,0 \\ \hline 5.3\,9 \end{array} \quad 11\% = 0.11$$

5.39 is 11% of 49.

A way of checking answers is by estimating as follows:

$$11\% \times 49 \approx 10\% \times 50 = 0.10 \times 50$$
$$= 5$$

Since 5 is close to 5.39, our answer is reasonable.

DO EXERCISE 7.

OBJECTIVES

After finishing Section 3.4, you should be able to:

■ Translate percent problems to equations.

■■ Translate percent problems to equations and solve.

Translate to an equation. Do not solve.

1. 12% of 50 is what?

   .12 · 50 =

2. What is 40% of $60?

   .40 × 60

3. $45 is 20% of what?

   45 = 20x   x = 45/20

4. 120% of what is 60?

   1.20 x = 60
   x = 60/1.20

5. 16 is what percent of 40?

   16 = x · 40
   16/40 = x

6. What percent of $9600 is $7104?

   x · 9600 = 7104

   7

7. Solve Exercise 6.

   74%

ANSWERS ON PAGE A–6

Solve

8. 64% of \$55 is what?

\$35.20

Example 5 120% of \$42 is what?

Solution *Translate:* 120% × 42 = *a*.

This tells us what to do.

$$\begin{array}{r} 42 \\ \times\ 1.2 \\ \hline 84 \\ 420 \\ \hline 50.4 \end{array} \qquad 120\% = 1.20 = 1.2$$

120% of \$42 is \$50.40.

DO EXERCISE 8.

Finding a Base

Example 6 5% of what is 20?

Solution *Translate:* 5% × *b* = 20.

To find the number we first divide by 5%.

$b = 20 \div 5\%$ We divide on both sides by 5%.

This tells us what to do. We convert 5% to decimal notation and divide.

$$\begin{array}{r} 400. \\ 0.05\overline{)20.00} \\ 2000 \\ \hline 0 \end{array} \qquad 5\% = 0.05$$

5% of 400 is 20.

Solve.

9. 20% of what is 45?

.20x = 45

225

DO EXERCISE 9.

Example 7 \$3 is 16% of what?

Solution *Translate:* 3 = 16% × *b*.

To find the number we first divide by 16%.

$3 \div 16\% = b$. We divide on both sides by 16%.

This tells us what to do. We convert 16% to decimal notation and divide.

ANSWERS ON PAGE A–6

3.4A PERCENT PROBLEMS

```
         1 8.7 5
0.1 6 ) 3.0 0 0 0
        1 6
        ─────
        1 4 0
        1 2 8
        ─────
          1 2 0
          1 1 2
          ─────
              8 0
              8 0
              ───
                0
```

$3 is 16% of $18.75.

DO EXERCISE 10.

Finding a Rate

Example 8   10 is what percent of 20?

Solution *Translate:*   10 = n % × 20.

Next we use the definition of percent.

   10 = n × 0.01 × 20

   10 = n × 0.2

To find the number we first divide by 0.2.

   10 ÷ 0.2 = n   We divide on both sides by 0.2.

This tells us what to do. We divide.

```
         5 0.
0.2 ) 1 0.0
      1 0 0
      ─────
          0
```

10 is 50% of 20.

Strictly speaking, the answer to this problem is 50, but we will consider either 50 or 50% correct.

DO EXERCISES 11.

Solve.

10. $60 is 120% of what?

60 = 1.20x

50

Solve.

11. 16 is what percent of 40?

16 = x · 40

40%

ANSWERS ON PAGE A–6

Solve.

12. What percent of $84 is $10.50?

RATIO AND PERCENT

Example 9   What percent of $50 is $16?

Solution Translate: $n \times \% \times 50 = 16$.

Next, we use the definition of percent.

$$n \times 0.01 \times 50 = 16$$
$$n \times 0.5 = 16$$

To find the number we first divide by 0.5.

$n = 16 \div 0.5$ We divide on both sides by 0.5.

This tells us what to do. We divide.

$$\begin{array}{r} 3\,2. \\ 0.5{\overline{\smash{\big)}\,1\,6.0}} \\ \underline{1\,5} \\ 1\,0 \\ \underline{1\,0} \\ 0 \end{array}$$

32% of $50 is $16.

DO EXERCISE 12.

EXERCISE SET 3.4A

● Translate to an equation. Do not solve.

1. What is 41% of 89?

2. 87% of 41 is what?

3. 89 is what percent of 100?

4. What percent of 25 is 8?

5. 13 is 25% of what?

6. 3.2% of what is 20?

●● Solve.

7. What is 120% of 75?

8. What is 65% of 480?

9. 150% of 30 is what?

   1.50

10. 100% of 13 is what?

11. What is 5% of $300?

12. What is 3% of $45?

13. 2.1% of 50 is what?

14. $33\frac{1}{3}$% of 240 is what?
    (Hint: $33\frac{1}{3}\% = \frac{1}{3}$.)

15. $12 is what percent of $50?

    $12 = x \cdot 50$

16. $15 is what percent of $60?

    $15 = x \cdot 60$

17. 20 is what percent of 10?

    $20 = x \cdot 10$

18. 90 is what percent of 30?

    $90 = x \cdot 30$

    $\frac{90}{30} = 3$

ANSWERS

1. $.41 \times 89 = x$
2. $.87 \times 41 = x$
3. $89 = x \cdot 100$
4. $8 = x \cdot 25$
5. $.25x = 13$
6. $3.2x = 20$
7. 90
8. 312
9. 45
10. 13
11. 15
12. 1.35
13. 1.05
14. 80
15. 24%
16. 25%
17. 200%
18. 300%

138

RATIO AND PERCENT

ANSWERS

19. 50%

20. 80%

21. 125%

22. 50%

23. 40

24. 225

25. 40

26. 89

27. 88

28. 78

29. 20

30. 50

31. $843.20

32. 64.5%

19. What percent of $300 is $150?

$150 = x \cdot 300$

20. What percent of $50 is $40?

$40 = x \cdot 50$

21. What percent of 80 is 100?

$100 = 80 \cdot x$

22. What percent of 30 is 15?

$15 = x \cdot 30$

23. 20 is 50% of what?

$20 = .50x$

24. 45 is 20% of what?

$45 = .20x$

25. 40% of what is $16?

$.40x = 16$

26. 100% of what is $89?

27. 56.32 is 64% of what?

$56.32 = .64x$

28. 34.32 is 44% of what?

$34.32 = .44x$

29. 70% of what is 14?

$.70x = 14$

30. 70% of what is 35?

$.70x = 35$

$35/70$

Solve.

31. What is 7.75% of $10,880?

Estimate _____

Calculate _____

32. 50,951.775 is what percent of 78,995?

Estimate _____

Calculate _____

3.4B SOLVING PERCENT PROBLEMS USING PROPORTIONS (Optional)*

■ TRANSLATING TO PROPORTIONS

A percent is a ratio of some number to 100. For example, 75% is the ratio $\frac{75}{100}$.

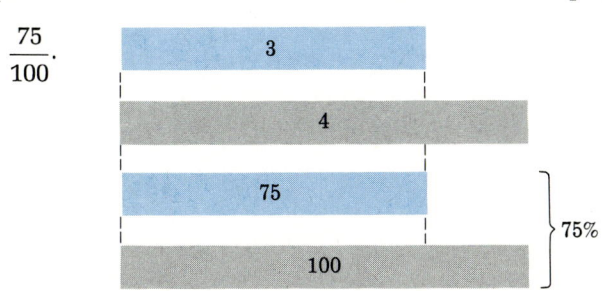

We also know that 3 and 4 have the same ratio as 75 and 100. Thus,

$$\frac{3}{4} = \frac{75}{100} = 75\%.$$

To solve a percent problem using a proportion we translate as follows.

Part is to *base* as *rate* is to 100.

$$\frac{a}{b} = \frac{n}{100}$$

For example,

75% of 40 is 30   *You might find it helpful to read this as "part is to whole as part is to whole."*

translates to

$$\frac{30}{40} = \frac{75}{100}.$$

A clue in translating is that the base, b, corresponds to 100 and usually follows the wording "percent of." Also, $n\%$ always translates to $n/100$.

Example 1 Translate to a proportion.

Solution

23% of 5 is what?
 rate   base part

$$\frac{a}{5} = \frac{23}{100}$$

Example 2 Translate to a proportion.

Solution

What is 11% of 49?
 part   rate base

$$\frac{a}{49} = \frac{11}{100}$$

DO EXERCISES 1 AND 2.

Note: The skills developed in this section are basically the same as those of Section 3.4A. Most problems are easier to set up using the ideas of Section 3.4A, but some students or instructors may find these same problems easier to set up using ratios, as illustrated in this section.

OBJECTIVES

After finishing Section 3.4B, you should be able to:

■ Translate percent problems to proportions.

■■ Solve percent problems.

Translate to a proportion. Do not solve.

1. 12% of 50 is what?

2. What is 40% of 60?

ANSWERS ON PAGE A–6

RATIO AND PERCENT

Translate to a proportion. Do not solve.

3. 45 is 20% of what?

4. 120% of what is 60?

Translate to a proportion. Do not solve.

5. 16 is what percent of 40?

6. What percent of 84 is 10.5?

Solve.

7. What is 12% of 50?

ANSWERS ON PAGE A-6

Example 3 Translate to a proportion.

Solution

3 is 10% of what?
part   rate   base

$$\frac{3}{b} = \frac{10}{100}$$

Example 4 Translate to a proportion.

Solution

45% of what is 23?
rate   base   part

$$\frac{23}{b} = \frac{45}{100}$$

DO EXERCISES 3 AND 4.

Example 5 Translate to a proportion.

Solution

10 is what percent of 20?
part   rate   base

$$\frac{10}{20} = \frac{n}{100}$$

Example 6 Translate to a proportion.

Solution

What percent of 50 is 7?
rate   base   part

$$\frac{7}{50} = \frac{n}{100}$$

DO EXERCISES 5 AND 6.

●● SOLVING PERCENT PROBLEMS

Example 7 What is 11% of 49?

Solution   part   rate   base

Translate: $\dfrac{a}{49} = \dfrac{11}{100}$

Solve: $a = 49 \cdot \dfrac{11}{100}$ Multiplying by 49

$a = \dfrac{49 \cdot 11}{100}$ The answer can be checked by estimating as before.

$a = \dfrac{539}{100}$

$a = 5.39$

5.39 is 11% of 49.

DO EXERCISE 7.

3.4B SOLVING PERCENT PROBLEMS USING PROPORTIONS

Example 8 120% of 42 is what?

Solution rate   base   part

Translate: $\dfrac{a}{42} = \dfrac{120}{100}$

Solve: $a = 42 \cdot \dfrac{120}{100}$ Multiplying by 42

$a = \dfrac{42 \cdot 120}{100}$

$a = \dfrac{5040}{100}$

$a = 50.4$

120% of 42 is 50.4.

DO EXERCISE 8.

Example 9 5% of what is $20?

Solution rate   base   part

Translate: $\dfrac{20}{b} = \dfrac{5}{100}$

Solve: $\dfrac{b}{20} = \dfrac{100}{5}$ Taking the reciprocal of both sides

$b = 20 \cdot \dfrac{100}{5}$ Multiplying by 20

$b = \dfrac{20 \cdot 100}{5}$

$b = \dfrac{2000}{5}$

$b = 400$

5% of $400 is $20.

DO EXERCISE 9.

Solve

8. 64% of 55 is what?

Solve.

9. 20% of what is $45?

ANSWERS ON PAGE A–6

Solve.

10. 60 is 120% of what?

RATIO AND PERCENT

Example 10 3 is 16% of what?

Solution part rate base

Translate: $\dfrac{3}{b} = \dfrac{16}{100}$

Solve: $\dfrac{b}{3} = \dfrac{100}{16}$ Taking the reciprocal of both sides

$b = 3 \cdot \dfrac{100}{16}$ Multiplying by 3

$b = \dfrac{3 \cdot 100}{16}$

$b = \dfrac{300}{16}$

$b = 18.75$

3 is 16% of 18.75

DO EXERCISE 10.

Example 11 $10 is what percent of $20?

Solution part rate base

Translate: $\dfrac{10}{20} = \dfrac{n}{100}$

Solve: $100 \cdot \dfrac{10}{20} = n$ Multiplying by 100

$\dfrac{1000}{20} = n$

$50 = n$

$10 is 50% of $20. The answer is 50%.

DO EXERCISE 11.

Solve.

11. $16 is what percent of $40?

Example 12 What percent of 50 is 16?

Solution rate base part

Translate: $\dfrac{16}{50} = \dfrac{n}{100}$

Solve: $100 \cdot \dfrac{16}{50} = n$ Multiplying by 100

$\dfrac{1600}{50} = n$

$32 = n$

32% of 50 is 16. The answer is 32%.

Solve.

12. What percent of 84 is 10.5?

DO EXERCISE 12.

EXERCISE SET 3.4B

NAME _____ CLASS _____ ANSWERS

EXERCISE SET 3.4B

■ Translate to a proportion. Do not solve.

1. What is 82% of 74?
2. 58% of 65 is what?

3. 4.3 is what percent of 5.9?
4. What percent of 6.8 is 5.3?

5. 14 is 25% of what?
6. 22.3% of what is 40?

■■ Solve.

7. What is 84% of $50?
8. What is 78% of $90?

9. 80% of 550 is what?
10. 90% of 740 is what?

11. What is 8% of 1000?
12. What is 9% of 2000?

13. 4.8% of 60 is what?
14. 63.1% of 80 is what?

15. $24 is what percent of $96?
16. $14 is what percent of $70?

17. 102 is what percent of 100?
18. 103 is what percent of 100?

1. _____
2. _____
3. _____
4. _____
5. _____
6. _____
7. _____
8. _____
9. _____
10. _____
11. _____
12. _____
13. _____
14. _____
15. _____
16. _____
17. _____
18. _____

RATIO AND PERCENT

19. What percent of $480 is $120?

20. What percent of $80 is $60?

21. What percent of 160 is 150?

22. What percent of 24 is 8?

23. $18 is 25% of what?

24. $75 is 20% of what?

25. 60% of what is 54?

26. 80% of what is 96?

27. 65.12 is 74% of what?

28. 63.7 is 65% of what?

29. 80% of what is 16?

30. 80% of what is 10?

Solve.

31. What is 8.85% of $12,640?

Estimate _____

Calculate _____

32. 78.8% of what is 9809.024?

Estimate _____

Calculate _____

ANSWERS

23. _____
24. _____
25. _____
26. _____
27. _____
28. _____
29. _____
30. _____
31. _____
32. _____
33. _____
34. _____
35. _____
36. _____

3.5 APPLICATION OF PERCENT

● PERCENT PROBLEMS

Applied problems involving percent are not always stated in a manner that is easily translated to a number sentence. In such cases it is helpful to restate the problem before translating. Sometimes it helps to draw a picture.

Example 1 The average family spends 26% of its income for food. A family earned $15,400 one year. How much was spent for food?

Solution We first draw a picture.

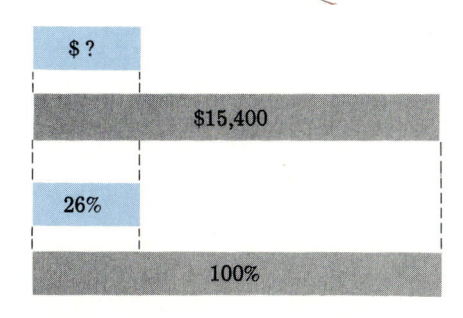

Method 1 Solve using an equation.

Restate: 26% of $15,400 is what?

Translate: 26% × $15,400 = p

Next we use the definition of percent.

0.26 × $15,400 = p

This sentence tells us what to do. We multiply 15,400 by 0.26.

```
      1 5,4 0 0
   ×       0.2 6
   ─────────────
        9 2 4 0 0
      3 0 8 0 0 0
   ─────────────
      4 0 0 4.0 0
```

The family spent $4004 for food.

DO EXERCISE 1.

OBJECTIVE

After finishing Section 3.5, you should be able to:

● Solve percent problems.

1. The average family spends 15% of its income for car expenses. A family earned $12,600 one year. How much was spent for car expenses?

15 × 12400

$1,890

ANSWER ON PAGE A–6

2. Do Exercise 1. Use Method 2.

Method 2* Solve using a proportion.

Restate: 26% of $15,400 is what?

Translate: $\dfrac{26}{100} = \dfrac{n}{15{,}400}$

Solve: $15{,}400 \cdot \dfrac{26}{100} = 15{,}400 \cdot \dfrac{n}{15{,}400}$

$\dfrac{400{,}400}{100} = n$

$4004 = n$

The family spent $4004 for food.

DO EXERCISE 2.

Example 2 The sales tax rate in California is 5%. On the purchase of a sofa the sales tax is $32. How much was the sofa before the sales tax (the purchase price)?

Solution We first draw a picture.

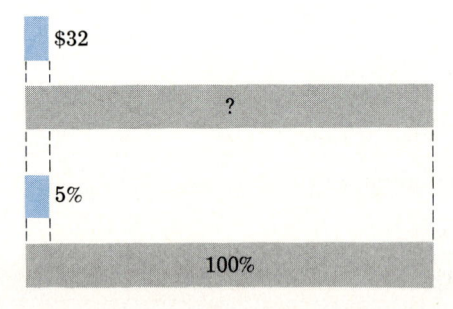

Method 1 Solve using an equation.

Restate: 5% of what is $32?

Translate: 5% × b = 32

Next we use the definition of percent.

0.05 × b = 32

Then we solve for b by dividing on both sides by 0.05.

b = 32 ÷ 0.05

---

* Note: If you skipped Section 3.4B, then you should ignore Method 2.

3.5 APPLICATION OF PERCENT

To find b we divide.

$$0.05\overline{\smash{\big)}3\,2.00}\;\;\underset{\wedge}{}640.$$

$$\begin{array}{r}
640. \\
0.05_{\wedge}\overline{\smash{\big)}3\,2.00_{\wedge}} \\
\underline{3\,0} \\
2\,0 \\
\underline{2\,0} \\
0
\end{array}$$

The purchase price was $640.

DO EXERCISE 3.

Method 2 Solve using a proportion.

Restate: 25% of what is $32?

Translate: $\dfrac{5}{100} = \dfrac{32}{b}$

Solve: $\dfrac{100}{5} = \dfrac{b}{32}$ Taking the reciprocal on both sides.

$$32 \cdot \dfrac{100}{5} = 32 \cdot \dfrac{b}{32}$$

$$\dfrac{3200}{5} = b$$

$$640 = b$$

The purchase price was $640.

DO EXERCISE 4.

Example 3 One year a consumer earns $15,000 and gets a $1200 raise. What percent of the year's salary was the raise?

Solution We first draw a picture.

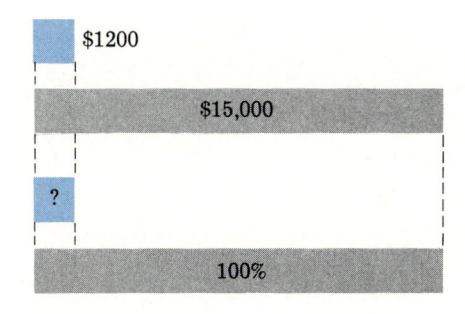

3. The sales tax rate in Indiana is **4%**. On the purchase of a calculator the sales tax was $3.52. How much was the purchase price?

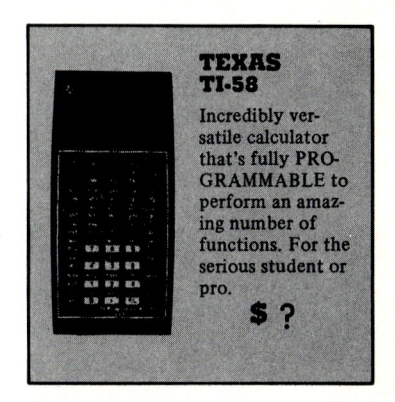

TEXAS TI-58
Incredibly versatile calculator that's fully PROGRAMMABLE to perform an amazing number of functions. For the serious student or pro.
$?

.04 y = 3.52
88
Tax = rate × cost

4. Do Exercise 3. Use Method 2.

ANSWER ON PAGE A-6

148

RATIO AND PERCENT

5. One year an investor has $12,000 in a savings account. The bank adds $1680 in interest to the account at the end of the year. What percent of the amount in the account is this?

[handwritten: 1680 = 12000 × x, 14%]

Method 1 Solve using an equation.

  Restate: $1200 is what percent of $15,000?

  Translate: 1200 = r% × 15,000

Next we use the definition of percent.

  $1200 = r \times 0.01 \times 15{,}000$

  $1200 = r \times 150$

Then we solve for r by dividing on both sides by 150.

  $1200 \div 150 = r$

To find r we carry out the division.

```
        8
150)1 2 0 0
    1 2 0 0
    ───────
          0
```

The raise was 8%.

DO EXERCISE 5.

6. Do Exercise 5. Use Method 2.

Method 2 Solve using a proportion.

  Restate: $1200 is what percent of $15,000?

  Translate: $\dfrac{n}{100} = \dfrac{1200}{15{,}000}$

  Solve: $100 \cdot \dfrac{n}{100} = 100 \cdot \dfrac{1200}{15{,}000}$

   $n = \dfrac{120{,}000}{15{,}000}$

   $n = 8$

The raise was 8%.

DO EXERCISE 6.

ANSWERS ON PAGE A–6

EXERCISE SET 3.5

■ Solve.

1. A corporation has a profit of $24,000 one year. It must pay 20% of this in federal taxes. How much is the federal tax?

1. 4800

2. A corporation has a profit of $18,500 one year. It must pay 20% of this in federal taxes. How much is the federal tax?

2. 3700

3. The sales tax rate in Arkansas is 3%. On the purchase of a refrigerator the sales tax is $14.70. How much is the purchase price?

$14.70 = .03x$

3. 490

4. The sales tax rate in Pennsylvania is 6%. On the purchase of a suit the sales tax is $10.80. How much is the purchase price?

$10.80 = .06x$

4. 180

5. On a business math test a student gets 7 out of 8 questions correct. What percent were correct?

5. 87.5%

6. A salesperson makes 40 calls to customers. Of these calls, 13 result in sales of a product. What percent were sales?

$\frac{13}{40}$

6. 32.5%

7. A quality-control inspector examines 100 stereos and finds 8 defective. What percent were defective? What percent were nondefective? At this rate, how many would be defective in a lot of 7500?

$\frac{8}{100} = \frac{x}{7500}$

8%

7. 600

8. A quality-control inspector examines 100 blouses and finds 9 defective. What percent were defective? What percent were nondefective? At this rate, how many would be defective in a lot of 8400?

$\frac{9}{100}$

9% 91%

8. 756

RATIO AND PERCENT

ANSWERS

9. **888**

10. **2190**

11. **9.1 %**

12. **15 %**

13. **25 %**

14. **7 %**

15. **239.76**

16. **27.5 %**

17. **$5784.96**

18. **49.96 %**

9. A study has revealed that 74% of all people who attend movies are in the 12-29 age group. A theater contained 1200 people for a showing of *Business Encounters of the Ninth Kind*. How many were in the 12-29 age group?

10. A study has revealed that most televisions are in use 25% of the time. Of the 8760 hours in a year, for how many would a television be in use?

11. One year an investor has $8600 in a savings account. The bank adds $782.60 in interest to the account. What percent of the amount in the account is this?

   $782.60 = x \cdot 8600$

12. One year a consumer earns $12,000 and gets an $1800 raise. What percent of the year's salary is this?

   $12,000 x = 1800$

13. Of the 8760 hours in a year most TV sets are on 2190 hours. What percent is this?

   $2190 = x \cdot 8760$

14. In a medical study it was determined that if 800 people kiss someone else who has a cold, only 56 will actually catch the cold. What percent is this?

   $56 = x \cdot 800$

15. Deming, New Mexico, claims to have the purest drinking water in the world. It is 99.9% pure. If you had 240 liters of water from Deming, how much of it, in liters, would be pure?

16. A baseball player gets 11 hits in 40 at bats. What percent are hits?

   $11 = 40 x$

17. A corporation has a profit of $28,567.98 one year. It must pay federal taxes of 20% on the first $25,000 and 22% on the amount that exceeds $25,000. How much is the federal tax? Round to the nearest cent.

18. One year a business has total sales of $55,000,000. Of this $27,480,235 is spent for manufacturing costs. What percent is this? Round to the nearest hundredth of a percent.

% increase or decrease = (amount of increase) / (original price)

3.6 PERCENT INCREASE AND DECREASE

■ PROBLEMS INVOLVING PERCENT INCREASE OR DECREASE

Percent is often used to state increases or decreases. Suppose the population of a town has *increased* 70%. This means the increase was 70% of the former population. The population of a town is 2340 and it increases 70%. The increase is 70% of 2340, or 1638. The new population is 2340 + 1638, or 3978. This is shown below.

What does it mean when one says that the price of Swiss cheese has decreased 8%? If the price was $1.00 a pound and it went down to $0.92 a pound, then the decrease is $0.08, which is 8% of the original price. This is shown below.

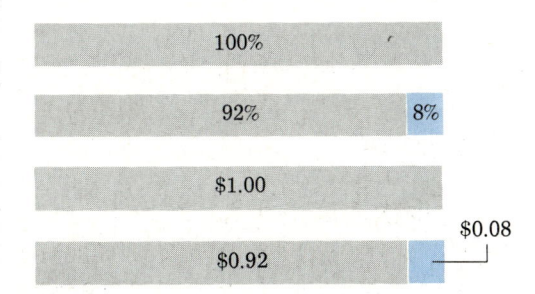

To find a percent of increase or decrease, find the amount of increase or decrease and then determine what percent this is of the original amount.

Example 1 The price of milk increased from 40¢ per liter to 45¢ per liter. What was the percent of increase?

Solution We first draw a picture.

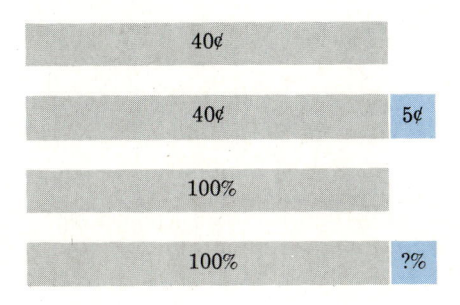

12.5

OBJECTIVE

After finishing Section 3.6, you should be able to

■ Solve problems involving percent increase or decrease.

Solve.

1. The price of an automobile increase from $5800 to $6322. What was the percent of increase?

   9 %

RATIO AND PERCENT

a) First, find the increase by subtracting.

$$\begin{array}{r} 4\ 5 \\ -4\ 0 \\ \hline 5 \end{array} \begin{array}{l} \text{New price} \\ \text{Original price} \\ \text{Increase} \end{array}$$

b) The increase is 5¢. Now we ask:

5 is what percent of 40 (the original price)?

(A common error is to use 45 instead of 40, the original amount.) To find out we use either of our two methods.

Method 1 Solve using a number sentence.

5 is what percent of 40?
↓   ↓   ↓   ↓
5 = n   % × 40

Next we use the definition of percent.

$5 = n \times 0.01 \times 40$

$5 = n \times 0.4$

To find the number we first divide by 0.4.

$5 \div 0.4 = n$ We divide on both sides by 0.4.

This tells us what to do. We divide.

$$\begin{array}{r} 12.5 \\ 0.4_\wedge\overline{)5.0_\wedge} \\ \underline{4} \\ 1\ 0 \\ \underline{8} \\ 2\ 0 \\ \underline{2\ 0} \\ 0 \end{array}$$

The percent of increase was 12.5%.

Method 2. Solve using a proportion.

Restate: 5 is what percent of 40?

Translate: $\dfrac{5}{40} = \dfrac{n}{100}$

$100 \cdot \dfrac{5}{40} = n$ Multiplying by 100

$\dfrac{500}{40} = n$

$12.5 = n$

The percent of increase was 12.5%.

DO EXERCISE 1.

ANSWER ON PAGE A–7

3.6 PERCENT INCREASE AND DECREASE

Example 2 By proper furnace maintenance a family that pays a monthly fuel bill of $88.00 can reduce it to $80.20. What is the percent of decrease? Round to the nearest tenth of a percent.

Solution We first draw a picture.

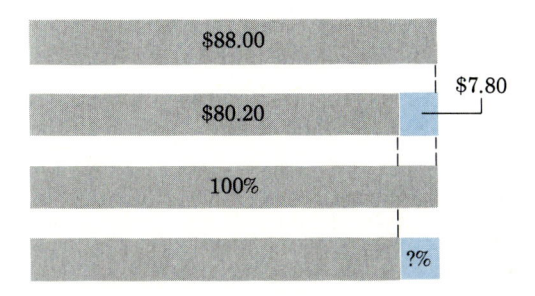

a) First, find the decrease.

$$\begin{array}{rl} 8\;8.0\;0 & \text{Original bill} \\ -8\;0.2\;0 & \text{New bill} \\ \hline 7.8\;0 & \text{Decrease} \end{array}$$

b) The decrease is $7.80. Now we ask:

7.80 is what percent of 88.00 (the original bill)?

(A common error is to use $80.20 instead of $88.00, the original amount.)

Method 1 Solve using a number sentence.

7.80 is what percent of 88.00?

$$7.80 = n \quad \% \quad \times \quad 88.00$$

Next we use the definition of percent.

$$7.8 = n \times 0.01 \times 88$$
$$7.8 = n \times 0.88$$

To find the number we first divide by 0.88.

$$7.8 \div 0.88 = n \qquad \text{We divide on both sides by 0.88.}$$

This tells us what to do. We divide.

```
            8.8 6
  0.8 8 ) 7.8 0 0 0
          7.0 4
          ─────
            7 6 0
            7 0 4
            ─────
              5 6 0
              5 2 8
              ─────
                3 2
```

We carry the division out to the hundredth place so the percent can be rounded to the nearest tenth. The percent of decrease is 8.9%.

Solve.

2. By using only cold water in a washing machine, a family that pays a monthly fuel bill of $88.00 can reduce it to $84.88. What is the percent of decrease? Round to the nearest tenth of a percent.

3.5% (handwritten)

Method 2 Solve using a proportion.

Restate: 7.80 is what percent of 88.00?

Translate: $\dfrac{7.80}{88.00} = \dfrac{n}{100}$

$100 \times \dfrac{7.80}{88.00} = n$ Multiplying by 100

$\dfrac{100 \times 7.80}{88.00} = n$

$\dfrac{780}{88} = n$

$8.9 = n$

The percent of decrease is 8.9%.

DO EXERCISE 2.

Example 3 A consumer earns $9700 one year and gets a 6% raise the next. What is the new salary?

Solution We first draw a picture.

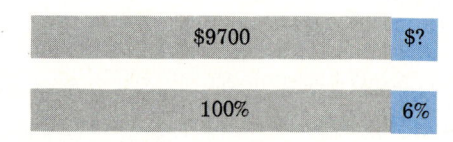

a) First, find the increase. We ask:

What is 6% of $9700?

Method 1 Solve using a number sentence.

What is 6% of 9700?

$a \;\; = 6\% \times 9700$

This tells us what to do. We convert 6% to decimal notation and multiply.

$$\begin{array}{r} 9700 \\ \times \; 0.06 \\ \hline 582.00 \end{array}$$ 6% = 0.06

The increase is $582.00

ANSWERS ON PAGE A–7

3.6 PERCENT INCREASE AND DECREASE

Method 2 Solve using a proportion.

Restate: What is 6% of 9700?

Translate: $\dfrac{a}{9700} = \dfrac{6}{100}$

$a = 9700 \cdot \dfrac{6}{100}$ Multiplying by 9700

$a = \dfrac{9700 \cdot 6}{100}$

$a = \dfrac{58{,}200}{100}$

$a = 582$

The increase is $582.00

b) The new salary is

$9700 + $582 = $10,282.

DO EXERCISE 3.

Example 4 One year the pilots of Pan American Airlines surprised the business world by taking an 11% decrease in salary. The former salary was $55,000. What was the new salary?

Solution We first draw a picture.

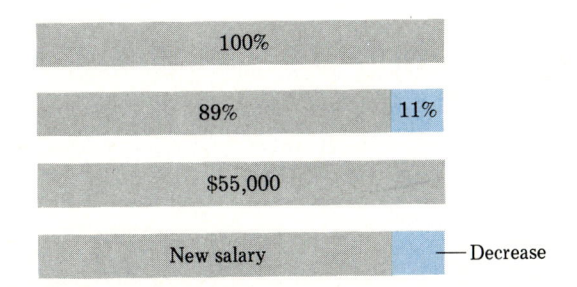

[Bar diagram: 100%; 89% | 11%; $55,000; New salary — Decrease]

a) First, find the decrease. We ask:

What is 11% of $55,000?

Method 1 Solve using an equation.

What is 11% of $55,000?

$p = 11\% \times 55{,}000$

Solve.

3. A consumer earns $9800 one year and gets a 9% raise the next. What is the new salary?

$10,682
$10,682

ANSWERS ON PAGE A–7

4. During a sale the price of a clock radio was decreased 25%. The original, or marked, price was $17.88. What was the new, or sale, price?

25% OFF Clock Radios
Wake up to savings on our Ken-Tech and Juliette digital clock radios. Orig. 17.88

RATIO AND PERCENT

This tells us what to do. We convert 11% to decimal notation and multiply.

$$\begin{array}{r} 55{,}000 \\ \times\ \ \ \ \ 0.11 \\ \hline 55000 \\ 55000\ \ \\ \hline 6050.00 \end{array}$$

The decrease is $6050.

Method 2 Solve using a proportion.

Restate: What is 11% of $55,000?

Translate: $\dfrac{a}{55{,}000} = \dfrac{11}{100}$

$a = 55{,}000 \cdot \dfrac{11}{100}$ Multiplying by 55,000

$a = \dfrac{605{,}000}{100}$

$a = 6050$

The decrease is $6050.

b) The new salary is found by subtracting the decrease from the former salary:

New salary = $55,000 − $6050 = $48,950

DO EXERCISE 4.

EXERCISE SET 3.6   **157**

NAME _____   CLASS _____   ANSWERS

EXERCISE SET 3.6

■ Solve.

1. An employee earns $18,940 one year, and gets an 8% raise the next. What is the new salary?

1. _20,455.20_

2. An employee earns $13,400 one year, and gets a 5% raise the next. What is the new salary?

2. _14,070_

3. The price of a coat is increased from $40 to $50. What is the percent of increase?

3. _25%_

4. The price of a radio was increased from $125 to $150. What was the percent of increase?

4. _20%_

5. The balance in a savings account increased from $400 to $436. What was the percent of increase?

5. _9%_

6. The population of a city increased from 8400 to 8820. What was the percent of increase?

6. _5%_

7. The value of a car decreased 30% one year. Its value the year before was $5600. What was its new value?

7. _3920_

8. The value of a machine decreased 12% one year. Its value the year before was $3200. What was its new value?

8. _2816_

9. A study has shown that a family that uses only cold water in its washing machine can reduce a monthly fuel bill of $86.00 to $82.56. What is the percent of decrease?

9. _4%_

10. A study has shown that a family that maintains its furnace properly can reduce a monthly fuel bill of $110 to $99. What is the percent of decrease?

10. _10%_

11. During a sale the price of a stereo was decreased from $399 to $369. What was the percent of decrease? Round to the nearest tenth of a percent.

11. _7.5%_

12. During a sale the price of round steak was decreased from $1.49 per pound to $1.39 per pound. What was the percent of decrease? Round to the nearest tenth of a percent.

12. _6.7%_

13. The price of a TV was increased from $500 to $520. What was the percent of increase?

13. _4%_

14. The price of a TV was decreased from $520 to $500. What was the percent of decrease? Round to the nearest tenth of a percent.

14. _3.8%_

15. Are the answers to Exercises 13 and 14 the same? Why?   no

15. _____

158 RATIO AND PERCENT

ANSWERS

16. 8%

17. 5%

18. 20%

19. 12%

20. $15540

21. $35,100

22. 4060

23. 4.084 bil.

24. $53 8.3%

25. $4836.21

26. .12%

---

16. The amount in a savings account increased from $200 to $216. What was the percent of increase?

17. The population of a small town increased from 840 to 882. What was the percent of increase?

18. During a sale a dress decreased in price from $35 to $28. What was the percent of decrease?

19. A person on a diet goes from a weight of 125 lb to a weight of 110 lb. What is the percent of decrease?

20. A person earns $14,800 one year and gets a 5% raise in salary. What is the new salary?

21. A person earns $32,500 one year and gets an 8% raise in salary. What is the new salary?

22. The value of a car typically decreases by 30% each year. A car is bought for $5800. What is its value one year later?

23. World population is increasing by 2.1% each year. In 1976 it was 4 billion. How much was it in 1977?

24. By increasing the thermostat from 72° to 78°, a family can reduce its cooling bill by 50%. If the cooling bill was $106.00, what would the new bill be? By what percent has the temperature been increased?

25. The original value of a car was $6856.95. During the first year its value decreased 29.47%. What was its new value? Round to the nearest cent.

26. In one year, the national debt increased from $746,945,000,000 to $747,828,000,000. What was the percent of increase? Round to the nearest hundredth of a percent.

159

NAME _____   SCORE _____   ANSWERS

TEST OR REVIEW — CHAPTER 3

[3.1, ●●●] 1. Solve: $\dfrac{x}{8} = \dfrac{7}{25}$.

1. 2.24

[3.2, ●] 2. If 4 cans of peaches cost $2.04, what is the cost of 11 cans?

2. 5.61

[3.3, ●●] 3. Convert to decimal notation: 87.4%.

3. .874

[3.3, ●●●] 4. Convert to percent notation: 0.31.

4. 31%

[3.3, ●●] 5. Convert to percent notation: $\dfrac{19}{20}$.

$\dfrac{19}{20} = \dfrac{x}{100} = \dfrac{95}{100}$

5. 95%

[3.3, ●●] 6. Convert to fractional notation: 9.5%.

$\dfrac{95}{1000} = \dfrac{19}{200}$

6. $\dfrac{95}{1000} = \dfrac{19}{200}$

[3.4A, ●●] Solve.
[3.4B, ●●] 7. What is 16% of 97?

7. 15.52

8. 97% of what is $1455?

$.97x = 1455$

8. 1500

160 RATIO AND PERCENT

ANSWERS

9. $980 is what percent of $1250?

$$980 = x \cdot 1250$$

9. 78.4%

[3.5, ●] Solve.

10. The sales tax rate in Maryland is 5%. On the purchase of a suit the sales tax is $6.60. How much was the purchase price?

$$.05x = 6.60$$

10. 132

11. One month a family spent 67% of their income for loan payments. Their income was $1100. How much was spent for loan payments?

11. 737

[3.6, ●] Solve.

12. An employee earns $12,300 one year and gets a 5.7% raise the following year. What is the new salary?

12. $13,001.10

13. The price of a calculator was increased from $25 to $27. What was the percent of increase?

$$\frac{2}{25}$$

13. 8%

14. The price of a calculator was decreased from $27 to $25. What was the percent of decrease? Round to the nearest tenth of a percent.

14. 7.4%

15. During a sale the price of a bottle of shampoo was decreased 50%. The original, or marked, price was $1.99. What was the sale price? Round to the nearest dollar.

.50

15. $1.00

Career: Financial Institution Management This is Gerald E. Resler. Gerald has a most compelling story of success. He took a course in business mathematics as part of a two-year accounting major at a business college. Apart from some economics and savings and loan courses taken in the summer, this is the extent of his higher education. Nevertheless, his aptitude, dedication, and willingness for hard work have led him to become Senior Vice-President and Chief Financial Officer of Railroadmen's Federal Savings and Loan.

As you can see in the photograph, interest rates are very much a part of Gerald's work. These interest rates apply to various types of savings accounts. Government laws used to control the maximum value, but the methods of compounding were allowed to vary. During those times, financial institutions used continuous compounding because it was the highest rate allowed. These laws were dropped late in 1982. Since then, interest has been compounded in periods such as daily, monthly, or quarterly, mainly because the public does not understand continuous compounding and because a financial institution can pay any rate it desires to be competitive with other financial institutions.

Interest rates for loans are also pertinent to Gerald's work. In fact, this is how a savings and loan makes money. Money is taken in through savings accounts and loaned out at higher rates. The difference is the basis for profit.

Gerald is in charge of three parts of the savings and loan—the savings department, the accounting department, and the mail department.

Gerald's hobbies include playing golf, watching basketball and baseball, woodworking, and photography.

4
INTEREST

INTEREST

READINESS CHECK: SKILLS FOR CHAPTER 4

Subtract.

1. $410.06 - 400$
2. $450 - 240.73$

Multiply.

3. 299×0.014889
4. 7500×0.73069

Round each to the nearest hundredth.

5. 4.451811
6. 5480.175

Evaluate.

7. 2^4
8. $(1.02)^2$

OBJECTIVES

After finishing Section 4.1, you should be able to:

- Find the interest earned.
- Solve for the rate in interest problems.
- Find the principal in interest problems.
- Find the interest in any payment.
- Determine the amount paid back.

4.1 SIMPLE INTEREST

Knowing about interest is important. For example, a knowledge of interest will help you to invest wisely and to borrow advantageously. Simply stated, *interest* is money paid for the use of money. When you have money in a bank you are paid for the use of your money. Likewise, when you borrow money you must pay for its use. Several types of interest will be studied in this chapter.

FINDING SIMPLE INTEREST

ENERGY SAVINGS BANK OF BRENTON LOANS

Insulate your home. Borrow $200 today at 14% Pay back $228 in 1 year.

At Energy Savings Bank you borrow $200 for one year. The amount borrowed ($200) is called the *principal*. The *interest rate* is 14%. This means that in addition to the principal you pay back 14% of the principal, which is

14% of $200, or $0.14 \times \$200$, or $28.

This $28 is simple interest. Interest paid on only the principal for the entire time is *simple interest*. If you had borrowed the money for $\frac{1}{4}$ of the year you would pay

$0.14 \times \$200 \times \frac{1}{4}$, or $7.00 in interest.

This leads us to the following *simple-interest* formula.

4.1 SIMPLE INTEREST

A formula for *simple interest* is

$I = P \times R \times T,$

where I is the interest, P is the principal (the amount borrowed or invested), R is the interest rate, and T is the time, in years or fractional parts of a year, that the principal is borrowed or invested.

Unless otherwise indicated the interest rate is an annual or yearly rate.

Example 1 A family borrows $400 on their CNA life insurance policy at 5% simple interest for one year. How much interest must be paid?

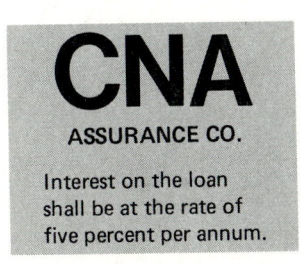

CNA ASSURANCE CO.
Interest on the loan shall be at the rate of five percent per annum.

Solution Substituting 400 for P, 0.05 for R, and 1 for T, we get

$I = P \times R \times T$
$= 400 \times 0.05 \times 1$
$= 20.$

An interest charge of $20 must be paid.

DO EXERCISE 1.

Example 2 A savings and loan certificate of deposit pays 12% simple interest. How much interest is earned in $1\frac{1}{2}$ years on $700?

Solution Substituting 700 for P, 0.12 for R, and 1.5 for T, we get

$I = P \times R \times T$
$= 700 \times 0.12 \times 1.5$
$= 126$

Interest earned is $126.

DO EXERCISE 2.

---

1. $800 is borrowed for two years at 15% simple interest. How much interest must be paid?

   240

2. A $500 municipal bond earns 11% simple interest. How much interest is earned in $4\frac{1}{2}$ years?

   $247.5

ANSWERS ON PAGE A–7

164

INTEREST

3. Some credit unions pay 4% simple interest on checking account average balances. What is the interest on a $300 average balance for 1 month?

Example 3 What is the simple interest earned on $250 for three months at 16%?

Solution Substituting 250 for P, 0.16 for R, and $\frac{3}{12}$ for T, we get

$I = P \times R \times T$

$= 250 \times 0.16 \times \frac{3}{12}$ 3 months is $\frac{3}{12}$ year

$= 10$

Interest earned is $10.00.

DO EXERCISE 3

▪▪▫ FINDING THE INTEREST RATE

We know that $I = P \times R \times T$. If we want a formula for R we can divide both sides of $I = P \times R \times T$, by $P \times T$, and we get

$R = \dfrac{I}{P \times T}.$

As a memory device you might remember $R = \dfrac{I}{P \times T}$ from the diagram

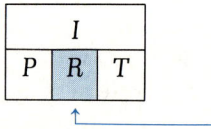

I
P	R	T

4. The simple interest for one month on a $4000 loan was $50. What was the rate?

Example 4 A $5000 savings certificate earned $1200 in simple interest in two years. What was the rate?

Solution Substitute 5000 for P, 2 for T, and 1200 for I, and solve for R.

$R = \dfrac{I}{P \times T}$

$R = \dfrac{1200}{5000 \times 2}$

$R = \dfrac{1200}{10{,}000}$ Dividing by 10,000 to get R

$R = 0.12$

The rate of interest was 12%.

DO EXERCISE 4.

▪▪▪ FIND THE PRINCIPAL

$I = P \times R \times T$, so to get a formula for P we divide both sides of $I = P \times R \times T$ by $R \times T$ and get

$P = \dfrac{I}{R \times T}.$

ANSWERS ON PAGE A–7

4.1 SIMPLE INTEREST

As a memory device you might remember $P = \dfrac{I}{R \times T}$ from the diagram

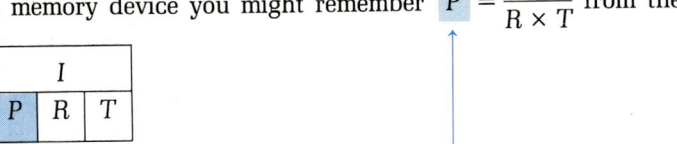

I	
P	R	T

Example 5 Last month on a 16% home mortgage loan the interest was $436.87. What was the amount owed at the beginning of last month?

Solution Substitute 0.16 for R, $\dfrac{1}{12}$ for T, and 436.87 for I, and solve for P.

$$P = \dfrac{I}{R \times T}$$

$$P = \dfrac{436.87}{0.16 \times 1/12}$$

$P = 32{,}765.26$ Rounded to nearest cent as throughout this chapter

The amount owed at the beginning of last month was $32,765.26.

DO EXERCISE 5.

INTEREST IN A PAYMENT

Interest you pay is deductible when you file your Federal Income Tax Return. It is helpful to know how much of each payment is interest.

Example 6 A mortgage balance was $26,434.29 one month and $26,193.56 the following month. A payment of $450 was made. How much of the $450 was interest?

Solution

a) Find the principal payment:

Principal payment = $26,434.29 − $26,193.56
  = $240.73.

b) Find the interest:

Interest = Total payment − Principal payment
  = $450 − $240.73
  = $209.27.

DO EXERCISE 6.

---

5. Short-term loans are available from the government at 5%. Suppose a student repaid a loan with one payment at the end of three months. The interest charge was $2.25. How much was borrowed?

I = PRT

$\dfrac{I}{R \cdot T} = P$

$\dfrac{2.25}{.05 \times \tfrac{1}{4}}$

$\$180$

6. The balance on a mobile home mortgage was $9348.62 one month and $9298.73 the next. A payment of $125 was made. How much interest was paid?

$\$75.11$

ANSWERS ON PAGE A–7

7. $500 is put in a bank paying 11% simple interest. How much is in the account after three years?

$665

INTEREST

8:8 AMOUNT PAID BACK

Consumers want to know the amount owed or in savings after a period of time. For example, when $200 is borrowed at 14% for one year the amount owed is $200 + $28 or $228. This leads us to the following formula:

$$A = P + I$$

where A is the amount owed or in savings, P is the principal, and I is the interest.

Example 7 A person borrows $800 at 15% simple interest for two years. How much is owed after two years?

Solution

a) Find the interest. We substitute 800 for P, 0.15 for R, and 2 for T in

$$I = P \times R \times T$$
$$= 800 \times 0.15 \times 2$$
$$= 240.$$

The interest is $240.

b) Find the amount owed. We substitute 800 for P and 240 for I in

$$A = P + I$$
$$= 800 + 240$$
$$= 1040.$$

The amount owed is $1040.

DO EXERCISE 7.

ANSWERS ON PAGE A–7

EXERCISE SET 4.1

■ Find the simple interest.

	Principal	Interest Rate	Time
1.	$500	13%	1 year
2.	$2000	16%	1 year
3.	$1700	15%	2 years
4.	$800	14%	$\frac{1}{2}$ year

5. A student loan for $1500 at 5% was repaid in one payment at the end of three years. How much interest was due at that time?

6. A $2800 loan at 14% was repaid at the end of 18 months. How much interest was due at that time?

7. A revolving charge account had a balance of $450 last month. The interest rate is 18% a year on the unpaid balance. How much interest was charged for the month?

8. A bank card account had a balance of $300 last month. If the interest rate was 15% a year on the unpaid balance, how much interest was due for the month?

■ ■ Find the rate.

	Principal	Interest	Time
9.	$900	$153	1 year
10.	$1800	$252	1 year
11.	$2400	$270	9 months
12.	$1600	$288	$1\frac{1}{2}$ years

13. The interest on a $2500 loan for $2\frac{1}{2}$ years was $687.50. What was the rate?

14. The interest on a $300 loan for two years was $84. What was the rate?

■ ■ ■ Find the principal.

	Interest	Interest Rate	Time
15.	$1260	18%	1 year
16.	$750	15%	1 year
17.	$133	14%	$\frac{1}{2}$ year
18.	$88	16%	3 months

19. The interest payment on a mobile home loan last month was $71.25 at 13%. How much was owed at the beginning of the month?

Answers:
1. 65
2. 320
3. 510
4. 56
5. 225
6. 588
7. 6.75
8. 3.75
9. 17%
10. 14%
11. 15%
12. 12%
13. 11%
14. 14%
15. 7000
16. 5000
17. 1900
18. 2200
19. 6576.94

168

INTEREST

$I = PRT \qquad P = \dfrac{I}{RT}$

ANSWERS

20. 2892.02
21. 1500
22. 100
23. 168.02
24. 352.08
25. 322.43
26. 455.15
27. 128.78
28. 25.18
29. 1610
30. 2912
31. 852
32. 4340
33. 1775
34. 2650
35.
36.
37.
38.

20. Interest on a 14% car loan last month was $33.75. How much was owed at the beginning of the month?

21. At the end of six months a bank pays you $90 interest on your 12% savings certificate. How much was the principal?

22. At the end of two years, $36 in interest was paid on an 18% loan. How much had been borrowed?

Find the interest in each payment.

	Payment	Old Balance	New Balance
23.	$450	$32,465.29	$32,183.31
24.	$625	$60,834.15	$60,561.23
25.	$586	$53,982.83	$53,719.26
26.	$941	$80,625.47	$80,139.62

27. Last month Cheryl owed $7426.18 on her car. After this month's $236.14 payment the balance is $7318.82. How much of the payment was interest?

28. Last month Mark owed $638.62 on his stereo. After this month's $75.27 payment the balance is $588.53. How much of the payment was interest?

Find the amount owed at the stated time.

	Principal	Interest Rate	Time
29.	$1400	15%	1 year
30.	$2600	12%	1 year
31.	$800	13%	½ year
32.	$3500	16%	1½ years

33. A person borrows $1250 at 14% for three years. How much will be owed after three years?

34. A person invests $2500 in a savings certificate paying 12% interest. How much is in the account after six months?

Complete the table for one-month payments on a $47,000 home mortgage loan balance.

	Interest	Rate	Loan Balance after a $500 payment
35.	$352.50	9%	46,852.50
36.	470	12%	46,970
37.	372	9.5%	$46,872.08
38.	489.58	12.5%	46,989.58

4.2 BANKER'S 360-DAY METHOD

◼ INTEREST

The banker's 360-day method is often used to compute simple interest when you borrow money from a bank. The method assumes that

a) a year has 360 days, and

b) the exact number of days from one day to another is used.

You pay more interest on your loan with this method.

Example 1 A customer borrowed $389 at 13% for 90 days to buy a Whirlpool range. How much interest was paid?

Solution Substituting 389 for P, 0.13 for R, and $\frac{90}{360}$ for T, we get

$$I = P \times R \times T$$

$$= 389 \times 0.13 \times \frac{90}{360}$$

$$= 12.64$$

An interest charge of $12.64 was paid.

DO EXERCISE 1.

A table may be used to find the time in days, as shown in Example 2.

Example 2 A customer borrowed $700 at 15% on April 17 and repaid it on September 5. How much interest was paid?

Solution

a) Find the number of days from April 17 to September 5.

OBJECTIVES

After finishing Section 4.2, you should be able to:

◼ Compute interest using the banker's 360-day method.

◼◼ Find the amount repaid with the banker's 360-day method.

1. A customer borrowed $389 at 13% for 130 days to buy a Whirlpool range. How much interest was paid?

ANSWER ON PAGE A–7

2. A customer borrowed $450 at 12% on June 26 and repaid it on October 7. How much interest was paid?

INTEREST

TABLE 4.1
DAY OF THE YEAR

April 17 is Day 107
September 5 is Day 248

DAY	JAN	FEB	MAR	APR	MAY	JUN	JUL	AUG	SEP	OCT	NOV	DEC
Days in month	31	28	31	30	31	30	31	31	30	31	30	31
DAY 1	1	32	60	91	121	152	182	213	244	274	305	335
DAY 2	2	33	61	92	122	153	183	214	245	275	306	336
DAY 3	3	34	62	93	123	154	184	215	246	276	307	337
DAY 4	4	35	63	94	124	155	185	216	247	277	308	338
DAY 5	5	36	64	95	125	156	186	217	248	278	309	339
DAY 6	6	37	65	96	126	157	187	218	249	279	310	340
DAY 7	7	38	66	97	127	158	188	219	250	280	311	341
DAY 8	8	39	67	98	128	159	189	220	251	281	312	342
DAY 9	9	40	68	99	129	160	190	221	252	282	313	343
DAY 10	10	41	69	100	130	161	191	222	253	283	314	344
DAY 11	11	42	70	101	131	162	192	223	254	284	315	345
DAY 12	12	43	71	102	132	163	193	224	255	285	316	346
DAY 13	13	44	72	103	133	164	194	225	256	286	317	347
DAY 14	14	45	73	104	134	165	195	226	257	287	318	348
DAY 15	15	46	74	105	135	166	196	227	258	288	319	349
DAY 16	16	47	75	106	136	167	197	228	259	289	320	350
DAY 17	17	48	76	107	137	168	198	229	260	290	321	351
DAY 18	18	49	77	108	138	169	199	230	261	291	322	352
DAY 19	19	50	78	109	139	170	200	231	262	292	323	353
DAY 20	20	51	79	110	140	171	201	232	263	293	324	354
DAY 21	21	52	80	111	141	172	202	233	264	294	325	355
DAY 22	22	53	81	112	142	173	203	234	265	295	326	356
DAY 23	23	54	82	113	143	174	204	235	266	296	327	357
DAY 24	24	55	83	114	144	175	205	236	267	297	328	358
DAY 25	25	56	84	115	145	176	206	237	268	298	329	359
DAY 26	26	57	85	116	146	177	207	238	269	299	330	360
DAY 27	27	58	86	117	147	178	208	239	270	300	331	361
DAY 28	28	59	87	118	148	179	209	240	271	301	332	362
DAY 29	29	0	88	119	149	180	210	241	272	302	333	363
DAY 30	30	0	89	120	150	181	211	242	273	303	334	364
DAY 31	31	0	90	0	151	0	212	243	0	304	0	365

ADD 1 DAY FOR LEAP YEAR IF FEBRUARY 29 FALLS BETWEEN THE TWO DATES

Number of days = 248 − 107   or   141

b) Find the interest.

Substituting 700 for P, 0.15 for R, and $\frac{141}{360}$ for T, we get

$I = P \times R \times T$

$= 700 \times 0.15 \times \frac{141}{360}$

$= 41.13.$

An interest charge of $41.13 was paid.

DO EXERCISE 2.

Time in days may be found without the use of a table, as shown in Example 3.

Example 3 A customer borrowed $590 at 11% on May 23 and repaid it on July 17. How much interest was paid?

4.2 BANKER'S 360-DAY METHOD

Solution

a) Find the number of days from May 23 to July 17.

8 days left in May (don't count the first day, May 23)
30 days in June
17 days in July (count the last day)
———
55 days

Remember: "30 days hath September, April, June, and November. All the rest have 31 except February (when not a leap year) which has 28."

b) Find the interest.

Substituting 590 for P, 0.11 for R, and $\frac{55}{360}$ for T, we get

$I = P \times R \times T$

$= 590 \times 0.11 \times \frac{55}{360} = 9.92$.

An interest charge of $9.92 was paid.

DO EXERCISE 3.

●● AMOUNT REPAID

Customers may want to know how much must be repaid on a loan. Example 4 answers this question.

Example 4 A customer borrowed $650 at 14% on March 19 and repaid it on May 5. How much was repaid?

Solution

a) Find the number of days from March 19 to May 5.

12 days in March
30 days in April
 5 days in May
———
47 days

b) Find the interest.

Substituting 650 for P, 0.14 for R, and $\frac{47}{360}$ for T, we get

$I = P \times R \times T$

$= 650 \times 0.14 \times \frac{47}{360} = 11.88$.

The interest was $11.88.

c) Find the amount repaid.

Substituting 650 for P and 11.88 for I, we get

$A = P + I$

$= 650 + 11.88 = 661.88$.

Thus, $661.88 was repaid.

DO EXERCISE 4.

---

3. A customer borrowed $650 at 11% on April 25 and repaid it on June 11. How much interest was paid?

4. A customer borrowed $1225 at 15% on August 21 and repaid it on October 9. How much was repaid?

ANSWERS ON PAGE A–7

172 INTEREST

1. Find the interest on $800 at 6% for 60 days.

SOMETHING EXTRA

Banker's 60-Day, 6% Interest

The following method permits quick interest calculation.

> **Banker's 60-Day, 6% Interest Method**
> To calculate interest move the decimal point 2 places to the left in the principal.

This method works because for $R = \dfrac{6}{100}$ and $T = \dfrac{1}{6}$, $\dfrac{60}{360}$ is $\dfrac{1}{6}$.

$$I = P \times \dfrac{\cancel{6}^{1}}{100} \times \dfrac{1}{\cancel{6}_{1}} \qquad \text{Cancel the 6's}$$

$$= \dfrac{P}{100} \qquad \text{(moves decimal point in } P \text{ 2 places to the left)}$$

Example 1 Find the interest on $500 at 6% for 60 days.

Solution Move the decimal point

5.00.

The interest is $5.00.

DO EXERCISE 1.

2. Find the interest on $800 for 180 days at 9%.

This method may be used for other rates and times.

Example 2 Find the interest on $500 for 120 days at 9%.

Solution

a) Move the decimal point two places to the left.

5.00.

So $5.00 is the interest on $500 at 6% for 60 days.

b) Multiply

Interest for 120 days = 2 × Interest for 60 days
= 2 × $5.00
= $10.00

3. Find the interest on $800 for 120 days at 12%.

c) Multiply

Interest at 9% = $\dfrac{3}{2}$ × Interest at 6% (since 9% is $\frac{3}{2}$ of 6%).

$= \dfrac{3}{2} \times \$10.00$

$= \$15.00$

The interest on $500 for 120 days at 9% is $15.

4. Find the interest on $800 for 90 days at 15%.

DO EXERCISES 2–4.

ANSWERS ON PAGE A–7

EXERCISE SET 4.2

■ Find the interest using the 360-day method.

	Principal	Interest Rate	Time (Days)
1.	$500	14%	30
2.	$1000	14%	30
3.	$900	12%	20
4.	$1500	12%	15
5.	$1200	18%	120
6.	$3000	16%	150
7.	$2300	15%	180
8.	$1600	15%	130

Solve using the 360-day method.

9. Find the interest due on an $800, 12% loan for 400 days.

10. Find the interest due on a $650, 14% loan for 580 days.

11. Find the interest due on a $250, 13% loan for 10 days.

12. Find the interest due on a $780, 11% loan for 25 days.

13. Find the interest due on an $825, 16% loan taken out September 14 and repaid on November 5.

14. Find the interest due on a $325, 12% loan taken out on March 4 and repaid on August 3.

ANSWERS

1. 5.83
2. 11.67
3. 6
4. 7.50
5. 72
6. 200
7. 172.50
8. 86.67
9. 106.67
10. 146.41
11. .90
12. 5.96
13. 19.07
14. 16.47

174 INTEREST

ANSWERS

15. A student took out a $500, 9% loan on September 5 and repaid it January 12. Find the interest.

15. _16.13_

16. A student took out a $700, 14% loan on October 11 and repaid it February 12. Find the interest.

16. _33.76_

17. A consumer borrowed $300 at 13% on March 17 and repaid it August 8. Find the interest.

17. _15.6_

18. A consumer borrowed $1250 at 17% on April 14 and repaid it July 23. Find the interest.

18. _59.03_

■■ Find the amount repaid using the 360-day method.

	Principal	Rate	Borrowed	Repaid
19.	$1300	14%	May 7	October 1
20.	$3500	11%	March 5	November 2
21.	$800	17%	May 9	July 2
22.	$900	16%	April 4	June 27

19. _1373.81_

20. _3758.81_

21. _820.40_

22. _933.60_

Solve using the 360-day method.

23. Find the amount repaid if $760 was borrowed June 1 at 12% and repaid August 14.

23. _778.75_

24. Find the amount repaid if $1050 was borrowed May 13 at 17% and repaid July 23.

24. _1085.20_

25. Find the amount repaid if $725 was borrowed September 22 at 13% and repaid on November 19.

25. _746.18_

26. Find the amount repaid if $800 was borrowed on June 17 at 11% and repaid on September 5.

26. _819.56_

4.3 EXACT INTEREST METHOD

◼ INTEREST

In many states recently enacted consumer protection laws require simple interest calculation using the *exact (accurate) interest method*. The method assumes that

a) a year has 365 days, and

b) the exact number of days is used.

Example 1 A customer borrowed $249.95 at 11% for 67 days to buy a Hitachi SR703 receiver. How much interest was paid?

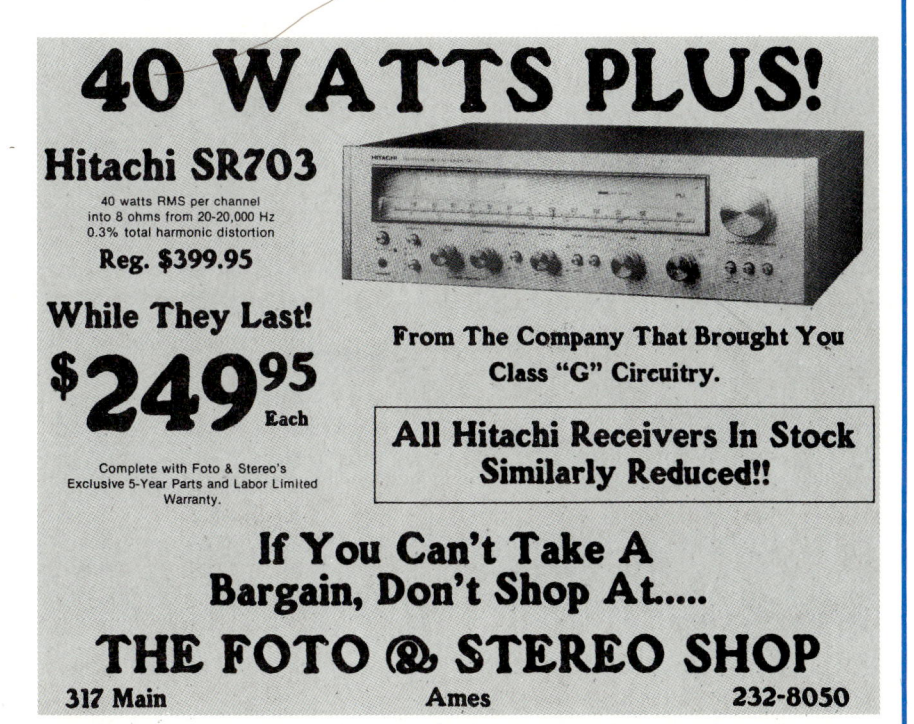

OBJECTIVES

After finishing Section 4.3, you should be able to:

◼ Compute interest using the exact interest method.

◼◼ Find the amount repaid using the exact interest method.

1. A customer borrowed $249.95 at 14% for 100 days to buy a Hitachi receiver. How much interest was paid?

9.59

40 WATTS PLUS!

Hitachi SR703
40 watts RMS per channel
into 8 ohms from 20-20,000 Hz
0.3% total harmonic distortion
Reg. $399.95

While They Last!
$249⁹⁵ Each

Complete with Foto & Stereo's
Exclusive 5-Year Parts and Labor Limited
Warranty.

From The Company That Brought You
Class "G" Circuitry.

All Hitachi Receivers In Stock Similarly Reduced!!

If You Can't Take A
Bargain, Don't Shop At.....

THE FOTO & STEREO SHOP
317 Main   Ames   232-8050

Solution Substituting 249.95 for P, 0.11 for R, and $\frac{67}{365}$ for T, we get

$$I = P \times R \times T$$

$$= 249.95 \times 0.11 \times \frac{67}{365}$$

$$= 5.05.$$

An interest charge of $5.05 was paid.

DO EXERCISE 1.

ANSWER ON PAGE A–7

2. A customer borrowed $295 at 16% for 135 days to buy a Honda Express. How much was repaid?

312.46

INTEREST

Note: If 360 days had been used in place of one year, then the interest charge would have been 249.95 × 0.11 × $\frac{67}{360}$, or $5.12. The banks would make *more* money. This is probably why a consumer protection law was enacted.

●● AMOUNT REPAID

Example 2 A customer borrowed $295 at 12% for 90 days to buy a Honda Express. How much was repaid?

Solution

a) Find the interest.

Substituting 295 for P, 0.12 for R, and $\frac{90}{365}$ for T, we get

$I = P \times R \times T$

$= 295 \times 0.12 \times \frac{90}{365}$

$= 8.73.$

An interest charge of $8.73 was paid.

b) Find the amount to be repaid.

Substituting 295 for P and 8.73 for I, we get

$A = P + I$

$= 295 + 8.73$

$= 303.73.$

Thus, $303.73 was repaid.

DO EXERCISE 2.

ANSWER ON PAGE A-7

EXERCISE SET 4.3

● Find the interest using the *exact* interest method.

	Principal	Interest Rate	Time (Days)
1.	$600	14%	90
2.	$800	15%	70
3.	$950	12%	15
4.	$890	17%	18
5.	$1200	16%	47
6.	$1500	13%	63
7.	$2240	13%	112
8.	$1780	10%	231
9.	$3675	12%	380
10.	$1375	19%	450

Solve using the *exact* interest method.

11. Find the interest on a $1250, 13% loan for 150 days.

12. Find the interest on a $1600, 17% loan for 190 days.

13. Find the interest on a $1575, 15% loan for 175 days.

14. Find the interest on a $2300, 19% loan for 180 days.

ANSWERS

1. 20.71
2. 23.07
3. 4.68
4. 7.46
5. 24.72
6. 33.64
7. 89.35
8. 112.65
9. 459.12
10. 322.09
11. 66.78
12. 141.59
13. 115.27
14. 215.51

178 INTEREST

ANSWERS

15. _16.44_

16. _24.66_

17. _10.38_

18. _4.52_

19. _456.04_

20. _614.79_

21. _812.48_

22. _507.40_

23. _748.32_

24. _504.13_

15. A student took out a $500 loan at 12% for 100 days. Find the interest.

16. A student took out a $1000 loan at 10% for 90 days. Find the interest.

17. A customer borrowed $550 at 13% for 53 days to buy a color television. How much interest was paid?

18. A customer borrowed $250 at 11% for 60 days to buy a drafting table. How much interest was paid?

■■ Find the amount repaid using the *exact* interest method.

	Principal	Rate	Days
19.	$450	14%	35
20.	$600	18%	50
21.	$780	19%	80
22.	$500	12%	45

23. A customer borrowed $700 at 14% for 180 days to buy a lawn tractor. How much was repaid?

24. A customer borrowed $485 at 16% for 90 days to buy a sewing machine. How much was repaid?

4.4 OTHER METHODS OF COMPUTING INTEREST

● 360-DAY, APPROXIMATE TIME INTEREST

In this section we study two more methods used to compute simple interest. Neither uses exact time. The first uses (1) a 360-day year, and (2) approximate time based on 30-day months.

Example 1 Find the interest on $400 borrowed on June 26 at 15% and repaid October 17.

Solution

a) Find the number of days based on 30-day months.

	Month	Day	
October 17	~~10~~ 9	~~17~~ 47	(change to 9 months, 47 days)
June 26	6	26	
Subtracting, we get	3	21	

Total days = 111 (3 months of 30 days and 21 days)

b) Find the interest.

Substituting 400 for P, 0.15 for R, and $\frac{111}{360}$ for T, we get

$I = P \times R \times T$

$= 400 \times 0.15 \times \frac{111}{360} = 18.50.$

The interest was $18.50.

DO EXERCISE 1.

●● 365-DAY, APPROXIMATE TIME INTEREST

Another method uses (1) a 365-day year, and (2) approximate time based on 30-day months.

OBJECTIVES

After finishing Section 4.4, you should be able to:

● Solve interest problems using a 360-day year and approximate time.

●● Solve interest problems using a 365-day year and approximate time.

1. A customer borrowed $850 on April 21 at 12% and repaid it July 5. How much interest was due?

$30.97

ANSWER ON PAGE A-8

180

INTEREST

2. Find the interest due on $600 borrowed April 27 at 15% and repaid August 21.

Example 2 A customer borrowed $500 at 14% on May 24 and repaid it on September 11. How much interest was due?

Solution

a) Find the number of days based on 30-day months.

	Month	Day
September 11	$\overset{8}{9}$	$\overset{41}{\cancel{11}}$
May 24	5	24
Subtracting, we get	3	17

Total days = 107 (3 months of 30 days and 17 days)

b) Find the interest.

Substituting 500 for P, 0.14 for R, and $\dfrac{107}{365}$ for T, we get

$I = P \times R \times T$

$= 500 \times 0.14 \times \dfrac{107}{365}$

$= 20.52.$

The interest was $20.52.

DO EXERCISE 2.

ANSWER ON PAGE A–8

EXERCISE SET 4.4

● Find the interest using the 360-day, approximate time method.

	Principal	Rate	Borrowed	Repaid
1.	$1400	15%	March 6	June 5
2.	$900	12%	May 12	August 8
3.	$2500	13%	April 23	November 24
4.	$1900	11%	June 21	December 14
5.	$1700	19%	May 17	October 27
6.	$1800	18%	July 6	September 7

Use a 360-day year and approximate time to find the interest on the following loans.

7. $1250 borrowed January 17 at 11% and repaid March 5

8. $1800 borrowed February 26 at 12% and repaid August 25

9. $2600 borrowed June 18 at 14% and repaid December 9

10. $2300 borrowed July 7 at 12% and repaid October 28

●● Find the interest using the 365-day, approximate time method.

	Principal	Rate	Borrowed	Repaid
11.	$850	13%	February 12	May 7
12.	$1875	15%	March 26	September 4
13.	$2300	14%	February 6	October 17
14.	$3500	17%	May 13	November 24

ANSWERS

1. 51.91
2. 25.80
3. 190.49
4. 100.44
5. $143.54
6. $54.90
7. $18.33
8. $107.40
9. 172.90
10. 85.1
11. 25.73
12. 121.75
13. 221.43
14. 331.34

182 INTEREST

ANSWERS

15. 33.48
16. 18.78
17. 173.44
18. 33.53
19. 90.78
20. 338.11
21. 158.09
22. 447.22
23. 22898.96
24. 26796.88
25. 15210.42
26. 46109.59

Find the 365-day, approximate time interest on a $479.99 Video Cassette Recorder loan using the rates and dates which follow.

SAVE $300
Magnavox 8-Hour VHS Video Cassette Recorder
479.99

Features electronic quartz digital clock, soft touch function controls, remote pause still, automatic fine tuning, more.

	Rate	Borrowed	Repaid
15.	19%	June 3	October 17
16.	21%	June 3	August 12
17.	13%	June 3	September 15
18.	15%	June 3	November 23

Use a 365-day year and approximate time to find the interest on the following loans.

19. $1560 borrowed February 15 at 12% and repaid August 12

20. $4300 borrowed March 22 at 14% and repaid October 17

21. $3699 borrowed October 24 at 15% and repaid February 8

22. $7610 borrowed September 27 at 13% and repaid March 12

Use a 360-day year and approximate time to find the interest on the following loans.

23. $650,000 borrowed September 7 at $14\frac{1}{4}$% and repaid December 6

24. $450,000 borrowed August 12 at $12\frac{1}{2}$% and repaid February 7

Use a 365-day year and approximate time to find the interest on the following loans.

25. $350,000 borrowed June 6 at $10\frac{1}{2}$% and repaid November 5

26. $750,000 borrowed July 9 at 12.75% and repaid January 5

4.5 SIMPLE INTEREST TABLES

■ 360-DAY SIMPLE INTEREST TABLES

In this section we find simple interest using tables. Examples 1 and 2 show how to use the table based on a 360-day year.

Example 1 A customer borrowed $549.88 at 16% for 180 days to buy a color console. How much interest was paid?

Solution

a) Find the interest on $100 from Table 4.2 (next page).

   The 180-day row and the 16% column meet at 8.000000. Thus, the interest on $100 at 16% for 180 days is $8.00.

b) Find the interest on $1.00 for 180 days at 16%.

   Move the decimal point in $8.00 two places to the left:

   0.08.00

   The interest on $1.00 for 180 days at 16% is $0.08.

c) Find the interest on $549.88.

   The interest on $1.00 is $0.08 so the interest on $549.88 is $43.99. (549.88 × 0.08).

DO EXERCISE 1.

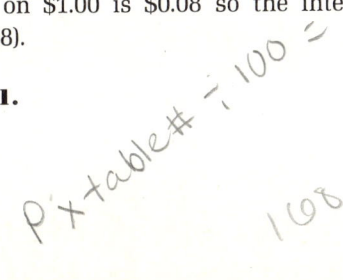

OBJECTIVES

After finishing section 4.5, you should be able to:

■ Use a 360-day simple interest table to find interest.

■ ■ Use a 365-day simple interest table to find interest.

1. A customer borrowed $399.50 at 16% for 240 days. How much interest was paid?

ANSWER ON PAGE A–8

TABLE 4.2
SIMPLE INTEREST ON $100, 360-DAY BASIS

DAY	16.00 % INTEREST	DAY	16.25 % INTEREST	DAY	16.50 % INTEREST	DAY	16.75 % INTEREST	DAY	17.00 % INTEREST	DAY	17.25 % INTEREST
1	0.044444	1	0.045139	1	0.045833	1	0.046528	1	0.047222	1	0.047917
2	0.088889	2	0.090278	2	0.091667	2	0.093056	2	0.094444	2	0.095833
3	0.133333	3	0.135417	3	0.137500	3	0.139583	3	0.141667	3	0.143750
4	0.177778	4	0.180556	4	0.183333	4	0.186111	4	0.188889	4	0.191667
5	0.222222	5	0.225694	5	0.229167	5	0.232639	5	0.236111	5	0.239583
6	0.266667	6	0.270833	6	0.275000	6	0.279167	6	0.283333	6	0.287500
7	0.311111	7	0.315972	7	0.320833	7	0.325694	7	0.330556	7	0.335417
8	0.355556	8	0.361111	8	0.366667	8	0.372222	8	0.377778	8	0.383333
9	0.400000	9	0.406250	9	0.412500	9	0.418750	9	0.425000	9	0.431250
10	0.444444	10	0.451389	10	0.458333	10	0.465278	10	0.472222	10	0.479167
11	0.488889	11	0.496528	11	0.504167	11	0.511806	11	0.519444	11	0.527083
12	0.533333	12	0.541667	12	0.550000	12	0.558333	12	0.566667	12	0.575000
13	0.577778	13	0.586806	13	0.595833	13	0.604861	13	0.613889	13	0.622917
14	0.622222	14	0.631944	14	0.641667	14	0.651389	14	0.661111	14	0.670833
15	0.666667	15	0.677083	15	0.687500	15	0.697917	15	0.708333	15	0.718750
16	0.711111	16	0.722222	16	0.733333	16	0.744444	16	0.755556	16	0.766667
17	0.755556	17	0.767361	17	0.779167	17	0.790972	17	0.802778	17	0.814583
18	0.800000	18	0.812500	18	0.825000	18	0.837500	18	0.850000	18	0.862500
19	0.844444	19	0.857639	19	0.870833	19	0.884028	19	0.897222	19	0.910417
20	0.888889	20	0.902778	20	0.916667	20	0.930556	20	0.944444	20	0.958333
21	0.933333	21	0.947917	21	0.962500	21	0.977083	21	0.991667	21	1.006250
22	0.977778	22	0.993056	22	1.008333	22	1.023611	22	1.038889	22	1.054167
23	1.022222	23	1.038194	23	1.054167	23	1.070139	23	1.086111	23	1.102083
24	1.066667	24	1.083333	24	1.100000	24	1.116667	24	1.133333	24	1.150000
25	1.111111	25	1.128472	25	1.145833	25	1.163194	25	1.180556	25	1.197917
26	1.155556	26	1.173611	26	1.191667	26	1.209722	26	1.227778	26	1.245833
27	1.200000	27	1.218750	27	1.237500	27	1.256250	27	1.275000	27	1.293750
28	1.244444	28	1.263889	28	1.283333	28	1.302778	28	1.322222	28	1.341667
29	1.288889	29	1.309028	29	1.329167	29	1.349306	29	1.369444	29	1.389583
30	1.333333	30	1.354167	30	1.375000	30	1.395833	30	1.416667	30	1.437500
31	1.377778	31	1.399306	31	1.420833	31	1.442361	31	1.463889	31	1.485417
32	1.422222	32	1.444444	32	1.466667	32	1.488889	32	1.511111	32	1.533333
33	1.466667	33	1.489583	33	1.512500	33	1.535417	33	1.558333	33	1.581250
34	1.511111	34	1.534722	34	1.558333	34	1.581944	34	1.605556	34	1.629167
35	1.555556	35	1.579861	35	1.604167	35	1.628472	35	1.652778	35	1.677083
36	1.600000	36	1.625000	36	1.650000	36	1.675000	36	1.700000	36	1.725000
37	1.644444	37	1.670139	37	1.695833	37	1.721528	37	1.747222	37	1.772917
38	1.688889	38	1.715278	38	1.741667	38	1.768056	38	1.794444	38	1.820833
39	1.733333	39	1.760417	39	1.787500	39	1.814583	39	1.841667	39	1.868750
40	1.777778	40	1.805556	40	1.833333	40	1.861111	40	1.888889	40	1.916667
41	1.822222	41	1.850694	41	1.879167	41	1.907639	41	1.936111	41	1.964583
42	1.866667	42	1.895833	42	1.925000	42	1.954167	42	1.983333	42	2.012500
43	1.911111	43	1.940972	43	1.970833	43	2.000694	43	2.030556	43	2.060417
44	1.955556	44	1.986111	44	2.016667	44	2.047222	44	2.077778	44	2.108333
45	2.000000	45	2.031250	45	2.062500	45	2.093750	45	2.125000	45	2.156250
46	2.044444	46	2.076389	46	2.108333	46	2.140278	46	2.172222	46	2.204167
47	2.088889	47	2.121528	47	2.154167	47	2.186806	47	2.219444	47	2.252083
48	2.133333	48	2.166667	48	2.200000	48	2.233333	48	2.266667	48	2.300000
49	2.177778	49	2.211806	49	2.245833	49	2.279861	49	2.313889	49	2.347917
50	2.222222	50	2.256944	50	2.291667	50	2.326389	50	2.361111	50	2.395833
30	1.333333	30	1.354167	30	1.375000	30	1.395833	30	1.416667	30	1.437500
60	2.666667	60	2.708333	60	2.750000	60	2.791667	60	2.833333	60	2.875000
90	4.000000	90	4.062500	90	4.125000	90	4.187500	90	4.250000	90	4.312500
120	5.333333	120	5.416667	120	5.500000	120	5.583333	120	5.666667	120	5.750000
150	6.666667	150	6.770833	150	6.875000	150	6.979167	150	7.083333	150	7.187500
180	8.000000	180	8.125000	180	8.250000	180	8.375000	180	8.500000	180	8.625000
210	9.333333	210	9.479167	210	9.625000	210	9.770833	210	9.916667	210	10.062500
240	10.666667	240	10.833333	240	11.000000	240	11.166667	240	11.333333	240	11.500000
270	12.000000	270	12.187500	270	12.375000	270	12.562500	270	12.750000	270	12.937500
300	13.333333	300	13.541667	300	13.750000	300	13.958333	300	14.166667	300	14.375000
330	14.666667	330	14.895833	330	15.125000	330	15.354167	330	15.583333	330	15.812500
360	16.000000	360	16.250000	360	16.500000	360	16.750000	360	17.000000	360	17.250000
365	16.222222	365	16.475694	365	16.729167	365	16.982639	365	17.236111	365	17.489583
366	16.266667	366	16.520833	366	16.775000	366	17.029167	366	17.283333	366	17.537500

Reprinted by permission from the *Thorndyke Encyclopedia of Banking and Financial Tables*, 1982 edition. Copyright © 1982 by Warren, Gorham, and Lamont, Inc., 210 South St., Boston MA 02111. All rights reserved.

INTERST TABLES

Freeze your food bargains and save... with this Whirlpool 12 cu. ft. power-saving upright freezer. Convenient super-storage door, built-in juice can rack. Fast-freeze shelves with cold coils. Power-saving heater control switch. Million Magnet® door. Defrost drain.

$299

See the complete selection of money saving freezers...

Example 2 A customer borrowed $299 at 16.75% for 67 days to purchase an upright freezer. How much interest was paid?

Solution

Find the interest on $100 from Table 4.2

a) The interest on $100 at 16.75% for

60 days is	2.791667
7 days is	0.325694
Interest on $100 for 67 days is	3.117361

b) Find the interest on $1.00 for 67 days at 16.75%.

Move the decimal point in 3.117361 two places to the left:

0.03.117361

The interest on $1.00 for 67 days at 16.75% is $0.03117361.

c) Find the interest on $299.

The interest on $1.00 is $0.03117361 so the interest on $299 is $9.32 (299 × 0.03117361).

DO EXERCISE 2.

●● 365-DAY SIMPLE INTEREST TABLES

Table 4.3 is based on a 365-day year and will be used for Example 3.

2. A customer borrowed $299 at 16.75% for 95 days to purchase an upright freezer. How much interest was paid?

ANSWER ON PAGE A–8

TABLE 4.3
SIMPLE INTEREST ON $100, 365-DAY BASIS

DAY	16.00 % INTEREST	DAY	16.25 % INTEREST	DAY	16.50 % INTEREST	DAY	16.75 % INTEREST	DAY	17.00 % INTEREST	DAY	17.25 % INTEREST
1	0.043836	1	0.044521	1	0.045205	1	0.045890	1	0.046575	1	0.047260
2	0.087671	2	0.089041	2	0.090411	2	0.091781	2	0.093151	2	0.094521
3	0.131507	3	0.133562	3	0.135616	3	0.137671	3	0.139726	3	0.141781
4	0.175342	4	0.178082	4	0.180822	4	0.183562	4	0.186301	4	0.189041
5	0.219178	5	0.222603	5	0.226027	5	0.229452	5	0.232877	5	0.236301
6	0.263014	6	0.267123	6	0.271233	6	0.275342	6	0.279452	6	0.283562
7	0.306849	7	0.311644	7	0.316438	7	0.321233	7	0.326027	7	0.330822
8	0.350685	8	0.356164	8	0.361644	8	0.367123	8	0.372603	8	0.378082
9	0.394521	9	0.400685	9	0.406849	9	0.413014	9	0.419178	9	0.425342
10	0.438356	10	0.445205	10	0.452055	10	0.458904	10	0.465753	10	0.472603
11	0.482192	11	0.489726	11	0.497260	11	0.504795	11	0.512329	11	0.519863
12	0.526027	12	0.534247	12	0.542466	12	0.550685	12	0.558904	12	0.567123
13	0.569863	13	0.578767	13	0.587671	13	0.596575	13	0.605479	13	0.614384
14	0.613699	14	0.623288	14	0.632877	14	0.642466	14	0.652055	14	0.661644
15	0.657534	15	0.667808	15	0.678082	15	0.688356	15	0.698630	15	0.708904
16	0.701370	16	0.712329	16	0.723288	16	0.734247	16	0.745205	16	0.756164
17	0.745205	17	0.756849	17	0.768493	17	0.780137	17	0.791781	17	0.803425
18	0.789041	18	0.801370	18	0.813699	18	0.826027	18	0.838356	18	0.850685
19	0.832877	19	0.845890	19	0.858904	19	0.871918	19	0.884932	19	0.897945
20	0.876712	20	0.890411	20	0.904110	20	0.917808	20	0.931507	20	0.945205
21	0.920548	21	0.934932	21	0.949315	21	0.963699	21	0.978082	21	0.992466
22	0.964384	22	0.979452	22	0.994521	22	1.009589	22	1.024658	22	1.039726
23	1.008219	23	1.023973	23	1.039726	23	1.055479	23	1.071233	23	1.086986
24	1.052055	24	1.068493	24	1.084932	24	1.101370	24	1.117808	24	1.134247
25	1.095890	25	1.113014	25	1.130137	25	1.147260	25	1.164384	25	1.181507
26	1.139726	26	1.157534	26	1.175342	26	1.193151	26	1.210959	26	1.228767
27	1.183562	27	1.202055	27	1.220548	27	1.239041	27	1.257534	27	1.276027
28	1.227397	28	1.246575	28	1.265753	28	1.284932	28	1.304110	28	1.323288
29	1.271233	29	1.291096	29	1.310959	29	1.330822	29	1.350685	29	1.370548
30	1.315068	30	1.335616	30	1.356164	30	1.376712	30	1.397260	30	1.417808
31	1.358904	31	1.380137	31	1.401370	31	1.422603	31	1.443836	31	1.465068
32	1.402740	32	1.424658	32	1.446575	32	1.468493	32	1.490411	32	1.512329
33	1.446575	33	1.469178	33	1.491781	33	1.514384	33	1.536986	33	1.559589
34	1.490411	34	1.513699	34	1.536986	34	1.560274	34	1.583562	34	1.606849
35	1.534247	35	1.558219	35	1.582192	35	1.606164	35	1.630137	35	1.654110
36	1.578082	36	1.602740	36	1.627397	36	1.652055	36	1.676712	36	1.701370
37	1.621918	37	1.647260	37	1.672603	37	1.697945	37	1.723288	37	1.748630
38	1.665753	38	1.691781	38	1.717808	38	1.743836	38	1.769863	38	1.795890
39	1.709589	39	1.736301	39	1.763014	39	1.789726	39	1.816438	39	1.843151
40	1.753425	40	1.780822	40	1.808219	40	1.835616	40	1.863014	40	1.890411
41	1.797260	41	1.825342	41	1.853425	41	1.881507	41	1.909589	41	1.937671
42	1.841096	42	1.869863	42	1.898630	42	1.927397	42	1.956164	42	1.984932
43	1.884932	43	1.914384	43	1.943836	43	1.973288	43	2.002740	43	2.032192
44	1.928767	44	1.958904	44	1.989041	44	2.019178	44	2.049315	44	2.079452
45	1.972603	45	2.003425	45	2.034247	45	2.065068	45	2.095890	45	2.126712
46	2.016438	46	2.047945	46	2.079452	46	2.110959	46	2.142466	46	2.173973
47	2.060274	47	2.092466	47	2.124658	47	2.156849	47	2.189041	47	2.221233
48	2.104110	48	2.136986	48	2.169863	48	2.202740	48	2.235616	48	2.268493
49	2.147945	49	2.181507	49	2.215068	49	2.248630	49	2.282192	49	2.315753
50	2.191781	50	2.226027	50	2.260274	50	2.294521	50	2.328767	50	2.363014
30	1.315068	30	1.335616	30	1.356164	30	1.376712	30	1.397260	30	1.417808
60	2.630137	60	2.671233	60	2.712329	60	2.753425	60	2.794521	60	2.835616
90	3.945205	90	4.006849	90	4.068493	90	4.130137	90	4.191781	90	4.253425
120	5.260274	120	5.342466	120	5.424658	120	5.506849	120	5.589041	120	5.671233
150	6.575342	150	6.678082	150	6.780822	150	6.883562	150	6.986301	150	7.089041
180	7.890411	180	8.013699	180	8.136986	180	8.260274	180	8.383562	180	8.506849
210	9.205479	210	9.349315	210	9.493151	210	9.636986	210	9.780822	210	9.924658
240	10.520548	240	10.684932	240	10.849315	240	11.013699	240	11.178082	240	11.342466
270	11.835616	270	12.020548	270	12.205479	270	12.390411	270	12.575342	270	12.760274
300	13.150685	300	13.356164	300	13.561644	300	13.767123	300	13.972603	300	14.178082
330	14.465753	330	14.691781	330	14.917808	330	15.143836	330	15.369863	330	15.595890
360	15.780822	360	16.027397	360	16.273973	360	16.520548	360	16.767123	360	17.013699
365	16.000000	365	16.250000	365	16.500000	365	16.750000	365	17.000000	365	17.250000
366	16.043836	366	16.294521	366	16.545205	366	16.795890	366	17.046575	366	17.297260

Reprinted by permission from the *Thorndyke Encyclopedia of Banking and Financial Tables*, 1982 edition. Copyright © 1982 by Warren, Gorham, and Lamont, Inc., 210 South St., Boston MA 02111. All rights reserved.

4.5 SIMPLE INTEREST TABLES 187

Example 3 A $329.99 loan for the drill press was paid for in 53 days at 16.25%. What was the interest?

Solution

a) Find the interest on $100 from Table 4.3.

The interest on $100 at 16.25% for

50 days is	2.226027
3 days is	0.133562
The interest on $100 for 53 days is	2.359589

b) Find the interest on $1.00 for 53 days at 16.25%.

Move the decimal point in 2.359589 two places to the left:

0.02.359589

The interest on $1.00 at 16.25% for 53 days is $0.02359589.

c) Find the interest on $329.99.

The interest on $1.00 is $0.02359589 so the interest on $329.99 is $7.79. (329.99 × $0.02359589).

DO EXERCISE 3.

3. A $329.99 loan for the drill press was paid for in 64 days at 17%. What was the interest?

ANSWER ON PAGE A–8

4. A $679 loan for the trip to Hawaii was paid for in 275 days at 16.50%. What was the interest?

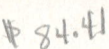

$84.41

INTEREST

HAWAII
VISIT 1-3-4 ISLANDS from $679

Example 4 A $679 loan for a trip to Hawaii was paid for in 335 days at 16%. What was the interest?

Solution

a) Find the interest on $100 from Table 4.3.

The interest on $100 at 16% for

| 330 days is | 14.465753 |
| 5 days is | 0.219178 |

The interest on $100

for 335 days is   14.684931   *Adding*

b) Find the interest on $1.00 for 335 days at 16%.

Move the decimal point in 14.684931 two places to the left:

.14.684931

The interest on $1.00 at 16% for 335 days is $0.14684931.

c) Find the interest on $679.

The interest on $1.00 is $0.14684931, so the interest on $679 is $99.71 (679 × $0.14684931).

DO EXERCISE 4.

ANSWER ON PAGE A–8

EXERCISE SET 4.5

● Find the interest using the 360-day table (Table 4.2).

	Principal	Rate	Days
1.	$5000	16%	360
2.	$3600	16%	150
3.	$4200	17%	210
4.	$3900	17%	240
5.	$4800	16%	330
6.	$2900	17%	300
7.	$4700	16.25%	322
8.	$3200	16.25%	186
9.	$2700	16.75%	123
10.	$5500	17.25%	151

Use the 360-day table (Table 4.2).

11. A customer borrowed $847.75 at 16% for 150 days to buy a used car. How much interest was paid?

12. A customer borrowed $1530 at 17% for 180 days to buy a computer. How much interest was paid?

13. A customer borrowed $499.99 at 16.75% for 93 days to buy a video camera. How much interest was paid?

14. A customer borrowed $725 at 17.25% for 187 days to buy a set of encyclopedias. How much interest was paid?

ANSWERS

1. 800
2. 240
3. 416.50
4. 442
5. 704
6. 410.83
7. 394.60
8. 268.67
9. 154.52
10. 397.95
11. 130.05
12. 21.63
13. 64.96
14.

190 INTEREST

ANSWERS

Find the interest using the 365-day table (Table 4.3).

	Principal	Rate	Days
15.	$5000	16%	360
16.	$3600	16%	150
17.	$4200	17%	210
18.	$3900	17%	240
19.	$4800	16%	330
20.	$2900	17%	300
21.	$4700	16.25%	322
22.	$3200	16.25%	186
23.	$2700	16.75%	123
24.	$5500	17.25%	151

15. 789.04
16. 236.71
17. 410.79
18. 435.95
19. 694.36
20. 410.83
21. 673.77
22. 264.99
23. 154.52
24. 397.95
25. 6.85
26. 223.6
27. 14.26
28. 591.24

Use the 365-day table (Table 4.3).

25. A $249 loan for a color television was paid for in 60 days at 16.50%. What was the interest?

26. A $2795 loan for a prebuilt garage was paid for in 180 days at 16%. What was the interest?

27. A $240 loan for a ceiling fan was paid for in 124 days at 17.25%. What was the interest?

28. A $5069 loan for a dining room set was paid for in 247 days at 17%. What was the interest?

4.6 COMPOUND INTEREST

SOLVING COMPOUND INTEREST PROBLEMS

Most forms of savings earn compound interest. *Compound interest* is interest paid on (1) principal, and (2) previously earned interest. Interest is usually compounded continuously, daily, monthly, quarterly, semiannually, or annually. The more often interest is compounded, the more interest your money earns.

Example 1 An employee invests $400 at 7% compounded quarterly in the General Motors Credit Union for six months. How much interest is earned?

Solution

a) Find the interest for the first quarter.

Substituting 400 for P, 0.07 for R, and $\frac{3}{12}$ for T, we get

$I = P \times R \times T$

$= 400 \times 0.07 \times \frac{3}{12}$

$= 7$

Interest earned during the first quarter is $7.00. Thus, the amount in savings is now $400 + $7 = $407.

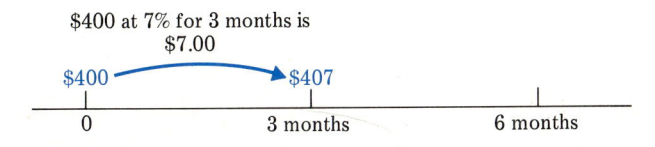

$400 at 7% for 3 months is $7.00

b) Going into the second quarter the principal is $407. Find the interest for the second quarter.

Substituting 407 for P, 0.07 for R, and $\frac{3}{12}$ for T, we get

$I = P \times R \times T$

$= 407 \times 0.07 \times \frac{3}{12}$

$= 7.12.$

Interest earned during the second quarter is $7.12. Thus, the total amount of interest earned is $14.12 ($7 + $7.12)

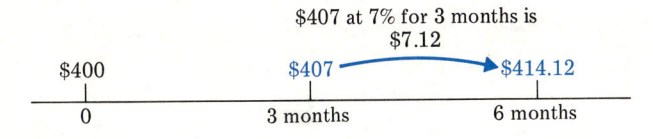

$407 at 7% for 3 months is $7.12

Simple interest earned would have been $14. The extra $0.12 is interest earned on interest.

DO EXERCISE 1.

OBJECTIVES

After finishing Section 4.6, you should be able to:

- Solve compound interest problems without a formula.
- Use a formula to solve compound interest problems.

1. A savings and loan institution pays 6% compounded quarterly. How much interest would $800 earn in six months?

ANSWER ON PAGE A–8

2. Use the formula to find the interest earned on $800 at 6% compounded quarterly for six months.

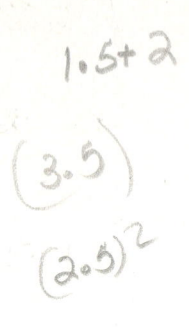

3. A customer invests $10,000 for one year at 14% compounded semiannually. Use the formula to find the amount and interest.

INTEREST

▣ A COMPOUND INTEREST FORMULA

Now we use a formula to solve compound interest problems.

> For compound interest, principal P grows to the amount A given by
>
> $$A = P \times (1 + i)^n$$
>
> where P is the principal, i is the rate per compounding period, n is the total number of compounding periods, and A is the amount after n compounding periods.

Example 2 An employee invests $400 at 7% compounded quarterly in the General Motors Credit Union for six months. Use the formula to find the amount and interest.

Solution Substituting 400 for P, $\dfrac{0.07}{4}$ for i, and 2 for n, we get

$A = P \times (1 + i)^n$ Remember: The order of operations is multiplication and division first from left to right and then addition and subtraction start with parenthesis.

$= 400 \times \left(1 + \dfrac{0.07}{4}\right)^2$

$= 400 \times (1 + 0.0175)^2$

$= 400 \times (1.0175)^2$

$= 400 \times 1.0353062$

$= 414.12.$

The amount after six months is $414.12. Hence, the interest is $14.12 ($414.12 − $400).

This agrees with the answer for Example 1.

DO EXERCISE 2.

Example 3 An employee invests $2000 for one year at 12% compounded semiannually. Use the formula to find the amount and interest.

Solution Substituting 2000 for P, $\dfrac{0.12}{2}$ for i, and 2 for n, we get

$A = P \times (1 + i)^n$

$= 2000 \times \left(1 + \dfrac{0.12}{2}\right)^2$

$= 2000 \times (1.06)^2$

$= 2000 \times 1.1236$

$= 2247.20$

The amount after 1 year is $2247.20, so the interest is $247.20 ($2247.20 − $2000).

DO EXERCISE 3.

ANSWERS ON PAGE A–8

EXERCISE SET 4.6

Find the compound interest without a formula.

	Principal	Rate	Compounded	Time
1.	$1000	12%	Quarterly	2 quarters
2.	$1000	18%	Quarterly	2 quarters
3.	$600	10%	Quarterly	2 quarters
4.	$900	8%	Quarterly	2 quarters
5.	$1400	14%	Semiannually	6 months
6.	$500	6%	Semiannually	6 months
7.	$1200	16%	Semiannually	1 year
8.	$1500	14%	Semiannually	1 year
9.	$1000	12%	Annually	1 year
10.	$1400	8%	Annually	1 year
11.	$1600	7%	Annually	2 years
12.	$1100	9%	Annually	2 years

13. Commercial Savings pays 12% compounded quarterly. How much interest would be earned on $1000 for six months?

14. National Thrift pays 8% compounded quarterly. How much interest would be earned on $1000 for six months?

ANSWERS

1. 60.90
2. 92.03
3. 30.38
4. 36.36
5. 32.67
6. 5.00
7. 64.85
8. 70.82
9. 120
10. 112
11. 231.84
12. 206.91
13. 60.90
14. 40.40

194

INTEREST

ANSWERS

15. AllSavers Bank pays 6% compounded semiannually. How much interest would be earned on $700 for one year?

16. Brenton Savings pays 14% compounded semiannually. How much interest would be earned on $900 for one year?

Use a formula to find the compound interest.

	Principal	Rate	Compounded	Time
17.	$2000	16%	Quarterly	3 quarters
18.	$1600	8%	Quarterly	2 quarters
19.	$1500	12%	Semiannually	6 months
20.	$1800	14%	Semiannually	1 year
21.	$1000	12%	Monthly	5 months
22.	$700	18%	Monthly	8 months

23. Pasadena Savings pays 8% compounded quarterly. Find the amount and interest on $1000 after three quarters.

24. Faribault Thrift pays 12% compounded quarterly. Find the amount and interest on $1000 after three quarters.

25. Thorp Investments pay 10% compounded semiannually. Find the amount and interest on $2500 after one year.

26. Financial Services pay 14% compounded semiannually. Find the amount and interest on $2800 after one year.

Use the y^x or similar key and the compound interest formula to find interest. Assume a 365-day year and daily compounding.

27. $10,000 at 12% for 180 days.

28. $5000 at 9% for 270 days.

4.7 COMPOUND-INTEREST TABLES

◉ COMPOUND INTEREST USING TABLES

Tables are often used to calculate compound interest. Appendix Table 4 (p. T–4) contains compound interest for various rates and time periods. Part of that table is shown below.

**Compound Interest
(Amount When $1.00 Is Compound)**

	INTEREST RATE EACH PERIOD					
Period	$1\frac{1}{4}\%$	$1\frac{1}{2}\%$	$1\frac{3}{4}\%$	2%	$2\frac{1}{2}\%$	3%
1	1.012500	1.017500	1.015000	1.020000	1.025000	1.030000
2	1.025156	1.030225	1.035306	1.040400	1.050625	1.060900
3	1.037970	1.045678	1.053424	1.061208	1.076891	1.092727
4	1.050945	1.061363	1.071859	1.082432	1.103813	1.125509
5	1.064082	1.077283	1.090617	1.104081	1.131408	1.159274
6	1.077383	1.093442	1.109703	1.126163	1.159693	1.194052
7	1.090850	1.109844	1.129123	1.148686	1.188685	1.229874
8	1.104486	1.126492	1.148883	1.171660	1.218402	1.266770
9	1.118292	1.143389	1.168988	1.195093	1.248862	1.304773
10	1.132271	1.160540	1.189445	1.218995	1.280084	1.343916

Example 1 How much interest is earned on $400 for six months at 7% compounded quarterly?

Solution

a) In the table above, find the $1\frac{3}{4}\%$ column (7% ÷ 4, since the interest is compounded quarterly).

b) Find 2 in the column headed Period (interest is compounded two times in six months).

c) The row containing 2 and the column for $1\frac{3}{4}\%$ meet at 1.035306. So $1.00 grows to $1.035306 at 7% after 6 months.

d) And $400 will grow to 400 × $1.035306 = $414.12 at 7% after 6 months.

e) The interest is $14.12 ($414.12 − $400).

Note that this answer agrees with the answer for Example 1, page 191.

DO EXERCISE 1.

Example 2 Find the amount after 10 years if $2000 is invested at 12% compounded semiannually.

Solution

a) In Table 4 (p. T–4) find the 6% column (12% ÷ 2, since the interest is compounded twice yearly).

b) Find 20 in the column headed Period (the interest is compounded 20 times in 10 years).

OBJECTIVE

After finishing Section 4.7, you should be able to:

◉ Solve compound interest problems using a table.

1. Find the interest on $1500 for two years at 10% compounded quarterly.

ANSWER ON PAGE A–8

196

INTEREST

2. Find the amount after four years if $250 is invested at 14% compounded semiannually.

[handwritten: 7]
[handwritten: 8]
[handwritten: 429.55]

c) The row containing 20 and the 6% column meet at 3.207139. So $1.00 grows to $3.207139 at 12% after 10 years.

d) And $2000 will grow to 2000 × $3.207139 = $6414.28 at 12% after 10 years.

DO EXERCISE 2.

Example 3 Find the amount after 10 years if $2000 is invested at 8% compounded annually.

Solution

a) In Table 4 (p. T–4) find the 8% column (8% ÷ 1, since the interest is compounded annually).

b) Find 10 in the column headed Period (the interest is compounded 10 times in 10 years).

c) The row containing 10 and the 8% column meet at 2.158924. So $1.00 grows to $2.158924 at 8% after 10 years.

d) And $2000 will grow to 2000 × $2.158924 = $4317.85 at 8% after 10 years.

DO EXERCISE 3.

3. Find the amount after 5 years if $800 is invested at 8% compounded annually.

[handwritten: 8]
[handwritten: 5]

ANSWERS ON PAGE A–8

EXERCISE SET 4.7

- Use Table 4 (p. T–4) to find the interest.

	Principal	Rate	Compounded	Time
1.	$500	8%	Quarterly	6 months
2.	$500	8%	Quarterly	1 year
3.	$700	10%	Quarterly	9 months
4.	$700	10%	Quarterly	1 year
5.	$1000	12%	Quarterly	18 months
6.	$1000	12%	Quarterly	2 years
7.	$800	14%	Semiannually	6 months
8.	$800	14%	Semiannually	1 year
9.	$600	16%	Semiannually	18 months
10.	$600	16%	Semiannually	2 years
11.	$1200	15%	Monthly	8 months
12.	$1200	15%	Monthly	1 year
13.	$1000	18%	Monthly	9 months
14.	$1000	18%	Monthly	2 years
15.	$5000	8%	Annually	1 year
16.	$5000	8%	Annually	2 years

ANSWERS

1. 20.20
2. 41.22
3. 53.82
4. 72.67
5. 194.05
6. 266.77
7. 56
8. 115.92
9. 155.83
10. 216.29
11. 141.95
12. 192.90
13. 143.39
14. 429.50
15. 400
16. 832

198 INTEREST

ANSWERS

17. 1105.71
18. 8337.86
19. 6097.88
20. 4635.86
21. 102.41
22. 346.85
23. 704.25
24. 1939.01
25. 546
26. 645.18
27. 375.55
28. 880.45
29. 333.27
30. 1887.31
31. 450.11
32. 929.60
33. 16,010.32
34. 11,475.23
35. 6312.39
36. 7503.66

Use Table 4 (p. T–4) to find the *interest*.

17. For 2 years on $3000 at 16% compounded quarterly
18. For 5 years on $7000 at 16% compounded quarterly.
19. For 12 years on $2000 at 12% compounded semiannually.
20. For 9 years on $2500 at 12% compounded semiannually.
21. For 15 months on $500 at 15% compounded monthly.
22. For 20 months on $1000 at 18% compounded monthly.
23. For 6 years on $1200 at 8% compounded annually.
24. For 8 years on $2700 at 7% compounded annually.

Use Table 4 (p. T-4) to find the amount.

	Time	Principal	Rate	Compounded
25.	2 years	$2500	10%	Quarterly
26.	4 years	$1100	12%	Quarterly
27.	3 years	$ 750	14%	Semiannually
28.	5 years	$1400	10%	Semiannually
29.	2 years	$2300	7%	Annually
30.	5 years	$4000	8%	Annually
31.	1 year	$2800	15%	Monthly
32.	2 years	$1800	21%	Monthly

33. An investor placed $10,000 in a money market certificate paying 16% compounded quarterly. How much money did the investor obtain upon cashing in the certificate three years later?

34. An investor placed $10,000 in a money market certificate paying 14% compounded quarterly. How much money did the investor obtain upon cashing in the certificate four years later?

35. An investor bought a $5000 bank certificate paying 12% compounded semiannually. How much money did the investor obtain upon cashing in the certificate two years later?

36. An investor bought a $5000 bank certificate paying 14% compounded semiannually. How much money did the investor obtain upon cashing in the certificate three years later?

4.8 DAILY AND CONTINUOUS COMPOUND INTEREST

◼ DAILY COMPOUND INTEREST

Inter-State Federal Savings compounds interest daily on a 365-day basis. Example 1 shows how to use Table 5 (page T–6) to find interest compounded daily.

Example 1 A customer invests $950 for 104 days at Inter-State Federal Savings. How much interest is earned?

Solution

a) Find the interest on $100 for 104 days.

From Table 5, we see that the interest is $1.507026.

b) Determine the interest on $950.

Since 950 is 9.5 × 100, the interest on $950 is $14.32 (9.5 × 1.507026).

DO EXERCISE 1.

The New York Bank for Savings compounds interest daily on a 360-day basis. Example 2 shows how to use the 360-day table (Table 6, p. T–7) to find interest compounded daily.

Example 2 A customer invests $950 at New York Bank for Savings for 104 days. How much interest is earned?

OBJECTIVES

After finishing Section 4.8, you should be able to:

◼ Use a table to solve daily compound interest problems.

◼◼ Use a table to solve continuous compound interest problems.

1. A customer invests $600 at Inter-State Federal Savings for 307 days. How much interest is earned?

   $29.09

ANSWER ON PAGE A–8

2. A customer invests $765 at New York Bank for Savings for 321 days. How much interest is earned?

$36.66

3. A customer invests $42,000 for 165 days at a bank paying 5% compounded daily. How much interest is earned?

973.52

4. If $42,000 is invested for 165 days at a bank paying 5% compounded continuously, how much interest is earned?

973.60

ANSWERS ON PAGE A–8

INTEREST

Solution

a) Find the interest on $100 for 104 days.

From Table 6, we see that the interest is $1.528114.

b) Determine the interest on $950.

Since 950 is 9.5 × 100, the interest on $950 is $14.52 (9.5 × 1.528114).

DO EXERCISE 2.

Example 3 A customer invests $12,362 for 178 days at a bank paying 5% compounded daily. How much interest is earned?

Solution

a) From Table 7 (p. T–8) we see that $1.00 becomes $1.025028 after 178 days.

b) Thus, $12,362 grows to $12,671.40 ($12,362 × 1.025028).

The interest earned is $309.40 ($12,671.40 − $12,362).

DO EXERCISE 3.

■■■ CONTINUOUS COMPOUND INTEREST

At some banks interest is compounded continuously (continuously accumulating). Example 4 shows how to use the 360-day table (Table 8, p. T–8) to find interest compounded continuously.

Example 4 If $12,362 is invested for 178 days at a bank paying 5% compounded continuously, how much interest is earned?

Solution

a) From Table 8, we see that $1.00 becomes $1.025030 after 178 days.

b) Thus, $12,362 grows to $12,671.42 ($12,362 × 1.025030).

The interest earned is $309.42 ($12,671.42 − $12,362).

Note that continuous compounding (Example 4) results in slightly more interest ($0.02) than daily compounding (Example 3). Unless very large amounts of money are invested the interest difference is very little.

DO EXERCISE 4.

EXERCISE SET 4.8

● Use Table 5 (p. T–6) to find the interest.

	Principal	Time (Days)
1.	$600	22
2.	$500	80
3.	$450	40
4.	$300	55

5. A customer had $400 in a checking account which paid 5.25% interest compounded daily. Use Table 5 to find the interest for 30 days.

6. A customer had $700 in a checking account which paid 5.25% interest compounded daily. Use Table 5 to find the interest for 28 days.

Use Table 6 (p. T–7) to find the interest.

	Principal	Time (Days)
7.	$250	25
8.	$375	42
9.	$725	70
10.	$630	50

11. A brokerage account pays 5.25% interest compounded daily on all balances to $2000. Use Table 6 to find the interest on a $900 balance for 20 days.

ANSWERS

1. 1.90
2. 5.79
3. 2.60
4. 2.38
5. 1.73
6. 2.82
7. .91
8. 2.30
9. 7.44
10. 4.61
11. 2.63

202 INTEREST

ANSWERS

12. **$4.38**

13. **$1.77**

14. **$1.21**

15. **$2.18**

16. **$3.07**

17. **$4.22**

18. **$1.03**

19. **$3.57**

20. ~~~~

12. A brokerage account pays 5.25% interest compounded daily on all balances to $2000. Use Table 6 (p. T–7) to find the interest on a $1200 balance for 25 days.

13. A credit union pays 5% interest compounded daily on all share draft account balances. Use Table 7 (p. T–8) to find the interest on a $425 balance for 30 days.

14. A credit union pays 5% interest compounded daily on all share draft account balances. Use Table 7 (p. T–8) to find the interest on a $310 balance for 28 days.

● ● Use Table 8 (p. T–8) to find the interest.

	Principal	Time (Days)
15.	$680	23
16.	$490	45
17.	$560	54
18.	$390	19

19. A passbook savings account pays 5% interest compounded continuously. Use Table 8 (p. T–8) to find the interest on $800 for 50 days.

20. A passbook savings account pays 5% interest compounded continuously. Use Table 8 (p. T–8) to find the interest on $690 for days.

4.9 NOMINAL AND EFFECTIVE INTEREST RATES

◼ EFFECTIVE INTEREST RATE

Financial institutions often compound interest several times each year. This has the effect of increasing the *nominal* (published) rate of interest. This increased rate of interest is called the *effective interest rate*. Suppose you invested $1000 at 8%, compounded annually for one year. At the end of one year you will have $1000(1 + 0.08)^1$, or $1080. If interest is compounded quarterly, you will have $1000(1 + 0.08/4)^4$, or $1082.43. The amount obtained from quarterly compounding is the same as if you had invested $1000 at 8.243%, compounded annually. That is, 8.243% is the effective interest rate corresponding to the nominal rate of 8%.

> A formula that relates *nominal* and *effective* rates is
>
> $$E = \left(1 + \frac{N}{n}\right)^n - 1,$$
>
> where E is the effective rate of interest, N is the nominal rate of interest, and n is the number of times the nominal rate is compounded **each year**.

Example 1 At Postal Thrift the nominal rate on passbook accounts is 6%. What is the effective rate?

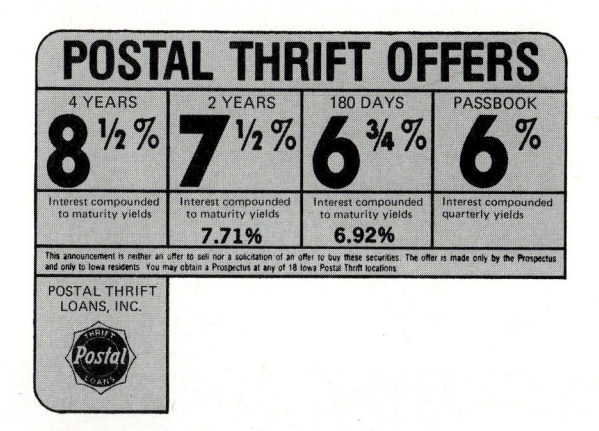

POSTAL THRIFT OFFERS

4 YEARS	2 YEARS	180 DAYS	PASSBOOK
8½%	7½%	6¾%	6%
Interest compounded to maturity yields	Interest compounded to maturity yields	Interest compounded to maturity yields	Interest compounded quarterly yields
	7.71%	6.92%	

POSTAL THRIFT LOANS, INC.

Solution Substituting 0.06 for N and 4 for n, we get

$$E = \left(1 + \frac{N}{n}\right)^n - 1$$
$$= \left(1 + \frac{0.06}{4}\right)^4 - 1$$
$$= (1 + 0.015)^4 - 1$$
$$= (1.015)^4 - 1$$
$$= 1.0613635 - 1 \quad \text{We find this power by multiplying or by using a calculator.}$$
$$= 0.0614. \quad \text{Subtracting and then rounding}$$

The effective rate is 6.14%.

DO EXERCISE 1.

OBJECTIVES

After finishing Section 4.9, you should be able to:

◼ Find the effective interest rate.

◼◼ Select the most favorable interest rate.

1. What is the effective rate on four-year certificates offered by Postal Thrift at $8\frac{1}{2}$% compounded quarterly?

$$\left(1 + \frac{.085}{4}\right)^4 - 1$$

ANSWER ON PAGE A-8

2. Which earns more interest, 12.75% compounded quarterly or 13% compounded semiannually?

▄▄ COMPARING INTEREST RATES

The effective rate allows consumers to compare and decide which interest rates are most favorable.

Example 2 One bank offers $5\frac{1}{4}$% compounded quarterly on their passbook accounts. Another offers $5\frac{1}{2}$% compounded semiannually. At which bank would you earn more interest?

Solution

a) For the $5\frac{1}{4}$% rate, we substitute 0.0525 for N and 4 for n to get

$$E = \left(1 + \frac{0.0525}{4}\right)^4 - 1$$

$$= (1 + 0.013125)^4 - 1$$

$$= (1.013125)^4 - 1$$

$$= 0.0535. \quad \text{We find this power by multiplying or by using a calculator.}$$

The effective rate is 5.35%.

b) For the $5\frac{1}{2}$% rate, we substitute 0.055 for N and 2 for n to get

$$E = \left(1 + \frac{0.055}{2}\right)^2 - 1$$

$$= (1.0275)^2 - 1$$

$$= 0.0558. \quad \text{We find this power by multiplying or by using a calculator.}$$

The effective rate is 5.58%.

Thus, more interest is earned at the bank that offers $5\frac{1}{2}$% compounded semiannually.

Note: The annual interest on $100 is $5.58 at $5\frac{1}{2}$% and $5.35 at $5\frac{1}{4}$%.

DO EXERCISE 2.

ANSWER ON PAGE A–8

NAME _____ CLASS _____ ANSWERS

EXERCISE SET 4.9

■ Find the effective interest rate.

	Nominal Rate	Compounded
1.	5%	Quarterly
2.	7%	Quarterly
3.	8%	Quarterly
4.	10%	Quarterly
5.	12%	Quarterly
6.	14%	Quarterly
7.	5%	Semiannually
8.	7%	Semiannually
9.	8%	Semiannually
10.	10%	Semiannually
11.	12%	Semiannually
12.	14%	Semiannually

$$E = \left(1 + \frac{N}{n}\right)^n - 1$$

13. At Postal Thrift, where interest is compounded quarterly, 180-day certificates pay a nominal rate of $6\frac{3}{4}$%. What is the effective rate?

$$\left(1 + \frac{.0675}{4}\right)^4 - 1$$

14. At Postal Thrift, where interest is compounded quarterly, 2-year certificates pay a nominal rate of $7\frac{1}{2}$%. What is the effective rate?

$$\left(1 + \frac{.0750}{4}\right)^4 - 1$$

1. 5.09%
2. 7.19%
3. 8.24%
4. 10.38%
5. 12.55%
6. 14.75%
7. 5.06%
8. 7.12%
9. 8.16%
10. 10.25%
11. 12.36%
12. 14.49%
13. 6.92%
14. 7.71%

206 INTEREST

ANSWERS

:: Tell which earns more interest.

15. 9% compounded monthly or $9\frac{1}{4}$% compounded quarterly.

9.38   9.58

15. _____

16. $7\frac{1}{4}$% compounded monthly or $7\frac{1}{2}$% compounded quarterly.

16. _____

17. $10\frac{1}{4}$% compounded monthly or $10\frac{1}{2}$% compounded quarterly.

11.07   10.92

17. _____

18. 12% compounded monthly or $12\frac{1}{4}$% compounded quarterly.

18. _____

19. 14% compounded monthly or $14\frac{1}{2}$% compounded semiannually.

14.93   14.74 70

19. _____

20. 11% compounded monthly or $11\frac{1}{4}$% compounded semiannually.

20. _____

21. Delaware Federal Bank offers 9% compounded monthly. Another bank offers $9\frac{1}{2}$% compounded semiannually. At which bank would you earn more interest?

21. _____

22. Hawkeye Savings offers $10\frac{1}{4}$% compounded monthly. Another bank offers $10\frac{1}{2}$% compounded semiannually. At which bank would you earn more interest?

22. _____

At Nevada Federal Savings and Loan interest is compounded daily. Use a 365-day year and the y^x or similar key to find the effective annual yield.

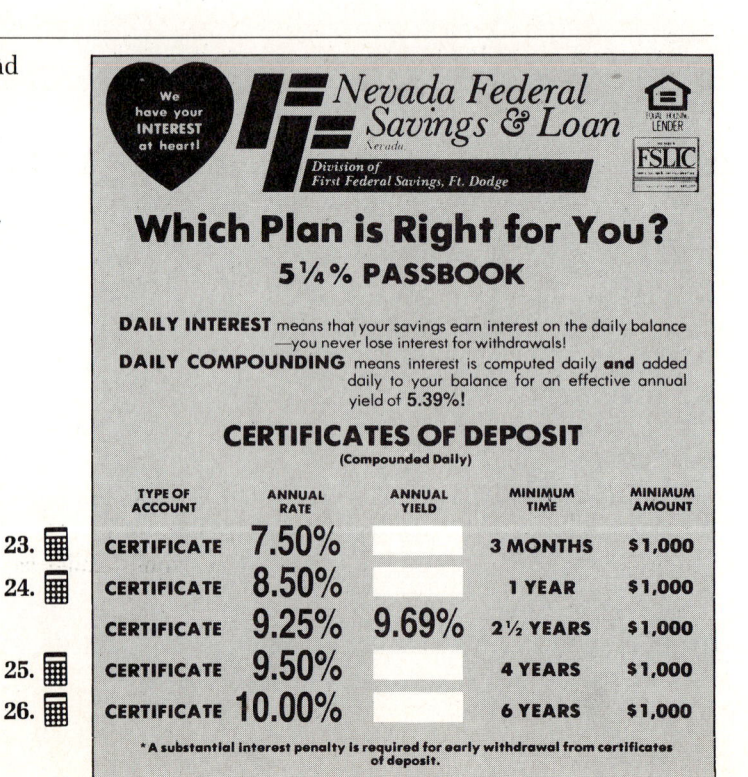

23. _____

24. _____

25. _____

26. _____

Nevada Federal Savings & Loan
Division of First Federal Savings, Ft. Dodge

We have your INTEREST at heart!

FSLIC

Which Plan is Right for You?

5¼% PASSBOOK

DAILY INTEREST means that your savings earn interest on the daily balance —you never lose interest for withdrawals!
DAILY COMPOUNDING means interest is computed daily **and** added daily to your balance for an effective annual yield of **5.39%**!

CERTIFICATES OF DEPOSIT
(Compounded Daily)

TYPE OF ACCOUNT	ANNUAL RATE	ANNUAL YIELD	MINIMUM TIME	MINIMUM AMOUNT
23. CERTIFICATE	7.50%		3 MONTHS	$1,000
24. CERTIFICATE	8.50%		1 YEAR	$1,000
CERTIFICATE	9.25%	9.69%	2½ YEARS	$1,000
25. CERTIFICATE	9.50%		4 YEARS	$1,000
26. CERTIFICATE	10.00%		6 YEARS	$1,000

*A substantial interest penalty is required for early withdrawal from certificates of deposit.

4.10 PRESENT VALUE

● FINDING THE PRESENT VALUE

A consumer wants $7500 four years from now to help purchase an automobile. How much must be invested now at 12% compounded semiannually so that $7500 will be available in four years? This type of problem is called a present value problem. Table 9 (p.T–9) contains present values for various rates and time periods. Part of that table is shown below.

Present Value of $1.00

Period	$3\frac{1}{2}$%	4%	5%	6%	7%	8%
1	.966183	.961538	.952380	.943396	.934579	.925925
2	.933510	.924556	.907029	.889996	.873438	.857338
3	.901942	.888996	.863837	.839619	.816297	.793832
4	.871442	.854804	.822702	.792093	.762895	.735029
5	.841973	.821927	.783526	.747258	.712986	.680583
6	.813500	.790314	.746215	.704960	.666342	.630169
7	.785990	.759917	.710681	.665057	.622749	.583490
8	.759411	.730690	.676839	.627412	.582009	.540268
9	.733731	.702586	.644608	.591898	.543933	.500248
10	.708918	.675564	.613913	.558394	.508349	.463193

Example 1 Find the present value of $7500 needed in four years at 12% compounded semiannually.

Solution

a) In the table above, find the 6% column (12% ÷ 2, since the interest is compounded semiannually).

b) Find 8 in the column headed Period (interest is compounded 8 times in 4 years).

c) The row containing 8 and the column for 6% meet at 0.627412. The present value of $1.00 at 12% compounded semiannually for 4 years is $0.627412.

d) Find the present value of $7500 at 12% compounded semiannually for 4 years.

Present Value of $7500 = Present Value of $1.00 × 7500
$$= \$0.627412 \times 7500$$
$$= \$4705.59$$

Therefore, $4705.59 invested now at 12% compounded semiannually will grow to $7500 in four years.

DO EXERCISE 1.

OBJECTIVE

After finishing Section 4.10, you should be able to:

● Find the present value.

1. Find the present value of $6300 needed in three years at 10% compounded semiannually.

ANSWER ON PAGE A–8

208

2. Find the present value of $12,000 needed in 5 years at 10% compounded quarterly.

INTEREST

Example 2 Find the present value of $20,000 needed in 10 years at 14% compounded quarterly.

Solution

a) In Table 9 (p. T–9) find the $3\frac{1}{2}$% column (14% ÷ 4, since the interest is compounded quarterly).

b) Find 40 in the column headed Period (interest is compounded 40 times in 10 years).

c) The row containing 40 and the column for $3\frac{1}{2}$% meet at 0.252572. The present value of $1.00 at 14% compounded quarterly for 10 years is $0.252572.

d) Find the present value of $20,000 at 14% compounded quarterly for 10 years.

$$\begin{aligned}\text{Present Value of } \$20{,}000 &= \text{Present Value of } \$1.00 \times 20{,}000 \\ &= \$0.252572 \times 20{,}000 \\ &= \$5051.44\end{aligned}$$

Therefore, $5051.44 invested now at 14% compounded quarterly will growth to $20,000 in 10 years.

DO EXERCISE 2.

ANSWER ON PAGE A–8

EXERCISE SET 4.10

■ Find the present value using Table 9 (p. T-9).

	Amount Needed	When Needed	Rate	Compounded
1.	$7000	3 years	12%	Quarterly
2.	$7000	3 years	12%	Semiannually
3.	$10,000	3 years	10%	Quarterly
4.	$10,000	3 years	18%	Monthly
5.	$20,000	4 years	12%	Semiannually
6.	$20,000	4 years	21%	Monthly
7.	$3000	2 years	16%	Quarterly
8.	$3000	2 years	15%	Monthly

9. Find the present value of $8760 needed in five years at 12% compounded semiannually.

10. Find the present value of $4590 needed in four years at 16% compounded semiannually.

11. Find the present value of $6780 needed in fourteen years at 8% compounded annually.

12. Find the present value of $9870 needed in nine years at 7% compounded annually.

ANSWERS

1. 4,909.65
2. 4934.72
3. 7435.55
4. 5850.89
5. 12,548.24
6. 8,697.16
7. 2192.07
8. 2226.59
9. 4891.53
10. 4954.08
11. 2308.33
12. 5368.62

210 INTEREST

ANSWERS

13. Find the present value of $1500 needed in five years at 10% compounded quarterly.

13. _915.41_

14. Find the present value of $5680 needed in seven years at 12% compounded quarterly.

14. _2482.59_

15. Find the present value of $4200 needed in four years at 15% compounded monthly.

15. _2313.60_

16. Find the present value of $8250 needed in three years at 18% compounded monthly.

16. _4826.98_

17. A traveler wants to have $5000 for a trip to Hawaii in five years. How much must be invested now at 10% compounded semiannually so the trip will be possible?

17. _3069.57_

18. A family needs $10,000 for a trip to Hawaii in five years. How much must be invested now at 12% compounded quarterly so the trip will be possible?

18. _8626.08_

TEST OR REVIEW—CHAPTER 4

If you miss an item, review the indicated section and objective.

[4.1, •] 1. A $5000 certificate of deposit pays 12% simple interest. How much interest is earned in 18 months?

[4.1, •••] 2. A homeowner paid $600 interest last month on a 12% mortgage. What was the amount owed at the beginning of last month?

[4.1, ••] 3. A policyholder borrowed $1000 from the insurance policy at 5%. In two years the loan was repaid. How much was repaid?

[4.2, •] 4. A consumer borrowed $850 at 16% on March 24 and repaid it July 1. Use the 360-day method to find how much interest was paid.

[4.3, •] 5. A consumer borrowed $575 at 11% on May 13 and repaid it September 5. Use the exact interest method to find how much interest was paid.

[4.4, ••] 6. A customer borrowed $785 at 15% on March 20 and repaid it June 7. Use 365-day and approximate time to find the interest.

[4.5, ••] 7. A $3500 loan for a Jacuzzi was paid for in 182 days at 16.50%. Use Table 3 (p. T–3) to find the interest.

[4.6, •] 8. An employee invests $700 at 8% compounded quarterly in the City Employees Credit Union for six months. Find the interest without using a formula or table.

[4.6, ••] 9. A customer invests $1000 at 12% compounded semiannually in a thrift certificate for two years. Find the interest with the use of a formula.

[4.6, ••] 10. A saver invests $2500 at 14% compounded semiannually in a certificate of deposit. Find the amount after two years with the use of a formula.

[4.7, •] 11. Thriftway Financial pays 18% compounded monthly. Use Table 4 (p. T-4) to find the amount after three years on a $10,000 investment.

ANSWERS

1. 900
2. 60,000
3. 100
4. 13.98
5. 18.20
6. 24.04
7. 287.96
8.
9. 1262.48
10. 3276.99
11. 7091.37

INTEREST

ANSWERS

[4.8, ●]

12. The New Haven Savings Bank compounds interest daily on a 360-day basis. Find the interest on $575 at 5.25% for 30 days using Table 6 (p.T–7).

12. 2.52

[4.8, ●●]

13. The Garden State Credit Union compounds interest continuously on share draft accounts. Find the interest on $380 at 5% for 30 days using Table 8 (p. T–8).

13. 1.59

[4.9, ●]

14. The Hawkeye State Credit Union compounds interest quarterly and pays 8% interest on savings accounts with balances to $2000. What is the effective rate?

$$E = P(1 + \frac{i}{n})^n - 1$$

14. 10¼

[4.9, ●●]

15. One bank offers $10\frac{1}{4}$% compounded semiannually on certificates of deposit. Another offers 10% compounded quarterly. Which earns more interest?

10.51 , 10.38

[4.10, ●]

15.

16. An individual wants to have $40,000 as a balloon mortgage payment in 5 years. How much must be invested now at 14% compounded quarterly so the payment may be paid? Use Table 9 (p. T-9).

20,102.06   19897.4

$I = 1(1 + $

Career: Data Processing/Bookkeeper This is Barbara Dickerson. Barbara works in a field known as Data Processing. Within Data Processing there are many kinds of jobs. Barbara's work is as a bookkeeper. She uses a computer to prepare ledger accounts, which record cash receipts and disbursements. She also uses a computer to prepare financial statements in conjunction with an accountant. One of the important benefits of Barbara's study of business mathematics is that it has enhanced her verbal skills. It is very important for her to be able to communicate in the language of the business world. For example, she must be able to communicate with accountants, with her employer, and with other employees. People who are successful in the type of work Barbara does make $15,000 to $18,000 per year.

PART II
PERSONAL FINANCE

5
CHECKING, SAVINGS, AND MONEY MARKET ACCOUNTS

READINESS CHECK — SKILLS FOR CHAPTER 5

Add.

1. $513.29 + $89.50
2. $590.88 + $579.69
3. $48.00 + $17.32 + $683.47 + $526.18 + $1437.95

Subtract.

4. $2712.92 − $267.50
5. $351.61 − $78.62
6. $739.54 − $2.50

OBJECTIVES

After finishing Section 5.1, you should be able to:

- Fill out a check for $17.95 written to Chuck's Records.
- Endorse a check.
- Identify information on a check.
- Identify the payee and the amount a bank will pay.
- Find the new balance.
- Find the net deposit.

5.1 PAYING BY CHECK

The nature of financial transactions has changed in recent years. For example, mortgage payments and transfers from checking to savings may be done automatically each month. Interest rates for loans and savings fluctuate since government regulations are now less restrictive.

In this chapter we discuss checking, savings, and money market accounts.

HOW TO WRITE A CHECK

We often write a check to pay bills. Our bank will then pay the amount on the check and deduct that amount from our account.

[Handwritten notes: Drawer — person writing check; Drawee — bank; Payee — person check is written to]

5.1 PAYING BY CHECK   **215**

Example 1 Fill out a check for $29.35 written to Electric Supply.

Solution

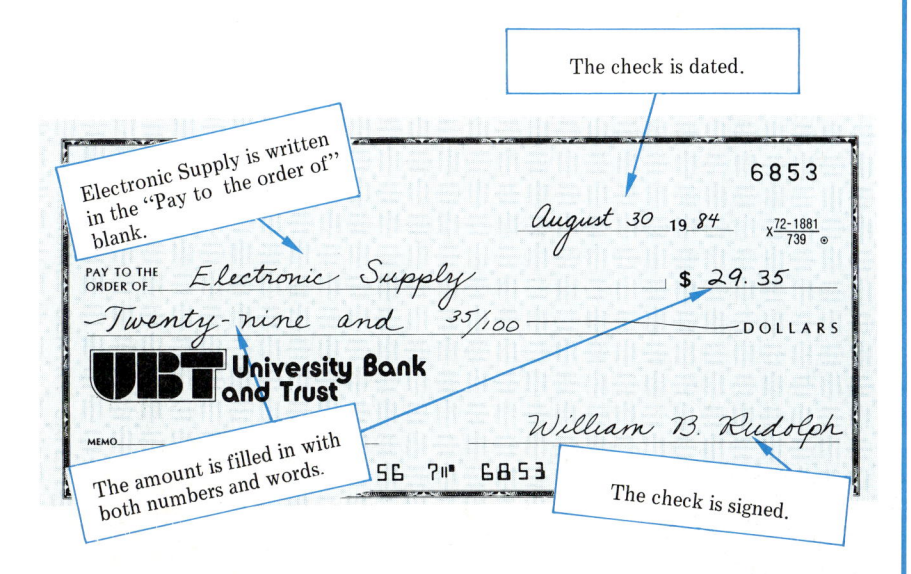

Electronic Supply is written in the "Pay to the order of" blank.

The check is dated.

The amount is filled in with both numbers and words.

The check is signed.

```
                                          6853
                        August 30, 19 84   x 72-1881/739

PAY TO THE
ORDER OF   Electronic Supply          $ 29.35
           Twenty-nine and 35/100 ———————— DOLLARS

UBT University Bank and Trust

MEMO                         William B. Rudolph
           ⋮56 7⋮  6853
```

DO EXERCISE 1.

■■ HOW TO ENDORSE A CHECK

The recipient of a check may either cash, deposit, or transfer the check. An endorsement on the back of the check will tell the bank what to do.

---

1. Fill out a check for $17.95 written to Chuck's Records.

```
                                    6854
                       19       x 72-1881/739
                                  $

                                  ———————— DOLLARS

UBT University Bank and Trust

PAY TO THE
ORDER OF
MEMO
  ⋮:0739⋮881⋮:  039 656 7⋮  6854
```

ANSWER ON PAGE A–9

216

CHECKING, SAVINGS, AND MONEY MARKET ACCOUNTS

2. You endorse a check written to you. Show the endorsements.

   a) The bank pays the amount written on the check.

   b) The bank deposits the amount written on the check into your account.

   c) The bank pays Joe Banks the amount written on the check.

Example 2 A check written to Clyde Williams is endorsed. Show some possible endorsements.

Solution *Blank Endorsement*

1. *Clyde Williams*

   The bank pays the amount written on the check.

2. *for deposit only
   Clyde Williams*

   Restrictive endorsement — protects rights of endorser

   The bank deposits the amount written on the check into Clyde William's account.

3. *Pay to the order of
   Suzanne Weber
   Clyde Williams*

   Special endorsement

   The bank pays Suzanne Weber the amount written on the check.

DO EXERCISE 2.

◼◼◼ THE INFORMATION ON A CHECK

Besides the typical information on a check there are several numbers that help a clearinghouse to sort and route checks. The canceled check on the next page illustrates these numbers.

ANSWER ON PAGE A–9

5.1 PAYING BY CHECK 217

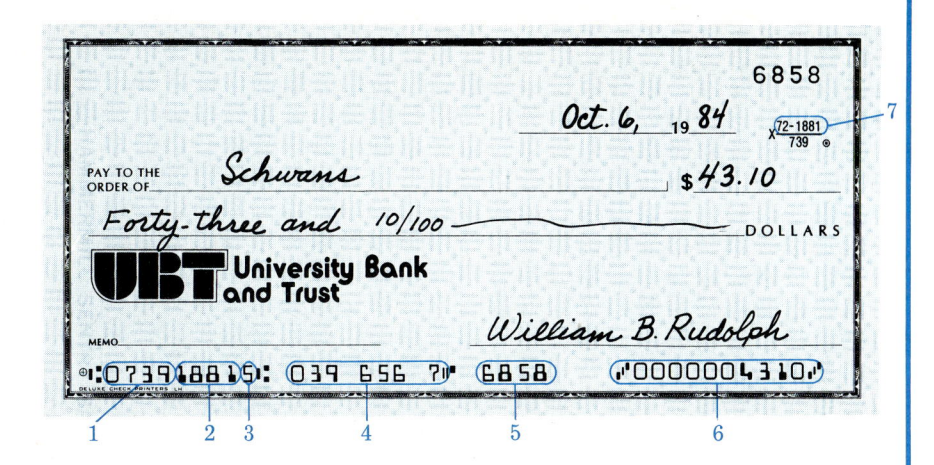

1 This is a Federal Reserve routing symbol, which identifies geographic areas. The first two digits (07) designate one of the Federal Reserve districts numbered 01–12; the third digit (3) the Federal Reserve Bank that serves the area; and the fourth digit (9) the state within the particular Federal Reserve district.

2 This number identifies the bank (1881).

3 This digit (5) enables computers to reconstruct an illegible digit among the other eight digits and to detect and reject misreads.

4 This number identifies the particular account in the bank (039 656 7).

5 This number (6858) is the check number. The number will not appear when the person who makes out the check must number each check (as in Example 3, on the next page).

6 This shows the amount of the check ($43.10). The decimal point is often read incorrectly by a computer so is omitted.

7 This is the American Bankers Association transit number. Banks want depositors to use this number (72-1881) to identify checks on deposit slips. Digits to the left of the hyphen (72) identify the large city or state in which the bank is located while the digit(s) to the right (1881) identify the bank.

218   CHECKING, SAVINGS, AND MONEY MARKET ACCOUNTS

3. Identify the account number and the amount of the check.

Example 3 Identify the account number and the amount of the check.

Solution

a) Identify the account number.

The account number is 0273 562.

b) Identify the amount of the check.

The amount of the check is $48.40.

DO EXERCISE 3.

■■ PAYEE AND CHECK AMOUNT

Check-writing pointers are given by a bank when an account is opened.

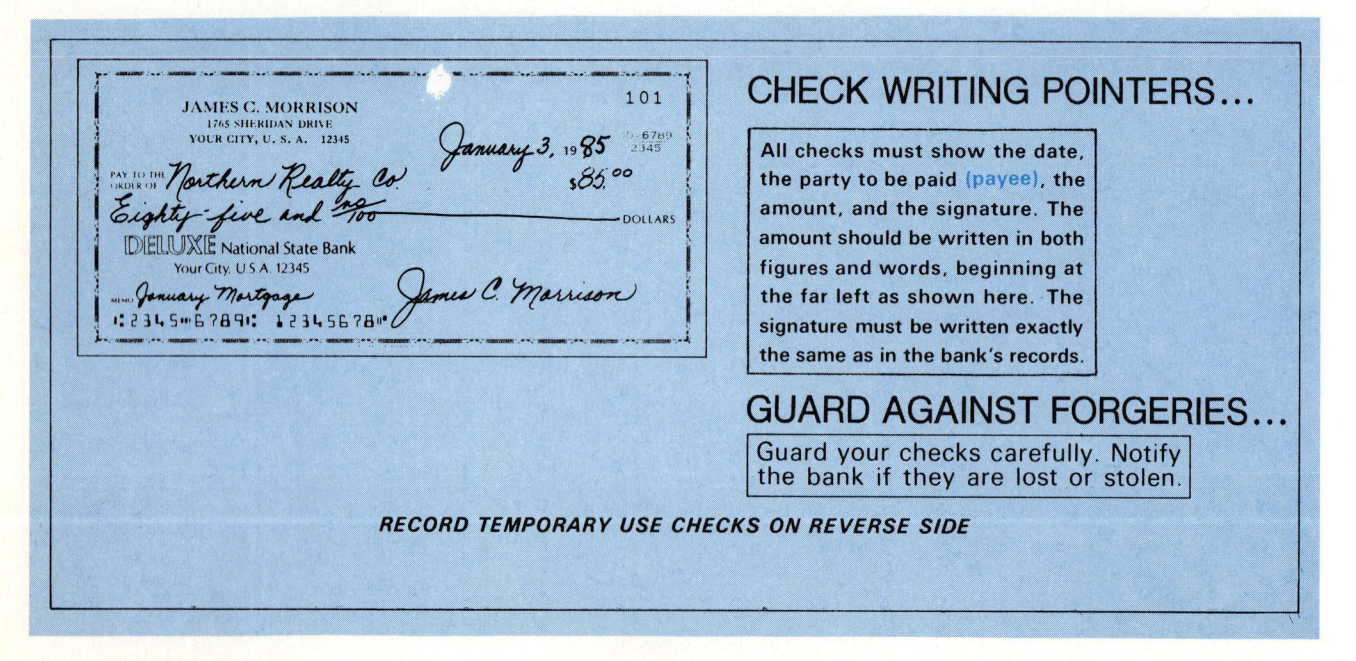

CHECK WRITING POINTERS...

All checks must show the date, the party to be paid (payee), the amount, and the signature. The amount should be written in both figures and words, beginning at the far left as shown here. The signature must be written exactly the same as in the bank's records.

GUARD AGAINST FORGERIES...

Guard your checks carefully. Notify the bank if they are lost or stolen.

RECORD TEMPORARY USE CHECKS ON REVERSE SIDE

ANSWER ON PAGE A–9

5.1 PAYING BY CHECK   219

When there is a discrepancy between the amounts written in figures and in words, the amount given in words will be paid.

Example 4 Identify the payee and the amount that the bank will pay.

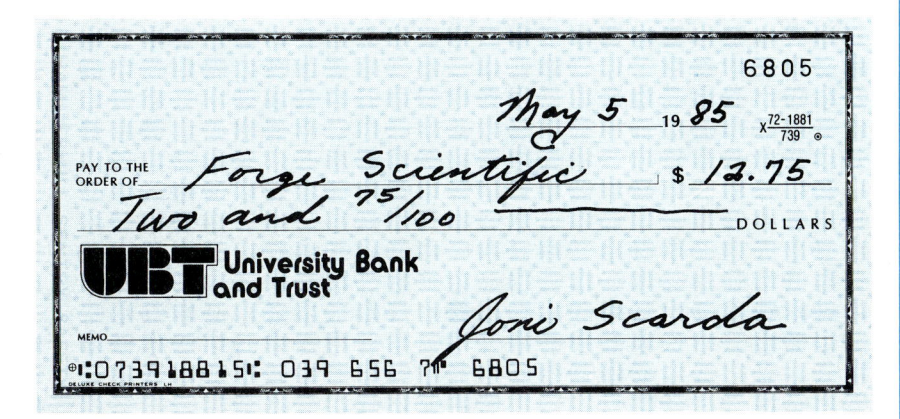

[Check #6805, May 5, 1985, Pay to the order of Forge Scientific, $12.75, "Two and 75/100 DOLLARS", University Bank and Trust, signed Joni Scarda]

Solution

a) Identify the payee.

The payee is Forge Scientific.

b) Identify the amount that the bank will pay.

The bank will pay the amount given in words, which is "Two and 75/100 dollars ($2.75)."

DO EXERCISE 4.

■■ FINDING THE NEW BALANCE

A check record book often attached to a checkbook is used to record information on checks written and deposits made.

CHECK NO	DATE	CHECKS ISSUED TO OR DESCRIPTION OF DEPOSIT	AMOUNT OF CHECK	√T	CHECK FEE (IF ANY)	AMOUNT OF DEPOSIT	BALANCE
							598 47
435	9/9/84	Nelson Electric	45 62				552 85
436	9/12/84	Fox Haven	156 50				396 35
437	9/15/84	Harlan Grocery	28 70				367 65
	9/18/84	Deposit				112 40	480 05
438	9/20/84	S & H Builders	52 80				427 25

Subtract to find the new balance after a check has been written.

New balance = Previous balance − Check amount

4. Identify the payee and the amount that the bank will pay.

[Check #6806, June 8, 1984, Pay to the order of Solar'n Concrete, $28.95, "Two and 29/100 DOLLARS", University Bank and Trust, signed Chris R. Rhodes]

ANSWERS ON PAGE A–9

5. Find the new balance.

CHECK NO	DATE	CHECKS ISSUED TO OR DESCRIPTION OF DEPOSIT	AMOUNT OF CHECK	✓T	CHECK FEE (IF ANY)	AMOUNT OF DEPOSIT	BALANCE
							872 24
181	5/5	Peterson's	47 93				824 31
182	5/7	Tricia's Bootery	96 14				

Example 5 Find the new balance of the checking account shown below.

CHECK NO	DATE	CHECKS ISSUED TO OR DESCRIPTION OF DEPOSIT	AMOUNT OF CHECK	✓T	CHECK FEE (IF ANY)	AMOUNT OF DEPOSIT	BALANCE
							392 70
822	5/6/85	Follette Repairs	14 60				378 10
823	5/7/85	Hops Linens	26 49				351 61
824	5/8/85	Toni's Lamps	78 62				

Solution

$$\text{New balance} = \text{Previous balance} - \text{Check amount}$$
$$= \$351.61 \quad - 78.62$$
$$= \$272.99$$

The new balance is $272.99.

DO EXERCISE 5.

Add to find the new balance after a deposit has been made.

> New balance = Previous balance + Deposit

Example 6 Find the new balance.

CHECK NO	DATE	CHECKS ISSUED TO OR DESCRIPTION OF DEPOSIT	AMOUNT OF CHECK	✓T	CHECK FEE (IF ANY)	AMOUNT OF DEPOSIT	BALANCE
							682 98
154	2/1/85	World Craft	147 89				535 09
155	2/3/85	Kral Cosmetics	21 80				513 29
	2/5/85	Deposit				89 50	

Solution

$$\text{New balance} = \text{Previous balance} + \text{Deposit}$$
$$= \$513.29 \quad + \$89.50$$
$$= \$602.79$$

The new balance is $602.79.

ANSWER ON PAGE A–9

5.1 PAYING BY CHECK

DO EXERCISE 6.

> **SUGGESTION**
>
> Shop around for a checking account. Shop for the lowest service charges. Some are free; some are free if you maintain a specified balance in a savings account; some have a Direct Deposit Plan through which your paycheck is deposited directly in your account by your employer; and some financial institutions offer free checking *and* pay interest on your balance.

THE DEPOSIT SLIP

Money (currency, coins, and checks) is put in a checking account using a deposit slip. The checks deposited are listed on the deposit slip by transit number (see p. 217).

Example 7 Find the net deposit.

Solution

a) Add the currency, coins, and checks.

Sum = $48.00 + $17.32 + $683.47 + $526.18 + $1437.95
    = $2712.92

b) Subtract the cash returned.

Net deposit = $2712.92 − $276.50
            = $2436.42

The net deposit is $2436.42.

DO EXERCISE 7.

---

6. Find the new balance.

7. Find the net deposit.

ANSWERS ON PAGE A–9

EXERCISE SET 5.1

■ Fill out each check as indicated. Put in today's date and sign your name.

1. To Ferber's for $29.99.

2. To Maude's Restaurant for $34.62.

3. To Jay Haus for $19.25.

CHECKING, SAVINGS, AND MONEY MARKET ACCOUNTS

4. To Stephanie Burns for $16.85.

Endorse a check for these situations.

5. *Carol Flynn*

The bank pays you the amount written on the check.

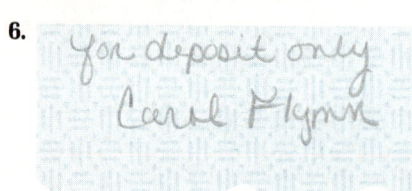

6. *For deposit only*
Carol Flynn

The bank deposits the amount written on the check into your account.

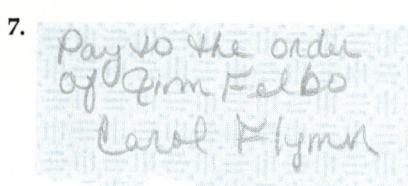

7. *Pay to the order of Jim Felbo*
Carol Flynn

The bank pays Jim Felbo the amount written on the check drawn from your account.

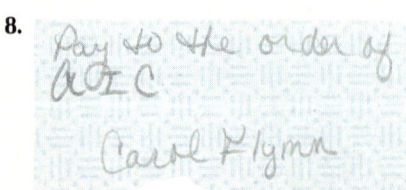

8. *Pay to the order of AIC*
Carol Flynn

The bank pays Academic Information Company the amount written on the check drawn from your account.

EXERCISE SET 5.1 **225**

▪▪▪ Identify the account number and the amount of the check.

ANSWERS

9.

10.

9. 400418
7.50

10. 435 1334
3.00

▪▪ Identify the payee and the amount that the bank will pay.

11.

11. 039 6567
4.87

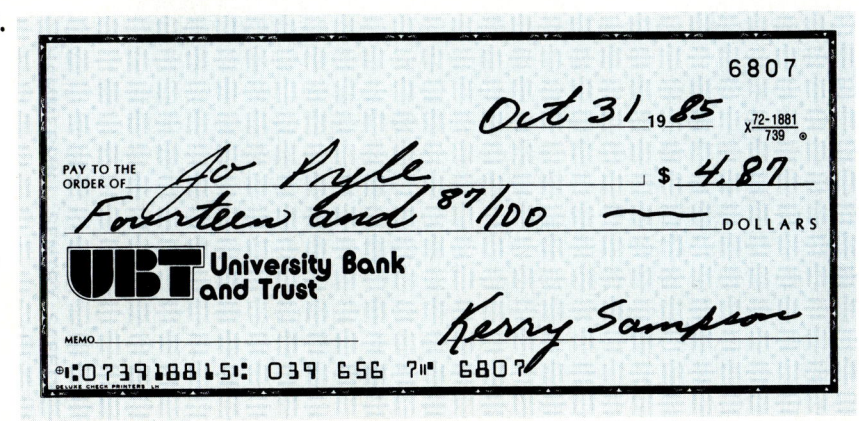

226   CHECKING, SAVINGS, AND MONEY MARKET ACCOUNTS

ANSWERS

12.

[Check #6808, May 4, 1985, Pay to the order of Fisher's, $20.38, Two and 38/100 dollars, University Bank and Trust, signed Stanlee Simms]

12. 0396567
    20.38

:: Find the new balance.

13.

CHECK NO	DATE	CHECKS ISSUED TO OR DESCRIPTION OF DEPOSIT	AMOUNT OF CHECK (−)	√T	CHECK FEE (IF ANY) (−)	AMOUNT OF DEPOSIT (+)	BALANCE
							731 19
432	12/3	Burr Wilbur	57 16				674 03
433	12/5	Pyle Photo	48 11				625 92
434	12/6	Lester's	95 16				

13. 530.76

14.

CHECK NO	DATE	CHECKS ISSUED TO OR DESCRIPTION OF DEPOSIT	AMOUNT OF CHECK (−)	√T	CHECK FEE (IF ANY) (−)	AMOUNT OF DEPOSIT (+)	BALANCE
							557 15
511	11/2	Central Roofing	68 14				489 01
512	11/3	Cooper Excavating	37 91				451 10
513	11/8	Sigler Printing	104 07				

14. 347.03

EXERCISE SET 5.1

ANSWERS

15.

CHECK NO.	DATE	CHECKS ISSUED TO OR DESCRIPTION OF DEPOSIT	AMOUNT OF CHECK (−)	√T	CHECK FEE (IF ANY) (−)	AMOUNT OF DEPOSIT (+)	BALANCE
							718 45
718	9/3	Harris TV	87 19				631 26
719	9/7	Unitog Rentals	62 17				569 09
	9/20	Deposit				381 14	

15. _950.23_

16.

CHECK NO.	DATE	CHECKS ISSUED TO OR DESCRIPTION OF DEPOSIT	AMOUNT OF CHECK (−)	√T	CHECK FEE (IF ANY) (−)	AMOUNT OF DEPOSIT (+)	BALANCE
							365 42
261	1/5	Kalyn Kennels	15 68				349 74
262	1/8	McDonald Mann	37 16				312 58
	1/12	Deposit				114 15	

16. _426.73_

Find the net deposit.

17.

CASH	CURRENCY	314 —
	COIN	16 38
LIST CHECKS SINGLY		
1-1887		462 20
72-15		132 50
TOTAL FROM OTHER SIDE		— —
TOTAL		
LESS CASH RECEIVED		— —
NET DEPOSIT		

17. _925.08_

18.

CASH	CURRENCY	217 —
	COIN	31 15
LIST CHECKS SINGLY		
2-14		314 17
27-8		416 32
TOTAL FROM OTHER SIDE		— —
TOTAL		
LESS CASH RECEIVED		— —
NET DEPOSIT		

18. _978.64_

19.

CASH	CURRENCY	321 —
	COIN	14 21
LIST CHECKS SINGLY		
7-21		468 31
93-121		548 56
TOTAL FROM OTHER SIDE		— —
TOTAL		
LESS CASH RECEIVED		410 25
NET DEPOSIT		

19. _941.83_

20.

CASH	CURRENCY	171 —
	COIN	13 21
LIST CHECKS SINGLY		
80-14		168 13
71-183		461 27
TOTAL FROM OTHER SIDE		— —
TOTAL		
LESS CASH RECEIVED		200 50
NET DEPOSIT		

20. _613.11_

228

CHECKING, SAVINGS, AND MONEY MARKET ACCOUNTS

ANSWERS

21. 2654.15

22. 4771.87

23. _____

24. _____

25. _____

26. _____

27. 213

28. 3206.52

29. 156.37

30. 2894.75

21. [Deposit slip: Currency 128—, Coin 46.02, Checks: 5-68 1468.15, 41-17 724.31, 3-162 608.17, Less Cash Received 320.50]

22. [Deposit slip: Currency 486—, Coin 14.02, Checks: 1-33 617.15, 12-14 1483.62, 37-182 2691.83, Less Cash Received 520.75]

■ Complete the check record.

CHECK NO.	DATE	CHECKS ISSUED TO OR DESCRIPTION OF DEPOSIT	AMOUNT OF CHECK (−)	√T	CHECK FEE (IF ANY)	AMOUNT OF DEPOSIT (+)	BALANCE 682 17
23. 611	8/7	Drury Well	47 18				634 99
24.	8/11	Deposit				161 34	796 33
25. 612	8/14	Sorenson Boutique	113 47				682 86
26.	8/17	Deposit				58 14	741

■ Complete the deposit slips.

27. [Deposit slip: Currency ___, Coin 14.38, Checks: 1-53 891.62, 14-3 763.35, 162-5 1324.17, Less Cash Received 368.25, Net Deposit 2838.27]

28. [Deposit slip: Currency 415—, Coin ___, Checks: 1-27 368.41, 42-63 489.15, 37-29 1622.19, Less Cash Received 523.25, Net Deposit 2527.87]

29. TOTAL

30. TOTAL

5.2 RECONCILING A BANK STATEMENT WITH A CHECK RECORD

■ BANK STATEMENT BALANCES

At regular intervals banks send depositors bank statements together with the canceled checks for the account. The depositor then uses these and the check record to see whether there are any errors.

OBJECTIVES

After finishing Section 5.2, you should be able to:

■ Verify bank statement balances.

■■ Reconcile a bank statement with a check record.

1. In the figure, the bank statement balance on 7/24 was $583.88. Verify that the balance on 8/2 was $1033.57.

UNIVERSITY BANK AND TRUST COMPANY
A FULL SERVICE BANK — FDIC

PAT DARCY
47 FLORA DRIVE
BIRMINGHAM, AL 35203

ACCOUNT NUMBER 498 – 54 – 9
PREVIOUS 07/21 CURRENT 08/21/84
STATEMENT DATE

HAVE YOU TRIED OUR 24-HOUR BANKING SERVICE YET

BEGINNING BALANCE	TOTAL CHECKS PAID	NO.	TOTAL DEPOSIT AMOUNT	NO.	SER. CHG.	BALANCE THIS STATEMENT
590.88	451.13	12	579.69	3	.00	719.44

CHECKS AND OTHER CHARGES		DEPOSITS AND OTHER CREDITS	DATE	BALANCE
7.00			07/24	583.88
		459.69	07/31	1,043.57
10.00			08/02	1,033.57
233.00			08/03	800.57
50.00		20.00	08/15	770.57
35.00			08/16	735.57
		100.00	08/17	835.57
8.50			08/18	827.07
4.00	4.90		08/21	
10.00	20.49			719.44
27.80	40.44			

Observe that:

1. To get each new balance figure, one adds any deposits to the previous balance then subtracts checks paid.

2. The beginning balance ($590.88 in the example above) and ending balance ($719.44) are given.

3. The total checks paid ($451.13) and total deposit ($579.69) amounts are given.

4. The dates of each transaction are given.

Example 1 The bank statement above shows that the balance on 8/3 was $800.57. Verify that the balance on 8/15 was $770.57.

Solution

New balance = Previous balance + Deposits − Checks
= $800.57 + 20.00 − $50.00
= $770.57

The balance on 8/15 was $770.57.

DO EXERCISE 1.

ANSWER ON PAGE A–10

CHECKING, SAVINGS, AND MONEY MARKET ACCOUNTS

2. Find the statement balance.

Beginning balance	$425.59
Deposits	378.21
Checks paid	287.75
Service charge	1.57

To find the statement balance,
1. Find the sum of the beginning balance and deposits, and then
2. Subtract the checks paid and the service charge (the amount that banks charge for check processing and record keeping).

Example 2 Verify that the statement balance in the figure on the preceding page is $719.44.

Solution

a) Find the sum of the beginning balance and deposits.

   Sum = $590.88 + $579.69
       = $1170.57

b) Subtract the checks paid and the service charge.

   Statement balance = Sum − Checks paid − Service charge
                     = $1170.57 − $451.13 − $0
                     = $719.44

The statement balance is $719.44

DO EXERCISE 2.

●● RECONCILING

The process comparing the bank statement with the check record is called *reconciling*.

Example 3 Reconcile the bank statement with the check record.

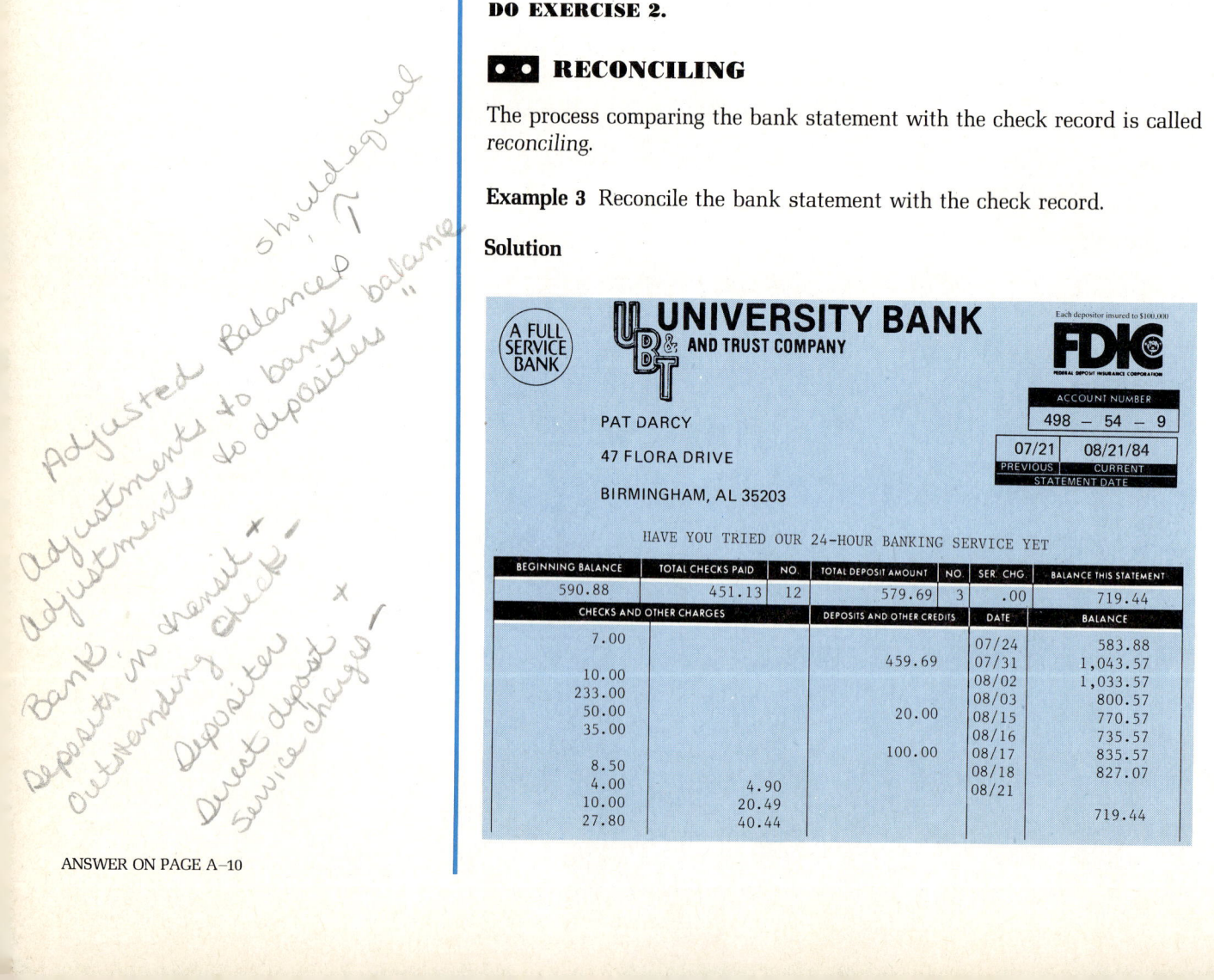

Solution

UNIVERSITY BANK AND TRUST COMPANY
A FULL SERVICE BANK — FDIC

PAT DARCY
47 FLORA DRIVE
BIRMINGHAM, AL 35203

ACCOUNT NUMBER 498 − 54 − 9
PREVIOUS 07/21 CURRENT 08/21/84
STATEMENT DATE

HAVE YOU TRIED OUR 24-HOUR BANKING SERVICE YET

BEGINNING BALANCE	TOTAL CHECKS PAID	NO.	TOTAL DEPOSIT AMOUNT	NO.	SER. CHG.	BALANCE THIS STATEMENT
590.88	451.13	12	579.69	3	.00	719.44

CHECKS AND OTHER CHARGES		DEPOSITS AND OTHER CREDITS	DATE	BALANCE
7.00			07/24	583.88
		459.69	07/31	1,043.57
10.00			08/02	1,033.57
233.00			08/03	800.57
50.00		20.00	08/15	770.57
35.00			08/16	735.57
		100.00	08/17	835.57
8.50			08/18	827.07
4.00	4.90		08/21	
10.00	20.49			
27.80	40.44			719.44

ANSWER ON PAGE A–10

5.2 RECONCILING A BANK STATEMENT WITH A CHECK RECORD

A typical bank-supplied reconciliation form is used. Under ① list the checks not yet paid by the bank. Deposits not yet credited on the statement are placed under ②.

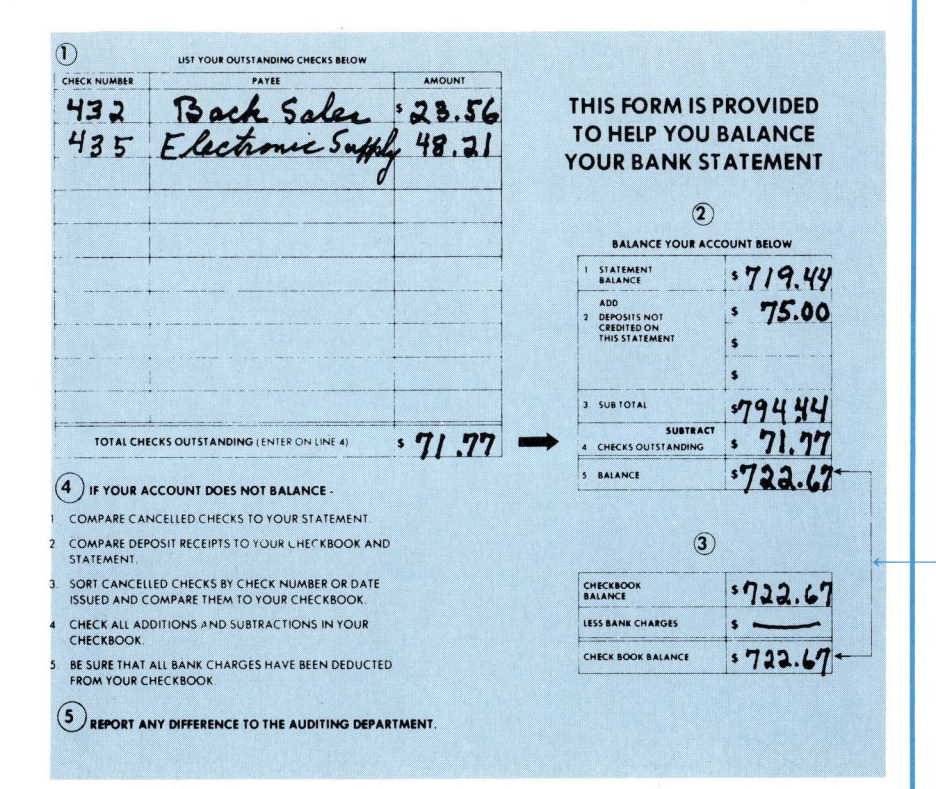

A √ in this column shows that the bank has paid the check.

These are equal, which shows that the bank statement and check record agree

3. Reconcile. Draw a form as in Example 3.

Check record balance	$516.84
Checks outstanding	62.17
	45.82
Deposits not recorded	167.98
Service charges	0.
Bank statement balance	456.85

456.85
+167.98
−62.17

562.66

516.84

DO EXERCISE 3.

ANSWER ON PAGE A 10

4. Reconcile.

Check record balance	$539.53
Checks outstanding	176.32
Deposits not recorded	78.19
Service charges	1.68
Bank statement balance	635.98

537.85

537.85

ANSWER ON PAGE A–10

CHECKING, SAVINGS, AND MONEY MARKET ACCOUNTS

Whenever there is a service charge, subtract it from the checkbook balance when reconciling.

Example 4 Reconcile.

Check record balance	$739.54
Checks outstanding	32.48
Deposits not recorded	312.78
Service charges	2.50
Bank statement balance	456.74

Solution

a) Find the adjusted statement balance.

$$\text{Adjusted statement balance} = \text{Statement balance} + \text{Deposits not recorded} - \text{Checks outstanding}$$
$$= \$456.74 + \$312.78 - \$32.48$$
$$= \$737.04$$

b) Find the adjusted check record balance.

$$\text{Adjusted check balance} = \text{Check record balance} - \text{Service charges}$$
$$= \$739.54 - \$2.50$$
$$= \$737.04$$

The adjusted statement balance and adjusted check record balance are equal, so the statement and check record are reconciled.

DO EXERCISE 4.

EXERCISE SET 5.2

• Find the balance

DATE	CHECKS AND OTHER DEBITS		DEPOSITS	BALANCE
07/28	10.00			51.40
07/30	8.00			43.40
1. 07/31	4.00		533.14	572.54
08/03	2.00	8.17		
	202.40			359.97
08/04	9.79	10.00		
	25.00	32.51		282.67
08/05	6.50	12.62		
	15.00	15.74		
2.	19.09			232.51
08/06	2.04	8.00		
	10.00			193.68
08/10	4.25	25.00		164.43
08/11	18.15	20.00		126.28
08/12	3.00			123.28
08/13	10.25			113.03
08/14	10.00			103.03
3. 08/17	1.03	10.00	247.69	339.69
08/18	2.06			337.63
08/19	15.00	18.22		
	20.00	100.00		184.41
08/20	31.38			153.03
08/24	5.22	24.00		
4.	43.40			108.41

Find the statement balance

5.
BALANCE LAST STATEMENT	NO	CHECKS AND DEBITS AMOUNT	NO	DEPOSITS AMOUNT	SERVICE CHARGE	BALANCE THIS STATEMENT
491.51	24	678.16	1	250.00	1.95	

6.
BALANCE LAST STATEMENT	NO	CHECKS AND DEBITS AMOUNT	NO	DEPOSITS AMOUNT	SERVICE CHARGE	BALANCE THIS STATEMENT
32.57	34	903.94	1	1,040.29	2.45	

7.
BALANCE LAST STATEMENT	NO	CHECKS AND DEBITS AMOUNT	NO	DEPOSITS AMOUNT	SERVICE CHARGE	BALANCE THIS STATEMENT
138.75	42	882.63	1	962.01	2.60	

8.
BALANCE LAST STATEMENT	NO	CHECKS AND DEBITS AMOUNT	NO	DEPOSITS AMOUNT	SERVICE CHARGE	BALANCE THIS STATEMENT
61.40	40	806.91	2	780.83	2.75	32.57

234   CHECKING, SAVINGS, AND MONEY MARKET ACCOUNTS

Reconcile. Draw a form as in Example 3.

	Check Record Balance	Checks Outstanding	Deposits not Recorded	Service Charges	Bank Statement Balance
9.	$340.81	$125.63 $462.13	$525.48	0	$403.09
10.	$424.47	$189.01	0	0	$613.48
11.	$765.92	$51.23 $79.96	$159.17	$0.72	$737.22
12.	$329.02	$91.15	0	$1.55	$418.62
13.	$1091.66	$42.63 $115.95	$426.83	0	$823.41
14.	$1162.85	$215.85 $463.21	$325.50 $463.75	$2.35	$1050.31
15.	$1194.22	$321.90	$527.80	$1.75	$986.57
16.	$1331.43	0	$648.26	0	$683.17

Fill in the bank statement where indicated.

	DATE	DESCRIPTION CHECKS/DEBITS	DEPOSITS/CREDITS	BALANCE
17.	08/25	20.65	30.00	288.58
	08/29	10.00	20.00	258.58
	08/30	7.00		251.58
	08/31	20.00	635.45	867.03
	09/01	233.00		634.03
	09/02	10.00	39.51	
		50.00		534.52
18.	09/06	25.00		
			136.25	681.93
19.	09/07	30.00	30.00	621.93
	09/08	42.96	231.14	347.83
	09/12	8.10		
		20.00	30.00	269.88
	09/13		425.81	695.69
	09/14	6.00	6.45	
		10.00	15.00	
		18.29		639.95
20.	09/15	9.00	15.00	615.95
	09/19	20.00	20.00	
		40.00		

5.3 OTHER FINANCIAL TRANSACTIONS

● SAVINGS

Financial institutions such as banks and savings and loans provide many services. Among the services are:

> Savings and Checking Accounts
> Certificates of Deposit (CD's)
> Retirement Accounts
> Loans
> Notary Services
> Safety Deposit Boxes
> Transmatic Service (automatic transfer between accounts and payment of certain bills)
> Payroll Deposit
> Direct Deposit of Government Checks
> Automatic Teller Machines (24-hour banking)

Interest computation methods vary. Examples 1 and 2 show that it is important to understand how your financial institution computes interest.*

Example 1 Newark Savings and Loan pays 12% interest compounded quarterly on the total amount in accounts having more than $2500. How much interest is earned on $3000 in one year?

Solution

We substitute $3000 for P, 0.03 for i, and 4 for n in

$$A = P \times (1 + i)^n$$
$$= \$3000 \times (1 + 0.03)^4$$
$$= \$3376.53 \quad \text{Use a calculator if you have one.}$$

The interest is $376.53 ($3376.53 − $3000).

DO EXERCISE 1.

---

*Many banks and savings and loans offer money market and SuperNow accounts (both allow writing of checks). If the average monthly balance drops below $2500 the account earns only $5\frac{1}{4}$% interest. The Depository Institutions Deregulation Committee is to phase out all restrictions on bank interest rates and balances by 1986.

OBJECTIVES

After finishing Section 5.3, you should be able to:

● Evaluate the interest on savings accounts.

●● Determine the amount in a money market mutual fund.

1. Birmingham Federal pays 11% interest compounded quarterly on the total amount in accounts having more than $2500. How much interest is earned on $4000 in one year?

455.48

ANSWER ON PAGE A–12

236

CHECKING, SAVINGS, AND MONEY MARKET ACCOUNTS

2. Forest City Savings and Loan pays 11% interest compounded quarterly on all amounts over $2500 and 5% compounded quarterly on the balance. How much interest is earned on $4000 in one year?

[handwritten: 2500 / 1500 / 171.93 / 127.38 / 299.31]

Example 2 Adelphi Savings and Loan pays 12% interest compounded quarterly on all amounts over $2500 and 6% compounded quarterly on the balance. How much interest is earned on $3000 in one year?

Solution

a) We substitute $500 ($3000 − $2500) for P, 0.03 for i, and 4 for n in

$$A = P \times (1 + i)^n$$
$$= \$500 \times (1 + 0.03)^4 \quad \text{Use a calculator if you have one.}$$
$$= \$562.75$$

The interest on $500 is $62.75 ($562.75 − $500).

b) We substitute $2500 for P, 0.015 for i, and 4 for n in

$$A = P \times (1 + i)^n$$
$$= \$2500 \times (1 + 0.015)^4 \quad \text{Use your calculator if you have one.}$$
$$= \$2653.41$$

The interest on $2500 is $153.41 ($2653.41 − $2500). From (a) and (b) we see that the total interest is

$62.75 + $153.41   or $216.16

DO EXERCISE 2.

⊙⊙ MONEY MARKET MUTUAL FUNDS

Money Market Mutual Funds are investment companies which pool investors' money to purchase large denomination (usually no less than $100,000) savings instruments. Interest rates are compounded daily and fluctuate. Investors have immediate access to their invested funds through check writing ($500 minimum) or phone redemption and there is no penalty for withdrawing money at any time. An initial investment of at least $1000 is

ANSWER ON PAGE A–12

often required with subsequent deposits of at least $100. The following table shows information on money market funds on a recent day.

```
                    Days    Yield Chg.
Money    Market:
AAA US      Gvt       21   7.58 + .01
AARP US     Gvt f     51   9.79 + .36
AetnaMMkt   ab        40  10.37 - .08
AlexBrownCash         30  10.50 - .35
AllianceCapRes f      33   9.64 - .29
AllianceGovtRes f     36   8.40 .........
AmerGenlMoney         26  10.53 - .40
AmerGenResrv b        36  10.82 + .29
AmerLiquidTrust       30   9.98 - .31
AmNatl      a         34  10.70 - .24
BabsonMoneyMkt        33  10.66 - .30
BirrWilson            23   9.87 - .95
BostonCoCash          38  10.66 - .33
CapitalCashMgt        25   9.41 - .13
CapitalPreservFd      31   8.26 - .47
CapitPreserv II        3   8.26 +1.31
CardinalGvtSec        10  15.03 +5.15
Carnegie GvtSecur     17   8.65 + .70
CashEquivIntMMkt      36  11.45 - .26
CashEquivIntPort      30   9.20 +1.04
CashMgmtTrAm b        19  10.05 + .05
CashResrvMgmt bf      30  10.16 - .35
CentennialMMTr        30  10.25 + .02
ChanclrGvt  b         40   8.93 - .28
Chanc. TaxFr   e      90   6.44 + .09
ColonialMMkt   a      23   9.66 - .25
ColumbDivIncm bf      23   9.89 - .33
CompositeCashMgmt     28  10.27 -1.16
CurrentInterest       34  10.54 - .29
DBL MM    Portfolio   36  11.25 - .21
DBL GvtSec            44   9.04 + .21
DailyCashAccum        26  10.00 - .10
DailyCashGovt         27   7.45 - .04
DailyIncomeFd         30  10.40 + .07
```

Money Market	Days	Yield	Chg.
Daily Cash Accum	26	10.00	−.10
1	**2**	**3**	**4**

1 The name of the money market fund. In this case it is the Daily Cash Accumulation Fund.

2 The average maturity in days for the savings instruments in the fund. In this case it is 26 days.

3 The previous seven-day annualized yield. In this case, 10.00%.

4 The change in yield from that of seven days ago. In this case the yield decreased by 0.10% over what it was seven days ago.

DO EXERCISES 3–5.

State the seven-day annualized yield for each fund.

3. American Liquid Trust Fund.

4. Capital Preservation Fund.

5. Cash Reserve Management Fund.

ANSWERS ON PAGE A–12

6. An investor had $10,000 in the American Liquid Trust Fund seven days ago. How much is in the fund now if the past seven-day annualized yield was 9.98%?

10,019.14

Example 3 An investor had $10,000 in the Daily Cash Accumulation Fund seven days ago. How much is in the fund now if the past seven-day annualized yield was 10.00%?

Solution

We substitute $10,000 for P, 0.10 for R, and $\frac{7}{365}$ for T in

$$I = P \times R \times T$$

$$= \$10{,}000 \times 0.10 \times \frac{7}{365}$$

$$= \$19.18$$

The amount now is $10,000 + $19.18, or $10,019.18.

DO EXERCISE 6.

COMMENT

There is some risk with most money market funds as the federal government does not insure investors against loss. Market Logic, an investment advisory letter, rates money market mutual funds for safety. Its address is 3471 North Federal Highway, Fort Lauderdale, Florida 33306.

---

your investment × yield × 7/365 = interest

EXERCISE SET 5.3

• Solve.

1. Clive Bank pays 12% interest compounded semiannually on the total amount in accounts having more than $2500. How much interest is earned on $5000 in one year?

   1. 618

2. Jackson Savings and Loan pays 10% compounded semiannually on the total amount in accounts having more than $2500. How much interest is earned on $5000 in one year?

   2. 512

3. Trenton Bank pays 12% interest compounded semiannually on all amounts over $2500 and 8% compounded semiannually on the balance. How much interest is earned on $5000 in one year?

   3. 513

4. Laramie Savings and Loan pays 10% compounded semiannually on all amounts over $2500 and 6% compounded semiannually on the balance. How much interest is earned on $5000 in one year?

   4. 408.50

5. Pittsburgh National Bank pays 12% interest compounded quarterly on the total amount in accounts having more than $2500. When the balance falls below $2500 the bank pays 6% compounded quarterly. How much interest is earned in one year on $3000 for nine months and $1500 for three months?

   5. 300.69

6. Faribault National Savings pays 10% interest compounded semiannually on the total amount in accounts having more than $2500. When the balance falls below $2500 the bank pays 6% compounded semiannually. How much interest is earned in one year on $4500 for six months and $2000 for six months?

   6. 285

240 CHECKING, SAVINGS, AND MONEY MARKET ACCOUNTS

ANSWERS

◉◉ Use the table to find the seven-day annualized yield.

7. Merrill Lynch Government Fund.

7. 9.22

8. Municipal Cash Reserves.

8. 6.66

9. Mutual of Omaha Money Market Fund.

9. 9.08

10. Phoenix Chase Fund.

10. 10.17

$15,000 was placed in each of the funds below seven days ago. How much is in each fund now? Use the table.

11. Massachusetts Cash Management Fund.

11. 15082.56

12. Money Market Management Fund.

12. 15030.32

13. Money Market Assets Fund.

13. 15031.47

14. National Cash Reserve Fund.

14. 15030.41

15. Paine Webber Cash Fund.

15. 15030.35

16. Plimoney Fund.

16. 15027.53

TEST OR REVIEW—CHAPTER 5

NAME _____   SCORE _____

TEST OR REVIEW—CHAPTER 5

If you miss an item, review the indicated section and objective.

[5.1, ●]   **1.** Fill out a check for $87.65 written to Foster's Clothing.

Check filled out:
- 6859
- 4-28 19 88
- Pay to the order of: Foster's Clothing $ 87.65
- eighty-seven and 65/100 DOLLARS
- Signed: Carol Flynn

[5.1, ● ●]   **2.** Endorse a check for these situations.

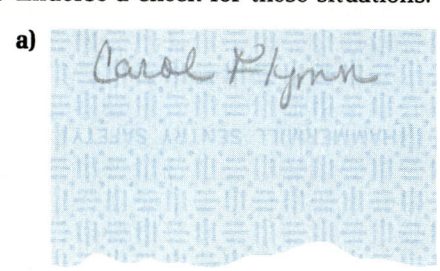

a) *Carol Flynn*

The bank pays you the amount written on the check.

b) *For deposit only / Carol Flynn*

The bank deposits the amount written on the check into your account.

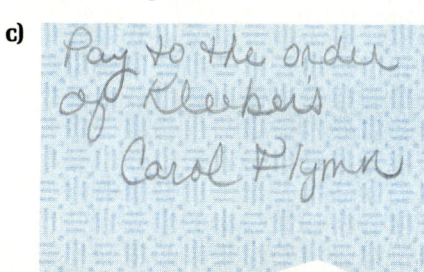

c) *Pay to the order of Kleeber's / Carol Flynn*

The bank pays Kleeber's the amount written on the check.

Copyright © 1984, by Addison-Wesley Publishing Company Inc. All rights reserved.

242 CHECKING, SAVINGS, AND MONEY MARKET ACCOUNTS

ANSWERS

[5.1, ●●●]   3. Identify the account number and the amount of this check.

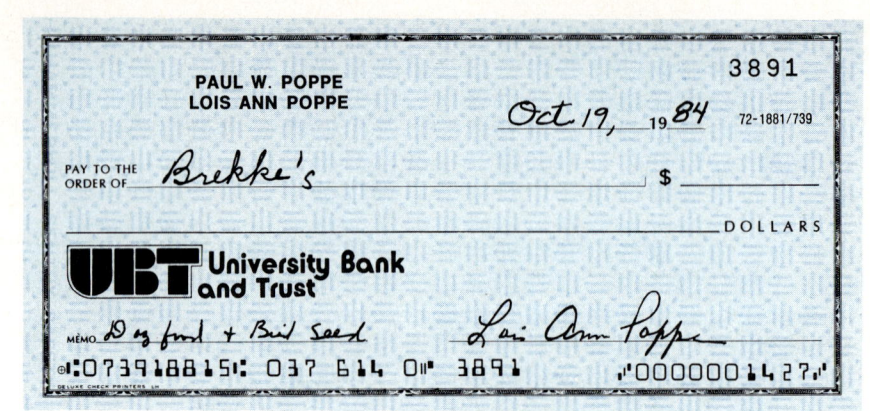

3. 037640
   14.27

[5.1, ●●]   4. Identify the payee and the amount that the bank will pay.

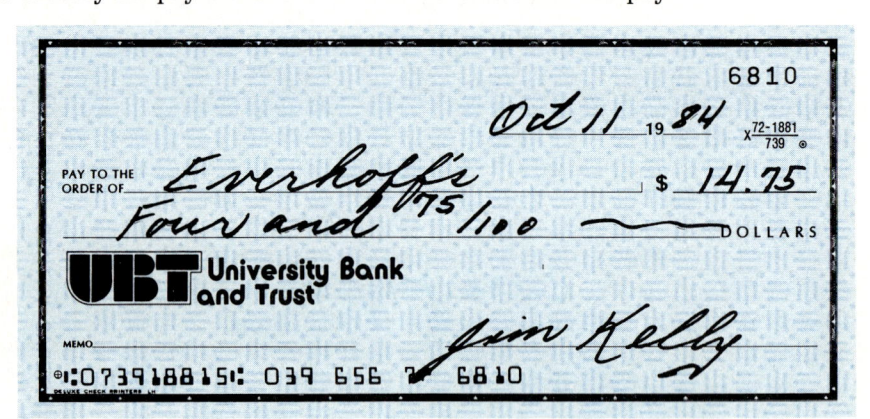

4. Everhoff's
   4.75

[5.1, ●●●]   5. Find the new balance.

5. 433.53

[5.1, ●●●]   6. Find the net deposit.

6. 685.86

TEST OR REVIEW—CHAPTER 5   **243**

[5.2, •]   Find the balance.   ANSWERS

BALANCE LAST STATEMENT	NO.	CHECKS AND DEBITS AMOUNT	NO.	DEPOSITS AMOUNT	SERVICE CHARGE	BALANCE THIS STATEMENT
7. 370.88	48	1,350.01	1	1,091.40	2.65	109.62

DATE	CHECKS AND OTHER DEBITS	DEPOSITS	BALANCE
10/27	15.00		355.88
10/28	10.00		345.88
8. 10/30	15.20	1,091.40	1422.08
11/02	1.54	4.12	
9.	202.40		1214.07

[5.2, ••] **10.** Reconcile on the form.

Check record balance $760.25
Checks outstanding   56.28, 14.96
Deposits not recorded   418.32
Service charges   0
Bank statement balance 413.17

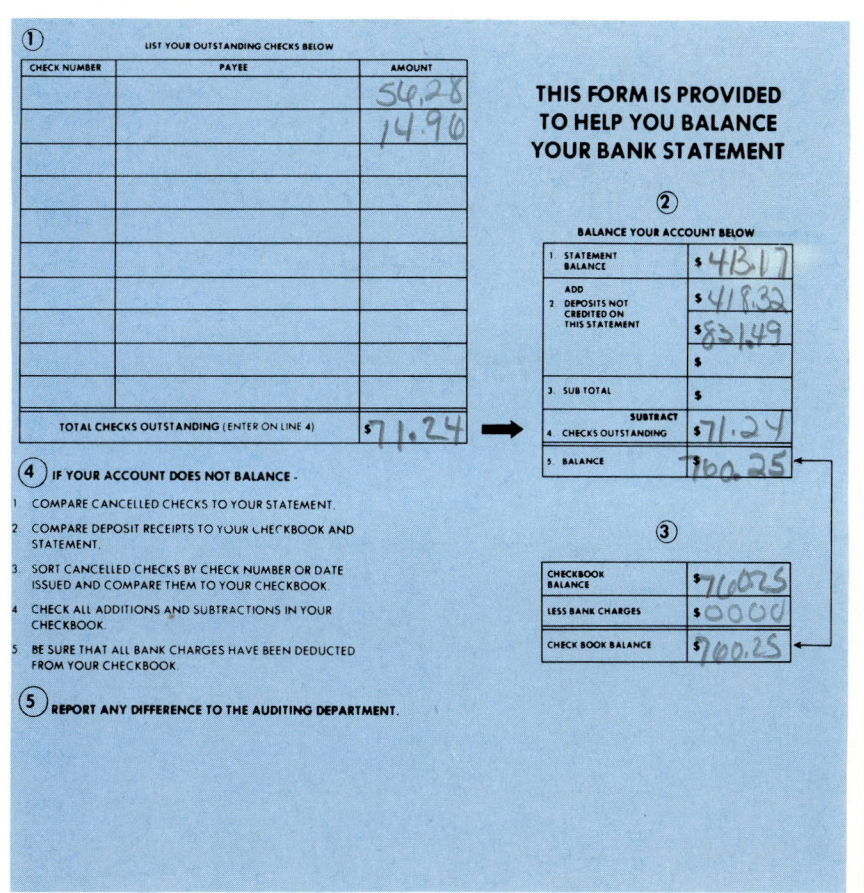

(form filled in:)
Outstanding checks: 56.28, 14.96
Total checks outstanding: $71.24

1. Statement Balance: $413.17
2. Deposits not credited: $418.32
   Subtotal: $831.49
4. Checks outstanding: $71.24
5. Balance: $760.25

Checkbook balance: $760.25
Less bank charges: $00.00
Check book balance: $760.25

[5.3, •]   **11.** Corning Federal pays 14% interest compounded quarterly on the total amount in accounts having more than $2500. How much interest is earned on $3500 in one year?   11. 516.32

[5.3, ••] **12.** An investor had $5000 in the Cash Equivalent Money Market Fund seven days ago. How much is in the fund now if the past seven-day annualized yield was 11.45%?

12. 5010.98

Career: Loan Officer This is James R. Bayless. Jim is partially paralyzed as a result of a stroke. With the help of vocational rehabilitation, Jim took several business and psychology courses and is now a loan officer for the small business administration. This is a federal agency which grants loans either directly through the government, or indirectly by guaranteeing loans through other financial institutions.

A direct loan can be as much as $150,000 and a guaranteed loan can be as much as $500,000. Thus there is great responsibility in Jim's work in determining the possibility of a loan. Many factors are considered, such as industry averages for the type of business seeking a loan and the credit rating of the owner of the business.

People who work for the government in a job such as Jim's are paid according to what is called a GS rating. One might begin with a GS-7, making $16,559, and through promotion and service advance to a GS-12, making $38,185.

Jim has many qualities which make for success. He likes people and is a friendly person. He also is a "stick-to-it" person who gets the job done. His hobbies include visiting friends, eating out, and watching golf tournaments.

6
LOANS AND ANNUITIES

LOANS AND ANNUITIES

READINESS CHECK—SKILLS FOR CHAPTER 6

Find the date.

1. 90 days from June 4.
2. 130 days from August 14.

Find I in $I = P \times R \times T$.

3. $P = \$1500$
   $R = 0.12$
   $T = 90/365$

4. $P = \$2000$
   $R = 0.15$
   $T = \frac{1}{4}$

Subtract.

5. $2171.25 - 565.35$
6. $2439.70 - 731.36$

OBJECTIVES

After finishing Section 6.1 you should be able to:

■ Calculate interest due on a note.
■ Determine the due date of a note.
■ Find the discount and proceeds of a note.

6.1 NOTES AND DISCOUNTS

From time to time individuals and businesses need a *loan* (to borrow money). Likewise regular savings is encouraged. Questions such as how payments are credited and the amount in savings after a time period arise.

These topics will be studied in this chapter.

■ INTEREST DUE ON A NOTE

Lenders often require borrowers to sign a note (*promissory note*) at the time a loan is made. By signing the note, the borrower promises to pay to the lender the amount borrowed plus a charge for the use of the money. Notes may be *interest bearing* (as in Example 1) or *noninterest bearing* (as in Example 2).

Example 1 Find the interest due at the end of six months on the following interest-bearing note.

$ 1,000.00   AMES, IOWA, March 27 19 84

Chris A. Hanson _____ after date, for value received I, we, or either of us promise to pay to the order of

UNIVERSITY BANK AND TRUST CO.   72-1881 / 713

One Thousand and 00/100 ——————————— DOLLARS

with interest thereon at the rate of 13 per cent annum from date, payable semi-annually, until paid
Payable at UNIVERSITY BANK & TRUST CO, Ames, Iowa. Should any of the principal or interest not be paid when due, it shall bear interest at the rate of 7 per cent per annum and the entire amount of principal and interest shall become due and collectible at once if any interest is not paid when due. The makers, endorsers and guarantors of this note agree to pay a reasonable attorney's fee if suit is brought or expense incurred hereon, and consent that any Justice of the Peace shall have jurisdiction of this note to the amount of $300, and hereby severally waive presentments for payment, notices of non-payment, protests and notices of protest and diligence in bringing suit against any party hereto, and consent that times of payment may be extended without notice. It is also agreed that should the holders of this note at any time deem themselves insecure they may demand such additional security as may seem to them necessary.

No. _____ Due September 27, 1984
P. O. Address _____

6.1 NOTES AND DISCOUNTS 247

Solution Find the interest due at the end of six months.

Substituting 1000 for P, 0.13 for R, and $\frac{6}{12}$ for T, we get

$$I = P \times R \times T$$
$$= 1000 \times 0.13 \times \frac{6}{12}$$
$$= 65.$$

The interest due is $65.

DO EXERCISE 1.

●● DUE DATE

For noninterest-bearing notes a charge (discount) is deducted at the time the loan is made. The amount on the face of the note is then due at maturity.

Example 2 Find the due date for this 90-day noninterest-bearing note.

$ 1,000.00   AMES, IOWA, May 15   19 84
Jo Phillips _____ after date, for value received I, we, or either of us promise to pay to the order of
UNIVERSITY BANK AND TRUST CO.   72-1881 / 713

One Thousand and 00/100 _____ DOLLARS
with interest thereon at the rate of **no** per cent per annum from date, payable semi-annually, until paid.
Payable at UNIVERSITY BANK & TRUST CO, Ames, Iowa. Should any of the principal or interest not be paid when due, it shall bear interest at the rate of 7 per cent per annum and the entire amount of principal and interest shall become due and collectible at once if any interest is not paid when due. The makers, endorsers and guarantors of this note agree to pay a reasonable attorney's fee if suit is brought or expense incurred hereon, and consent that any Justice of the Peace shall have jurisdiction of this note to the amount of $300, and hereby severally waive presentments for payment, notices of non-payment, protests and notices of protest and diligence in bringing suit against any party hereto, and consent that times of payment may be extended without notice. It is also agreed that should the holders of this note at any time deem themselves insecure they may demand such additional security as may seem to them necessary.

No._____ Due_____
P. O. Address_____

Solution The note is for 90 days, and 90 days from May 15 is

May 15–31	16 days
June 1–30	30 days
July 1–31	31 days
August 1–13	13 days
Total	90 days

Thus, the note is due August 13.

DO EXERCISE 2.

---

1. Find the interest due on $1000 at the end of six months if the rate is 15%.

$1000 \times .15 \times 6/12$

2. If the note in Example 2 is for 135 days, what is its due data?

Aug 13 (31)   45
             −18
     18   ──
              27
     30
   Sept 27

ANSWERS ON PAGE A–14

3. A three-year noninterest-bearing note for $6000 was presented to a bank using an 11% discount rate. Find the discount and proceeds.

DISCOUNT AND PROCEEDS

As mentioned, a lender may deduct a loan charge (*discount*) at the time a loan is obtained. This discount is often considered interest paid in advance.

> A formula for finding the discount is
> $$D = M \times R \times T,$$
> where $D =$ the discount, $M =$ the amount due at maturity, $R =$ the discount rate, and $T =$ the time.

The amount the borrower receives is the *proceeds*.

> A formula for finding the proceeds is
> $$P = M - D,$$
> where $P =$ the proceeds, $M =$ the amount due at maturity, and $D =$ the discount.

Example 3 A $2295 two-year noninterest-bearing note for money to purchase a two-car garage was presented to a bank that uses a 14% discount rate. Find the discount and proceeds.

Solution

a) Find the discount.

Substituting 2295 for M, 0.14 for R, and 2 for T, we get

$D = M \times R \times T$

$ = 2295 \times 0.14 \times 2$

$ = 642.60.$ The amount of money the bank charges for the loan.

The discount is $642.60.

b) Find the proceeds.

Substituting 2295 for M and 642.60 for D, we get

$P = M - D$

$ = 2295 - 642.60$

$ = 1652.40.$ The amount received by the borrower.

The proceeds are $1652.40.

DO EXERCISE 3.

6.1 NOTES AND DISCOUNTS   249

Sometimes a businessperson is given a note and converts the note to cash at a bank before its maturity date. Example 4 illustrates the process and assumes a 365-day year.

Example 4 A three-month noninterest-bearing note for $500 dated March 24 was converted to cash at a bank at which the discount rate is 13% on May 19. Find the discount and proceeds.

Solution

a) Find the number of days from the date that the note was converted to cash to the maturity date.

From Table 1 (p. T–1) we find that the number of days between June 24 (maturity date) and May 19 is 175 − 139, or 36.

b) Find the discount.

Substituting 500 for M, 0.13 for R, and $\frac{36}{365}$ for T, we get

$D = 500 \times 0.13 \times \frac{36}{365}$

$= 6.41.$

The discount is $6.41.

c) Find the proceeds.

Substituting 500 for M and 6.41 for D, we get

$P = 500 − 6.41$
$= 493.59.$

The proceeds are $493.59.

DO EXERCISE 4.

The notes in Examples 3 and 4 are noninterest-bearing notes. Example 5 illustrates the process if the note is interest bearing.

Example 5 A four-month 15% note dated March 28 for $500 was sold to a bank on June 5 where it was discounted at 10%. What were the proceeds of the note?

Solution

a) Find the amount due at maturity.

Substituting 500 for P, 0.15 for R, and $\frac{4}{12}$ for T, we get

$I = P \times R \times T$

$= 500 \times 0.15 \times \frac{4}{12}$

$= 25.$

The amount due at maturity is $525 ($500 + $25).

b) Find the number of days that the bank held the note.

4. A 90-day nointerest-bearing note for $600 dated July 7 was converted to cash at a bank at which the discount rate is 12% on August 12. Find the discount and proceeds.

ANSWER ON PAGE A–14

250 LOANS AND ANNUITIES

5. A three-month 12% note dated August 7 for $700 was sold to a bank on October 4 where it was discounted at 10%. What were the proceeds of the note?

From Table 1 (p. T–1) we find that the number of days from July 28 (maturity date) to June 5 is 209 − 156, or 53.

c) Find the discount.

Substituting 525 for M, 0.10 for R, and $\frac{53}{365}$ for T, we get

$$D = 525 \times 0.10 \times \frac{53}{365}$$

$$= 7.62.$$

d) Find the proceeds.

We substitute 525 for M and 7.62 for D and get

$$P = 525 - 7.62$$
$$= 517.38.$$

The proceeds are $517.38.

DO EXERCISE 5.

The individual in the advertisement to the left needs $5000. If this money is borrowed under the discount method, then more than $5000 must be borrowed.

> The
> Amount borrowed = $\dfrac{\text{Amount needed}}{1 - (\text{Rate} \times \text{Time})}$

Personals

Would like to borrow $5000 on secured loan above bank interest rates, have credit references. If interested, call to set up appointment.

Example 6 The individual described in the advertisement wants $5000. How much must be borrowed at 11% discount if the loan is to be repaid in nine months?

Solution Substituting 5000 for the Amount Needed, 0.11 for the Rate, and $\frac{9}{12}$ for the Time, in

$$\text{Amount borrowed} = \frac{\text{Amount needed}}{1 - (\text{Rate} \times \text{Time})}$$

we get

$$\text{Amount borrowed} = \frac{5000}{1 - \left(0.11 \times \dfrac{9}{12}\right)}$$

$$= 5449.59.$$

Thus, $5449.59 must be borrowed.

DO EXERCISE 6.

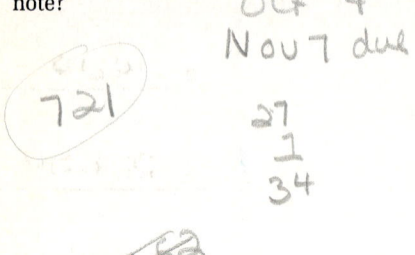

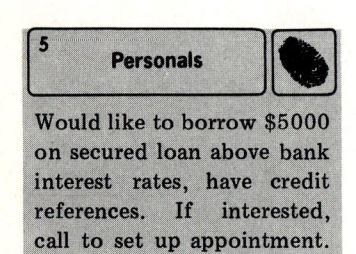

6. A customer needs $7500. How much must be borrowed at 13% discount if the loan is to be repaid in seven months? Round divisor to three decimal places before dividing.

EXERCISE SET 6.1

● **Solve.**

1. Find the interest due at the end of eight months on an 11% note for $450.

2. Find the interest due at the end of three months on a 10% note for $568.

3. Find the interest due at the end of two years on a 13% note for $825.

4. Find the interest due at the end of two years on a 14% note for $780.

5. Find the interest due at the end of three years on a 12% note for $1500.

6. Find the interest due at the end of seven months on a 15% note for $2000.

●● **Solve.**

7. Find the due date on a 90-day noninterest-bearing note dated July 5.

8. Find the due date on a 90-day noninterest-bearing note dated May 2.

9. Find the due date on a 190-day noninterest-bearing note dated August 4.

10. Find the due date on a 270-day noninterest-bearing note dated June 3.

11. Find the due date on a 180-day noninterest-bearing note dated June 2.

12. Find the due date on a 100-day noninterest-bearing note dated March 1.

●●● **Find the discount and proceeds.**

13. A $3500 two-year note with discount rate 11%

14. An $8700 three-year note with discount rate 12%

15. A $450 note for 120 days with discount rate 10% (assume a 360-day year)

16. A $1400 note for 150 days with discount rate 13% (assume a 360-day year)

17. A four-month note dated April 7 for $750 that was converted to cash at a discount rate of 9% on May 15 (assume a 365-day year)

ANSWERS

1. 33
2. 14.20
3. 214.50
4. 218.40
5. 540
6. 175
7. Oct 3
8. July 31
9. Feb 10
10. Feb 28
11. Nov 29
12. June 9
13. 770, 2730
14. 3132, 5568
15. 15, 435
16. 75.83, 1324.17
17. 15.53, 743.47

252 LOANS AND ANNUITIES

ANSWERS

18. 19.38, 830.62

19. 4.40, 888.10

20. 31.31, 1498.44

21. 4545.45

22. 3977.27

23. 4736.84

24. 1973.68

25. 2577.32

26. 4375

27. 6463.29

28. 5615.14

29. 40.41

30. 208.28

31. 756 / 143.65

32. 4656.32 / 4668.20

33. 4803.36

34. 6594.94

---

18. A six-month note dated June 3 for $850 that was converted to cash at a discount rate of 8% on August 21 (assume a 365-day year)

19. A three-month 8% note dated May 5 for $875 and converted to cash on July 6 at a discount rate of 6% (assume a 365-day year)

20. A six-month 11% note dated August 14 for $1450 and converted to cash on November 23 at a discount rate of 9% (assume a 365-day year)

Find the amount borrowed at 12% discount if:

21. $4000 is needed for one year.

22. $3500 is needed for one year.

23. $3600 is needed for two years.

24. $1500 is needed for two years.

25. $2500 is needed for 90 days (assume a 360-day year).

26. $4200 is needed for 120 days (assume a 360-day year).

27. $6250 is needed for 100 days (assume a 365-day year). Round divisor to three decimal places before dividing.

28. $5340 is needed for 150 days (assume a 365-day year). Round divisor to three decimal places before dividing.

---

29. Find the interest due on a $648.75 note at the end of 195 days if the rate is $11\frac{1}{2}$%. (Assume a 360-day year.)

30. Find the interest due on a $4562.45 note at the end of 155 days if the rate is $10\frac{3}{4}$%. (Assume a 365-day year.)

Find the discount and proceeds.

31. A five-month $15\frac{1}{2}$% note dated May 28 for $768.67 and converted to cash on August 24 at a discount rate of $12\frac{1}{4}$% (assume a 360-day year)

32. A seven-month 11.75% note dated May 14 for $4503.25 and converted to cash on September 11 at a discount rate of 11.35% (assume a 365-day year)

33. How much must be borrowed at $13\frac{1}{4}$% discount if $4568 is needed for 132 days? (Assume a 360-day year.) Round divisor to three decimal places before dividing.

34. How much must be borrowed at $12\frac{3}{4}$% discount if $6285 is needed for 135 days? (Assume a 365-day year.)

6.2 THE UNITED STATES RULE

◆ APPLYING THE UNITED STATES RULE

A borrower will often make several payments on a note before it is due. *The United States Rule* is one method used to apply partial payments toward the principal of a note. It is the method accepted in most states. Lending institutions may use either a 365- or 360-day year. Examples 1 and 2 illustrate the process, on the basis of a 360-day year.

Example 1 A customer borrowed $2500 on February 2, 1985, for two years at 12%. The following payments were made: $450 on August 15, 1985; $675 on March 5, 1986; and $900 on October 12, 1986. How much was due on February 2, 1987? How much was the total interest?

Solution Steps (a) through (d) show how the first payment was applied toward paying off the loan.

a) Find the number of days from February 2 to August 15, 1985.

From Table 1 (p. T–1) we find there were 194 days.

b) Find the interest due on August 15, 1985.

Substituting 2500 for P, 0.12 for R, and $\frac{194}{360}$ for T, we get

$I = P \times R \times T$

$= 2500 \times 0.12 \times \frac{194}{360}$

$= 161.67.$

c) Find the principal payment.

Principal payment = Payment − Interest
$= 450 - 161.67$
$= 288.33$

d) New balance = Old balance − Principal payment
$= 2500 - 288.33$
$= 2211.67$

Steps (e) through (h) show how the second payment was applied toward paying off the loan.

e) Find the number of days from August 15, 1985, to March 5, 1986.

From Table 1 (p. T–1), we find there were 202 days (March 5 = 64 + 365 = 429, and August 15 = 227; and 429 − 227 = 202 days).

f) Find the interest due on March 5, 1986.

Substituting 2211.67 for P, 0.12 for R, and $\frac{202}{360}$ for T, we get

$I = P \times R \times T$

$= 2211.67 \times 0.12 \times \frac{202}{360}$

$= 148.92.$

OBJECTIVES

After finishing Section 6.2, you should be able to:

◆ Use the United States Rule to apply partial payments to a note.

1. A customer borrowed $2000 on March 5, 1983, for one year at 11%. Payments of $350 on July 17, $560 on October 25, and $450 on January 3 were made. How much was due on March 5, 1984 (1984 was a leap year, assume a 360-day year)?

g) Find the principal payment.

Principal payment = Payment − Interest
= 675 − 148.92
= 526.08

h) Find the new balance.

New balance = Old balance − Principal payment
= 2211.67 − 526.08
= 1685.59

The procedure for the third and fourth payments is similar. Remember that for the third payment the principal is $1685.59, and for the fourth payment it is $909.76. The following table summarizes the results.

Payment Number	Payment Date	Amount	Days	Interest to Payment Date	Principal Payment	Balance Owed After Payment
	February 2, 1985					$2500.00
1	August 15, 1985	$450.00	194	$161.67	$288.33	$2211.67
2	March 5, 1986	$675.00	202	$148.92	$526.08	$1685.59
3	October 12, 1986	$900.00	221	$124.17	$775.83	$ 909.76
4	February 2, 1987	$944.03	113	$ 34.27	$909.76	0

The amount due on February 2, 1987, was

$909.76 + $34.27   or $944.03.

The total interest was $161.67 + $148.92 + $124.17 + 34.27 or $469.03.

DO EXERCISE 1.

Example 2 shows the process when some payments are smaller than the interest due. When this is the case, the payment is held until future payments added to it are greater than the interest due. To illustrate, in Example 2, the second payment (for $200) is smaller than the interest due ($308.25). Consequently, the principal payment of $674.19 ($200 + $900 − $308.25 − $117.56) is not made until the time of the next payment.

Example 2 You borrow $3000 on May 11, 1984, for two years at 12%. The following payments are to be made: $400 on November, 1984; $200 on October 3, 1985, and $900 on February 7, 1986. How much is due on May 11, 1986?

Solution The computations are similar to those used in Example 1. Steps (a) through (d) show how the first payment is applied to paying off the loan.

6.2 THE UNITED STATES RULE

a) Find the number of days from May 11 to November 4, 1984.

From Table 1 (p. T–1), we find that there are 177 days.

b) Find the interest due on November 4, 1984.

Substituting 3000 for P, 0.12 for R, and $\frac{177}{360}$ for T, we get

$I = P \times R \times T$

$ = 3000 \times 0.12 \times \frac{177}{360}$

$ = 177.$

c) Find the principal payment.

Principal payment = Payment − Interest
$ = 400 - 177$
$ = 223$

d) Find the new balance

New balance = Old balance − Principal payment
$ = 3000 - 223$
$ = 2777$

A similar procedure is used to show how payments 2, 3, and 4 are applied toward paying off the loan.

The following table summarizes the results.

Payment Number	Payment Date	Amount	Days	Interest to Payment Date	Principal Payment	Balance Owed After Payment
	May 11, 1984					$3000.00
1	November 4, 1984	$ 400.00	177	$177.00	$ 223.00	$2777.00
2	October 3, 1985	$ 200.00	333	$308.25	0	$2777.00
3	February 7, 1986	$ 900.00	127	$117.56	$ 674.19	$2102.81
4	May 11, 1986	$2168.00	93	$ 65.19	$2102.81	0

The amount due on May 11, 1986, is

$2102.81 + $65.19, or $2168.00.

DO EXERCISE 2.

The following example is based on a 365-day year.

Example 3 A student borrowed $3200 on April 15, 1984, for two years at 15%. The following payments were made: $500 on July 2, 1984; $300 on December 14, 1984; and $200 on March 23, 1985. How much was due on April 15, 1986?

2. A customer borrows $2800 on March 1, 1984, for two years at 14%. The following payments were made: $100 on November 5, 1984; $700 on January 2, 1985; and $1500 on September 29, 1985. How much is due on March 1, 1986 (assume a 360-day year)?

ANSWER ON PAGE A–14

LOANS AND ANNUITIES

3. A customer borrowed $4500 on January 12, 1985, for two years at 13%. The following payments were made: $800 on March 15, 1985; $1000 on October 1, 1985; and $1800 on April 2, 1986. How much was due on January 12, 1987 (assume a 365-day year)?

Solution The table below shows how each payment was applied to paying off the loan.

Payment Number	Payment Date	Amount	Days	Interest to Payment Date	Principal Payment	Balance Owed After Payment
	April 15, 1984					$3200.00
1	July 2, 1984	$ 500.00	78	$102.58	$ 397.42	$2802.58
2	December 14, 1984	$ 300.00	165	$190.04	$ 109.96	$2692.62
3	March 23, 1985	$ 200.00	99	$109.55	$ 90.45	$2602.17
4	April 15, 1986	$3017.09	388	$414.92	$2602.17	0

The amount due on April 15, 1986, was

$2602.17 + $414.92   or $3017.09.

DO EXERCISE 3.

ANSWER ON PAGE A–14

EXERCISE SET 6.2

● Use the United States Rule when applying partial payments.

Complete the table for a $4000 one-year loan made May 1, 1984, at 11% (assume a 360-day year).

	Payment Number	Payment Date	Amount	Days	Interest to Payment Date	Principal Payment	Balance Owed After Payment
		May 1, 1984					$4000.00
1.	1	August 2, 1984	$ 300.00	93	113.67	186.33	3813.67
2.	2	November 30, 1984	$ 500.00	120	139.83	360.17	3453.50
3.	3	February 4, 1985	$2000.00	66	69.65	1930.35	1523.15
4.	4	May 1, 1985	1563.18	86	40.02	1523.15	

Complete the table for a $5000 two-year loan made July 2, 1984, at 14% (assume a 360-day year).

	Payment Number	Payment Date	Amount	Days	Interest to Payment Date	Principal Payment	Balance Owed After Payment
		July 2, 1984					$5000.00
5.	1	December 1, 1984	$450.00	152	295.56	154.44	4845.56
6.	2	October 5, 1985	$240.00	308	580.39	0	4845.56
7.	3	January 12, 1986	$960.00	99	186.55	433.06	4412.50
8.	4	July 2, 1986	4705.93	171	293.43	4412.50	

9. A consumer borrows $4500 on March 5, 1984, for one year at 15%. The following payments are made: $600 on October 13; $1500 on February 3, 1985; and $700 on February 26, 1985. How much is due on March 5, 1985 (assume a 360-day year)?

10. A consumer borrows $3200 on April 11, 1984, for one year at 11%. The following payments are made: $1000 on July 5; $950 on November 3; and $700 on February 12, 1985. How much is due on April 11, 1985 (assume a 360-day year)?

11. Jan Seitz borrows $5000 on March 1, 1985, for two years at 14%. The following payments are made: $600 on June 2, 1985; $350 on February 7, 1986; and $1500 on October 13, 1986. How much is due on March 1, 1987 (assume a 360-day year)?

12. Sam Shaw borrows $6000 on June 3, 1984, for two years at 15%. The following payments are made: $700 on October 3, 1984; $200 on April 7, 1985; and $2500 on February 1, 1986. How much is due on June 3, 1986 (assume a 360-day year)?

258

LOANS AND ANNUITIES

Complete the table for a $4000 one-year loan made May 1, 1984, at 11% (assume a 365-day year).

	Payment Number	Payment Date	Amount	Days	Interest to Payment Date	Principal Payment	Balance Owed After Payment
		May 1, 1984					$4000.00
13.	1	August 2, 1984	$100.00				
14.	2	November 30, 1984	$700.00				
15.	3	February 4, 1985	$ 50.00				
16.	4	May 1, 1985					

17. A customer borrowed $7000 on May 2, 1985, for one year at 13%. The following payments were made: $1450 on August 17, 1985, and $2700 on February 5, 1986. How much was due on May 2, 1986 (assume a 365-day year)?

18. A customer borrowed $5700 on June 8, 1984, for one year at 16%. The following payments were made: $2000 on October 5, 1984, and $3000 on March 29, 1985. How much was due on June 8, 1985 (assume a 365-day year)?

19. Upon graduation on May 31, 1985, a student borrowed $9000 for two years at 11%. The following payments were made: $400 on December 5, 1985, and $6000 on August 1, 1986. How much was due on May 31, 1987 (assume a 365-day year)?

20. A small business borrowed $7500 on July 7, 1985, for two years at 12%. The following payments were made: $300 on February 10, 1986, and $5000 on May 3, 1987. How much was due on July 7, 1987 (assume a 365-day year)?

Complete the table for an $11\frac{1}{2}$% $3200 loan taken out June 2, 1984, for two years (assume a 365-day year.

	Payment Number	Payment Date	Amount	Days	Interest to Payment Date	Principal Payment	Balance Owed After Payment
		June 2, 1984					$3200.00
21.	1	September 5, 1984	$ 450.00				
22.	2	January 1, 1985	$ 300.00				
23.	3	February 2, 1986	$2000.00				
24.	4	June 2, 1986					

6.3 THE MERCHANT'S RULE

● APPLYING THE MERCHANT'S RULE

Lenders sometimes apply partial payments on a note using the *Merchant's Rule*. The process involves:

1. Calculating interest and adding it to the amount borrowed, and
2. Finding interest on each payment from the payment date to the note due date. Then the sum of interest and payment is subtracted from the balance due.

Example 1 illustrates this process based on a 360-day year. The same example was used to illustrate how partial payments are applied using the United States Rule.

Example 1 A customer borrowed $2500 on February 2, 1985, for two years at 12%. The following payments were made: $450 on August 15, 1985; $675 on March 5, 1986; and $900 on October 12, 1986. How much was due on February 2, 1987? What was the total interest paid?

Solution

a) Find the interest on the amount borrowed.

Substituting 2500 for P, 0.12 for R, and 2 for T, we get

$I = P \times R \times T$
$ = 2500 \times 0.12 \times 2$
$ = 600.$

The interest is $600.00.

b) Add the interest to the amount borrowed.

Total amount = Interest + Amount borrowed
$ = \$600 + \$2500$
$ = \$3100$

c) Find the number of days from August 15, 1985, to February 2, 1987.

Using the methods discussed in Section 4.2, we find that the number of days was 536.

d) Find the interest on the first payment from the payment date to the note due date.

$I = P \times R \times T$
$ = 450 \times 0.12 \times \dfrac{536}{360}$
$ = 80.40$

e) Add payment and interest.

Payment + Interest = 450 + 80.40
$ = 530.40$

f) Find the new balance.

New Balance = Total amount − (Payment + Interest)
$ = 3100 - 530.40$
$ = 2569.60$

OBJECTIVE

After finishing Section 6.3, you should be able to:

● Use the Merchant's Rule to apply partial payments to a note.

LOANS AND ANNUITIES

1. A customer borrowed $2000 on March 5, 1983, for one year at 11%. The following payments were made: $350 on July 17; $560 on October 25; and $450 on January 3, 1984. How much was due on March 5, 1984 (assume a 360-day year and remember 1984 was a leap year)?

Similarly, steps (g) through (j) illustrate how the second payment was applied toward paying off the loan.

g) Find the number of days from March 5, 1986, to February 2, 1987.

Using the methods discussed in Section 5.2, we find that the number of days is 334.

h) Find the interest on the second payment from the payment date to the note due date.

$$I = P \times R \times T$$

$$= 675 \times 0.12 \times \frac{334}{360}$$

$$= 75.15$$

i) Add payment and interest.

Payment + Interest = 675 + 75.15

= 750.15

j) Find the new balance.

New balance = 2569.60 − 750.15

= 1819.45

The table below shows similar information for all payments.

Payment Number	Payment Date	Amount	Days to Due Date	Interest on Payment to Due Date	Payment + Interest	New Balance
	February 2, 1985					$3100.00
1	August 15, 1985	$450.00	536	$80.40	$530.40	$2569.60
2	March 5, 1986	$675.00	334	$75.15	$750.15	$1819.45
3	October 12, 1986	$900.00	113	$33.90	$933.90	$ 885.55
4	February 2, 1987	$885.55				0

The amount due on February 2, 1987, is $885.55.

The total interest = $600 − ($80.40 + $75.15 + $33.90)

= $410.55

Note that the final payment ($885.55) and the total interest paid ($410.55) using the Merchant's Rule is less than the final payment ($944.03) and the total interest paid ($469.03) using the United States Rule. Using the Merchant's Rule results in lower interest and a smaller final payment than using the United States Rule.

DO EXERCISE 1.

ANSWER ON PAGE A–14

Example 2 shows how payments are applied using a 365-day year.

Example 2 A customer borrowed $3200 on April 15, 1984, for two years at 15%. The following payments were made: $500 on July 2, 1984; $300 on December 14, 1984; and $200 on March 23, 1985. How much was due on April 15, 1986?

Solution The table shows how each payment was applied to the principal.

Payment Number	Payment Date	Amount	Days to Due Date	Interest on Payment to Due Date	Payment + Interest	New Balance
	April 15, 1984					$4160.00
1	July 2, 1984	$ 500.00	652	$133.97	$633.97	$3526.03
2	December 14, 1984	$ 300.00	487	$ 60.04	$360.04	$3165.99
3	March 23, 1985	$ 200.00	388	$ 31.89	$231.89	$2934.10
4	April 15, 1986	$2934.10				0

The amount due on April 15, 1986 was $2934.10.

DO EXERCISE 2.

2. A customer borrowed $4500 on January 12, 1985 for two years at 13%. The following payments were made: $800 on March 15, 1985; $1000 on October 1, 1985; and $1800 on April 2, 1986. How much was due on January 12, 1987 (assume a 365-day year)?

ANSWER ON PAGE A–14

EXERCISE SET 6.3

■ Use the Merchant's Rule when applying partial payments.

Complete the table for a $4000 11% loan made May 1, 1984, payable over one year (assume a 360-day year).

	Payment Number	Payment Date	Amount	Days to Due Date	Interest on Payment to Due Date	Payment + Interest	New Balance
1.		May 1, 1984					4440
2.	1	August 2, 1984	$ 300.00	272	24.93	324.93	4115.07
3.	2	November 30, 1984	$ 500.00	152	23.22	523.22	3591.85
4.	3	February 4, 1985	$2000.00	86	52.55	2052.55	1539.30
5.	4	May 1, 1985	1539.30				

Complete the table for a $5000 two-year loan made July 2, 1984, at 14% (assume a 365-day year).

	Payment Number	Payment Date	Amount	Days to Due Date	Interest on Payment to Due Date	Payment + Interest	New Balance
6.		July 2, 1984					6400
7.	1	December 1, 1984	$450.00	578	99.76	549.76	5860.24
8.	2	October 5, 1985	$240.00	270	24.85	264.85	5585.38
9.	3	January 12, 1986	$960.00	171	62.96	1022.97	4562.41
10.	4	July 2, 1986	4562.41				

11. A consumer borrows $4500 on March 5, 1984, for one year at 15%. The following payments are made: $600 on October 13; $1500 on February 3, 1985; and $700 on February 26, 1985. How much is due on March 5, 1985? (Assume a 360-day year.)

11. _____

12. A consumer borrows $3200 on April 11, 1984, for one year at 11%. The following payments are made: $1000 on July 5; $950 on November 3; and $700 on February 12, 1985. How much is due on April 11, 1985? (Assume a 360-day year.)

12. _____

264 LOANS AND ANNUITIES

Complete the table for a $4000 11% loan made May 1, 1984, payable over one year (assume a 365-day year).

Payment Number	Payment Date	Amount	Days to Due Date	Interest on Payment to Due Date	Payment + Interest	New Balance
13.	May 1, 1984					4440
14. 1	August 2, 1984	$100.00	272	8.20	108.20	4331.80
15. 2	November 30, 1984	$700.00	152	32.07	732.07	3599.73
16. 3	February 4, 1985	$ 50.00	86	1.30	51.30	3548.43
17. 4	May 1, 1985	3548.43				

18. A customer borrowed $7000 on May 2, 1985, for one year at 13%. The following payments were made: $1450 on August 17, 1985, and $2700 on February 5, 1986. How much was due on May 2, 1986 (assume a 365-day year)?

19. A customer borrowed $5700 on June 8, 1984, for one year at 16%. The following payments were made: $2000 on October 5, 1984, and $3000 on March 29, 1985. How much was due on June 8, 1985 (assume a 365-day year)?

20. Upon graduation on May 31, 1985, a student borrowed $9000 for two years at 11%. The following payments were made: $400 on December 5, 1985, and $6000 on August 1, 1986. How much was due on May 31, 1987 (assume a 365-day year)?

21. A small business borrowed $7500 on July 7, 1985, for two years at 12%. The following payments were made: $300 on February 10, 1986, and $5000 on May 3, 1987. How much was due on July 7, 1987 (assume a 365-day year)?

Complete the table for an $11\frac{1}{2}$% $3200 loan taken out June 2, 1984, for two years (assume a 365-day year).

Payment Number	Payment Date	Amount	Days to Due Date	Interest on Payment to Due Date	Payment + Interest	New Balance
22.	June 2, 1984					3936
23. 1	September 5, 1984	$ 450.00	635	90.03	540.03	3395.97
24. 2	January 1, 1985	$ 300.00	518	48.96	348.96	3047.01
25. 3	February 2, 1986	$2000.00	120	75.62	2075.62	971.39
26. 4	June 2, 1986	971.39				

6.4 ANNUITIES

Equal payments over time are *annuities*. Examples include equal deposits into savings over a period of time or periodic payments from an insurance company after retirement.

ORDINARY ANNUITIES

An annuity in which payments are made at the end of a time period is an *ordinary annuity*. The following figure shows an ordinary annuity situation where $1.00 is deposited at the end of each of three years in an account paying 12% interest compounded annually. The solid line represents the interest earning period.

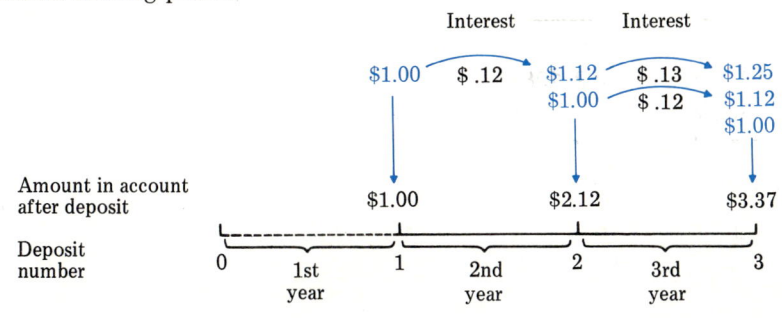

	Interest		Interest	
	$1.00 → $.12 →	$1.12	$.13 →	$1.25
		$1.00 →	$.12 →	$1.12
				$1.00

Amount in account after deposit: $1.00, $2.12, $3.37

Deposit number: 0 — 1st year — 1 — 2nd year — 2 — 3rd year — 3

Note that after three yearly $1.00 deposits earning 12% compounded annually the total amount in the account is $3.37. The first $1.00 deposit earns $0.25 interest in two years, the second $1.00 deposit earns $0.12 in one year and the third $1.00 deposit earns no interest although it is included in the total amount.

An ordinary annuity table may also be used to find how much will be in the account after three payments. Part of the ordinary annuity table (Table 10, p. T–11) appears below.

$S_{\overline{n}|i}$
Amount of Annuity

n	Rate 11%	Rate 12%
1	1.00000000	1.00000000
2	2.11000000	2.12000000
3	3.34210000	3.37440000
4	4.70973100	4.77932800
5	6.22780141	6.35284736
6	7.91285957	8.11518904
7	9.78327412	10.08901173
8	11.85943427	12.29969314
9	14.16397204	14.77565631
10	16.72200896	17.54873507
11	19.56142995	20.65458328
12	22.71318724	24.13313327

$S_{\overline{n}|i}$ is the amount accumulated after n $1.00 payments at $i\%$ interest for each payment period. In this problem we want to find $S_{\overline{3}|12}$.

OBJECTIVES

After finishing Section 6.4, you should be able to:

- Find the accumulated amount in an ordinary annuity.
- Find the accumulated amount in an annuity due.

LOANS AND ANNUITIES

Find the amount accumulated after n $1.00 payments at 12% interest for each payment period. The n value is

1. 5   *6.35*

2. 6   *8.12*

3. 9   *14.78*

4. You deposit $700 at the end of every three months into your credit union account which pays 11% compounded quarterly. How much is in your account after the 50th payment?

73,368.19

ANSWERS ON PAGE A–14

Read down the n column to 3 and across that row to the 12% column. The answer is $3.37 (rounded) as before.

DO EXERCISES 1–3.

For regular deposits of $P the total accumulation A is

$$A = P \times S_{\overline{n}|i}$$

Example 1 At the end of every quarter you deposit $500 into your credit union account, which pays 12% compounded quarterly. How much is in your account after the 40th payment?

Solution We find $S_{\overline{40}|3}$.   3% = 12% ÷ 4

Read down the n column of Table 10 (p. T–11) to 40 and across that row to the 3% column.

$$S_{\overline{40}|3} = 75.40125973$$

We substitute $500 for P and 75.40125973 for $S_{\overline{40}|3}$ in

$$A = P \times S_{\overline{40}|3}$$
$$= \$500 \times 75.40125973$$
$$= \$37{,}700.63.$$

The accumulated amount is $37,700.63.

DO EXERCISE 4.

⚀ ANNUITIES DUE

An annuity in which payments are made at the beginning of a time period is an *annuity due*. The following figure shows an annuity due situation where $1.00 is deposited at the beginning of each of three years in an account paying 12% interest compounded annually. The solid line represents the interest earning period.

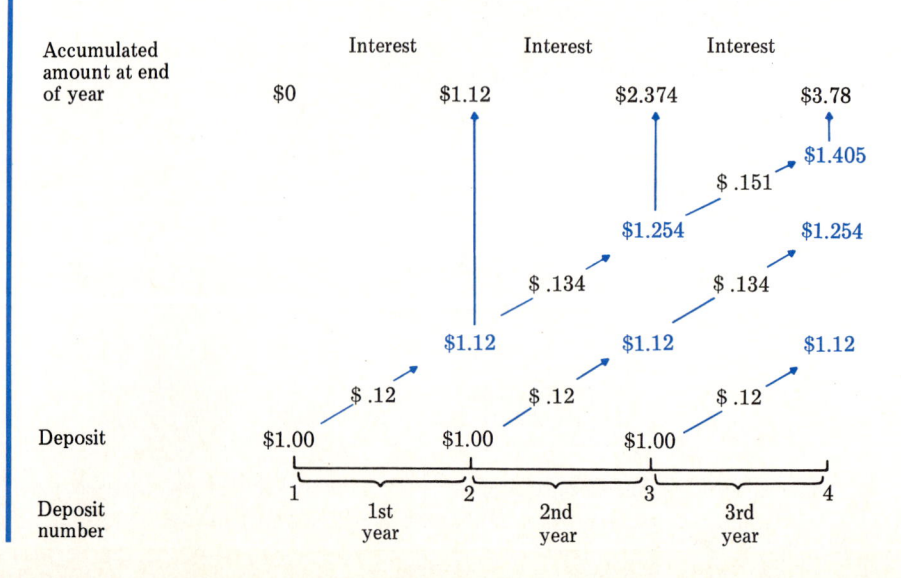

Accumulated amount at end of year	$0	Interest → $1.12	Interest → $2.374	Interest → $3.78
				$1.405
			$.151	
		$1.254	$1.254	
		$.134	$.134	
	$1.12	$1.12	$1.12	
	$.12	$.12	$.12	
Deposit	$1.00	$1.00	$1.00	
Deposit number	1 1st year	2 2nd year	3 3rd year	4

6.4 ANNUITIES

Note that at the end of the year in which the third $1.00 deposit was made the accumulated amount was $3.78. The first $1.00 deposit grows to $1.12 after one year, $1.254 after two years, and $1.405 after three years. Similarly the other two $1.00 deposits grow to $1.254 and $1.12. The total amount does not include any deposit made at the beginning of the fourth year.

Even though this is an annuity due situation an ordinary annuity table (Table 10, p. T–11) may be used to find the accumulated amount at the end of the third year. To do this:

We add 1 to n.

n is 3 so n + 1 is 4

We find $S_{\overline{4}|12}$.

$S_{\overline{4}|12} = 4.77932800$

We subtract 1 and round.

4.77932800 − 1 = 3.78

The answer is $3.78 (rounded) as before.

Notice 4.77932800 is the accumulated amount immediately after the fourth deposit. When we subtract 1 (the fourth deposit) we get the amount immediately before the fourth deposit, that is, the amount at the end of three years.

DO EXERCISES 5–7.

For regular deposits of $P in an annuity due situation the total accumulation A is

$$A = P \times (S_{\overline{n+1}|i} - 1)$$

Example 2 You deposit $500 at the beginning of every quarter into your credit union account which pays 12% compounded quarterly. How much is is in your account at the end of the 40th quarter, that is, immediately before the 41st payment?

Solution We add 1 to n.

n is 40 so n + 1 is 41

We find $S_{\overline{41}|3}$, 3% = 12% ÷ 4   Use Table 10, p. T–11.

$S_{\overline{41}|3} = 78.66329753$

We subtract 1 and round.

78.66329753 − 1 = 77.6633

We find A by substituting $500 for P and 77.6633 for $(S_{\overline{n+1}|i} - 1)$ in

$A = P \times (S_{\overline{n+1}|i} - 1)$
$ = \$500 \times 77.6633$
$ = \$38{,}831.65.$

The accumulated amount is $38,831.65.

DO EXERCISE 8.

Find the accumulated amount at the end of the nth year where $1.00 deposits are made at the beginning of each year in an account paying 12% compounded yearly. The n value is

5. 5

6. 6

7. 9

8. You deposit $700 at the beginning of every quarter into your credit union account, which pays 11% compounded quarterly. How much is in your account at the end of the 30th quarter?

ANSWERS ON PAGE A–14

SOMETHING EXTRA—ERROR PATTERNS

1. Find the error.

You deposit $2000 at the beginning of each of 25 successive years into a retirement account which pays 12% compounded annually. How much is the accumulated amount at the end of the 25th year?

Solution We find $S_{\overline{25}|12}$.

$$S_{\overline{25}|12} = 133.33387006$$

We subtract 1 and round.

$$133.33387006 - 1 = 132.3339$$

We find A by substituting $2000 for P and 132.3339 for $S_{\overline{n+1}|i} - 1$ in

$$A = P \times (S_{\overline{n+1}|i} - 1)$$
$$= \$2000 \times 132.3339$$
$$= \$264{,}667.80.$$

The accumulated amount is $264,667.80.

2. Find the error.

You deposit $400 at the end of each quarter in your credit union account, which pays 12% compounded quarterly. How much is in your account immediately after the 20th payment?

Solution We find $S_{\overline{20}|12}$.

$$S_{\overline{20}|12} = 72.05244244$$

We substitute $400 for P and 72.05244244 for $S_{\overline{20}|12}$ in

$$A = P \times S_{\overline{20}|12}$$
$$= \$400 \times 72.05244244$$
$$= \$28{,}820.98.$$

The accumulated amount is $28,820.98.

EXERCISE SET 6.4

NAME _____ For monday   CLASS _____   ANSWERS

Use Table 10 (p. T–11) for this exercise set.

● Find the accumulated amount immediately after the last payment. Assume each payment occurs at the end of a period.

	Amount of Each Payment	Payment and Compounding Period	Rate	Number of Payments
1.	$1.00	annually	14%	10
2.	$1.00	annually	14%	25
3.	$100	semiannually	14%	20
4.	$100	semiannually	14%	50
5.	$200	annually	14%	10
6.	$200	annually	14%	25
7.	$50	monthly	12%	48
8.	$50	monthly	15%	48
9.	$125	monthly	12%	30
10.	$125	monthly	15%	30
11.	$150	quarterly	11%	28
12.	$150	quarterly	12%	28
13.	$400	quarterly	11%	40
14.	$400	quarterly	12%	40

15. You deposit $300 at the end of every quarter into your savings account, which pays 11% compounded quarterly. How much is in your account after the 36th payment?

16. You deposit $500 at the end of every quarter into your savings account, which pays 12% compounded quarterly. How much is in your account after the 16th payment?

Answers:
1. 19.337
2. 181.871
3. 4099.549
4. 40652.893
5. 18204.985
6. 36374.164
7. 3061.130
8. 3261.419
9. 4187.862
10. 4516.134
11. 6204.146
12. 6439.638
13. 28507.258
14. 30160.50
15. 18059.973
16. 10078.441

270

LOANS AND ANNUITIES

ANSWERS

17. 7346.71

18. 4312.70

19. 4386.52

20. 21360.96

21. 4408.90

22. 20753.68

23. 4391.59

24. 4572.59

25. 6374.76

26. 6632.83

27. 29291.21

28. 31065.32

29. 49618.74

30. 90965.74

17. Your parents loan you $120 at the end of each of the 48 months you attend college. The interest rate is 12% compounded monthly. How much do you owe them immediately after the 48th payment?

18. Your parents loan you $75 at the end of each of the 48 months you attend college. The interest rate is 9% compounded monthly. How much do you owe them immediately after the 48th payment?

●● Find the accumulated amount at the end of the last payment period. Assume each payment occurs at the beginning of the period.

	Amount of Each Payment	Payment and Compounding Period	Rate	Number of Payments
19.	$100	semiannually	14%	20
20.	$100	semiannually	14%	40
21.	$200	annually	14%	10
22.	$200	annually	14%	20
23.	$125	monthly	12%	30
24.	$125	monthly	15%	30
25.	$150	quarterly	11%	28
26.	$150	quarterly	12%	28
27.	$400	quarterly	11%	40
28.	$400	quarterly	12%	40

29. You deposit $1200 at the beginning of every six months in your savings account, which pays 13% compounded semiannually. How much is in your account at the end of 10 years?

30. You deposit $900 at the beginning of every six months in your savings account, which pays 14% compounded semiannually. How much is in your account at the end of 15 years?

6.5 INDIVIDUAL RETIREMENT ACCOUNTS AND KEOGH PLANS

Many individuals regularly invest some of their current income on a tax deferred basis in *Individual Retirement Accounts* and *Keogh Plans*. Because taxes are not paid on this money, such plans exemplify what are called *tax shelters*. The tax is due when this money and the earnings from it are paid (usually during retirement).

● INDIVIDUAL RETIREMENT ACCOUNTS

An Individual Retirement Account (IRA) is an example of an annuity. A deposit made into an IRA may be deducted from gross income, thereby reducing current federal income tax. For example, a $2000 IRA deposit will decrease current federal income taxes $800 for those in the 40% tax bracket. (40% of $2000 is $800).

DO EXERCISES 1-3.

In effect no current federal income taxes are paid on IRA deposits (nor the income earned on the deposits) until the money is withdrawn after age $59\frac{1}{2}$. Then the money is taxed at ordinary income tax rates. If money is withdrawn prior to age $59\frac{1}{2}$ the total amount withdrawn is taxed in the year in which it is received and there is also a 10% penalty. For example, if you withdraw $20,000 from your IRA account at age 50 and are in the 40% tax bracket you pay the federal government

$8000	Tax (40% of $20,000)
$2000	Penalty (10% of $20,000)
$10,000	Total paid to the federal government.

DO EXERCISES 4-6.

OBJECTIVES

After finishing Section 6.5, you should be able to:

■ Find the accumulated amount in an IRA account.

■ ■ Find the accumulated amount in a Keogh account.

Calculate the decrease in federal income tax for a $2000 IRA deposit for those in the

1. 30% tax bracket.

2. 50% tax bracket.

3. 47% tax bracket.

Calculate the total amount paid to the federal government for early withdrawal of $50,000 from an IRA for someone in the

4. 50% tax bracket.

5. 35% tax bracket.

6. 45% tax bracket.

ANSWERS ON PAGE A-14

The Dreyfus IRA is one example of an IRA.

The Dreyfus IRA

IRAs are now for everyone—and Dreyfus does it all for you!

How Dreyfus can help you take full advantage of the new, liberalized tax law provisions on Individual Retirement Accounts:

It is now possible for you to open an IRA of your own, even though you may be covered under tax-qualified plans (including Keogh plans), government plans or certain annuities.

An IRA is a hedge against inflation.

Accumulating money for your future is a serious business. More and more, the responsibility of providing for the future is in your own hands.

The IRA provides a way for you to save in a tax-favored environment. What is equally important is where to invest these dollars for maximum growth and protection from inflation.

The maximum annual IRA contribution has been raised to $2,000. An IRA is tax deductible and its earnings are tax deferred. The tax savings are substantial: $2,000 put into an IRA is completely free of Federal tax. If a husband and wife both work and each contributes $2,000, the joint deduction from taxable income is $4,000.

If your spouse is not employed, a separate IRA may still be opened and between the two plans you may contribute and deduct 100% of income up to $2,250.

The compounding of interest, dividends or gains tax deferred in an IRA plan can really add up. Even if you only put in small amounts now, the amount you can accumulate over time, because of compounding, becomes very significant. For example, if your overall average return is 12%, your money will double in 6 years. If the overall return is higher your money grows even faster. Here's what you would accumulate toward retirement at only 12% after various periods of time, compounded annually:

\$2,000 a year in an IRA Plan Hypothethical 12% Return	
After	Amount in Plan
5 years	$ 14,230
10	39,309
15	83,506
20	161,397
25	298,668
30	540,585
40	1,718,284

Note: If both you and your spouse work, each may open an IRA providing up to $4,000 annual deduction. After 20 years, earning 12%, you and your spouse could have a total nest egg of $322,794.94. And this can be done, even if you or your spouse works part-time.

If you work part-time, you can contribute the $2,000 maximum.

This example is calculated on a fixed interest rate compounded annually and assumes no fluctuation in the value of the principal. While no return is guaranteed, the 12% rate was chosen for illustrative purposes.

Let's see how you may become a millionaire after 40 years by investing in the Dreyfus IRA.

Example 1 How much is the accumulated amount in the Dreyfus IRA at the end of the 40th year if $2000 is invested at the beginning of each year at 12% compounded annually?

6.5 INDIVIDUAL RETIREMENT ACCOUNTS AND KEOGH PLANS

Solution This is an annuity due situation as payments are at the beginning of each year (not clear from the ad).

We add 1 to n.

n is 40 so $n + 1$ is 41

We find $S_{\overline{41}|12}$.

$S_{\overline{41}|12} = 860.14239079$ (Table 10, p. T–11)

We substract 1 and round.

$860.14239079 - 1 = 859.142$

We find A by substituting $2000 for P and 859.142 for $(S_{\overline{(n+1)}|i} - 1)$ in

$A = P \times (S_{\overline{(n+1)}|i} - 1)$
$= \$2000 \times 859.142$
$= \$1,718,284.$

At the end of 40 years your accumulated amount is $1,718,284.

DO EXERCISE 7.

Amounts contributed regularly at the end of a year (ordinary annuity) will result in a smaller accumulated amount. Financial institutions use annuity due situations when advertising IRAs because the results look better.

KEOGH PLAN

Self-employed individuals are eligible to contribute the lesser of $30,000 or 25% of annual earned income on a tax deferred basis into a Keogh Plan for retirement. For example, if your income from self employment is $56,000 then you may contribute $14,000 (25% of $56,000) on a tax deferred basis into a Keogh Plan for retirement.

DO EXERCISES 8–10.

---

7. How much is the accumulated amount in the Dreyfus IRA at the end of the 30th year if $2000 is invested at the beginning of each year at 12% compounded annually?

State the maximum amount you may contribute annually to your Keogh Plan if you are self employed and have earned income of

8. $80,000

9. $60,000

10. $120,000

ANSWERS ON PAGE A–14

How much will a $12,000 deposit in a Keogh Plan reduce current federal income taxes for a person in the

11. 48% tax bracket?

12. 50% tax bracket?

13. 30% tax bracket?

14. How much is the accumulated amount in a Keogh Plan after the 30th annual end of year payment of $4000 into a 11% compounded annually account?

ANSWERS ON PAGE A–14

LOANS AND ANNUITIES

As with an IRA a deposit in a Keogh Plan may be deducted from gross income, thereby reducing current federal income taxes. For example, a $14,000 Keogh Plan deposit will decrease federal income taxes $5600 for those in the 40% tax bracket (40% of $14,000 is $5600).

DO EXERCISES 11–13.

At retirement, periodic payments from a Keogh Plan are taxed as ordinary income. However, a participant may select a lump-sum withdrawal which is subject to a 10-year income averaging method.

Example 2 How much is the accumulated amount in a Keogh Plan after the 20th annual end-of-year payment of $6000 into a 12% compounded annually account?

Solution This is an ordinary annuity situation as payments are made at the end of the year.

We find $S_{\overline{20}|12}$.

$$S_{\overline{20}|12} = 72.05244244$$

We substitute $6000 for P and 72.05244244 for $S_{\overline{20}|12}$ in

$$A = P \times S_{\overline{20}|12}$$
$$= \$6000 \times 72.05244244$$
$$= \$432{,}314.65.$$

The accumulated amount is $432,314.65.

DO EXERCISE 14.

EXERCISE SET 6.5

Use Table 10 (p. T–11) for these exercises.

● For each find the equity (accumulated amount) immediately before your 65th birthday. Assume deposits are made on the day you reach each age and the interest rate is 12% compounded annually. Round to the nearest dollar.

Chart shows appreciation of funds in an Individual Retirement Account at various ages.

	Age	Amount saved per year	Equity at age 65
1.	55	$2,000	
2.	45	2,000	
3.	35	2,000	
4.	34	2,000	
5.	32	2,000	
6.	30	2,000	
7.	26	2,000	
8.	24	2,000	
9.	22	2,000	
10.	20	2,000	

11. How much is the accumulated amount in an IRA at the end of the 30th year if $1300 is invested at the beginning of each year at 14% compounded annually?

12. How much is the accumulated amount in an IRA at the end of the 25th year if $1400 is invested at the beginning of each year at 14% compounded annually?

13. How much is the accumulated amount in an IRA immediately after the 30th payment if $1300 is invested at the end of each year at 14% compounded annually?

14. How much is the accumulated amount in an IRA immediately after the 25th payment if $1400 is invested at the end of each year at 14% compounded annually?

276 LOANS AND ANNUITIES

ANSWERS

●● Find the accumulated amount in each Keogh Plan immediately after the last payment. Assume equal payments are made at the end of each payment period. Round to the nearest dollar.

	Deposit	Number of Deposits	Payment Period	Rate	Compounding Period
15.	$3000	30	annually	13%	annually
16.	$4500	35	annually	14%	annually
17.	$2200	40	semiannually	13%	semiannually
18.	$1500	44	semiannually	14%	semiannually
19.	$1000	40	quarterly	11%	quarterly
20.	$1800	20	quarterly	12%	quarterly
21.	$350	48	monthly	12%	monthly
22.	$425	36	monthly	15%	monthly

15. _____

16. _____

17. _____

18. _____

19. _____

20. _____

21. _____

22. _____

23. A person deposited $15,000 at the end of each of five successive years into a Keogh Plan paying 14% compounded annually. How much is the accumulated amount immediately after the fifth payment?

23. _____

24. A person deposited $8,000 at the end of each of five successive years into a Keogh Plan paying 13% compounded annually. How much is the accumulated amount immediately after the fifth payment?

24. _____

25. You deposit $500 at the end of each month into a Keogh Plan paying 15% compounded monthly. How much is the accumulated amount immediately after the 36th payment?

25. _____

26. You deposit $200 at the end of each month into a Keogh Plan paying 12% compounded monthly. How much is the accumulated amount immediately after the 36th payment?

26. _____

6.6 PRESENT VALUE OF AN ANNUITY

Suppose we want to know how much we must invest now at 12% compounded annually so that a certain amount will be paid to us for each of the next five years with no money left over after the 5th payment. This is a present value of an annuity problem. The *present value of an annuity* is the sum of the present value of each of the payments. Present value of annuity problems will be studied in this section.

◼ PRESENT VALUE OF AN ORDINARY ANNUITY

The present value of an ordinary annuity situation arises when a certain amount invested now results in equal payments at the end of a series of equal time periods. The following figure shows the present value of an ordinary annuity situation where a certain amount invested now at 12% compounded annually results in $1.00 payments at the end of the first and second years with no money left over after the second payment.

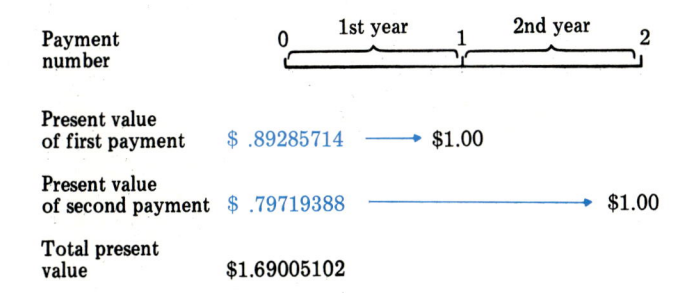

Payment number	0 1st year 1 2nd year 2
Present value of first payment	$ .89285714 ⟶ $1.00
Present value of second payment	$ .79719388 ⟶ $1.00
Total present value	$1.69005102

From the figure we see that

$0.79719388 grows to $1.00 at the end of two years.

This follows when we substitute $1.00 for A, 0.12 for i, and 2 for n in

$$A = P(1 + i)^n \quad \text{Compound Interest Formula}$$

$$\$1.00 = P(1 + 0.12)^2$$

$$\$1.00 = P(1.12)^2$$

$$\$1.00 = P(1.2544)$$

$$.79719388 = P \quad \text{Dividing on both sides by 1.2544}$$

OBJECTIVES

After finishing Section 6.6, you should be able to:

◼ Solve present value of ordinary annuity problems.

◼◼ Solve present value of annuity due problems.

How much must be invested now at 12% compounded annually so that $1.00 withdrawals at the end of each of the next n years are possible? The value of n is

1. 5

2. 7

3. 10

4. You need $3000 at the end of each of the next five years. To do this how much must be invested now at 12% compounded annually?

10,814.33

ANSWERS ON PAGE A–14

LOANS AND ANNUITIES

Likewise $0.89285714 grows to $1.00 at the end of one year. To find the total investment now we add

.79719388
.89285714
1.69005102

An investment of a little over $1.69 now at 12% compounded annually will permit annual payments of $1.00 each for the next two years.

A present value of an ordinary annuity table (Table 11, p. T–13) may also be used to solve this problem. From Table 11 we find values of $A_{n|i}$ where $A_{n|i}$ is the amount which must be invested now at i% per payment period so n $1.00 payments (withdrawals) are possible. In this problem we find $A_{\overline{2}|12}$.

$A_{\overline{2}|12} = 1.69005102$

The answer is $1.69005102 as before.

DO EXERCISES 1–3.

For regular withdrawals of $P the total amount A which must be invested now is

$$A = P \times A_{\overline{n}|i}$$

Example 1 You need $5000 at the end of each of the next four years. To do this how much must be invested now at 12% compounded annually?

Solution We find $A_{\overline{4}|12}$.

$A_{\overline{4}|12} = 3.03734935$

We find A by substituting $5000 for P and 3.03734935 for $A_{\overline{4}|12}$ in

$A = P \times A_{\overline{4}|12}$
$= \$5000 \times 3.03734935$
$= \$15{,}186.75.$

If $15,186.75 is invested now at 12% compounded annually then we may withdraw $5000 for each of the next four years.

DO EXERCISE 4.

PRESENT VALUE OF AN ANNUITY DUE

For present value of an annuity due situations equal withdrawals start immediately and continue at the beginning of each subsequent time period. The following figure shows a present value of an annuity due situation where a certain amount invested now at 12% compounded annually results in $1.00 payments now and at the beginning of each of the next two years with no money left over after the third payment.

Payment number	1	2	3
Present value of first payment	$1.00		
Present value of second payment	$.89285714 ⟶	$1.00	
Present value of third payment	$.79719388 ⟶		$1.00
Total present value	$2.69005102		

An investment now of a little over $2.69 at 12% compounded annually will permit an immediate $1.00 withdrawal as well as $1.00 withdrawals at the beginning of each of the next two years. Even though this is a present value of an annuity due situation, the present value of an ordinary annuity table (Table 11, p. T–13) may be used to solve it. To do this

We subtract 1 from n. n is 3 so $n - 1$ is 2.
We find $A_{\overline{2}|12}$. $A_{\overline{2}|12} = 1.69005102$.
We add 1. $1.69005102 + 1 = 2.69005102$.

The answer is $2.69005102 as before.

DO EXERCISES 5–7.

In present value of annuity due situations where equal withdrawals of $P start immediately, the amount A which must be invested now is

$$A = P \times (A_{\overline{n-1}|i} + 1)$$

How much must be invested now at 12% compounded annually to receive n $1.00 payments starting today? The value of n is

5. 5

6. 7

7. 10

ANSWERS ON PAGE A–14

8. How much must you invest today at 12% compounded monthly to meet your next 12 monthly $230 car payments, the first of which is due now?

Example 2 You will travel overseas for the next year. How much should you now invest at 12% compounded monthly to meet your next twelve $620 monthly house payments where the first payment is due today?

Solution We subtract 1 from n. n is 12 so $n - 1$ is 11.

Find $A_{\overline{11}|i}$ 12% ÷ 12

$A_{\overline{11}|i} = 10.36762825$ Table 11, p. T–13

Add 1 to $A_{\overline{11}|i}$ $10.36762825 + 1 = 11.36762825$

To find A we substitute $620 for P and 11.36762825 for $(A_{\overline{n-1}|i} + 1)$ in

$A = P \times (A_{\overline{n-1}|i} + 1)$
$= \$620 \times 11.36762825$
$= \$7047.93.$

If $7047.93 is invested today your next 12 $620 house payments can be made.

DO EXERCISE 8.

EXERCISE SET 6.6

Use Table 11 (p. T–13) for these exercises.

• Solve.

1. When you retire you plan to buy an annuity which pays you $14,000 at the end of each of 10 years. How much should you pay for the annuity if interest is 13% compounded annually?

2. When you retire you plan to buy an annuity which pays you $9000 at the end of each of 15 years. How much should you pay for the annuity if interest is 11% compounded annually?

3. You are the winner in a Sweepstakes that pays you $20,000 at the end of each of the next 10 years. Contest rules require the sponsor to deposit the money now. How much does the sponsor need to deposit now at 12% compounded annually?

4. You are the winner in a Sweepstakes that pays you $15,000 at the end of each of the next 20 years. Contest rules require the sponsor to deposit the money now. How much does the sponsor need to deposit now at 11% compounded annually?

5. The highway commission buys some of your land. For tax purposes you want $7000 payments at the end of each of the next five years. How much should the highway commission deposit now at 14% compounded annually to meet this obligation?

6. The highway commission buys some of your land. For tax purposes you want $10,000 payments at the end of each of the next four years. How much should the highway commission deposit now at 12% compounded annually to meet this obligation?

7. You must pay a neighbor $175 at the end of each of the next 12 months. How much should you deposit now at 15% compounded monthly to meet this obligation?

8. You must pay a neighbor $500 at the end of each of the next 20 months. How much should you deposit now at 18% compounded monthly to meet this obligation?

9. A salesperson tells you the monthly payments for a Delorean car are only $576.39 for 48 months at 12% compounded monthly. How much does the Delorean cost? Round to the nearest dollar.

10. A salesperson tells you the monthly payments for a Delorean car are only $553.50 for 48 months at 15% compounded monthly. How much does the Delorean cost? Round to the nearest dollar.

11. Your property taxes are $635 semiannually. How much should you invest now at 12% compounded semiannually to pay the next two installments?

12. Your property taxes are $430 semiannually. How much should you invest now at 11% compounded semiannually to pay the next two installments?

ANSWERS

1. 75,967.41

2. 64,297.78

3. 113004.46

4. 119,449.92

5. 24031.57

6. 29157.123

7. 1938.88

8. 8584.32 / 9469.68

9. 21887.81

10. 19888.07

11. 1144.20

12. 739.92

282 LOANS AND ANNUITIES

ANSWERS

13. 32298.79
14. 18242.38
15. 34006.79
16. 15588.89
17. 23469.00
18. 31398.49
19. 26445.50
20. 20383.03
21. 16608.16
22. 10205.49
23. 13447.92
24. 3445.75
25. 1233.96
26. 1023.09
27. 7670.74
    8762.36

Solve.

How much must you invest now at the given rate to make these withdrawals beginning immediately?

	Each Withdrawal	Number of Withdrawals	Withdrawal and Rate Period	Rate
13.	$8000	5	Annually	12%
14.	$5000	4	Annually	13%
15.	$3000	20	Semiannually	14%
16.	$1200	25	Semiannually	13%
17.	$1500	20	Quarterly	11%
18.	$1800	24	Quarterly	12%
19.	$700	36	Monthly	15%
20.	$950	24	Monthly	12%

21. Your parents plan to give you $5000 at the start of each of the next four years for college expenses. How much must they invest today at 14% compounded annually so payments may start immediately?

22. Your parents plan to give you $3000 at the start of each of the next four years for college expenses. How much must they invest today at 12% compounded annually so payments may start immediately?

23. Your estimated federal income taxes are $3500 each quarter to be paid at the beginning of each of the next four quarters starting with the first payment now. How much must you invest today at 11% compounded quarterly to meet this obligation?

24. Your estimated federal income taxes are $900 each quarter to be paid at the beginning of each of the next four quarters starting with the first payment now. How much must you invest today at 12% compounded quarterly to meet this obligation?

25. You are on a budget balancing account with the utility company so that each monthly bill is $110. How much must you invest today at 15% compounded monthly to meet this obligation for the next 12 months where the first payment is due today?

26. You are on a budget balancing account with the utility company so that each monthly bill is $90. How much must you invest today at 12% compounded monthly to meet this obligation for the next 12 months where the first payment is due today?

27. Starting immediately, an insurance company must pay $200 at the beginning of each of the next 48 months to a claimant on disability. How much should the insurance company invest today at 12% compounded monthly to meet this obligation?

28. Starting immediately, an insurance company must pay $300 at the beginning of each of the next 36 months to a claimant on disability. How much should the insurance company invest today at 15% compounded monthly to meet this obligation?

TEST OR REVIEW — CHAPTER 6

If you miss an item, review the indicated section and objective.

[6.1, ●]   **1.** Find the interest due at the end of nine months on a $750 14% note.

[6.1, ●●]   **2.** Find the due date on a 120-day noninterest-bearing note dated May 7.

[6.1, ●●●]   **3.** A six-month note for $4200 was discounted at 11%. What were the discount and proceeds?

[6.2, ●]   **4.** Use the United States Rule to find the amount due at maturity on a 12%, three-month, $2000 note dated May 21, if partial payments of $450 and $370 were made on July 28 and August 2, respectively. (Assume a 365-day year.)

[6.3, ●]   **5.** Use the Merchant's Rule to find the amount due at maturity on a 12%, three-month, $2000 note dated May 21, if partial payments of $450 and $370 were made on July 28 and August 2, respectively. (Assume a 365-day year.)

Use Table 10 (p. T–11) for 6–9.

[6.4, ●]   **6.** You deposit $150 at the end of every month into your savings account which pays 12% compounded monthly. How much is in your account after the 48th payment?

284 LOANS AND ANNUITIES

[6.4, ■] **7.** You deposit $120 at the beginning of each month in savings account paying 15% compounded monthly. How much is in your account at the end of the 18th month?

[6.5, ■] **8.** How much is the accumulated amount in an IRA at the end of the 40th year if $2000 is invested at the beginning of each year at 11% compounded annually?

[6.5, ■] **9.** How much is the accumulated amount in a Keogh Plan after the 15th annual end of year payment of $2500 into a 14% compounded annually account?

Use Table 11 (p. T–13) for 10–12.

[6.6, ■] **10.** You plan to give your parents $3500 at the end of each of the next four years. To do this how much must be invested now at 12% compounded annually?

11. A snowmobile salesperson tells you the monthly payments for a snowmobile are only $98.23 at the end of each of the next 36 months at 12% compounded monthly. How much does the snowmobile cost? Round to the nearest dollar.

[6.6, ■] **12.** Your parents plan to give you $8000 at the start of each of the next five years for your new business. How much must they invest today at 13% compounded annually so payments may start immediately?

Career: Business Consultant This is Henry M. Taylor. Henry took a course like the one this text is used for while studying for a BS degree in Business Education at Indiana Central University. He also received an MA in Economics.

Henry is presently Executive Director of the Indianapolis Business Development Foundation, a not-for-profit organization. The purpose of this organization, and of Henry's work as a Business Consultant, is to help new minority enterprises get started and assist them in development, as well as to help existing minority firms grow. These firms now gross over $60 million annually.

In Henry's role as a business consultant, he must frequently make decisions about the capability of a business to receive and pay off a loan. He may also advise a business regarding their granting credit to potential customers.

Other material in this book which is important is that on ratio and percent, interest, and statistics. For example, the ratio of a company's assets to liabilities may be used in financial planning and loan decisions. People who are successful in Henry's type of work usually earn from $30,000 to $80,000 annually.

Henry's hobbies include gardening, listening to music, and art.

7
INSTALLMENT AND CONSUMER CREDIT

READINESS CHECK — SKILLS FOR CHAPTER 7

Solve for x.

1. $\dfrac{220.48}{2000} = \dfrac{x}{100}$

2. $\dfrac{x}{0.25} = \dfrac{0.3}{0.5}$

Divide.

3. $\$4067.58 \div 48$

4. $\$178,250 \div 360$

Find.

5. $\dfrac{6}{78} \times \$60$

6. $\dfrac{45}{406} \times \$153$

7.1 THE ANNUAL PERCENTAGE RATE (APR)

Intelligent buying requires not only an awareness of product quality but also a good knowledge of borrowing costs. In this chapter we study consumer financing of purchases so you will have the necessary information for intelligent buying.

■ FINANCE CHARGE

The federal Truth-in-Lending Law requires all lenders to state

1. the finance charge, and
2. the annual percentage rate (APR).

Consumers use this information to tell how much loans actually cost.

Example 1 Cecile borrowed $2000 from University Bank to buy a car. Her monthly payment will be $92.52 for 24 months. Find the finance charge.

Solution

$$\begin{aligned}
\text{Finance Charge} &= \text{Number of Payments} \times \text{Monthly Payment} - \text{Amount of Loan} \\
&= (24 \times \$92.52) - \$2000 \\
&= \$2220.48 - \$2000 \\
&= \$220.48
\end{aligned}$$

The finance charge was $220.48.

DO EXERCISE 1.

OBJECTIVES

After finishing Section 7.1, you should be able to:

■ Determinine finance charges.

■■ Use a table to find the APR.

■■■ Calculate APR using a formula.

1. Diego borrowed $4000 for 36 months from University Bank. His monthly payment will be $129.53. Find the finance charge.

ANSWERS ON PAGE A–15

7.1 THE ANNUAL PERCENTAGE RATE (APR)

●● FINDING THE ANNUAL PERCENTAGE RATE

The APR is the effective interest rate paid when you borrow money.

Let's consider two loans, Loan A and Loan B.

Loan A Jane Richardson borrowed $100 for one year. At the end of one year she repaid Twin Cities Bank $114, in a single payment.

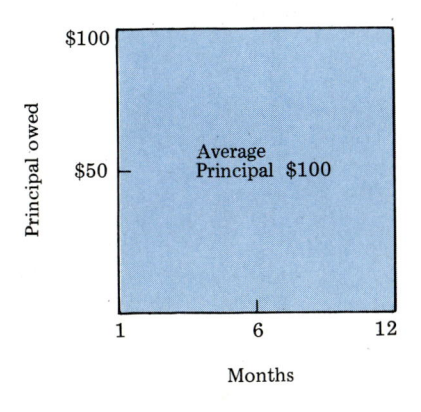

Start of Month	Principal Owed
1	$100
2	$100
3	$100
4	$100
5	$100
6	$100
7	$100
8	$100
9	$100
10	$100
11	$100
12	$100
Sum	**$1200**

$$\frac{\text{Average}}{\text{Principal}} = \frac{\$1200}{12} \quad \text{or} \quad \$100$$

$14.00 interest was paid at the end of one year. To find the rate (APR) substitute 100 for P, 1 for T, and 14 for I.

$$I = P \times R \times T$$
$$14 = 100 \times R \times 1$$
$$\frac{14}{100} = R$$
$$0.14 = R$$

The interest rate (APR) is 14%.

INSTALLMENT AND CONSUMER CREDIT

Loan B Stuart Wills borrowed $100 for one year from Twin Cities Bank. He repaid the loan in 12 monthly payments of $9.50.

Start of Month	Principal Owed	Payment Amount	Applied Toward Principal	Applied Toward Interest
1	$100.00	$9.50	$7.42	$2.08
2	$92.58	$9.50	$7.58	$1.92
3	$85.00	$9.50	$7.74	$1.76
4	$77.26	$9.50	$7.90	$1.60
5	$69.36	$9.50	$8.06	$1.44
6	$61.30	$9.50	$8.23	$1.27
7	$53.07	$9.50	$8.40	$1.10
8	$44.67	$9.50	$8.57	$0.93
9	$36.10	$9.50	$8.75	$0.75
10	$27.35	$9.50	$8.93	$0.57
11	$18.42	$9.50	$9.12	$0.38
12	$9.30	$9.50	$9.30	$0.20
Sum	$674.41	$114.00	$100.00	$14.00

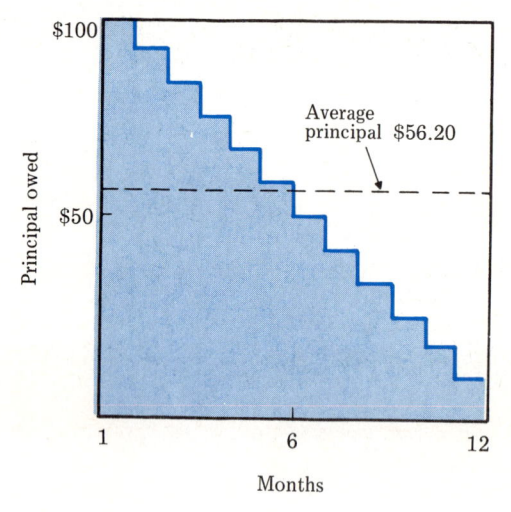

$$\frac{\text{Average}}{\text{Principal}} = \frac{\$674.41}{12} \quad \text{or} \quad \$56.20$$

To find the rate (APR) substitute 56.20 for P, 1 for T, and 14 for I.

$$I = P \times R \times T$$
$$14 = 56.20 \times R \times 1$$
$$\frac{14}{56.20} = R$$
$$0.2491 = R$$

The interest rate (APR) is 24.91%.

7.1 THE ANNUAL PERCENTAGE RATE (APR)

The interest paid on both loans was $14. However, the effective interest rate was different. Jane had the use of the entire $100 for a whole year. Stuart had the use of his money for the first month only.

The APR is based on the average principal.

$$\text{Average Principal} = \frac{\text{Sum of Amount Owed Each Month}}{\text{Total Number of Payments}}$$

For Loan A the average principal was $100, and the APR was 14%. For Loan B the average principal was $56.20, and the APR was 24.91%.

Table 12 (p. T–15) contains APR values. Part of that table appears as Table 7.1 on p. 290.

Example 2 A student borrowed $2000 from University Bank to buy a car. The loan is to be repaid over 24 months. Find the APR.

Solution

a) Find the finance charge per $100 of the amount borrowed. From the ad we see the total interest is $220.48.

$$\frac{220.48}{2000} = \frac{x}{100}$$

$$100 \times \frac{220.48}{2000} = x \quad \text{Multiplying on both sides by 100}$$

$$11.024 = x$$

b) Find 24 in the column headed Number of Payments in Table 7.1 and read across the row until the value nearest 11.024 is found (11.02 in this example).

c) The rate at the top of the column containing 11.02 is 10.25%. The APR is thus 10.25%.

DO EXERCISE 2.

2. Find the APR for the $4000 University Bank auto loan payable over 36 months.

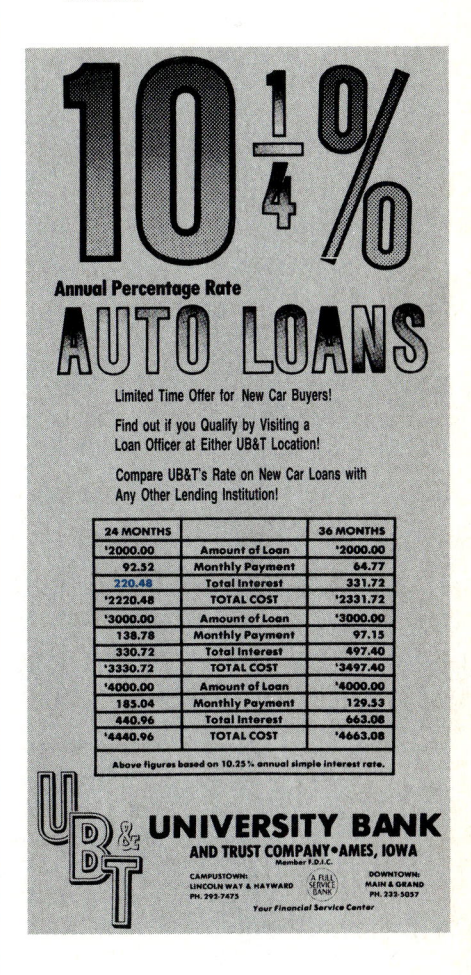

10¼% Annual Percentage Rate AUTO LOANS

Limited Time Offer for New Car Buyers!

Find out if you Qualify by Visiting a Loan Officer at Either UB&T Location!

Compare UB&T's Rate on New Car Loans with Any Other Lending Institution!

24 MONTHS			36 MONTHS
$2000.00	Amount of Loan		$2000.00
92.52	Monthly Payment		64.77
220.48	Total Interest		331.72
$2220.48	TOTAL COST		$2331.72
$3000.00	Amount of Loan		$3000.00
138.78	Monthly Payment		97.15
330.72	Total Interest		497.40
$3330.72	TOTAL COST		$3497.40
$4000.00	Amount of Loan		$4000.00
185.04	Monthly Payment		129.53
440.96	Total Interest		663.08
$4440.96	TOTAL COST		$4663.08

Above figures based on 10.25% annual simple interest rate.

UB&T UNIVERSITY BANK AND TRUST COMPANY • AMES, IOWA
Member F.D.I.C.

CAMPUSTOWN: LINCOLN WAY & HAYWARD PH. 292-7475

DOWNTOWN: MAIN & GRAND PH. 232-5057

Your Financial Service Center

ANSWERS ON PAGE A–15

TABLE 7.1
ANNUAL PERCENTAGE RATE TABLE FOR MONTHLY PAYMENT PLANS

NUMBER OF PAYMENTS	10.00%	10.25%	10.50%	10.75%	11.00%	11.25%	11.50%	11.75%	12.00%	12.25%	12.50%	12.75%	13.00%	13.25%	13.50%	13.75%
(FINANCE CHARGE PER $100 OF AMOUNT FINANCED)																
1	0.83	0.85	0.87	0.90	0.92	0.94	0.96	0.98	1.00	1.02	1.04	1.06	1.08	1.10	1.12	1.15
2	1.25	1.28	1.31	1.35	1.38	1.41	1.44	1.47	1.50	1.53	1.57	1.60	1.63	1.66	1.69	1.72
3	1.67	1.71	1.76	1.80	1.84	1.88	1.92	1.96	2.01	2.05	2.09	2.13	2.17	2.22	2.26	2.30
4	2.09	2.14	2.20	2.25	2.30	2.35	2.41	2.46	2.51	2.57	2.62	2.67	2.72	2.78	2.83	2.88
5	2.51	2.58	2.64	2.70	2.77	2.83	2.89	2.96	3.02	3.08	3.15	3.21	3.27	3.34	3.40	3.46
6	2.94	3.01	3.08	3.16	3.23	3.31	3.38	3.45	3.53	3.60	3.68	3.75	3.83	3.90	3.97	4.05
7	3.36	3.45	3.53	3.62	3.70	3.78	3.87	3.95	4.04	4.12	4.21	4.29	4.38	4.47	4.55	4.64
8	3.79	3.88	3.98	4.07	4.17	4.26	4.36	4.46	4.55	4.65	4.74	4.84	4.94	5.03	5.13	5.22
9	4.21	4.32	4.43	4.53	4.64	4.75	4.85	4.96	5.07	5.17	5.28	5.39	5.49	5.60	5.71	5.82
10	4.64	4.76	4.88	4.99	5.11	5.23	5.35	5.46	5.58	5.70	5.82	5.94	6.05	6.17	6.29	6.41
11	5.07	5.20	5.33	5.45	5.58	5.71	5.84	5.97	6.10	6.23	6.36	6.49	6.62	6.75	6.88	7.01
12	5.50	5.64	5.78	5.92	6.06	6.20	6.34	6.48	6.62	6.76	6.90	7.04	7.18	7.32	7.46	7.60
13	5.93	6.08	6.23	6.38	6.53	6.68	6.84	6.99	7.14	7.29	7.44	7.59	7.75	7.90	8.05	8.20
14	6.36	6.52	6.69	6.85	7.01	7.17	7.34	7.50	7.66	7.82	7.99	8.15	8.31	8.48	8.64	8.81
15	6.80	6.97	7.14	7.32	7.49	7.66	7.84	8.01	8.19	8.36	8.53	8.71	8.88	9.06	9.23	9.41
16	7.23	7.41	7.60	7.78	7.97	8.15	8.34	8.53	8.71	8.90	9.08	9.27	9.46	9.64	9.83	10.02
17	7.67	7.86	8.06	8.25	8.45	8.65	8.84	9.04	9.24	9.44	9.63	9.83	10.03	10.23	10.43	10.63
18	8.10	8.31	8.52	8.73	8.93	9.14	9.35	9.56	9.77	9.98	10.19	10.40	10.61	10.82	11.03	11.24
19	8.54	8.76	8.98	9.20	9.42	9.64	9.86	10.08	10.30	10.52	10.74	10.96	11.18	11.41	11.63	11.85
20	8.98	9.21	9.44	9.67	9.90	10.13	10.37	10.60	10.83	11.06	11.30	11.53	11.76	12.00	12.23	12.46
21	9.42	9.66	9.90	10.15	10.39	10.63	10.88	11.12	11.36	11.61	11.85	12.10	12.34	12.59	12.84	13.08
22	9.86	10.12	10.37	10.62	10.88	11.13	11.39	11.64	11.90	12.16	12.41	12.67	12.93	13.19	13.44	13.70
23	10.30	10.57	10.84	11.10	11.37	11.63	11.90	12.17	12.44	12.71	12.97	13.24	13.51	13.78	14.05	14.32
24	10.75	11.02	11.30	11.58	11.86	12.14	12.42	12.70	12.98	13.26	13.54	13.82	14.10	14.38	14.66	14.95
25	11.19	11.48	11.77	12.06	12.35	12.64	12.93	13.22	13.52	13.81	14.10	14.40	14.69	14.98	15.28	15.57
26	11.64	11.94	12.24	12.54	12.85	13.15	13.45	13.75	14.06	14.36	14.67	14.97	15.28	15.59	15.89	16.20
27	12.09	12.40	12.71	13.03	13.34	13.66	13.97	14.29	14.60	14.92	15.24	15.56	15.87	16.19	16.51	16.83
28	12.53	12.86	13.18	13.51	13.84	14.16	14.49	14.82	15.15	15.48	15.81	16.14	16.47	16.80	17.13	17.46
29	12.98	13.32	13.66	14.00	14.33	14.67	15.01	15.35	15.70	16.04	16.38	16.72	17.07	17.41	17.75	18.10
30	13.43	13.78	14.13	14.48	14.83	15.19	15.54	15.89	16.24	16.60	16.95	17.31	17.66	18.02	18.38	18.74
31	13.89	14.25	14.61	14.97	15.33	15.70	16.06	16.43	16.79	17.16	17.53	17.90	18.27	18.63	19.00	19.38
32	14.34	14.71	15.09	15.46	15.84	16.21	16.59	16.97	17.35	17.73	18.11	18.49	18.87	19.25	19.63	20.02
33	14.79	15.18	15.57	15.95	16.34	16.73	17.12	17.51	17.90	18.29	18.69	19.08	19.47	19.87	20.26	20.66
34	15.25	15.65	16.05	16.44	16.85	17.25	17.65	18.05	18.46	18.86	19.27	19.67	20.08	20.49	20.90	21.31
35	15.70	16.11	16.53	16.94	17.35	17.77	18.18	18.60	19.01	19.43	19.85	20.27	20.69	21.11	21.53	21.95
36	16.16	16.58	17.01	17.43	17.86	18.29	18.71	19.14	19.57	20.00	20.43	20.87	21.30	21.73	22.17	22.60
37	16.62	17.06	17.49	17.93	18.37	18.81	19.25	19.69	20.13	20.58	21.02	21.46	21.91	22.36	22.81	23.25
38	17.08	17.53	17.98	18.43	18.88	19.33	19.78	20.24	20.69	21.15	21.61	22.07	22.52	22.99	23.45	23.91
39	17.54	18.00	18.46	18.93	19.39	19.86	20.32	20.79	21.26	21.73	22.20	22.67	23.14	23.61	24.09	24.56
40	18.00	18.48	18.95	19.43	19.90	20.38	20.86	21.34	21.82	22.30	22.79	23.27	23.76	24.25	24.73	25.22
41	18.47	18.95	19.44	19.93	20.42	20.91	21.40	21.89	22.39	22.88	23.38	23.88	24.38	24.88	25.38	25.88
42	18.93	19.43	19.93	20.43	20.93	21.44	21.94	22.45	22.96	23.47	23.98	24.49	25.00	25.51	26.03	26.55
43	19.40	19.91	20.42	20.94	21.45	21.97	22.49	23.01	23.53	24.05	24.57	25.10	25.62	26.15	26.68	27.21
44	19.86	20.39	20.91	21.44	21.97	22.50	23.03	23.57	24.10	24.64	25.17	25.71	26.25	26.79	27.33	27.88
45	20.33	20.87	21.41	21.95	22.49	23.03	23.58	24.12	24.67	25.22	25.77	26.32	26.88	27.43	27.99	28.55
46	20.80	21.35	21.90	22.46	23.01	23.57	24.13	24.69	25.25	25.81	26.37	26.94	27.51	28.08	28.65	29.22
47	21.27	21.83	22.40	22.97	23.53	24.10	24.68	25.25	25.82	26.40	26.98	27.56	28.14	28.72	29.31	29.89
48	21.74	22.32	22.90	23.48	24.06	24.64	25.23	25.81	26.40	26.99	27.58	28.18	28.77	29.37	29.97	30.57
49	22.21	22.80	23.39	23.99	24.58	25.18	25.78	26.38	26.98	27.59	28.19	28.80	29.41	30.02	30.63	31.24
50	22.69	23.29	23.89	24.50	25.11	25.72	26.33	26.95	27.56	28.18	28.80	29.42	30.04	30.67	31.29	31.92
51	23.16	23.78	24.40	25.02	25.64	26.26	26.89	27.52	28.15	28.78	29.41	30.05	30.68	31.32	31.96	32.60
52	23.64	24.27	24.90	25.53	26.17	26.81	27.45	28.09	28.73	29.38	30.02	30.67	31.32	31.98	32.63	33.29
53	24.11	24.76	25.40	26.05	26.70	27.35	28.00	28.66	29.32	29.98	30.64	31.30	31.97	32.63	33.30	33.97
54	24.59	25.25	25.91	26.57	27.23	27.90	28.56	29.23	29.91	30.58	31.25	31.93	32.61	33.29	33.98	34.66
55	25.07	25.74	26.41	27.09	27.77	28.44	29.13	29.81	30.50	31.18	31.87	32.56	33.26	33.95	34.65	35.35
56	25.55	26.23	26.92	27.61	28.30	28.99	29.69	30.39	31.09	31.79	32.49	33.20	33.91	34.62	35.33	36.04
57	26.03	26.73	27.43	28.13	28.84	29.54	30.25	30.97	31.68	32.39	33.11	33.83	34.56	35.28	36.01	36.74
58	26.51	27.23	27.94	28.66	29.37	30.10	30.82	31.55	32.27	33.00	33.74	34.47	35.21	35.95	36.69	37.43
59	27.00	27.72	28.45	29.18	29.91	30.65	31.39	32.13	32.87	33.61	34.36	35.11	35.86	36.62	37.37	38.13
60	27.48	28.22	28.96	29.71	30.45	31.20	31.96	32.71	33.47	34.23	34.99	35.75	36.52	37.29	38.06	38.83

7.1 THE ANNUAL PERCENTAGE RATE (APR)

Example 3 Find the APR for the Buick Opel loan.

Solution

a) Find the amount financed.

$$\underset{\text{Cash price}}{\$3348} - \underset{\text{Down payment}}{\$348} = \underset{\text{Amount financed}}{\$3000}$$

b) Find the total of all payments.

$$\$87.68 \times 42 = \$3682.56$$

c) Find the finance charge.

$$\$3682.56 - \$3000 = \$682.56$$

d) Find the finance charge per $100.

$$\frac{682.56}{3000} = \frac{x}{100}$$

$$x = 22.752$$

e) Find 42 in the column headed Number of Payments in Table 7.1 and read across the row until the value nearest 22.752 is found (22.96 in this example).

f) The rate at the top of the column containing 22.96 is 12%. The APR is 12%.

Note that the ad gives the APR as 11.90%. The Federal Reserve System requires the estimated APR to be within $\frac{1}{8}$% of the actual APR so 12% would meet that requirement.

DO EXERCISE 3.

Intermediate values may be obtained from a table by interpolation. The process is explained in Example 4.

Example 4 Use interpolation to show that the APR for financing the Buick Opel is 11.90%.

Solution

a) From Example 3, we know that the finance charge per 100 is 22.752.

b) In the row containing 42 in Table 7.1, we find that 22.752 is between 22.45 and 22.96.

c) The rate for the column with 22.45 is 11.75% and for 22.96 is 12.00%.

d) This is represented by

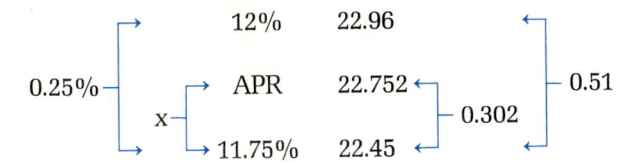

$$0.25\% \begin{cases} x \begin{cases} 12\% & 22.96 \\ \text{APR} & 22.752 \\ 11.75\% & 22.45 \end{cases} 0.302 \end{cases} 0.51$$

3. After a down payment an auto is financed for $3342.80 at $89.27 per month for 48 months. Find the APR.

ANSWERS ON PAGE A–15

4. Use interpolation to find the APR of the following.

MONTE CARLO
$121.94 PER MO.
Stk. no. 3973, automatic, air, AM radio. Sale Priced $5262 with $662 down. Finance $4600 for 48 months. Deferred price $6515, APR

5. Use the formula to estimate the APR for the Pinto.

PINTO RUNABOUT
$77.11 PER MO. OR $3492
Limited Edition pkg. A78x13 WSW tires, AM radio, tinted glass complete. $500 down, finance $2992 for 48 months. Deferred payment price $4201.28, WAC Stk. No. 940.

e) The APR = 11.75% + x% and

$$\frac{x}{0.25} = \frac{0.302}{0.51}$$

$$x = 0.25 \cdot \frac{0.302}{0.51} \quad \text{Multiplying on both sides by 0.25}$$

$$x = 0.15$$

The APR is 11.90% (11.75% + 0.15%).

DO EXERCISE 4.

▪▪▪ A FORMULA FOR ESTIMATING THE ANNUAL PERCENTAGE RATE

A good estimate of the APR* is given by

$$APR = \frac{72I}{3P(n+1) + I(n-1)},$$

where I = the interest (finance charge), P = the principal, and n = the number of monthly payments.

Example 5 Estimate the APR on a loan to buy the Monarch.

Solution
a) Find I, P, and n.
$I = 36(100.63) - 3030$
$\quad = 3622.68 - 3030$
$\quad = 592.68;$
$P = 3030;$
$n = 36.$

MONARCH 2 Door Coupe "Red"
$100.63 Mo.
$3530 Cash
$500 down, 36 mo. APR 11.99 Deferred Price

b) Substituting 592.68 for I, 3030 for P, and 36 for n, we get

$$APR = \frac{72(592.68)}{3(3030)(37) + (592.68)(35)}$$

$$= 0.1195.$$

The APR is about 11.95%.

Note that the actual APR is 11.99%. The formula is more complicated than others frequently used but provides greater accuracy as required by the Federal Reserve System when updating the Truth-in-Lending Law.

DO EXERCISE 5.

---
*Constantine D. Kazarinoff showed this formula is a better approximation than the often used.

$$APR = \frac{24I}{P(n+1)} \quad \text{or} \quad APR = \frac{24I}{(P+I)(n+1)}.$$

ANSWERS ON PAGE A–15

NAME _____ CLASS _____ ANSWERS

EXERCISE SET 7.1

■ Find the finance charge for each of 1–4.

	Amount Financed	Monthly Payment	Number of Payments
1.	$5,000	$108.04	84
2.	$10,000	$186.67	120
3.	$15,000	$280.00	120
4.	$25,000	$466.67	120

We can give you the approval you want in just a matter of days — even on very large amounts.

HOW DO YOU APPLY? Just phone. When you see for yourself how fast we say "yes," you'll wonder why you waited so long! Call today!

CREDITHRIFT OF AMERICA — We've got your loan

■■ Use Table 12 (p. T–15) to find the APR to the nearest $\frac{1}{4}$%.

5. HAMMOND ORGAN
WITH EXCLUSIVE ELECTRONIC FEATURES! ALL IT TAKES IS TWO FINGERS FOR INSTANT FUN AND MUSICAL ACCOMPLISHMENT. COME IN TODAY, SEE HOW EASY IT IS TO PLAY!
$1999 Cash Price (Not Including Sales Tax)
$56.62 Monthly Payment
48 MONTHS

6. KIMBALL PIANO
A PIANO CREATED TO SATISFY YOUR HIGH STANDARDS FOR MUSICAL SOUND WITH RICH, RESONANT TONE, QUALITY AND SUPERIOR HAND-CRAFTED STYLING. THIS IS A PIANO THAT WILL PROVIDE MAXIMUM MUSICAL PLEASURE.
$999 Cash Price (Not Including Sales Tax)
$36.06 Monthly Payment
36 MONTHS

7. NEW KIMBALL Grand PIANO
$2999 Cash Price (Not Including Sales Tax)
$71.64 Monthly Payment
60 MONTHS

8. USED ORGAN
$599 Cash Price (Not Including Sales Tax)
$29.95 Monthly Payment
24 MONTHS

9. COUGAR $5416
2-dr., silver metallic, automatic trans., power and air conditioning. List price $5873; $416 down payment. Finance $5,000 at $134.22 per month for 48 months.

10. SUBARU 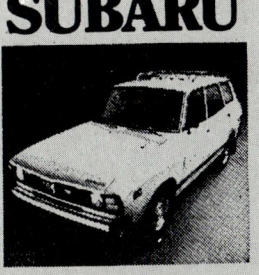
ONLY **$104.85** per/mo
with qualified credit, $4393 cash, or $343 down, 48 mo.

294 INSTALLMENT AND CONSUMER CREDIT

11.
CUTLASS SUPREME
AT-PS-AC
Vinyl Roof
$58.72 Mo.
$1687 Cash
$500 Down 24 mo. APR
Deferred price $1909.28

12.
MUSTANG II
Coupe
Vinyl Roof
$103.63 Mo.
$3100 Cash
$500 Down 30 mo. APR
Deferred price $3608.90

▮▮▮ Use the formula to estimate the APR to the hundredths position in Exercises 13–22.

	Amount Borrowed	Monthly Payment	Number of Payments
13.	$3000	$155	24
14.	$4600	$230	24
15.	$6000	$155	48
16.	$7500	$195	48
17.	$4200	$1125	4
18.	$1700	$460	4

19.
VW BEETLE
Low Miles
Like New
$80.19 Mo.
$2495
$500 Down 30 mo.

20.
MALIBU CLASSIC
$121⁹⁴ PER MO.
Malibu Classic, Stk. No. 4196, 6 cyl., power steering, air, automatic. Sale price $5170 with $570 down. Finance $4600 for 48 months.

21.
CUTLASS SUPREME
AT-PS-AC
NICE CAR
$85.24 Mo.
$2973 Cash
$500 down, 36 mo. APR
Deferred Price $3563.64

22.
MERCURY
4-DR
AT-PS-AC
LIKE NEW
$62.22 Mo.
$2268 Cash
$500 down, 36 mo.

23. 🖩 Use the formula to find the amount borrowed if the APR is 26%, the number of monthly payments 24, and the interest $430.

24. 🖩 Use the formula to find the amount borrowed if the APR is 19%, the number of monthly payments 36, and the interest $940.

ANSWERS

11. _____
12. _____
13. _____
14. _____
15. _____
16. _____
17. _____
18. _____
19. _____
20. _____
21. _____
22. _____
23. _____
24. _____

7.2 FINDING THE PAYMENT AMOUNT

When considering a purchase a consumer often wants to know the monthly payments and how much of each payment is for principal and interest. This information enables the consumer to determine whether the purchase is affordable. In this section we study these topics.

◦ MONTHLY PAYMENTS

Example 1 Find the monthly payment for a $3000 Industrial Investment Company loan payable over 60 months.

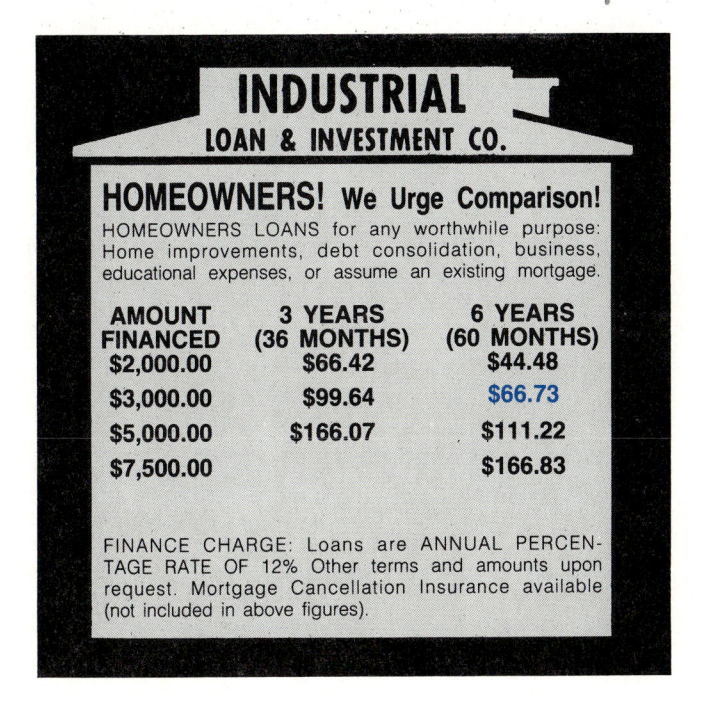

INDUSTRIAL LOAN & INVESTMENT CO.

HOMEOWNERS! We Urge Comparison!
HOMEOWNERS LOANS for any worthwhile purpose: Home improvements, debt consolidation, business, educational expenses, or assume an existing mortgage.

AMOUNT FINANCED	3 YEARS (36 MONTHS)	6 YEARS (60 MONTHS)
$2,000.00	$66.42	$44.48
$3,000.00	$99.64	$66.73
$5,000.00	$166.07	$111.22
$7,500.00		$166.83

FINANCE CHARGE: Loans are ANNUAL PERCENTAGE RATE OF 12% Other terms and amounts upon request. Mortgage Cancellation Insurance available (not included in above figures).

Solution

a) Find the finance charge per $100.

Read down the column headed Number of Payments in Table 12 (p. T–15) to 60 and across that row to the 12% column.

The finance charge per $100 is $33.47.

b) A proportion gives the finance charge for the loan:

$$\frac{33.47}{100} = \frac{x}{3000}$$

$x = 1004.10.$

The finance charge is $1004.10.

c) Find the total to be paid.

$1004.10 + $3000 = $4004.10.

d) The monthly payment is $66.73, or $4004.10 ÷ 60.

DO EXERCISE 1.

OBJECTIVES

After finishing Section 7.2, you should be able to:

◦ Calculate monthly payments.

◦◦ Find the amount of each payment which is applied to interest and principal.

1. Find the monthly payment on a $7500 Industrial Investment Comapny loan payable for 36 months.

ANSWER ON PAGE A–15

2. An 11.25% home mortgage loan of $65,000 was taken out for 26 years. What were the monthly payments?

3. An 11.00% home mortgage loan of $65,000 was taken out for 25 years. What were the monthly payments?

ANSWERS ON PAGE A–15

INSTALLMENT AND CONSUMER CREDIT

"He hates me. I've got a house mortgage at 6¼ per cent which still has ten years to go!"

The interest rate for a mortgage and the price of homes have risen substantially in recent years. Loans extending over a long time period in which all payments are equal are called *amortized loans*. Real estate, automobile, and other large loans are often amortized loans.

Example 2 An 11.5% home mortgage loan of $50,000 is taken out for 30 years (360 months). What are the finance charge and the monthly payment?

Solution

a) Find the finance charge per $100.

Read down the column headed Number of Payments in Table 12 (p. T–15) to 360 and across that row to the 11.5% column.

The finance charge per $100 is $256.50.

b) A proportion gives the finance charge for the loan:

$$\frac{\$256.50}{100} = \frac{x}{50{,}000}$$

$x = \$128{,}250.$

The finance charge is $128,250.

c) Find the total amount to be paid.

$128,250 + $50,000 = $178,250

d) The monthly payment is $495.15, or $178,250 ÷ 360.

Note that the finance charge is over twice the amount of the loan.

DO EXERCISE 2.

Amortization tables exist, from which the payments may be found directly. Table 13 (p. T–22) is an amortization table. Part of that table is shown on the next page as Table 7.2.

Example 3 Suppose you took out an 11.5% home mortgage loan of $50,000 for 30 years. What were the monthly payments?

Solution Read down the column headed Amount in Table 7.2 to 50,000 and across that row to the 30-year column. The monthly payment is $495.15.

DO EXERCISE 3.

TABLE 7.2
MONTHLY PAYMENT REQUIRED TO AMORTIZE A LOAN

11.500%

TERM AMOUNT	15 Years	16 Years	17 Years	18 Years	19 Years	20 Years	21 Years	22 Years	23 Years	24 Years	25 Years	30 Years	35 Years	40 Years
5	.06	.06	.06	.06	.06	.06	.06	.06	.06	.06	.06	.05	.05	.05
10	.12	.12	.12	.11	.11	.11	.11	.11	.11	.11	.11	.10	.10	.10
15	.18	.18	.17	.17	.17	.16	.16	.16	.16	.16	.16	.15	.15	.15
25	.30	.29	.28	.28	.28	.27	.27	.27	.26	.26	.26	.25	.25	.25
50	.59	.58	.56	.55	.55	.54	.53	.53	.52	.52	.51	.50	.49	.49
75	.88	.86	.84	.83	.82	.80	.80	.79	.78	.77	.77	.75	.74	.73
100	1.17	1.15	1.12	1.10	1.09	1.07	1.06	1.05	1.04	1.03	1.02	1.00	.98	.97
200	2.34	2.29	2.24	2.20	2.17	2.14	2.11	2.09	2.07	2.05	2.04	1.99	1.96	1.94
300	3.51	3.43	3.36	3.30	3.25	3.20	3.17	3.13	3.10	3.08	3.05	2.98	2.93	2.91
400	4.68	4.57	4.48	4.40	4.33	4.27	4.22	4.17	4.14	4.10	4.07	3.97	3.91	3.88
500	5.85	5.71	5.60	5.50	5.41	5.34	5.27	5.22	5.17	5.13	5.09	4.96	4.89	4.85
600	7.01	6.85	6.71	6.59	6.49	6.40	6.33	6.26	6.20	6.15	6.10	5.95	5.86	5.81
700	8.18	7.99	7.83	7.69	7.57	7.47	7.38	7.30	7.23	7.17	7.12	6.94	6.84	6.78
800	9.35	9.13	8.95	8.79	8.65	8.54	8.43	8.34	8.27	8.20	8.14	7.93	7.81	7.75
900	10.52	10.28	10.07	9.89	9.74	9.60	9.49	9.39	9.30	9.22	9.15	8.92	8.79	8.72
1000	11.69	11.42	11.19	10.99	10.82	10.67	10.54	10.43	10.33	10.25	10.17	9.91	9.77	9.69
2000	23.37	22.83	22.37	21.97	21.63	21.33	21.08	20.85	20.66	20.49	20.33	19.81	19.53	19.37
3000	35.05	34.24	33.55	32.95	32.44	32.00	31.61	31.28	30.98	30.73	30.50	29.71	29.29	29.05
4000	46.73	45.65	44.73	43.94	43.25	42.66	42.15	41.70	41.31	40.97	40.66	39.62	39.05	38.74
5000	58.41	57.06	55.91	54.92	54.07	53.33	52.68	52.12	51.63	51.21	50.83	49.52	48.81	48.42
6000	70.10	68.47	67.09	65.90	64.88	63.99	63.22	62.55	61.96	61.45	60.99	59.42	58.57	58.10
7000	81.78	79.89	78.27	76.89	75.69	74.66	73.76	72.97	72.29	71.69	71.16	69.33	68.33	67.78
8000	93.46	91.30	89.45	87.87	86.50	85.32	84.29	83.39	82.61	81.93	81.32	79.23	78.09	77.47
9000	105.14	102.71	100.63	98.85	97.31	95.98	94.83	93.82	92.94	92.17	91.49	89.13	87.85	87.15
10000	116.82	114.12	111.81	109.83	108.13	106.65	105.36	104.24	103.26	102.41	101.65	99.03	97.62	96.83
11000	128.51	125.53	123.00	120.82	118.94	117.31	115.90	114.67	113.59	112.65	111.82	108.94	107.38	106.52
12000	140.19	136.94	134.18	131.80	129.75	127.98	126.43	125.09	123.91	122.89	121.98	118.84	117.14	116.20
13000	151.87	148.36	145.36	142.78	140.56	138.64	136.97	135.51	134.24	133.13	132.15	128.74	126.90	125.88
14000	163.55	159.77	156.54	153.77	151.38	149.31	147.51	145.94	144.57	143.37	142.31	138.65	136.66	135.56
15000	175.23	171.18	167.72	164.75	162.19	159.97	158.04	156.36	154.89	153.61	152.48	148.55	146.42	145.25
16000	186.92	182.59	178.90	175.73	173.00	170.63	168.58	166.78	165.22	163.85	162.64	158.45	156.18	154.93
17000	198.60	194.00	190.08	186.72	183.81	181.30	179.11	177.21	175.54	174.09	172.80	168.35	165.94	164.61
18000	210.28	205.41	201.26	197.70	194.62	191.96	189.65	187.63	185.87	184.33	182.97	178.26	175.70	174.30
19000	221.96	216.83	212.44	208.68	205.44	202.63	200.18	198.06	196.20	194.57	193.13	188.16	185.47	183.98
20000	233.64	228.24	223.62	219.66	216.25	213.29	210.72	208.48	206.52	204.81	203.30	198.06	195.23	193.66
21000	245.32	239.65	234.81	230.65	227.06	223.96	221.26	218.90	216.85	215.05	213.46	207.97	204.99	203.34
22000	257.01	251.06	245.99	241.63	237.87	234.62	231.79	229.33	227.17	225.29	223.63	217.87	214.75	213.03
23000	268.69	262.47	257.17	252.61	248.69	245.28	242.33	239.75	237.50	235.53	233.79	227.77	224.51	222.71
24000	280.37	273.88	268.35	263.60	259.50	255.95	252.86	250.17	247.82	245.77	243.96	237.67	234.27	232.39
25000	292.05	285.30	279.53	274.58	270.31	266.61	263.40	260.60	258.15	256.01	254.12	247.58	244.03	242.08
26000	303.73	296.71	290.71	285.56	281.12	277.28	273.94	271.02	268.48	266.25	264.29	257.48	253.79	251.76
27000	315.42	308.12	301.89	296.54	291.93	287.94	284.47	281.45	278.80	276.49	274.45	267.38	263.55	261.44
28000	327.10	319.53	313.07	307.53	302.75	298.61	295.01	291.87	289.13	286.73	284.62	277.29	273.32	271.12
29000	338.78	330.94	324.25	318.51	313.56	309.27	305.54	302.29	299.45	296.97	294.78	287.19	283.08	280.81
30000	350.46	342.35	335.43	329.49	324.37	319.93	316.08	312.72	309.78	307.21	304.95	297.09	292.84	290.49
31000	362.14	353.77	346.61	340.48	335.18	330.60	326.61	323.14	320.11	317.45	315.11	307.00	302.60	300.17
32000	373.83	365.18	357.80	351.46	345.99	341.26	337.15	333.56	330.43	327.69	325.28	316.90	312.36	309.86
33000	385.51	376.59	368.98	362.44	356.81	351.93	347.69	343.99	340.76	337.93	335.44	326.80	322.12	319.54
34000	397.19	388.00	380.16	373.43	367.62	362.59	358.22	354.41	351.08	348.17	345.60	336.70	331.88	329.22
35000	408.87	399.41	391.34	384.41	378.43	373.26	368.76	364.84	361.41	358.41	355.77	346.61	341.64	338.90
36000	420.55	410.82	402.52	395.39	389.24	383.92	379.29	375.26	371.73	368.65	365.93	356.51	351.40	348.59
37000	432.24	422.24	413.70	406.37	400.06	394.58	389.83	385.68	382.06	378.89	376.10	366.41	361.16	358.27
38000	443.92	433.65	424.88	417.36	410.87	405.25	400.36	396.11	392.39	389.13	386.26	376.32	370.93	367.95
39000	455.60	445.06	436.06	428.34	421.68	415.91	410.90	406.53	402.71	399.37	396.43	386.22	380.69	377.63
40000	467.28	456.47	447.24	439.32	432.49	426.58	421.44	416.95	413.04	409.61	406.59	396.12	390.45	387.32
41000	478.96	467.88	458.42	450.31	443.30	437.24	431.97	427.38	423.36	419.85	416.76	406.02	400.21	397.00
42000	490.64	479.29	469.61	461.29	454.12	447.91	442.51	437.80	433.69	430.09	426.92	415.93	409.97	406.68
43000	502.33	490.71	480.79	472.27	464.93	458.57	453.04	448.23	444.01	440.33	437.09	425.83	419.73	416.37
44000	514.01	502.12	491.97	483.25	475.74	469.23	463.58	458.65	454.34	450.57	447.25	435.73	429.49	426.05
45000	525.69	513.53	503.15	494.24	486.55	479.90	474.11	469.07	464.67	460.81	457.42	445.64	439.25	435.73
46000	537.37	524.94	514.33	505.22	497.37	490.56	484.65	479.50	474.99	471.05	467.58	455.54	449.01	445.41
47000	549.05	536.35	525.51	516.20	508.18	501.23	495.19	489.92	485.32	481.29	477.75	465.44	458.78	455.10
48000	560.74	547.76	536.69	527.19	518.99	511.89	505.72	500.34	495.64	491.53	487.91	475.34	468.54	464.78
49000	572.42	559.18	547.87	538.17	529.80	522.56	516.26	510.77	505.97	501.77	498.07	485.25	478.30	474.46
50000	584.10	570.59	559.05	549.15	540.61	533.22	526.79	521.19	516.30	512.01	508.24	495.15	488.06	484.15
55000	642.51	627.65	614.96	604.07	594.67	586.54	579.47	573.31	567.92	563.21	559.06	544.67	536.86	532.56
60000	700.92	684.70	670.86	658.98	648.74	639.86	632.15	625.43	619.55	614.41	609.89	594.18	585.67	580.97
65000	759.33	741.76	726.77	713.90	702.80	693.18	684.83	677.55	671.18	665.61	660.71	643.69	634.47	629.39
70000	817.74	798.82	782.67	768.81	756.86	746.51	737.51	729.67	722.81	716.81	711.53	693.21	683.28	677.80
75000	876.15	855.88	838.58	823.73	810.92	799.83	790.19	781.79	774.44	768.01	762.36	742.72	732.09	726.22
80000	934.56	912.94	894.48	878.64	864.98	853.15	842.87	833.90	826.07	819.21	813.18	792.24	780.89	774.63
85000	992.97	970.00	950.39	933.56	919.04	906.47	895.55	886.02	877.70	870.41	864.00	841.75	829.70	823.04
90000	1051.38	1027.05	1006.29	988.47	973.10	959.79	948.14	938.14	929.33	921.61	914.83	891.27	878.50	871.46
95000	1109.79	1084.11	1062.20	1043.39	1027.16	1013.11	1000.90	990.26	980.96	972.81	965.65	940.78	927.31	919.87
100000	1168.19	1141.17	1118.10	1098.30	1081.22	1066.43	1053.58	1042.38	1032.59	1024.01	1016.47	990.30	976.11	968.29

297

4. A 10.75% home mortgage loan of $52,350 was taken out for 25 years. What were the monthly payments and the finance charge?

Example 4 A 10.75% home mortgage loan of $62,500 was taken out for 35 years (420 months). What were the monthly payments and the finance charge?

Solution

a) Find the monthly payment.

From Table 13, (p. T–22) we find that the monthly payment for

$60,000 is $550.51
$ 2,000 is $ 18.36
$ 500 is $ 4.59.

So for $62,500 the monthly payment is $573.46 (adding).

b) Find the finance charge.

$$\begin{aligned}\text{Finance charge} &= \text{Total amount paid} - \text{Amount borrowed} \\ &= (\$573.46 \times 420) - \$62{,}500 \\ &= \$178{,}353.20\end{aligned}$$

DO EXERCISE 4.

INTEREST AND PRINCIPAL PAYMENTS

Lending institutions can provide a borrower with an amortization schedule on request. The schedule shows how much of each payment is interest and how much is principal. In addition, the interest rate, loan amount, and balance of the loan are given. Part of an amortization schedule, based on a 360-day year and 30-day month, is shown below.

SCHEDULE OF DIRECT REDUCTION LOAN

CUSTOMER NAME: KELIN ABBOTT
LOAN NUMBER: 6375
CUSTOMER NUMBER: 721881
ORDER NUMBER: 732801
PAYMENT: $687.25
RATE: 13.500%
LOAN: $60,000.00

Payment Number	Interest	Due Date—Paid To	Principal	Total Payment	Balance of Loan	Date Paid
1	675.00	1-1-85	12.25	687.25	59,987.75	
2	674.86	2-1-85	12.39	687.25	59,975.36	
3	674.72	3-1-85	12.53	687.25	59,962.83	
4	674.58	4-1-85	12.67	687.25	59,950.16	
5	674.44	5-1-85	12.81	687.25	59,937.35	
6	674.30	6-1-85	12.95	687.25	59,924.40	
7	674.15	7-1-85	13.10	687.25	59,911.30	
8	674.00	8-1-85	13.25	687.25	59,898.05	
9	673.85	9-1-85	13.40	687.25	59,884.65	
10	673.70	10-1-85	13.55	687.25	59,871.10	
11	673.55	11-1-85	13.70	687.25	59,857.40	
12	673.40	12-1-85	13.85	687.25	59,843.55	

7.2 FINDING THE PAYMENT AMOUNT 299

Example 5 How much of payment 6 in the figure on p. 302 is interest? How much is principal? What is the new balance?

Solution

a) Find the amount of interest.

   Read down the payment column to 6 and across to the column headed Interest.

   The interest is $674.30.

b) Find the amount of principal.

   Read down the payment column to 6 and across to the column headed Principal.

   The principal is $12.95.

c) Find the new balance.

   Read down the payment column to 6 and across to the column headed Balance of Loan.

   The new balance is $59,924.40.

DO EXERCISE 5.

A borrower can find how much of each payment is interest and how much is principal without the use of an amortization schedule. Example 6 illustrates the process for payment 6.

Example 6 The amount owed on a 13.5% loan is $59,937.35. How much of the $687.25 monthly payment is interest? How much is principal? What is the new balance? Assume a 360-day year and 30-day month.

Solution

a) Find the interest.

   Substituting $59,937.35 for P, 0.135 for R, and $\frac{30}{360}$ for T, we get

   $I = P \times R \times T$

   $= \$59{,}937.35 \times 0.135 \times \frac{30}{360}$

   $= \$674.30.$

   The interest is $674.30.

b) Find the amount of principal.

   Amount of principal = Total payment − Interest

                            = $687.25   − $674.30

                            = $12.95

   The amount of principal is $12.95.

5. How much of payment 8 is interest? How much is principal? What is the new balance?

ANSWER ON PAGE A–15

INSTALLMENT AND CONSUMER CREDIT

6. The amount owed on a 10.5% loan is $59,828.60. How much of the $548.85 monthly payment is interest? How much is principal? What is the new balance? Assume a 360-day year and 30-day month.

c) Find the new balance.

New balance = Previous balance − Principal payment
= $59,937.35 − $12.95
= $59,924.40

The new balance is $59,924.40.

DO EXERCISE 6.

ANSWER ON PAGE A–15

NAME _____ CLASS _____ ANSWERS

EXERCISE SET 7.2

● You are having difficulty deciding which car to buy. Use Table 12 (p. T–15) to find the monthly payments.

1.
VOLKWAGEN
Four Speed, BEETLE
$20.00 DOWN
PER MONTH
24 Months, Cash Price, $802.18, Time Sale Price, Interest Rate, 26.00%
CALL 553-6900 For Credit OK
SUNSET AUTOS
With Qualified Credit

2.
MARQUIS COUPE
AT-PS-AC
Double Sharp
Mo.
$3468 Cash
$500 down, 36 mo. APR 12.00%
Deferred Price

3.
VEGA
HATCHBACK, Automatic.
$20.00 DOWN
PER MONTH
24 Months, Cash Price, $802.18, Time Sale Price, Interest Rate, 26.25%
CALL 553-6900 For Credit Approval
SUNSET AUTOS
5115 CENTER ST.
With Qualified Credit

4.
PONTIAC
GRAND VILLE SEDAN, All Power, Factory Air,.
$20.00 DOWN
PER MONTH
24 Months, Cash Price, $887.68, Time Sale, Price, Interest Rate, 24.5%
CREDIT OK BY PHONE, 553-6900
SUNSET AUTOS
5115 CENTER
With Qualified Credit

5.
IMPALA FOUR DOOR
PER MO.
Stk. no. 4174, V8, cruise, tilt, air conditioned. Sale Price $5367 with $567 down. Finance $4800 for 48 months.
Deferred price
APR 12%.

6.
MAVERICK
4 Door Sedan
AT-PS-PB-AC
Mo.
$3450 Cash
$500 down, 36 mo. APR 12.00%
Deferred price

7.
LTD
PER MO.
OR $5224
Dk. blue metallic with paint stripes, bumper guards & much more. Other colors at this price & many more with all the options. 4 door, V-8, automatic transmission, factory air conditioning, power steering, power brakes, tinted glass, white wall radials, remote control mirrors, Finance 48 monthly payments of ____ per mo. with only $500 down at 11% APR. & Deferred payment price

8.
OLDS
VISTA CRUISER WAGON
$10.00 DOWN
PER MONTH
24 Months, Cash Price, $507.85, Time Sale Price, Interest Rate, 28%.
Credit OK BY Phone, 553-6900
SUNSET AUTOS
5115 CENTER
With Qualified Credit

1. _____
2. _____
3. _____
4. _____
5. _____
6. _____
7. _____
8. _____

INSTALLMENT AND CONSUMER CREDIT

Use Table 13 (p. T-22) to find the monthly payments.

9. On a 20-year 11.25% loan for $80,000.

10. On a 25-year 11% loan for $55,000.

11. On a 30-year 11.5% loan for $53000 to buy the Montego home.

THE MONTEGO
The Montego offers 1306 sq. ft. of finished living area with 3 full sized bedrooms and 1¾ baths, formal dining room and an eat-in kitchen with breakfast bar

Use the following amortization schedule to answer Exercises 12–13.

SCHEDULE OF DIRECT REDUCTION LOAN

CUSTOMER NAME: KELIN ABBOTT
LOAN NUMBER: 6375
CUSTOMER NUMBER: 721881
ORDER NUMBER: 732801
PAYMENT: $687.25
RATE: 13.500%
LOAN: $60,000.00

Payment Number	Interest	Due Date—Paid To	Principal	Total Payment	Balance of Loan	Date Paid
46	666.98	10-1-88	20.27	687.25	59,267.19	
47	666.76	11-1-88	20.49	687.25	59,246.70	
48	666.53	12-1-88	20.72	687.25	59,225.98	

12. How much of payment 47 is interest? How much is principal? What is the new balance?

13. How much of payment 48 is interest? How much is principal? What is the new balance?

14. The amount owed on a 10.5% loan is $57,710.02. How much of the $548.85 monthly payment is interest? How much is principal? What is the new balance? (Assume a 360-day year and 30-day month.)

15. The amount owed on a 10.5% loan is $57,253.45. How much of the $548.85 monthly payment is interest? How much is principal? What is the new balance? (Assume a 360-day year and 30-day month.)

7.3 INTEREST ON OTHER LOANS

In this section we study how interest is computed on several different types of loans.

ADD-ON INTEREST

At the time of purchase interest is often added on to the amount borrowed. For example, $600 borrowed at 15% add-on for 12 months means that 15% of $600 (or $90) is added on to the $600 borrowed as interest, and $690 must be repaid. Interest computed in this manner is called *add-on interest*.

Example 1 Laura Seborg, a recent graduate, used a 9% add-on loan for 36 months to purchase a seven-piece bedroom suite. How much interest was charged?

COMPLETE 7-PC. GROUPS INCLUDE MATTRESS & BOXSPRING
TRIPLE DRESSER
MIRROR • CHEST
HEADBOARD • FRAME
MATTRESS AND
BOXSPRING
333⁰⁰

Solution Substituting 333 for P, 0.09 for R, and 3 for T, we get

$I = P \times R \times T$
$= 333 \times 0.09 \times 3$
$= 89.91.$

The interest charged was $89.91.

DO EXERCISE 1.

On this type of loan the interest is added on to the amount borrowed and then the monthly payments are computed.

Example 2 Find the monthly payments for the 9% add-on loan for the bedroom suite.

Solution

a) Find the amount borrowed plus interest.

Amount borrowed + interest = $333 + $89.91
$= $422.91

b) Find the monthly payment.

Monthly payment = $422.91 ÷ 36
$= $11.75

DO EXERCISE 2.

OBJECTIVES

After finishing Section 7.3, you should be able to:

• Compute add-on interest.
•• Find the APR for add-on interest.
••• Compute installment plan interest.

1. Compute the interest if a loan to purchase the seven-piece bedroom suite is at an 11% add-on rate for 36 months.

2. Find the monthly payment for an 11% add-on loan for 36 months for the bedroom suite.

ANSWERS ON PAGE A–15

●●● THE APR FOR ADD-ON INTEREST

Since the amount borrowed was paid back over 36 months, the borrower did not have the use of it for the entire time. As a result, the APR is greater than the add-on interest rate.

Example 3 Compute the APR for a 9% add-on loan for the furniture.

Solution

a) Find the finance charge per $100 of the amount borrowed.

$$\frac{89.91}{333} = \frac{x}{100}$$

$$x = 27$$

b) Find 36 in the column headed Number of Payments in Table 7.3 and read across the row until the value nearest 27 is found (27.01 in this example).

TABLE 7.3
ANNUAL PERCENTAGE RATE TABLE FOR MONTHLY PAYMENT PLANS

NUMBER OF PAYMENTS	14.00%	14.25%	14.50%	14.75%	15.00%	15.25%	15.50%	15.75%	16.00%	16.25%	16.50%	16.75%	17.00%	17.25%	17.50%	17.75%
	(FINANCE CHARGE PER $100 OF AMOUNT FINANCED)															
1	1.17	1.19	1.21	1.23	1.25	1.27	1.29	1.31	1.33	1.35	1.37	1.40	1.42	1.44	1.46	1.48
2	1.75	1.78	1.82	1.85	1.88	1.91	1.94	1.97	2.00	2.04	2.07	2.10	2.13	2.16	2.19	2.22
3	2.34	2.38	2.43	2.47	2.51	2.55	2.59	2.64	2.68	2.72	2.76	2.80	2.85	2.89	2.93	2.97
4	2.93	2.99	3.04	3.09	3.14	3.20	3.25	3.30	3.36	3.41	3.46	3.51	3.57	3.62	3.67	3.73
5	3.53	3.59	3.65	3.72	3.78	3.84	3.91	3.97	4.04	4.10	4.16	4.23	4.29	4.35	4.42	4.48
6	4.12	4.20	4.27	4.35	4.42	4.49	4.57	4.64	4.72	4.79	4.87	4.94	5.02	5.09	5.17	5.24
7	4.72	4.81	4.89	4.98	5.06	5.15	5.23	5.32	5.40	5.49	5.58	5.66	5.75	5.83	5.92	6.00
8	5.32	5.42	5.51	5.61	5.71	5.80	5.90	6.00	6.09	6.19	6.29	6.38	6.48	6.58	6.67	6.77
9	5.92	6.03	6.14	6.25	6.35	6.46	6.57	6.68	6.78	6.89	7.00	7.11	7.22	7.32	7.43	7.54
10	6.53	6.65	6.77	6.88	7.00	7.12	7.24	7.36	7.48	7.60	7.72	7.84	7.96	8.08	8.19	8.31
11	7.14	7.27	7.40	7.53	7.66	7.79	7.92	8.05	8.18	8.31	8.44	8.57	8.70	8.83	8.96	9.09
12	7.74	7.89	8.03	8.17	8.31	8.45	8.59	8.74	8.88	9.02	9.16	9.30	9.45	9.59	9.73	9.87
13	8.36	8.51	8.66	8.81	8.97	9.12	9.27	9.43	9.58	9.73	9.89	10.04	10.20	10.35	10.50	10.66
14	8.97	9.13	9.30	9.46	9.63	9.79	9.96	10.12	10.29	10.45	10.62	10.78	10.95	11.11	11.28	11.45
15	9.59	9.76	9.94	10.11	10.29	10.47	10.64	10.82	11.00	11.17	11.35	11.53	11.71	11.88	12.06	12.24
16	10.20	10.39	10.58	10.77	10.95	11.14	11.33	11.52	11.71	11.90	12.09	12.28	12.46	12.65	12.84	13.03
17	10.82	11.02	11.22	11.42	11.62	11.82	12.02	12.22	12.42	12.62	12.83	13.03	13.23	13.43	13.63	13.83
18	11.45	11.66	11.87	12.08	12.29	12.50	12.72	12.93	13.14	13.35	13.57	13.78	13.99	14.21	14.42	14.64
19	12.07	12.30	12.52	12.74	12.97	13.19	13.41	13.64	13.86	14.09	14.31	14.54	14.76	14.99	15.22	15.44
20	12.70	12.93	13.17	13.41	13.64	13.88	14.11	14.35	14.59	14.82	15.06	15.30	15.54	15.77	16.01	16.25
21	13.33	13.58	13.82	14.07	14.32	14.57	14.82	15.06	15.31	15.56	15.81	16.06	16.31	16.56	16.81	17.07
22	13.96	14.22	14.48	14.74	15.00	15.26	15.52	15.78	16.04	16.30	16.57	16.83	17.09	17.36	17.62	17.88
23	14.59	14.87	15.14	15.41	15.68	15.96	16.23	16.50	16.78	17.05	17.32	17.60	17.88	18.15	18.43	18.70
24	15.23	15.51	15.80	16.08	16.37	16.65	16.94	17.22	17.51	17.80	18.09	18.37	18.66	18.95	19.24	19.53
25	15.87	16.17	16.46	16.76	17.06	17.35	17.65	17.95	18.25	18.55	18.85	19.15	19.45	19.75	20.05	20.36
26	16.51	16.82	17.13	17.44	17.75	18.06	18.37	18.68	18.99	19.30	19.62	19.93	20.24	20.56	20.87	21.19
27	17.15	17.47	17.80	18.12	18.44	18.76	19.09	19.41	19.74	20.06	20.39	20.71	21.04	21.37	21.69	22.02
28	17.80	18.13	18.47	18.80	19.14	19.47	19.81	20.15	20.48	20.82	21.16	21.50	21.84	22.18	22.52	22.86
29	18.45	18.79	19.14	19.49	19.83	20.18	20.53	20.88	21.23	21.58	21.94	22.29	22.64	22.99	23.35	23.70
30	19.10	19.45	19.81	20.17	20.54	20.90	21.26	21.62	21.99	22.35	22.72	23.08	23.45	23.81	24.18	24.55
31	19.75	20.12	20.49	20.87	21.24	21.61	21.99	22.37	22.74	23.12	23.50	23.88	24.26	24.64	25.02	25.40
32	20.40	20.79	21.17	21.56	21.95	22.33	22.72	23.11	23.50	23.89	24.28	24.68	25.07	25.46	25.86	26.25
33	21.06	21.46	21.85	22.25	22.65	23.06	23.46	23.86	24.26	24.67	25.07	25.48	25.88	26.29	26.70	27.11
34	21.72	22.13	22.54	22.95	23.37	23.78	24.19	24.61	25.03	25.44	25.86	26.28	26.70	27.12	27.54	27.97
35	22.38	22.80	23.23	23.65	24.08	24.51	24.94	25.36	25.79	26.23	26.66	27.09	27.52	27.96	28.39	28.83
36	23.04	23.48	23.92	24.35	24.80	25.24	25.68	26.12	26.57	27.01	27.46	27.90	28.35	28.80	29.25	29.70
37	23.70	24.16	24.61	25.06	25.51	25.97	26.42	26.88	27.34	27.80	28.26	28.72	29.18	29.64	30.10	30.57
38	24.37	24.84	25.30	25.77	26.24	26.70	27.17	27.64	28.11	28.59	29.06	29.53	30.01	30.49	30.96	31.44
39	25.04	25.52	26.00	26.48	26.96	27.44	27.92	28.41	28.89	29.38	29.87	30.36	30.85	31.34	31.83	32.32
40	25.71	26.20	26.70	27.19	27.69	28.18	28.68	29.18	29.68	30.18	30.68	31.18	31.68	32.19	32.69	33.20

c) The rate at the top of the column containing 27.01 is 16.25%. The APR is 16.25%.

DO EXERCISE 3.

●●● INSTALLMENT PLAN INTEREST

Buying on an *installment plan* means paying for goods and services over a period of time. Expensive items such as major appliances, televisions, and stereo equipment, and even medical bills are sometimes paid for using the installment plan.

CITIZEN SMITH   **By Dave Gerard**

"We could break up your bill into installments — pay one every four hours!"

Example 4 You purchased a $695 stereo for $50 down and $57 a month for 12 months. What was the finance charge?

Solution

a) Find the amount of the loan.

Amount of loan = Purchase price − Down payment
= 695 − 50
= 645

b) Find the total amount paid.

Total amount paid (excluding down payment) = Number of payments × Amount of each payment
= 12 × 57
= 684

c) Find the finance charge.

Finance charge = Total amount paid − Amount of loan
= 684 − 645
= 39

The finance charge was $39.

DO EXERCISE 4.

3. Find the APR for an 11% add-on loan for 36 months for the bedroom suite. Give your answer to the nearest 0.25%.

4. An $870 medical bill was paid for with $50 down and $75 a month for 12 months. What was the finance charge?

ANSWERS ON PAGE A–15

5. A $325 sewing machine is paid for in five monthly installments of $65 plus $1\frac{1}{4}$% each month on the unpaid balance. What is the finance charge?

Example 5 A $450 television was paid for in three monthly installments of $150 plus $1\frac{1}{2}$% each month on the unpaid balance. What was the finance charge?

Solution

a) Find the finance charge for each month.

Month	Unpaid balance	Finance charge
1	$450	$450 × 0.015, or $6.75
2	$300	$300 × 0.015, or $4.50
3	$150	$150 × 0.015, or $2.25

b) Find the total finance charge.

$$\text{Total finance charge} = \text{Sum of monthly finance charges}$$
$$= \$6.75 + \$4.50 + \$2.25$$
$$= \$13.50$$

The total finance charge was $13.50.

DO EXERCISE 5.

> A formula for finding the finance charge on installment loans is
> $$I = \frac{n(n+1)}{2}(P)(i)$$
> where I = the finance charge, n = the number of payments, P = the monthly payment, and i = the interest rate charged on the unpaid balance.

The following example, identical to Example 5, uses this formula to compute the finance charge.

Example 6 A $450 television was paid for in three monthly installments of $150 plus $1\frac{1}{2}$% each month on the unpaid balance. What was the finance charge?

Solution

Substituting 3 for n, 150 for P, and 0.015 for i in

$$I = \frac{n(n+1)}{2}(P)(i)$$

we get

$$I = \frac{3(3+1)}{2}(150)(0.015)$$

$$= 13.50.$$

The finance charge was $13.50.

DO EXERCISE 6.

6. A $445 freezer was paid for in five monthly installments of $89 plus 2% each month on the unpaid balance. What was the finance charge?

NAME _____ CLASS _____ ANSWERS

EXERCISE SET 7.3

■ Solve.

1. An 8% add-on loan for $3500 for 36 months was used to purchase furniture. How much was the interest?

2. A 7% add-on loan for $5600 for 24 months was used to purchase applicances. How much was the interest?

3. A 9% add-on loan for $4000 for 12 months was used to purchase a security system. How much was the interest?

4. An 8% add-on loan for $3000 for 24 months was used to purchase a septic system. How much was the interest?

5. Find the monthly payments for the furniture in 1.

6. Find the monthly payments for the appliances in 2.

7. Find the monthly payments for the security system in 3.

8. Find the monthly payments for the septic system in 4.

■■ Use Table 12 (p. T–15) to find the APR to the nearest $\frac{1}{4}$ percent.

9. For the furniture in 1.

10. For the appliances in 2.

11. For the security system in 3.

12. For the septic system in 4.

1. _____

2. _____

3. _____

4. _____

5. _____

6. _____

7. _____

8. _____

9. _____

10. _____

11. _____

12. _____

INSTALLMENT AND CONSUMER CREDIT

Complete. Use Table 12 (p. T–15) and give answer to the nearest $\frac{1}{4}$%.

	Amount of Loan	Add-on-Rate	Interest	Monthly Payment	Payments	APR
13.	$ 500	$6\frac{1}{2}$%			24	
14.	$ 399	8%			18	
15.	$ 950		$242.25		36	
16.	$ 700		$140.00		24	
17.	$1200			$34.00	48	
18.	$1000			$50.83	24	
19.		$6\frac{1}{2}$%	$ 58.50		24	
20.		$7\frac{1}{2}$%	$390.00		48	
21.			$120.00	$24.00	30	
22.			$101.20	$16.70	36	

Find the finance charge on each of these purchases for your new home.

23. A $379 freezer is purchased for $75 down and $28 a month for twelve months.

24. A $285 dishwasher is purchased for $25 down and $47 a month for six months.

25. A $320 washer is purchased for $45 down and $42 a month for seven months.

26. A $700 riding mower is purchased for $80 down and $55 a month for twelve months.

27. A $595 amplifier is paid for in seven monthly installments of $85 plus 2% each month on the unpaid balance.

28. A $430 range is paid for in five monthly payments of $86 plus $2\frac{1}{2}$% each month on the unpaid balance.

29. A $492 color television is paid for in six monthly installments of $82 plus 3% each month on the unpaid balance.

30. An $1104 video cassette recorder is paid for in six monthly installments of $184 plus $1\frac{1}{2}$% each month on the unpaid balance.

31. A $511.92 microwave oven is paid for in twelve equal monthly payments plus $1\frac{3}{4}$% each month on the unpaid balance. Find the finance charge.

32. A $317.10 chord organ is paid for in six equal monthly payments plus $1\frac{1}{4}$% each month on the unpaid balance. Find the finance charge.

7.4 EARLY PAYMENT OF A LOAN

Consumers may wish to pay off an installment plan loan early. They may then be entitled to an interest rebate. The *Rule of 78* is used to find the interest rebate (unearned interest).

INTEREST REBATE

Example 1 A waste disposal loan is being repaid in three equal monthly payments of $50 each. The total amount of interest is $18. At the end of the second month the loan is paid in full. How much is the interest rebate?

Solution Let x be the interest for the third month. Then 2x is the interest for the second month (since twice as much is owed ($100) at the end of month 2) and 3x is the interest for the first month (since three times as much is owed ($150) at the end of month 1).

Sum of interest charges = Total interest charge

$$x + 2x + 3x = \$18$$
$$(1 + 2 + 3)x = \$18$$
$$6x = \$18$$

So $x = \$3$.

The interest rebate is $3, since this would have been the interest charged for the third month.

DO EXERCISE 1.

Note in Example 1 that the interest on $150 for one month ($9) is the same as the interest on $50 for three months.

The following example illustrates a general procedure for finding the interest rebate.

Example 2 A loan is being repaid in twelve equal monthly payments. At the end of the eighth month the loan is paid in full. What fraction of the total interest need not be paid?

OBJECTIVES

After finishing Section 7.4, you should be able to:

- Determine the interest rebate.
- Calculate the final payment.

1. A loan is being repaid in three monthly payments of $75 each. The total amount of interest is $30. The loan is paid in full at the end of the second month. How much is the interest rebate?

ANSWER ON PAGE A–16

2. A loan is being repaid in twelve equal monthly payments. At the end of the seventh month the loan is paid in full. What fraction of the total interest charge need not be paid?

Solution

a) Find the interest for the twelfth month.

Let x be the interest for the twelfth month; then

2x is the interest for the eleventh month, and

. . .
. . .
. . .

12x is the interest for the first month.

Sum of interest charges = Total interest charge

$$x + 2x + \cdots + 12x = I$$
$$(1 + 2 + \cdots + 12)x = I$$
$$78x = I \quad \text{Adding up the numbers 1 through 12*}$$
$$x = \frac{1}{78} \cdot I \quad \text{Multiplying by } \frac{1}{78}$$

The interest charge for the twelfth month is $\frac{1}{78}$ of the total interest charge, I.

b) Find the interest charges for each of the last four months.

The interest charges for each of the last 4 months are

x,   2x,   3x,   and   4x   or

$$\frac{1}{78}I, \quad \frac{2}{78}I, \quad \frac{3}{78}I, \quad \text{and} \quad \frac{4}{78}I$$

and we know that

$$\frac{1}{78}I + \frac{2}{78}I + \frac{3}{78}I + \frac{4}{78}I = \frac{10}{78}I,$$

so $\frac{10}{78}$ of the total interest charges, I, are paid during the last four months.

Thus $\frac{10}{78}$ of the total interest charges need not be paid.

DO EXERCISE 2.

Note in Example 2 that the interest for one year is divided into 78 increments, with $\frac{12}{78}$ due at the end of the first month, $\frac{11}{78}$ due at the end of the second month, and so forth. Consequently, the method is named the **Rule of 78**.

---

* A quick way to find the sum of the numbers 1 through n is to use the formula

$$1 + 2 + 3 + \cdots + n = \frac{n \times (n+1)}{2};$$

thus

$$1 + 2 + 3 + \cdots + 12 = \frac{12 \times 13}{2} = 78.$$

●● FINAL PAYMENT

Example 3 A twelve-month refrigerator installment loan with $70 payments and an interest charge of $60 was paid in full at the end of nine months. How much was the final payment?

Solution

a) Find the unearned part of the interest charges.

$$\frac{1}{78}I + \frac{2}{78}I + \frac{3}{78}I = \frac{6}{78}I$$

b) Find the unearned interest charge.

$$\text{Unearned interest charge} = \frac{6}{78} \times 60$$
$$= 4.62$$

The interest rebate was $4.62.

c) Find the final payment.

$$\begin{aligned}\text{Final payment} &= \text{Amount still owed} - \text{Interest rebate} \\ &= (3 \times 70) - 4.62 \\ &= 205.38\end{aligned}$$

The final payment was $205.38.

DO EXERCISE 3.

The rebate for early payment of an installment loan for other than twelve months is illustrated in Example 4.

Example 4 A 28-month installment loan with $80 payments and an interest charge of $153 was paid in full at the end of 19 months. How much was the final payment?

Solution

a) Find the number of interest increments.

Using the formula from Example 2, we find that the number of increments is

$$\frac{n \times (n+1)}{2} = \frac{28 \times 29}{2} \text{ or } 406.$$

b) Find the number of interest increments in the remaining nine, or (28 − 19), months.

Using the formula from Example 2, we find that the number of remaining increments is

$$\frac{n \times (n+1)}{2} = \frac{9 \times 10}{2} \text{ or } 45.$$

3. A twelve-month installment loan having an interest charge of $48 and monthly payments of $72 was paid in full at the end of seven months. How much were the interest rebate and the final payment?

ANSWER ON PAGE A–16

4. A 36-month installment loan with $90 payments and an interest charge of $162 was paid in full at the end of 21 months. How much were the interest rebate and the final payment?

c) Find the interest rebate.

$$\text{Interest rebate} = \frac{\text{Increments remaining}}{\text{Total increments}} \times \text{Interest}$$

$$= \frac{45}{406} \times \$153$$

$$= \$16.96$$

d) Find the final payment.

Final payment = (Number of payments remaining × Payments) − Rebate

$= (9 \times \$80) - \$16.96$

$= \$703.04$

DO EXERCISE 4.

NAME	CLASS	ANSWERS

EXERCISE SET 7.4

■ You win the Publishers Clearing House Sweepstakes and pay off these loans early. Find the interest rebate.

1. Twelve monthly payments of $60, interest of $45, and paid in full at the end of four months

2. Twelve monthly payments of $60, interest of $32, and paid in full at the end of ten months

3. Four monthly payments of $25, interest of $14, and paid in full at the end of three months

4. Four monthly payments of $25, interest of $20, and paid in full at the end of two months

5. Fifteen monthly payments of $70, interest of $68, and paid in full at the end of twelve months

6. Fifteen monthly payments of $70, interest of $85, and paid in full at the end of thirteen months

7. Nine monthly payments of $45, interest of $56, and paid in full at the end of five months

8. Nine monthly payments of $45, interest of $62, and paid in full at the end of three months

9. A loan is being repaid in five equal monthly payments of $80 each. The total amount of interest is $43. At the end of the third month the loan is paid in full. How much is the interest rebate?

10. A loan is being repaid in seven equal monthly payments of $125 each. The total amount of interest is $95. At the end of the second month the loan is paid in full. How much is the interest rebate?

11. A 30-month installment loan with $140 monthly payments and an interest charge of $230 was paid in full at the end of 23 months. How much was the interest rebate?

12. An 18-month installment loan with $106 monthly payments and an interest charge of $270 was paid in full at the end of 15 months. How much was the interest rebate?

ANSWERS

1. _____
2. _____
3. _____
4. _____
5. _____
6. _____
7. _____
8. _____
9. _____
10. _____
11. _____
12. _____

314 INSTALLMENT AND CONSUMER CREDIT

ANSWERS

⚃ Determine the final payment.

13. For the loan in 1.

14. For the loan in 2.

15. For the loan in 3.

16. For the loan in 4.

17. For the loan in 5.

18. For the loan in 6.

19. For the loan in 7.

20. For the loan in 8.

21. For the loan in 9.

22. For the loan in 10.

23. For the loan in 11.

24. For the loan in 12.

🖩 Find the interest rebate and the final payment.

25. 24 monthly payments of $90.55, interest of $288.77, and paid in full at the end of 19 months

26. 48 monthly payments of $90.55, interest of $486.33, and paid in full at the end of 36 months

27. 36 monthly payments of $125.34, interest of $356.94, and paid in full at the end of 23 months

28. 30 monthly payments of $125.33, interest of $304.56, and paid in full at the end of 21 months

7.5 CHARGE CARDS

Credit cards have become very much a part of our daily lives. We charge purchases, receive monthly statements, and make payments regularly. In this section we study this form of credit.

REVOLVING CREDIT

A charge account in which amounts for new purchases are added to existing amounts owed is a *revolving credit plan*. Annual percentage rates used in computing finance charges vary depending on the amount owed and the customer's state of residence, as do methods for finding minimum payments due. A monthly statement for a J. R. Nickel revolving credit plan appears below. The method for computing finance charges appears in the lower left corner of the statement.

Example 1 Find the finance charge for the J. R. Nickel statement.

Solution The finance charge is $1\frac{1}{2}\%$ per month (for amounts up to $500) of the average daily balance.

Finance charge = 0.015 × 108.69
             = 1.63

The finance charge is $1.63.

DO EXERCISE 1.

OBJECTIVES

After finishing Section 7.5, you should be able to:

- Determine the finance charge, new balance, and minimum payment for revolving credit plans.
- Calculate the costs for bank card use.

1. The average daily balance on a J. R. Nickel statement was $435.97. What was the finance charge?

ANSWER ON PAGE A–16

2. Find the finance charge on a J. R. Nickel statement in which the average daily balance was $698.67.

For average daily balances in excess of $500 the finance charge is $1\frac{1}{4}\%$ of the excess and $1\frac{1}{2}\%$ of $500.

Example 2 Find the finance charge for a J. R. Nickel statement in which the average daily balance was $823.75.

Solution

a) Find the finance charge on the amount over $500.

The amount over $500 is $323.75 ($823.75 − $500), so

Finance charge = 0.0125 × 323.75
(amount over $500)

= 4.05.

b) Find the finance charge on $500.

Finance charge = 0.015 × 500
(on $500)

= 7.50

c) Find the total finance charge.

Total finance charge = 4.05 + 7.50

= 11.55

The total finance charge was $11.55.

DO EXERCISE 2.

The following example shows the computation needed to find the new balance.

Example 3 Find the new balance for the J. R. Nickel statement on the preceding page.

Solution

New balance = Previous balance + Purchases + Finance charge − Payment

= 199.28 + 22.70 + 1.63 − 100.00

= 123.61

The new balance is $123.61.

DO EXERCISE 3.

3. Find the new balance for a J. R. Nickel statement in which the previous balance was $246.89, purchases totaled $54.67, the finance charge was $2.38, and the payment was $45.

ANSWERS ON PAGE A–16

The table below shows the minimum payment for J. R. Nickel charge accounts.

New Balance (less insurance premiums)	Minimum Payment
11.00 or less	Balance
11.01–200	$10
200.01–250	15
250.01–300	20
300.01–350	25
350.01–400	30
400.01–450	35
450.01–500	40
Over $500	1/10 of Balance

Example 4 Find the minimum payment for the J. R. Nickel statement on p. 315.

Solution Since the new balance is $123.61, the minimum payment is $10.00.

DO EXERCISE 4.

◉◉ BANK CARDS

Bank cards have made credit purchases readily available. MasterCard and Visa are two examples of widely used bank cards.

These cards may be used to purchase goods and services in both the United States and foreign countries. For this service the banks usually charge both the business (about 5% of the purchase amount) and the purchaser a finance charge. In addition, an annual fee may be charged to the cardholder. The fee may vary but is typically about $15.00.

Example 5 MasterCard purchases by patrons of a business amounted to $4000. How much did the business pay MasterCard?

Solution The amount paid by the business is 5% of the amount of the purchases, so

Amount paid = 0.05 × 4000
            = 200

The business paid MasterCard $200.

DO EXERCISE 5.

---

4. Find the minimum payment for a J. R. Nickel statement having a new balance of $385.67.

5. MasterCard purchases amounted to $8000 for a business. How much did the business pay to MasterCard?

ANSWERS ON PAGE A–16

Here is a typical MasterCard statement.

ACCOUNT NUMBER	CREDIT LIMIT	AVAILABLE CREDIT	DAYS IN BILLING CYCLE	STATEMENT DATE	PAYMENT DUE DATE	MINIMUM PAYMENT DUE
5173 0062 4703 04	500	52	29	11/17/84	12/12/84	22.00

TELEPHONE NO. (See Reverse Side): Iowa Residents 1-800-622-8252 / All Others 1-800-247-8101 / Local 245-3157

DATE OF TRANS.	POST.	REFERENCE NUMBER	CHARGES, PAYMENTS AND CREDITS SINCE LAST STATEMENT	AMOUNT
0924	1021	*7548024LX2XAMDY24	SINCLAIR MRKTNG=400001 SIOUX FALLS SD	19.00
1021	1026	*7541117MU02RUTDFM	ROBO CAR WASH SIOUX FALLS SD	25.00
1026	1101	*7528200MYVP9MBU6E	CALIF 6 MOTELS 34 HAYWARD CA	24.39
1027	1102	*7528200N1VNV5LNK6	CALIF 6 MOTELS 34 HAYWARD CA	24.39
1103	1103	7531700N41NMNEKYX	PAYMENT = THANK YOU	58.88−
1107	1111	*7520400NA2Y5A7GD8	KNOTTS BERRY FARM BUENA PARK CA	16.90
1105	1111	*7525400N900NHKTNB	VILLA MOTEL BUENA PARK CA	31.80
		FINANCE CHARGE *PURCHASES $5.97 *CASH ADVANCE $0.00		5.97

PREVIOUS BALANCE	PAYMENTS	CREDITS	PURCHASES AND CASH ADVANCES	DEBIT ADJUSTMENTS	FINANCE CHARGE	NEW BALANCE
358.88	58.88	0.00	141.48	0.00	5.97	447.45

AN AMOUNT FOLLOWED BY A MINUS SIGN (−) IS A CREDIT OR A CREDIT BALANCE UNLESS OTHERWISE INDICATED.

Send Billing Error Notices To: MASTERCARD DEPARTMENT P.O. BOX 522 DES MOINES IOWA 50302

	UNDER RATE CHANGE POINT	DOLLAR POINT AT WHICH RATES CHANGE	OVER RATE CHANGE POINT	1. Average Daily Balance of Previous Balance	2. Average Daily Balance of Current Cash Advances
ANNUAL PERCENTAGE RATES	% 18.00		% 15.00	321.17	0.00
MONTHLY PERIODIC RATES	% 1.500	500	% 1.250	3. Average Daily Balance of Current Purchases 77.68	4. Average Daily Balance subject to FINANCE CHARGE 398.85

MasterCard 2I

To avoid additional finance charges, payment in full of the new balance must be received at the address for receipt of payment by 12:00 noon of the payment due date.

NOTICE: See reverse side for important information.

We will find the new balance.

Example 6 Find the new balance.

Solution

$$\text{New Balance} = \text{Previous Balance} + \text{Purchases and Cash Advances} + \text{Finance Charges} - \text{Payments}$$

$$= \$358.88 + \$141.48 + \$5.97 - \$58.88$$

$$= \$447.45$$

The new balance is $447.45.

DO EXERCISE 6.

Next we find the finance charge.

Example 7 Determine the finance charge.

Solution

a) Find the average daily balance of the previous balance (Box 1).

The previous balance

10/19–11/2   There are 29 days in the billing cycle and 10/19 is 29 days before 11/17.

14 days at $343.85 ($358.88 − $15.03*) $4813.90

11/3–11/17

15 days at $300 ($358.88 − $58.88) $4500.00
Daily Balance (Previous balance) $9313.90

$$\text{Average Daily Balance (Previous balance)} = \frac{\$9313.90}{29}$$

$$= \$321.17$$

b) Find the average daily balance of current cash advances (Box 2).

There was no money borrowed, so 0 is in Box 2.

c) Find the average daily balance of current purchases (Box 3).

Charge	Posted	Days to 11/17	Amount	Amount × Days
Sinclair	10/21	28	$19.00	$532.00
Robo	10/26	23	25.00	575.00
Motel	11/1	17	24.39	414.63
Motel	11/2	16	24.39	390.24
Knotts	11/11	7	16.90	118.30
Villa Motel	11/11	7	31.80	222.60

Daily Balance (Current purchases) $2252.77

$$\text{Average Daily Balance (Current purchases)} = \frac{\$2252.77}{29}$$

$$= \$77.68$$

*The previous month's finance charge was $15.03 and no interest is charged on interest.

6. Find the new balance if the purchases were $183.26. Assume same finance charge.

ANSWER ON PAGE A-16

7. Determine the finance charge if an additional purchase of $36.95 was posted on 11/5.

d) Find the finance charge.

Add entries in Boxes 1, 2, and 3.

$321.17 + 0 + $77.68 = $398.85

Multiply by 1.5% (For amounts less than $500).

Finance charge = 0.015 × $398.85
= $5.97

The finance charge was $5.97.

DO EXERCISE 7.

The computations for Visa are similar.

ANSWER ON PAGE A–16

EXERCISE SET 7.5

NAME _____ / _____ CLASS _____ ANSWER

EXERCISE SET 7.5

1. Fill in the finance charge, new balance, and minimum payment where indicated.

Sears Charge — Sears, Roebuck and Co.

You may pay by mail or at any Sears Store. If you pay by mail, please send only the top portion of your statement with your payment. If you pay at any Sears Store, please bring the entire statement with you. Your payment will be credited as of the date received if you use the enclosed self-addressed envelope. Payment made in any other manner will be processed promptly but could result in up to a 5 day delay in crediting your account. PLEASE MAKE ADDRESS CHANGE OR CORRECTIONS IN ADDRESS AREA BELOW.

If state of residence changes, your account will be transferred, as required, for servicing.

3 47601 57893 4

Francis T. Hoyt
321 Edge Rd.
Sumner, IA 50103

Thank You for Shopping at Sears
Amount Due

OFFICE USE ONLY

$ _____ AMOUNT PAID

347601578934

MAIL ANY BILLING ERROR NOTICE TO Sears Credit Department at address shown below. Direct other inquiries to nearest Sears store.

Mo.	Day	Reference	TRANSACTION DESCRIPTION See reverse for detailed description of department numbers indicated below.	CHARGES	PAYMENTS & CREDITS
**			FINANCE CHARGE**ON AVG DAILY BAL OF $346.85		
11	03	5314	PAYMENT		50.00
11	08	DR02	HOUSEWARES 11	10.28	
11	15	DR06	AUTOMOTIVE ACCESSORIES 28	36.96	

PLEASE MENTION THIS ACCOUNT NUMBER WHEN ORDERING OR WRITING	BILLING DATE	PREVIOUS BALANCE	NEW BALANCE	MINIMUM PAYMENT
3 47601 57893 4	Nov 21, 1984	$376.28	$	$

If the FINANCE CHARGE exceeds 50¢, the ANNUAL PERCENTAGE RATE is 18% on the first $500 of the AVERAGE DAILY BALANCE and 15% on that part of the AVERAGE DAILY BALANCE in excess of $500. The AVERAGE DAILY BALANCE excludes any purchases added during the monthly billing period and any unpaid FINANCE CHARGE.

To avoid a FINANCE CHARGE next month, pay this amount within 30 days from Billing Date.

If you prefer to pay in installments, pay this amount or more within 30 days from Billing Date. The sooner you pay and the more you pay, the smaller your FINANCE CHARGE.

14351-161 7/1/78   NOTICE: SEE REVERSE SIDE FOR IMPORTANT INFORMATION.

If your highest "New Balance" is:	Your Minimum Payment will be:	If your highest "New Balance" is:	Your Minimum Payment will be:	If your highest "New Balance" is:	Your Minimum Payment will be:
$ .01 to $ 8.00	Balance	$240.01 to $260.00	$13.00	$440.01 to $470.00	$19.00
8.01 to 160.00	$ 8.00	260.01 to 290.00	14.00	470.01 to 500.00	20.00
160.01 to 180.00	9.00	290.01 to 340.00	15.00	Over $500.00..1/25th of Highest Account Balance rounded to next higher whole dollar amount	
180.01 to 200.00	10.00	340.01 to 380.00	16.00		
200.01 to 220.00	11.00	380.01 to 410.00	17.00		
220.01 to 240.00	12.00	410.01 to 440.00	18.00		

2. Find the finance charge for a Sears statement having an average daily balance of $645.

2. _____

INSTALLMENT AND CONSUMER CREDIT

ANSWERS

3. _____

4. _____

3. Find the new balance for a Sears statement in which the previous balance was $436, the purchases totaled $32, the payment was $50, and the finance charge was $6.35.

4. Find the minimum payment for a Sears statement having a new balance of $476.85.

5. Fill in where indicated.

There was no finance charge the previous month.

TELEPHONE NO. (See Reverse Side): Iowa Residents 1-800-622-8252
All Others 1-800-247-8101   Local 245-3157

ACCOUNT NUMBER	CREDIT LIMIT	AVAILABLE CREDIT	DAYS IN BILLING CYCLE	STATEMENT DATE	PAYMENT DUE DATE	MINIMUM PAYMENT DUE
	1700	1387	29	11/12/84	12/07/84	15.00

DATE OF TRANS.	POST.	REFERENCE NUMBER	CHARGES, PAYMENTS AND CREDITS SINCE LAST STATEMENT	AMOUNT
1010	1015	*7533340MF00002LE0	CENTRAL HARDWARD #41 COLUMBUS OH	42.15
1004	1018	*7523300MG3JE3GM04	STANTONS SHEET MUSIC COLUMBUS OH	15.80
1015	1022	*7541130MN0HNPWGB9	OSU BOOKSTORE COLUMBUS OH	18.94
1009	1022	*7523300MN3JFWR0RA	STANTONS SHEET MUSIC COLUMBUS OH	24.65
1021	1027	*7541130MV0J5ZALZ2	OSU BOOKSTORE COLUMBUS OH	21.10
1110	1110	7531700NC1NMKETGC	PAYMENT — THANK YOU	400.00−

FINANCE CHARGE   *PURCHASES   *CASH ADVANCE $0.00

PREVIOUS BALANCE	PAYMENTS	CREDITS	PURCHASES AND CASH ADVANCES	DEBIT ADJUSTMENTS	FINANCE CHARGE	NEW BALANCE
580.47	400.00	0.00	122.64	0.00		

AN AMOUNT FOLLOWED BY A MINUS SIGN (−) IS A CREDIT OR A CREDIT BALANCE UNLESS OTHERWISE INDICATED.

Send Billing Error Notices To: MASTERCARD DEPARTMENT P.O. BOX 522 DES MOINES IOWA 50302

	UNDER RATE CHANGE POINT	DOLLAR POINT AT WHICH RATES CHANGE	OVER RATE CHANGE POINT	1. Average Daily Balance of Previous Balance	2. Average Daily Balance of Current Cash Advances
ANNUAL PERCENTAGE RATES	% 18.00	500	% 15.00	539.09	0.00
MONTHLY PERIODIC RATES	% 1.500		% 1.250	3. Average Daily Balance of Current Purchases	4. Average Daily Balance subject to FINANCE CHARGE

MasterCard 2I

To avoid additional finance charges, payment in full of the new balance must be received at the address for receipt of payment by 12:00 noon of the payment due date.

NOTICE: See reverse side for important information.

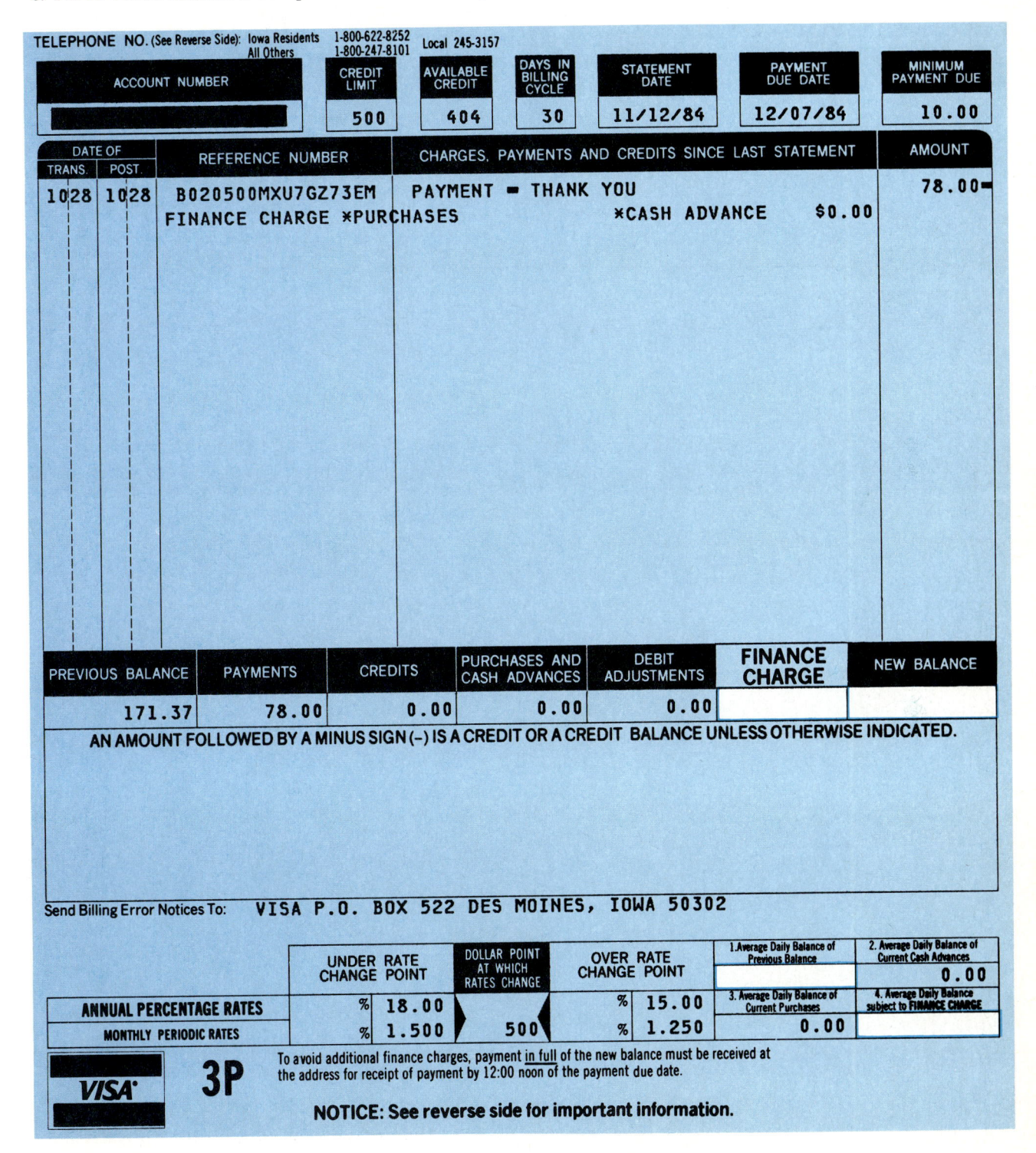

6. Fill in where indicated. The previous finance charge was $3.69.

TELEPHONE NO. (See Reverse Side):	Iowa Residents 1-800-622-8252	All Others 1-800-247-8101	Local 245-3157				
ACCOUNT NUMBER		CREDIT LIMIT	AVAILABLE CREDIT	DAYS IN BILLING CYCLE	STATEMENT DATE	PAYMENT DUE DATE	MINIMUM PAYMENT DUE
		500	404	30	11/12/84	12/07/84	10.00

DATE OF TRANS.	POST.	REFERENCE NUMBER	CHARGES, PAYMENTS AND CREDITS SINCE LAST STATEMENT	AMOUNT
10 28	10 28	B020500MXU7GZ73EM	PAYMENT — THANK YOU	78.00—
		FINANCE CHARGE *PURCHASES *CASH ADVANCE	$0.00	

PREVIOUS BALANCE	PAYMENTS	CREDITS	PURCHASES AND CASH ADVANCES	DEBIT ADJUSTMENTS	FINANCE CHARGE	NEW BALANCE
171.37	78.00	0.00	0.00	0.00		

AN AMOUNT FOLLOWED BY A MINUS SIGN (−) IS A CREDIT OR A CREDIT BALANCE UNLESS OTHERWISE INDICATED.

Send Billing Error Notices To: VISA P.O. BOX 522 DES MOINES, IOWA 50302

	UNDER RATE CHANGE POINT	DOLLAR POINT AT WHICH RATES CHANGE	OVER RATE CHANGE POINT	1. Average Daily Balance of Previous Balance	2. Average Daily Balance of Current Cash Advances
ANNUAL PERCENTAGE RATES	% 18.00		% 15.00		0.00
MONTHLY PERIODIC RATES	% 1.500	500	% 1.250	3. Average Daily Balance of Current Purchases 0.00	4. Average Daily Balance subject to FINANCE CHARGE

VISA 3P

To avoid additional finance charges, payment in full of the new balance must be received at the address for receipt of payment by 12:00 noon of the payment due date.

NOTICE: See reverse side for important information.

7. Fill in where indicated. The previous finance charge was $14.98.

TELEPHONE NO. (See Reverse Side): Iowa Residents 1-800-622-8252 All Others 1-800-247-8101 Local 245-3157						
ACCOUNT NUMBER	CREDIT LIMIT	AVAILABLE CREDIT	DAYS IN BILLING CYCLE	STATEMENT DATE	PAYMENT DUE DATE	MINIMUM PAYMENT DUE
	600	74	30	11/10/84	12/05/84	26.00

DATE OF TRANS.	POST.	REFERENCE NUMBER	CHARGES, PAYMENTS AND CREDITS SINCE LAST STATEMENT	AMOUNT
10/19	10/20	*7531700MM1EP7MGDV	TARGET #171 BILLINGS BILLINGS MT	33.24
10/25	10/25	7531700MV1N3M9P53	PAYMENT — THANK YOU	52.00−
		FINANCE CHARGE *PURCHASES	*CASH ADVANCE $0.00	

PREVIOUS BALANCE	PAYMENTS	CREDITS	PURCHASES AND CASH ADVANCES	DEBIT ADJUSTMENTS	FINANCE CHARGE	NEW BALANCE
536.24	52.00	0.00	33.24	0.00		

AN AMOUNT FOLLOWED BY A MINUS SIGN (−) IS A CREDIT OR A CREDIT BALANCE UNLESS OTHERWISE INDICATED.

Send Billing Error Notices To: **MASTERCARD DEPARTMENT P.O. BOX 522 DES MOINES IOWA 50302**

	UNDER RATE CHANGE POINT	DOLLAR POINT AT WHICH RATES CHANGE	OVER RATE CHANGE POINT	1. Average Daily Balance of Previous Balance	2. Average Daily Balance of Current Cash Advances
ANNUAL PERCENTAGE RATES	% 18.00	500	% 15.00		0.00
MONTHLY PERIODIC RATES	% 1.500		% 1.250	3. Average Daily Balance of Current Cash Advances	4. Average Daily Balance subject to FINANCE CHARGE

MasterCard 2I

To avoid additional finance charges, payment in full of the new balance must be received at the address for receipt of payment by 12:00 noon of the payment due date.

NOTICE: See reverse side for important information.

TEST OR REVIEW—CHAPTER 7

NAME _____ SCORE _____ ANSWERS

If you miss an item, review the indicated section and objective.

[7.1, •] 1. A consumer borrowed $3500 to buy a Jacuzzi. Her monthly payments were $123.50 for 36 months. Find the finance charge.

1. _____

[7.1, • •] 2. Find the APR (to the nearest 0.25%) on a $4000 auto loan payable over 36 months with payments of $135 (Table 12).

2. _____

[7.1, • • •] 3. Use the APR formula to estimate the APR for a $3600 loan payable over 24 months with payments of $170.

3. _____

[7.2, •] 4. Find the monthly payments on a $5600 loan payment over 48 months at an APR of $11\frac{1}{4}$% (Table 12).

4. _____

[7.2, • •] 5. Use the amortization schedule below to find how much of payment 91 is interest, how much is principal, and what the new balance is.

SCHEDULE OF DIRECT REDUCTION LOAN

BANK A COUNT — RUDOLPH, WI 54475 — 715-435-3131

CUSTOMER NAME: KELIN ABBOTT — LOAN NUMBER: 6375
CUSTOMER NUMBER: 721881 — ORDER NUMBER: 732801 — PAYMENT: $687.25 — RATE: 13.500% — LOAN: $60,000.00

PAYMENT NUMBER	INTEREST	DUE DATE–PAID TO	PRINCIPAL	TOTAL PAYMENT	BALANCE OF LOAN	DATE PAID
90	654.10	6-1-87	33.15	687.25	58,108.65	
91	653.72	7-1-87	33.53	687.25	58,075.12	
92	653.35	8-1-87	33.90	687.25	58,041.22	
93	652.96	9-1-87	34.29	687.25	58,006.93	

5. _____

[7.3, •] 6. An 11% add-on loan for $5200 over 24 months was used to buy furniture. How much interest was charged?

6. _____

[7.3, • •] 7. Find the APR (to the nearest 0.25%) for an $1800 7% add-on loan payable over 24 months (Table 12).

7. _____

[7.3, • • •] 8. An $845 stereo is purchased for $75 down and $68 a month for 12 months. What is the finance charge?

8. _____

[7.4, •] 9. A 12-month installment loan with $95 payments and an interest charge of $68 was paid in full at the end of eight months. How much was the interest rebate?

9. _____

[7.4, • •] 10. Find the final payment in 9.

10. _____

[7.5, •] 11. Find the finance charge for a J. R. Nickel statement in which the average daily balance is $764.96.

11. _____

325

[7.5, ●●] **12.** Complete where indicated. The previous finance charge was $2.85.

ACCOUNT NUMBER	CREDIT LIMIT	AVAILABLE CREDIT	DAYS IN BILLING CYCLE	STATEMENT DATE	PAYMENT DUE DATE	MINIMUM PAYMENT DUE
	500	222	32	11/09/84	12/04/84	13.00

DATE OF TRANS.	POST	REFERENCE NUMBER	CHARGES, PAYMENTS AND CREDITS SINCE LAST STATEMENT	AMOUNT
10 20	10 22	*7531700MPU7FR5DGZ	CASH ADVANCE MINNEAPOLIS MN	50.00
11 03	11 03	7531700N41N3JG6WA	PAYMENT — THANK YOU	30.00—
			FINANCE CHARGE *PURCHASES *CASH ADVANCE	

PREVIOUS BALANCE	PAYMENTS	CREDITS	PURCHASES AND CASH ADVANCES	DEBIT ADJUSTMENTS	FINANCE CHARGE	NEW BALANCE
253.27	30.00	0.00	50.00	0.00		

AN AMOUNT FOLLOWED BY A MINUS SIGN (−) IS A CREDIT OR A CREDIT BALANCE UNLESS OTHERWISE INDICATED.

Send Billing Error Notices To: MASTERCARD DEPARTMENT P.O. BOX 522 DES MOINES IOWA 50302

	UNDER RATE CHANGE POINT	DOLLAR POINT AT WHICH RATES CHANGE	OVER RATE CHANGE POINT
ANNUAL PERCENTAGE RATES	18.00 %	500	15.00 %
MONTHLY PERIODIC RATES	1.500 %		1.250 %

1. Average Daily Balance of Previous Balance:
2. Average Daily Balance of Current Cash Advances: 29.68
3. Average Daily Balance of Current Purchases: 0.00
4. Average Daily Balance subject to FINANCE CHARGE:

MasterCard 2I

To avoid additional finance charges, payment in full of the new balance must be received at the address for receipt of payment by 12:00 noon of the payment due date.

NOTICE: See reverse side for important information.

Career: Stockbroker/Financial Consultant *This is Clarence W. Schnicke. He is a very successful stockbroker and Financial Consultant for Shearson/ American Express. Clarence enjoys mathematics and finds that on a day-to-day basis all of Chapters 1–14 and 16 are necessary to his work.*

Usual salaries for people in his field are from $20,000 to $60,000, with a few people at $100,000. These salaries come after being registered at state and national levels and a period of about five years to build up clientele.

Clarence received a BS in Zoology from Wheaton College, but near the end of his studies counselors discovered an aptitude for business. He took several business courses while at Wheaton and went on to study stocks, bonds, and other financial subjects at the University of Chicago.

A Financial Consultant's job is to help others achieve financial security or benefits. A consultant must develop confidence between the client and himself. A detailed interview with the client is necessary to determine their personal financial needs. Both consultant and client must realize that there are pitfalls in investing which must be avoided, if possible. No action should ever be taken on the impulse of the moment. The consultant must understand the client's financial standing. For example, does the client have a will? Does the client have sufficient insurance? Is the client a salaried worker? Has the client built up an estate? The answers to all of these questions help the Consultant meet the needs of the client.

The Financial Consultant should be cordial and outgoing. The consultant must keep abreast of economic trends and maintain the confidentiality of each clients and all of that client's business.

Clarence's hobbies are travel, gardening, and musical activities.

8
STOCKS AND BONDS

STOCKS AND BONDS

READINESS CHECK—SKILLS FOR CHAPTER 8

Multiply.

1. 200 × $297.50

2. 15 × $1018.75

3. What is 2% of $1687.50?

Add.

4. $1687.50 + $33.75

Subtract.

5. $1653.50 − $33.75

Divide and round to the nearest hundredth.

6. $\dfrac{1.30}{16.875}$

Divide and round to the nearest tenth.

7. $\dfrac{297.75}{18.61}$

OBJECTIVES

After finishing Section 8.1, you should be able to:

■ Find the total cost of a purchase of stock.

■■ Find the total return on the sale of stock.

8.1 STOCKS AND COMMISSIONS

When you own a share of stock in a corporation, you own part of the company. A stock exchange is like a supermarket in which stocks are bought and sold. The following table shows some quotations for a recent day on the New York Stock Exchange.

8.1 STOCKS AND COMMISSIONS

Here is how we read a typical listing:

52 Weeks High	Low	Stock	Div.	Yld %	P-E Ratio	Sales 100s	High	Low	Close	Net Chg.
$21\frac{3}{8}$	$15\frac{5}{8}$	Goodyr	1.30	7.8	7	399	$16\frac{3}{4}$	$16\frac{3}{8}$	$16\frac{5}{8}$	$-\frac{1}{8}$
1.	2.	3.	4.	5.	6.	7.	8.	9.	10.	11.

1. The highest price per share of the stock during the preceding 52 weeks.
2. The lowest price of the stock during the preceding 52 weeks.
3. The abbreviated name of the corporation. In this case, it is *The Goodyear Tire and Rubber Company*.
4. The yearly dividend per share that the company is paying. In this case, it is $1.30 per share.
5. The yield per share. We will explain this later.
6. The price-earnings ratio. We will explain this later. Both the yield and price-earnings ratio are indicators of the quality of the stock, but there are other indicators.
7. The sales in 100s on that day. In this case, 39,900 shares were sold.
8. The highest selling price per share of the stock that day. In this case, it was $16\frac{3}{4}$, or $16.75 per share.
9. The lowest selling price per share of the stock that day. In this case, it was $16\frac{3}{8}$, or $16.375 per share.
10. The selling price per share for the last sale of the day (the closing price). In this case, it was $16\frac{5}{8}$, or $16.625 per share.
11. The difference between the closing price on this day and the closing price the day before. In this case, it is $-\$\frac{1}{8}$ or $-\$0.125$ per share. The minus sign means that the price on this day was lower than the price the day before.

■ BUYING STOCKS

Suppose you see a listing such as the one shown above for *Goodyr* and decide you want to buy 100 shares. What should you have to pay? From the listing you can get only an idea of the cost. On the actual day that you tell your broker to buy the stock, a representative goes to a person dealing in Goodyr stock and makes a bid, say $16\frac{3}{4}$. If it is accepted, you pay $100 \times \$16\frac{3}{4}$ *plus* commission. However, the bid may not be accepted. Whatever is finally agreed on is the *selling price*.

Commission rates depend on the brokerage firm. The following is a way to approximate commission. We assume that

Value of purchase = Number of shares × Price per share

Price per share	Commission
Less than or equal to $47 per share	2% of the value of the purchase
More than $47 per share	$0.85 × the number of shares

STOCKS AND BONDS

1. Find the total cost of purchasing 100 shares.

Stock	Selling price
GTE	$28\frac{5}{8}$

   2919.75

Example 1 Find the total cost of purchasing 100 shares.

Solution

Stock	Selling price
Goodyr	$16\frac{7}{8}$

a) Find the value of the purchase.

   Value = Number of shares × Price per share

   $= 100 \times \$16\frac{7}{8}$

   $= 100 \times \$16.875$

   $= \$1687.50$

b) Find the commission.

   Commission = 2% of the value   *Since the price per share is less than $47*
   $= 0.02 \times \$1687.50$
   $= \$33.75$

c) Add the value and the commission. This is the total cost.

   Total cost = Value + Commission
   $= \$1687.50 + \$33.75$
   $= \$1721.25$

DO EXERCISE 1.

Example 2 Find the total cost of purchasing 200 shares.

Stock	Selling price
IBM	$297\frac{1}{2}$

Solution

a) Find the value of the purchase.

   Value = Number of shares × Price per share

   $= 200 \times \$297\frac{1}{2}$

   $= 200 \times \$297.50$

   $= \$59{,}500$

2. Find the total cost of purchasing 300 shares.

Stock	Selling price
IndiM	$109\frac{1}{4}$

   33,030

b) Find the commission.

   Commission = $0.85 × Number of shares   *Since the price per share is more than $47*
   $= \$0.85 \times 200$
   $= \$170$

c) Find the total cost.

   Total cost = Value + Commission
   $= \$59{,}500 + \$170$
   $= \$59{,}670$

ANSWERS ON PAGE A–18

DO EXERCISE 2.

8.1 STOCKS AND COMMISSIONS

●●● SELLING STOCKS

Suppose you own 100 shares of Goodyear stock and want to sell them. If the selling price is $\$16\frac{7}{8}$, your *return* is $100 \times \$16\frac{7}{8}$ minus the commission. Note that a commission is paid by the buyer on the purchase of stock and also by the seller on the sale of stock. Commission is computed as before.

Example 3 Find the total return on the sale of 100 shares.

Stock	Selling price
Goodyr	$16\frac{7}{8}$

Solution

a) Find the value of the sale.

Value = Number of shares × Price per share

$= 100 \times \$16\frac{7}{8}$

$= 100 \times \$16.875$

$= \$1687.50$

b) Find the commission.

Commission = 2% of the value   *Since the price per share*
$= 0.02 \times \$1687.50$ *is less than $47*
$= \$33.75$

c) Subtract the commission from the value. This is the total return.

Total return = Value − Commission
$= \$1687.50 − \$33.75$
$= \$1653.75$

DO EXERCISE 3.

Example 4 Find the total return on the sale of 200 shares.

Stock	Selling price
IBM	$297\frac{1}{2}$

Solution

a) Find the value of the purchase.

Value = Number of shares × Price per share

$= 200 \times \$297\frac{1}{2}$

$= 200 \times \$297.50$

$= \$59,500$

b) Find the commission.

Commission = $0.85 × Number of shares   *Since the price per*
$= \$0.85 \times 200$ *share is more than $47*
$= \$170$

---

3. Find the total return on the sale of 100 shares.

Stock	Selling price
GTE	$28\frac{5}{8}$

2805.25

Return = MV − C

ANSWER ON PAGE A–18

4. Find the total return on the sale of 300 shares.

Stock	Selling price
IndiM	$109\frac{1}{4}$

32625.14

c) Find the total return.

Total return = Value − Commission
= $59,500 − $170
= $59,330

DO EXERCISE 4.

Stocks sold in multiples of 100 are called *round lots*. These would be lots such as 100 shares, 400 shares, and 3000 shares. Other sales are called *odd lots*, such as 97 shares, 142 shares, and so on. Usually the method of computing commission that we discussed in this section can be used, but in some cases commission per share is higher—$\frac{1}{8}$ to $\frac{1}{2}$ of a dollar.

Who Should Buy Stock?

One should never buy stock unless he or she can afford to lose the money. It is a high risk investment. One rule of thumb is to have one year's salary in a savings account before considering a stock purchase.

Most brokerage firms charge a rather high commission, say 10%, when the value of the purchase is below $300. Thus, if you have only a small amount to invest, it might be put to better use elsewhere. However, in recent years discount brokers, with lower charges, have appeared. They provide a less expensive alternative for the independent investor. Many businesses have pension and retirement plans that invest money in stock for their employees. These plans are managed by people with experience in the stock market and they can be good investments.

What Is the Advantage of Stock over a Savings Account?

If you invest $1000 in a savings account at 8% simple interest, you get $1080 back at the end of a year. If you invest $1000 in a stock, you *might* get a dividend of $80 and the value of the stock *might* go up $140. Your investment would be worth roughly (excluding commission) $1220, or $1080 + $140. The extra $140, called a *capital gain*, is the advantage of investing in stock rather than a savings account. But keep in mind that you could also *lose* $140 if the stock declines in value.

The Dow-Jones Industrial Average

The Dow-Jones Industrial Average is but one of many indicators, or barometers, of trends in the stock market. It can be thought of as an average of 30 selected stocks. An average of 800 is considered low, whereas an average of 1000 is high. A graph such as the one below shows the Dow-Jones average over several weeks and indicates whether the market is rising, falling, or stabilized.

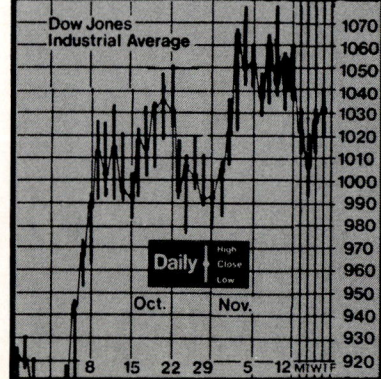

EXERCISE SET 8.1

■ Find the total cost of purchasing 100 shares.

	Stock	Selling price
1.	GMot	$65\frac{3}{4}$

1. 6666.00

2.	Bendix	$77\frac{1}{8}$

2. 7797.50

3.	GPU	$18\frac{3}{8}$

3. 1874.25

4.	GnRefr	$7\frac{1}{4}$

4. 739.5

Find the total cost of purchasing 200 shares.

	Stock	Selling price
5.	IngerR	$58\frac{1}{2}$

5. 11,870

6.	GTFI	94

6. 18,970

7.	AHome	$131\frac{1}{8}$

7. 26395

8.	NEG	$100\frac{7}{8}$

8. 20,335

STOCKS AND BONDS

ANSWERS

Find the total return on the sale of 100 shares.

Stock	Selling price
9. Chrysler	$11\frac{1}{4}$
10. ColGas	$27\frac{1}{2}$
11. CnDt	48
12. McDnld	53

9. 1162.50

10. 2695

11. 4715

12. 5215

Find the total return on the sale of 500 shares.

Stock	Selling price
13. Pndrosa	$23\frac{5}{8}$
14. Purex	$16\frac{5}{8}$
15. TexInst	$82\frac{7}{8}$
16. TrG	$99\frac{3}{8}$

13. 11516.25

14. 8146.25

15. 41012.50

16. 49262.50

17. Find the total cost of purchasing 6000 shares.

Stock	Selling price
ATT	$62\frac{7}{8}$

17. 382,350

18. Find the total return on the sale of 8000 shares.

Stock	Selling price
Exxon	$45\frac{3}{8}$

18. 355,740

8.2 STOCKS: YIELD AND PRICE-EARNINGS RATIO

YIELD

Suppose a company has earnings of $500,000 in one year. They may elect to pay part of this, say $300,000, to their stockholders. If there are 10,000 shares of stock, they would pay $30 per share in what are called *dividends*. It is helpful to know what percent the yearly dividend is of the price per share. This percent is called the *yield*.

$$\text{Yield} = \frac{\text{Yearly dividend}}{\text{Price per share}}$$

Example 1 Find the yield.

Stock	Dividend	Price per share
Goodyr	$1.30	$16\frac{7}{8}$

Solution

$$\text{Yield} = \frac{\text{Yearly dividend}}{\text{Price per share}}$$

$$= \frac{\$1.30}{\$16\frac{7}{8}}$$

$$= \frac{\$1.30}{\$16.875}$$

≈ 0.077 Divide and round to the nearest thousandth.

$= 7.7\%$ Convert to percent.

The yield is 7.7%.

DO EXERCISES 1 AND 2.

To interpret yield, compare it with what you might get in a savings account, say 7%. Thus, the yield in Example 1 is good, but a yield of 1.9% might not be too profitable. This is not the only consideration, however. Remember the capital gain. The yield on a stock might be low, but it still may have gained considerably in value.

PRICE-EARNINGS RATIO

If a company has earnings of $500,000 in one year, and there are 10,000 shares of stock, the earnings per share is $50. Note that this is not dividends per share. A company may not elect to pay any dividends, but the earnings per share can still be considered. The *price-earnings ratio*, *P/E*, is the price per share of the stock divided by the earnings per share.

OBJECTIVES

After finishing Section 8.2, you should be able to:

• Find the yield of a stock.

•• Find the price-earnings ratio of a stock.

Find the yield.

1. *Stock:* GTE
   Dividend: $2.24
   Price per share: $28\frac{5}{8}$

2. *Stock:* IndiM
   Dividend: $12
   Price per share: $109\frac{1}{4}$

ANSWERS ON PAGE A–18

Find the price-earnings ratio.

3. *Stock:* K mart

Price per share: $29

Earnings per share: $2.50

11.6

4. *Stock:* Mobil

Price per share: 60\frac{1}{8}$

Earnings per share: $9.40

6.4

ANSWERS ON PAGE A-18

STOCKS AND BONDS

$$\text{Price-earnings ratio} = \frac{P}{E} = \frac{\text{Price per share}}{\text{Earnings per share}}$$

Example 2 Find the price-earnings ratio.

Stock	Price per share	Earnings per share
IBM	297\frac{3}{4}$	$18.61

Solution

$$\frac{P}{E} = \frac{\text{Price per share}}{\text{Earnings per share}}$$

$$= \frac{\$297\frac{3}{4}}{\$18.61}$$

$$= \frac{\$297.75}{\$18.61}$$

≈ 16.0 Divide and round to the nearest tenth.

DO EXERCISES 3 AND 4.

To interpret price-earnings ratio, one might think of 6 as low and 20 as high. Generally speaking, the lower the price-earnings ratio, the better. Again, there are other things to consider. A low price-earnings ratio sometimes indicates a time to buy. In Example 2, one might think that the price-earnings ratio of 16 for IBM is poor, but this has been a stock with lots of growth potential. On the other hand, a low price-earnings ratio might indicate faulty management. A stock with increasing price will have an increasing price-earnings ratio, but if you bought the stock before the price started increasing, you would be quite pleased that the price-earnings ratio is getting larger. In conclusion, we can say that all indicators of the quality of a stock are relative. Learn as much as you can from your stock broker before making a sale or purchase.

EXERCISE SET 8.2

Find the yield.

	Stock	Dividend	Price per share	Answer
1.	GMot	$5	$65 3/4	7.6%
2.	Bendix	$3	$77 1/8	3.9%
3.	CBS	$2.40	$53 5/8	4.5%
4.	AriP	$9.50	$112 7/8	8.4%
5.	NCR	$1	$55 3/8	1.8%
6.	GAF	$0.60	$13 1/2	4.4%

STOCKS AND BONDS

ANSWERS

◉◉ Find the price-earnings ratio.

Stock	Price per share	Earnings per share
7. McDnld	$53	$3.53
8. BakrInt	$30 5/8	$2.36
9. ContAir	$13 3/4	$1.96
10. duPont	$116 1/4	$12.92
11. ARA	$40 1/8	$4.00
12. MGM	$38 7/8	$3.00

7. 15

8. 13

9. 7

10. 9

11. 10

12. 13

---

13. 🖩 Find the yield.

Stock	Dividend	Price per share
PacGE	$2.16	$23 7/8

14. 🖩 Find the price-earnings ratio.

Stock	Price per share	Earnings per share
MMM	$59 3/8	$3.96

13. 9 %

14. 15

8.3 BONDS AND COMMISSIONS

Some corporations sell *bonds*, which are a way of borrowing money from the general public. The owner of a bond has somewhat more security than the owner of a stock in a corporation. If you are a bondholder, you are a creditor and as such have priority in getting your money if the corporation folds. You also get a fixed amount of interest on your investment as opposed to stock dividends, which a corporation can decide to change. The price of a bond is affected, as with stocks, by supply and demand. The following table shows some quotations from a recent day on the New York Exchange.

OBJECTIVES

After finishing Section 8.3, you should be able to:

- Find the total cost of a bond purchase.
- Find the current yield of a bond.

A bond listing differs from a stock listing. Here is how we read a bond listing:

Bonds	Cur Yld	Vol	High	Low	Close	Net Chg
Kellog $8\frac{5}{8}$–85	8.7	2	$99\frac{3}{8}$	$99\frac{3}{8}$	$99\frac{3}{8}$	$-\frac{5}{8}$
1.	2.	3.	4.	5.	6.	7. 8.

1. The name of the company.

2. The $8\frac{5}{8}$ is the interest rate paid per year. The basic value of a bond is usually $1000. This is also called *par value*. In one year interest of $8\frac{5}{8}\% \times \$1000$, or $86.25, is paid on the bond. The 85 is an abbreviation for 1985, the year in which the bond *matures* (is paid off). If the listing had said $8\frac{5}{8}$s85, it would mean that interest is paid semiannually.

3. The current yield. We will explain this later.

4. The volume is the number of bonds sold that day, in thousands. In this case it is 2000.

5. The high and low for the day, but this is not given in dollars. It is a per-
6. centage of $1000. Thus if the selling price is $99\frac{3}{8}$, it means that the bond sold for $99\frac{3}{8}\% \times \$1000$, or $993.75. Thus a bond that sells for 102, or $1020, is more in demand than this one.

340 STOCKS AND BONDS

1. Find the total cost of purchasing three bonds.

Bond	Selling price
CnPw $5\frac{7}{8}$96	$68\frac{1}{2}$

7. The closing price, which is the selling price for the last sale of the day.

8. The difference between the closing price on this day and the closing price on the previous day. For this bond, it is $-\frac{5}{8}$. The minus sign means that this is lower than the price the day before.

■ BUYING BONDS

Suppose you see the above listing and decide that you want to buy some *Kellog* bonds; the selling price is $99\frac{3}{8}$. Each bond you buy costs $99\frac{3}{8}\% \times \$1000$ *plus* commission. Again, commission rates vary with the brokerage firm. Here is a method of computing approximate commission.

Number of bonds	Commission
1–3	$25
4 or more	$7.50 × Number of bonds

Example 1 Find the total cost of purchasing two bonds.

Bond	Selling price
Kellog $8\frac{5}{8}$85	$99\frac{3}{8}$

Solution

a) Find the value.

Value = Number of bonds × Selling price

$= 2 \times 99\frac{3}{8}\% \times \$1000$

$= 2 \times \$993.75$

$= \$1987.50$

b) Find the commission.

Commission = $25   Since there are only two bonds purchased

c) Add the value and the commission.

Total cost = Value + Commission

$= \$1987.50 + \$25$

$= \$2012.50$

DO EXERCISE 1.

Example 2 Find the total cost of purchasing 15 bonds.

Bond	Selling price
CrdF $10\frac{1}{8}$91	$101\frac{7}{8}$

ANSWER ON PAGE A–18

8.3 BONDS AND COMMISSIONS

Solution

a) Find the value of the purchase.

Value = Number of bonds × Selling price

$= 15 \times 101\frac{7}{8}\% \times \$1000$

$= 15 \times \$1018.75$

$= \$15,281.25$

b) Find the commission.

Commission = $7.50 × Number of bonds   *Since more than four are bought*

$= \$7.50 \times 15$

$= \$112.50$

c) Find the total cost.

Total cost = Value + Commission

$= 15,281.25 + \$112.50$

$= \$15,393.75$

DO EXERCISE 2.

CURRENT YIELD

For the Kellog company we have noted that interest paid per year is $86.25 for each bond. For two bonds the interest would be 2 × $86.25, or $172.50. We found in Example 1 that the total cost of two bonds is $2012.50. Any investor wants to know what percent of the amount spent is returned. That is,

$172.50 is what percent of $2012.50?

This is given by

$\dfrac{\$172.50}{\$2012.50} \approx 0.086 \quad \text{or} \quad 8.6\%.$

In the stock listing it says that the current yield is 8.7%. We did not get the 8.7% because we used a different method of computing commission. At least, you can think of current yield in a bond listing as an approximation for the return on your investment.

$$\text{Current yield} = \frac{\text{Total annual interest}}{\text{Total cost}}$$

Example 3 Find the current yield if 15 bonds are purchased.

Bond	Selling price
CrdF $10\frac{1}{8}$91	$101\frac{7}{8}$

2. Find the total cost of purchasing 18 bonds.

Bond	Selling price
McyCr $9\frac{1}{4}$90	$100\frac{1}{8}$

ANSWER ON PAGE A–18

3. Find the current yield if three bonds are purchased.

Bond	Selling price
CnPw $5\frac{7}{8}$ 96	$68\frac{1}{2}$

Solution

a) Find the total cost. See Example 2. The total cost is $15,393.75.

b) Find the total annual interest.

$$\text{Total annual interest} = 10\frac{1}{8}\% \times \text{Number of bonds} \times \$1000$$

$$= 0.10125 \times 15 \times \$1000$$

$$= \$1518.75$$

c) Find the current yield.

$$\text{Current yield} = \frac{\text{Total annual interest}}{\text{Total cost}}$$

$$= \frac{\$1518.75}{\$15,393.75}$$

$$\approx 0.099 \quad \text{or} \quad 9.9\%$$

DO EXERCISES 3 AND 4.

4. Find the current yield if 18 bonds are purchased.

Bond	Selling price
McyCr $9\frac{1}{4}$ 90	$100\frac{1}{8}$

ANSWERS ON PAGE A–18

EXERCISE SET 8.3

● Find the total cost of purchasing two bonds.

	Bond	Selling price	
1.	ATT $8\frac{3}{4}$00	$99\frac{5}{8}$	625
2.	Arco 8.70s91	$99\frac{3}{4}$	
3.	OcciP 11s92	$106\frac{1}{4}$	
4.	TWA 11s86	$102\frac{7}{8}$	

Find the total cost of purchasing ten bonds.

	Bond	Selling price
5.	Woolw 9s99	97
6.	Xerox 6s95	87
7.	UAL 8s03	$146\frac{1}{8}$
8.	PorG $9\frac{7}{8}$s85	$103\frac{1}{8}$
9.	Sears 8s06	$91\frac{3}{4}$
10.	MGM 10s94	$95\frac{5}{8}$

ANSWERS

1. 2017.50
2. 2020
3. 2150
4. 2082.50
5. 9775
6. 8775
7. 14687.50
8. 10387.50
9. 9250
10. 9637.50

344   STOCKS AND BONDS

ANSWERS

📼 Find the current yield if two bonds are purchased.

	Bond	Selling price
11.	ATT $8\frac{3}{4}$00	$99\frac{5}{8}$
12.	Arco 8.70s91	$99\frac{3}{4}$
13.	OcciP 11s92	$106\frac{1}{4}$
14.	TWA 11s86	$102\frac{7}{8}$

11. 8.7 %

12. 8.6 %

13. 10.2 %

14. 10.6 %

Find the current yield if ten bonds are purchased.

	Bond	Selling price
15.	Woolw 9s99	97
16.	Xerox 6s95	87
17.	UAL 8s03	$146\frac{1}{8}$
18.	PorG $9\frac{7}{8}$s85	$103\frac{1}{8}$
19.	Sears 8s06	$91\frac{3}{4}$
20.	MGM 10s94	$95\frac{5}{8}$

15. 9.2 %

16. 6.8 %

17. 5.4 %

18. 9.5 %

19. 8.6 %

20. 10.4 %

21. 🖩 Find the total cost and current yield if 328 bonds are purchased.

     Bond   Selling price

     RCA 10.2s92 $106\frac{7}{8}$

21. _____

22. 🖩 Find the total cost and current yield if 679 bonds are purchased.

     Bond   Selling price

     Sinclr $4\frac{3}{8}$s86 $130\frac{3}{8}$

22. _____

345

NAME _____ SCORE _____ ANSWERS

TEST OR REVIEW—CHAPTER 8

If you miss an item, review the indicated section and objective.

[8.1, •] Find the total cost of purchasing 100 shares.

	Stock	Selling price
1.	Comsat	$42\frac{1}{8}$
2.	EsKod	$56\frac{1}{4}$

1. $4296.75

2. $5633.5

[8.1, ••] Find the total return on the sale of 100 shares.

	Stock	Selling price
3.	Comsat	$42\frac{1}{8}$
4.	EsKod	$56\frac{1}{4}$

3. $4128.25

4. $5616.50

[8.2, •] Find the yield.

	Stock	Dividend	Price per share
5.	EsKod	$1.72	$56\frac{1}{4}$

5. 3.1%

[8.2, ••] Find the price-earnings ratio.

	Stock	Price per share	Earnings per share
6.	EsKod	$56\frac{1}{4}$	$4.33

6. 13

Copyright © 1984, by Addison-Wesley Publishing Company Inc. All rights reserved.

STOCKS AND BONDS

[8.3, ◐] Find the total cost of purchasing three bonds.

Bond	Selling price
7. GnEl $6\frac{1}{4}$89	$97\frac{7}{8}$

Find the total cost of purchasing 14 bonds.

Bond	Selling price
8. PAA $10\frac{1}{2}$01	$121\frac{1}{2}$

[8.3, ◐◐] Find the current yield if three bonds are purchased.

Bond	Selling price
9. GnEl $6\frac{1}{4}$89	$97\frac{7}{8}$

Find the current yield if 14 bonds are purchased.

Bond	Selling price
10. PAA $10\frac{1}{2}$01	$121\frac{1}{2}$

Career: Life Insurance Agent *Barton L. Kaufman, a Life Insurance Agent, is the President and Chief Executive Officer of the Kaufman Financial Corporation. Bart took a course such as this while preparing for a BS degree in Life Insurance at Indiana University. He also has a Law degree from the same university and has earned the title, CLU, Chartered Life Underwriter. A CLU has taken specialized training in life insurance.*

Should you be considering a career in life insurance, keep in mind that you do not have to have this amount of preparation. Bart is at the top of his profession both in terms of educational preparation and performance. In most states, one can sell life insurance upon the passing of a state test, but it is advisable to have more preparation, such as becoming a Chartered Life Underwriter.

Clearly, the mathematics in this chapter is the most relevant to Bart's work. Other important material is ratio and percent.

There are many qualities, apart from mathematical knowledge, which make for an excellent life insurance agent. The most important is the ability to work on your own. You must be a self-starter. You should like people. In truth, many people resist the purchase of life insurance. It is easy to procrastinate. You must be able to help them understand that there is a need. There is a great range of salaries in the field. Some make $20,000 to $25,000. Others make $50,000 to $100,000. People who are very successful can earn over $300,000 per year.

9
INSURANCE

READINESS CHECK: SKILLS FOR CHAPTER 9

How many hundreds are in

1. 75,000
2. 20,000

How many thousands are in

3. 1,341,000
4. 67,000

Multiply.

5. 20% × $56,000
6. $815 × 25
7. 28.80 × 1.95
8. 46.80 × 1.95
9. $\frac{3}{4}$ × 50,000
10. $\frac{3}{5}$ × 80,000

Subtract.

11. 700 − 280
12. 1400 − 250

9.1 BUSINESS AND HOMEOWNER'S INSURANCE

Prudent planning for financial investments protects you against future financial hardship. In much the same way, insurance protects you and your family against financial loss due to accidents, sickness, liability, death, and other unexpected occurrences. We discuss insurance coverage and its cost in this chapter.

■ BUSINESS OWNER'S FIRE INSURANCE

Business owners pay far less for fire insurance when their businesses are in fire resistant buildings. Three types of construction are:

1. *Frame:* Exterior walls are predominantly wood or stucco or other combustible materials, and the floors and roof are wood or steel frame.

2. *Incombustible:* Exterior walls, floors, and roof are constructed of—and supported by—metal, asbestos, gypsum, or other noncombustible materials.

3. *Fire resistive:* Walls are of reinforced concrete or structural steel encased in masonry or concrete materials with fire-proofed floors and roof decks and their supports.

The following table lists the annual fire insurance *premiums* (payment for coverage) for each $100 of building-and-contents replacement cost.

	Frame	Incombustible	Fire-resistive
Building	$0.68	$0.29	$0.06
Contents	$2.32	$1.97	$0.96

Example 1 A business is in a frame building which would cost $75,000 to replace. What is the annual fire insurance premium for the building?

OBJECTIVES

After finishing Section 9.1, you should be able to:

■ Compute a business owner's fire insurance premiums.

■■ Find the amount of a loss a homeowner's insurer will pay.

■■■ Determine the premium for homeowner's insurance.

9.1 BUSINESS AND HOMEOWNER'S INSURANCE

Solution

Total Premium = Premium per $100 × Replacement Cost (in hundreds)
= $0.68 × 750   There are 750 hundreds in 75,000
= $510

The total premium is $510.

DO EXERCISE 1.

Example 2 The contents in a fire-resistive building would cost $20,000 to replace. What is the annual fire insurance premium on the contents?

Solution

Total Premium = Premium per $100 × Replacement Cost (in hundreds)
= $0.96 × 200   There are 200 hundreds in 20,000
= $192

The total premium is $192.

DO EXERCISE 2.

Other types of insurance businessowners might consider include income loss from temporary business interruption and liability. Coverage and premiums vary greatly.

∴ HOMEOWNER'S INSURANCE

Homeowners can purchase fire insurance providing protection against

Fire    Lightning    Damage due to extinguishing fire

or one of three types of homeowner's policies (see the following page).

Each type provides the coverage shown for the preceding policy as well as the protection indicated in the figure. For example, the broad type provides protection against the perils listed as well as the protection provided by the basic and fire policies. In addition, all three homeowner's policies provide:

Comprehensive personal liability

Medical payments (other than to insureds)

Physical damage to property of others

All costs of defending suits (whether you are liable or not)

Additional living expense when home is not habitable

---

1. A business is in a fire resistive building which would cost $75,000 to replace. What is the annual fire insurance premium for the building?

2. The contents in a frame building would cost $20,000 to replace. What is the annual fire insurance premium on the contents?

ANSWERS ON PAGE A–18

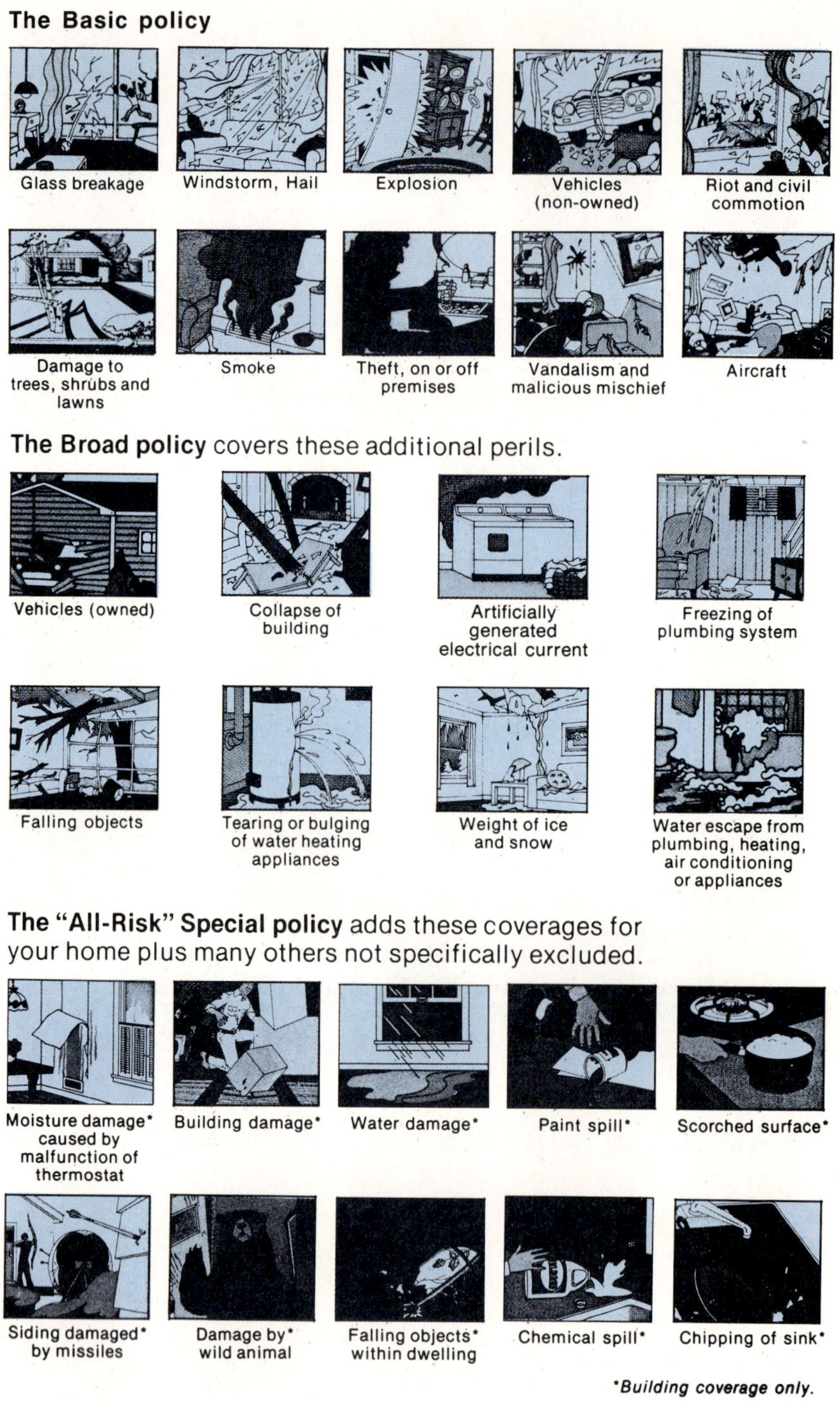

INSURANCE

The Basic policy

Glass breakage · Windstorm, Hail · Explosion · Vehicles (non-owned) · Riot and civil commotion · Damage to trees, shrubs and lawns · Smoke · Theft, on or off premises · Vandalism and malicious mischief · Aircraft

The Broad policy covers these additional perils.

Vehicles (owned) · Collapse of building · Artificially generated electrical current · Freezing of plumbing system · Falling objects · Tearing or bulging of water heating appliances · Weight of ice and snow · Water escape from plumbing, heating, air conditioning or appliances

The "All-Risk" Special policy adds these coverages for your home plus many others not specifically excluded.

Moisture damage* caused by malfunction of thermostat · Building damage* · Water damage* · Paint spill* · Scorched surface* · Siding damaged* by missiles · Damage by* wild animal · Falling objects* within dwelling · Chemical spill* · Chipping of sink*

Building coverage only.

The amount of coverage for complete loss of dwelling is the insurance amount carried or the replacement cost of the home, whichever is smaller.

Example 3 A broad-form homeowner's policy for $50,000 is taken out on a home that would cost $60,000 to replace. A tornado destroys the home. How much is paid by the insurance company?

9.1 BUSINESS AND HOMEOWNER'S INSURANCE

Solution The insurance company pays the amount of insurance carried ($50,000).

DO EXERCISE 3.

Full coverage is provided for partial loss of dwelling whenever the amount of insurance carried is 80% or more of the dwelling's *replacement cost*. The replacement cost is the present value of the house less the value of the land and basement.

Inflation riders keyed to the Composite Construction Cost Index of the U.S. Department of Commerce keep the 80% or more coverage current as property values increase.

Example 4 An all-risk homeowner's policy for $52,000 is taken out on a home whose replacement cost is $60,000. A nonowned automobile does $5000 damage to the house. How much does the insurance company pay?

Solution

a) Find out if the insurance coverage is at least 80%.

$$\text{Replacement cost feature} = 80\% \times \$60,000$$
$$= 0.80 \times \$60,000$$
$$= \$48,000$$

The insurance coverage ($52,000) is greater than 80%.

b) Find the amount that the insurance company pays.

The insurance company pays the total loss ($5000), since the insurance carried ($52,000) is more than the minimum 80% coverage ($48,000).

DO EXERCISE 4.

Full coverage is not provided for the partial loss of a dwelling whenever the insurance carried is less than 80% of the replacement cost. This *coinsurance* means the insurer and policyowner both pay certain amounts when a loss occurs.

Example 5 An all-risk homeowner's policy for $30,000 is taken out on a home that would cost $50,000 to replace. Water damage to the home from an open window during a storm is $6000. How much is paid by the insurance company?

Solution

a) Find 80% of $50,000.

$$\text{Replacement cost feature} = 80\% \times \$50,000$$
$$= 0.80 \times \$50,000$$
$$= \$40,000$$

The amount of insurance carried ($30,000) is *not* 80% of the replacement cost ($40,000), so not all of the loss is covered by the insurance company.

---

3. A broad-form homeowner's policy for $65,000 is taken out on a home that would cost $70,000 to replace. A fire destroys the home. How much is paid by the insurance company?

4. A broad-form homeowner's policy for $45,000 is taken out on a home whose replacement cost is $56,000. A fire does $10,000 damage to the house. How much does the insurance company pay?

ANSWERS ON PAGE A–18

5. A basic-form homeowner's policy for $45,000 is taken out on a home that would cost $85,000 to replace. Lightning damage is $10,000. How much is paid by the insurance company?

b) Find the amount that the insurance company pays.

$$\text{Amount insurance pays} = \frac{\text{Insurance carried}}{80\% \text{ of replacement cost}} \times \text{Loss}$$

$$= \frac{30,000}{40,000} \times \$6,000$$

$$= \$4,500$$

The insurance company pays $4,500.

Note that the loss was coinsured, as the company pays $4500 and the policyowner pays $1500.

DO EXERCISE 5.

Homeowner's policies also provide coverage on the contents (up to 50% of dwelling coverage) and living expenses (up to 20% of dwelling coverage) should the house become uninhabitable because of a covered loss.

Example 6 An all-risk homeowner's policy for $56,000 is taken out on a house. How much coverage is provided for contents and living expenses?

Solution

a) Find the coverage for contents.

$$\text{Coverage for contents} = 50\% \times \text{Dwelling coverage}$$

$$= 0.50 \times \$56,000$$

$$= \$28,000$$

Contents loss is covered up to $28,000.

b) Find the coverage for living expenses.

$$\text{Coverage for living expenses} = 20\% \times \text{Dwelling coverage}$$

$$= 0.20 \times \$56,000$$

$$= \$11,200$$

The family in Example 6 would have as much as $11,200 to live on after their house was damaged or destroyed.

DO EXERCISE 6.

6. A basic-form homeowner's policy for $48,000 is taken out on a house. How much coverage is provided for contents and living expenses?

The 80% feature applies only to the dwelling and not to the contents or living expenses.

SUGGESTION

The 80% feature is calculated on the replacement cost, *not* the present value of the house. For example, a house with a present value of $65,000 may have a replacement cost of $50,000 since the replacement cost would not include the value of land or an unfinished basement. The 80% feature on $65,000 indicates that at least $52,000, or 80% of $65,000, of insurance must be purchased on the house. However, only $40,000, or 80% of $50,000, of insurance need be purchased to qualify for the 80% feature. The consumer can save on premium dollars by insuring only on the replacement cost and *not* the present value.

Contents on which there is a loss are first evaluated on the basis of replacement cost and then depreciated according to industry guidelines. Industry guidelines for depreciation appear in Table 14 (T–26). Most insurance companies use straight-line depreciation (see p. 460) to determine reimbursement for loss.

Example 7 A basic-form homeowner's policy for $58,000 is taken out on a house. A stereo purchased for $500 four years ago was stolen. The comparable model costs $700 today. How much of the loss will the insurance company pay?

Solution

a) Find the coverage on the contents.

Coverage on contents = 50% × Dwelling coverage
= 0.50 × $58,000
= $29,000

Losses up to $29,000 are covered.

b) Find straight-line depreciation on the comparable model.

From Table 14 (p. T–26), we see that depreciation is 7–10 years. Suppose the stereo is a good model and therefore would last 10 years.

Depreciation for four years = Depreciation for one year × 4
= (700 ÷ 10) × 4
= 70 × 4
= 280

The depreciation is $280.

c) Find the amount after depreciation (the trade-in value).

Amount after depreciation = Comparable model cost − Depreciation
= 700 − 280
= 420

The insurance company will pay $420 since this amount does not exceed the maximum coverage.

DO EXERCISE 7.

Some insurers do not depreciate contents, that is, the full replacement cost is paid. This coverage is available to consumers whose homes have fire extinguishers, smoke alarms, and deadbolt locks and which were built since 1955.

▪▪▪ THE COST OF HOMEOWNER'S INSURANCE

The cost of homeowner's insurance depends on several factors. Among them are the type of construction (frame, masonry, or other), roof type (composition or wood shingles), distance from fire station, type of fire department (volunteer or professional), and location (for example, windstorm damage is more likely in certain sections of the country than others). Table 15 (p. T–29) lists the annual premiums (costs) for one home insurer. Form 1 is the basic policy, Form 2 the broad-form policy, and Form 3 the all-risk policy.

7. An all-risk homeowner's policy for $42,000 is taken on a house. A man's overcoat purchased for $200 one year ago was ruined in a fire. The comparable coat costs $250 today. How much of the loss will the insurance company pay?

ANSWER ON PAGE A–18

INSURANCE

Example 8 Find the annual premium for a $36,000 Form 2, $100 all-peril deductible homeowner's policy on a frame house in Zone 1, Protection Class 2.

TABLE 9.1

Zone I
Protection Class: 1-4   **Annual Premiums**

	$50 All-Peril Deductible							$100 All-Peril Deductible					
	Masonry or Mas. Veneer			Frame			Masonry or Mas. Veneer			Frame		
	Form			Form			Form			Form		
Amount	1	2	3	1	2	3	1	2	3	1	2	3
$ 5,000*	41	47	48	41	48	49	37	43	44	37	44	45
7,000*	43	49	50	43	49	51	39	45	46	39	45	46
8,000	44	50	51	44	50	52	40	45	46	40	45	47
10,000	45	51	53	45	52	54	41	46	48	41	47	49
12,000	46	53	54	46	54	55	42	48	49	42	49	50
14,000	49	56	57	49	56	58	45	51	52	45	51	53
15,000	50	57	58	50	58	59	45	52	53	45	53	54
16,000	52	59	61	52	60	62	47	54	55	47	55	56
17,000	54	61	62	54	62	63	49	55	56	49	56	57
18,000	55	63	64	55	64	65	50	57	58	50	58	59
19,000	58	65	66	58	65	66	53	59	60	53	59	60
20,000	59	66	68	59	67	69	54	60	62	54	61	63
21,000	61	69	70	61	70	71	55	63	64	55	64	65
22,000	63	71	72	63	71	73	57	65	66	57	65	66
23,000	65	73	74	65	74	75	59	66	67	59	67	68
24,000	68	76	78	68	78	79	62	69	71	62	71	72
25,000	72	80	82	72	81	83	65	73	75	65	74	75
26,000	75	84	85	75	85	86	68	76	77	68	77	78
27,000	78	87	89	78	89	90	71	79	81	71	81	82
28,000	81	91	92	81	93	94	74	83	84	74	85	86
29,000	84	93	95	84	95	96	76	85	86	76	86	87
30,000	86	97	98	86	99	100	78	88	89	78	90	91
31,000	90	101	103	90	103	104	82	92	94	82	94	95
32,000	94	105	107	94	107	108	85	95	97	85	97	98
33,000	97	109	111	97	111	112	88	99	101	88	101	102
34,000	101	113	115	101	115	117	92	103	105	92	105	106
35,000	104	116	118	104	118	119	95	105	107	95	107	108
36,000	107	120	122	107	122	123	97	109	111	97	111	112
37,000	111	124	126	111	126	128	101	113	115	101	115	116
38,000	114	128	130	114	130	131	104	116	118	104	118	119
39,000	118	132	134	118	134	136	107	120	122	107	122	124
40,000	122	136	138	122	138	140	111	124	125	111	125	127
42,000	129	144	146	129	146	148	117	131	133	117	133	135
44,000	136	152	154	136	154	156	124	138	140	124	140	142
46,000	143	160	163	143	163	165	130	145	148	130	148	150
48,000	150	168	171	150	171	173	136	153	155	136	155	157
50,000	158	177	179	158	179	182	144	161	163	144	163	165
60,000	194	217	220	194	221	223	176	197	200	176	201	203
70,000	230	257	261	230	262	264	209	234	237	209	238	240
80,000	266	297	301	266	304	305	242	270	274	242	276	277
90,000	302	337	342	302	346	347	275	306	311	275	315	316

Solution In Table 9.1 read down the amount column to $36,000 and across to the column headed $100 all-peril deductible, frame, Form 2. The annual premium is $111.

DO EXERCISE 8.

The premium for a homeowner's policy falling between two table entries can be found by *interpolation*. For example, if the amount of insurance needed is halfway between two entries, then the premium charged is halfway between the corresponding premiums.

Example 9 Find the annual premium for a $47,000 Form 3, $50 all-peril deductible homeowner's policy on a masonry house in Zone 1, Protection Class 8.

Solution

a) Find the premium for the entries between which $47,000 falls.

From Table 15 (p. T-29) we see that the premium for $46,000 is $177 and for $48,000 is $185.

b) Find the premium for $47,000.

Since $47,000 is halfway between the two entries, the premium will be halfway between the corresponding entries:

$$\text{Premium} = \frac{177 + 185}{2}$$

$$= 181.$$

The annual premium for the $47,000 policy is $181.

DO EXERCISE 9.

The premium for a homeowner's policy with coverage greater than $200,000 can be found by adding the appropriate $10,000-premium increments to the premium for $200,000.

Example 10 Find the annual premium for a $240,000 Form 3, $50 all-peril deductible homeowner's policy on a masonry veneer house in Zone 1, Protection Class 11.

Solution

a) Find the premium for $200,000.

From Table 15 (p. T-29) we see that the premium is $1559.

b) Find the premium for each $10,000 increment.

From Table 15 (p. T-29) we find that the premium for each $10,000 increment is $81.

c) Find the premium for four $10,000 increments.

Premium for four increments = 4 × Premium for one increment

= 4 × 81

= 324

The premium for the additional $40,000 is $324.

8. Using Table 9.1, find the annual premium for a $70,000 Form 3, $100 all-peril deductible homeowner's policy on a frame house in Zone 1, Protection Class 4.

9. Find the annual premium for an $85,000 Form 2, $100 all-peril deductible homeowner's policy on a frame house in Zone 1, Protection Class 9.

ANSWERS ON PAGE A-18

10. Find the annual premium for a $230,000 Form 2, $100 all-peril deductible homeowner's policy on a frame house in Zone 1, Protection Class 3.

d) Find the total premium.

Total premium = Premium for $200,000 + Premium for increment
= 1559 + 324
= 1883

The total premium is $1883.

DO EXERCISE 10.

NAME _____ CLASS _____ ANSWERS

EXERCISE SET 9.1

■ Find the business owner's fire insurance premiums. Use the table on p. 354.

1. A business is in a frame building which would cost $125,000 to replace. What is the annual fire insurance premium for the building?

2. A business is in an incombustible building which would cost $125,000 to replace. What is the annual fire insurance premium for the building?

3. A business is in a fire resistive building which would cost $250,000 to replace. What is the annual fire insurance premium for the building?

4. A business is in an incombustible building which would cost $250,000 to replace. What is the annual fire insurance premium for the building?

5. A business is in a frame building which would cost $90,000 to replace. What is the annual fire insurance premium for the building?

6. A business is in a fire resistive building which would cost $90,000 to replace. What is the annual fire insurance premium for the building?

■■ Solve.

7. Fire destroys a house having a $45,000 broad-form homeowner's policy on it. The replacement cost of the home is $80,000. How much does the insurance company pay?

8. An airplane destroys a house having a $52,000 basic-form homeowner's policy on it. The replacement cost of the home is $58,000. How much does the insurance company pay?

9. An all-risk policy for $35,000 is taken out on a house with a replacement cost of $43,000. A chemical spill does $5000 in damage to the floors. How much does the insurance company pay?

10. A broad-form policy for $62,000 is taken out on a house with a replacement cost of $77,500. Part of the house collapses, causing $8000 damage. How much does the insurance company pay?

11. A basic-form policy for $30,000 is taken out on a house with a replacement cost of $55,000. A nonowned vehicle does $6000 in damage to the house. How much does the insurance company pay?

12. A broad-form policy for $75,000 is taken out on a house with replacement cost of $100,000. A falling tree limb does $1500 in damage to the house. How much does the insurance company pay?

1. _____

2. _____

3. _____

4. _____

5. _____

6. _____

7. _____

8. _____

9. _____

10. _____

11. _____

12. _____

358 INSURANCE

ANSWERS

13. A basic-form policy for $37,000 is taken out on a house. How much coverage is provided for contents and living expenses?

14. An all-risk policy for $49,000 is taken out on a house. How much coverage is provided for contents and living expenses?

15. A broad-form policy for $80,000 is taken out on a house. Silverware purchased ten years ago for $600 was stolen. The cost to replace it today is $1400. How much of the loss will the insurance company pay? Use Table 14 (p. T–26).

16. A basic-form policy for $43,000 is taken out on a house. A basic evening dress purchased two years ago for $40 was ruined in a fire. The cost to replace it today is $50. How much of the loss will the insurance company pay? Use Table 14 (p. T–26).

••• Solve. Use Table 15 (p. T–29).

17. An insurance agent determines that a potential customer needs $90,000 protection for a masonry home in Protection Class 10, Zone 1. What is the annual homeowner's premium for a Form 2, $100 all-peril deductible policy?

18. An insurance agent determines that a potential customer needs $48,000 protection for a frame home in Protection Class 8, Zone 1. What is the annual homeowner's premium for a Form 3, $100 all-peril deductible policy?

Find the annual premium.

	Amount of Insurance	Deductible	Construction Type	Form	Zone	Class
19.	$ 24,000	$ 50	Frame	2	1	4
20.	$ 32,000	$ 50	Frame	2	1	4
21.	$ 37,000	$100	Masonry	3	1	7
22.	$ 44,000	$100	Masonry	3	1	7
23.	$ 70,000	$ 50	Masonry veneer	1	1	9
24.	$ 90,000	$ 50	Masonry veneer	1	1	9
25.	$ 65,000	$100	Frame	2	1	10
26.	$ 55,000	$100	Frame	2	1	10
27.	$220,000	$100	Masonry	3	1	4
28.	$230,000	$100	Masonry	3	1	4

9.2 AUTOMOBILE INSURANCE

Drivers can purchase automobile insurance, which protects them and others driving their automobile against loss. Table 9.2 lists coverage descriptions.

● AMOUNT OF THE LOSS PAYABLE

Example 1 A motorist has 100,000/300,000 bodily injury liability coverage. What is the maximum coverage when two or more people are injured in an accident?

Solution The second limit (300,000) is the maximum coverage when two or more people are injured in one accident. The insurance company will pay up to $300,000 for bodily injuries.

DO EXERCISE 1.

TABLE 9.2
COVERAGE DESCRIPTIONS

1. **Bodily Injury and Property Damage Liability**

   Pays damages for which you are liable arising from injuries or death, or from damage to property of others. Includes defense of suits and bail bonds. Pays up to the first limit for any one person and up to the second limit for two or more people injured or killed. Pays up to the limit shown for damage to property of others.

   A minimum of $50,000/$100,000 Bodily Injury and $25,000 Property Damage is suggested due to today's high claim cost. In fact even higher limits are needed in many cases.

2. **Uninsured Motorists**

   Protects you and occupants of your car for personal injuries if caused by an uninsured motorist or unknown hit-and-run driver.

   You must carry Bodily Injury and Property Damage to obtain this coverage.

3. **Comprehensive**

   Pays loss by fire, theft, accidental damage, and glass damage, less any deductible.
   Note the significant savings you can enjoy by taking $50 deductible instead of full coverage.
   Usually required if car is financed.
   Note CB owners! CB radios not covered. Coverage available at extra cost.

   Collision

   Again you can reduce your premium quite a few dollars by taking a higher deductible.
   Pays for damage to your car, less your deductible, for collision with another object or upset.
   Usually required if car is financed.

4. **Towing and Labor**

   Pays towing and labor repair costs at place of disablement up to $50 ($25 in Texas).

5. **Personal Injury Protection—(No Fault) Medical Payments**

   Must carry Bodily Injury and Property Damage to buy these coverages. Many states offer Personal Injury Protection, a form of "No Fault" coverage in place of or with Medical Payments coverage.

(continued)

OBJECTIVES

After finishing Section 9.2, you should be able to:

● Determine the loss payable by the insurer and the policyowner.

●● Figure the cost of automobile insurance.

1. A motorist has 50,000/100,000 bodily injury liability coverage. What is the maximum coverage when two or more people are injured in an accident?

ANSWER ON PAGE A–19

2. A motorist with 25,000/50,000/10,000 coverage does $12,435 damage to a Lincoln. How much does the motorist pay?

INSURANCE

TABLE 9.2 (*continued*)

In fact, PIP is required by the state in Colorado, Kansas, Nevada, North Dakota, Oregon, Utah. Also in Texas unless rejected in writing. It's recommended in Washington.

PIP offers in addition to Medical and Hospital benefits, weekly income, loss of services and funeral benefits. Some variations also offer survivors benefits.

Medical Payments coverage is available in other states.

Pays medical and/or funeral expenses for each family member and other passengers in your car who are injured or killed. Pays up to limits shown except when other insurance policies pay all or part of such expenses.

It is also available as an optional coverage in some PIP states. If so it is an "excess" coverage and would pay only if the coverage limits under PIP are exceeded.

Be sure and read your policy for complete details.

6. **Travel Accident** (Not available in Kansas or Texas)

Pays up to $5,000 (or $10,000) for injury, disability or death from accidents involving land, sea, or air travel. You can add this extra protection to your auto policy by filling in the name or names of persons applying. Anyone between ages 14 and 70 may apply.

Beneficiary

Your standard TA beneficiary provision reads as follows:

Unless otherwise requested, the benefits on the death of any person insured shall be paid to the Applicant, if living, otherwise to the spouse of the Applicant, if living, otherwise equally to the Applicant's then living lawful children, including stepchildren and adopted children, if any, otherwise equally to the Applicant's then living parents, otherwise to the estate of the Applicant.

Example 2 A motorist with 50,000/100,000/25,000 (sometimes abbreviated 50/100/25) coverage does $25,678 damage to a house. How much does the motorist pay?

Solution

a) Find the maximum property damage coverage.

The maximum property damage coverage is the third limit ($25,000).

b) Find the amount that the motorist pays.

Amount motorist pays = Total damage − Amount insurance pays
$$= 25,678 - 25,000$$
$$= 678$$

The motorist pays $678.

DO EXERCISE 2.

Uninsured motorist coverage is often 10,000/20,000, which means that, if hit by an uninsured motorist, the motorist and occupants are protected for personal injuries up to $10,000 for one person and up to $20,000 for each occurrence.

Example 3 A motorist with 10,000/20,000 uninsured motorist coverage is injured by a hit-and-run driver and has medical expenses of $11,560. How much does the motorist pay?

9.2 AUTOMOBILE INSURANCE

Solution

a) Find the maximum coverage.

The maximum coverage for one person is $10,000.

b) Find the amount that the motorist pays.

Amount motorist pays = Total damage − Amount insurance pays
= 11,560 − 10,000
= 1560

The motorist pays $1560.

DO EXERCISE 3.

Example 4 A rock breaks the car windshield of a motorist with $50 deductible comprehensive coverage. How much does the insurance company pay of the $175 needed to replace the windshield?

Solution Find the amount that the insurance company pays.

Amount insurance pays = Amount of damage − Deductible
= 175 − 50
= 125

The insurance company pays $125.

DO EXERCISE 4.

Collision coverage pays up to the value of the automobile less the deductible. After the policyowner pays the deductible the company pays the smaller of either the repair cost or the automobile's value.

Example 5 A motorist with $250 deductible collision coverage and a car worth $1400 has an accident that requires $2000 in repairs. How much does the insurance company pay?

Solution

The car's value is $1400. The insurance company will pay $1150, or $1400 − $250.

DO EXERCISE 5.

> **SUGGESTION**
>
> Don't file collision claims that are just over your deductible. Otherwise the insurance company may raise your premium. Pay the expense yourself.

Towing and labor coverage does not pay for parts or gasoline that may be required in case of a breakdown.

---

3. A motorist with 10,000/20,000 uninsured-motorist coverage is injured by a hit-and-run driver and has medical expenses of $13,632. How much does the motorist pay?

4. A car worth $3500 is stolen from a motorist who has $250 deductible comprehensive coverage. How much does the insurance company pay?

5. A motorist with $100 deductible collision coverage and a car worth $2650 has an accident that requires $700 in repairs. How much does the insurance company pay?

ANSWERS ON PAGE A–19

INSURANCE

6. A motorist with towing and labor coverage up to $25 is charged $35 by the mechanic who repairs the car. The $35 includes a $10 towing fee, $11 for service, and $14 for parts. How much does the insurance company pay?

Example 6 A motorist with towing and labor coverage up to $25 is charged by the mechanic who repairs the car. The $22 includes a $15 service fee, $4 for parts, and $3 for gasoline. How much does the insurance pay?

Solution Find the amount that the insurance company pays.

Amount insurance pays = Total charge
  − Amount for gasoline and parts
  = 22 − (4 + 3)
  = 15

The insurance company pays $15.

DO EXERCISE 6.

A passenger riding with you at the time of an accident can be reimbursed for medical expenses under the medical-payments coverage.

Example 7 A motorist with medical-payments coverage to a maximum of $5000 for each person is involved in an accident that injures one passenger. The passenger has $6235 in medical expenses. How much does the passenger pay?

Solution Find the amount that the passenger pays.

Amount passenger pays = Amount of expenses
  − Amount insurance pays
  = 6235 − 5000
  = 1235

The passenger pays $1235.

7. A motorist with medical-payments coverage to a maximum of $2500 for each person is involved in an accident that injures one passenger. The passenger has $4368 in medical expenses. How much does the passenger pay?

DO EXERCISE 7.

■■ THE COST OF AUTOMOBILE INSURANCE

The cost of automobile insurance depends on several factors. Among them are the kind of car, the location and use of the car, and the age, sex, driving record, and marital status of the driver. A basic premium table and a rating factor table, Tables 16 and 17 (pp. T–33 and T–34) for one insurer are used in Example 8.

Example 8 A single female, age 18, with a medium-size 1984 car selects the following coverage:

Liability	100/300/50
Medical	25,000
Comprehensive	Actual cash value (ACV)
Collision	100 deductible
Uninsured motorist	25/50

Find the premium for six months.

ANSWERS ON PAGE A–19

Solution

Find the basic premium and rating factor for each coverage from Tables 16 and 17 (pp. T–33 and T–34).

	Basic premium	Rating factor	Premium
Liability	28.80	1.95	28.80 × 1.95 or 56.16
Medical	6.60	1.95	6.60 × 1.95 or 12.87
Comprehensive	27.40	1.95	27.40 × 1.95 or 53.43
Collision	46.80	1.95	46.80 × 1.95 or 91.26
Uninsured motorist	2.30	1.00	2.30 × 1.00 or 2.30
TOTAL			216.02 (adding)

The premium for six months is $216.02.

DO EXERCISE 8.

Note that uninsured motorist coverage is the only coverage in which the rating factor is not used (in effect, it is 1.00). The motorist who drives carelessly and gets tickets or is involved in an accident in which the insurance company pays over $100 can expect to pay even higher premiums. For example, an accident in which the insurance company pays over $100 may result in at least a 10% premium increase during each of the following three to five years.

SUGGESTION

You will want to get bids from several reputable car insurers, using a form like the one below, before deciding which company to choose.

Coverage	Limits	Six-month rate
Bodily injury	100/300	_____
Property damage	50	_____
Medical	5000	_____
Comprehensive	ACV	_____
Collision	100 deductible	_____
Uninsured motorist	10/20	_____

---

8. A single male, age 18, with a medium-size 1984 car selects the following coverage:

Liability	100/300/50
Medical	25,000
Comprehensive	ACV
Collision	100 deductible
Uninsured motorist	25/50

Find the premium for six months.

ANSWER ON PAGE A–19

NAME _____ CLASS _____ ANSWERS

EXERCISE SET 9.2

A motorist has the coverages and limits shown below.

```
         COVERAGES/LIMITS/PREMIUM
AB  BODILY INJ/PROP DAMAGE
    100,000/300,000/25,000
C   MEDICAL PAYMENTS    5,000
D   COMPREHENSIVE (ACV)
G   100 DEDUCT COLLISION
U   UNINSURED MOTOR VEHICLE
    10,000/20,000
H   EMERGENCY ROAD SERVICE
```

■ Find the amounts (a) that the motorist pays and (b) that the insurance company pays for each loss.

1. A bodily injury suit by one person, in which the award by the jury was $106,250.

2. A bodily injury suit by three people in which the award by the jury was $432,000.

3. Property damage of $238 to a telephone pole.

4. Property damage of $21,628 to a building.

5. Medical payments of $8679 to one injured passenger.

6. Medical payments of $4568 to one injured passenger and of $6782 to another.

7. Theft of an automobile valued at $5675.

8. Windstorm damage of $567 to an automobile.

9. Repair work of $3546 (for accident-caused damage) to the motorist's car, valued at $6580.

10. Repair work of $2587 (for accident-caused damage) to the motorist's car, valued at $1785.

A motorist has the coverage and limits shown below.

```
         COVERAGES/LIMITS/PREMIUM
AB  BODILY INJ/PROP DAMAGE
    300,000/500,000/50,000
C   MEDICAL PAYMENTS    5,000
D   COMPREHENSIVE (ACV)
G   500 DEDUCT COLLISION
U   UNINSURED MOTOR VEHICLE
    10,000/20,000
H   EMERGENCY ROAD SERVICE
```

Find the amounts (a) the motorist pays and (b) the insurance company pays for each loss.

11. A bodily injury suit by one person in which the award by the jury was $275,000.

366

INSURANCE

ANSWERS

12. A bodily injury suit by two people in which the award by the jury was $615,000.

13. Property damage of $52,000 to an expensive sport car.

14. Property damage of $635 to a fire hydrant.

15. Medical payments of $4200 to one injured passenger.

16. Medical payments of $1287 to one injured passenger and $7300 to another.

17. Repair of windshield damage of $317.

18. Theft of an automobile valued at $9254.

19. Repair work of $780 (for accident-caused damage) to the motorist's car, valued at $9490.

20. Repair work of $4342 (for accident-caused damage) to the motorist's car, valued at $3500.

Use Tables 16 and 17 (pp. T–33 and T–34) to find the six-month premiums for these medium-size cars. All have actual cash value comprehensive and $100 deductible collision coverage.

	Sex	Age	Miles/Week Work	Marital Status	Car Year	Liability	Medical	Uninsured Motorist
21.	M	26	50	S	1983	50/100/10	5,000	25/50
22.	M	26	50	M	1983	50/100/10	5,000	25/50
23.	F	22	70	S	1984	25/50/10	5,000	100/300
24.	F	19	0	S	1984	100/300/50	5,000	10/20
25.	M	24	0	S	1982	100/300/50	25,000	25/50
26.	F	24	0	S	1982	100/300/50	25,000	25/50
27.	M	18	0	S	1981	25/50/10	5,000	10/20
28.	F	18	0	S	1981	25/50/10	5,000	10/20
29.	M	27	120	M	1984	50/100/10	25,000	100/300
30.	F	27	120	M	1984	50/100/10	25,000	100/300

One insurance company had to pay jury awards for policyholders with the following coverages.

Total award by jury	Policyholder's coverage	Number of injured persons
$325,876.50	250,000/500,000	3
$172,564.75	50,000/100,000	1
$567,892.25	100,000/300,000	2
$467,985.50	200,000/400,000	1

31. What is the total amount that the insurance company paid?

32. What is the total amount that the policyholders paid?

9.3 LIFE INSURANCE

Life insurance provides financial protection in the event of the insured's death. The two most common types of policies are known as *term* and *permanent* insurance. Their features appear in Table 9.3.

TABLE 9.3

Basic type	Features	Comments
Term	Provides benefits only when the insured dies within a specified period. If the specified period may be extended without new medical evidence, the policy is *renewable*. If the policy can be exchanged for permanent insurance without new medical evidence, the policy is *convertible*. If the amount of insurance remains constant, the policy is known as *level term*, whereas if the amount of insurance becomes less according to some type of schedule, the policy may be known as *decreasing, declining,* or *diminishing term*.	The most common term policies are the one-year renewable and convertible policy, the five-year renewable and convertible policy, and various durations of decreasing term insurance, with the most popular being 15, 20, or 25 years. The premium for level term insurance is constant only until renewal, whereas the premium for decreasing term insurance remains level as the face amount of the policy becomes less.
Permanent	Provides benefits without regard to the date when the insured dies. This type of insurance may also be known as *ordinary life, whole life,* or *cash value insurance*. The premium remains level and payable until the insured's death. The policy develops a subsidiary account within the contract that is known as *cash value*.	If the premium paying period is designed to be less than the insured's lifetime, the policy is known as a *limited pay policy*. A common type of this contract is a 20 payment life or a life paid up at 65 contract. If the insurance benefit payable to the insured at a specified date while he or she is living is equal to that which would have been paid if he or she had died, the policy is known as an *endowment*.

OBJECTIVES

After finishing Section 9.3, you should be able to:

- Find the amount of coverage after a certain number of years.
- Determine the cash value of an insurance policy.
- Find extended term coverage.
- Determine reduced paid up coverage.
- Calculate the cost of life insurance.

AMOUNT OF COVERAGE

A decreasing term policy is often purchased to pay off a home mortgage at the insured's death. The death benefit and mortgage balance decrease each year. The year the insured dies is important in determining exactly how large a death benefit the insurance company will pay. Table 9.4 (next page) lists the coverage for each year in a 15-year decreasing term policy.

1. An insured with a $35,000 15-year decreasing term policy dies during the ninth policy year. How much does the insurance company pay?

INSURANCE

Example 1 The insured has a $25,000 15-year decreasing term policy and dies during the fifth policy year. How much will the insurance company pay?

TABLE 9.4

Schedule of Insurance

The Amount payable per $1,000 of Initial Face Amount will be determined at the corresponding Policy Year at death. Policy Year 1 begins on the Date of Issue, Policy Year 2 begins one year after the Date of Issue, etc.

Policy Year	Amount per $1000 of Initial Face Amount	Policy Year	Amount per $1000 of Initial Face Amount	Policy Year	Amount per $1000 of Initial Face Amount
1	$1000	6	$761	11	$438
2	958	7	704	12	361
3	913	8	643	13	278
4	865	9	579	14	191
5	815	10	511	15	99

Solution

a) Find the amount payable per $1000.

Read down to 5 in the policy year column of Table 9.4 and across to the column headed Amount per $1000 of Initial Face Amount. The amount payable for each $1000 is $815.

b) Since the initial policy was issued for $25,000, the total amount payable will be

Amount payable per $1000 × Number of thousands = $815 × 25

= $20,375.

The amount paid by the insurance company was $20,375.

DO EXERCISE 1.

CASH VALUE

Permanent insurance has a cash value, which permits the insured to borrow against the policy. If the insured elects to do so he or she will be charged an interest rate that has been specified in the policy. Frequently this interest rate is lower than the interest rates charged for personal loans by commercial lenders. The major disadvantage of borrowing from one's policy is that upon death the amount of the loan that may remain unpaid is deducted from the face amount of coverage and the result is a death benefit much lower than the one originally issued. A second disadvantage of borrowing from one's insurance is that if the loan becomes large the loan interest required may equal or even exceed the premium charged. Table 9.5 (p. 370) lists the cash values for insurance policies.

Example 2 After a $10,000 permanent insurance policy that was issued at age 22 has been in force for 12 years, the insured wants to borrow on the policy. How much is available?

ANSWER ON PAGE A–19

9.3 LIFE INSURANCE

Solution

a) Determine the amount available to be borrowed per $1000 of insurance.

Locate the box headed Age 22 At Issue on Table 9.5 and read down to 12 in the column headed Years in Force with all Due Premiums Paid. Read across to the column headed Guaranteed Cash or Loan Value. The amount per $1000 is $148.00.

b) Since the policy was issued for $10,000, the total amount available is
Amount available per $1000 × Number of thousands = $148.00 × 10
= $1480.

The amount available to be borrowed is $1480.

DO EXERCISE 2.

••• EXTENDED TERM COVERAGE

Permanent insurance offers other options upon surrender of the policy in addition to surrendering the policy for cash. An insured may elect to exchange the policy for extended term insurance, which provides the original amount of insurance to be kept in force without any additional premium payments for a limited time. Table 9.5 (p. 370) lists the benefits.

Example 3 An insured purchased a $15,000 permanent insurance policy at age 26. After he has paid premiums for 14 years, what will his extended term insurance option be?

Solution Determine the period of time that the insurance company will continue the policy on the extended term basis.

Locate the box headed Age 26 at Issue on Table 9.5 and read down to 14 in the column headed Years in Force with all Due Premiums Paid. Read across to the column headed Extended Term Insurance. The extended term insurance option is 21 years, 185 days. If the insured wishes to cease paying premiums, the insurance company will keep the policy in force on an extended term insurance basis for the next 21 years, 185 days; however, if the insured dies after that time period the insurance company is under no further obligation.

DO EXERCISE 3.

◊◊ REDUCED PAID UP COVERAGE

Another option that permanent insurance offers upon surrender of the policy in addition to either surrendering the policy for cash or accepting extended term insurance is that of reduced paid up insurance. This provision permits the insured to keep the policy in force until death without any further premium payments on a reduced face amount basis. Whereas the extended term insurance option keeps the policy going without further premium payments for a certain specified period for the full face amount, the reduced paid up insurance option keeps the policy going indefinitely without further premium payments but for a lesser amount. Table 9.5 (p. 370) lists the benefits.

2. An insured with a $26,000 permanent insurance policy wants to know its cash value after 15 years. The insured was 24 when she bought the policy. What is the policy's cash value?

3. An insured purchased a $15,000 permanent insurance policy at age 23. After he has paid premiums for 19 years, what will his extended term insurance option be?

ANSWERS ON PAGE A–19

369

TABLE 9.5

Guaranteed Cash or Loan Value, Reduced Paid-up Insurance, Extended Term Insurance
Applicable to a Policy without Either Paid-up Additions or Dividend Accumulations and without Indebtedness
Values at end of years other than those shown will be quoted on request.

Years In Force with all Due Premiums Paid	Age 20 Guaran-teed Cash or Loan Value	Age 20 Reduced Paid-up Insurance	Age 20 Extended Term Yrs.	Age 20 Extended Term Days	Age 21 Guaran-teed Cash or Loan Value	Age 21 Reduced Paid-up Insurance	Age 21 Extended Term Yrs.	Age 21 Extended Term Days	Age 22 Guaran-teed Cash or Loan Value	Age 22 Reduced Paid-up Insurance	Age 22 Extended Term Yrs.	Age 22 Extended Term Days	Age 23 Guaran-teed Cash or Loan Value	Age 23 Reduced Paid-up Insurance	Age 23 Extended Term Yrs.	Age 23 Extended Term Days	Age 24 Guaran-teed Cash or Loan Value	Age 24 Reduced Paid-up Insurance	Age 24 Extended Term Yrs.	Age 24 Extended Term Days	Years In Force with all Due Premiums Paid
1/2	–	–	0	60	–	–	0	60	–	–	0	60	–	–	0	60	–	–	0	60	1/2
1	–	–	0	60	–	–	0	60	–	–	0	60	–	–	0	60	–	–	0	60	1
2	$1	$3	0	141	$1	$3	0	136	$1	$3	0	131	$1	$3	0	126	$1	$3	0	122	2
3	12	33	4	139	13	35	4	205	13	34	4	140	14	36	4	189	15	38	4	228	3
4	25	67	8	180	26	68	8	166	27	70	8	143	29	73	8	209	30	74	8	166	4
5	39	102	12	60	40	103	11	336	42	106	11	330	44	109	11	309	45	109	11	195	5
6	53	136	15	41	55	138	14	335	56	138	14	176	59	143	14	164	61	145	14	66	6
7	67	169	17	164	69	170	17	36	71	172	16	266	74	175	16	188	76	177	16	40	7
8	81	200	19	113	84	203	19	2	87	206	18	243	90	209	18	113	92	209	17	287	8
9	96	232	20	344	99	234	20	186	102	237	20	23	105	239	19	217	109	243	19	90	9
10	111	263	22	86	114	265	21	258	118	269	21	107	122	272	20	314	125	274	20	107	10
11	125	290	23	49	129	294	22	238	133	297	22	57	137	300	21	235	141	303	21	44	11
12	139	316	23	305	143	319	23	104	148	324	22	303	152	326	22	93	157	330	21	280	12
13	154	344	24	175	158	346	23	318	163	350	23	127	168	353	22	297	173	357	22	98	13
14	169	370	24	356	173	371	24	114	178	374	23	269	184	380	23	87	189	383	22	234	14
15	184	395	25	124	189	398	24	264	194	400	24	37	200	405	23	201	205	407	22	333	15
16	198	417	25	187	203	419	24	313	209	423	24	101	215	427	23	251	221	431	23	33	16
17	212	437	25	219	218	441	24	363	224	445	24	137	230	448	23	274	236	451	23	44	17
18	226	457	25	226	232	461	24	358	238	464	24	121	245	469	23	273	252	473	23	57	18
19	240	477	25	209	247	481	24	357	254	486	24	135	260	488	23	251	267	492	23	26	19
20	255	497	25	198	262	501	24	335	269	505	24	103	276	509	23	234	283	512	23	0	20
to Age 60	566	788	19	131	562	783	19	67	557	776	18	352	552	769	18	278	546	761	18	188	to Age 60
to Age 65	642	837	17	78	638	831	17	14	634	826	16	320	629	820	16	248	625	815	16	191	to Age 65

NONFORFEITURE FACTOR FOR EACH $1,000 OF FACE AMOUNT (See "Basis of Values" on page 7)

First 10 Years	11th Through 15th Year	First 10 Years	11th Through 15th Year	First 10 Years	11th Through 15th Year	First 10 Years	11th Through 15th Year	First 10 Years	11th Through 15th Year
$15.36	$14.19	$15.80	$14.58	$16.26	$15.00	$16.73	$15.43	$17.23	$15.89

Years In Force with all Due Premiums Paid	Age 25 Guaran-teed Cash or Loan Value	Age 25 Reduced Paid-up Insurance	Age 25 Extended Term Yrs.	Age 25 Extended Term Days	Age 26 Guaran-teed Cash or Loan Value	Age 26 Reduced Paid-up Insurance	Age 26 Extended Term Yrs.	Age 26 Extended Term Days	Age 27 Guaran-teed Cash or Loan Value	Age 27 Reduced Paid-up Insurance	Age 27 Extended Term Yrs.	Age 27 Extended Term Days	Age 28 Guaran-teed Cash or Loan Value	Age 28 Reduced Paid-up Insurance	Age 28 Extended Term Yrs.	Age 28 Extended Term Days	Age 29 Guaran-teed Cash or Loan Value	Age 29 Reduced Paid-up Insurance	Age 29 Extended Term Yrs.	Age 29 Extended Term Days	Years In Force with all Due Premiums Paid
1/2	–	–	0	60	–	–	0	60	–	–	0	60	–	–	0	60	–	–	0	60	1/2
1	–	–	0	60	–	–	0	60	–	–	0	60	–	–	0	60	–	–	0	60	1
2	$1	$3	0	117	$1	$3	0	112	$1	$3	0	112	$1	$3	0	107	$1	$3	0	102	2
3	16	40	4	258	17	41	4	278	18	43	4	291	19	45	4	295	20	46	4	293	3
4	31	75	8	115	33	78	8	143	34	79	8	78	35	80	8	8	37	83	8	4	4
5	47	112	11	155	49	114	11	104	50	114	10	342	52	116	10	276	54	118	10	203	5
6	63	146	13	325	65	148	13	213	67	150	13	95	70	153	13	29	72	155	12	264	6
7	79	180	15	308	82	183	15	202	84	184	15	39	87	187	14	285	90	190	14	160	7
8	95	212	17	144	98	215	16	363	102	219	16	253	105	221	16	94	108	223	15	296	8
9	112	245	18	274	116	249	18	133	119	251	17	310	123	254	17	157	127	257	17	2	9
10	129	277	19	303	133	280	19	129	137	283	18	317	141	286	18	135	146	290	17	349	10
11	145	305	20	213	149	308	20	16	154	312	19	213	158	314	19	10	163	318	18	199	11
12	161	332	21	64	166	336	20	242	171	340	20	53	176	343	19	224	181	346	19	29	12
13	178	360	21	259	183	364	21	53	188	366	20	209	193	369	19	364	199	374	19	177	13
14	194	385	22	15	200	390	21	185	205	392	20	326	211	396	20	126	217	400	19	278	14
15	211	411	22	125	217	415	21	280	223	419	21	68	229	422	20	218	235	425	20	3	15
16	227	434	22	176	233	437	21	319	239	441	21	94	246	445	20	257	252	448	20	31	16
17	242	454	22	177	249	459	21	333	256	463	21	121	262	466	20	251	269	470	20	37	17
18	258	475	22	180	265	480	21	326	272	483	21	104	279	487	20	247	287	492	20	44	18
19	274	496	22	163	282	501	21	321	289	504	21	91	297	509	20	245	304	512	20	14	19
20	291	517	22	150	298	520	21	278	306	525	21	60	314	529	20	207	322	533	19	353	20
to Age 60	540	752	18	98	535	745	18	23	528	735	17	288	522	727	17	203	515	717	17	105	to Age 60
to Age 65	620	808	16	119	615	801	16	48	610	795	15	343	605	788	15	278	599	781	15	200	to Age 65

NONFORFEITURE FACTOR FOR EACH $1,000 OF FACE AMOUNT (See "Basis of Values" on page 7)

First 10 Years	11th Through 15th Year	First 10 Years	11th Through 15th Year	First 10 Years	11th Through 15th Year	First 10 Years	11th Through 15th Year	First 10 Years	11th Through 15th Year
$17.75	$16.36	$18.29	$16.86	$18.85	$17.38	$19.44	$17.92	$20.06	$18.49

After the year for which a value is first shown, values as of any time during a policy year will be determined by the Company with allowance for the time elapsed in such year, and for any period in such year for which due premiums have been paid. However, if payment is made prior to the end of the period for which due premiums have been paid, the amount of such payment will be the Guaranteed Cash Value as of the end of that period less interest (at the effective rate of 5% per year) from the date of payment to the end of the period.

Example 4 The insured has a $40,000 permanent insurance policy, which she bought at age 29. She wants to know how much the policy will be for on a reduced paid up basis at age 60.

Solution

a) To determine the amount of the reduced paid up insurance, locate the box headed Age 29 at Issue on Table 9.5 and read down to Age 60 in the column headed Years in Force with all Due Premiums Paid. Read across to the column headed Reduced Paid Up Insurance. The amount of insurance that will be in force on a Reduced Paid Up basis at age 60 for the duration of the insured's life would be $717 per $1000.

b) Since the policy was issued for $40,000, the total amount of reduced paid up insurance is

Amount per $1000 × Number of thousands = $717 × 40 = $28,680.

DO EXERCISE 4.

4. An insured purchased a $30,000 permanent insurance policy at age 24. How much reduced paid up insurance will she have in 16 years if she wishes to stop paying her premiums at that time?

THE COST OF LIFE INSURANCE

Life insurance companies levy charges known as premiums to the insured. Premiums are based on several variables, including the age and sex of the insured (women are considered as having a life expectancy that is three years longer than men), the type of insurance applied for, the amount of insurance requested, and the addition of any optional features known as *riders*. The unisex issue (now in the courts) will most likely change the costs and benefits of life insurance.

Example 5 The insured, who is male and age 25, wishes to buy a $10,000 permanent insurance policy. How much is the premium?

Solution

a) Find the premium payable for $1000 for a male, age 25.

Read down to age 25 on Table 9.6 (next page) and across to Life-M. The amount payable for each $1000 is $13.46.

b) Since the initial policy is to be issued for $10,000, the total amount payable will be

Amount payable per $1000 × Number of thousands = $13.46 × 10
= $134.60.

The amount charged by the insurance company is $134.60.

DO EXERCISE 5.

5. A 30-year-old female wishes to buy a $20,000 permanent insurance policy. How much is the premium?

Many life insurance companies offer the insured the option of adding an *accidental death benefit* to the basic policy. This feature, which is also known as *double indemnity*, will customarily double the face amount of the policy in the event that the insured's death results from an accident.

Example 6 A 35-year-old male wishes to purchase a $15,000 policy with double indemnity. How much is his premium?

ANSWERS ON PAGE A–19

INSURANCE

Solution

a) Find the premium payable for $1000 for a male, age 35.

Read down to age 35 on Table 9.6 and across to Life-M. The amount payable for each $1000 is $19.06.

TABLE 9.6
ORDINARY LIFE (PER $1000)

Age At Issue	Life-M	Life-F	Non-Smokers	W.P.	A.D.B.	Years To Pay Up W/Divs.	Total Mo. Inc. At 65 Male	Total Mo. Inc. At 65 Female	Interest Adj. Cost Index* 10 Yrs.	Interest Adj. Cost Index* 20 Yrs.
0	$ 7.77	$ 7.58		$ .20	$ .64	24	$15.24	$14.04	$ 3.46	$ 2.01
1	7.77	7.58		.20	.66	24	14.96	13.77	2.88	1.72
2	7.89	7.69		.21	.69	24	14.64	13.48	2.82	1.67
3	8.03	7.82		.21	.72	24	14.34	13.20	2.77	1.65
4	8.17	7.95		.22	.75	24	14.04	12.92	2.73	1.66
5	8.32	8.09		.22	.78	24	13.72	12.63	2.70	1.64
6	8.49	8.25		.23	.79	24	13.41	12.35	2.69	1.65
7	8.66	8.42		.23	.81	24	13.10	12.06	2.68	1.63
8	8.84	8.59		.24	.82	24	12.79	11.78	2.76	1.65
9	9.03	8.78		.24	.84	24	12.49	11.50	2.77	1.68
10	9.23	8.97		.25	.86	24	12.19	11.22	2.79	1.69
11	9.44	9.17		.25	.87	24	11.89	10.95	2.83	1.72
12	9.65	9.37		.26	.89	24	11.60	10.66	2.87	1.75
13	9.88	9.59		.26	.91	25	11.31	10.41	2.93	1.80
14	10.12	9.82		.27	.92	25	11.02	10.15	3.00	1.83
15	10.36	10.05		.28	.94	25	10.75	9.90	3.07	1.89
16	10.61	10.29		.28	.94	25	10.50	9.66	3.07	1.89
17	10.87	10.53		.29	.94	25	10.23	9.42	3.16	1.89
18	11.15	10.79		.30	.94	25	10.00	9.21	3.19	1.92
19	11.43	11.04		.31	.93	25	9.75	8.98	3.22	1.95
20	11.72	11.29	$ 11.42	.32	.91	25	9.51	8.76	3.25	1.96
21	12.04	11.58	11.72	.33	.90	25	9.31	8.57	3.23	2.00
22	12.37	11.88	12.02	.34	.89	25	9.09	8.37	3.30	2.02
23	12.72	12.20	12.35	.35	.88	25	8.88	8.17	3.31	2.06
24	13.08	12.53	12.68	.37	.87	25	8.67	7.98	3.41	2.11
25	13.46	12.87	13.03	.38	.88	25	8.46	7.79	3.45	2.18
26	13.91	13.28	13.46	.40	.88	25	8.29	7.63	3.54	2.25
27	14.38	13.70	13.92	.41	.88	25	8.11	7.46	3.56	2.38
28	14.88	14.15	14.40	.43	.89	25	7.93	7.30	3.70	2.47
29	15.39	14.61	14.89	.45	.90	25	7.75	7.13	3.85	2.64
30	15.93	15.10	15.42	.48	.91	25	7.57	6.97	3.95	2.77
31	16.50	15.61	15.97	.50	.92	24	7.39	6.81	4.06	2.95
32	17.09	16.13	16.53	.53	.93	24	7.23	6.66	4.26	3.14
33	17.72	16.69	17.14	.56	.94	24	7.05	6.49	4.43	3.37
34	18.37	17.26	17.77	.59	.96	24	6.87	6.32	4.62	3.59
35	19.06	17.86	18.43	.63	.97	24	6.69	6.16	4.84	3.89
36	19.79	18.50	19.13	.67	.98	24	6.50	5.99	5.13	4.23
37	20.57	19.19	19.89	.72	1.00	24	6.31	5.81	5.46	4.58
38	21.38	19.90	20.67	.77	1.01	24	6.12	5.64	5.82	5.00
39	22.22	20.64	21.48	.82	1.02	24	5.93	5.46	6.14	5.42
40	23.12	21.44	22.34	.88	1.04	24	5.72	5.27	6.59	5.93
41	24.05	22.26	23.24	.95	1.06	24	5.54	5.10	6.97	6.40
42	25.03	23.12	24.18	1.02	1.07	23	5.35	4.93	7.48	6.96
43	26.06	24.02	25.17	1.11	1.09	23	5.15	4.74	7.96	7.54
44	27.15	24.99	26.20	1.20	1.11	23	4.95	4.56	8.50	8.20
45	28.29	26.01	27.29	1.30	1.13	23	4.74	4.36	9.10	8.89
46	29.47	27.06	28.42	1.42	1.14	23	4.56	4.20	9.55	9.44
47	30.71	28.17	29.60	1.55	1.16	23	4.37	4.02	10.06	10.09
48	32.02	29.35	30.85	1.69	1.18	22	4.18	3.85	10.64	10.77
49	33.40	30.60	32.18	1.85	1.20	22	3.97	3.66	11.21	11.55
50	34.86	31.93	33.58	2.04	1.22	22	3.76	3.46	11.95	12.42
51	36.40	33.34	35.06	2.24	1.25	22	3.50	3.22	12.69	13.33
52	38.03	34.84	36.63	2.46	1.27	21	3.30	3.04	13.45	14.29
53	39.74	36.41	38.28	2.71	1.29	21	3.10	2.86	14.36	15.38
54	41.56	38.09	40.04	2.98	1.32	21	2.89	2.66	15.31	16.53
55	43.83	39.87	41.91	3.27	1.35	21	2.68	2.46	16.35	17.82
56	45.53	41.79	43.87	3.58	1.38	20	2.44	2.24	17.47	19.12
57	47.71	43.84	45.97	3.87	1.41	20	2.18	2.00	18.72	20.57
58	50.01	46.01	48.18	4.16	1.45	20	1.91	1.75	20.00	22.12
59	52.45	48.33	50.51	4.42	1.48	19	1.63	1.50	21.51	23.84
60	55.03	50.79	53.03		1.52	19	1.35	1.24	23.23	25.69
61	57.79	53.37	55.79		1.56	19	1.06	.97	24.93	27.64
62	60.71	56.08	58.71		1.59	19	.75	.69	26.87	29.74
63	63.81	58.96	61.81		1.64	18	.44	.40	28.99	32.02
64	67.09	62.04	65.09		1.68	18	.10	.10	31.29	34.52
65	70.57	65.30	68.57		1.72	18			33.71	37.18
66	74.35	68.86	72.35			18	10 Yrs and		36.45	40.10
67	78.34	72.62	76.34			17	Life Alt		39.33	43.23
68	82.55	76.59	80.55			17	Larger Inc		42.42	46.54
69	86.99	80.78	84.99			17	Incl Guar CV		45.75	50.08
70	91.66	85.20	89.66			17	+ Term Div +		49.30	53.82
71	96.80	90.08	94.80			16	CV of Pd Up		53.06	
72	102.22	95.24	100.22			16	Addns		57.17	
73	107.95	100.70	105.95			16			61.59	
74	114.05	106.52	112.05			15			66.38	
75	120.57	112.76	118.57			15			71.67	

*Figures are for basic male rates. Adjust as necessary for policy fee, non-smoker discount, female discount
Minimum Policy Ages 0–14 $1,500. Ages 15–75 $2,000. Non-Smokers $10,000.
TERMINAL DIVIDENDS, IF ANY, ARE INCLUDED IN THE LAST FOUR COLUMNS ABOVE

9.3 LIFE INSURANCE

b) Since the initial policy is to be issued with the accidental death benefit, or double indemnity, we must add in the charge for this rider. Read down to Age 35 Male on Table 9.6 and across to the column headed A.D.B. The charge for the accidental death benefit is $0.97 per $1000.

c) The charge for the basic policy is, therefore, $19.06 + $0.97 = $20.03 per $1000. Since the initial policy is to be issued for $15,000, to find the cost of the policy we multiply:

Base rate × Number of thousands = $20.03 × 15
= $300.45.

The premium is thus $300.45.

DO EXERCISE 6.

The *disability waiver of premium* benefit is another rider that can be added to a policy. This rider waives all premiums in the event that the insured is totally disabled for a period of six months.

Example 7 A 32-year-old male wishes to purchase an $18,000 policy with a waiver of premium benefit. How much is the premium?

Solution

a) Find the premium payable for $1000 for a male, age 32.

Read down to age 32 on Table 9.6 and across to Life-M. The amount payable for each $1000 is $17.09.

b) Since the initial policy is to be issued with the waiver of premium benefit, we must add in the charge for this rider. Read down to age 32 on Table 9.6 and across to the column headed W.P. The charge for the waiver of premium rider is $0.53 per $1000. The charge for the basic policy is, therefore, $17.09 plus $0.53 = $17.62 per $1000. Since the initial policy is to be issued for $18,000, to find the cost of the policy, we multiply:

Base rate × Number of thousands = $17.62 × 18
= $317.16.

The premium is thus $317.16.

DO EXERCISE 7.

Frequently, insurance premiums are paid on an other-than-annual basis; however, the most common methods now are semiannual, quarterly, monthly, and automatic bank draft. If premiums are paid on a semiannual basis, the company sends notices twice a year. When premiums are paid quarterly, the insurance company sends four separate bills, three months apart. Monthly billing means that the insurance company sends notices each month. One of the most popular methods of paying premiums in recent years has been the automatic bank draft method. The insurance company automatically withdraws the amount of the premium from the insured's bank on a monthly basis.

---

6. A female, age 37, wishes to purchase a $25,000 policy with double indemnity. How much is the premium?

7. A female, age 40, wishes to purchase a $30,000 policy with a waiver of premium benefit. How much is the premium?

ANSWERS ON PAGE A–19

8. It is determined that an insurance premium is $300.45 per year, but the insured wants to pay monthly. (a) What is the monthly premium? (b) What is the total paid for the year?

INSURANCE

Premiums that are paid more frequently than annually are increased. The reasons include the greater expense of collection, the loss of interest on the policyholder's money, and a greater tendency toward lapse. Typical charges for premium methods other than annual are shown below.

Semiannual	51.000%
Quarterly	26.000%
Automatic bank draft	8.417%
Regular momthly	8.833%

Example 8 It is determined that an insurance premium is $317.16 per year, but the insured wants to pay quarterly. (a) What is the quarterly premium? (b) What is the total paid for the year?

Solution

a) According to the list above, for a quarterly payment, we take 26% of the annual premium, which is $317.16.

$$26\% \times \$317.16 = 0.26 \times \$317.16.$$
$$= \$82.46$$

b) Total paid = Amount each quarter × Number of payments
= $82.46 × 4
= $329.84

Note that the actual amount paid for the year is $329.84 − $317.16, or $12.68 more by paying in four payments rather than by paying the entire $317.16 at the beginning of the year.

DO EXERCISE 8.

ANSWER ON PAGE A–19

EXERCISE SET 9.3

For these exercises use Tables 18, 19, and 20 (pp. T–34, T–35, and T–36).

● Find the amount payable.

1. An insured with an $80,000 15-year decreasing term policy dies during the twelfth policy year.

2. An insured with a $125,000 15-year decreasing term policy dies during the second policy year.

3. An insured with a $40,000 15-year decreasing term policy dies during the tenth policy year.

4. An insured with a $50,000 15-year decreasing term policy dies during the fourth policy year.

●● Solve.

5. After a $50,000 permanent insurance policy that was issued at age 20 had been in force for 17 years, the insured wanted to borrow on the policy. How much was available?

6. After a $40,000 permanent insurance policy that was issued at age 21 had been in force for 11 years, the insured wanted to borrow on the policy. How much was available?

7. After a $20,000 permanent insurance policy that was issued at age 27 had been in force for nine years, the insured wanted to borrow on the policy. How much was available?

8. After a $35,000 permanent insurance policy that was issued at age 25 had been in force for four years, the insured wanted to borrow on the policy. How much was available?

●●● Solve.

9. Premium payments are stopped after 20 years on a $40,000 permanent policy bought at age 24. How long will the insurance policy be continued under the extended term option?

10. Premium payments are stopped after 18 years on a $60,000 permanent policy bought at age 28. How long will the insurance policy be continued under the extended term option?

11. The insured has a $25,000 permanent insurance policy bought at age 28 on which premiums have been paid for 18 years. Premium payments are stopped. How long will the insurance company continue coverage under the extended term insurance option?

12. The insured has a $40,000 permanent insurance policy bought at age 20 on which premiums have been paid for 10 years. Premium payments are stopped. How long will the insurance company continue coverage under the extended term insurance option?

376 INSURANCE

ANSWERS

⠲ Solve.

13. A $40,000 permanent policy was bought at age 23. What will be the reduced paid up value at 60?

14. A $70,000 permanent policy was bought at age 26. What will be the reduced paid up value at 65?

15. The insured has a $35,000 permanent insurance policy bought at age 27. How much will the policy be for on a reduced paid up basis at age 65?

16. The insured has a $40,000 permanent insurance policy bought at age 24. How much will the policy be for on a reduced paid up basis at age 60?

⠲ Determine the cost.

17. A 21-year-old female wishes to buy a $35,000 permanent insurance policy. How much is the premium?

18. A 21-year-old male wishes to buy a $35,000 permanent insurance policy. How much is the premium?

19. A female, age 24, wishes to purchase a $30,000 policy with double indemnity. How much is the premium?

20. A male, age 24, wishes to purchase a $30,000 policy with double indemnity. How much is the premium?

21. A female, age 23, wishes to purchase a $25,000 policy with a waiver of premium benefit. How much is the premium?

22. A male, age 23, wishes to purchase a $25,000 policy with a waiver of premium benefit. How much is the premium?

23. It is determined that an insurance premium is $458.68 per year, but the insured wants to pay quarterly. What is the quarterly premium? What is the total paid for the year?

24. It is determined that an insurance premium is $679.54 per year, but the insured wants to pay quarterly. What is the quarterly premium? What is the total paid for the year?

25. An insured with a $235,000 15-year decreasing term policy dies during the twelfth policy year. How much does the insurance company pay?

26. For a $110,000 permanent policy bought at age 28, find the cash value after 19 years; the extended term coverage after 15 years; and the reduced paid up value at age 65.

27. Find the automatic bank draft monthly premium for a $56,000 permanent insurance policy with double indemnity and waiver of premium riders purchased by a 31-year-old female.

28. Find the quarterly premium for a $47,000 permanent insurance policy with double indemnity and waiver of premium riders purchased by a 27-year-old male.

TEST OR REVIEW—CHAPTER 9

If you miss an item, review the indicated section and objective.

[9.1, ● ●] 1. An all-risk homeowner's policy for $60,000 is taken out on a home whose replacement cost is $80,000. A water heater breaks doing $5000 damage. How much is paid by the insurance company?

2. A basic-form homeowner's policy for $70,000 is taken out on a house. A stereo bought two years ago was stolen. The comparable stereo today costs $2400 while the one stolen cost $1600. It was expected to last eight years. How much does the insurance pay? Use Table 14.

[9.1, ● ● ●] 3. Find the annual premium for a $60,000 Form 3, $50 all-peril deductible homeowner's policy on a masonry house in Zone 1, Protection Class 3. Use Table 15 (p. T–29).

[9.2, ●] 4. A motorist with 75,000/150,000/25,000 coverage does $28,500 damage to a building. How much does the motorist pay?

5. A motorist with 100,000/300,000/50,000 coverage loses a lawsuit brought by an injured person for $142,000. How much does the insurance company pay?

6. A motorist with medical-payments coverage up to $5000 for each person is involved in an accident that injures one passenger. The passenger has $7450 in medical expenses. How much does the passenger pay?

[9.2, ● ●] 7. A single male, age 17, with a medium-size 1984 car, selects 100/300/50 liability, 5000 medical, ACV comprehensive, $100 deductible collision, and 10/20 uninsured-motorist coverage. Find the six-month premium. Use Tables 16 and 17 (pp. T–33 and T–34).

[9.3, ●] 8. The insured has a $45,000 15-year decreasing term policy and dies during the fifth policy year. How much will the insurance company pay? Use Table 18 (p. T–34).

Use Table 19 (T–35) for 9–11.

[9.3, ● ●] 9. After a $35,000 permanent insurance policy that was issued at age 23 had been in force for 14 years, the insured wanted to borrow on the policy. How much was available?

[9.3, ● ● ●] 10. An insured purchased a $30,000 permanent policy at age 27. After she has paid premiums for 11 years, what will her extended term insurance be?

[9.3, ⋮⋮] 11. The insured has a $50,000 permanent insurance policy bought at age 26. How much will the policy be for on a reduced paid up basis at age 65?

ANSWERS

1. _____

2. _____

3. _____

4. _____

5. _____

6. _____

7. _____

8. _____

9. _____

10. _____

11. _____

INSURANCE

Use Table 20 (p. T–36, 37) for 12–14.

[9.3, ■]

12. The insured, who is female and age 24, wishes to buy a $15,000 permanent insurance policy. What is the premium?

13. A 22-year old female wishes to purchase a $40,000 policy with double indemnity. How much is the premium?

14. A 25-year old male wishes to purchase a $30,000 policy with a waiver of premium benefit. How much is the premium?

10
TAXES

Career: Personal Trust Administrator *This is Elizabeth McCord. Liz is a personal trust administrator for a large financial institution in Chicago. The path she has traveled to her present position is impressive. She first received a Bachelor's Degree in French, but then a took a three-month course of study in a Lawyer's Assistant (Paralegal) Program at Roosevelt University, specializing in estates, trusts, and wills. After completion of this program, she obtained a position in a law firm. From there she went to her present employer, where she first worked as an income tax preparer and analyst. She was promoted in the company, first as an administrative assistant, then to a supervisor, and finally to her present position as Trust Officer.*

A trust is a fund of money which serves many purposes. For example, one can put a block of money away for a child. The income from the money is then taxed in a different way which saves taxes. The money and/or its income can be used for the child's education or other expenses. Through a will, a trust can also be set up on a person's death. A trust officer, such as Liz, then helps make decisions about the appropriate use of the money in the trust. Thus business mathematics comes into play quite often. For example, what percentage of interest is the fund making? By what percent will an expense deplete the fund? Will an expense deplete the fund so much that future financial needs, for which the fund was set up, cannot be met?

People in Liz's kind of work can make between $20,000 and $30,000 per year. Liz is an organized, inquisitive person who enjoys working with people.

380

TAXES

READINESS CHECK—SKILLS FOR CHAPTER 10

Find.

1. 3% of 69¢
2. 27% of $65,000

Add.

3. $28.95 + $1.16
4. $23,700 + $320.00

Divide.

5. 4317 ÷ 1.03
6. 635,747 ÷ 42,091,402

OBJECTIVES

After finishing Section 10.1, you should be able to

■ Calculate sales tax.
■■ Determine sales.

1. Find the sales tax on a 78¢ purchase in a 5% sales tax state. Use the major fraction rule.

10.1 SALES TAX

Taxes provide money for governmental services. Our taxes are used for social programs, research, defense, education, police, fire protection and many other services. In this chapter we study sales, property, and federal income taxes.

■ FINDING THE SALES TAX

State and local governments often tax goods and services. The taxes (expressed as percents) are *sales taxes*. Rates vary among states. The *sales tax* is a percentage added on to the purchase price.

Various methods are used to compute sales tax. For example, some states use the *major fraction rule*. For this method any fraction of a cent less than $\frac{1}{2}$ is disregarded, whereas for fractions greater than or equal to $\frac{1}{2}$, another penny is added.

Example 1 Find the sales tax on one furnace filter in a 3% sales tax state. Use the major fraction rule.

FURNACE FILTERS
Only 69¢
Sizes In Stock

Solution The filter costs 69¢ so the sales tax is

3% × 69¢ = 2.07¢

The sales tax is 2¢.

DO EXERCISE 1.

There are several states that do not use the major fraction rule. Table 10.1 lists several of them together with their method of computation.

ANSWER ON PAGE A–19

10.1 SALES TAX

TABLE 10.1						
State	Rate	1¢	2¢	3¢	4¢	5¢
Iowa	4%	13–37	38–62	63–87		
Georgia	3%	11–35	36–66	67–1.00†		
Pennsylvania	6%	11–17	18–34	35–50	51–67	68–84†

* Use the major fraction rule for any larger amount.
† Any fraction is treated as a cent on larger amounts. For example, the sales tax on $23.42 is 70.26¢, which is treated as 71¢.

Example 2 Find the sales tax if the 69¢ furnace filter is bought in Georgia.

Solution From Table 10.1 we see that any purchase from 67¢ to $1.00 in Georgia has a 3¢ sales tax.

Thus, the Georgia sales tax on the 69¢ furnace filter is 3¢.

DO EXERCISE 2.

Many states that do not use the major fraction rule for small amounts do use it for larger purchases.

Example 3 Find the sales tax on the $28.95 battery in a 4% sales tax state. Use the major fraction rule.

Solution The price is $28.95 and

$$4\% \times \$28.95 = \$1.158.$$

Thus, the sales tax is $1.16.

DO EXERCISE 3.

To find the total cost the sales tax and the price of the article are added.

Example 4 Find the total cost for a $28.95 battery in a 4% sales tax state. Use the major fraction rule.

---

2. Find the sales tax on a 47¢ purchase made in Pennsylvania.

3. Find the sales tax on a $567.25 freezer in a 5% sales tax state. Use the major function rule.

ANSWERS ON PAGE A–19

4. Find the total cost of a $4562 automobile in a 5% sales tax state. Use the major fraction rule.

TAXES

Solution

a) Find the sales tax.

From Example 3 we know that the sales tax is $1.16.

b) Find the total cost.

Total cost = Price + Sales tax
= $28.95 + $1.16
= $30.11

The total cost is $30.11.

DO EXERCISE 4.

●● SALES

Business people collect the sales tax and send it to the government periodically. Often only the total amount of each sale is recorded, so the amount of sales tax due the government must be determined at the time that the tax is sent.

Example 5 A business had receipts of $4317, which include a 3% sales tax. How much were sales?

Solution Let x be the sales. Then

100% of sales + 3% of sales is 4317

$$1.00 \cdot x + 0.03 \cdot x = 4317$$
$$1.03x = 4317$$
$$x = 4191.26. \quad \text{Dividing both sides by 1.03}$$

Thus sales were $4191.26.

DO EXERCISE 5.

5. A business had receipts of $7689, which include a 4% sales tax. How much were sales?

ANSWERS ON PAGE A–19

EXERCISE SET 10.1   **383**

NAME _____   CLASS _____   ANSWERS

EXERCISE SET 10.1

■ Find the sales tax. Use Table 10.1 when necessary.   1. _____

1. An $0.86 purchase in a state having a 4% sales tax. Use the major fraction rule.

                                                                               2. _____

2. A $0.76 purchase in a state having a 3% sales tax. Use the major fraction rule.

                                                                               3. _____

3. A $1.14 purchase in Iowa.

                                                                               4. _____

4. An $0.82 purchase in Pennsylvania.

5. A $0.72 purchase in Georgia.
                                                                               5. _____

6. A $0.72 purchase in Iowa.
                                                                               6. _____

7. A $149.95 purchase in a state with a 5% sales tax. Use the major fraction rule.
                                                                               7. _____

8. A $645.49 lawn tractor in a state with a 3% sales tax. Use the major fraction rule.

                                                                               8. _____
9. Find the total cost of an $1879 motorcycle in a state with a 4% sales tax. Use the major fraction rule.

                                                                               9. _____
10. Find the total cost of a $6238 automobile in a state with a 6% sales tax. Use the major fraction rule.

                                                                               10. _____

Find the sales tax on these items purchased in Georgia.

11.   12.
   JON BOAT, 14', deck, swival   35' PARK MODEL Travel Trail-
   seat, carpeting, Balko trailer, 15   er, Roll out awnings, air, many
   hp electric start Johnson, 12   extras. Must sell this week,   11. _____
   hours $1,650. 864-2798 after 5 $8500. Can be seen at Kennedy
                                            Park.

                                                                               12. _____

Copyright © 1984, by Addison-Wesley Publishing Company Inc. All rights reserved.

384 TAXES

ANSWERS

13.

14.

13. A 16' x 32' Swimming Pool $8400 INSTALLED
- Steel Walls
- 3' Concrete Deck
- Diving Board & Ladder
- Deluxe Filtration System with Heater
- Maint. Kit & Chemicals

10 YEARS EXPERIENCE
"Quality For Less"
PETERSON POOLS

14. $29.88 SONY MODEL ICF-700
AM/FM, AC/DC
Portable Radio AC Adaptor Included

Solve.

15. A business has $6789 in receipts, which include a 5% sales tax. How much were sales?

16. A business has $9875 in receipts, which include a 6% sales tax. How much were sales?

17. A business has $9802 in receipts, which include a 4% sales tax. How much were sales?

18. A business has $7690 in receipts, which include a 6% sales tax. How much were sales?

19. A business has $3780 in receipts, which include a 4% sales tax. How much was the sales tax?

20. A business has $7540 in receipts, which include a 5% sales tax. How much was the sales tax?

Complete. Use the major fraction rule.

	Purchase	Price	Rate	Sales Tax	Total Cost
21.	Scanner	$ 289.95	4%		
22.	Chain saw		5%		$ 68.24
23.	Radial saw			$ 6.90	$236.89
24.	Cutlass	$3894.75		$233.69	

10.2 PROPERTY TAX

◼ ASSESSED VALUE

Local governments tax real estate and personal property to pay for schools and other governmental services. These taxes are *property taxes* and vary nationwide. Property taxes are based on the *assessed value* (determined by a tax assessor) of the property.

Example 1 The current market value of a home is $65,000 and the assessment rate is 27%. Find the assessed value.

Solution

$$\begin{aligned}\text{Assessed value} &= 27\% \times \$65,000 \\ &= 0.27 \times \$65,000 \\ &= \$17,550\end{aligned}$$

The assessed value is $17,550.

DO EXERCISE 1.

◼◼ TAX RATE

The tax rate (*levy*) is determined by dividing the amount of money needed (stated in the budget) by the total assessed value of property (the sum of all property assessments) within the governmental boundaries.

$$\text{Tax rate} = \frac{\text{Money needed}}{\text{Total assessed value}}$$

Example 2 A school district needs $635,747 in property tax revenue and has property assessed at $42,091,402 within its boundaries. What is the tax rate?

Solution Substitute 635,747 for money needed and 42,091,402 for total assessed value in

$$\begin{aligned}\text{Tax rate} &= \frac{\text{Money needed}}{\text{Total assessed value}} \\ &= \frac{635{,}747}{42{,}091{,}402} \\ &= 0.015104.\end{aligned}$$

The tax rate is 1.5104% or 1.5104¢ per dollar; thus,

$$\$1.5104 \text{ per } \$100 \left(\frac{1.5104}{\$1} \cdot \frac{100}{100} = \frac{151.04¢}{\$100} = \frac{\$1.5104}{\$100}\right)$$

or $15.104 per $1000 (often expressed as 15.104 mills, where a *mill is one-thousandth of a dollar*).

DO EXERCISE 2.

OBJECTIVES

After finishing Section 10.2, you should be able to:

◼ Determine assessed value.

◼◼ Compute the tax rate.

◼◼◼ Determine the tax.

1. The current market value of a home is $52,000. Find the assessed value if the assessment rate is 43%.

2. A town needs $342,000 from property taxes and has property assessed at $27,454,103 within its boundaries. What is the tax rate in mills?

ANSWERS ON PAGE A–19

3. Find the tax for city expenses on a home assessed at $47,000 where the tax rate is 2.364 mills.

◼◼◼ AMOUNT OF TAX

The tax rate is used to find the tax on each property within the boundaries of the governmental body.

> Tax = Assessed value × Tax rate

Example 3 Find the tax for schools on a home assessed at $62,000 where the tax rate is 17.445 mills.

Solution Substitute 62,000 for assessed value and 0.017445 for tax rate in

Tax = Assessed value × Tax rate
   = 62,000 × 0.017445
   = 1081.59

The tax is $1081.59.

DO EXERCISE 3.

EXERCISE SET 10.2

● Solve.

1. The current market value of a home is $53,875. Find the assessed value if the assessment rate is 58%.

2. The current market value of a home is $48,000. Find the assessed value if the assessment rate is 40%.

3. The current market value of a home is $67,500. Find the assessed value if the assessment rate is 55%.

4. The current market value of a home is $85,000. Find the assessed value if the assessment rate is 60%.

5. The assessment rate is 64% of the current market value. Find the assessed value of a home with market value $58,500.

6. The assessment rate is 72% of the current market value. Find the assessed value of a home with market value $87,600.

●● Solve.

7. A county needs $346,780 from property taxes and has $83,567,765 of assessed property within its boundaries. What is the tax rate (in mills)?

8. A town needs $1,250,000 from property taxes and has $215,654,900 of assessed property within its boundaries. What is the tax rate (in mills)?

9. A township needs $560,870 from property taxes and has $45,789,000 of assessed property within its boundaries. What is the tax rate (as a percent)?

10. A school district needs $867,905 from property taxes and has $93,684,500 of assessed property within its boundaries. What is the tax rate (as a percent)?

●●● Solve.

11. Find the tax for county roads on a home assessed at $43,000 where the tax rate is 1.6035%.

12. Find the tax for county roads on a home assessed at $57,800 where the tax rate is 2.0168%.

13. Find the tax for county operations on a home assessed at $28,000 where the tax rate is 9.0345 mills.

14. Find the tax for schools on a home assessed at $32,000 where the tax rate is 17.035 mills.

Complete the table for a home assessed at $46,387.

Taxing body	Rate in mills	Amount
15. County	6.6258	
16. Water district		$ 18.85
17. School		$699.87
18. Township	0.3255	

10.3 FEDERAL INCOME TAX

A federal income tax return must be filed once each year by most Americans. Once a return is filed, you are on the Internal Revenue Service mailing list.

OBJECTIVES

After finishing Section 10.3, you should be able to:

■ Prepare Form 1040EZ.

■■ Prepare Form 1040A.

Many taxpayers' sources of income and deductions are not complicated. They should consider preparing their own tax returns. In this section we study the preparation of Federal Income Tax Forms 1040EZ and 1040A. A third, Form 1040, will not be studied as it is quite lengthy and may require additional supporting schedules.

■ FORM 1040EZ

Individuals who meet these conditions may file Form 1040EZ.

> **You can use Form 1040EZ for:**
>
> Single filing status only
>
> Your own personal exemption only
>
> No dependents
>
> Income from:
>   Wages, salaries, tips
>   Interest income ($400 or less)
>   No dividend income
>   Less than $50,000 in taxable income
>
> Partial charitable contributions deduction
>
> No tax credits

A completed Form 1040EZ appears in Example 1.

Example 1 Complete.

Department of the Treasury—Internal Revenue Service
Form 1040EZ Income Tax Return for Single filers with no dependents (0)

OMB No. 1545-0675

Instructions are on the back of this form.
Tax Table is in the 1040EZ and 1040A Tax Package.

Name and address

Use the IRS mailing label. If you don't have a label, print or type:

Name (first, initial, last): Joyce T Owens
Social security number: 484-30-5678
Present home address: 1418 Fifth Ave
City, town or post office, State, and ZIP code: Chesterland, OH 44026

Presidential Election Campaign Fund
Check this box ☑ if you want $1 of your tax to go to this fund.

Figure your tax

Attach Copy B of Forms W-2 here

1	Wages, salaries, and tips. Attach your W-2 form(s).	1 23,700.—
2	Interest income of $400 or less. If more than $400, you cannot use Form 1040EZ.	2 320.—
3	Add line 1 and line 2. This is your **adjusted gross income**.	3 24,020.—
ⓘ 4	Allowable part of your charitable contributions. Complete the worksheet on page 18. Do not write more than $25.	4 20.—
5	Subtract line 4 from line 3.	5 24,000.—
6	Amount of your personal exemption.	6 1,000.00
7	Subtract line 6 from line 5. This is your **taxable income**.	7 23,000.—
⑧	Enter your Federal income tax withheld. This is shown on your W-2 form(s).	8 4,800.—
⑨	Use the tax table on pages 26-31 to find the **tax** on your taxable income on line 7.	9 4,690.—

Refund or amount you owe

10	If line 8 is larger than line 9, subtract line 9 from line 8. Enter the amount of your **refund**.	10 110.—

Attach tax payment here

11	If line 9 is larger than line 8, subtract line 8 from line 9. Enter the **amount you owe**. Attach check or money order for the full amount payable to "Internal Revenue Service."	11

Sign your return

I have read this return. Under penalties of perjury, I declare that to the best of my knowledge and belief, the return is correct and complete.

Your signature: X Joyce T. Owens
Date: April 12, 1984

For Privacy Act and Paperwork Reduction Act Notice, see page 34.

*Circled numbers explained on next page.

Comments on lines of Form 1040EZ.

4

Use the worksheet below to figure your charitable contributions deduction:	
A. Cash contributions	A. $80.00
B. Contributions other than cash	B.+ —0.—
C. Add lines A and B. Do not write more than $100 ($50 if married filing separately).	C.= 80.00
D. Multiply the amount on line C by 25% (.25).	D. x .25
*E. Write your answer here and on line 13 of Form 1040A (or on line 4 of Form 1040EZ).	E.= $20.00

*Maximum allowable is $25.00

8 Amount withheld this year from earnings.
9 First find the $23,000–$23,050 income line in Table 10.2 on p. 392. (This is part of Table 21, p. T–38.) Next, find the column headed "Single" and read down the column. The amount where the income line row and Single column meet is $4,690. This is the tax.

DO EXERCISE 1 (P. 393).

TABLE 10.2

If 1040A, line 16, OR 1040EZ, line 7 is—		And you are—			
At least	But less than	Single	Married filing jointly	Married filing separately	Head of a house-hold
			Your tax is—		
16,250	16,300	2,674	2,074	3,224	2,515
16,300	16,350	2,688	2,085	3,241	2,527
16,350	16,400	2,701	2,096	3,257	2,538
16,400	16,450	2,715	2,107	3,274	2,550
16,450	16,500	2,728	2,118	3,290	2,561
16,500	16,550	2,742	2,129	3,307	2,573
16,550	16,600	2,755	2,140	3,323	2,584
16,600	16,650	2,769	2,151	3,340	2,596
16,650	16,700	2,782	2,162	3,356	2,607
16,700	16,750	2,796	2,173	3,373	2,619
16,750	16,800	2,809	2,184	3,389	2,630
16,800	16,850	2,823	2,195	3,406	2,642
16,850	16,900	2,836	2,206	3,422	2,653
16,900	16,950	2,850	2,217	3,439	2,665
16,950	17,000	2,863	2,228	3,455	2,676
17,000						
17,000	17,050	2,877	2,239	3,472	2,688
17,050	17,100	2,890	2,250	3,488	2,699
17,100	17,150	2,904	2,261	3,505	2,711
17,150	17,200	2,917	2,272	3,521	2,722
17,200	17,250	2,931	2,283	3,538	2,734
17,250	17,300	2,944	2,294	3,554	2,745
17,300	17,350	2,958	2,305	3,571	2,757
17,350	17,400	2,971	2,316	3,587	2,768
17,400	17,450	2,985	2,327	3,604	2,780
17,450	17,500	2,998	2,338	3,620	2,791
17,500	17,550	3,012	2,349	3,637	2,803
17,550	17,600	3,025	2,360	3,653	2,814
17,600	17,650	3,039	2,371	3,671	2,826
17,650	17,700	3,052	2,382	3,691	2,837
17,700	17,750	3,066	2,393	3,710	2,849
17,750	17,800	3,079	2,404	3,730	2,860
17,800	17,850	3,093	2,415	3,749	2,872
17,850	17,900	3,106	2,426	3,769	2,883
17,900	17,950	3,120	2,437	3,788	2,895
17,950	18,000	3,133	2,448	3,808	2,906
18,000						
18,000	18,050	3,147	2,459	3,827	2,918
18,050	18,100	3,160	2,470	3,847	2,929
18,100	18,150	3,174	2,481	3,866	2,941
18,150	18,200	3,187	2,492	3,886	2,952
18,200	18,250	3,202	2,503	3,905	2,965
18,250	18,300	3,217	2,514	3,925	2,979
18,300	18,350	3,233	2,525	3,944	2,993
18,350	18,400	3,248	2,536	3,964	3,007
18,400	18,450	3,264	2,547	3,983	3,021
18,450	18,500	3,279	2,558	4,003	3,035
18,500	18,550	3,295	2,569	4,022	3,049
18,550	18,600	3,310	2,580	4,042	3,063
18,600	18,650	3,326	2,591	4,061	3,077
18,650	18,700	3,341	2,602	4,081	3,091
18,700	18,750	3,357	2,613	4,100	3,105
18,750	18,800	3,372	2,624	4,120	3,119
18,800	18,850	3,388	2,635	4,139	3,133
18,850	18,900	3,403	2,646	4,159	3,147
18,900	18,950	3,419	2,657	4,178	3,161
18,950	19,000	3,434	2,668	4,198	3,175

If 1040A, line 16, OR 1040EZ, line 7 is—		And you are—			
At least	But less than	Single	Married filing jointly	Married filing separately	Head of a house-hold
			Your tax is—		
19,000						
19,000	19,050	3,450	2,679	4,217	3,189
19,050	19,100	3,465	2,690	4,237	3,203
19,100	19,150	3,481	2,701	4,256	3,217
19,150	19,200	3,496	2,712	4,276	3,231
19,200	19,250	3,512	2,723	4,295	3,245
19,250	19,300	3,527	2,734	4,315	3,259
19,300	19,350	3,543	2,745	4,334	3,273
19,350	19,400	3,558	2,756	4,354	3,287
19,400	19,450	3,574	2,767	4,373	3,301
19,450	19,500	3,589	2,778	4,393	3,315
19,500	19,550	3,605	2,789	4,412	3,329
19,550	19,600	3,620	2,800	4,432	3,343
19,600	19,650	3,636	2,811	4,451	3,357
19,650	19,700	3,651	2,822	4,471	3,371
19,700	19,750	3,667	2,833	4,490	3,385
19,750	19,800	3,682	2,844	4,510	3,399
19,800	19,850	3,698	2,855	4,529	3,413
19,850	19,900	3,713	2,866	4,549	3,427
19,900	19,950	3,729	2,877	4,568	3,441
19,950	20,000	3,744	2,888	4,588	3,455
20,000						
20,000	20,050	3,760	2,899	4,607	3,469
20,050	20,100	3,775	2,910	4,627	3,483
20,100	20,150	3,791	2,921	4,646	3,497
20,150	20,200	3,806	2,932	4,666	3,511
20,200	20,250	3,822	2,943	4,685	3,525
20,250	20,300	3,837	2,956	4,705	3,539
20,300	20,350	3,853	2,968	4,724	3,553
20,350	20,400	3,868	2,981	4,744	3,567
20,400	20,450	3,884	2,993	4,763	3,581
20,450	20,500	3,899	3,006	4,783	3,595
20,500	20,550	3,915	3,018	4,802	3,609
20,550	20,600	3,930	3,031	4,822	3,623
20,600	20,650	3,946	3,043	4,841	3,637
20,650	20,700	3,961	3,056	4,861	3,651
20,700	20,750	3,977	3,068	4,880	3,665
20,750	20,800	3,992	3,081	4,900	3,679
20,800	20,850	4,008	3,093	4,919	3,693
20,850	20,900	4,023	3,106	4,939	3,707
20,900	20,950	4,039	3,118	4,958	3,721
20,950	21,000	4,054	3,131	4,978	3,735
21,000						
21,000	21,050	4,070	3,143	4,997	3,749
21,050	21,100	4,085	3,156	5,017	3,763
21,100	21,150	4,101	3,168	5,036	3,777
21,150	21,200	4,116	3,181	5,056	3,791
21,200	21,250	4,132	3,193	5,075	3,805
21,250	21,300	4,147	3,206	5,095	3,819
21,300	21,350	4,163	3,218	5,114	3,833
21,350	21,400	4,178	3,231	5,134	3,847
21,400	21,450	4,194	3,243	5,153	3,861
21,450	21,500	4,209	3,256	5,173	3,875
21,500	21,550	4,225	3,268	5,192	3,889
21,550	21,600	4,240	3,281	5,212	3,903
21,600	21,650	4,256	3,293	5,231	3,917
21,650	21,700	4,271	3,306	5,251	3,931
21,700	21,750	4,287	3,318	5,270	3,945

If 1040A, line 16, OR 1040EZ, line 7 is—		And you are—			
At least	But less than	Single	Married filing jointly	Married filing separately	Head of a house-hold
			Your tax is—		
21,750	21,800	4,302	3,331	5,290	3,959
21,800	21,850	4,318	3,343	5,309	3,973
21,850	21,900	4,333	3,356	5,329	3,987
21,900	21,950	4,349	3,368	5,348	4,001
21,950	22,000	4,364	3,381	5,368	4,015
22,000						
22,000	22,050	4,380	3,393	5,387	4,029
22,050	22,100	4,395	3,406	5,407	4,043
22,100	22,150	4,411	3,418	5,426	4,057
22,150	22,200	4,426	3,431	5,446	4,071
22,200	22,250	4,442	3,443	5,465	4,085
22,250	22,300	4,457	3,456	5,485	4,099
22,300	22,350	4,473	3,468	5,504	4,113
22,350	22,400	4,488	3,481	5,524	4,127
22,400	22,450	4,504	3,493	5,543	4,141
22,450	22,500	4,519	3,506	5,563	4,155
22,500	22,550	4,535	3,518	5,582	4,169
22,550	22,600	4,550	3,531	5,602	4,183
22,600	22,650	4,566	3,543	5,621	4,197
22,650	22,700	4,581	3,556	5,641	4,211
22,700	22,750	4,597	3,568	5,660	4,225
22,750	22,800	4,612	3,581	5,680	4,239
22,800	22,850	4,628	3,593	5,699	4,253
22,850	22,900	4,643	3,606	5,719	4,267
22,900	22,950	4,659	3,618	5,740	4,281
22,950	23,000	4,674	3,631	5,762	4,295
23,000						
23,000	23,050	4,690	3,643	5,784	4,309
23,050	23,100	4,705	3,656	5,806	4,323
23,100	23,150	4,721	3,668	5,828	4,337
23,150	23,200	4,736	3,681	5,850	4,351
23,200	23,250	4,752	3,693	5,872	4,365
23,250	23,300	4,767	3,706	5,894	4,379
23,300	23,350	4,783	3,718	5,916	4,393
23,350	23,400	4,798	3,731	5,938	4,407
23,400	23,450	4,814	3,743	5,960	4,421
23,450	23,500	4,829	3,756	5,982	4,435
23,500	23,550	4,846	3,768	6,004	4,450
23,550	23,600	4,863	3,781	6,026	4,466
23,600	23,650	4,881	3,793	6,048	4,482
23,650	23,700	4,898	3,806	6,070	4,498
23,700	23,750	4,916	3,818	6,092	4,514
23,750	23,800	4,933	3,831	6,114	4,530
23,800	23,850	4,951	3,843	6,136	4,546
23,850	23,900	4,968	3,856	6,158	4,562
23,900	23,950	4,986	3,868	6,180	4,578
23,950	24,000	5,003	3,881	6,202	4,594
24,000						
24,000	24,050	5,021	3,893	6,224	4,610
24,050	24,100	5,038	3,906	6,246	4,626
24,100	24,150	5,056	3,918	6,268	4,642
24,150	24,200	5,073	3,931	6,290	4,658
24,200	24,250	5,091	3,943	6,312	4,674
24,250	24,300	5,108	3,956	6,334	4,690
24,300	24,350	5,126	3,968	6,356	4,706
24,350	24,400	5,143	3,981	6,378	4,722
24,400	24,450	5,161	3,993	6,400	4,738
24,450	24,500	5,178	4,006	6,422	4,754

1. Provide the necessary information in the white spaces. Cash contributions were $60.00.

Department of the Treasury—Internal Revenue Service
Form 1040EZ Income Tax Return for Single filers with no dependents (0)

OMB No. 1545-0675

Instructions are on the back of this form.
Tax Table is in the 1040EZ and 1040A Tax Package.

Name and address

Use the IRS mailing label. If you don't have a label, print or type:

Name (first, initial, last): Jerry K. Reid
Social security number: 356 13 2684
Present home address: 17 Northwestern Ave.
City, town or post office, State, and ZIP code: Burlingame, CA 94010

Presidential Election Campaign Fund
Check this box ☑ if you want $1 of your tax to go to this fund.

Figure your tax

1 Wages, salaries, and tips. Attach your W-2 form(s). ... 1 | 20,225.00
2 Interest income of $400 or less. If more than $400, you cannot use Form 1040EZ. 2 | 250.00

Attach Copy B of Forms W-2 here

3 Add line 1 and line 2. This is your **adjusted gross income**. 3 |
4 Allowable part of your charitable contributions. Complete the worksheet on page 18. Do not write more than $25. 4 |
5 Subtract line 4 from line 3. 5 |
6 Amount of your personal exemption. 6 | 1,000.00
7 Subtract line 6 from line 5. This is your **taxable income**. 7 |
8 Enter your Federal income tax withheld. This is shown on your W-2 form(s). 8 | 4,010.00
9 Use the tax table on pages 26-31 to find the **tax** on your taxable income on line 7. 9 |

Refund or amount you owe

10 If line 8 is larger than line 9, subtract line 9 from line 8. Enter the amount of your **refund**. 10 |

Attach tax payment here

11 If line 9 is larger than line 8, subtract line 8 from line 9. Enter the **amount you owe**. Attach check or money order for the full amount payable to "Internal Revenue Service." 11 |

Sign your return

I have read this return. Under penalties of perjury, I declare that to the best of my knowledge and belief, the return is correct and complete.

Your signature: X Jerry K. Reid
Date: April 5, 1984

For Privacy Act and Paperwork Reduction Act Notice, see page 34.

◉◉ FORM 1040A

Individuals who meet these conditions may file Form 1040A.

> **You can use Form 1040A for:**
> Any of four filing statuses
> All exemptions you are entitled to
> All qualified dependents
> Income from:
>   Wages, salaries, tips
>   Interest and dividends
>   Unemployment compensation
>   Less than $50,000 in taxable income
> Partial charitable contributions deduction
> Deduction for a married couple when both work
> Partial credit for political contributions
> Earned income credit

Those who file Form 1040A may have any one of four filing statuses. These are:

> **Filing status:**
> Single, married filing joint, married filing separate, or head of household

A completed Form 1040A appears in Example 2.

Comments on lines of Form 1040A.

11

Use the following worksheet to figure your deduction:	(a) You	(b) Your Spouse
A. Wages, salaries, tips (from line 6 of Form 1040A).	A. $ 22580.—	$ 1780.—
B. Write amount from column (a) or (b) above, whichever is smaller.		B. $ 1780.—
C. Multiply the amount on line B by 5% (.05).	C.	x .05
D. Write your answer here and on line 11 of Form 1040A.	D. $	89.—

13 Use same form as 4 on p. 391.
19a Use Table 10.2 (p. 392).

DO EXERCISE 2 (P. 396).

Example 2 Complete.

Department of the Treasury—Internal Revenue Service
Form 1040A US Individual Income Tax Return (0) OMB No. 1545-0085

Step 1 Name and address
Use the IRS mailing label. Otherwise, print or type.

Your first name and initial (if joint return, also give spouse's name and initial): **Janice M and Jim W** Last name: **Hunter**
Your social security no.: **167-50-2849**
Present home address: **416 Edge Road**
Spouse's social security no.: **261-35-2431**
City, town or post office, State, and ZIP code: **Lewisburg PA 17837**
Your occupation: **Merchandiser**
Spouse's occupation: **Toolmaker**

Presidential Election Campaign Fund
Do you want $1 to go to this fund? ☒ Yes ☐ No
If joint return, does your spouse want $1 to go to this fund? ☒ Yes ☐ No

Step 2 Filing status (Check only one) and Exemptions

1. ☐ Single (See if you can use Form 1040EZ.)
2. ☒ Married filing joint return (even if only one had income)
3. ☐ Married filing separate return. Enter spouse's social security no. above and full name here. _____
4. ☐ Head of household (with qualifying person). If the qualifying person is your unmarried child but not your dependent, write this child's name here. _____

Always check the exemption box labeled Yourself. Check other boxes if they apply.
5a ☒ Yourself ☐ 65 or over ☐ Blind
  b ☒ Spouse   ☐ 65 or over ☐ Blind
Write number of boxes checked on 5a and b: **2**

c First names of your dependent children who lived with you **Ted**
Write number of children listed on 5c: **1**

Attach Copy B of Forms W-2 here

d Other dependents: (1) Name (2) Relationship (3) Number of months lived in your home. (4) Did dependent have income of $1,000 or more? (5) Did you provide more than one-half of dependent's support?
Write number of other dependents listed on 5d: ☐

e Total number of exemptions claimed .... Add numbers entered in boxes above: **3**

Step 3 Adjusted gross income

6. Wages, salaries, tips, etc. (Attach Forms W-2) .... 6 **24360 —**
7. Interest income (Complete page 2 if over $400 or you have any All-Savers interest) ... 7 **170 —**
8a. Dividends ____ (Complete page 2 if over $400) 8b Exclusion ____ Subtract line 8b from 8a: 8c
9a. Unemployment compensation (insurance). Total from Form(s) 1099-UC
  b. Taxable amount, if any, from worksheet on page 16 of Instructions ... 9b
10. Add lines 6, 7, 8c, and 9b. This is your total income. .... 10 **24530 —**
(11). Deduction for a married couple when both work. Complete the worksheet on page 17. ... 11 **89 —**
12. Subtract line 11 from line 10. This is your adjusted gross income. ... 12 **24441 —**

Step 4 Taxable income

(13). Allowable part of your charitable contributions. Complete the worksheet on page 18 ... 13 **25 —**
14. Subtract line 13 from line 12 .... 14 **24416 —**
15. Multiply $1,000 by the total number of exemptions claimed in box 5e ... 15 **3000 —**
16. Subtract line 15 from line 14. This is your taxable income. ... 16 **21416 —**

Step 5 Tax, credits, and payments
Attach check or money order here

17a. Partial credit for political contributions. See page 19 .... 17a
  b. Total Federal income tax withheld, from W-2 form(s). (If line 6 is more than $32,400, see page 19.) ... 17b **3380 —**
  Stop Here and Sign Below if You Want IRS to Figure Your Tax
  c. Earned income credit, from worksheet on page 21 .... 17c
18. Add lines 17a, b, and c. These are your total credits and payments ... 18 **3380 —**
(19a). Find tax on amount on line 16. Use tax table, pages 26-31 ... 19a **3243 —**
  b. Advance EIC payment (from W-2 form(s)) 19b
20. Add lines 19a and 19b. This is your total tax. .... 20 **3243 —**

Step 6 Refund or amount you owe

21. If line 18 is larger than line 20, subtract line 20 from line 18. Enter the amount to be **refunded to you** .... 21 **137 —**
22. If line 20 is larger than line 18, subtract line 18 from line 20. Enter the **amount you owe**. Attach payment for full amount payable to "Internal Revenue Service." ... 22

Step 7 Sign your return

I have read this return and any attachments filed with it. Under penalties of perjury, I declare that to the best of my knowledge and belief, the return and attachments are correct and complete.

Your signature: *Janice Hunter* Date: *April 1, 1984* Spouse's signature (If filing jointly, BOTH must sign): *Jim W Hunter*

Paid preparer's signature _____ Date _____ Check if self-employed ☐ Preparer's social security no. _____
Firm's name (or yours, if self-employed) _____ E.I. no. _____
Address and Zip code _____

For **Privacy Act and Paperwork Reduction Act Notice,** see page 34.

*Circled numbers explained on preceding page.

2. Provide the necessary information in the white spaces. Your wages were $35,520 and your spouse's $1500. Use your name and a fictitious spouse (if not married). Use Table 21 (p. T–38).

Department of the Treasury—Internal Revenue Service
Form 1040A US Individual Income Tax Return (0)
OMB No. 1545-0085

Step 1 — Name and address
Use the IRS mailing label. Otherwise, print or type.

Your first name and initial (if joint return, also give spouse's name and initial) | Last name | Your social security no.
Present home address | | Spouse's social security no.
City, town or post office, State, and ZIP code | Your occupation
 | Spouse's occupation

Presidential Election Campaign Fund
Do you want $1 to go to this fund? ☐ Yes ☐ No
If joint return, does your spouse want $1 to go to this fund? ☐ Yes ☐ No

Step 2 — Filing status (Check only one) **and Exemptions**

1. ☐ Single (See if you can use Form 1040EZ.)
2. ☒ Married filing joint return (even if only one had income)
3. ☐ Married filing separate return. Enter spouse's social security no. above and full name here. _____
4. ☐ Head of household (with qualifying person). If the qualifying person is your unmarried child but not your dependent, write this child's name here. _____

Always check the exemption box labeled Yourself. Check other boxes if they apply.

5a ☒ Yourself   ☐ 65 or over   ☐ Blind
 b ☒ Spouse   ☐ 65 or over   ☐ Blind

Write number of boxes checked on 5a and b: **2**

 c First names of your dependent children who lived with you _____
Write number of children listed on 5c: ☐

 d Other dependents: (1) Name (2) Relationship (3) Number of months lived in your home (4) Did dependent have income of $1,000 or more? (5) Did you provide more than one-half of dependent's support?
Write number of other dependents listed on 5d: ☐

Attach Copy B of Forms W-2 here

 e Total number of exemptions claimed . . . . Add numbers entered in boxes above: **2**

Step 3 — Adjusted gross income

6. Wages, salaries, tips, etc. (Attach Forms W-2) . . . . 6 | **37020 —**
7. Interest income (Complete page 2 if over $400 or you have any All-Savers interest) . . . 7 | **110 —**
8a. Dividends _____ (Complete page 2 if over $400)   8b Exclusion _____   Subtract line 8b from 8a   8c
9a. Unemployment compensation (insurance). Total from Form(s) 1099-UC _____
 b. Taxable amount, if any, from worksheet on page 16 of Instructions . . . 9b
10. Add lines 6, 7, 8c, and 9b. This is your total income 10
11. Deduction for a married couple when both work. Complete the worksheet on page 17 . . . 11
12. Subtract line 11 from line 10. This is your adjusted gross income . . . 12

Step 4 — Taxable income

13. Allowable part of your charitable contributions. Complete the worksheet on page 18 . . . 13 | **15 —**
14. Subtract line 13 from line 12 . . . 14
15. Multiply $1,000 by the total number of exemptions claimed in box 5e . . . 15
16. Subtract line 15 from line 14. This is your taxable income . . . 16

Step 5 — Tax, credits, and payments

Attach check or money order here

17a. Partial credit for political contributions. See page 19 . . . ■ 17a
 b. Total Federal income tax withheld, from W-2 form(s). (If line 6 is more than $32,400, see page 19.) . . . 17b | **8300 —**

Stop Here and Sign Below if You Want IRS to Figure Your Tax

 c. Earned income credit, from worksheet on page 21 . . . 17c
18. Add lines 17a, b, and c. These are your total credits and payments . . . 18
19a. Find tax on amount on line 16. Use tax table, pages 26-31 . . . 19a
 b. Advance EIC payment (from W-2 form(s)) . . . 19b
20. Add lines 19a and 19b. This is your total tax . . . 20

Step 6 — Refund or amount you owe

21. If line 18 is larger than line 20, subtract line 20 from line 18. Enter the amount to be **refunded to you** . . . 21
22. If line 20 is larger than line 18, subtract line 18 from line 20. Enter the **amount you owe**. Attach payment for full amount payable to "Internal Revenue Service." . . . 22

Step 7 — Sign your return

I have read this return and any attachments filed with it. Under penalties of perjury, I declare that to the best of my knowledge and belief, the return and attachments are correct and complete.

Your signature _____ Date _____ Spouse's signature (If filing jointly, BOTH must sign) _____

Paid preparer's signature _____ Date _____ Check if self-employed ☐   Preparer's social security no. _____

Firm's name (or yours, if self-employed) _____   E.I. no. _____
Address and Zip code _____

For **Privacy Act and Paperwork Reduction Act Notice,** see page 34.

NAME _____   CLASS _____

EXERCISE SET 10.3

▪ Provide the necessary information in the white spaces. Use Table 21 (p. T–38) and your own name and address.

1. **Department of the Treasury — Internal Revenue Service**
   Form 1040EZ Income Tax Return for Single filers with no dependents (0)
   OMB No. 1545-0675

   Instructions are on the back of this form.
   Tax Table is in the 1040EZ and 1040A Tax Package.

   Name and address
   Use the IRS mailing label. If you don't have a label, print or type:

Name (first, initial, last)	Social security number
Present home address	
City, town or post office, State, and ZIP code	

   Presidential Election Campaign Fund
   Check this box ☐ if you want $1 of your tax to go to this fund.

   Figure your tax

1	Wages, salaries, and tips. Attach your W-2 form(s).	1	14780.—
2	Interest income of $400 or less. If more than $400, you cannot use Form 1040EZ.	2	70.—
3	Add line 1 and line 2. This is your **adjusted gross income**.	3	.
4	Allowable part of your charitable contributions. Complete the worksheet on page 18. Do not write more than $25.	4	15.—
5	Subtract line 4 from line 3.	5	.
6	Amount of your personal exemption.	6	1,000.00
7	Subtract line 6 from line 5. This is your **taxable income**.	7	.
8	Enter your Federal income tax withheld. This is shown on your W-2 form(s).	8	2340.—
9	Use the tax table on pages 26-31 to find the **tax** on your taxable income on line 7.	9	.

   Attach Copy B of Forms W-2 here

   Refund or amount you owe

10	If line 8 is larger than line 9, subtract line 9 from line 8. Enter the amount of your **refund**.	10	.
11	If line 9 is larger than line 8, subtract line 8 from line 9. Enter the **amount you owe**. Attach check or money order for the full amount payable to "Internal Revenue Service."	11	.

   Attach tax payment here

   Sign your return
   I have read this return. Under penalties of perjury, I declare that to the best of my knowledge and belief, the return is correct and complete.
   Your signature _____ Date _____
   X
   For **Privacy Act and Paperwork Reduction Act Notice**, see page 34.

Copyright © 1984, by Addison-Wesley Publishing Company Inc. All rights reserved.

2.

Department of the Treasury — Internal Revenue Service

Form 1040EZ Income Tax Return for Single filers with no dependents (0)

OMB No. 1545-0675

Instructions are on the back of this form.
Tax Table is in the 1040EZ and 1040A Tax Package.

Name and address

Use the IRS mailing label. If you don't have a label, print or type:

Name (first, initial, last)	Social security number
Present home address	
City, town or post office, State, and ZIP code	

Presidential Election Campaign Fund
Check this box ☐ if you want $1 of your tax to go to this fund.

Figure your tax

Attach Copy B of Forms W-2 here

1	Wages, salaries, and tips. Attach your W-2 form(s).	1 27810.—
2	Interest income of $400 or less. If more than $400, you cannot use Form 1040EZ.	2 130.—
3	Add line 1 and line 2. This is your **adjusted gross income.**	3
4	Allowable part of your charitable contributions. Complete the worksheet on page 18. Do not write more than $25.	4 15.—
5	Subtract line 4 from line 3.	5
6	Amount of your personal exemption.	6 1,000.00
7	Subtract line 6 from line 5. This is your **taxable income.**	7
8	Enter your Federal income tax withheld. This is shown on your W-2 form(s).	8 6270.—
9	Use the tax table on pages 26-31 to find the **tax** on your taxable income on line 7.	9

Refund or amount you owe

Attach tax payment here

10	If line 8 is larger than line 9, subtract line 9 from line 8. Enter the amount of your **refund.**	10
11	If line 9 is larger than line 8, subtract line 8 from line 9. Enter the **amount you owe.** Attach check or money order for the full amount payable to "Internal Revenue Service."	11

Sign your return

I have read this return. Under penalties of perjury, I declare that to the best of my knowledge and belief, the return is correct and complete.

Your signature   Date
X

For **Privacy Act and Paperwork Reduction Act Notice,** see page 34.

:: Provide the necessary information in the white spaces. Use Table 21 (p. T–38), your name (and a fictitious spouse when needed).

3.

Department of the Treasury — Internal Revenue Service

Form 1040A US Individual Income Tax Return (0)

OMB No. 1545-0085

Step 1
Name and address
Use the IRS mailing label. Otherwise, print or type.

Your first name and initial (if joint return, also give spouse's name and initial) | Last name | Your social security no.

Present home address | Spouse's social security no.

City, town or post office, State, and ZIP code | Your occupation
| Spouse's occupation

Presidential Election Campaign Fund
Do you want $1 to go to this fund?................☐ Yes ☐ No
If joint return, does your spouse want $1 to go to this fund? ☐ Yes ☐ No

Step 2
Filing status
(Check only one)
and Exemptions

1. ☐ Single (See if you can use Form 1040EZ.)
2. ☑ Married filing joint return (even if only one had income)
3. ☐ Married filing separate return. Enter spouse's social security no. above and full name here. _____
4. ☐ Head of household (with qualifying person). If the qualifying person is your unmarried child but not your dependent, write this child's name here. _____

Always check the exemption box labeled Yourself. Check other boxes if they apply.

5a ☑ Yourself   ☐ 65 or over   ☐ Blind   Write number of boxes checked on 5a and b **2**
 b ☑ Spouse   ☐ 65 or over   ☐ Blind

 c First names of your dependent children who lived with you _____
   JEFF, Jill   Write number of children listed on 5c **2**

Attach Copy B of Forms W-2 here

 d Other dependents:
   (1) Name | (2) Relationship | (3) Number of months lived in your home. | (4) Did dependent have income of $1,000 or more? | (5) Did you provide more than one-half of dependent's support?

   Write number of other dependents listed on 5d ☐

 e Total number of exemptions claimed................. Add numbers entered in boxes above **4**

Step 3
Adjusted gross income

6 Wages, salaries, tips, etc. (Attach Forms W-2)........... 6 **48260.—**
7 Interest income (Complete page 2 if over $400 or you have any All-Savers interest)....... 7 **140.—**
8a Dividends _____ (Complete page 2 if over $400) 8b Exclusion _____ Subtract line 8b from 8a 8c _____
9a Unemployment compensation (insurance). Total from Form(s) 1099-UC _____
 b Taxable amount, if any, from worksheet on page 16 of Instructions............. 9b _____
10 Add lines 6, 7, 8c, and 9b. This is your total income.......... 10 _____
11 Deduction for a married couple when both work. Complete the worksheet on page 17.... 11 **170.—**
12 Subtract line 11 from line 10. This is your adjusted gross income........ 12 _____

Step 4
Taxable income

13 Allowable part of your charitable contributions. Complete the worksheet on page 18..... 13 **20.—**
14 Subtract line 13 from line 12.......... 14 _____
15 Multiply $1,000 by the total number of exemptions claimed in box 5e....... 15 _____
16 Subtract line 15 from line 14. This is your taxable income............ 16 _____

Step 5
Tax, credits, and payments

Attach check or money order here

17a Partial credit for political contributions. See page 19...... ■ 17a _____
 b Total Federal income tax withheld, from W-2 form(s). (If line 6 is more than $32,400, see page 19.)............. 17b **8271.—**
   Stop Here and Sign Below if You Want IRS to Figure Your Tax
 c Earned income credit, from worksheet on page 21.......... 17c _____
18 Add lines 17a, b, and c. These are your total credits and payments......... 18 _____
19a Find tax on amount on line 16. Use tax table, pages 26-31....... 19a _____
 b Advance EIC payment (from W-2 form(s)) .... 19b _____
20 Add lines 19a and 19b. This is your total tax............ 20 _____

Step 6
Refund or amount you owe

21 If line 18 is larger than line 20, subtract line 20 from line 18. Enter the amount to be **refunded to you**............. 21 _____
22 If line 20 is larger than line 18, subtract line 18 from line 20. Enter the **amount you owe**. Attach payment for full amount payable to "Internal Revenue Service."....... 22 _____

Step 7
Sign your return

I have read this return and any attachments filed with it. Under penalties of perjury, I declare that to the best of my knowledge and belief, the return and attachments are correct and complete.

▶ _____   ▶ _____
Your signature   Date   Spouse's signature (If filing jointly, BOTH must sign)

Paid preparer's signature _____ Date _____ Check if self-employed ☐   Preparer's social security no. _____

Firm's name (or yours, if self-employed) _____   E.I. no. _____
Address and Zip code _____

For **Privacy Act and Paperwork Reduction Act Notice,** see page 34.

Copyright © 1984, by Addison-Wesley Publishing Company Inc. All rights reserved.

400

4.

Department of the Treasury—Internal Revenue Service
Form 1040A US Individual Income Tax Return (0)
OMB No. 1545-0085

Step 1
Name and address
Use the IRS mailing label. Otherwise, print or type.

Your first name and initial (if joint return, also give spouse's name and initial) | Last name | Your social security no.

Present home address | Spouse's social security no.

City, town or post office, State, and ZIP code | Your occupation
 | Spouse's occupation

Presidential Election Campaign Fund
Do you want $1 to go to this fund? .... ☐ Yes ☐ No
If joint return, does your spouse want $1 to go to this fund? ☐ Yes ☐ No

Step 2
Filing status
(Check only one)
and Exemptions

1. ☑ Single (See if you can use Form 1040EZ.)
2. ☐ Married filing joint return (even if only one had income)
3. ☐ Married filing separate return. Enter spouse's social security no. above and full name here. ____
4. ☐ Head of household (with qualifying person). If the qualifying person is your unmarried child but not your dependent, write this child's name here. ____

Always check the exemption box labeled Yourself. Check other boxes if they apply.

5a ☑ Yourself ☐ 65 or over ☐ Blind | Write number of boxes checked on 5a and b | **1**
b ☐ Spouse ☐ 65 or over ☐ Blind | Write number of children listed on 5c | ☐
c First names of your dependent children who lived with you ____

Attach Copy B of Forms W-2 here

d Other dependents:
(1) Name | (2) Relationship | (3) Number of months lived in your home. | (4) Did dependent have income of $1,000 or more? | (5) Did you provide more than one-half of dependent's support?
ETHEL | MOTHER | 12 | NO | YES

Write number of other dependents listed on 5d | **1**

e Total number of exemptions claimed .... | Add numbers entered in boxes above | **2**

Step 3
Adjusted gross income

6. Wages, salaries, tips, etc. (Attach Forms W-2) .... 6 | **25100 —**
7. Interest income (Complete page 2 if over $400 or you have any All-Savers interest) ...... 7 | **225 —**
8a. Dividends ____ (Complete page 2 if over $400) 8b Exclusion ____ Subtract line 8b from 8a 8c
9a. Unemployment compensation (insurance). Total from Form(s) 1099-UC ____
   b. Taxable amount, if any, from worksheet on page 16 of Instructions 9b
10. Add lines 6, 7, 8c, and 9b. This is your total income. 10
11. Deduction for a married couple when both work. Complete the worksheet on page 17 11
12. Subtract line 11 from line 10. This is your adjusted gross income. 12

Step 4
Taxable income

13. Allowable part of your charitable contributions. Complete the worksheet on page 18 .... 13 | **10 —**
14. Subtract line 13 from line 12. 14
15. Multiply $1,000 by the total number of exemptions claimed in box 5e 15
16. Subtract line 15 from line 14. This is your taxable income. 16

Step 5
Tax, credits, and payments

17a. Partial credit for political contributions. See page 19 ...... ■ 17a
  b. Total Federal income tax withheld, from W-2 form(s). (If line 6 is more than $32,400, see page 19.) .... 17b **4705 —**

Stop Here and Sign Below if You Want IRS to Figure Your Tax

Attach check or money order here

  c. Earned income credit, from worksheet on page 21 ...... 17c
18. Add lines 17a, b, and c. These are your total credits and payments 18
19a. Find tax on amount on line 16. Use tax table, pages 26-31 ...... 19a
  b. Advance EIC payment (from W-2 form(s)) 19b
20. Add lines 19a and 19b. This is your total tax. 20

Step 6
Refund or amount you owe

21. If line 18 is larger than line 20, subtract line 20 from line 18. Enter the amount to be **refunded to you** 21
22. If line 20 is larger than line 18, subtract line 18 from line 20. Enter the **amount you owe.** Attach payment for full amount payable to "Internal Revenue Service." 22

Step 7
Sign your return

I have read this return and any attachments filed with it. Under penalties of perjury, I declare that to the best of my knowledge and belief, the return and attachments are correct and complete.

▶ Your signature | Date | ▶ Spouse's signature (If filing jointly, BOTH must sign)

Paid preparer's signature | Date | Check if self-employed ☐ | Preparer's social security no.

Firm's name (or yours, if self-employed) | E.I. no.
Address and Zip code

For **Privacy Act and Paperwork Reduction Act Notice,** see page 34.

TEST OR REVIEW—CHAPTER 10

If you miss an item, review the indicated section and objective.

[10.1, •] **1.** Find the sales tax on the $29.88 clock radio in a 5% sales tax state. Use the major fraction rule.

[10.1, ••] **2.** A business had receipts of $9862, which include a 4% sales tax. How much were sales?

[10.2, •] **3.** The current market value of a home is $54,000 and the assessment rate is 31%. Find the assessed value.

[10.2, ••] **4.** A school district needs $982,460 in property tax revenue and has property assessed at $92,872,450 within its boundaries. What is the tax rate in mills?

[10.2, •••] **5.** Find the tax for schools on a home assessed at $47,000 where the tax rate is 14.324 mills.

[10.3, ●]   **6.** Provide the necessary information in the white spaces. Use your own name and Table 21 (p. T–38).

Department of the Treasury — Internal Revenue Service
Form 1040EZ Income Tax Return for Single filers with no dependents (0)

OMB No. 1545-0675

Instructions are on the back of this form.
Tax Table is in the 1040EZ and 1040A Tax Package.

Name and address

Use the IRS mailing label. If you don't have a label, print or type:

Name (first, initial, last)	Social security number

Present home address

City, town or post office, State, and ZIP code

Presidential Election Campaign Fund
Check this box ☐ if you want $1 of your tax to go to this fund.

Figure your tax

1. Wages, salaries, and tips. Attach your W-2 form(s). **1** 24820.—

2. Interest income of $400 or less. If more than $400, you cannot use Form 1040EZ. **2** 70.—

Attach Copy B of Forms W-2 here

3. Add line 1 and line 2. This is your **adjusted gross income**. **3**

4. Allowable part of your charitable contributions. Complete the worksheet on page 18. Do not write more than $25. **4** 25.—

5. Subtract line 4 from line 3. **5**

6. Amount of your personal exemption. **6** 1,000.00

7. Subtract line 6 from line 5. This is your **taxable income**. **7**

8. Enter your Federal income tax withheld. This is shown on your W-2 form(s). **8** 5200.—

9. Use the tax table on pages 26-31 to find the **tax** on your taxable income on line 7. **9**

Refund or amount you owe

10. If line 8 is larger than line 9, subtract line 9 from line 8. Enter the amount of your **refund**. **10**

Attach tax payment here

11. If line 9 is larger than line 8, subtract line 8 from line 9. Enter the **amount you owe**. Attach check or money order for the full amount payable to "Internal Revenue Service." **11**

Sign your return

I have read this return. Under penalties of perjury, I declare that to the best of my knowledge and belief, the return is correct and complete.

Your signature   Date

X

For **Privacy Act and Paperwork Reduction Act Notice**, see page 34.

[10.3, ● ●] **7.** Provide the necessary information in the white spaces. Use your name (and a fictitious spouse if not married) and Table 21 (p. T–38).

Department of the Treasury — Internal Revenue Service
Form 1040A US Individual Income Tax Return (0)
OMB No. 1545-0085

Step 1 — Name and address
Use the IRS mailing label. Otherwise, print or type.

Your first name and initial (if joint return, also give spouse's name and initial) | Last name | Your social security no.

Present home address | Spouse's social security no.

City, town or post office, State, and ZIP code | Your occupation | Spouse's occupation

Presidential Election Campaign Fund
Do you want $1 to go to this fund?.................. ☐ Yes ☐ No
If joint return, does your spouse want $1 to go to this fund? ☐ Yes ☐ No

Step 2 — Filing status (Check only one) and Exemptions

1. ☐ Single (See if you can use Form 1040EZ.)
2. ☑ Married filing joint return (even if only one had income)
3. ☐ Married filing separate return. Enter spouse's social security no. above and full name here. ____
4. ☐ Head of household (with qualifying person). If the qualifying person is your unmarried child but not your dependent, write this child's name here. ____

Always check the exemption box labeled Yourself. Check other boxes if they apply.

5a ☑ Yourself   ☐ 65 or over   ☐ Blind   Write number of boxes checked on 5a and b: **2**
 b ☑ Spouse   ☐ 65 or over   ☐ Blind

c First names of your dependent children who lived with you ____
  SARA   Write number of children listed on 5c: **1**

d Other dependents: (1) Name (2) Relationship (3) Number of months lived in your home. (4) Did dependent have income of $1,000 or more? (5) Did you provide more than one-half of dependent's support?
                                                                  Write number of other dependents listed on 5d: ____

Attach Copy B of Forms W-2 here

e Total number of exemptions claimed........ Add numbers entered in boxes above: **3**

Step 3 — Adjusted gross income

6. Wages, salaries, tips, etc. *(Attach Forms W-2)*................ 6 | **27460.—**
7. Interest income *(Complete page 2 if over $400 or you have any All-Savers interest)*....... 7 | **210.—**
8a. Dividends ____ *(Complete page 2 if over $400)* 8b Exclusion ____ Subtract line 8b from 8a 8c ____
9a. Unemployment compensation (insurance). Total from Form(s) 1099-UC ____
 b. Taxable amount, if any, from worksheet on page 16 of Instructions........... 9b ____
10. Add lines 6, 7, 8c, and 9b. This is your total income............ 10 ____
11. Deduction for a married couple when both work. Complete the worksheet on page 17..... 11 | **112.—**
12. Subtract line 11 from line 10. This is your adjusted gross income......... 12 ____

Step 4 — Taxable income

13. Allowable part of your charitable contributions. Complete the worksheet on page 18..... 13 | **20.—**
14. Subtract line 13 from line 12............................ 14 ____
15. Multiply $1,000 by the total number of exemptions claimed in box 5e....... 15 ____
16. Subtract line 15 from line 14. This is your taxable income........... 16 ____

Step 5 — Tax, credits, and payments

17a. Partial credit for political contributions. See page 19....... 17a ____
 b. Total Federal income tax withheld, from W-2 form(s). *(If line 6 is more than $32,400, see page 19.)*.... 17b | **3540.—**

Stop Here and Sign Below if You Want IRS to Figure Your Tax

Attach check or money order here

 c. Earned income credit, from worksheet on page 21........ 17c ____
18. Add lines 17a, b, and c. These are your total credits and payments........ 18 ____
19a. Find tax on amount on line 16. Use tax table, pages 26-31...... 19a ____
 b. Advance EIC payment *(from W-2 form(s))*............. 19b ____
20. Add lines 19a and 19b. This is your total tax............. 20 ____

Step 6 — Refund or amount you owe

21. If line 18 is larger than line 20, subtract line 20 from line 18. Enter the amount to be **refunded to you**............................ 21 ____
22. If line 20 is larger than line 18, subtract line 18 from line 20. Enter the **amount you owe**. Attach payment for full amount payable to "Internal Revenue Service."...... 22 ____

Step 7 — Sign your return

I have read this return and any attachments filed with it. Under penalties of perjury, I declare that to the best of my knowledge and belief, the return and attachments are correct and complete.

Your signature | Date | Spouse's signature (If filing jointly, BOTH must sign)

Paid preparer's signature | Date | Check if self-employed ☐ | Preparer's social security no.

Firm's name (or yours, if self-employed) ____ | E.I. no. ____
Address and Zip code ____

For **Privacy Act and Paperwork Reduction Act Notice,** see page 34.

Copyright © 1984, by Addison-Wesley Publishing Company Inc. All rights reserved.

8. Provide the necessary information in the white spaces. Use your name and Table 21 (p. T–38).

Department of the Treasury — Internal Revenue Service
Form 1040A US Individual Income Tax Return (0)   OMB No. 1545-0085

Step 1 — Name and address
Use the IRS mailing label. Otherwise, print or type.

Your first name and initial (if joint return, also give spouse's name and initial) | Last name | Your social security no.
Present home address | | Spouse's social security no.
City, town or post office, State, and ZIP code | Your occupation
 | Spouse's occupation

Presidential Election Campaign Fund
Do you want $1 to go to this fund? ☐ Yes ☐ No
If joint return, does your spouse want $1 to go to this fund? ☐ Yes ☐ No

Step 2 — Filing status (Check only one) **and Exemptions**

1 ☐ Single (See if you can use Form 1040EZ.)
2 ☐ Married filing joint return (even if only one had income)
3 ☐ Married filing separate return. Enter spouse's social security no. above and full name here. _____
4 ☒ Head of household (with qualifying person). If the qualifying person is your unmarried child but not your dependent, write this child's name here. _____

Always check the exemption box labeled Yourself. Check other boxes if they apply.

5a ☒ Yourself   ☐ 65 or over   ☐ Blind | Write number of boxes checked on 5a and b | **1**
 b ☐ Spouse   ☐ 65 or over   ☐ Blind |
 c First names of your dependent children who lived with you LORA | Write number of children listed on 5c | **1**
 d Other dependents:
   (1) Name (2) Relationship (3) Number of months lived in your home. (4) Did dependent have income of $1,000 or more? (5) Did you provide more than one-half of dependent's support? | Write number of other dependents listed on 5d |
 e Total number of exemptions claimed . . . . | Add numbers entered in boxes above | **2**

Step 3 — Adjusted gross income

6   Wages, salaries, tips, etc. (Attach Forms W-2). 6   **15280.—**
7   Interest income (Complete page 2 if over $400 or you have any All-Savers interest). 7   **40.—**
8a Dividends _____ (Complete page 2 if over $400)   8b Exclusion _____   Subtract line 8b from 8a   8c
9a Unemployment compensation (insurance). Total from Form(s) 1099-UC _____
 b Taxable amount, if any, from worksheet on page 16 of Instructions. 9b
10 Add lines 6, 7, 8c, and 9b. This is your total income. 10
11 Deduction for a married couple when both work. Complete the worksheet on page 17. 11
12 Subtract line 11 from line 10. This is your adjusted gross income. 12

Step 4 — Taxable income

13 Allowable part of your charitable contributions. Complete the worksheet on page 18. 13   **10.—**
14 Subtract line 13 from line 12. 14
15 Multiply $1,000 by the total number of exemptions claimed in box 5e. 15
16 Subtract line 15 from line 14. This is your taxable income. 16

Step 5 — Tax, credits, and payments
Attach check or money order here

17a Partial credit for political contributions. See page 19. . . . . . . ■ 17a
  b Total Federal income tax withheld, from W-2 form(s). (If line 6 is more than $32,400, see page 19.). . . . . 17b **1590.—**
    Stop Here and Sign Below if You Want IRS to Figure Your Tax
  c Earned income credit, from worksheet on page 21. . . . . . 17c
18 Add lines 17a, b, and c. These are your total credits and payments. 18
19a Find tax on amount on line 16. Use tax table, pages 26-31. . . . 19a
  b Advance EIC payment (from W-2 form(s)). 19b
20 Add lines 19a and 19b. This is your total tax. 20

Step 6 — Refund or amount you owe

21 If line 18 is larger than line 20, subtract line 20 from line 18. Enter the amount to be **refunded to you** 21
22 If line 20 is larger than line 18, subtract line 18 from line 20. Enter the **amount you owe.** Attach payment for full amount payable to "Internal Revenue Service." 22

Step 7 — Sign your return

I have read this return and any attachments filed with it. Under penalties of perjury, I declare that to the best of my knowledge and belief, the return and attachments are correct and complete.

Your signature _____ Date _____ | Spouse's signature (If filing jointly, BOTH must sign) _____
Paid preparer's signature _____ Date _____ | Check if self-employed ☐ | Preparer's social security no.
Firm's name (or yours, if self-employed) _____ | E.I. no.
Address and Zip code _____

For **Privacy Act and Paperwork Reduction Act Notice,** see page 34.

404

PART III
RETAILING/ ACCOUNTING

11
FINANCIAL STATEMENTS

Career: Business Administration *This is Ray Carucci. Ray took Business Mathematics at Florida Southern College, where he received a BS degree in Business Administration. The chapters in this book which are relevant to his work are 1–11, 13, 15, and 16, but the most important chapter, on Financial Statements, is the one you are about to study.*

Ray is currently employed as the Executive Director of the Memorial Clinic of Indianapolis. In this capacity, Ray is directly responsible for all the business affairs of 30 physicians. People who are successful in this field, as Ray is, can expect to make a salary between $40,000 and $50,000 a year.

Ray has an interesting employment background. Upon graduation from Florida Southern he served in the U.S. Army, where he held many key positions in the areas of personnel administration and management. In one such position he was directly responsible for establishing the first School of Administration in Saudi Arabia. While in college, Ray acted as Assistant General Manager for the Lakeland Pilots, a minor league baseball team in the Florida State League.

Ray's hobbies include watching all kinds of sports and playing tennis.

FINANCIAL STATEMENTS

READINESS CHECK: SKILLS FOR CHAPTER 11

Subtract.

1. $7825 − $4985
2. $3200 − $2840

Add.

3.
```
   7,000
  13,000
  28,000
+ 41,000
```

4.
```
   5,200
   9,800
  20,000
+ 43,000
```

Divide and change to a percent (nearest tenth).

5. $\dfrac{9,000}{140,000}$
6. $\dfrac{4,000}{105,000}$

11.1 PROFIT AND LOSS

Owners, managers, and investors want to know whether a business is making a profit or incurring a loss. A financial picture of a business is often obtained by looking at income statements and balance sheets. These topics will be studied in this chapter.

◼ GROSS PROFIT

A retailer can calculate *gross profit* (or loss) by subtracting the cost of goods sold from the *net sales* (revenue brought in by the sale of the goods less returns and adjustments).

> Gross profit = Net sales − Cost

Example 1 A retailer bought clothes for $2567 and sold them for $4589. There were no adjustments or returns. What was the gross profit?

Solution Find the gross profit.

Gross profit = Net sales − Cost
             = $4589 − $2567
             = $2022

The retailer's gross profit was $2022.

DO EXERCISE 1.

OBJECTIVES

After finishing Section 11.1, you should be able to:

◼ Compute gross profit.

◼◼ Determine net income.

1. A retailer bought hardware for $8765 and sold it for $12,645. There were no adjustments or returns. What was the gross profit?

ANSWER ON PAGE A–27

11.1 PROFIT AND LOSS

For a retailer, *revenue* is income from sales. Consumers sometimes return unsatisfactory items. As mentioned above, when computing gross profit these sales returns are subtracted from revenue (sales) to get *net sales*.

> Net sales = Revenue − Returns

Example 2 A retailer sold clothing costing $4525 for $6895. Returns were $345. How much was the gross profit?

Solution

a) Find the net sales.

Net sales = Revenue − Returns
= $6895 − $345
= $6550

b) Find the gross profit.

Gross profit = Net sales − Cost
= $6550 − $4525
= $2025

The gross profit was $2025.

DO EXERCISE 2.

○○ NET INCOME

Net income, sometimes called *net profit*, is the final amount remaining after all deductions. Retailers incur certain expenses such as rent, utilities, labor, and some miscellaneous expenses in doing business. The net income is found by subtracting the sum of these expenses from the gross profit.

> Net income = Gross profit − Expenses

Example 3 A retailer had a gross profit of $4589. His expenses were $135 for utilities, $250 for rent, and $165 for miscellaneous items. What was the net income?

Solution

a) Find the sum of the expenses.

Sum of expenses = $135 + $250 + $165
= $550

b) Find the net income.

Net income = Gross profit − Expenses
= $4589 − $550
= $4039

The net income was $4039.

DO EXERCISE 3.

---

2. A retailer sold furniture costing $6785 for $9875. Returns were $987. How much was the gross profit?

3. A retailer had a gross profit of $7895. Her expenses were $348 for utilities, $785 for rent, and $1395 for labor. What was the net income?

ANSWERS ON PAGE A–27

4. An automobile repair shop earned $3567 one month and had $1475 in expenses. What was the net income?

FINANCIAL STATEMENTS

For a service business, the net income is found by subtracting the expenses from the revenue (amount earned).

> **Net income = Revenue − Expenses**

Example 4 An appliance repair shop earned $1875 one month and had $325 in expenses. What was the net income?

Solution Find the net income.

$$\begin{aligned} \text{Net income} &= \text{Revenue} - \text{Expenses} \\ &= \$1875 - \$325 \\ &= \$1550 \end{aligned}$$

The net income was $1550.

DO EXERCISE 4.

The net income (loss) can be calculated in several steps. Example 5 illustrates the procedure.

Example 5 A retailer earned $7825 from sales, paid $4985 for the goods sold, and had expenses of $3200. What was the net income (loss)? There were no adjustments or returns.

Solution

a) Find the gross profit.

$$\begin{aligned} \text{Gross profit} &= \text{Net sales} - \text{Cost} \\ &= \$7825 - \$4985 \\ &= \$2840 \end{aligned}$$

b) $\begin{aligned} \text{Net income} &= \text{Gross profit} - \text{Expenses} \\ &= \$2840 - \$3200 \\ &= -\$360 \quad \text{Subtract \$2840 from \$3200 and put a minus sign in front of the answer to show a loss.} \end{aligned}$

The loss was $360.

DO EXERCISE 5.

Parentheses are also used to show a loss. In Example 5 the loss of $360 is written ($360), or ⟨$360⟩.

---

5. A retailer earned $6578 from sales, paid $4360 for the goods sold, and had expenses of $2564. There were no adjustments or returns. What was the net income (loss)?

ANSWERS ON PAGE A–27

NAME _____ CLASS _____ ANSWERS

EXERCISE SET 11.1

■ Solve.

1. A retailer bought yard goods for $3642 and sold them for $4875. There were no adjustments or returns. What was the gross profit?

2. A civic group bought fruit for $1468 and sold it for $3125. There were no adjustments or returns. What was the gross profit?

3. A retailer sold lighting fixtures costing $1568 for $2379. Returns were $142. How much was the gross profit?

4. A retailer sold cookery costing $2275 for $3865. Returns were $567. How much was the gross profit?

5. A garden supply store bought $4378 of plants and supplies and sold them for $6582. How much was the gross profit?

6. An electronics store bought $10,635 of merchandise and sold it for $14,379. How much was the gross profit?

7. An appliance store sold goods that cost $4390 for $6807. What was the gross profit?

8. A hobby shop sold products that cost $1560 for $2300. What was the gross profit?

■■ Solve.

9. A flower shop had a gross profit of $2568. Its expenses were $876 for utilities, $500 for rent, and $235 for miscellaneous items. What was the net income?

10. A sporting goods store had a gross profit of $7685. Its expenses were $1385 for labor, $876 for rent, and $567 for miscellaneous items. What was the net income?

11. A computer store had a gross profit of $12,336. Its expenses were $2865 for personnel, $537 for rent, and $321 for miscellaneous items. What was the net income?

12. An automobile repair shop had a gross profit of $7654. Its expenses were $3895 for labor, $390 for utilities, and $123 for miscellaneous. What was the net income?

13. A plumber earned $2895 one month and had $643 in expenses. What was the net income?

14. An electrician earned $2645 one month and had $458 in expenses. What was the net income?

1. _____

2. _____

3. _____

4. _____

5. _____

6. _____

7. _____

8. _____

9. _____

10. _____

11. _____

12. _____

13. _____

14. _____

Copyright © 1984, by Addison-Wesley Publishing Company Inc. All rights reserved.

15. A retailer earned $4798 from sales, paid $2375 for the goods sold, and had expenses of $568. What was the net income (loss)?

16. A retailer earned $6789 from sales, paid $3568 for the goods sold, and had expenses of $4389. What was the net income (loss)?

Find the gross profit and net income (loss).

17.	Net sales	$8925.68	**18.**	Net sales	$7896.58
	Cost of goods	$3679.87		Cost of goods	$2564.94
	Expenses	$5699.87		Expenses	$1567.98

11.2 INCOME STATEMENTS

Profit and loss figures are displayed on *income statements* (sometimes called earnings reports or profit and loss statements). The statement shows how much the business made or lost and is quite useful. For example, we may examine sales, profits and expenses for comparable periods (monthly, quarterly, annually).

ENTRIES ON THE INCOME STATEMENT

Income statements aren't all exactly alike but most are similar. An income statement for Axtel Company appears below.

OBJECTIVES

After finishing Section 11.2, you should be able to:

- Find entries on an income statement.
- Analyze an income statement.

AXTEL COMPANY
FARMINGTON, VIRGINIA

	Income Statement	1985	1984
1	Net Sales	140,000	105,000
	Cost of sales and operating expenses		
2	Cost of goods sold	102,000	80,000
3	Depreciation	5,000	2,000
4	Selling and administrative expenses	24,000	19,000
5	Operating profit	9,000	4,000
6	Other income		
	Dividends and Interest	4,000	1,500
7	Total income	13,000	5,500
8	Less bond interest	3,500	3,500
9	Income before federal tax	9,500	2,000
10	Federal tax	1,400	300
11	Net profit for year	8,100	1,700

Net Sales

The primary revenue source is always listed first on the income statement. For Axtel Company, a manufacturer, it is net sales, while for a utility company it would be operating revenues. A comparison of net sales shows Axtel had more sales in 1985 than 1984.

1	Net sales	140,000	105,000

Cost of Sales and Operating Expenses

For a manufacturer like Axtel Company this includes all costs incurred from the raw materials to the finished product. Included are raw materials, labor, overhead expenses, and depreciation.

Cost of Goods Sold

The largest item (listed first) under cost of sales and operating expenses is cost of goods sold.

FINANCIAL STATEMENTS

1. Verify the operating profit for 1984.

| 2 | Cost of goods sold | 102,000 | 80,000 |

Depreciation

Depreciation (see Chapter 13) is an expense since it represents a decline in the useful life of an asset (such as machinery) due to wear and tear.

| 3 | Depreciation | 5,000 | 2,000 |

2. Verify the operating profit for 1985.

Selling and Administrating Expenses

This item includes salaries and commissions for salespeople, travel, entertainment, advertising, and executives salaries.

| 4 | Selling and administrative expenses | 24,000 | 19,000 |

We subtract all previous expenses from net sales to get operating profit.

| 5 | Operating profit | 9,000 | 4,000 |

3. Verify the total income for 1984.

DO EXERCISES 1–2.

Other Income

Companies may invest in stocks and bonds. Interest and dividends obtained are considered other income.

| 6 | Other income
Dividends and Interest | 4,000 | 1,500 |

We add operating profit and other income to get total income.

4. Verify the total income for 1985.

| 7 | Total income | 13,000 | 5,500 |

DO EXERCISES 3–4.

Bond Interest

This item is a fixed expense as it must be paid each year. Axtel Company's bonds pay 10% interest on $35,000 so the interest expense is $3,500.

| 8 | Less bond interest | 3,500 | 3,500 |

ANSWERS ON PAGE A–27

We subtract bond interest from total income to get income before federal income tax.

| 9 | Income before federal tax | 9,500 | 2,000 |

DO EXERCISES 5–6.

Federal Income Tax

The federal income tax on companies with no more than $25,000 income before tax is 15%. The 1985 federal income tax for Axtel Company is 15% of $9500 or $1400 (rounded).

| 10 | Federal tax | 1,400 | 300 |

DO EXERCISE 7.

Net Profit

This item is obtained when all expenses have been subtracted from all income. For Axtel Company, after we subtract federal tax from income before tax we get net profit.

| 11 | Net profit for year | 8,100 | 1,700 |

DO EXERCISES 8–9.

◉◉ ANALYZING THE INCOME STATEMENT

Comparisons are useful for investors. One example is the *operating margin of profit*. For Axtel Company, 1985 sales were $140,000 and operating profit $9,000, so the

$$\text{Operating margin of profit} = \frac{\text{Operating profit}}{\text{Net sales}}$$

$$= \frac{9{,}000}{140{,}000}$$

$$= 6.4\%.$$

This figure shows that after operating expenses, 6.4¢ of every $1 of sales was still available to the company. Similarly, in 1984

$$\text{Operating margin of profit} = \frac{4{,}000}{105{,}000}$$

$$= 3.8\%.$$

Comparing these figures indicates that Axtel Company is becoming more profitable. This increased profitability might be attributable to more efficient operating procedures, new product lines, or an increased customer base.

---

5. Verify the income before federal tax for 1984.

6. Verify the income before federal tax for 1985.

7. Verify the federal tax for 1984.

8. Verify the net profit for 1984.

9. Verify the net profit for 1985.

ANSWERS ON PAGE A–27

FINANCIAL STATEMENTS

10. Calculate the 1984 net profit ratio for Axtel Company.

Another useful comparison is the *net profit ratio*. For Axtel Company in 1985, sales were $140,000 and net profit $8,100, so the

$$\text{Net profit ratio} = \frac{\text{Net profit}}{\text{Net sales}}$$

$$= \frac{8,100}{140,000}$$

$$= 5.8\%.$$

In 1985, for every $1 in sales, 5.8¢ went to the company.

DO EXERCISE 10.

A comparison of these figures from year to year and with similar figures from other companies in the same product line will enable us to better evaluate profit progress.

Another analysis technique (called *vertical analysis*) tells us how each sales dollar was spent. We find the percent of net sales of each entry on the income statement. For example, in 1984 the cost of goods sold was 72.9% $\left(\frac{102,000}{140,000}\right)$ of net sales for Axtel Company.

11. In 1985, federal tax was what percent of net sales for Axtel Company?

DO EXERCISE 11.

An income statement may not supply figures for two years as we have done. However, these figures permit use of *horizontal analysis* to study a company's finances. Horizontal analysis is a method used to compare figures for two or more time intervals and helps us to spot trends. It enables us to ask such questions as: What is the gain (loss) in sales, expenses, or profit from year to year? The method involves finding the percent increase (decrease) for each item on the income statement. For example, to find the percentage gain in sales from 1984 to 1985 we find

a) the sales gain

Sales gain = 140,000 − 105,000
= 35,000

and then

12. For 1985 find to the nearest tenth the percent increase (decrease) in selling and administrating expenses from 1984 for Axtel Company.

b) divide by the 1984 sales.

$$\frac{35,000}{105,000} = .33 \text{ or } 33\%$$

The sales increase from 1984 to 1985 was 33%.

The figure in the denominator is always taken from the earlier time period.

DO EXERCISE 12.

Vertical and horizontal analysis are applicable to the balance sheet, which will be discussed in the next section.

ANSWERS ON PAGE A−27

EXERCISE SET 11.2

1. Complete where indicated.

TRAUX COMPANY
MARBLEBORO, MASSACHUSETTS

Income Statement	1986	1985
Net sales	250,000	210,000
Cost of sales and operating expenses		
Cost of goods sold	187,000	163,000
Depreciation	9,000	6,000
Selling and administrating expenses	43,000	38,000
Operating profit		
Other income		
Dividends and interest	12,000	8,000
Total income		
Less bond interest	6,000	6,000
Income before federal tax		
Federal tax	2,550	750
Net profit for year		

2. Fill in the boxes.

MICROELECTRONICS
SUNNYVALE, CALIFORNIA

Income Statement	1986	Percent of Net Sales
Net sales	530,000	
Cost of sales and operating expenses		
Cost of goods sold	260,000	
Depreciation	25,000	
Selling and administrating expenses	80,000	
Operating profit	165,000	
Other income		
Dividends and interest	20,000	
Total income	185,000	
Less bond interest	42,000	
Income before federal tax	143,000	
Federal tax	25,000	
Net profit for year	118,000	

FINANCIAL STATEMENTS

3. Fill in the boxes with the percent increase (decrease).

HUSKY TOOLS
PORTSMOUTH, MAINE

Income Statement	Percent Change	1986	1985
Net sales		370,000	315,000
Cost of sales and operating expenses			
Cost of goods sold		230,000	160,000
Depreciation		10,000	10,000
Selling and administrating expenses		50,000	45,000
Operating profit		80,000	100,000
Other income			
Dividends and interest		30,000	5,000
Total income		110,000	105,000
Less bond interest		20,000	20,000
Income before federal tax		90,000	85,000
Federal tax		16,000	14,000
Net profit for year		74,000	71,000

4. Find the operating margin of profit for the indicated year for

	1986	1985
Traux Company		
Microelectronics		no
Husky Tools		

5. Find the net profit ratio for the indicated year for

	1986	1985
Traux Company		
Microelectronics		no
Husky Tools		

11.3 BALANCE SHEETS

Balance sheets provide a financial picture of a company at a particular time. On a balance sheet assets are generally on the left while liabilities and owners equity are on the right. However, sometimes these components appear at the top and bottom (respectively) of the balance sheet.

◼ ENTRIES ON THE BALANCE SHEET

Balance sheets aren't all exactly alike but most are similar. The left side of a balance sheet for the Axtel Company appears below.

AXTEL COMPANY
FARMINGTON, VIRGINIA

Balance Sheet—December 31, 1985

	Assets	1985	1984
	Current Assets		
1	Cash	7,000	5,200
2	Marketable securities at cost (1985–$15,000, 1984–$12,000)	13,000	9,800
3	Accounts receivable (1985–$2000, 1984–$1500)	28,000	20,000
4	Inventories	41,000	43,000
5	Total current assets	89,000	78,000
6	Fixed Assets		
	Land	6,000	6,000
	Buildings	48,000	45,000
	Machinery	14,000	11,000
	Office equipment	2,000	1,500
		70,000	63,500
7	Less accumulated depreciation	14,000	11,500
8	Net fixed assets	56,000	52,000
9	Prepayments and deferred charges	2,000	1,000
10	Intangibles	1,000	1,000
11	Total assets	148,000	132,000

Current Assets

Included in current assets are cash and other assets which will be converted to cash within a year.

Cash

Cash means bills, silver, and bank deposits.

1	Cash	7,000	5,200

OBJECTIVES

After finishing Section 11.3, you should be able to:

◼ Find entries on a balance sheet.
◼◼ Analyze the balance sheet.

1. Verify the total current assets on December 31, 1984.

2. Verify the total current assets on December 31, 1985.

Marketable Securities

Examples of marketable securities include treasury bills, certificates of deposit, and commercial paper. These securities are readily convertible to cash. Listed values are at cost with current values in parentheses.

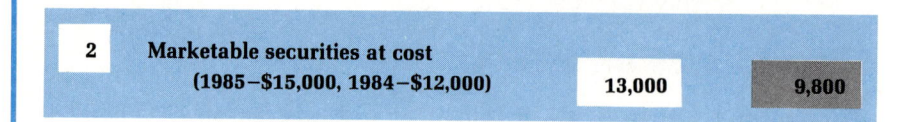

| 2 | Marketable securities at cost (1985–$15,000, 1984–$12,000) | 13,000 | 9,800 |

Accounts Receivable

This item is for goods already shipped to customers, the payment for which has not yet been received. The figure represents the receivable amount after an allowance for bad debts of $2,000 in 1985 and $1,500 in 1984.

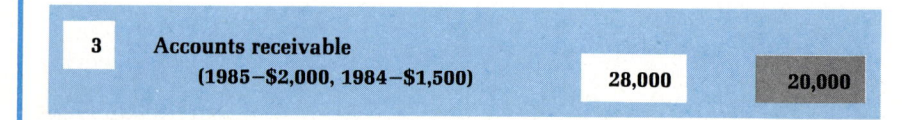

| 3 | Accounts receivable (1985–$2,000, 1984–$1,500) | 28,000 | 20,000 |

Inventories

Inventory valuation (see Chapter 12) assigns a value to the materials on hand.

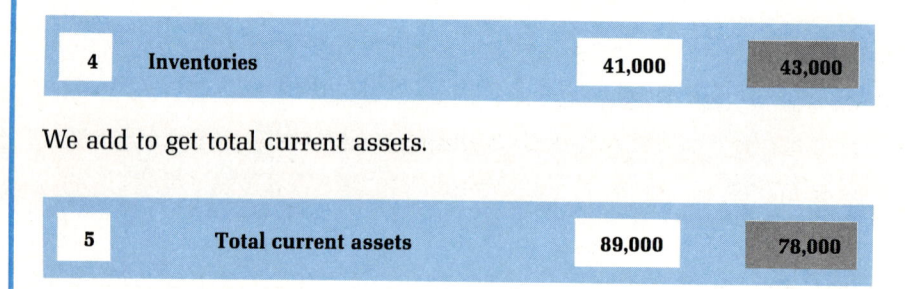

| 4 | Inventories | 41,000 | 43,000 |

We add to get total current assets.

| 5 | Total current assets | 89,000 | 78,000 |

DO EXERCISES 1–2.

Fixed Assets

These assets are not generally sold and are used in the manufacturing process. Included are land, property, machinery, and equipment.

11.3 BALANCE SHEETS

6	Fixed Assets		
	Land	6,000	6,000
	Buildings	48,000	45,000
	Machinery	14,000	11,000
	Office equipment	2,000	1,500

We add to get total fixed assets 70,000 and 63,500

DO EXERCISES 3–4.

Depreciation

This item represents a decline in useful life of an asset (excluding land) due to wear and tear. Depreciation is discussed in Chapter 13.

7	Less accumulated depreciation	14,000	11,500

We subtract accumulated depreciation from the total of fixed assets to get net fixed assets.

8	Net fixed assets	56,000	52,000

DO EXERCISES 5–6.

Prepayments and Deferred Charges

Prepayments occur when charges are paid in advance. For example, insurance premiums and leasing arrangements are sometimes paid for several years in advance. These benefits have not yet been used and therefore are assets. Likewise, expenditures for activities like research and development have benefits which extend over several years and are assets. They are called deferred charges.

9	Prepayments and deferred charges	2,000	1,000

Intangibles

This type of asset has no physical existence but does have value. For example, the exclusive privilege of a microcomputer manufacturer to market its products in the schools of a state would be an intangible.

10	Intangibles	1,000	1,000

3. Verify the total fixed assets on December 31, 1984.

4. Verify the total fixed assets on December 31, 1985.

5. Verify net fixed assets on December 31, 1984.

6. Verify net fixed assets on December 31, 1985.

ANSWERS ON PAGE A–28

FINANCIAL STATEMENTS

7. Verify the total assets on December 31, 1984.

We add all of the assets to get total assets.

11	Total assets	148,000	132,000

DO EXERCISES 7–8.

The right side of the balance sheet for Axtel Company appears below.

AXTEL COMPANY
FARMINGTON, VIRGINIA

	Liabilities	1985	1984
	Current liabilities		
12	Accounts payable	25,000	21,000
13	Notes payable	8,000	9,000
14	Accrued expenses payable	6,700	2,000
15	Federal income tax payable	1,300	1,000
16	Total current liabilities	41,000	33,000
	Long term liabilities		
17	Bonds: 10% interest due 1998	35,000	35,000
18	Total liabilities	76,000	68,000
	Stockholders Equity		
	Capital stock		
19	Common stock, $10 par value each, 3300 shares	33,000	33,000
20	Capital surplus	9,000	9,000
21	Accumulated retained earnings	30,000	22,000
22	Total stockholders equity	72,000	64,000
23	Total liabilities and stockholders equity	148,000	132,000

8. Verify the total assets on December 31, 1985.

Current Liabilities

Included in this item are debts payable during the coming year.

Accounts Payable

This item includes the amount payable to creditors from whom the company purchased goods.

12	Accounts payable	25,000	21,000

ANSWERS ON PAGE A–28

Notes Payable

Money owed to a financial institution or other lender is included in this item. A note signed by a company official is given to the lender.

| 13 | Notes payable | 8,000 | 9,000 |

Accrued Expenses Payable

This item represents the amount the company owes to its employees, for interest, and for legal services as well as similar items.

| 14 | Accrued expenses payable | 6,700 | 2,000 |

Federal Income Tax Payable

This is similar to items listed under accrued expenses but listed separately because of its importance.

| 15 | Federal income tax payable | 1,300 | 1,000 |

We add all amounts under current liabilities to get total current liabilities.

| 16 | Total current liabilities | 41,000 | 33,000 |

DO EXERCISES 9–10.

Long-Term Liabilities

Liabilities due in more than a year from the date on the balance sheet are in this category.

Bonds

These are long-term securities on which the company pays interest regularly (see Chapter 8). Axtel Company issued $35,000 in bonds due in 1998 on which 10% interest is paid.

| 17 | Bonds: 10% interest due in 1998 | 35,000 | 35,000 |

9. Verify the total current liabilities on December 31, 1984.

10. Verify the total current liabilities on December 31, 1985.

422

11. Verify the total liability on December 31, 1984.

FINANCIAL STATEMENTS

We add current and long-term liabilities to get total liabilities.

| 18 | Total liabilities | 76,000 | 68,000 |

DO EXERCISES 11–12.

Capital Stock

This item represents ownership of Axtel Company. Each shareholder owns a certain proportionate amount of the company.

Common Stock

Common stock and its features are discussed in Chapter 8.

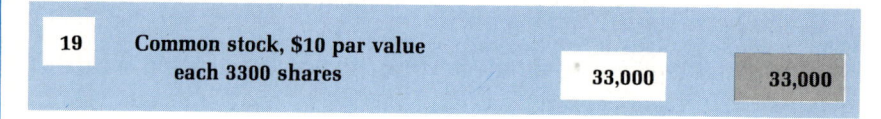

| 19 | Common stock, $10 par value each 3300 shares | 33,000 | 33,000 |

Capital Surplus

This item is the amount over the par value that stockholders paid. For example, suppose stockholders of Axtel Company paid a total of $42,000 for 3300 shares of $10 par value common stock. The $42,000 of shareholder equity is then allocated to capital stock and capital surplus.

| 20 | Capital surplus | 9,000 | 9,000 |

12. Verify the total liability on December 31, 1985.

Accumulated Retained Earnings

To explain this term suppose that during its first year Axtel Company has $10,000 of profit and pays out $6,600 in stock dividends. At the end of the first year accumulated retained earnings are $3,400 ($10,000 − $6,600), as the company had no accumulated earnings prior to the start of business. On December 31, 1985 accumulated retained earnings (sometimes called earned surplus) were $30,000.

| 21 | Accumulated retained earnings | 30,000 | 22,000 |

ANSWERS ON PAGE A–28

11.3 BALANCE SHEETS

We add the amount in the above three items to get total stockholders equity.

22	Total stockholders equity	72,000	64,000

DO EXERCISES 13–14.

To obtain the total liabilities and stockholders equity we add the amounts for these items.

23	Total liabilities and stockholders equity	148,000	132,000

DO EXERCISES 15–16.

Note that total assets equal total liabilities and stockholders equity, hence the name "balance sheet."

◉◉ ANALYZING THE BALANCE SHEET

Balance sheet figures provide opportunities to evaluate a company. For example, working capital is needed for business expansion and new opportunities. Working capital is the difference between total current assets and current liabilities. For Axtel Company

$$\text{Working capital} = \text{Current assets} - \text{Current liabilities}$$
$$= \$89,000 - \$41,000$$
$$= \$48,000.$$

An investor may ask whether this is an adequate amount of working capital for Axtel Company. The *current ratio* helps answer this question. It is the ratio of current assets to current liabilities. For Axtel Company

$$\text{Current ratio} = \frac{\text{Current assets}}{\text{Current liabilities}}$$
$$= \frac{\$89,000}{\$41,000} = \frac{2.2}{1} \quad \text{or} \quad 2.2 \text{ to } 1.$$

This means that for each $2.20 of current assets there is $1.00 of current liabilities. Many investors feel the current ratio should be at least 2 to 1. However, the current ratio is just one of several tests which aid the decision making process.

DO EXERCISE 17.

---

13. Verify the total stockholders equity on December 31, 1984.

14. Verify the total stockholders equity on December 31, 1985.

15. Verify the total liabilities and stockholders equity on December 31, 1984.

16. Verify the total liabilities and stockholders equity on December 31, 1985.

AJAX COMPANY	
Inventories	$80,000
Current assets	$300,000
Current liabilities	$127,000

For Ajax Company find

17. Current ratio.

ANSWERS ON PAGE A–28

For Ajax Company find

18. Quick assets ratio.

FINANCIAL STATEMENTS

Often investors use the *quick assets ratio* (sometimes called the *acid test ratio*), which eliminates inventories as they are not necessarily quickly convertible to cash.

$$\text{Quick assets ratio} = \frac{\text{Current assets} - \text{Inventories}}{\text{Current liabilities}}$$

$$= \frac{\$89,000 - \$41,000}{\$41,000}$$

$$= \frac{1.2}{1} \quad \text{or} \quad 1.2 \text{ to } 1$$

Investors find a quick assets ratio of 1 to 1 acceptable, as a company then has the ability to quickly meet its obligations.

DO EXERCISE 18.

EXERCISE SET 11.3

1. Fill in the boxes.

MARLAX INDUSTRIES
McALLEN, TEXAS

Balance Sheet-December 31, 1985

Assets	1985
Current Assets	
Cash	25,000
Marketable securities at cost ($19,000)	15,000
Accounts receivable ($1500)	32,000
Inventories	48,000
Total current assets	☐
Fixed Assets	
Land	12,000
Buildings	80,000
Machinery	42,000
Office equipment	8,000
	☐
Less accumulated depreciation	16,000
Net fixed assets	☐
Prepayments and deferred charges	3,000
Intangibles	2,000
Total assets	☐

FINANCIAL STATEMENTS

2. Fill in the boxes.

MARLAX INDUSTRIES

Liabilities	1985
Current liabilities	
Accounts payable	15,000
Notes payable	20,000
Accrued expenses payable	5,000
Federal income tax payable	3,000
Total current liabilities	☐
Long-term liabilities	
Bonds: 12% interest due 2004	25,000
Total liabilities	☐
Stockholders Equity	
Capital stock	
Common stock, $5 par value each, 12,000 shares	60,000
Capital surplus	45,000
Accumulated retained earnings	78,000
Total stockholders equity	☐
Total liabilities and stockholders equity	☐

For Marlax Industries find the

3. Working capital.

4. Current ratio.

5. Quick assets ratio.

TEST OR REVIEW—CHAPTER 11

If you miss an item, review the indicated section and objective.

[11.1, •] **1.** A retailer bought appliances for $12,686 and sold them for $17,499. There were no adjustments or returns. What was the gross profit?

[11.1, ••] **2.** A retailer had a gross profit of $5789. Her expenses were $135 for utilities, $425 for rent, and $768 for labor. What was the net income?

[11.2, • ••] **3.** Complete where indicated.

HARBISON WALKER
PITTSBURGH, PENNSYLVANIA

Income Statement	1986	Percent of Net Sales
Net sales	205,000	
Cost of sales and operating expenses		
Cost of goods sold	110,000	
Depreciation	18,000	
Selling and administrative expenses	37,000	
Operating profit	____	____
Other income		
Dividends and interest	5,000	
Total income	____	____
Less bond interest	15,000	
Income before federal tax	____	
Federal tax	4,600	
Net profit for year	____	____

ANSWERS

1. _____

2. _____

FINANCIAL STATEMENTS

[11.2, ●●]   **4.** Complete where indicated.

TELEX INDUSTRIES
TULSA, OK

Income Statement	Percent Change	1986	1985
Net sales		315,000	270,000
Cost of sales and operating expenses			
Cost of goods sold		170,000	145,000
Depreciation		30,000	25,000
Selling and administrating expenses		80,000	70,000
Operating profit		35,000	30,000
Other income			
Dividends and interest		15,000	12,000
Total income		50,000	42,000
Less bond interest		10,000	10,000
Income before federal tax		40,000	32,000
Federal tax		6,400	5,000
Net profit for year		33,600	27,000

[11.2, ●●]   **5.** Find the 1986 margin of profit for Telex Industries.

6. Find the 1986 net profit ratio for Telex Industries.

[11.3, ●]   **7.** Complete as indicated.

ARMSTRONG COMPANY
ELY, NEVADA

Balance Sheet—December 31, 1985

Assets	1985
Current Assets	
Cash	12,000
Marketable securities at cost ($35,000)	26,000
Accounts receivable ($3200)	51,000
Inventories	63,000
Total current assets	☐
Fixed Assets	
Land	21,000
Buildings	93,000
Machinery	49,000
Office equipment	8,000
	☐
Less accumulated depreciation	18,000
Net fixed assets	☐
Prepayments and deferred charges	27,000
Intangibles	4,000
Total assets	☐

FINANCIAL STATEMENTS

[11.3, ●]   **8.** Complete as indicated.

<table>
<tr><th colspan="2">ARMSTRONG COMPANY</th></tr>
<tr><th>Liabilities</th><th>1985</th></tr>
<tr><td>Current liabilities
   Accounts payable
   Notes payable
   Accrued expenses payable
   Federal income tax payable</td><td>34,000
13,000
46,000
11,000</td></tr>
<tr><td>Total current liabilities</td><td></td></tr>
<tr><td>Long-term liabilities
   Bonds: 11% interest due 2005</td><td>60,000</td></tr>
<tr><td>Total liabilities</td><td></td></tr>
<tr><th colspan="2">Stockholders Equity</th></tr>
<tr><td>Capital stock
   Common stock, $5 par value each, 25,000 shares</td><td>125,000</td></tr>
<tr><td>Capital surplus</td><td>28,000</td></tr>
<tr><td>Accumulated retained earnings</td><td>19,000</td></tr>
<tr><td>Total stockholders equity</td><td></td></tr>
<tr><td>Total liabilities and stockholders equity</td><td></td></tr>
</table>

[11.3, ● ●]   For Armstrong Company find the

9. Working capital.

10. Current ratio.

11. Quick assets ratio.

Career: Management This is Dixie Chavis Theodorou. She is an American Indian, born of the Lumbee Tribe in North Carolina. She is now the President of Dixie Painting Co., Inc., which specializes in industrial painting and sandblasting.

Dixie was a housewife for a number of years, but, thanks to the encouragement of her husband, became president of her own company. What would Dixie like to say to math students today? Her answer is, "Stay in school and take all the math you can get. You will be surprised at the many ways you will need it, even around the household."

How is math used in the painting business? The most critical part of the business is the ability to make an estimate of the cost. One needs to figure the number of square feet to be covered. Usually one gallon of paint will cover anywhere from 200 to 450 square feet. Once the cost of paint is figured one must add supplies, the number of work-hours required for the job, and overhead costs such as office space and equipment. Once the estimate is determined, an increase of from 20% to 40% is built in for profit.

What qualities make Dixie a success? She is patient and not afraid to ask questions. If she does not know the answer to a question, she is quite willing to make a trip to the library or call other people for information. She continues to educate herself, taking courses in blueprint reading, paint estimating, and mathematics.

12 PURCHASING AND INVENTORY

READINESS CHECK—SKILLS FOR CHAPTER 12

Translate into an equation.

1. What percent of 25 is 15?
2. What percent of 83 is 47?

Multiply.

3. 30% × $24.99
4. 20% × $124.20

Divide. Write the answer as a percent.

5. 17 ÷ 42.5
6. 10.8 ÷ 18

Change the answer to a percent.

7. 0.90 × 0.70
8. 0.90 × 0.80 × 0.60

OBJECTIVES

After finishing Section 12.1, you should be able to:

◼ Solve problems involving trade discount and net price.

◼ Solve problems involving discount rate and list price.

1. The list price of a microcomputer is $1530 and the net price is $1117. What is the trade discount?

12.1 DISCOUNT AND PRICE

In order to stay in business a retailer must pay expenses and make a profit. To do this, a retailer sells merchandise for more than was paid for it. In this chapter we will discuss (a) the difference between what a retailer pays for merchandise and what it is sold for and (b) inventory methods.

◼ TRADE DISCOUNT

Merchandise is sold to retailers by manufacturers and wholesalers at a lower price than the consumer pays. This *trade discount* helps retailers to make a profit.

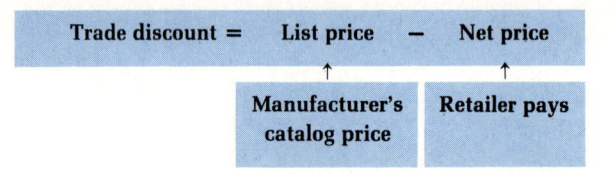

Trade discount = List price − Net price
                   ↑   ↑
           Manufacturer's   Retailer pays
           catalog price

Example 1 The list price of a color television is $409.98, the net price $325.50. What is the trade discount?

Solution

Trade discount = List price − Net price
               = $409.98 − $325.50
               = $84.48

The trade discount is $84.48.

DO EXERCISE 1.

It is common practice for manufacturers to quote a trade discount as a percent of the list price.

Trade discount = Discount rate × List price

ANSWER ON PAGE A–31

12.1 DISCOUNT AND PRICE

Example 2 The list price of a radio is $24.99. A manufacturer gives a 30% discount to all retailers. What is the trade discount?

Solution

Trade discount = Discount rate × List price
$$= 30\% \times \$24.99$$
$$= 0.30 \times \$24.99$$
$$= \$7.50$$

The trade discount is $7.50.

DO EXERCISE 2.

Retailers can find the net price when the list price and trade discount are known.

> Net price = List price − Trade discount

Example 3 A manufacturer gives a 28% discount on a refrigerator with a list price of $468.99. What is the net price?

Solution

a) Find the trade discount.

Trade discount = 28% × $468.99
$$= 0.28 \times \$468.99$$
$$= \$131.32$$

b) Find the net price.

Net price = List price − Trade discount
$$= \$468.99 - \$131.32$$
$$= \$337.67$$

The net price is $337.67.

DO EXERCISE 3.

●● DISCOUNT RATE

Suppose a manufacturer's net price is $10.50 for a calculator with a list price of $16.99. The trade discount is $6.49. What percent of the list price is the trade discount? To find out we translate as follows.

What percent of the list price is the trade discount?
$$x \qquad \$16.99 = \qquad \$6.49$$

To find the missing number, we divide:

$$x = \frac{\$6.49}{\$16.99}$$

$$x = 0.38 = 38\%$$

2. The list price of a stereo is $349.98. A manufacturer gives a 35% discount to all retailers. What is the trade discount?

3. A manufacturer gives a 20% discount on a rototiller with a list price of $645. What is the net price?

ANSWERS ON PAGE A-31

4. A manufacturer's net price is $98.95 for a fan with a list price of $122.99. What is the discount rate to the nearest percent?

PURCHASING AND INVENTORY

We can formalize this as follows:

> **To find the discount rate,**
> 1. Find the trade discount;
> 2. Divide the trade discount by the list price; and
> 3. Convert to a percent.

Example 4 A manufacturer's net price is $10.50 for a calculator with a list price of $16.99. What is the discount rate?

Solution

1. Trade discount = $16.99 − $10.50   *Find the trade discount.*
   = $6.49

2. Discount rate = $\dfrac{\$6.49}{\$16.99}$ *Divide by the list price.*

   = 0.38
3. = 38%   *Convert to a percent.*

The discount rate is 38%.

DO EXERCISE 4.

A manufacturer may want to find the list price for merchandise when the net price and discount rate are known.

> List Price = $\dfrac{\text{Net Price}}{1 - \text{Discount Rate}}$

Example 5 A manufacturer sets the net price of a range at $295.50 and offers a 40% discount. What is the list price?

Solution

$$\text{List Price} = \dfrac{\text{Net Price}}{1 - \text{Discount Rate}}$$

$$= \dfrac{\$295.50}{1 - 0.40}$$

$$= \dfrac{\$295.50}{0.60}$$

$$= \$492.50$$

The list price is $492.50.

DO EXERCISE 5.

5. A manufacturer sets the net price of a vacuum sweeper at $59.30 and offers a 21% discount. What is the list price?

ANSWERS ON PAGE A−31

NAME _____ CLASS _____ ANSWERS

EXERCISE SET 12.1

● Solve.

1. The list price of a lamp is $121.99, the net price $87.50. What is the trade discount?

2. The list price of a vase is $14.95, the net price $9.25. What is the trade discount?

3. The list price of a car is $7847. The manufacturer gives a 20% discount to all dealers. What is the trade discount?

4. The list price of a dishwasher is $249.99. The manufacturer gives a 25% discount to all retailers. What is the trade discount?

Find the trade discount.

5. TWIN SIZE MATRESS AND BOX $109.95
   Net Price $74.95

6. FULL SIZE MATTRESS AND BOX $119.95
   Net Price $79.95

7. BRAND NEW CHROME FRAME STENO POSTURE CHAIR... 69.95
   Discount 45%

8. BRAND NEW WALNUT GRAIN 62x18 MATCHING CREDENZA... 189.95
   Discount 40%

9. A manufacturer gives a 30% discount on a couch with a list price of $899.98. What is the net price?

10. A manufacturer gives a 40% discount on all kitchen appliances. The list price of a disposal is $159.99. What is the net price?

Find the net price. The list price and discount are given.

11. JAYMAR GOLF SLACKS 18.95
    Discount 27%

12. MEN'S GOLF SHOES Foot Joy & Etonic 39.95
    Discount 35%

●● Solve.

13. A publisher's net price is $13.20 for a book with a list price of $16.50. What is the discount rate?

1. _____
2. _____
3. _____
4. _____
5. _____
6. _____
7. _____
8. _____
9. _____
10. _____
11. _____
12. _____
13. _____

PURCHASING AND INVENTORY

14. A manufacturer's net price is $4.95 for a clock with a list price of $7.50. What is the discount rate?

What is the discount rate to the nearest percent? The list and net prices are given.

15. OLYMPUS XA1 — The 35mm you don't have to set — $69.95

Net Price $41.97

16. NIKON EM — 9 PIECE 3 LENS OUTFIT (with FLASH) — $179.95
- Totally automatic
- Super lightweight
- Nikon quality at a low price
- EM body
- 50mm 1.8 Nikon lens
- 135 aux. tele. lens
- 28mm aux. wide angle
- Electronic flash
- Lens cap
- Body cap
- Color film
- Lens tissue

Net Price $71.98

17. A manufacturer sets the net price of a freezer at $287.45 and offers a 30% discount. What is the list price?

18. A manufacturer sets the net price of an end table at $47.75 and offers a 28% discount. What is the list price?

19. A manufacturer sets the net price of a computer at $398 and offers a 32% discount. What is the list price?

20. A manufacturer sets the net price of a large screen television at $1850 and offers a 25% discount. What is the list price?

Complete.

21.	Item	Microwave oven
	List	$498.99
	Less $27\frac{1}{2}$%	
	Net	

22.	Item	Gold locket
	List	
	Less 35.8%	
	Net	$89.50

23.	Item	Round tray
	List	$15.00
	Less	
	Net	$9.80

24.	Item	Tray table
	List	$59.95
	Less $33\frac{1}{3}$%	
	Net	

12.2 SEVERAL TRADE DISCOUNTS

■ SEVERAL DISCOUNTS

Manufacturers may give additional discounts (sometimes called *chain* or *series discounts*) to move their products quickly. Example 1 illustrates the process.

Example 1 A shoe manufacturer offers a trade discount of 5% in addition to a previously offered discount of 20%. Find the net price for a pair of shoes that lists for $36.95.

Solution

a) Apply the first discount to the list price.

   Discount = 20% × $36.95
             = 0.20 × $36.95
             = $7.39

b) Find the net price after the first discount.

   Net price = $36.95 − $7.39
             = $29.56

c) Apply the second discount to this price.

   Discount = 5% × $29.56
            = 0.05 × $29.56
            = $1.48

d) Find the net price after the second discount.

   Net price = $29.56 − $1.48
             = $28.08

The net price is $28.08.

DO EXERCISE 1.

Example 2 illustrates another method for solving this problem called the *method of complements*. It involves finding the *complement* of each percent (the percent which when added to the given percent results in 100%).

Example 2 A shoe manufacturer offers a trade discount of 5% in addition to a previously offered discount of 20%. Find the net price for a pair of shoes that lists for $36.95.

Solution

a) Subtract each percent from 100%.

   100% − 20% = 80% = 0.80

   100% − 5% = 95% = 0.95

OBJECTIVE

After finishing Section 12.2, you should be able to:

■ Solve problems which involve several discounts.

1. A dress manufacturer offers a trade discount of 7% in addition to a previously offered discount of 32%. Find the net price for a dress that lists for $62.49.

ANSWER ON PAGE A−31

2. A dress manufacturer offers a trade discount of 7% in addition to a previously offered discount of 32%. Using the method of complements, find the net price for a dress that lists for $62.49.

3. A dress manufacturer offers a trade discount of 39%. Find the net price for a dress that lists for $62.49.

4. A manufacturer offers successive discounts of 25%, 7%, and 8% during August. Find the net price of an end table that lists for $149.95.

ANSWERS ON PAGE A–31

---

b) Find the net price.

Net price = 0.80 × 0.95 × $36.95

= $28.08

The net price is $28.08.

DO EXERCISE 2.

The following example illustrates that a single discount of 25% is better for the retailer than a discount of 20% followed by a discount of 5%.

Example 3 A shoe manufacturer offers a trade discount of 25%. Find the net price of a pair of shoes that lists for $36.95.

Solution

a) Find the discount.

Discount = 25% × $36.95

= $9.24

b) Find the net price.

Net price = $36.95 − $9.24

= $27.71

The net price is $27.71.

Note that $27.71 is less than the $28.08 given in Example 2.

DO EXERCISE 3.

A procedure similar to that used in Example 2 may be used for any number of discounts.

Example 4 A manufacturer offers successive discounts of 20%, 10%, and 5% during July. Find the net price of a filing cabinet that lists for $119.88.

Solution

a) Subtract each percent from 100%.

100% − 20% = 80% = 0.80

100% − 10% = 90% = 0.90

100% − 5% = 95% = 0.95

b) Find the net price.

Net price = 0.80 × 0.90 × 0.95 × $119.88

= $82.00

The net price is $82.00.

DO EXERCISE 4.

NAME _____ CLASS _____ ANSWERS

EXERCISE SET 12.2

• Solve.

1. A camera manufacturer offers a 5% trade discount in addition to a previously offered discount of 16%. Find the net price of the Minolta Camera.

MINOLTA X700 — 9 PIECE 3 LENS OUTFIT (with FLASH)
- Manual option
- Shutter weighted program system
- Aperture and shutter automation
- X700 body
- w/ 50 mm f.2 Rokkor X lens
- 135 mm aux. tele lens
- 28mm aux. wide angle lens
- Electronic flash
- Lens cap
- Body cap
- Color film
- Lens tissue

$279.95

1. _____

2. A camera manufacturer offers a 10% trade discount in addition to a previously offered discount of 26%. Find the net price of the Canon Camera.

Canon AE-1 PROGRAM — 9 PIECE 3 LENS OUTFIT (with FLASH)
- Shutter priority automation
- Programmed automation
- Compact, lightweight
- Program body
- 50mm 1.8 Canon lens
- 135mm aux. tele lens
- 28mm aux. wide angle lens
- Electronic flash
- Lens cap
- Body cap
- Color film
- Lens tissue

$289.95

3. A computer software manufacturer offers a 5% trade discount in addition to a previously offered discount of 20%. Find the net price of Mattel's Space Armada.

2. _____

INTELLIVISION — SPACE ARMADA
Mattel Electronics™ Space Armada™
Defend the planet Earth against the attack of alien warlords with lethal bombs and guided missiles. Two skill levels. #3759.

$24.99

3. _____

ANSWERS

4. _____

5. _____

6. _____

7. _____

8. _____

9. _____

10. _____

11. _____

12. _____

4. A computer software manufacturer offers a 10% trade discount in addition to a previously offered discount of 30%. Find the net price of the Mattel Star Strike.

Mattel Electronics™ Star Strike™
Maneuver your spaceship through a trench to destroy alien forces. If you crash or are hit too many times, your planet is destroyed. #5161

$29.99

5. A shirt manufacturer offers a trade discount of 8% in addition to a previously offered discount of 15%. Find the net price of a shirt that lists for $13.50.

6. A suit manufacturer offers a trade discount of 10% in addition to a previously offered discount of 6%. Find the net price of a suit that lists for $225.99.

7. A power tool manufacturer offers a trade discount of 32% in addition to a previously offered discount of 9%. Find the net price of a power drill that lists for $54.49.

8. A baby clothes manufacturer offers a trade discount of 6% in addition to a previously offered discount of 5%. Find the net price of a one-piece sleeper that lists for $4.44

9. A power tool manufacturer offers a trade discount of 41%. Find the net price of a power drill that lists for $54.49.

10. A baby clothes manufacturer offers a trade discount of 11%. Find the net price of a one-piece sleeper that lists for $4.44.

11. A manufacturer offers successive discounts of 8%, 7%, and 10% in June. Find the net price of a lightweight jacket that lists for $27.00.

12. A manufacturer offers successive discounts of 9%, 5%, and 12% in September. Find the net price of a storage building that lists for $319.99.

Complete

Item	List Price	Discount Rate	Net Price	Trade Discount
13. Chair	$115.99	17%, 3%, and 5%		
14. Radio	$ 36.99	12%, 4%, and 2%		
15. Lamp	$ 98.99	8%, 5%, 6%, and 3%		
16. Fan	$117.95	12%, 9%, 5%, and 6%		

12.3 CHANGING SEVERAL DISCOUNT RATES TO A SINGLE RATE

◼ SINGLE RATE EQUIVALENT OF SEVERAL RATES

Computation is easier when several discount rates are changed to a single rate.

> To change several discount rates to a single rate,
> 1. Subtract each discount rate from 100% and convert to a decimal;
> 2. Multiply and convert back to a percent;
> 3. Subtract from 100%.

Example 1 Find the single discount rate for a 10% discount followed by a 30% discount.

Solution

1. $100\% - 10\% = 90\% = 0.90$ Subtract from 100% and convert to a decimal.
   $100\% - 30\% = 70\% = 0.70$

2. $0.90 \times 0.70 = 0.63 = 63\%$ Multiply and convert back to a percent.

3. $100\% - 63\% = 37\%$ Subtract from 100%.

The single discount rate is 37%.

DO EXERCISE 1.

Example 2 Find the single discount rate and trade discount on a lawn tractor with a list price of $2985 and successive discounts of 10%, 8%, and 12%.

Solution

a) Find the single discount rate.

1. $100\% - 10\% = 90\% = 0.90$
   $100\% - 8\% = 92\% = 0.92$ Subtract from 100% and convert to a decimal.
   $100\% - 12\% = 88\% = 0.88$

2. $0.90 \times 0.92 \times 0.88 = 0.729 = 72.9\%$ Mutiply and convert back to a percent.

3. $100\% - 72.9\% = 27.1\%$ Subtract from 100%.

The single discount rate is 27.1%.

b) Find the trade discount.

   Trade discount $= 27.1\% \times \$2985$
   $= 0.271 \times \$2985 = \$808.94$

The trade discount is $808.94.

DO EXERCISE 2.

OBJECTIVES

After finishing Section 12.3, you should be able to:

◼ Change several discount rates to a single rate.

◼◼ Compare discount rates to determine the best buy.

1. Find the single discount rate for a 10% discount followed by a 20% discount.

2. Find the single discount rate and trade discount on a hydraulic lift with a list price of $9875 and successive discounts of 15%, 7%, and 11%.

ANSWER ON PAGE A–32

3. One manufacturer offers a dishwasher at discounts of 12% and 8%, while another manufacturer offers a comparable dishwasher for the same list price at discounts of 15% and 5%. Which is the better buy?

COMPARING RATES

Finding the single discount rate can be helpful for comparison when retailers make purchases.

Example 3 One manufacturer offers a sofa at discounts of 10% and 30%, while another manufacturer offers a comparable sofa for the same list price at discounts of 25% and 15%. Which is the better buy?

Solution

a) Find the single discount for the first manufacturer.

1. $100\% - 10\% = 90\% = 0.90$ Subtract from 100% and
   $100\% - 30\% = 70\% = 0.70$ convert to a decimal.

2. $0.90 \times 0.70 = 0.63 = 63\%$ Multiply and convert back to a percent.

3. $100\% - 63\% = 37\%$ Subtract from 100%.

The single discount rate for the first manufacturer is 37%.

b) Find the single discount rate for the second manufacturer.

1. $100\% - 25\% = 75\% = 0.75$ Subtract from 100% and
   $100\% - 15\% = 85\% = 0.85$ convert to a decimal.

2. $0.75 \times 0.85 = 0.63\frac{3}{4} = 63\frac{3}{4}\%$ Multiply and convert back to to a percent.

3. $100\% - 63\frac{3}{4}\% = 36\frac{1}{4}\%$ Subtract from 100%.

The single discount rate for the second manufacturer is $36\frac{1}{4}\%$.

c) The larger discount, and therefore the better buy, is obtained from the first manufacturer.

DO EXERCISE 3.

NAME _____ CLASS _____ ANSWERS

EXERCISE SET 12.3

■ Find the single discount rate equivalent to the first discount followed by the second discount. Round to the nearest percent.

	First Discount	Second Discount
1.	10%	25%
2.	25%	10%
3.	14%	5%
4.	15%	12%
5.	18%	4%
6.	20%	15%
7.	30%	4%
8.	40%	5%

9. Find the single discount rate for a 20% discount followed by a 5% discount.

10. Find the single discount rate for a 10% discount followed by a 10% discount.

11. Find the single discount rate to the nearest tenth of a percent for successive discounts of 5%, 10%, and 15%.

12. Find the single discount rate to the nearest tenth of a percent for successive discounts of 7%, 8%, and 12%.

13. Find the single discount rate to the nearest tenth of a percent for successive discounts of 10%, 4%, and 5%.

14. Find the single discount rate to the nearest tenth of a percent for successive discounts of 15%, 12%, and 5%.

15. Use the single discount rate to find the trade discount on a luggage set with a list price of $275 and discounts of 13% and 5%.

16. Use the single discount rate to find the trade discount on a stereo with a list price of $525 and discounts of 20% and 7%.

444 PURCHASING AND INVENTORY

ANSWERS

17. Use the single discount rate to find the trade discount on a computer with a list price of $2750 and discounts of 30% and 10%.

17. _____

18. Use the single discount rate to find the trade discount on a computer with a list price of $595 and discounts of 25% and 10%.

■■ Solve.

19. One manufacturer offers a blender at discounts of 15% and 9%, while another manufacturer offers a comparable model for the same list price at discounts of 20% and 4%. Which is the better buy?

18. _____

20. One manufacturer offers a piano at discounts of 25% and 7%, while another manufacturer offers a comparable model for the same list price at discounts of 20% and 12%. Which is the better buy?

19. _____

21. One manufacturer offers a bedroom set at discounts of 20% and 7%, while another manufacturer offers a comparable set for the same list price at discounts of 25% and 2%. Which is the better buy?

20. _____

22. One manufacturer offers a range at discounts of 23% and 8%, while another manufacturer offers a comparable range for the same list price at discounts of 30% and 1%. Which is the better buy?

21. _____

Complete.

Item	List Price	Discount Rates	Single Rate	Trade Discount
23. Ring	$399.98	20%, 8%, and 14%		
24. Table	$795.99	$33\frac{1}{2}$%, $4\frac{1}{4}$%, and 5%		

22. _____

12.4 CASH DISCOUNTS

■ RETAILER COST

Manufacturers and wholesalers often give a discount for early payment. The cash discount is subtracted after trade discount(s) but before transportation charges are added.

OBJECTIVE

After finishing Section 12.4, you should be able to:

■ Find the retailer cost after trade and cash discounts.

1. On the Foster's invoice, suppose that each jacket cost $31.25 and payment is made on June 11. How much is paid?

[Order Blank from Foster's Supply Co., 4562 Longnecker Drive-St. Louis, Mo. 63105. Date 6/5/85. Name: Lee Whaley. Address: 518 Welch. City & State: Aiken SC. Zip Code: 29801. Terms: 2/10, n/30. 6 Each, Cat No. 502, Pg No. 23, Down Insulated Jacket, Unit Price $28.75 Each, Total Price $172.50. Less 20% and 10%, $48.30. $124.20. Transportation $4.06. $128.26.]

2% discount for payments made by June 15 (10 days from invoice date).

Net due from June 16 through July 5 (thereafter, interest may be charged).

Example 1 Lee Whaley pays the invoice on June 8. How much does he pay?

Solution

a) Find the amount paid excluding transportation charges. The 2% discount applies since payment was made before June 15.

Discount = 2% × $124.20
= 0.02 × $124.20 = $2.48

Amount (excluding transportation) = $124.20 − $2.48 = 121.72

b) Add transportation charges.

Total paid = $121.72 + $4.06 = $125.78

The total paid is $125.78.

DO EXERCISE 1.

ANSWER ON PAGE A–32

2. On the Brook's Tools invoice, suppose each leverage cutter was $21.49 and each expansive bit was $7.85. The goods were received March 20 and the bill was paid March 28. How much was paid?

PURCHASING AND INVENTORY

Table 12.1 lists other notations for cash discount appearing on invoices.

TABLE 12.1

Terms	Meaning
3/10 1/30, n/60	3% discount within 10 days of invoice date, 1% discount from 11th to 30th day, and net from 31st to 60th day.
2/10, E.O.M.	2% discount within 10 days of beginning of next month (E.O.M. means End Of Month).
n/30	Net within 30 days of invoice date.
3/10, n/30, R.O.G.	3% within 10 days of Receipt Of Goods (R.O.G.), net from 11th to 30th day.

Example 2 The goods listed on the Brook's Tools invoice were received on March 25 and the bill was paid on April 2. How much was paid?

Brook's Tools, Inc.
Weirton, WV 26062

Date: March 12, 1985   Invoice No. 807
Ship To: Fremont Bros.
         Millard, NE 68137
Shipped: Yellow Freight   Terms: 4/10, n/30, R.O.G.

Quantity	Description	Unit Price	Amount
40	Leverage Cutters	18.95	758.00
50	Expansive Bit	6.95	347.50
	Subtotal		1105.50
	Less 30% and 10%		409.04
	Balance		696.46
	Freight		29.85
	Total		726.31

Solution

a) Find the amount paid excluding freight charges. The 4% discount applies since payment was made within 10 days of receipt of goods.

Discount = 4% × $696.46
= 0.04 × $696.46
= $27.86

Amount (excluding freight) = $696.46 − 27.86
= $668.60

b) Add the freight charges.

Total paid = $668.60 + $29.85
= $698.45

The total paid was $698.45.

DO EXERCISE 2.

EXERCISE SET 12.4

● Find the retailer's cost.

1. Date received: May 7, 1985; date paid: June 1, 1985.

Balance	$1286
Freight	$ 168
Total	$1454
Date	May 3, 1985
Terms	4/10, 2/30, n/60

2. Date received: May 9, 1985; date paid: May 14, 1985.

Balance	$2700
Freight	$ 305
Total	$3005
Date	May 5, 1985
Terms	5/10, 1/30, n/60

3. Date received: August 15, 1985; date paid: September 11, 1985.

Balance	$3685
Freight	$ 426
Total	$4111
Date	August 3, 1985
Terms	5/15, E.O.M.

4. Date received: December 4, 1985; date paid: December 19, 1985.

Balance	$4736
Freight	$ 396
Total	$5132
Date	November 30, 1985
Terms	5/10, n/30, R.O.G.

5. Date received: January 24, 1985; date paid: February 2, 1985.

Balance	$ 987
Freight	$ 36
Total	$1023
Date	January 5, 1985
Terms	3/10, 1/30, n/60

448

ANSWERS

PURCHASING AND INVENTORY

6. Date received: May 17, 1985; date paid: June 5, 1985.

> Balance $1568
> Freight $ 112
> Total $1680
> Date   May 9, 1985
> Terms   3/10, 2/30, n/60

6. _____

7. Date received: June 4, 1985; date paid: July 9, 1985.

> Balance $2586
> Freight $ 162
> Total $2748
> Date   June 1, 1985
> Terms   2/10, E. O. M.

7. _____

8. Date received: September 5, 1985; date paid: October 7, 1985.

> Balance $5682
> Freight $ 318
> Total $6000
> Date   September 2, 1985
> Terms   3/10, E. O. M.

8. _____

9. Date received: October 1, 1985; date paid: October 9, 1985.

> Balance $8531
> Freight $ 623
> Total $9154
> Date   September 28, 1985
> Terms   4/10, n/30, R. O. G.

9. _____

10. Date received: December 3, 1985; date paid: December 28, 1985.

> Balance $5241
> Freight $ 316
> Total $5557
> Date   November 25, 1985
> Terms   3/10, n/30, R. O. G

10. _____

12.5 INVENTORY

We know

> Gross Profit = Net Sales − Cost of the Goods Sold

Inventory helps a business to determine the cost of the goods sold, and it will be studied in this section.

◖ COST OF THE GOODS

Businesses take inventory (they count and price their goods) at regular intervals—usually monthly, quarterly, semiannually, or annually. The inventory sheet for Computonics shows how the cost is found.

INVENTORY SHEET

Computonics
Sunnyvale, CA

Date June 30, 1985

QUANTITY	DESCRIPTION	PRICE	UNIT	EXTENSIONS
20	Sinclair Computers	$67.25	ea	$1345.00
35	Apple Disc Drives	375.00	ea	
500	Floppy Discs	2.50	ea	

1 "Price" is the unit cost to the business.

2 "Extensions" is the price times the quantity.

For example, 20 Sinclair Computers were purchased at $67.25 each for a total cost of $1345. That is,

$$\underbrace{\$1345}_{\text{Total cost}} = \underbrace{20}_{\substack{\text{Number of}\\\text{computers}}} \times \underbrace{\$67.25}_{\substack{\text{Cost of each}\\\text{computer}}}$$

Example 1 Find the total cost of the disc drives on the Computonics Inventory Sheet.

Solution

Total Cost = Number of Units × Cost of each Unit
        =   35   × $375
        = $13,125

The total cost of 35 disc drives is $13,125.

DO EXERCISE 1.

OBJECTIVES

After finishing Section 12.5, you should be able to:

◖ Calculate the cost of goods.

◖◖ Find the cost of goods sold.

1. Find the total cost of the floppy discs on the Computonics Inventory Sheet.

ANSWER ON PAGE A–32

2. Find the inventory on December 31, 1984 for General Appliance if 25 freezers which cost $340 each are in stock in addition to items in Example 2.

PURCHASING AND INVENTORY

When we add the total cost for each product we obtain the total cost of all items on hand. This sum is the inventory at that time.

Example 2 Find the inventory on December 31, 1984 for General Appliances.

Solution

INVENTORY SHEET
General Appliances
Athens, GA

Date December 31, 1984

QUANTITY	DESCRIPTION	✓	PRICE	UNIT	EXTENSIONS
12	Hotpoint Ranges		$410.00	ea	$4920.00
15	Amana Radar Ranges		285.00	ea	4275.00
18	Whirlpool Refrigerators		550.00	ea	9900.00

Adding the total cost for each product we obtain

$4920 + $4275 + $9900

or

$19,095

The inventory on December 31, 1984 is $19,095.

DO EXERCISE 2.

■■ COST OF THE GOODS SOLD

To find the cost of the goods sold, use

Cost of Goods Sold = Beginning Inventory + Purchases − Ending Inventory

Example 3 What was the cost of the goods sold for Stanfords?

Solution

STANFORD'S

Beginning Inventory	$8000
Purchases	$6500
Ending Inventory	$5000

3. What would the cost of goods sold for Stanford's have been if the ending inventory was $2600?

a) Add the Beginning Inventory and Purchases

$8000 + $6500 = $14,500

b) Subtract the Ending Inventory

$14,500 − $5000 = $9500

The cost of the goods sold was $9500.

DO EXERCISE 3.

EXERCISE SET 12.5

● Find the cost of the quantity of each item on the inventory sheet.

INVENTORY SHEET

The Sharper Image
Baton Rouge, LA

Date May 1, 1985

	QUANTITY	DESCRIPTION	√	PRICE	UNIT
1.	3	Captain's Clock		$140.00	ea
2.	15	Cordless Muraphone		95.25	ea
3.	4	Float to Relax Tank		2750.00	ea
4.	12	Phone Dialer		62.50	ea
5.	5	Biofeedback Earphones		119.75	ea
6.	30	Sanyo Flashlights		18.00	ea
7.	18	Citizen's Travel Clock		32.45	ea
8.	25	Compact Paper Shredder		107.50	ea

INVENTORY SHEET

Eddie Bauer
Denver, CO

Date September 30, 1985

	QUANTITY	DESCRIPTION	√	PRICE	UNIT
9.	16	Ridgeline Parka		$123.00	ea
10.	14	Blizzard Master Vest		87.00	ea
11.	36	Thinsulate Deerskin Gloves		24.25	ea
12.	50	Polypropylene Underwear		15.65	ea
13.	24	Chino Pants		14.75	ea
14.	10	Gore-Tex Down Jacket		122.45	ea
15.	40	Turtleneck Pullovers		11.50	ea
16.	8	Ragg Wool Sweater		21.75	ea

17. Find the inventory on May 1, 1985 for The Sharper Image (Exercises 1–8 above).

18. Find the inventory on September 30, 1985 for Eddie Bauer (Exercises 9–16 above).

●● Find the cost of the goods sold.

19. **HECKEL'S**

Beginning Inventory $9,847
Ending Inventory $2,347

452

PURCHASING AND INVENTORY

ANSWERS

20. BABE'S
Beginning Inventory $12,809
Ending Inventory $ 4,975

20. _____

21. COSBY FARMS
Beginning Inventory $23,586
Ending Inventory $11,905

21. _____

22. FORGIONE'S
Beginning Inventory $14,280
Ending Inventory $ 6,907

22. _____

23. RACHAEL'S
Beginning Inventory $46,302
Purchases $ 7,328
Ending Inventory $12,694

23. _____

24. THE WHIRLWIND
Beginning Inventory $43,256
Purchases $13,507
Ending Inventory $25,892

24. _____

25. LACKAWANNA PARTS
Beginning Inventory $67,367
Purchases $18,000
Ending Inventory $31,794

25. _____

26. STONE'S
Beginning Inventory $32,786
Purchases $ 9,680
Ending Inventory $17,329

26. _____

12.6 SPECIAL INVENTORY METHODS

■ INVENTORY VALUATION

OBJECTIVES

After finishing Section 12.6, you should be able to:

■ Evaluate inventory.

■■ Find gross profit.

In practice the same item may be purchased several times in an inventory period at a different cost each time. For example, suppose two identical Betamax Video Recorders were purchased by a retailer at different times. The purchase price for the first was $624 and the second $710. One of the units is sold. Which one remains? The method used to take ending inventory answers this question. Ending inventory methods include the *First In, First Out* (*FIFO*); *Last In, First Out* (*LIFO*); or weighted average methods. Different inventory valuation methods result in different financial pictures and therefore different tax consequences.

To illustrate, suppose the retailer sold the Betamax for $900. If it was the first purchased, the gross profit was $276.

$900	Net sales
624	Cost to retailer
$276	Gross profit

However, if it was the second purchased, the gross profit was $190.

$900	Net sales
710	Cost to retailer
$190	Gross profit

The gross profit in the first case looks much better. However, this more favorable financial picture may result in increased taxes. Example 1 provides a detailed illustration.

Example 1 A retailer purchased quantities of the same model television set three times during an inventory period. The first purchase was 32 sets at $335.30 each; the second, 21 sets at $374.80 each; and the third, 25 at $406.75 each. In all, 44 sets were sold (34 sets were in inventory). Evaluate the ending inventory by the FIFO, LIFO, and weighted average methods.

Solution

a) Evaluate using FIFO.

The 34 sets in inventory are the last 25 and 9 from the second purchase.

25 @ $406.75 = $10,168.75
9 @ $374.80 = $ 3,373.20
$13,541.95 Ending inventory value at cost using FIFO

b) Evaluate using LIFO.

The 34 sets in inventory are the first 32 and 2 from the second purchase.

32 @ $335.30 = $10,729.60
2 @ $374.80 = $ 749.60
$11,479.20 Ending inventory value at cost using LIFO

c) Evaluate using the weighted average method.

Find the cost of each purchase.

First	32 @ $335.30 = $10,729.60
Second	21 @ $374.80 = $ 7,870.80
Third	25 @ $406.75 = $10,168.75
Total number 78	$28,769.15 Total cost

1. Evaluate the ending inventory in Example 1 by the FIFO, LIFO, and weighted average methods if 40 sets were sold (38 sets were in inventory).

Find the average cost.

$$\text{Average cost} = \frac{\text{Total cost}}{\text{Total number}}$$

$$= \frac{\$28{,}769.15}{78}$$

$$= \$368.84 \quad \text{Rounding; see Section 2.4.}$$

$$\text{Ending inventory value at cost using weighted average} = \text{Number of items in inventory} \times \text{Average cost}$$

$$= 34 \qquad \$368.84$$

$$= \$12{,}540.56$$

DO EXERCISE 1.

◼◼ GROSS PROFIT

The following example illustrates how to calculate gross profit using each of the three inventory methods.

Example 2 Net sales in Example 1 were $24,935. Find the gross profit using the FIFO, LIFO, and weighted average methods.

Solution

a) Find the gross profit using FIFO.

Cost of televisions sold = Total cost − FIFO inventory value
= $28,769.15 − $13,541.95
(From Example 1c) (From Example 1a)
= $15,227.20

So

Gross profit = Net sales − Cost
= $24,935 − $15,227.20
= $9707.80

b) Find the gross profit using LIFO.

Cost of televisions sold = Total cost − LIFO inventory value
= $28,769.15 − $11,479.20
= $17,289.95

So

Gross profit = Net sales − Cost
= $24,935 − $17,289.95
= $7645.05

c) Find the gross profit using weighted averages.

Cost of televisions sold = Total cost − Weighted average inventory value
= $28,769.15 − $12,540.56
= $16,228.59

So

Gross profit = Net sales − Cost
= $24,935 − $16,228.59
= $8706.41

2. Net sales in Example 1 were $27,460. Find the gross profit using the FIFO, LIFO, and weighted average methods.

DO EXERCISE 2.

NAME _____ CLASS _____ ANSWERS

EXERCISE SET 12.6

■ Solve.

A retailer purchased quantities of the same model stereo three times during an inventory period. The first purchase was 37 stereos at $246.80 each; the second, 26 at $264.50 each; and the third, 31 at $294.60 each. In all, 38 stereos were sold (56 stereos were in inventory). Net sales were $11,856. Find.

1. The ending inventory by FIFO

2. The ending inventory by LIFO

3. The ending inventory by the weighted average method

A retailer purchased quantities of the same model camera four times during an inventory period. The first purchase was 7 cameras at $256.30 each; the second, 11 at $263.75 each; the third, 9 at $276.70 each; and the fourth, 8 at $295.40 each. In all, 26 cameras were sold (9 cameras were in inventory). Net sales were $10,918. Find.

4. The ending inventory by FIFO

5. The ending inventory by LIFO

6. The ending inventory by the weighted average method

A retailer purchased the same model computer three times during an inventory period. The first purchase was 20 computers at $99.95 each; the second, 25 at $102.50 each; the third, 15 at $105.80 each. In all, 43 computers were sold. Net sales were $6256. Find.

7. The ending inventory by FIFO

8. The ending inventory by LIFO

9. The ending inventory by the weighted average method

■■ Find the gross profit.

10. Using FIFO for the stereo purchases (Exercises 1–3)

11. Using LIFO for the stereo purchases (Exercises 1–3)

12. Using the weighted average method for the stereo purchases (Exercises 1–3)

13. Using FIFO for the camera purchases (Exercises 4–6)

1. _____

2. _____

3. _____

4. _____

5. _____

6. _____

7. _____

8. _____

9. _____

10. _____

11. _____

12. _____

13. _____

456

PURCHASING AND INVENTORY

ANSWERS

14. _____

15. _____

16. _____

17. _____

18. _____

19. _____

20. _____

21. _____

22. _____

23. _____

24. _____

14. Using LIFO for the camera purchases (Exercises 4–6)

15. Using the weighted average method for the camera purchases (Exercises 4–6)

16. Using FIFO for the computer purchases (Exercises 7–9)

17. Using LIFO for the computer purchases (Exercises 7–9)

18. Using the weighted average method for the computer purchases (Exercises 7–9)

A retailer purchased quantities of the same calculator seven times during an inventory period. The first purchase was 23 calculators at $7.90 each; the second, 14 at $6.95 each; the third, 19 at $6.75 each; the fourth, 25 at $6.60 each; the fifth, 30 at $6.50 each; the sixth, 18 at $6.35 each; and the seventh, 29 at $6.15 each. In all, 97 calculators were sold (61 were in inventory). Net sales were $1139.75. Find the following.

19. The ending inventory by FIFO

20. The gross profit using FIFO

21. The ending inventory by LIFO

22. The gross profit using LIFO

23. The ending inventory by the weighted average method

24. The gross profit using the weighted average method

TEST OR REVIEW—CHAPTER 12

NAME _____   SCORE _____   ANSWERS

If you miss an item, review the indicated section and objective.

[12.1, •]   **1.** Find the trade discount for the wine rack.

TWELVE BOTTLE WINE RACK BY RIVERSIDE
Solid antique pine and brass   **$98**

Net Price $65

1. _____

[12.1, ••]   **2.** A manufacturer's net price is $1350 for a hot tub with a list price of $1800. What is the discount rate?

2. _____

[12.2, •]   **3.** A manufacturer offers discounts of 15%, 10%, and 5% during June. Find the net price of a radial snow tire that lists for $54.99.

[12.3, •]   **4.** Find the single discount rate for a 15% discount followed by a 10% discount.

3. _____

[12.3, ••]   **5.** One manufacturer offers lawn furniture at discounts of 15% and 5%, while another manufacturer offers comparable furniture for the same list price at discounts of 10% and 10%. Which is the better buy?

4. _____

[12.4, •]   **6.** Find the amount paid on the invoice shown below if the date received was May 18, 1985, and the date paid was May 24, 1985.

Balance	$1457
Freight	$ 149
Total	$1606
Date	May 15, 1985
Terms	3/10, 2/30, n/60

5. _____

[12.5, •]   **7.** Find the inventory on December 31, 1985 for Beane and Company.

6. _____

INVENTORY SHEET

Beane and Company
Greenville, NC

Date December 31, 1985

QUANTITY	DESCRIPTION	√	PRICE	UNIT
15	Moccasins		$ 26.00	ea
20	Corduroy Skirt		31.50	ea
8	Icelandic Jackets		119.75	ea

7. _____

8. Find the cost of the goods sold.

FREDRICK'S	
Beginning Inventory	$25,752
Purchases	$ 8,945
Ending Inventory	$11,563

A retailer purchased quantities of the same digital watch three times during an inventory period. The first purchase was 17 watches at $26.50 each; the second, 10 at $29.75 each; and the third, 16 at $31.80 each. In all, 18 watches were sold (25 watches were in inventory). Net sales were $855.

9. Evaluate the ending inventory by FIFO.

10. Find the gross profit using FIFO.

Career: Accountant/Certified Public Accountant This is Maria Gamboa Farrell. She is a Certified Public Accountant (CPA). To become a CPA you must study and pass a special CPA test. You also need work experience. The rewards are great. You become more valuable to others and can obtain a salary from $30,000 to an almost unlimited amount.

All of the mathematics in this book is relevant to Maria's work, but the most important concepts are those of ratio and interest. Maria has always enjoyed mathematics as it has played a vital role in her business and personal life. A firm background in mathematics allows her to make confident, informed decisions regarding financial statements, investments, and taxes. Maria is more qualified mathematically than most CPAs as she has a BS degree in Mathematics. She also has an MS degree in Accounting and a Master's degree in Business Administration.

Maria thinks that the computer will be used more and more in the future to improve productivity. She advises anyone considering accounting as a career to take as many computer courses as possible.

13
DEPRECIATION

READINESS CHECK—SKILLS FOR CHAPTER 13

Add.

1. $911.11
   797.22
+ 683.33

Subtract.

2. $4687.50 − $512.50

3. Multiply.   0.14 × $2925

4. Multiply.   Round the answer to the nearest cent.   0.25 × $2193.75

5. What is 12% of $5500?

13.1 DEPRECIATION: THE STRAIGHT-LINE METHOD

OBJECTIVE

After finishing Section 13.1, you should be able to:

■ Prepare a depreciation schedule using the straight-line method.

As defined by the American Institute of Certified Public Accountants, *depreciation* is "an accounting principle which aims to distribute the cost of tangible capital assets, less salvage value (if any), over the estimated useful life of the asset in a systematic and rational manner. It is a process of allocation of cost, not of valuation."

Let us try to comprehend this somewhat complicated definition in terms of an example. A company buys an office machine for $5200 on January 1 of a given year. The machine is expected to last for eight years after which its *trade-in value*, or *salvage value*, will be $1100. Over its lifetime it declines in value or *depreciates* $5200 − $1100, or $4100. The decline in value from $5200 to $1100 can occur in many ways, as shown below.

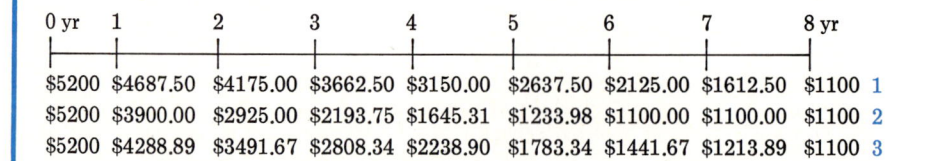

0 yr	1	2	3	4	5	6	7	8 yr	
$5200	$4687.50	$4175.00	$3662.50	$3150.00	$2637.50	$2125.00	$1612.50	$1100	1
$5200	$3900.00	$2925.00	$2193.75	$1645.31	$1233.98	$1100.00	$1100.00	$1100	2
$5200	$4288.89	$3491.67	$2808.34	$2238.90	$1783.34	$1441.67	$1213.89	$1100	3

For financial accounting purposes, there are several frequently used methods to compute depreciation. In the above table, Method 1 is called the *straight-line method*, Method 2 the *double declining-balance method*, and Method 3 the *sum-of-the-years'-digits method*. We shall consider these and others.

■ THE STRAIGHT-LINE METHOD

Suppose, for the machine above, the company figures the decline in value to be the *same* each year, that is $\frac{1}{8}$ or 12.5% of $4100, which is $512.50. After one year the *salvage value*, or simply *value*, is

$5200 − $512.50, or $4687.50.

After two years it is

$4687.50 − $512.50, or $4175.00

13.1 DEPRECIATION: THE STRAIGHT-LINE METHOD

After three years it is

$4175.00 − $512.50, or $3662.50,

and so on.

> For straight-line depreciation,
>
> a) The total depreciation = Cost − Salvage value.
>
> b) The annual depreciation = $\dfrac{\text{Cost} - \text{Salvage value}}{\text{Expected life}}$.
>
> c) The rate of depreciation = $\dfrac{\text{Annual depreciation}}{\text{Total depreciation}}$.

Example 1 For the following item, find the total depreciation, annual depreciation, and rate of depreciation:

Item: Office machine;
Cost = $5200;
Expected life = 8 years:
Salvage value = $1100.

Solution

a) The total depreciation = Cost − Salvage value
= $5200 − $1100
= $4100

b) The annual depreciation = $\dfrac{\text{Cost} - \text{Salvage value}}{\text{Expected life}}$

$= \dfrac{\$5200 - \$1100}{8}$

$= \dfrac{\$4100}{8}$

= $512.50

c) The rate of depreciation = $\dfrac{\text{Annual depreciation}}{\text{Total depreciation}}$

$= \dfrac{\$512.50}{\$4100}$

= 0.125, or 12.5%

In many cases salvage values are considered to be $0, but not always.

DO EXERCISE 1.

A depreciation schedule gives a complete list of the values and total depreciation throughout the life of an item.

Example 2 Prepare a depreciation schedule for the office machine discussed in Example 1.

---

1. For the following item, find the total depreciation, annual depreciation, and rate of depreciation:

   Item: Automobile
   Cost = $8700
   Expected life = 5 years
   Salvage value = $1600

ANSWER ON PAGE A–32

2. Prepare a depreciation schedule for the automobile discussed in Margin Exercise 1, using the blank table below. Round answers to the nearest cent.

Year	Rate of depreciation	Annual depreciation	Value	Total depreciation
0				
1				
2				
3				
4				
5				

DEPRECIATION

Solution

Year	Rate of depreciation	Annual depreciation	Value	Total depreciation
0			$5200	
1	$\frac{1}{8}$ or 12.5%	$512.50	4687.50	$ 512.50
2	12.5%	512.50	4175.00	1025.00
3	12.5%	512.50	3662.50	1537.50
4	12.5%	512.50	3150.00	2050.00
5	12.5%	512.50	2637.50	2562.50
6	12.5%	512.50	2125.00	3075.00
7	12.5%	512.50	1612.50	3587.50
8	12.5%	512.50	1100.00	4100.00

1. The rate of depreciation is the same each year.

2. The annual depreciation is the same each year.

3. We find the values by starting with the initial cost, $5200, and successively subtracting $512.50. For example, $5200 − $512.50 = $4687.50. Then $4687.50 − $512.50 = $4175.00, and so on.

4. We find the total depreciations by starting with $512.50 after the first year and successively adding $512.50. For example, $512.50 + $512.50 = $1025.00. Then $1025.00 + $512.50 = $1537.50, and so on.

DO EXERCISE 2.

Why do we call this *straight-line depreciation*? If we make a graph relating values to time, we see that the values lie in a straight line.

ANSWER ON PAGE A–32

13.1 DEPRECIATION: THE STRAIGHT-LINE METHOD

NAME _____ CLASS _____ ANSWERS

EXERCISE SET 13.1

■ For each item given below, (a) find the total depreciation, and (b) find the annual depreciation.

1. Item: Automobile
   Cost = $8000
   Expected life = 4 years
   Salvage value = $2000

2. Item: Automobile
   Cost = $12,000
   Expected life = 3 years
   Salvage value = $4800

3. Item: Postage machine
   Cost = $450
   Expected life = 8 years
   Salvage value = $0

4. Item: Typewriter
   Cost = $2500
   Expected life = 6 years
   Salvage value = $0

5. Item: Building
   Cost = $50,000
   Expected life = $33\frac{1}{3}$ years
   Salvage value = $0

6. Item: Building
   Cost = $100,000
   Expected life = 40 years
   Salvage value = $0

Prepare a depreciation schedule for the situation in:

7. Exercise 1.

Year	Rate of depreciation	Annual depreciation	Value	Total depreciation
0				
1				
2				
3				
4				

8. Exercise 2.

Year	Rate of depreciation	Annual depreciation	Value	Total depreciation
0				
1				
2				
3				

1. _____

2. _____

3. _____

4. _____

5. _____

6. _____

DEPRECIATION

9. Exercise 3.

Year	Rate of depreciation	Annual depreciation	Value	Total depreciation
0				
1				
2				
3				
4				
5				
6				
7				
8				

10. Exercise 4.

Year	Rate of depreciation	Annual depreciation	Value	Total depreciation
0				
1				
2				
3				
4				
5				
6				

11. For the situation in Exercise 5, find the total depreciation, annual depreciation, and values after the first and second years.

12. For the situation in Exercise 6, find the total depreciation, annual depreciation, and values after the first and second years.

13.2 DEPRECIATION: THE DECLINING-BALANCE METHOD

■ DOUBLE DECLINING BALANCE

A company buys a machine for $5200. The machine is expected to last for eight years after which its salvage value will be $1100. The straight-line rate of depreciation would be $\frac{1}{8}$, or 12.5%. Depreciation can be deducted as a business expense when a business computes its taxes. When a business is starting out it has many expenses and less income and therefore needs all the tax advantages it can get. For this, and other reasons, the Internal Revenue Service has allowed certain assets to be depreciated at a rate that is larger than the straight-line rate, but *no more* than twice the straight-line rate. (Such a rate could be, for example, $1\frac{1}{4}$, $1\frac{1}{2}$, or 2 times the straight-line rate.) Suppose for the above that the rate is $2 \cdot \frac{1}{8}$, or 25%. This is called the *double declining-balance method*. Then the value after one year is

$5200 - (25\% \times \$5200)$ We subtract 25% of the initial value.
$= \$5200 - (0.25 \times \$5200)$
$= \$5200 - \$1300$
$= \$3900.$

After two years it is

$\$3900 - (0.25 \times \$3900)$ We subtract 25% of the preceding value.
$= \$3900 - \$975$
$= \$2925.$

After three years it is

$\$2925 - (0.25 \times \$2925)$
$= \$2925 - \$731.25$
$= \$2193.75.$

After four years it is

$\$2193.75 - (0.25 \times \$2193.75)$
$= \$2193.75 - \$548.44$ Rounded to the nearest cent
$= \$1645.31,$

and so on.

Example 1 Prepare a depreciation schedule for the situation below. Use the double declining-balance method.

    Item: Office machine
    Cost = $5200
    Expected life = 8 years
    Salvage value = $1100

OBJECTIVE

After finishing Section 13.2, you should be able to:

■ Prepare a depreciation schedule using the double declining-balance method.

468   DEPRECIATION

1. Prepare a depreciation schedule for the item below. Use the double declining-balance method.

Item: Automobile

Cost = $8700

Expected life = 5 years

Salvage value = $1600

Year	Rate of depreciation	Annual depreciation	Value	Total depreciation
0				
1				
2				
3				
4				
5				

ANSWER ON PAGE A-33

Solution

Year	Rate of depreciation	Annual depreciation	Value	Total depreciation
0			$5200	
1	$\frac{2}{8}$ or 25%	$1300.00	3900.00	$1300
2	25%	975.00	2925.00	2275
3	25%	731.25	2193.75	3006.25
4	25%	548.44	1645.31	3554.69
5	25%	411.33	1233.98	3966.02
6		133.98	1100.00	4100.00
7		0 *	1100.00 *	4100.00 *
8		0	1100.00	4100.00

1. The rate of depreciation is the same each year: twice the straight-line rate.

2. We find the values by starting with the initial cost, $5200, and successively subtracting 0.25 times the value. For example, $5200 − (0.25 × $5200) = $3900. Then, $3900 − (0.25 × $3900) = $2925, and so on.

3. We find the annual depreciations when we multiply each successive value by 0.25. For example, 0.25 × $5200 = $1300, and 0.25 × $3900 = $975.

DO EXERCISE 1.

---

* Note that

$1233.98 − (0.25 × $1233.98) = $1233.98 − $308.50
= $925.48,

but the value cannot drop below the salvage value. Thus, after $1233.98 the next value becomes $1100.00, and the annual depreciation for that year is $1233.98 − $1100.00, or $133.98.

EXERCISE SET 13.2

■ Prepare a depreciation schedule for each situation. Use the double declining-balance method.

1. *Item:* Automobile
   Cost = $8000
   Expected life = 4 years
   Salvage value = $2000

Year	Rate of depreciation	Annual depreciation	Value	Total depreciation
0				
1				
2				
3				
4				

2. *Item:* Automobile
   Cost = $12,000
   Expected life = 3 years
   Salvage value = $4800

Year	Rate of depreciation	Annual depreciation	Value	Total depreciation
0				
1				
2				
3				

3. *Item:* Typewriter
   Cost = $2500
   Expected life = 6 years
   Salvage value = $0

Year	Rate of depreciation	Annual depreciation	Value	Total depreciation
0				
1				
2				
3				
4				
5				
6				

DEPRECIATION

4. *Item:* Postage machine
Cost = $450
Expected life = 8 years
Salvage value = $0

Year	Rate of depreciation	Annual depreciation	Value	Total depreciation
0				
1				
2				
3				
4				
5				
6				
7				
8				

5. *Item:* Computer
Cost = $5400
Expected life = 5 years
Salvage value = $1000

Year	Rate of depreciation	Annual depreciation	Value	Total depreciation
0				
1				
2				
3				
4				
5				

For each item given below, find the annual depreciation, the rate of depreciation, and the values after the first and second years. Use the declining-balance method and a rate that is $1\frac{1}{2}$ times the straight-line rate.

6. *Item:* Building
Cost = $50,000
Expected life = $33\frac{1}{3}$ years
Salvage value = $0

7. *Item:* Building
Cost = $100,000
Expected life = 40 years
Salvage value = $0

13.3 DEPRECIATION: THE SUM-OF-THE-YEARS'-DIGITS METHOD

◻ DEPRECIATION FRACTIONS

Another method of depreciation, which allows larger amounts of depreciation in early years and smaller amounts in later years, is the *sum-of-the-years'-digits method*. Each year a different rate (a fraction) of depreciation is used.

Example 1 For the item below, (a) find the depreciation fractions, and (b) find the depreciation and values after one year and after two years.

    Item: Office machine   Expected life = 8 years
           Cost = $5200   Salvage value = $1100

Solution

a) To find the depreciation we first find the sum-of-the-years' digits:

$8 + 7 + 6 + 5 + 4 + 3 + 2 + 1 = 36$*

The number 36 will be the denominator of each fraction. We then find the depreciation fractions (rates) by dividing each number in the sum by 36:

$$\frac{8}{36}, \frac{7}{36}, \frac{6}{36}, \frac{5}{36}, \frac{4}{36}, \frac{3}{36}, \frac{2}{36}, \frac{1}{36}.$$

b) The total depreciation is $5200 − $1100, or $4100. The depreciation the first year is

$$\frac{8}{36} \times \$4100 = \frac{8 \times \$4100}{36} = \frac{\$32{,}800}{36}$$

              = $911.11.   Round to the nearest cent

The value after one year is

$5200 − $911.11,   or $4288.89.

The depreciation the second year is

$$\frac{7}{36} \times \$4100 = \frac{7 \times \$4100}{36} = \frac{\$28{,}700}{36} = \$797.22.$$

The value after two years is

$4288.89 − $797.22,   or $3491.67.

DO EXERCISE 1.

---

*There is a formula for doing this faster (*n* represents the expected life):

$$n + \cdots + 3 + 2 + 1 = \frac{n \cdot (n + 1)}{2}.$$

Thus, $8 + 7 + 6 + 5 + 4 + 3 + 2 + 1 = (8 \cdot 9)/2 = 72/2 = 36$; multiply the expected life by one more than the expected life and divide by 2.

OBJECTIVES

After finishing Section 13.3, you should be able to:

◻ Find the depreciation fractions for a sum-of-the-years'-digits method.

◼◻ Prepare a depreciation schedule using the sum-of-the-years'-digits method.

1. For the item below, (a) find the depreciation fractions, and (b) find the depreciation and values after one year, two years, and three years.

   Item: Automobile
   Cost = $8700
   Expected life = 5 years
   Salvage value = $1600

ANSWER ON PAGE A–34

472

2. Prepare a depreciation schedule for the situation below. Use the sum-of-the-years'-digits method.

Cost = $8700

Expected life = 5 years

Salvage value = $1600

Year	Rate of depreciation	Annual depreciation	Value	Total depreciation
0				
1				
2				
3				
4				
5				

DEPRECIATION

●● SUM-OF-THE-YEARS'-DIGITS METHOD

Example 2 Prepare a depreciation schedule for the situation below. Use the sum-of-the-years'-digits method.

Cost = $5200

Expected life = 8 years

Salvage value = $1100

Solution

Year	Rate of depreciation	Annual depreciation	Value	Total depreciation
0			$5200	
1	$\frac{8}{36}$ or 22.2%	$911.11	4288.89	$ 911.11
2	$\frac{7}{36}$ or 19.4%	797.22	3491.67	1708.33
3	$\frac{6}{36}$ or 16.7%	683.33	2808.34	2391.66
4	$\frac{5}{36}$ or 13.9%	569.44	2238.90	2961.10
5	$\frac{4}{36}$ or 11.1%	455.56	1783.34	3416.66
6	$\frac{3}{36}$ or 8.3%	341.67	1441.67	3758.33
7	$\frac{2}{36}$ or 5.6%	227.78	1213.89	3986.11
8	$\frac{1}{36}$ or 2.8%	113.89	1100.00	4100.00

1. The rate of depreciation gets lower each year.

2. We find the annual depreciations first. To do this we multiply the total depreciation by each fraction. For example, $\frac{8}{36} \times \$4100 = \$911.11$, $\frac{7}{36} \times \$4100 = \$797.22$, and so on.

3. We find the values by subtracting each annual depreciation in succession. For example, $5200 - $911.11 = $4288.89, $4288.89 - $797.22 = $3491.67, and so on.

DO EXERCISE 2.

ANSWER ON PAGE A-34

EXERCISE SET 13.3

■ For each situation described below, find the depreciation factions. Use the sum-of-the-years'-digits method.

1. *Item:* Automobile
   Cost = $8000
   Expected life = 4 years
   Salvage value = $2000

2. *Item:* Automobile
   Cost = $12,000
   Expected life = 3 years
   Salvage value = $4800

3. *Item:* Postage machine
   Cost = $450
   Expected life = 8 years
   Salvage value = $0

4. *Item:* Typewriter
   Cost = $2500
   Expected life = 6 years
   Salvage value = $0

■ ■ Use the sum-of-the-years'-digits method to prepare a depreciation schedule for the situation in:

5. Exercise 1.

Year	Rate of depreciation	Annual depreciation	Value	Total depreciation
0				
1				
2				
3				
4				

6. Exercise 2.

Year	Rate of depreciation	Annual depreciation	Value	Total depreciation
0				
1				
2				
3				

474 DEPRECIATION

ANSWERS

7. Exercise 3.

Year	Rate of depreciation	Annual depreciation	Value	Total depreciation
0				
1				
2				
3				
4				
5				
6				
7				
8				

8. Exercise 4.

Year	Rate of depreciation	Annual depreciation	Value	Total depreciation
0				
1				
2				
3				
4				
5				
6				

For each situation, find the depreciation fractions, the annual depreciation, and the values after the first and second years. Use the sum-of-the-years'-digits method.

9. Item: Building
Cost = $80,000
Expected life = 25 years
Salvage value = $0

10. Item: Building
Cost = $100,000
Expected life = 40 years
Salvage value = $0

13.4 DEPRECIATION: ACRS AND FEDERAL TAXES

How does a company go about choosing a depreciation method? The following comments may be helpful.

Straight-Line Method. This method is the most often used. It allows for consistent yearly depreciation over the life of the asset, and has an advantage over the accelerated methods in that it allows for higher profits (before taxes) in the early years of a business.

Declining Balance Method and Sum-of-the-Years'-Digits Method. These methods are used when management wants a large depreciation expense in the beginning years of an asset's life. The reason for this could be to write off more depreciation on a machine that will be more efficient when it is new. Another reason could be the tax advantage of having a larger expense in the early years of an asset's life, thus less income tax in those early years, when a new business is usually struggling.

Units of Production Method. Other "consistent" methods are allowed. Suppose, for example, that an automobile manufacturer buys a machine and knows that it will be good for the production of 100,000 units of a part regardless of the number of years it will be used. If in the first year 40,000 units are produced, depreciation will be 40,000 ÷ 100,000, or 40% of the machine's cost.

ACRS AND TAX DEPRECIATION

The *1981 Economic Recovery Act* completely changed depreciation write-off as applied to taxes. The *Accelerated Cost Recovery System (ACRS)* has replaced other depreciation methods for those assets placed in service after 1980. ACRS places all depreciable assets in one of four categories:

3-Year Property: autos, light equipment, race horses.

5-Year Property: heavy trucks, most manufacturing equipment.

10-Year Property: certain public utility property as well as manufactured homes, railroad tank cars, certain coal utilization property of public utilities.

15-Year Property: most real estate and certain other utility property.

The Act sets laws regarding percentages to be used to write off the cost recovery (depreciation) of the asset.

It should be noted that ACRS is for tax purposes and the results can differ greatly between ACRS and the other methods discussed. ACRS was "invented" in an attempt to encourage private sector businesses to invest in new assets and therefore help the economy rebound from recession. Examples 1 and 2 will demonstrate the differing results. ACRS is, simply stated, a special write-off method involving declining balance and straight-line depreciation.

OBJECTIVE

After finishing Section 13.4, you should be able to:

- Prepare a depreciation schedule using ACRS.

DEPRECIATION

1. Prepare a depreciation schedule for the item listed below. Use ACRS.

Item: Race horse
Cost = $300,000
Expected life = 3 years (by law)

Year	Rate of depreciation	Annual depreciation	Value	Total depreciation
0				
1				
2				
3				

Below is a table of the percentages for three- and five-year property.

Year	3-Year Property	5-Year Property
1	25%	15%
2	38%	22%
3	37%	21%
4	—	21%
5	—	21%

The Act specifies that the salvage value will be $0.

Example 1 Prepare a depreciation schedule for the item discussed below. Use ACRS.

Item: Automobile
Cost = $10,000
Expected life = 3 years (by law)

Solution

a) First, look for the percentages on the 3-year table.

b) Then, multiply the percentages by the $10,000 cost.

Year 1: 0.25 × $10,000 = $ 2500
Year 2: 0.38 × $10,000 = $ 3800
Year 3: 0.37 × $10,000 = $ 3700
Total Cost Recovery $10,000

The depreciation schedule is as follows.

Year	Rate of depreciation	Annual depreciation	Value	Total depreciation
0			$10,000	
1	25%	$2,500	7,500	$2,500
2	38%	3,800	3,700	6,300
3	37%	3,700	0	10,000

DO EXERCISE 1.

Example 2 Prepare a depreciation schedule for the item discussed below. Use ACRS.

Item: Machine which molds engine blocks
Cost = $250,000
Expected life = 5 years (by law)

ANSWER ON PAGE A–35

13.4 DEPRECIATION: ACRS AND FEDERAL TAXES

Solution

a) First, look for the percentages on the 5-year table.

b) Then, multiply the percentages by the $250,000 cost.

Year 1: 0.15 × $250,000 = $ 37,500
Year 2: 0.22 × $250,000 = $ 55,000
Year 3: 0.21 × $250,000 = $ 52,500
Year 4: 0.21 × $250,000 = $ 52,500
Year 5: 0.21 × $250,000 = $ 52,500
Total Cost recovery $250,000

The depreciation schedule is as follows.

Year	Rate of depreciation	Annual depreciation	Value	Total depreciation
0			$250,000	
1	15%	$37,500	212,500	$ 37,500
2	22%	55,000	157,500	92,500
3	21%	52,500	105,000	145,000
4	21%	52,500	52,500	197,500
5	21%	52,500	0	250,000

DO EXERCISE 2.

The following are the percentages for 10-Year property and 15-Year property.*

10-Year Property

1st year	8%
2nd year	14%
3rd year	12%
4th through 6th year	10%
7th through 10th year	9%

15-Year Utility Property

1st year	5%
2nd year	10%
3rd year	9%
4th year	8%
5th and 6th year	7%
7th through 15th year	6%

2. Prepare a depreciation schedule. Use ACRS.

   Item: Heavy truck
   Cost = $200,000
   Expected life = 5 years (by law)

Year	Rate of depreciation	Annual depreciation	Value	Total depreciation
0				
1				
2				
3				
4				
5				

ANSWER ON PAGE A–35

---

* There are many details of qualification that will not be gone into here. For example, the tables change after Dec 31, 1984. Also, some tables and computations depend on the month property goes into service.

NAME _____ CLASS _____

EXERCISE SET 13.4

■ Prepare a depreciation schedule for each situation. Use ACRS.

1. *Item:* Automobile
   Cost = $15,000
   Expected life = 3 years (by law)

Year	Rate of depreciation	Annual depreciation	Value	Total depreciation
0				
1				
2				
3				

2. *Item:* Race horse
   Cost = $280,000
   Expected life = 3 years (by law)

Year	Rate of depreciation	Annual depreciation	Value	Total depreciation
0				
1				
2				
3				

3. *Item:* Heavy truck
   Cost = $210,000
   Expected life = 5 years (by law)

Year	Rate of depreciation	Annual depreciation	Value	Total depreciation
0				
1				
2				
3				
4				
5				

4. *Item:* Molding machine
   Cost: $80,000
   Expected Life = 5 years (by law)

Year	Rate of depreciation	Annual depreciation	Value	Total depreciation
0				
1				
2				
3				
4				
5				

5. *Item:* Manufactured home
   Cost: $130,000
   Expected Life = 10 years (by law)

Year	Rate of depreciation	Annual depreciation	Value	Total depreciation
0				
1				
2				
3				
4				
5				
6				
7				
8				
9				
10				

TEST OR REVIEW—CHAPTER 13

Consider this situation when answering each question below:

Item: Manufacturing equipment
Cost: $8500,
Expected life = 5 years
Salvage value = $0

[13.1, ●]   **1.** Prepare a depreciation schedule. Use the straight-line method.

Year	Rate of depreciation	Annual depreciation	Value	Total depreciation
0				
1				
2				
3				
4				
5				

[13.2, ●]   **2.** Prepare a depreciation schedule. Use the double declining-balance method.

Year	Rate of depreciation	Annual depreciation	Value	Total depreciation
0				
1				
2				
3				
4				
5				

[13.3, ●]   **3.** Find the depreciation fractions for the sum-of-the-years'-digits method.

482   DEPRECIATION

[13.3, ●●]   **4.** Prepare a depreciation schedule. Use the sum-of-the-years'-digits method.

Year	Rate of depreciation	Annual depreciation	Value	Total depreciation
0				
1				
2				
3				
4				
5				

[13.4, ●]   **5.** Prepare a depreciation schedule. Use ACRS.

Year	Rate of depreciation	Annual depreciation	Value	Total depreciation
0				
1				
2				
3				
4				
5				

Career: Merchandising This is Michael Daryanani. Michael is the Manager of the downtown Indianapolis store of L. Strauss and Co, which sells men's and women's clothing.

Michael's work is in the field of merchandising. This field entails preparing a product for sale, pricing, cost markup, cost markdown, and sales forecasting. His work as manager also includes preparing work schedules of employees, as well as determining sales quotas.

People who work in the sale of clothing usually receive a base salary, but their income can be increased indefinitely by a bonus system. Each sale they make yields a commission, perhaps 6.8%. If, for a certain period of time, the total commission exceeds the base salary, then the employee receives the commission. If the total commission is less then the base salary, then the employee receives the base salary. This can result in a strong motivation to work for a higher pay through commisions.

Michael's life indeed portrays the self-made man. Business mathematics is very important in his work. His parents are from India, but he was born and raised in Hong Kong. It was there that he began working in clothing sales. He moved to this country and began work as a sales clerk for his present employer. From that position he has been promoted to manager of the firm's largest store. What is the secret of his success? The answer is hard work and dedication.

Michaels's hobbies include bowling and watching tennis, baseball, and football.

14
PRICING

READINESS CHECK—SKILLS FOR CHAPTER 14

Find

1. $63.29 − $49.95
2. $199.95 − $129.95
3. 0.20 × $110
4. 0.40 × $12.00
5. $12.00 ÷ 1.40
6. $229 ÷ 0.60
7. What percent of $289 is $109?
8. What is 25% of $579?

14.1 PRICING GOODS: COST PRICE BASIS

The pricing of goods and services is important. Prices must be competitive, yet assure the business person a profit. In this chapter we study methods of pricing.

■ MARKUP

The difference between the selling price and the cost of an article to a retailer is the *markup*.

> Markup = Selling price − Cost

Example 1 A retailer's cost for a mattress was $47.25. The mattress sold for $68.88. What was the markup?

Solution Find the markup.

Markup = Selling price − Cost
= $68.88 − $47.25 = $21.63

The markup was $21.63.

DO EXERCISE 1.

■■ RETAILER'S COST

Transportation charges are considered part of the retailer's cost.

Example 2 A retailer pays $349.97 for a stereo receiver and $3.74 in transportation charges. What is the retailer's cost?

OBJECTIVES

After finishing Section 14.1, you should be able to:

■ Find the markup.
■■ Determine the retailer's cost.
■■■ Express markup as a percent of cost.
■■■■ Calculate selling price.
■■■■■ Find the most a retailer should pay for goods.

1. A retailer's cost for a digital watch was $48.75. The watch sold for $72.30. What was the markup?

ANSWER ON PAGE A–36

Solution Find the retailer's cost.

Retailer's cost = Transportation charges + Cost of article
= $3.74 + $349.97 = $353.71

The retailer's cost is $353.71.

DO EXERCISE 2.

2. A retailer pays $22 for an attaché case and $1.05 in transportation charges. What is the retailer's cost?

••• MARKUP AS A PERCENT OF COST

Sometimes markup is stated as a percent of cost. Suppose a retailer sells a black and white television that costs $54.75 for $79.95. The markup is $25.20. What percent of the cost is the markup? To find out we translate:

What percent of the cost is the markup?
$$x \cdot \$54.75 = \$25.20$$

To find the missing number, we divide:

$$x = \frac{\$25.20}{\$54.75} = 0.46 = 46\%.$$

We can formalize this as follows:

To find markup as a percent of cost,

a) **Find the markup;**

b) **Divide the markup by the cost; and**

c) **Convert to percent notation.**

Example 3 uses this procedure to solve the problem.

Example 3 A retailer sells a television that costs $54.75 for $79.95. What is the percent of markup based on cost?

Black & White TV
Quick start picture tube, solid state chassis, and much more. A terrific value! #21T63.

79⁹⁵

3. A retailer sells a color television that costs $342 for $520. What is the percent of markup based on cost?

Solution

a) Markup = Selling price − Cost
= $79.95 − $54.75   *Find the markup.*
= $25.20

b) $\dfrac{\text{Markup}}{\text{Cost}} = \dfrac{\$25.20}{\$54.75}$ *Divide the markup by the cost.*

= 0.46

c) = 46%   *Convert to percent notation.*

The percent of markup based on cost is 46%.

DO EXERCISE 3.

ANSWERS ON PAGE A−36

4. A retailer's cost for an electric griddle is $26.56. The retailer wants a 70% markup based on cost. What is the selling price?

5. A retailer knows that consumers will pay at most $5.00 for a tie and wants a 35% markup based on cost. What is the maximum cost that the retailer can pay for the tie?

ANSWERS ON PAGE A–36

PRICING

PRICING

A retailer may apply markup based on cost to set prices. Example 4 illustrates the procedure.

Example 4 A retailer's cost for a basketball is $10.15. The retailer wants an 80% markup based on cost. What is the selling price?

Solution

a) Find the markup based on cost.

Markup based on cost = Markup percent × Cost
= 80% × $10.15
= 0.80 × $10.15
= $8.12

b) Find the selling price.

Selling price = Cost + Markup based on cost
= $10.15 + $8.12
= $18.27

The selling price is $18.27.

DO EXERCISE 4.

RETAILER COST

When buying merchandise a retailer often knows from past experience how much consumers will pay for an item. When the selling price and markup based on cost are known, then the retailer can find the maximum cost that he or she can pay for the merchandise.

> **To find the maximum cost for a retailer.**
> a) Add 100% to the percent markup;
> b) Convert the answer from Step (a) to decimal notation;
> c) Divide the selling price by the answer to (b).

Example 5 A retailer knows that consumers will pay at most $12.00 for a shirt and wants a 40% markup based on cost. What is the maximum cost that the retailer can pay for the shirt?

Solution

a) 100% + 40% = 140%   Add 100% to the percent markup.

b)   140% = 1.40   Convert to decimal notation.

c) $\dfrac{\text{Selling price}}{1.40} = \dfrac{\$12.00}{1.40}$ Divide the selling price by 1.40.

= $8.57

The maximum cost that the retailer can pay is $8.57.

DO EXERCISE 5.

NAME _____ CLASS _____ ANSWERS

EXERCISE SET 14.1

■ Find the markup.

1.
Oldsmobile
Omega Brougham Sedan

Tinted glass, bucket seats, body side mouldings, rear defrost, air conditioning, sport mirrors, paint stripe, cruise control, tilt wheel, white wall tires, AM/FM stereo. #22598

$9495

Retailer's cost: $7596

2.
Oldsmobile
Firenza S

Coupe, tinted glass, sport mirrors, paint stripe, power steering, power brakes, super stock wheels, AM/FM stereo, 4 speed, front wheel drive, #22727

$7595

Retailer's cost: $5848

3.
WATERBED
LOWEST PRICE
IN TOWN
COMPLETE
175⁰⁰

Retailer's cost: $96

4.
ELECTRIC
BED
$695⁰⁰
Lifetime Guar.
Mattress

Retailer's cost: $452

5. A retailer's cost for an electric blanket was $21.88. It sold for $41.95. What was the markup?

6. A retailer's cost for a rug shampooer was $34.43. It sold for $44.95. What was the markup?

7. A retailer's cost for a ring was $235. It sold for $537. What was the markup?

8. A retailer's cost for a hot tub was $764. It sold for $1067. What was the markup?

■■ Find the retailer's cost.

9. A retailer pays $37.09 for a vacuum cleaner and $2.10 in transportation charges. What is the retailer's cost?

10. A retailer pays $7.75 for a digital alarm clock and $0.88 in transportation charges. What is the retailer's cost?

11. Skeii Pontiac pays $6400 for a Pontiac Phoenix and transportation charges of $350. What is Skeii Pontiac's cost?

1. _____

2. _____

3. _____

4. _____

5. _____

6. _____

7. _____

8. _____

9. _____

10. _____

11. _____

Copyright © 1984, by Addison-Wesley Publishing Company Inc. All rights reserved.

488 PRICING

ANSWERS

12. _____

13. _____

14. _____

15. _____

16. _____

17. _____

18. _____

19. _____

20. _____

21. _____

22. _____

12. Gabus Ford pays $4300 for a Ford Escort and $360 transportation charges. What is Gabus Ford's cost?

■■■ What is the percent of markup based on cost? Round to the nearest percent.

13.
MAGNAVOX 13" COLOR TV
WHILE 20 LAST
Model 4038
ONLY 1 PER CUSTOMER
100% Solid-State 13"
Diagonal Portable TV
$199

Retailer's cost: $145

14.
5 ONLY
PHILCO 19" COLOR
PORTABLE TV
Deluxe Features
No Dealers
$249

Retailer's cost: $180

15.
HOWARD MILLER FLOOR CLOCK
This contemporary floor clock is made of Carpathian olive ash burl and accented with chrome.
$571

Retailer's cost: $385

16.
CONTEMPORARY LOVESEAT
Striped Herculon in colors of gold, beige and brown. Oak wood trim with cane insert at base.
$349

Retailer's cost: $255

17. A retailer sells a travel alarm that costs $8.04 for $12.95. What is the percent of markup based on cost (to the nearest percent)?

18. A retailer sells an electric typewriter that costs $196.28 for $289.75. What is the percent of markup based on cost (to the nearest percent)?

■■ Find the selling price.

19.
MALIBU
Classic 2 Dr. V-8, auto, PS, PB, A/C, Tutone, extra nice.

Dealer's cost: $6780
Markup based on cost: 21%

20.
COUGAR
XR-7, V-8, auto, PS, PB, A/C, vinyl top, cloth seats.

Dealer's cost: $5975
Markup based on cost: 18%

21.
LYNX
4 cyl, 4 speed, PS, Like New.

Dealer's cost: $6490
Markup based on cost: 20%

22.
ZEPHYR
4 door, 6 cyl, auto, PS, PB, A/C, vinyl top.

Dealer's cost: $5200
Markup based on cost: 26%

EXERCISE SET 14.1

23. A retailer's cost for a black and white television is $124.28. The retailer would like a 28% markup based on cost. What is the selling price?

24. A retailer's cost for a can opener is $9.04. The retailer would like a 32% markup based on cost. What is the selling price?

Find the most a dealer should pay for these items. The selling price and markup based on cost are given.

25. NEW SHARP VX1184 PRINT & DISPLAY CALCULATOR 109.95
35%

26. BRAND NEW SELF-CORRECT ELEC. PORT. TYPEWRITERS 239.95
27%

27. BRAND NEW SINGLE ELEMENT ELECTRIC TYPEWRITERS 495.00
32%

28. NEW SILVER-REED PRINT & DISPLAY CALCULATOR 69.95
28%

CHAIRS..

29. BRAND NEW CHROME FRAME UPHOLSTERED SWIVEL ARM 89.95
19%

30. BRAND NEW CHROMCRAFT HI-BACK SWIVEL ARM 219.95
26%

DESKS..

31. BRAND NEW WALNUT GRAIN 30x60 EXECUTIVE DESK 189.95
22%

32. BRAND NEW WALNUT GRAIN SECRETARIAL L-UNIT 269.95
31%

33. A retailer knows that consumers will pay at most $8.00 for a scarf and wants a 35% markup based on cost. What is the maximum cost that the retailer can pay for the scarf?

34. A retailer knows that consumers will pay at most $14.00 for jogging shorts and wants a 42% markup based on cost. What is the maximum cost that the retailer can pay for the shorts?

Complete the following table.

Item	Basic Cost for Retailer	Transportation Cost	Retailer's Cost	Selling Price	Markup Based on Cost
35. Iron	$12.99		$14.04	$20.98	
36. Crock pot		$1.57	$16.80		96%
37. Waffle grill	$13.56	$1.14		$25.25	
38. Fondue set		$1.14		$28.95	73%

ANSWERS

23. _____
24. _____
25. _____
26. _____
27. _____
28. _____
29. _____
30. _____
31. _____
32. _____
33. _____
34. _____
35. _____
36. _____
37. _____
38. _____

14.2 PRICING GOODS: SELLING PRICE BASIS

■ MARKUP AS A PERCENT OF SELLING PRICE

Sometimes markup is stated as a percent of the selling price. Suppose a retailer sells a microwave oven that costs $180 for $289. The markup is $109. What percent of the selling price is the markup? To find out we translate as follows:

What percent of the selling price is the markup?

$$x \cdot \$289 = \$109$$

To find the missing number, we divide:

$$x = \frac{\$109}{\$289} = 0.377 = 37.7\%$$

We can formalize this as follows:

> **To find markup as a percent of selling price,**
> a) **Find the markup;**
> b) **Divide the markup by the selling price; and**
> c) **Convert to percent notation.**

Example 1 uses this procedure to solve the problem.

Example 1 A retailer sells a microwave oven that costs $180 for $289. What is the percent of markup based on selling price (to the nearest percent)?

Solution

a) Markup = Selling price − Cost
       = $289 − $180   *Find the markup.*
       = $109

OBJECTIVES

After finishing Section 14.2, you should be able to:

■ Solve markup as a percent of selling price problems.
■■ Find the selling price.
■■■ Calculate dealer cost.

1. A retailer sold a color television that cost $342 for $520. What was the percent of markup based on the selling price (to the nearest percent)?

PRICING

b) $\dfrac{\text{Markup}}{\text{Selling price}} = \dfrac{\$109}{\$289}$ Divide the markup by the selling price

  $= 0.377$

c) $= 37.7\%$ Convert to percent notation.

The percent of markup based on the selling price is 38%.

DO EXERCISE 1.

Suppose a retailer sells a color television for $579. The markup based on the selling price is 25%. What is the markup; that is, what is 25% of the selling price? To find out we translate as follows:

What is 25% of the selling price?

x = 25% · $579

   = 0.25 · $579

   = $144.75

We can formalize this as follows:

To find the markup when the selling price and the percent of markup on the selling price are known,

a) **Convert the percent of markup to decimal notation;**

b) **Multiply this decimal by the selling price.**

Example 2 uses this procedure to solve the problem.

Example 2 The percent of markup based on the selling price of a color television was 25%. The selling price was $579. What was the markup?

2. The percent of markup based on the selling price of a refrigerator was 30%. The selling price was $580. What was the markup?

23″ diagonal measure Color TV
Early American styling in a beautiful Maple woodgrain finish. Features Chromacolor picture tube, Titan chassis with power sentry, color sentry, EVG electronic video guard tuning system, and 1 knob channel selector.

$579.00

Solution

a) 25% = 0.25   Convert the percent of markup to a decimal.

b) Markup = 0.25 × $579

           = $144.75   Multiply by the selling price.

The markup based on the selling price was $144.75.

DO EXERCISE 2.

ANSWERS ON PAGE A–36

14.2 PRICING GOODS: SELLING PRICE BASIS

●● SELLING PRICE

A retailer may apply markup based on the selling price to set prices. That is, if the retailer's cost and the percent of markup based on the selling price are known, then the selling price may be found.

> **To find the selling price when the cost and the percent of markup based on the selling price are known,**
> a) Subtract the percent of markup from 100%;
> b) Convert the answer from Step (a) to decimal notation;
> c) Divide the cost by this decimal.

Example 3 A retailer's cost for an electric typewriter is $229. The retailer wants a 40% markup based on the selling price. What is the selling price?

Solution

a) $100\% - 40\% = 60\%$ Subtract from 100%.

b) $60\% = 0.60$ Convert to decimal notation.

c) Selling price $= \dfrac{\$229}{0.60}$ Divide the cost by 0.60.

$\quad\quad\quad\quad\quad = \$381.67$

The selling price is $381.67.

DO EXERCISE 3.

●●● DEALER COST

When buying merchandise a retailer often knows how much customers will pay for an item. When the selling price and the markup based on the selling price are known, then the retailer can determine the maximum cost that he or she can pay for the merchandise.

> **To find the maximum cost for a retailer,**
> a) Find the markup;
> b) Subtract the markup from the selling price.

Example 4 A retailer knows that consumers will pay at most $12.00 for a shirt and wants a 40% markup based on the selling price. What is the maximum cost that the retailer may pay for the shirt?

Solution

a) Markup $= 40\% \times$ Selling price
$\quad\quad\quad\quad = 0.40 \times \$12.00$ Find the markup.
$\quad\quad\quad\quad = \$4.80$

b) Maximum cost $= \$12.00 - \$4.80$
$\quad\quad\quad\quad\quad\quad = \$7.20$ Subtract the markup from the selling price.

The maximum cost that the retailer can pay is $7.20.

DO EXERCISE 4.

---

3. A retailer's cost for a down jacket is $53.90. The retailer wants a 38% markup based on the selling price. What is the selling price?

4. A retailer knows that consumers will pay at most $5.00 for a tie and wants a 35% markup based on the selling price. What is the maximum cost that the retailer can pay for the tie?

ANSWERS ON PAGE A-36

NAME _____ CLASS _____

EXERCISE SET 14.2

■ Find the percent of markup to the nearest percent based on selling price. The retailer's cost is below each ad.

1. LADIES' ETONIC SKIRTS 18^{95}
   $14.97

2. MEN'S GOLF SHOES Etonic & Green Joys 19^{95}
   $13.96

3. UMBRELLAS 3^{95}
   $2.37

4. LADIES' #7 WOOD $$14^{95}$
   $10.00

Round the percent answers to the nearest percent.

5. A retailer sold a pack tent that cost $43.95 for $72.95. What was the percent of markup based on the selling price?

6. A retailer sold a desk lamp that cost $8.75 for $12.50. What was the percent of markup based on the selling price?

7. A retailer sold a rocking chair that cost $98.00 for $159.00. What was the percent of markup based on the selling price?

8. A retailer sold a telescope that cost $52.75 for $82.50. What was the percent of markup based on the selling price?

9. The percent of markup based on the selling price of a slide projector was 40%. The selling price was $122.50. What was the markup?

10. The percent of markup based on the selling price of a camera was 55%. The selling price was $419.95. What was the markup?

11. The percent of markup based on the selling price of a radio was 32%. The selling price was $69.95. What was the markup?

12. The percent of markup based on the selling price of a stereo was 27%. The selling price was $369.95. What was the markup?

ANSWERS

1. _____
2. _____
3. _____
4. _____
5. _____
6. _____
7. _____
8. _____
9. _____
10. _____
11. _____
12. _____

496 PRICING

Complete the table.

	Retailer's Cost	Markup Based on Selling Price	Selling Price
13.	$ 27.50	35%	
14.	$112	26%	
15.	$476	19%	
16.	$625	28%	

17. A retailer's cost for a calculator is $16.00. The retailer wants a 30% markup based on the selling price. What is the selling price?

18. A retailer's cost for a blender is $19.80. The retailer wants a 65% markup based on the selling price. What is the selling price?

Below each ad is the markup based on selling price. What is the most a dealer should pay for each item?

19.
TRUNDLE BED. COMP.
$279.95
VERY STURDY 312 COIL MATTRESSES

35%

20.
KING SIZE
$289.95
MATTRESS & BOX

40%

21.
HIDEABED MATTRESS
$49.95

45%

22.
WATER BED SHEETS
$34.95

42%

23. A retailer knows that consumers will pay at most $4.50 for a meat thermometer and wants a 17% markup based on the selling price. What is the maximum cost that the retailer can pay for the thermometer?

24. A retailer knows that consumers will pay at most $25.50 for a humidifier-vaporizer and wants a 28% markup based on the selling price. What is the maximum cost that the retailer can pay for the humidifier-vaporizer?

25. A retailer has $600 with which to buy shirts. Consumers will pay $11.99 for each shirt. The markup based on the selling price for each shirt is to be $33\frac{1}{3}$%. How many shirts can be purchased? How much is left over?

26. A retailer has $200 with which to buy neckties. Consumers will pay $4.99 for each tie. The markup based on the selling price is to be 29%. How many neckties can be purchased? How much is left over?

14.3 MARKDOWN

14.3 MARKDOWN

▪ MARKDOWN PROBLEMS

Sometimes businesses have sales. At that time merchandise is marked down. *Markdown* is the difference between the regular price and the sale price.

> Markdown = Regular price − Sale price

Example 1 A casting reel regularly priced at $63.29 is on sale for $49.95. What is the markdown?

Solution

$$\begin{aligned}\text{Markdown} &= \text{Regular price} - \text{Sale price}\\ &= \$63.29 - \$49.95\\ &= \$13.34\end{aligned}$$

The markdown is $13.34.

DO EXERCISE 1.

Markdown is sometimes stated as a percent. The markdown is the product of the percent of markdown and the regular price.

> Markdown = Percent of markdown × Regular price

Example 2 In the bookstore advertisement the markdown is 20%. The regular price of a book is $17.50. What is the markdown on the book?

Solution

$$\begin{aligned}\text{Markdown} &= \text{Percent of markdown} \times \text{Regular price}\\ &= 20\% \times \$17.50\\ &= 0.20 \times \$17.50\\ &= \$3.50\end{aligned}$$

The markdown is $3.50.

DO EXERCISE 2.

OBJECTIVES

After finishing Section 14.3, you should be able to:

▪ Find markdown.

▪▪ Determine the sale price.

▪▪▪ Calculate percent markdown on regular price.

▪▪▪▪ Calculate percent markdown on sale price.

1. A smoke detector regularly priced at $24.99 is on sale for $18.99. What is the markdown?

2. The regular price of a book is $23.00. What is the markdown when the percent of markdown is 20%?

ANSWERS ON PAGE A–36

497

3. An automobile is on sale at 15% off the regular price of $6578. What is the sale price?

PRICING

◉◉ SALE PRICE

Sale price = Regular price − Markdown

To find the sale price,
a) Find the markdown;
b) Subtract the markdown from the regular price.

Example 3 A suit is on sale at 20% off the regular price of $110. What is the sale price?

20% off our Quad® suit. Sale $88

Reg. $110. A highly versatile four-piece vested suit tailored in polyester double-knit. Classic styling includes a soft shoulder jacket with flapped patch pockets, reversible vest and two pairs of coordinating slacks. Fashion colors in regular, short and long sleeves.

Solution

a) Markdown = 20% × $110
            = 0.20 × $110   *Find the markdown.*
            = $22

b) Sale price = $110 − $22   *Subtract the markdown from the regular price.*
             = $88

The sale price is $88.

DO EXERCISE 3.

◉◉◉ MARKDOWN AS A PERCENT OF REGULAR PRICE

® Stereo Receiver
Reg. 199.95
129⁹⁵

ANSWER ON PAGE A–36

Suppose a retailer sold a stereo receiver regularly priced at $199.95 for $129.95. The markdown was $70.00. What percent of the regular price was the markdown? To find out we translate as follows:

What percent of the regular price is the markdown?
$$x \cdot \$199.95 = \$70.00$$

To find the missing number, we divide:

$$x = \frac{\$70.00}{\$199.95}$$

$$x = 0.35 = 35\%$$

We can formalize this as follows:

> **The percent of markdown on the regular price can be found by**
> a) **Finding the markdown;**
> b) **Dividing the markdown by the regular price.**

Example 4 uses this procedure to solve the problem.

Example 4 Find the percent of markdown on the regular price for the stereo receiver.

Solution

a) Markdown = $199.95 − $129.95
    = $70   *Find the markdown.*

b) Percent of markdown = $\frac{\$70}{\$199.95}$ *Divide by the regular price.*

    = 0.35
    = 35%

The percent of markdown on the regular price is 35%.

DO EXERCISE 4.

▞▞ MARKDOWN AS A PERCENT OF SALE PRICE

Suppose a retailer sold a stereo receiver regularly priced at $199.95 for $129.95. The markdown was $70.00. What percent of the sale price was the markdown? To find out we translate as follows:

What percent of the sale price is the markdown?
$$x \cdot \$129.95 = \$70.00$$

To find the missing number we divide:

$$x = \frac{\$70.00}{\$129.95}$$

$$x = 0.54 = 54\%$$

4. Find the percent of markdown on the regular price for the scanner (to the nearest percent).

UHF/VHF Scanner*
Reg. 169.95   **119⁹⁵**

ANSWER ON PAGE A–36

WASHER
18 lb. capacity Heavy duty, fabric softener & bleach, dispenser, 4 wash & rinse temp., Magic Clean lint filter, 4 wash cycles, 2 speeds.
Reg. $579 $368

5. Find the percent of markdown on the sale price for the washer (to the nearest percent).

PRICING

We can formalize this as follows:

> The percent of markdown on the sale price can be found by
> a) Finding the markdown;
> b) Dividing the markdown by the sale price.

Example 5 uses this procedure to solve the problem.

® Stereo Receiver
Reg. 199.95
129.95

Example 5 Find the percent of markdown on the sale price for the stereo receiver.

Solution

a) Markdown = $199.95 − $129.95
   = $70   *Find the markdown.*

b) Percent of markdown = $\dfrac{\$70}{\$129.95}$ *Divide by the sale price.*

   = 0.54
   = 54%

The percent of markdown on the sale price is 54%.

DO EXERCISE 5.

Examples 4 and 5 show that, while the markdown may be the same, it is advantageous for the retailer to advertise percent of markdown based on the sale price rather than on the regular price. A 54% markdown seems larger than a 35% markdown to the consumer.

EXERCISE SET 14.3

● Find the markdown.

1. reg. $189.50 CORNER SOLID OAK ETAGERE BY BUTLER. $148

2. reg. $229.50 COLONIAL SWIVEL ROCKER
Tufted back with wood trim, adjustable swivel base. Nylon cream color velvet. $168

3. reg. $789.50 SECRETARY DESK BY RIVERSIDE
For the small space, 26" wide. Solid oak and oak veneers, lighted top. $598

4. reg. $359.50 SOFA GAME TABLE BY LANE
Flip-top opens to expose backgammon game. $189

5. Clip & bring this coupon to Sunderland's Home Gallery
30% OFF Mannington JT88® Duracon® Never-wax Vinyl Flooring

Regular price: $456

6. Clip & bring this coupon to Sunderland's Home Gallery
40% OFF Merillat® Kitchen Cabinets

Regular price: $1850

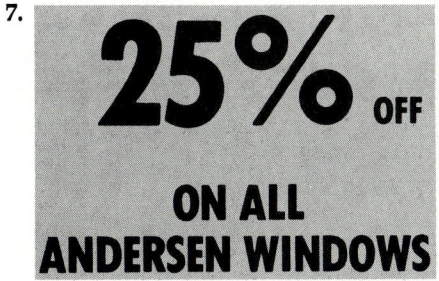

7. 25% OFF ON ALL ANDERSEN WINDOWS

Regular price: $387

8. 50% Off Henri Fountains & Bird Baths

Regular price: $26.00

9. A maintenance-free automobile battery regularly priced at $49.99 is on sale for $42.99. What is the markdown?

10. A spa regularly priced at $1695 is on sale for $1495. What is the markdown?

11. The regular price of patio furniture is $840. The sale price is 25% off the regular price. What is the markdown?

PRICING

12. The regular price of a tree fern is $6.98. The sale price is 29% off the regular price. What is the markdown?

▪▪ What is the sale price?

35% OFF OF SELECTED BICYCLES

13. Regular price: $460

14. Regular price: $285

15. A 14-piece cookware set is on sale at 30% off the regular price of $147.90. What is the sale price?

16. A sleeping bag is on sale at 35% off the regular price of $142.95. What is the sale price?

▪▪▪ Find the markdown as a percent of the regular price. Round to the nearest percent.

17. **DOUGLAS® POST HOLE DIGGER** REGULAR 15.99 — **12.88**
Wood handle. Perfect tool for putting up fences, mail boxes, clothesline poles and more.

18. **HEDGE TRIMMER** REGULAR 39.99 — **29.88**
Double insulated 13" hedge trimmer. 2.2 amp motor. Three position safety switch. 8118.

19. The regular price of an egg cooker is $17.90 and the sale price is $13.50. Find the percent of markdown on the regular price.

20. The regular price of a deep-fat fryer is $26.95 and the sale price is $18.75. Find the percent of markdown on the regular price.

▪▪ Find the markdown as a percent of the sale price. Round to the nearest percent.

21. **ATARI® 400 Personal Computer System** 268.99 Reg. 299.00

22. **commodore VIC-20** 188.99 Reg. 229.00

23. The regular price of a whirlpool bath is $249.95 and the sale price is $199.95. Find the percent of markdown on the sale price.

24. The regular price of a toaster is $22.95 and the sale price is $16.95. Find the percent of markdown on the sale price.

TEST OR REVIEW—CHAPTER 14

If you miss an item, review the indicated section and objective.

[14.1, •] **1.** A retailer's cost for the Toshiba is $52. What is the markup?

TOSHIBA KTS-3
FM Stereo and cassette player w/headset
$69.95

[14.1, •••] **2.** For the Toshiba find the percent of markup based on cost (round to the nearest percent).

[14.1, ••••] **3.** A retailer's cost for a bicycle is $87.88. The retailer wants a 37% markup based on the cost. What is the selling price?

[14.1, ••••] **4.** A retailer knows that customers will pay at most $35 for a sweater and wants a 40% markup based on cost. What is the most the retailer should pay for the sweater?

[14.2, •] **5.** A retailer's cost for the Sony is $525. Find the percent of markup based on selling price (round to the nearest percent).

SONY PORTABLE RECORDER
SL2000
• Slow-fast motion • Lightweight-9lbs.
• 5 hour beta • Auto rewind
• Audio dub
$759.95

[14.2, •] **6.** The percent of markup based on the selling price of the sofa was 34%. What was the markup?

BROYHILL TRADITIONAL SOFA
Crescent shaped with cinnamon background, blue and rust mini-print. 100% Scotchgard cotton.
$588

ANSWERS

1. _____

2. _____

3. _____

4. _____

5. _____

6. _____

504

PRICING

ANSWERS

[14.2, ●●] **7.** A retailer's cost for golf shoes is $6.50. The retailer wants a 42% markup based on the selling price. What is the selling price?

[14.2, ●●●] **8.** A dealer wants 42% markup based on selling price for the bedroom suite. What is the most the dealer should pay?

DIXIE BEDROOM SUITE
Traditional honey pine ... consists of dresser, chest and bookcase headboard and matching two drawer nightstand. **$939**

7. _____

8. _____

[14.3, ●] **9.** A Baldwin Piano regularly priced at $2695 is on sale for $1347.50. What is the markdown?

PIANOS
WAS   NOW
Baldwin built piano 2695 $1347.50

[14.3, ●●] **10.** A tub enclosure regularly priced at $238 is on sale at 25% off its regular price. What is the sale price?

9. _____

[14.3, ●●●] **11.** Find the percent markdown on the regular price for an Oxford Cloth shirt. (round to the nearest percent).

FAMOUS LABEL CLASSIC BUTTON DOWN
OXFORD CLOTH SHIRTS!
• COTTON-POLY BLENDS!
• WHITE, PASTELS!
• FINE LINE STRIPES!
• RUFFLE NECKS!
19⁹⁰
REG. $24

10. _____

11. _____

[14.3, ●●●●] **12.** Find the percent of markdown on the sale price for the mink coat (round to the nearest percent).

Natural Blackglama® mink coats. Originally $5,995. Now $3,995.

12. _____

15
PAYROLL

Career: Realtor This is Patty Sanchez Wignall. Patty is a realtor, selling homes for the F. C. Tucker Realty Company of Carmel, Indiana. Raised in Trinidad, Colorado, she moved to Evansville, Indiana, where she attended Lockyears Business College to take a Real Estate Sales course. Patty is firm in her belief that mathematics is very important to her work.

Patty's salary is based strictly on a commission basis. If she does not sell any houses, she does not make any money. Suppose you wanted to sell your home and you asked Patty and her real estate firm to represent you. Patty and her firm are then said to have your listing. You would agree on a commission on the sale of your house, say 7%. When the house is sold, you must pay this commission. If Patty and her firm actually sell the house for you, then Patty receives 55% of the 7%, and her firm receives 45%. Suppose another firm actually sells the home. In such a case that firm receives half of the 7%, and Patty's firm receives half. Patty would then receive half of half, or one-fourth of the commission. Thus, fractions and percents are quite pertinent to a realtor.

What makes Patty a top-notch realtor? She is a good listener, is willing to spend lots of time and effort, and goes the extra mile to satisfy her clients. She is a person of high integrity, looks and acts successful, and continues to study finance, mathematics, and other related subjects to improve herself.

A realtor can have a wide range of salaries, from $0 to $20,000 to $80,000 per year, depending on one's effort and success. Patty feels that for the limited amount of education required, this field offers excellent potential income.

Patty's hobbies include golfing, water polo, fishing, dancing, knitting, and water skiing.

READINESS CHECK — SKILLS FOR CHAPTER 15

Add.

1. $23.12 + $14.71 + $16.25
2. $202.30 + $80.33

Subtract.

3. $247.20 − $220
4. $276 − $28.80

Find.

5. 6.7% of $34,000
6. 9.35% of $35,200

Divide.

7. $16,800 ÷ 12
8. $9000 ÷ 26

15.1 EMPLOYEE WAGES

What you earn may be figured on an hourly, production unit, salary, commission, or other basis. You receive paychecks for your earnings less deductions. These important financial matters will be studied in this chapter.

GROSS EARNINGS

The amount of money earned before deductions is called *gross earnings*. Working time up to and including 40 hours a week is *regular time*.

Example 1 Find the gross earnings of a person who accepts the job shown below and works 36 hours.

> Sales-No sales skills necessary
> **EARN $4/HR**
> Flexible hours to distribute Zip Code Directories in own area. Over 18 years. CALL 280-3770 8 to 5 PM.

Solution

Gross earnings = Hourly wage × Hours worked
= $4.00 × 36
= $144.00

The gross earnings are $144.00.

DO EXERCISE 1.

The Fair Labor Standards Act requires a company that does business in more than one state to pay employees time and a half for overtime. This means that an employee is paid $1\frac{1}{2}$ times the hourly rate for every hour worked over 40 in one week.

OBJECTIVE

After finishing Section 15.1, you should be able to:

■ Calculate gross earnings for regular and overtime work.

1. Find the gross earnings for an individual who accepts the job of medical records transcriptionist and works 29 hours.

> **Employment**
> MEDICAL RECORDS transcriptionist, parttime, hours flexible, experience preferred. $2.98 an hour. Story County Hospital, Nevada, An Equal Opportunity Employer.

ANSWER ON PAGE A–37

15.1 EMPLOYEE WAGES

507

Example 2 Find the gross earnings for an electrical worker who accepts the interstate job shown below and works 50 hours a week.

A/C ELECTRICAL WORKER
$6.60 per hour

Solution

a) Find the earnings for regular time.

Regular time earnings = Regular time worked × Regular rate
= 40 × $6.60
= $264.00

b) Find the earnings for overtime.

Earnings for overtime = Overtime hours worked × Overtime rate
= 10 × (1.5 × 6.60)
= $99.00

c) Find the gross earnings.

Gross earnings = Regular earnings + Overtime earnings
= $264.00 + $99.00
= $363.00

The electrical worker earned $363.00 for the 50 hours worked.

DO EXERCISE 2.

In addition to time-and-a-half pay for Saturdays, double time is often paid for work on Sundays and holidays. Moreover, some employee contracts require that time and a half be paid for hours worked over eight daily, regardless of the number worked each week. The following example illustrates this.

Example 3 Find the gross earnings for a preservation packager who accepts the job shown below and works six hours on each of Monday, Tuesday, and Wednesday, ten hours on each of Thursday and Friday, five hours Saturday, and four hours Sunday.

PRESERVATION PACKAGER
$5.95 per hour

Solution

a) Find the gross earnings for regular time.

Regular time earnings = Regular time worked × Regular rate
= 34 × $5.95
= $202.30

---

2. Find the gross earnings for an electroplating worker who accepts the interstate job listed below and works a 56-hour week.

**ELECTROPLATING WORKER
(CLEANING AND COATING)**
$6.37 per hour

ANSWER ON PAGE A–37

3. Find the gross earnings for a mechanic who accepts the job shown below and works nine hours on each of Monday through Thursday, seven hours on Friday, eight hours on Saturday, and five hours on Sunday.

A/C MECHANIC (RUBBER)
$6.37 per hour

b) Find the gross earnings for time-and-a-half overtime.

$$\text{Earnings for time and a half} = \text{Overtime hours worked} \times \text{Overtime rate}$$
$$= 9 \times (1.5 \times 5.95)$$
$$= \$80.33$$

c) Find the gross earnings for double time.

$$\text{Earnings for double time} = \text{Hours worked double time} \times \text{Rate}$$
$$= 4 \times (2 \times 5.95)$$
$$= \$47.60$$

d) Find the total gross earnings.

$$\text{Total gross earnings} = \text{Regular earnings} + \text{Time-and-a-half earnings}$$
$$+ \text{Double-time earnings}$$
$$= \$202.30 + \$80.33 + \$47.60$$
$$= \$330.23$$

The total gross earnings are $330.23.

DO EXERCISE 3.

EXERCISE SET 15.1

• Find the gross earnings for Exercises 1–10.

	Rate	Hours at Regular Rate	Hours at Time-and-a-Half Rate	Hours at Double Rate
1.	$6.50	40	8	0
2.	$8.16	40	8	0
3.	$7.50	36	7	0
4.	$7.30	38	8	0
5.	$8.46	32	12	6
6.	$7.90	36	11	4
7.	$8.32	39	7	3
8.	$7.72	39	6	5
9.	$7.40	40	0	8
10.	$7.64	40	0	8

Calculate gross earnings for a regular 40-hour week.

11. TYPIST-Recept.P/T,6hr/day 10-4 or 11-5 $6/hr, will train on word proc. immed Robin Castler P.O. Box 92911 LA 90009

12. TEL. SALES   ADV. SPECIALTIES
$8 PER HOUR
or high comm. bonuses. Make orders easily without selling.   AM/PM
Joe   213/466-2198

13. **SECURITY GUARD**
Armed security officer needed. Immediate opening for prestigious position at Century Plaza Hotel. $5 hour starting salary and excellent benefits after 90 days. Valid Weapons Permit required. For appt. call Usps
(213) 543-1610 or 543-1619
Equal Opportunity Employer M/F

14. ★ **WAREHOUSE** ★
TENT INSTALLERS
Must be over 21 with valid Driver's License. On job training. Advancement opportunity. $4.25/hour. Apply in person between 11 a.m. & 2 p.m.
627 Hazel Street, Glendale

ANSWERS

1. _____
2. _____
3. _____
4. _____
5. _____
6. _____
7. _____
8. _____
9. _____
10. _____
11. _____
12. _____
13. _____
14. _____

510 PAYROLL

ANSWERS

15. **SERVICE PERSON.** Install & maintain air conditioners, dishwashers, washer & dryers & refrigerators. 3yrs exper. $6.25/hr. Report in person to Hollywood Job Service, 6725 Santa Monica Bl, LA. Re order #1242463/827261-010. Ad pd by Er

16. **TELEPHONE INV PROD. FULL TIME**
★ **QUALIFIERS** ★
No selling $4/hr. to start, raises bonuses. Prestigious Beverly Hills office. Call Mr. Johnson   213/273-5465

15. _____

16. _____

Calculate gross earnings for a person who works a total of 40 hours at regular rate, 7 hours at time-and-a-half rate, and 5 hours at double rate.

17. **SUPERVISOR** night psych brd/care facil. 1AM-9AM $4/hr   213/450-1748

18. ★ **SECRETARIES $9.00** ★
STAR TEMPS   213/480-0617

17. _____

18. _____

19. Sign maker $9.30/hr, form sign base, reinforce, install electrical components, make individual letters. Must have knowledge of working metal. 1 yr. exp. as asst. sign maker. Job in Wilmington. Send this ad and resume to Job #91948, P.O. Box 15102, LA 90015 no later than Aug. 21

20. **UPHOLSTERER** $8.25/hr. 1 yr as upholsterer or 1 yr in creative design construction. Read blue prints, cut material, fit each individual piece. Job in Sun Valley. Send this ad & resume to Job #91916, PO Box 15102, LA 90015 no later than Aug. 21.

19. _____

20. _____

21. **P/T SWITCHBOARD OPER**
Hours 10-4 in busy real estate office. Grand Central area. $6.00/hr. 682-2300 x204

22. **PHYSICIAN-CARDIOLOGIST**
BC IM/BE Cardio.   Fee Paid
$30.HR. Part Time-Prvt Pract.
LARKIN MEDICAL
25 W. 43st/off 5/agency   695-2668

21. _____

22. _____

23. 🖩 An employee who earns $6.15 an hour worked 32 hours regular time, 8.5 hours at time and a half, and 12.25 hours at double time. Find the gross earnings.

24. 🖩 An employee who earns $7.19 an hour worked 40 hours regular time, 7.5 hours at time and a half, and 3.25 hours at double time. Find the gross earnings.

23. _____

24. _____

15.2 PIECEWORK PLANS

Employees are sometimes paid for the number of units they produce. Such a pay plan is called a *piecework plan*. If the employee is paid a fixed amount for each unit, then the plan is a *straight piecework plan*.

● STRAIGHT PIECEWORK EARNINGS

A certain minimum amount is guaranteed for workers on the piecework plan. Otherwise when production equipment failed wages would be lost at no fault of the worker.

Example 1 A press operator in a brick refractory is paid $0.07 for each brick produced, with $50 guaranteed daily. In one day 816 bricks were produced. How much was earned?

Solution Find the amount earned.

Amount earned = Number produced × Earnings each unit
= 816 × $0.07
= $57.12

The amount earned was $57.12, since it was more than the guaranteed amount.

DO EXERCISE 1.

●● DIFFERENTIAL PIECEWORK EARNINGS

A *differential piecework plan* is used to provide employees with an incentive to produce more units. Under this plan the employee is paid an increased rate per unit as the number of units produced increases.

Example 2 A microprocessor assembler is paid according to the number of soldering connections made. The differential pay scale is shown in the chart below. How much was earned if 300 soldering connections were made?

Differential Pay Scale For Soldering	
Soldering connections made	Rate per connection
200 or fewer	$0.11
201–250	$0.13
251 or more	$0.15

Solution

a) Find the rate per connection.

From the chart we see that the rate per connection is $0.15.

b) Find the amount earned.

Amount earned = Rate per connection × Number of connections
= $0.15 × 300
= $45.00

The amount earned was $45.00.

DO EXERCISE 2.

OBJECTIVES

After finishing Section 15.2, you should be able to:

● Compute straight piecework earnings.

●● Compute differential piecework earnings.

●●● Compute earnings with piecework overtime.

1. A machine assembler is paid $0.04 for each part assembled with $45 guaranteed daily. In one day 1500 parts were assembled. How much was earned?

2. In Example 2, how much was earned if 223 connections were made?

ANSWERS ON PAGE A–37

PAYROLL

3. An employee on piecework earns $2.15 for each unit produced and produced 195 units in one 43-hour week. Calculate the gross earnings.

▰▰▰ OVERTIME PIECEWORK EARNINGS

Piecework plans where employees work in excess of 40 hours weekly also pay overtime wages. In this situation we:

    First, find earnings for piecework completed.
    Next, find an equivalent hourly wage, and
    Finally, compute gross earnings for regular and overtime hours.

Example 3 An employee on piecework earns $3.80 for each unit produced and produced 125 units in one 44-hour week. Calculate the gross earnings.

Solution We find earnings for piecework completed.

$$\text{Piecework Earnings} = \text{Units} \times \text{Rate per Unit}$$
$$= 125 \times \$3.80$$
$$= \$475$$

Next we find an equivalent hourly rate.

$$\text{Hourly Rate} = \text{Amount Earned} \div \text{Hours Worked}$$
$$= \$475 \div 44$$
$$= \$10.80$$

Finally, we calculate gross earnings.

Regular earnings	40 × $10.80 =	$432.00
Overtime earnings	4 × $10.80 × 1.5 =	$64.80
Gross earnings		$496.80 Adding

The employee's gross earnings were $496.80.

DO EXERCISE 3.

ANSWER ON PAGE A–37

EXERCISE SET 15.2

■ Find the amount earned where $220 is guaranteed.

	Units Produced	Rate per Unit
1.	60	$3.92
2.	83	$2.95
3.	500	$0.39
4.	728	$0.34
5.	460	$0.96
6.	92	$4.07

7. A parts assembler is paid $4.26 for each part assembled, with $385 guaranteed weekly. In one week 93 parts were assembled. How much was earned?

8. A hydropump assembly plant pays an employee $1.57 for each bearing with $425 guaranteed weekly. In one week 280 bearings were placed on motor shafts. How much was earned?

9. A transmission assembly plant pays an employee $3.61 for each differential gear assembled, with $535 guaranteed weekly. In one week 127 differential gears were assembled. How much was earned?

10. An engraving firm pays an employee $5.05 for each stamping, with $362 guaranteed weekly. In one week 65 stampings were made. How much was earned?

■ ■ Use the chart at the right to find the amount earned.

	Units Produced
11.	22
12.	29
13.	15
14.	33
15.	31
16.	38

Differential Pay Scale

Units produced	Rate per unit
16 or fewer	$17.00
17–19	$17.50
20–25	$18.00
26–35	$18.75
36 or over	$19.75

PAYROLL

ANSWERS

Solve.

17. An employee on piecework earns $1.37 for each unit produced and produced 367 units in one 45-hour week. Calculate the gross earnings.

18. An employee on piecework earns $2.85 for each unit produced and produced 165 units in one 42-hour week. Calculate the gross earnings.

19. An employee produced 231 units in one 48-hour week at $2.10 for each unit. Calculate the gross earnings.

20. An employee produced 416 units in one 46-hour week at $1.35 for each unit. Calculate the gross earnings.

Complete. Use the chart at the right for the differential pay rate.

Amount Earned

	Units produced	Straight piecework plan at 3.5¢ per unit	Differential piecework using table
21.	942		
22.	1056		
23.	876		
24.	1023		

Differential Pay Scale

Units produced	Rate per unit
950 or fewer	3.25¢
951–975	3.65¢
976–1000	3.85¢
1001 or over	4.01¢

15.3 SALARIED EMPLOYEES

Salaried employees' earnings are usually given as weekly, monthly, or annual amounts. For example, a dental nurse who accepts the position shown below would earn at least $700 salary each month.

> **DENTAL NURSE**
> Exper. only. RDA preferred w/X-Ray cert. & knowledge of expanded duties. Super professionally motivated staff. Salary $700+ depending on qualifications. Benefits. Call 474-4695

■ AMOUNT OF PAY

Pay periods may be weekly, biweekly, semimonthly, or monthly. Example 1 shows how to compute the weekly pay.

Example 1 Find the weekly pay for the dental nurse who earns $700 a month.

Solution

a) Find the annual salary.

Annual salary = Monthly salary × 12
= $700 × 12 = $8400

b) Find the weekly pay.

$$\text{Weekly pay} = \frac{\text{Annual salary}}{52}$$

$$= \frac{\$8400}{52} = \$161.54$$

> **Reminder:**
> Weekly ⟶ 52 times/yr.
> Biweekly ⟶ 26 times/yr.
> Semimonthly ⟶ 24 times/yr.
> Monthly ⟶ 12 times/yr.

The weekly pay is $161.54.

DO EXERCISE 1.

Note that weekly earnings cannot be found by dividing the earnings each month by four since there are more than four weeks in a month. Individuals paid biweekly are paid every other week (a total of 26 pay periods each year).

Example 2 Find the biweekly pay for a keypunch operator who accepts the position shown below and earns $750 each month.

> **KEYPUNCH OPERS TO $750**

Solution

a) Find the annual salary.

Annual salary = Monthly salary × 12
= $750 × 12 = $9000

b) Find the biweekly pay.

$$\text{Biweekly pay} = \frac{\text{Annual salary}}{26}$$

$$= \frac{\$9000}{26} = \$346.15$$

The biweekly pay is $346.15.

DO EXERCISE 2.

OBJECTIVE

After finishing Section 15.3, you should be able to:

■ Determine the earnings for several pay periods.

1. Find the weekly pay for the bank teller who accepts the position shown below and earns $650 each month.

> **BANK TELLER**
> Position available for a full time commercial & savings teller, 1k yr recent teller exper req. Must be service oriented well groomed & able to deal professionally with public. Salary to $650 downtown location, full Xbenefits- + parking subsidy
> **UNION BAPK 238-7006**
> An Equal Opportunity Employer

2. Find the biweekly pay for an office clerk who accepts the position shown below and earns $640 each month.

> **OFFICE CLERK $640**
> KEARNY MESA AREA
> EMPLOYER PAID FEE
> Skills needed are 10 key add machine by touch, lite bkkpng.
> FEE JOBS ALSO
> El Cajon EMPLOYMENT AGENCY
> 905 W. Main at Richfield   44 6176

ANSWERS ON PAGE A–37

PAYROLL

3. Find the semimonthly pay for a computer programmer who accepts the position shown below and earns $30,000 annually.

> DATA PROCESSING
> COMPUTER PRGRS TO $30,000

An individual who is paid semimonthly (twice each month) has 24 pay periods each year (2 each month × 12 months).

Example 3 Find the semimonthly pay for a claims adjustor trainee who accepts the position shown below and earns $10,000 annually.

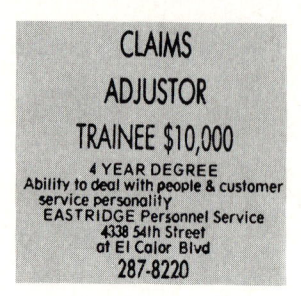

> CLAIMS
> ADJUSTOR
> TRAINEE $10,000
> 4 YEAR DEGREE
> Ability to deal with people & customer service personality
> EASTRIDGE Personnel Service
> 4338 54th Street
> at El Cajon Blvd
> 287-8220

Solution Find the semimonthly pay.

$$\text{Semimonthly pay} = \frac{\text{Annual pay}}{24}$$

$$= \frac{\$10,000}{24}$$

$$= \$416.67$$

The semimonthly pay is $416.67.

DO EXERCISE 3.

A person paid monthly has 12 pay periods annually.

Example 4 Find the monthly pay for a civil engineer who accepts the position shown below and earns $16,800 annually.

4. Find the monthly pay for a food service manager who accepts the position shown below and earns $17,000 annually.

> FOOD SERVICER MGR.
> Experienced, or qualifications of chief commissaryman, S.D. area. Advancement opportunity, send resume to I.M.I. - 32591N 53rd St. San Diego, Ca. 92105

> CIVIL ENGINEER
> Trainee to $16,800
> FEE NEGOTIABLE. Prefer BSE degree tho would consider AA degree in civil engineering. Estimating, drafting or construction exper. helpful.
> 287-0800   5381 El Cajon Blvd.
> THE WESTBROOKE AGENCY

Solution Find the monthly pay.

$$\text{Monthly pay} = \frac{\text{Annual pay}}{12}$$

$$= \frac{\$16,800}{12}$$

$$= \$1400$$

The monthly pay is $1400.00.

ANSWERS ON PAGE A-37

DO EXERCISE 4.

EXERCISE SET 15.3

NAME _____ CLASS _____ ANSWERS

EXERCISE SET 15.3

■ Find monthly and annual pay for people hired for these positions.

1. **JEWELRY**
Posit avail. Handmaking all items of jewelry. Highly skilled & specialized training in mounting all kinds of precious stones in platinum & 18kt gold jewelry. Ability in use of jewelry making tools. Ability in the cart of invisible setting. Min 3 yrs exp. & 10 yrs exp. $560/wkly. 40 hrs. Work Mon-Fri, 8:30-5 pm. Call 212-371-8580, 1-5 pm.

2. **RESTAURANT—MANAGER**
Coordinates food srvc activs, estimates food & bev costs, purchases supplies, plans menus incl Yugoslav specialties such as: Cevapcici, Raznjici, Djuvec, Tripice. Directs hiring & assignment of personnel. Min 4 yrs exper, college deg reqd, refs. 40 hrs, $400/wk. Apply in person, Aug. 4, 4-6 PM: Nikola Rebraka, Panarella Restaurant, 513 Columbus Ave NYC.

3. **MEDICAL SECRETARY**
P/T, typing & short hand, M-W-F, 9:30-3 PM 874-1867, $150/wk.

4. ★ SHOE SALESMAN (m/f), F/T. Shoe exp. nec. $285/wk. guar. for quali. + med. ins. 213/864-4422

5. Exchange Coordinator-coord xchange for antique British & American toys. 5 yrs exp. 40 hrs $300/wk, call Ehrlich-Bober & Co.-80 Pine St-NY 212-480-0750

6. BUYER-To purchase fabrics & raw textiles; using knowledge of materials & salability, to inspect, grade & order materials. Arrange for transportation, or payment & delivery of goods & its return if necessary. Requirements: BA deg or equivalency + 3 yrs exp; work week 35 hrs/wk, 5 days/wk, salary $350/wk. Job order #8852395 DOT code 162.157.038 Contact NYS Employment Service, 25 W. 34 St, Rm 1607, NY NY 10001

Find weekly and semimonthly pay for people hired for these positions.

7. SECTY—Bilingual to perform secretarial & administration functions for int'l. trade co. loc. in L.A. Receive incoming telephone, sched. appts., dispenses information, prepare corres. & business documentation & oper. typewr., telex & related keyboard & transcribing eqpmt. Knowl. of acctg. principles, type 55 wpm, read, write, speak Chinese. 1 yr. exp. Sal. $1386/mo. Send this ad & your resume to Job #4-1656, P.O. Box 15102, L.A., Ca. 90015 no later than 8/23/82.

8. **SECRETARY—PART TIME**
Secy/Recept. for WLA offc. Tues, Wed. & Thurs. 9-5 Good typing skills. Exp. only. $725 per mo. Call Pearl 213/273-1850

Copyright © 1984, by Addison-Wesley Publishing Company Inc. All rights reserved.

518 PAYROLL

9. WORD PROCESSING SPECIALISTS
$20,000
Exclusive position avail in Int'l Investment firm for a profsl word processor w/exp on any type of system. Work in the Controllers Office of this Park Avenue firm. Some stat typg involved. Call:
MARTY FELIX 962-4020
STANTON AGENCY   189 B'WAY

10. LIGHTING DESIGN CONSULTANT- Designs and implements lighting for use in institutional displays (primarily for jewelry and art) using advanced color-corrective lighting devices. Supervises quality control of lamps manufactured for contracts, 4 yrs exp required, thorough knowledge of lighting designs, techniques & color coordinated lamps & proven ability to create lighting concepts to meet clients display needs. 40 hr/wk; $40,000/yr. Send resume to Box NT 2035, 810 7th Ave, NYC 10019

Complete.

	Position	Weekly	Biweekly	Semimonthly	Monthly	Annual salary
11.	Accountant					$14,000
12.	Electronic technician					$12,500
13.	Advertising assistant				$ 900	
14.	Buyer				$1300	
15.	Loan processor		$650			
16.	Respiratory therapist		$550			
17.	Nursing supervisor			$625		
18.	Escrow officer			$725		
19.	Machinist	$225				
20.	Physical therapist	$275				

Find the weekly, biweekly, semimonthly, and monthly pay for individuals who earn the following annual salaries.

21. A legal secretary who earns $14,565.50.

22. A customer service agent who earns $13,685.75.

23. A store manager who earns $21,535.85.

24. A propane-gas truck driver who earns $19,856.75.

15.4 COMMISSIONS

Some employees earn a straight *commission*. This means that the employees are paid a certain amount (usually a percent) of sales made. The rate (percent) of commission depends on the product being sold, the ease of selling the product, and any additional benefits for the employee. Commissions act as an incentive to salespeople; the more sold, the more money earned.

■ EARNINGS

Example 1 A real estate salesperson had sales of $1.6 million in a recent year. The commission rate was 7%. How much was earned?

> BOB VAN DOREN,
> 1.6 Million

Solution

$$\begin{aligned} \text{Earnings} &= \text{Sales} \times \text{Rate} \\ &= \$1{,}600{,}000 \times 0.07 \\ &= \$112{,}000 \end{aligned}$$

The earnings were $112,000.

DO EXERCISE 1.

Sometimes a salesperson will earn a salary plus commission.

Example 2 The saleswoman who accepts the position shown below earns $250 each week plus a commission of 8% on the clothing sold. The saleswoman sold $1875 in clothing last week. What were her earnings?

> SALES LADY, personable, mature, & dependable, full time, sal I + comm. for Women's clothing store, exper. 3 yrs or more only, 234-1311

Solution

$$\begin{aligned} \text{Earnings} &= \text{Salary} + \text{Commission} \\ &= \$250 + (0.08 \times \$1875) \\ &= \$250 + \$150 \\ &= \$400 \end{aligned}$$

Her earnings were $400.00.

DO EXERCISE 2.

Sometimes a sales supervisor will earn a straight commission on sales plus a commission on sales of those he or she supervises. This additional commission on the earnings of those supervised is called an *override*.

Example 3 A sales supervisor sold $65,000 of machinery at 5% commission and was paid a 2% commission on $125,000 sold by the employees supervised. Find the supervisor's earnings.

OBJECTIVES

After finishing Section 15.4, you should be able to:

■ Calculate commission earnings.

■ ■ Compute commission overtime.

1. A real estate salesperson had sales of $1 million in a recent year. The commission rate was 7%. How much was earned?

> SHARON HOGLE, Million Dollars in sales

2. A sales representative earned $200 plus 7% commission on $3000 in sales last week. What were the representative's earnings?

ANSWERS ON PAGE A–37

3. A sales representative earns 8% commission on personal sales and 3% on sales of employees supervised. Personal sales were $22,000 and employees' sales $74,000. Find the earnings.

4. The sports sales position shown below pays $200 a week plus 4% on sales above $1500. If a person who accepts one of the positions sells $2300 in equipment one week, what are the earnings?

MERCHANDISING
SPORTS SALES
EMPLOYMENT OPENINGS
1. ATHLETIC EQUIPMENT
   SALES TRAINEE
   (BASEBALL/BASKETBALL)
2. TENNIS/RACQUETBALL
   EQUIPMENT
   SALES TRAINEE
3. FISHING/CAMPING
   EQUIPMENT
   SALES TRAINEE

— SALESMEN — $18 to $28,000 a year + bonus, xlnt management future, leads furn., car req'd. 272-4902

ANSWERS ON PAGE A–37

PAYROLL

Solution

$$\text{Earnings} = (0.05 \times \$65{,}000) + (0.02 \times \$125{,}000)$$
$$= \$3250 + \$2500$$
$$= \$5750$$

The earnings were $5750.00.

DO EXERCISE 3.

Some employees are paid a bonus in addition to a salary. The bonus may be paid for additional sales above a certain goal called a *quota*.

Example 4 The person who accepted the canvasser position shown below earned $250 a week plus 5% on orders received in excess of $3000. If $3700 in orders were taken, what were the canvasser's earnings?

CANVASSERS
$250 week. Salary & Bonuses.
Call Bob Rogers 292-8233

Solution

a) Find the amount in excess of the quota.

$$\text{Excess} = \text{Amount ordered} - \text{Quota}$$
$$= \$3700 - \$3000$$
$$= \$700$$

b) Find the bonus earned.

$$\text{Bonus earned} = \text{Rate} \times \text{Excess}$$
$$= 0.05 \times \$700$$
$$= \$35$$

c) Find the total earnings.

$$\text{Total earnings} = \text{Salary} + \text{Bonus}$$
$$= \$250 + \$35$$
$$= \$285$$

The earnings were $285.00.

DO EXERCISE 4.

To encourage additional sales, an employer sometimes pays a salary and a graduated bonus. The greater the sales, the greater the bonus rate.

Example 5 The salesperson accepting the position shown to the left earns $21,000 each year plus a bonus of 1% on sales to $500,000, 2% on sales from $500,000 to $800,000, and 4% on sales over $800,000. Find the earnings if sales were $900,000.

Solution

a) Find the total bonus.

$$\text{Bonus on first } \$500{,}000 = \text{Rate} \times \$500{,}000$$
$$= 0.01 \times \$500{,}000$$
$$= \$5000$$

Bonus on next $300,000 = Rate × $300,000
$$= 0.02 × \$300,000$$
$$= \$6000$$

Bonus on remaining $100,000 = Rate × $100,000
$$= 0.04 × \$100,000$$
$$= \$4000$$

Total bonus = $5000 + $6000 + $4000 = $15,000

b) Find the total earnings.

Total earnings = Salary + Total bonus
$$= \$21,000 + \$15,000$$
$$= \$36,000$$

The total amount earned was $36,000.

DO EXERCISE 5.

Sometimes an employee is paid a *draw* against commission. The salesperson is paid an amount based on expected sales. Excess sales earn additional money for the salesperson and earnings are adjusted upward. Likewise, sales not meeting expectations result in the draw being reduced. A draw permits a salesperson to plan better financially for a short period of time. However, the draw is periodically adjusted upward or downward based on sales.

Example 6 The salesperson who accepts the position shown below is given a $350 weekly draw and earns a 9% commission on sales. If sales were $5000, how much did commission differ from draw?

SALES large printing & direct mail co. is seeking exper. sales person. Draw + comm. & expenses. Xlnt opportunities for the right person. Call 222-0535

Solution

a) Find the commission.

Commission = Rate × Sales
$$= 0.09 × \$5000$$
$$= \$450$$

b) Find the difference between commission and draw.

Difference = Commission − Draw
$$= \$450 − \$350$$
$$= \$100$$

The salesperson would earn an additional $100 above draw.

DO EXERCISE 6.

5. A salesperson earns $600 in monthly salary plus a bonus of 1% on sales up to $12,000, 3% on sales from $12,000 to $20,000, and 5% on sales over $20,000. Find the earnings if sales were $23,000.

6. A salesperson accepts a position paying $275 a week draw and earns 8% commission on all sales. If sales were $4200, how much did commission differ from draw?

ANSWERS ON PAGE A–37

7. An electronics salesperson earns $290 for a 40-hour week plus a commission of 5% on sales. Last week sales were $4700 and hours worked were 47. How much was earned?

PAYROLL

▣ COMMISSION OVERTIME

The Fair Labor Standards Act requires salespeople who work on a commission basis be paid for overtime (salespeople working away from the business location are excluded).

Example 7 A hardware salesperson earns $325 for a 40-hour workweek plus a commission of 7% on sales. Last week sales were $3288.50 and hours worked were 48. How much was earned?

Solution Find the salary and commission.

Salary	$325.00	
Commission	$230.20	7% of $3288.50
Total	$555.20	

The equivalent hourly wage is

$$\text{Hourly wage} = \$555.20 \div 40$$
$$= \$13.88$$

Find

Regular earnings	40 × $13.88	= $555.20
Overtime earnings	8 × 1.5 × $13.88	= $166.56
Total earnings		$721.76

In total $721.76 was earned.

DO EXERCISE 7.

ANSWER ON PAGE A–37

NAME _____ CLASS _____ ANSWERS

EXERCISE SET 15.4

■ Solve.

1. A real estate agent sold a home for $68,000 and earned a 7% commission. How much was earned?

   1. _____

2. A car salesperson sold a car for $6300 and earned a 4% commission. How much was earned?

   2. _____

3. A sales agent earns $300 a week plus a 5% commission on sales. Sales were $4000. How much was earned?

   3. _____

4. A shoe salesperson earns $175 a week plus 7% on sales. Sales were $900. How much was earned?

   4. _____

5. A sales representative earns 9% commission on personal sales and 2% on sales of employees supervised. Personal sales were $10,000 and employee sales were $35,000. How much was earned?

   5. _____

6. A sales supervisor earns 8% commission on personal sales and 3% on sales of employees supervised. Personal sales were $40,000 and employee sales were $94,000. How much was earned?

   6. _____

7. A salesperson earns $150 weekly plus 6% of sales in excess of $4000. Sales were $4700. How much was earned?

   7. _____

8. A salesperson earns $600 in monthly salary plus 5% on sales in excess of $19,000. Sales were $23,000. How much was earned?

   8. _____

9. A machinery parts salesperson earns $225 weekly plus a bonus of 1% on sales to $5000, 2% on sales from $5000 to $8000, and 3% on sales over $8000. Sales were $8400. How much was earned?

   9. _____

10. A book salesperson is given a $300 draw and earns a 10% commission on sales. If sales were $5200, how much did commission differ from draw?

    10. _____

524

PAYROLL

ANSWERS

11. A lumberyard salesperson earns $230 weekly plus a bonus of 3% on sales to $2000 and 5% on sales over $2000. Sales were $2700. How much was earned?

11. _____

12. A plumbing salesperson is given a $400 draw and earns a 12% commission on sales. If sales were $5700, how much did commission differ from draw?

12. _____

■ ■ Solve.

13. A shoe salesperson earns $280 for a 40-hour workweek plus a commission of 20% on sales. Last week sales were $800 and hours worked were 54. How much was earned?

13. _____

14. A clothing salesperson earns $240 for a 40-hour workweek plus a commission of 8% on sales. Last week sales were $1700 and hours worked were 50. How much was earned?

14. _____

15. An appliance salesperson earns $210 for a 40-hour workweek plus a commission of 9% on sales. Last week sales were $3400 and hours worked were 46. How much was earned?

15. _____

16. A book salesperson earns $175 for a 40-hour workweek plus a commission of 10% on sales. Last week sales were $1050 and hours worked were 45. How much was earned?

16. _____

15.5 WITHHOLDING OF FEDERAL INCOME TAX

Employers are required by law to withhold federal income tax from employees' paychecks. Each year an income tax form is filed (see Section 10.3, pp. 389–396) and the difference between what was withheld and what is owed is determined. Then either a refund check is mailed to the taxpayer or the taxpayer sends the Internal Revenue Service a check for the balance of tax owed. One method used to determine the income tax withheld is the *percentage method*.

● THE PERCENTAGE METHOD

Example 1 A married taxpayer earns $1255 each month and claims three exemptions. How much is withheld for federal income tax?

Solution

a) Find the amount of one exemption from Table 15.1

TABLE 15.1

Percentage Method Income Tax Withholding Table

Payroll Period	One withholding allowance
Weekly	$19.23
Biweekly	38.46
Semimonthly	41.66
Monthly	83.33
Quarterly	250.00
Semiannually	500.00
Annually	1,000.00
Daily or miscellaneous (each day of the payroll period)	3.85

The payroll period is monthly so the amount of one exemption is $83.33

b) Find the amount of three exemptions.

$$\text{Amount of 3 exemptions} = \text{Amount of 1 exemption} \times \text{Number of exemptions}$$
$$= \$83.33 \times 3$$
$$= \$249.99$$

c) Subtract the exemption amount from the total wages.

Total wages − Exemption amount = $1255 − $249.99
$$= \$1005.01$$

d) Use Table 15.2 on p. 526 to find the amount of tax withheld from $1005.01

From the table we see that the tax withheld is $115.44 + 19% of the excess over $998.

Tax withheld = $115.44 + 0.19 × ($1005.01 − $998) = $116.77

The tax withheld is $116.77

DO EXERCISE 1.

OBJECTIVES

After finishing Section 15.5, you should be able to:

● Determine the amount withheld using the percentage method.

●● Determine the amount withheld using the wage bracket method.

1. A married taxpayer earns $1627 each month and claims four exemptions. How much is withheld for federal income tax?

ANSWER ON PAGE A–37

2. A single taxpayer earns $218 each week and claims three exemptions. How much is withheld for federal income tax?

PAYROLL

TABLE 15.2
IF THE PAYROLL PERIOD WITH RESPECT TO AN EMPLOYEE IS MONTHLY

(a) SINGLE person—including head of household:			(b) MARRIED person—		
If the amount of wages is:	The amount of income tax to be withheld shall be:		If the amount of wages is:	The amount of income tax to be withheld shall be:	
Not over $117 0			Not over $200 0		
Over— But not over—		of excess over—	Over— But not over—		of excess over—
$117 —$267	12%	—$117	$200 —$506	12%	—$200
$267 —$742	$18.00 plus 16%	—$267	$506 —$998	$36.72 plus 16%	—$506
$742 —$1,042	$94.00 plus 20%	—$742	$998 —$1,545	$115.44 plus 19%	—$998
$1,042 —$1,408	$154.00 plus 24%	—$1,042	$1,545 —$1,967	$219.37 plus 24%	—$1,545
$1,408 —$1,875	$241.84 plus 30%	—$1,408	$1,967 —$2,408	$320.65 plus 27%	—$1,967
$1,875 —$2,317	$381.94 plus 34%	—$1,875	$2,408 —$2,850	$439.72 plus 32%	—$2,408
$2,317	$532.22 plus 37%	—$2,317	$2,850	$581.16 plus 37%	—$2,850

Example 2 A single taxpayer earns $276 each week and claims two exemptions. How much is withheld for federal income tax?

Solution

a) Find the amount of one exemption from Table 15.1. The payroll period is weekly so the amount of one exemption is $19.23

b) Find the amount of two exemptions.

$$\text{Amount of 2 exemptions} = \text{Amount of 1 exemption} \times \text{Number of exemptions}$$
$$= \$19.23 \times 2$$
$$= \$38.46$$

c) Subtract the exemption amount from the total wages.

$$\text{Total wages} - \text{Exemption} = \$276 - \$38.46$$
$$= \$237.54$$

d) Use Table 15.3 below to find the amount of tax withheld on $237.54

TABLE 15.3
IF THE PAYROLL PERIOD WITH RESPECT TO AN EMPLOYEE IS WEEKLY

(a) SINGLE person—including head of household:			(b) MARRIED person—		
If the amount of wages is:	The amount of income tax to be withheld shall be:		If the amount of wages is:	The amount of income tax to be withheld shall be:	
Not over $27 0			Not over $46 0		
Over— But not over—		of excess over—	Over— But not over—		of excess over—
$27 —$62	12%	—$27	$46 —$117	12%	—$46
$62 —$171	$4.20 plus 16%	—$62	$117 —$230	$8.52 plus 16%	—$117
$171 —$240	$21.64 plus 20%	—$171	$230 —$356	$26.60 plus 19%	—$230
$240 —$325	$35.44 plus 24%	—$240	$356 —$454	$50.54 plus 24%	—$356
$325 —$433	$55.84 plus 30%	—$325	$454 —$556	$74.06 plus 27%	—$454
$433 —$535	$88.24 plus 34%	—$433	$556 —$658	$101.60 plus 32%	—$556
$535	$122.92 plus 37%	—$535	$658	$134.24 plus 37%	—$658

From the table we see that the amount withheld is $21.64 + 20% of the excess over $171.

$$\text{Tax withheld} = \$21.64 + 0.20 \times (\$237.54 - \$171)$$
$$= \$34.95$$

The tax withheld is $34.95.

ANSWER ON PAGE A–37

DO EXERCISE 2.

15.5 WITHHOLDING OF FEDERAL INCOME TAX

⚆⚆ THE WAGE BRACKET METHOD

Another method used to determine the income tax withheld is the *wage bracket method*. This method is used in Examples 3 and 4, which are identical to Examples 1 and 2.

Example 3 A married taxpayer earns $1255 each month and claims three exemptions. How much is withheld for federal income tax?

Solution

a) Read down the left column of Table 15.4 on p. 528 (Table 24, p. T–52) until the wage bracket containing 1255 is located.

   The location is in the bracket reading "at least 1240 but less than 1280."

b) Read across that row to the column headed 3.

The tax withheld is $117.70

DO EXERCISE 3.

Example 4 A single taxpayer earns $276 each week and claims two exemptions. How much is withheld for federal income tax?

Solution

a) Read down the left column of Table 24 (p. T–47) until the wage bracket containing 276 is located.

   The location is in the bracket reading "at least 270 but less than 280."

b) Read across that row to the column headed 2.

The tax withheld is $34.80.

DO EXERCISE 4.

Do you see that the two withholding tax methods result in approximately the same amount being withheld from pay?

---

3. A married taxpayer earns $1430 each month and claims four exemptions. How much is withheld for federal income tax?

4. A single taxpayer earns $218 each week and claims three exemptions. How much is withheld for federal income tax?

TABLE 15.4
MARRIED PERSONS—MONTHLY PAYROLL PERIOD

And the wages are—		And the number of withholding allowances claimed is—										
At least	But less than	0	1	2	3	4	5	6	7	8	9	10 or more
					The amount of income tax to be withheld shall be—							
$0	$200	$0	$0	$0	$0	$0	$0	$0	$0	$0	$0	$0
200	204	.20	0	0	0	0	0	0	0	0	0	0
204	208	.70	0	0	0	0	0	0	0	0	0	0
208	212	1.20	0	0	0	0	0	0	0	0	0	0
212	216	1.70	0	0	0	0	0	0	0	0	0	0
216	220	2.20	0	0	0	0	0	0	0	0	0	0
220	224	2.60	0	0	0	0	0	0	0	0	0	0
224	228	3.10	0	0	0	0	0	0	0	0	0	0
228	232	3.60	0	0	0	0	0	0	0	0	0	0
232	236	4.10	0	0	0	0	0	0	0	0	0	0
236	240	4.60	0	0	0	0	0	0	0	0	0	0
240	248	5.30	0	0	0	0	0	0	0	0	0	0
248	256	6.20	0	0	0	0	0	0	0	0	0	0
256	264	7.20	0	0	0	0	0	0	0	0	0	0
264	272	8.20	0	0	0	0	0	0	0	0	0	0
272	280	9.10	0	0	0	0	0	0	0	0	0	0
280	288	10.10	.10	0	0	0	0	0	0	0	0	0
288	296	11.00	1.00	0	0	0	0	0	0	0	0	0
296	304	12.00	2.00	0	0	0	0	0	0	0	0	0
304	312	13.00	3.00	0	0	0	0	0	0	0	0	0
312	320	13.90	3.90	0	0	0	0	0	0	0	0	0
320	328	14.90	4.90	0	0	0	0	0	0	0	0	0
328	336	15.80	5.80	0	0	0	0	0	0	0	0	0
336	344	16.80	6.80	0	0	0	0	0	0	0	0	0
344	352	17.80	7.80	0	0	0	0	0	0	0	0	0
352	360	18.70	8.70	0	0	0	0	0	0	0	0	0
360	368	19.70	9.70	0	0	0	0	0	0	0	0	0
368	376	20.60	10.60	.60	0	0	0	0	0	0	0	0
376	384	21.60	11.60	1.60	0	0	0	0	0	0	0	0
384	392	22.60	12.60	2.60	0	0	0	0	0	0	0	0
392	400	23.50	13.50	3.50	0	0	0	0	0	0	0	0
400	420	25.20	15.20	5.20	0	0	0	0	0	0	0	0
420	440	27.60	17.60	7.60	0	0	0	0	0	0	0	0
440	460	30.00	20.00	10.00	0	0	0	0	0	0	0	0
460	480	32.40	22.40	12.40	2.40	0	0	0	0	0	0	0
480	500	34.80	24.80	14.80	4.80	0	0	0	0	0	0	0
500	520	37.40	27.20	17.20	7.20	0	0	0	0	0	0	0
520	540	40.60	29.60	19.60	9.60	0	0	0	0	0	0	0
540	560	43.80	32.00	22.00	12.00	2.00	0	0	0	0	0	0
560	580	47.00	34.40	24.40	14.40	4.40	0	0	0	0	0	0
580	600	50.20	36.80	26.80	16.80	6.80	0	0	0	0	0	0
600	640	55.00	41.60	30.40	20.40	10.40	.40	0	0	0	0	0
640	680	61.40	48.00	35.20	25.20	15.20	5.20	0	0	0	0	0
680	720	67.80	54.40	41.10	30.00	20.00	10.00	0	0	0	0	0
720	760	74.20	60.80	47.50	34.80	24.80	14.80	4.80	0	0	0	0
760	800	80.60	67.20	53.90	40.60	29.60	19.60	9.60	0	0	0	0
800	840	87.00	73.60	60.30	47.00	34.40	24.40	14.40	4.40	0	0	0
840	880	93.40	80.00	66.70	53.40	40.00	29.20	19.20	9.20	0	0	0
880	920	99.80	86.40	73.10	59.80	46.40	34.00	24.00	14.00	4.00	0	0
920	960	106.20	92.80	79.50	66.20	52.80	39.50	28.80	18.80	8.80	0	0
960	1,000	112.60	99.20	85.90	72.60	59.20	45.90	33.60	23.60	13.60	3.60	0
1,000	1,040	119.60	105.60	92.30	79.00	65.60	52.30	39.00	28.40	18.40	8.40	0
1,040	1,080	127.20	112.00	98.70	85.40	72.00	58.70	45.40	33.20	23.20	13.20	3.20
1,080	1,120	134.80	119.00	105.10	91.80	78.40	65.10	51.80	38.40	28.00	18.00	8.00
1,120	1,160	142.40	126.60	111.50	98.20	84.80	71.50	58.20	44.80	32.80	22.80	12.80
1,160	1,200	150.00	134.20	118.30	104.60	91.20	77.90	64.60	51.20	37.90	27.60	17.60
1,200	1,240	157.60	141.80	125.90	111.00	97.60	84.30	71.00	57.60	44.30	32.40	22.40
1,240	1,280	165.20	149.40	133.50	117.70	104.00	90.70	77.40	64.00	50.70	37.40	27.20
1,280	1,320	172.80	157.00	141.10	125.30	110.40	97.10	83.80	70.40	57.10	43.80	32.00
1,320	1,360	180.40	164.60	148.70	132.90	117.10	103.50	90.20	76.80	63.50	50.20	36.80
1,360	1,400	188.00	172.20	156.30	140.50	124.70	109.90	96.60	83.20	69.90	56.60	43.20
1,400	1,440	195.60	179.80	163.90	148.10	132.30	116.40	103.00	89.60	76.30	63.00	49.60
1,440	1,480	203.20	187.40	171.50	155.70	139.90	124.00	109.40	96.00	82.70	69.40	56.00
1,480	1,520	210.80	195.00	179.10	163.30	147.50	131.60	115.80	102.40	89.10	75.80	62.40
1,520	1,560	218.40	202.60	186.70	170.90	155.10	139.20	123.40	108.80	95.50	82.20	68.80

EXERCISE SET 15.5

■ Use the percentage method (Tables 22 and 23 on pp. T–44 and T–45).

1. A married taxpayer earns $2348 each month and claims four exemptions. How much is withheld for federal income tax?

2. A married taxpayer earns $957 each month and claims two exemptions. How much is withheld for federal income tax?

3. A single taxpayer earns $2186 each month and claims three exemptions. How much is withheld for federal income tax?

4. A single taxpayer earns $1348 each month and claims two exemptions. How much is withheld for federal income tax?

5. A married taxpayer earns $429 weekly and claims four exemptions. How much is withheld for federal income tax?

6. A single taxpayer earns $459 weekly and claims three exemptions. How much is withheld for federal income tax?

PAYROLL

◉◉ Use the wage bracket method (Table 24 on p. T–46).

7. A married taxpayer earns $2348 each month and claims four exemptions. How much is withheld for federal income tax?

8. A married taxpayer earns $957 each month and claims two exemptions. How much is withheld for federal income tax?

9. A single taxpayer earns $2186 each month and claims three exemptions. How much is withheld for federal income tax?

10. A single taxpayer earns $1348 each month and claims two exemptions. How much is withheld for federal income tax?

11. A married taxpayer earns $429 weekly and claims four exemptions. How much is withheld for federal income tax?

12. A single taxpayer earns $459 weekly and claims three exemptions. How much is withheld for federal income tax?

15.6 SOCIAL SECURITY*

■ EMPLOYEES TAX

The social security tax was established with the passage of the Federal Insurance Contributions Act (FICA) and provides old-age, survivor, disability, and hospitalization insurance for employees. The maximum taxable earnings change as the average wage level changes. Table 15.5 lists the maximum taxable earnings and rate for several years.

TABLE 15.5 SOCIAL SECURITY RATES FOR EMPLOYEES

Year	Maximum Taxable Earnings	Rate
1984	$36,000*	6.7%
1985	$38,100*	7.05%*
1986	$40,200*	7.15%*
1987	$42,600*	7.15%*

* Social Security Administration estimates

Example 1 An employee earned $18,600 in 1984. How much was paid by the employee in social security tax?

Solution Since $18,600 does not exceed the maximum taxable earnings ($36,000) for 1984, the entire amount was taxed.

Social security tax = $18,600 × 6.7%
$\qquad$ = $18,600 × 0.067
$\qquad$ = $1246.20

The social security tax was $1246.20.

DO EXERCISE 1.

Earnings in excess of the maximum taxable earnings are not subject to the social security tax.

Example 2 An employee earns $37,000 in 1984. How much is paid by the employee in social security tax?

Solution The maximum taxable earnings in 1984 are $36,000, so there is no social security tax on $37,000 − $36,000, or $1000.

Social security tax = $36,000 × 6.7%
$\qquad$ = $2412

The social security tax is $2412.

DO EXERCISE 2.

Employers are required by law to match their employees' social security contributions. To illustrate, a $2000 employee contribution in 1985 would

---

OBJECTIVES

After finishing Section 15.6, you should be able to:

■ Compute social security tax for employees.

■ ■ Compute social security tax for self employed people.

1. An employee earns $23,500 in 1984. How much social security tax does the employee pay?

2. An employee earns $39,000 in 1984. How much is paid by the employee in social security tax?

---

* Information in this section, although current at time of writing, tends to be changed frequently.

ANSWERS ON PAGE A–38

3. During 1985, an employee earns $2137 each month. How much is deducted from each paycheck for social security tax?

be matched by a $2000 employer contribution. Therefore the 1985 contribution to the employee's social security account would be $2000 + $2000, or $4000. The social security tax (contributions of employee and employer) is deposited periodically in a local bank and then forwarded to a Federal Reserve Bank (some employers deposit directly in a Federal Reserve Bank). Earnings are then credited to the employee's social security account. Social security taxes are deducted from each paycheck that an employee receives until the maximum taxable earnings are exceeded.

Example 3 During 1984 an employee earns $725.80 biweekly. How much is deducted from each paycheck for social security tax?

Solution Find the amount deducted.

$$\begin{aligned} \text{Amount deducted} &= \text{Rate} \times \text{Earnings} \\ &= 6.7\% \times \$725.80 \\ &= 0.067 \times \$725.80 \\ &= \$48.63 \end{aligned}$$

Thus, $48.63 is deducted for social security tax.

DO EXERCISE 3.

●● SELF-EMPLOYED PERSONS TAX

Self-employed persons pay a different rate than employees do. However, the amount of maximum taxable earnings is the same as for employees. The rates for self-employed persons are shown in Table 15.6.

4. A self-employed person earns $23,200 in 1985. How much social security tax is paid?

**TABLE 15.6
SOCIAL SECURITY RATES FOR SELF-EMPLOYED PERSONS**

Year	Rate
1984	11.3%
1985	11.8%*
1986	12.3%*
1987	12.3%*

* Effective rates after a tax credit.

Example 4 A self-employed person earns $38,000 in 1984. How much social security tax is paid?

Solution

The amount of maximum taxable earnings in 1984 is $36,000, so there is no social security tax on $38,000 − $36,000, or $2000.

$$\begin{aligned} \text{Social security tax} &= \$36,000 \times 11.3\% \\ &= \$36,000 \times 0.113 \\ &= \$4068 \end{aligned}$$

The social security tax is $4068.

ANSWERS ON PAGE A–38

DO EXERCISE 4.

NAME _____ CLASS _____ ANSWERS

EXERCISE SET 15.6

● Find the social security tax for these employees.

1. A machinist with $23,780 in 1985 earnings.

2. A drill press operator with $27,900 in 1985 earnings.

3. A pharmacist with $32,000 in 1985 earnings.

4. A receptionist with $15,890 in 1984 earnings.

5. A college president with $85,000 in 1986 earnings.

6. A chemist with $47,000 in 1984 earnings.

7. A physical therapist with $23,490 in 1985 earnings.

8. An occupational therapist with $19,760 in 1984 earnings.

9. A mechanic with $21,650 in 1986 earnings.

10. A data processor with $27,400 in 1985 earnings.

11. A purchasing agent with $18,670 in 1984 earnings.

12. A service station employee with $15,600 in 1984 earnings.

13. A legal secretary with $25,900 in 1985 earnings.

14. A policewoman with $17,490 in 1984 earnings.

15. A wholesale manager with $27,200 in 1985 earnings.

16. An accountant with $43,000 in 1986 earnings.

1. _____
2. _____
3. _____
4. _____
5. _____
6. _____
7. _____
8. _____
9. _____
10. _____
11. _____
12. _____
13. _____
14. _____
15. _____
16. _____

Copyright © 1984, by Addison-Wesley Publishing Company Inc. All rights reserved.

PAYROLL

ANSWERS

●● Find the social security tax for these self-employed people.

17. A writer with $56,000 in 1985 earnings.

17. _____

18. A consultant with $72,000 in 1986 earnings.

18. _____

19. A contractor with $83,000 in 1985 earnings.

19. _____

20. A sales representative with $31,000 in 1986 earnings.

20. _____

21. An independent insurance agent with $57,300 in 1986 earnings.

21. _____

22. An automobile body shop owner with $34,000 in 1984 earnings.

22. _____

23. A painter with $25,700 in 1985 earnings.

23. _____

24. A gardener with $29,800 in 1984 earnings.

24. _____

25. An appliance repair person with $23,800 in 1987 earnings.

25. _____

26. A RotoRooter owner with $37,000 in 1985 earnings.

26. _____

27. An upholsterer with $24,750 in 1987 earnings.

27. _____

28. A cabinet maker with $31,400 in 1986 earnings.

28. _____

29. A sheetrock specialist with $29,620 in 1986 earnings.

29. _____

30. A carpet installer with $21,300 in 1987 earnings.

30. _____

15.7 PAYROLL   535

15.7 PAYROLL

■ NET PAY

A payroll clerk computes the *net pay* an employee earns as well as gross earnings. Net pay is often called *take-home pay*. It is the amount of money an employee receives after deductions. Deductions include income taxes, social security taxes, insurance (group life, automobile, and medical), contributions, stock purchase plans, and savings. Many companies (especially small ones) calculate payroll manually. A time clock records when an employee starts and finishes work, a weekly time ticket is completed, and a payroll register (journal) is used to record information on each employee.

Example 1 Compute the net pay for Lu Ahman who is married and claims three exemptions.

WEEKLY TIME TICKET

JOB NAME OR NO.	KIND OF WORK DONE	S	M	T	W	T	F	S	HRS	RATE	AMOUNT
36824	Assembly		4	6	3	2	5		20	6.	120 00
47815	Labor		1.5	1	1.5	1.3			5.3	6.	31 80
63219	Labeling		1.8	1	3	4	1		10.8	6.	64 80
58739	Trouble Shooting	0.7		0.5	0.7	2			3.9	6.	23 40

Employee's Name: Lu Ahman   Week Ending: May 16, 1984

Total Regular Time: 8 8 8 8 8   40 6. 240 00

Approved: aLT

Deductions — Withhold $19.80, F.I.C.A. $16.08, State WH INS. $16.25
Total Earnings: 240 00
Total Deductions: 52 13
Net Pay: 187 87
Date Paid 5/19/84 Check No. 397

Solution

a) Find the total deductions.

Total deductions = Withholding + Social security + Insurance
= $19.80 + $16.08 + $16.25
= $52.13

b) Find the net pay.

Net pay = Total earnings − Total deductions
= $240.00 − $52.13
= $187.87

The net pay was $187.87.

DO EXERCISE 1 ON THE NEXT PAGE.

OBJECTIVES

After finishing Section 15.7, you should be able to:

■ Compute net pay.

■■ Find the total and net wages from a payroll journal.

■■■ Read computer printout for payroll.

536

PAYROLL

1. Compute the net pay for Lee Fisk, who is single and claims two exemptions. The weekly time card is shown on the right.

WEEKLY TIME TICKET

EMPLOYEE'S NAME: Lee Fisk NO. ___ WEEK ENDING: July 18, 1984

JOB NAME OR NO.	KIND OF WORK DONE	S	M	T	W	T	F	S	HRS.	RATE	AMOUNT
83516	Inventory		1.3	2	0.6	2.5	1.9		8.3	5.50	45.65
49718	Handling		0.8	1.4		1.4	0.7		4.3	5.50	23.65
63492	Stiching		3.8	2.9	2.5	1.7	2.5		13.4	5.50	73.70
47815	Labor			1.7	0.8	0.9	1.6		5.0	5.50	27.50
36824	Assembly		2.1		4.1	1.5	1.3		9.0	5.50	49.50

Total Regular Time: 8 8 8 8 8 40.0 5.50 220.00

Total Overtime

APPROVED: AT
DEDUCTIONS: WITHHOLD 24.80 S.D.I. F.I.C.A. 14.74 STATE WH. SAVINGS 18.75
Total Earnings 220.00
Total Deductions
NET PAY

4K 409 Rediform Date Paid 7/21/84 Check No. 568

ANSWER ON PAGE A-38

PAYROLL JOURNAL

A payroll journal (register) is used to record payroll information for each employee. The payroll journal provides the employer with information on total payroll costs and deductions.

Example 2 Compute the total wages and net wages for the payroll journal.

PAYROLL JOURNAL SHEET NO. 5

WORK WEEK, BEGINS—DAY: Monday TIME OF DAY: 8 a.m. DATE OF PAYMENT: May 19, 1984

EMPLOYEE'S NAME	EXEMP-TIONS FED. STATE	S	M	T	W	T	F	S	TOTAL HOURS	REGULAR RATE OF PAY	AT REGULAR RATE FOR TOTAL HOURS WORKED	EXTRA FOR OVERTIME	OTHER WAGES	TOTAL WAGES	F.O.A.B. TAX	FED. WITH-HOLDING TAX	STATE WITH-HOLDING TAX	INS	CONT	SAV	TOTAL DEDUC-TIONS	NET CASH WAGES PAID
Lu Ahman (M)	3		8	8	8	8	8		40	6.00/hr.	240.00			240.00	16.08	19.80		16.25			52.13	187.87
Orpha Grap (M)	2		8	8	8	8	8		40	5.85/hr.	234.00			234.00	15.68	21.20			7.00		43.88	190.12
Alva Hope (S)	3		8	8	8	8	8		40	4.90/hr.	196.00			196.00	13.13	16.30				12.00	41.43	154.57
Fran Lynn (M)	4		8	8	8	8	8		40	6.45/hr.	258.00			258.00	17.29	18.30		16.25	11.00		51.84	206.16
Stanlee Ort (S)	2		8	8	8	8	8		40	5.75/hr.	230.00			230.00	15.41	26.80			9.00		51.28	178.79

EFFICIENCY LINE NO. 3000

(1) REQUIRED ONLY WHEN EMPLOYEE WORKS OVERTIME.
(2) REQUIRED ONLY WHERE CASH WAGE ACTUALLY PAID IS LESS THAN MINIMUM WAGE REQUIRED BY THE ACT.

Solution

a) Find the total wages.

Total wages = Sum of wages paid each employee
= \$240 + \$234 + \$196 + \$258 + \$230
= \$1158

Total wages were \$1158.

b) Find the net wages.

Net wages = Sum of net wages paid each employee
= \$187.87 + \$190.12 + \$154.57 + \$206.16 + \$178.79
= \$917.51

Net wages were \$917.51.

DO EXERCISE 2.

••• COMPUTERIZED PAYROLL

Many large companies use computers for payroll and increasingly small businesses are using microcomputers for payroll. This section shows one procedure where the employee completes a time record (see Fig. 15.1), the information is put in computer format by keypunch operators, and the computer processes and prints out payroll information for each employee on a register (see Fig. 15.2). Finally, the employee is paid by check (see Fig. 15.3).

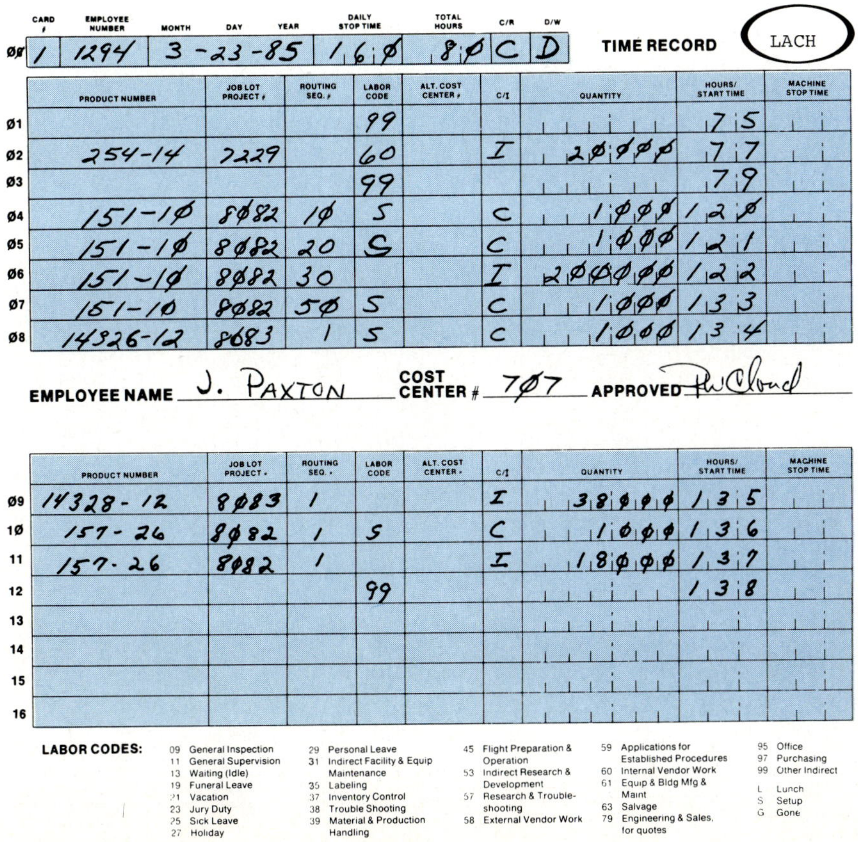

TIME RECORD

LACH

	CARD #	EMPLOYEE NUMBER	MONTH DAY YEAR	DAILY STOP TIME	TOTAL HOURS	C/R	D/W
ØØ	1	1294	3-23-85	16Ø	8Ø	C	D

	PRODUCT NUMBER	JOB LOT PROJECT #	ROUTING SEQ. #	LABOR CODE	ALT. COST CENTER #	C/I	QUANTITY	HOURS/ START TIME	MACHINE STOP TIME
Ø1				99				75	
Ø2	254-14	7229		60		I	2ØØØØ	77	
Ø3				99				79	
Ø4	151-1Ø	8Ø82	1Ø	S		C	1ØØØ	12Ø	
Ø5	151-1Ø	8Ø82	20	S		C	1ØØØ	121	
Ø6	151-1Ø	8Ø82	30			I	2ØØØØØ	122	
Ø7	151-1Ø	8Ø82	5Ø	S		C	1ØØØ	133	
Ø8	14326-12	8Ø83	1	S		C	1ØØØ	134	

EMPLOYEE NAME J. PAXTON COST CENTER # 7Ø7 APPROVED R.W. Cloud

	PRODUCT NUMBER	JOB LOT PROJECT #	ROUTING SEQ. #	LABOR CODE	ALT. COST CENTER #	C/I	QUANTITY	HOURS/ START TIME	MACHINE STOP TIME
Ø9	14328-12	8Ø83	1			I	38ØØØ	135	
1Ø	157-26	8Ø82	1	S		C	1ØØØ	136	
11	157-26	8Ø82	1			I	18ØØØ	137	
12				99				138	
13									
14									
15									
16									

LABOR CODES:
09 General Inspection
11 General Supervision
13 Waiting (Idle)
19 Funeral Leave
21 Vacation
23 Jury Duty
25 Sick Leave
27 Holiday
29 Personal Leave
31 Indirect Facility & Equip Maintenance
35 Labeling
37 Inventory Control
38 Trouble Shooting
39 Material & Production Handling
45 Flight Preparation & Operation
53 Indirect Research & Development
57 Research & Trouble-shooting
58 External Vendor Work
59 Applications for Established Procedures
60 Internal Vendor Work
61 Equip & Bldg Mfg & Maint
63 Salvage
79 Engineering & Sales, for quotes
95 Office
97 Purchasing
99 Other Indirect
L Lunch
S Setup
G Gone

FIGURE 15.1

2. Compute the total wages and net wages for the payroll journal if an additional employee is hired and is paid gross wages of \$245 and net wages of \$193.76.

ANSWER ON PAGE A–38

3. Find the starting time and quantity for product number 14328-12 in Fig. 15.1.

ANSWER ON PAGE A-38

PAYROLL

Examples 3, 4, and 5 show the procedure for J. T. Paxton (employee number 1294) from the time record to the computer printout of payroll and finally to the paycheck.

Example 3 From Fig. 15.1, determine the hours worked, the quantity of product 254-14 made, and the starting time for employee 1294.

Solution

a) Find the hours worked.

The top boxed row shows that 8 hours were worked.

b) Find the quantity of product 254-14 made.

Row 02 lists 20 as the quantity.

c) Find the starting time.

The starting time is given in row 01 as 7.5. Thus, the starting time is 7:30.

DO EXERCISE 3.

Figure 15.2 lists part of a register that gives payroll information for employee 1294.

Example 4 Find the regular rate of pay for employee 1294.

Lach CHEMICAL COMPANY CURRENT AND YTD EARNINGS REGISTER *PAYR05* PAGE 8
DATE PROCESSED 3/29/85 BEGIN DATE 3/12/85 END DATE 3/25/85 CHECK DATE 3/31/85
*** HOURLY ***

EMP C/C	REGULAR	PREMIUM	VAC	SICK	P/L	HOL	GONE	VAC LEFT	VAC USED	P/L LEFT	P/L USED	PAY ADJ AMT	CHECK NO.
1285/707	64.0							80.0		54.2	8.0		62281
	282.88												

FIC GROSS	GROSS	FEDERAL	STATE	DISAB	FICA	MEDICAL	STOCK	AUTO	SAVINGS	OTHER	NET	
282.88	282.88	26.49	6.92		17.11						232.36	C/E
2324.92	2360.28	290.17	61.26		140.64	25.68					1842.53	YTD

EMP C/C	REGULAR	PREMIUM	VAC	SICK	P/L	HOL	GONE	VAC LEFT	VAC USED	P/L LEFT	P/L USED	PAY ADJ AMT	CHECK NO.
1294/707	68.0		8					104.0	16.0	49.2	4.0		62282
	314.16		36.96										

FIC GROSS	GROSS	FEDERAL	STATE	DISAB	FICA	MEDICAL	STOCK	AUTO	SAVINGS	OTHER	NET	
351.12	351.12	52.26	8.83		21.24						268.79	C/E
2544.23	2544.23	418.20	63.69		153.92	30.48				.62	1877.32	YTD

EMP C/C	REGULAR	PREMIUM	VAC	SICK	P/L	HOL	GONE	VAC LEFT	VAC USED	P/L LEFT	P/L USED	PAY ADJ AMT	CHECK NO.
1409/722	72.0	6.0	8					48.0	32.0	12.2	9.0		62284
	424.08	53.04	47.12										

FIC GROSS	GROSS	FEDERAL	STATE	DISAB	FICA	MEDICAL	STOCK	AUTO	SAVINGS	OTHER	NET	
524.24	524.24	43.94	17.85		31.72				10.48		420.25	C/E
3385.62	3397.40	294.44	106.86		204.83	64.74			67.92		2658.61	YTD

FIGURE 15.2

15.7 PAYROLL   539

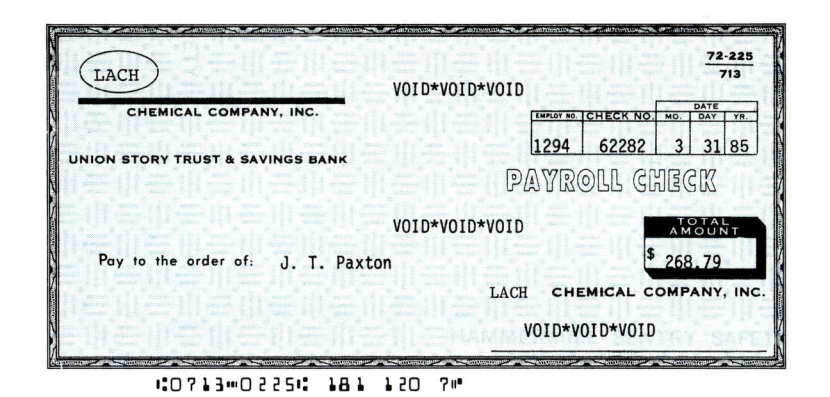

FIGURE 15.3

Solution

a) Find the regular hours worked.

The regular hours worked are 68.

b) Find the hourly wage.

$$\text{Hourly wage} = \frac{\text{Amount earned for regular hours}}{\text{Regular hours worked}}$$

$$= \frac{314.16}{68}$$

$$= 4.62$$

The hourly wage is $4.62.

DO EXERCISE 4.

The payroll check lists a statement of earnings and the net earnings for J. T. Paxton (employee 1294). It appears in Fig. 15.3.

Example 5 Verify that the net pay is correct for J. T. Paxton.

Solution

Net pay = Gross pay − Deductions
     = $351.12 − ($52.26 + $8.83 + $21.24)
     = $268.79

The net pay is $268.79.

DO EXERCISE 5.

---

4. Find the gross current earnings and amount withheld for federal, state, and social security taxes for employee 1294.

5. Find the net pay for J. T. Paxton if the gross pay had been $394.36 and the deductions the same as in Example 5.

ANSWERS ON PAGE A-38

EXERCISE SET 15.7

■ Complete weekly time tickets. The number of exemptions claimed and the marital status of each employee are given. Use Table 24 (p. T–46) and Table 15.5 to compute withholding and social security tax.

1. Married with five exemptions

WEEKLY TIME TICKET

EMPLOYEE'S NAME: Dana Garner   NO.   WEEK ENDING: July 24, 1984

JOB NAME OR NO.	KIND OF WORK DONE	S	M	T	W	T	F	S	HRS.	RATE	AMOUNT
36824	Assembly		3	4	1.7	2	5			6.50	
47895	Maintenance		2.4	1.8	5.4	3.3	0.6			6.50	
18462	Troubleshooting		0.9	1.1		1.8	1.8			6.50	
49183	Press Work		1.7	1.1	0.9	0.9	0.6			6.50	

APPROVED: apt

DEDUCTIONS — WITHHOLD / S.D.I. / F.I.C.A. / STATE WH. / SAVINGS 18.75

Total Earnings / Total Deductions / NET PAY

Date Paid 7/27/84   Check No. 2395

2. Single with two exemptions

WEEKLY TIME TICKET

EMPLOYEE'S NAME: Dale Farrar   NO.   WEEK ENDING: July 24, 1984

JOB NAME OR NO.	KIND OF WORK DONE	S	M	T	W	T	F	S	HRS.	RATE	AMOUNT
36824	Assembly		2	1.4	5	4	1			6.75	
47895	Maintenance		1.8	5.1		0.3	4			6.75	
62171	Glazing		3.7		2.1	2	2.5			6.75	
49183	Press Work		0.5	1.5	0.9	1.7	2.5			6.75	

APPROVED: apt

DEDUCTIONS — WITHHOLD / S.D.I. / F.I.C.A. / STATE WH. / CONT. 5.50

Total Earnings / Total Deductions / NET PAY

Date Paid 7/27/84   Check No. 2396

3. Married with two exemptions

WEEKLY TIME TICKET

EMPLOYEE'S NAME: Stanlee Ott   NO.   WEEK ENDING: July 24, 1984

JOB NAME OR NO.	KIND OF WORK DONE	S	M	T	W	T	F	S	HRS.	RATE	AMOUNT
47895	Maintenance		0.5	1.5	2.2	3	2.5			5.75	
18263	Welding		1.2	3.2	5.1	0.6	3.1			5.75	
18462	Troubleshooting		5.1	2.7	0.2	0.7	1.6			5.75	
49183	Press Work			1.6	0.4	0.5	0.4			5.75	
62171	Glazing		1.2		0.1	3.2	0.4			5.75	

APPROVED: apt

DEDUCTIONS — WITHHOLD / S.D.I. / F.I.C.A. / STATE WH. / INS. 20.50

Total Earnings / Total Deductions / NET PAY

Date Paid 7/27/84   Check No. 2397

542 PAYROLL

4. Single with one exemption

WEEKLY TIME TICKET

EMPLOYEE'S NAME: TRACEY STOLTZ   NO. _____   WEEK ENDING: JULY 24, 1984

JOB NAME OR NO.	KIND OF WORK DONE	S	M	T	W	T	F	S	HRS.	RATE	AMOUNT
18263	WELDING		4.6	3.9	6.3	5.4	4.7			6.25	
47895	MAINTENANCE		2.8	2.7		1.8	2.1			6.25	
49183	PRESS WORK		0.6	1.4	1.7	0.8	1.2			6.25	

Total Regular Time
Total Overtime

APPROVED: apt
DEDUCTIONS: WITHHOLD | S.D.I. | F.I.C.A. | STATE WH.
Total Earnings
Total Deductions

4K 409 Rediform   Date Paid 7/27/84   Check No. 2398   NET PAY

5. Complete the payroll journal. Determine the total wages and net wages.

PAYROLL JOURNAL   SHEET NO. _____

WORK WEEK, BEGINS—DAY: MONDAY   TIME OF DAY: _____   DATE OF PAYMENT: July 27, 1984

EMPLOYEE'S NAME	EXEMPTIONS FED./STATE	HOURS OF WORK S M T W T F S TOTAL	REGULAR RATE OF PAY	EARNINGS: AT REGULAR / EXTRA FOR OVERTIME / OTHER WAGES / TOTAL WAGES	DEDUCTIONS: F.O.A.B. TAX / FED. WITHHOLDING TAX / STATE WITHHOLDING TAX / OTHER DEDUCTIONS / TOTAL DEDUCTIONS	NET CASH WAGES PAID
DANA GARNER (M)						
DALE FARRAR (S)						
STANLEE OTT (M)						
TRACEY STOLTZ (S)						

For each of employees 1284 and 411, list the

6. _____   **6.** Current (C/E) gross earnings   **7.** Federal income tax withheld
7. _____
8. _____   **8.** State income tax withheld   **9.** Social security tax paid
9. _____
10. _____   **10.** Net earnings   **11.** Year-to-date (YTD) net earnings
11. _____

EMP	C/C	REGULAR	PREMIUM	VAC	SICK	P/L	HOL	GONE	VAC LEFT	VAC USED	P/L LEFT	P/L USED	PAY ADJ AMT	CHECK NO.
1284	830	80.0 251.20	1.3 6.12								6.6			62280

FIG GROSS	GROSS	FEDERAL	STATE	DISAB	FICA	MEDICAL	STOCK	AUTO	SAVINGS	OTHER	NET	
257.32	257.32	21.90	5.98		15.57						213.87	C/E
1216.27	1216.27	76.17	21.58		73.59						1044.93	YTD

EMP	C/C	REGULAR	PREMIUM	VAC	SICK	P/L	HOL	GONE	VAC LEFT	VAC USED	P/L LEFT	P/L USED	PAY ADJ AMT	CHECK NO.
411	780	44.0 137.28												62285

FIG GROSS	GROSS	FEDERAL	STATE	DISAB	FICA	MEDICAL	STOCK	AUTO	SAVINGS	OTHER	NET	
137.28	137.28	11.48	1.67		8.31						115.82	C/E
199.68	199.68	11.48	2.09		12.00						174.02	YTD

TEST OR REVIEW — CHAPTER 15

If you miss an item, review the indicated section and objective.

[15.1, •] **1.** Find the gross earnings of the person who accepts the sewing machine operator position and work 35 hours a week.

> SEWING MACHINE OP Operate semi-automatic short-cycle buttonhole, stitching mach. Position garments, adjust stitch'h cutt'g mechanism. Familiar w/semi-automatic short-cycle machine reqd. 2 yrs exp. $4.50/hr. 35/hrs/wk 924-2262

[15.2, •] **2.** A machine assembler is paid $4.65 for each unit assembled. Find the amount earned in one day if eight units are assembled.

[15.2, •••] **3.** An employee on piecework earns $4.10 for each unit produced and produced 105 in one 45-hour week. Calculate the gross earnings.

[15.3, •] **4.** Find the biweekly pay for an employee whose salary is $1300 a month.

[15.3, •] **5.** Find the weekly pay for a Registered Nurse who earns $1475 a month.

[15.4, •] **6.** A sales representative earns a 10% commission on sales made and a 3% commission on supervised employees sales. Sales for the representative were $30,000 and for supervised employees were $98,000. How much was the sales representative's commission?

[15.4, ••] **7.** A utility salesperson earns $310 for a 40 hour workweek plus a commission of 5% on sales. Utility sales last week were $2700 and hours worked 42. How much was earned?

544

PAYROLL

ANSWERS

[15.5, ●]

8. Use the percentage method to find the amount of federal income tax withheld weekly from the pay of a single taxpayer earning $330 a week and claiming three exemptions. Use Tables 22 and 23, pp. T–44 and T–45.

8. _____

[15.5, ●●]

9. Use the wage bracket method to find the amount of federal income tax withheld monthly from the pay of a married taxpayer earning $1500 a month and claiming four exemptions. Use Table 24, p. T–46.

9. _____

[15.6, ●]

10. An employee earns $39,000 in 1985. How much social security tax will be paid by the employee if the maximum taxable earnings are $38,100 and the rate is 7.05%?

10. _____

[15.6, ●●]

11. A self-employed person earns $47,000 in 1985. How much social security tax will be paid by the person if the maximum taxable earnings are $38,100 and the rate is 9.9%?

[15.7, ●]

12. Compute the net pay for a married employee who earns $245 weekly and claims six exemptions. The only deductions are for federal income tax and social security (6.7%). Use Table 24, p. T–46.

12. _____

[15.7, ●●●]

For the payroll data list shown below, find

13. _____

13. The current gross pay.

14. _____

14. The current social security tax.

EMP C/C	REGULAR	PREMIUM	VAC	SICK	P/L	HOL	GONE	VAC LEFT	VAC USED	P/L LEFT	P/L USED	PAY ADJ AMT	CHECK NO.
295/701	76.0				4			120.0		25.2	20.0		62283
	385.32				20.28								

FIC GROSS	GROSS	FEDERAL	STATE	DISAB	FICA	MEDICAL	STOCK	AUTO	SAVINGS	OTHER	NET	
405.60	405.60	70.52	13.00		24.54				24.34		273.20	C/E
2805.48	2846.04	447.88	86.72		169.73	59.55			170.79		1911.37	YTD

PART IV
STATISTICS

16
STATISTICS AND GRAPHS

Career: Data Processing/Teletype Operator *This is Toni Venezia. Toni operates a computer-oriented teletype machine which transmits stock and bond orders to the New York stock exchanges. Mathematics is quite relevant in Toni's job. Topics in this text which have bearing on her job include: fractions, ratios, percent, interest, taxes, financial statements, and statistics. The material on stocks and bonds in Chapter 8 is the most important.*

Toni received a BS degree in Business and Marketing from Indiana University. She has about two years of experience in the brokerage business. During that time she has worked as a sales assistant, cashier, and teletype operator. Toni has many attributes which contribute to her work. She is dedicated, enjoys working with people, and likes to take on new responsibilities.

Her hobbies include water skiing, tennis, swimming, and aerobic exercise.

STATISTICS AND GRAPHS

READINESS CHECK — SKILLS FOR CHAPTER 16

Divide. Write decimal notation.

1. $1142 \div 4$
2. $\dfrac{252}{5}$

Divide. Round to three decimal places.

3. $\dfrac{1193}{238}$

16.1 AVERAGES, MEDIANS, AND MODES

In this chapter we discuss various ways to organize data into graphs. We also learn to analyze data with measures of central tendency such as averages, medians, and modes.

● AVERAGES

Suppose we have a set of data and we wanted to pick one number which is representative, typical, or "central." There are several kinds of such numbers. One is called the *average*.

Suppose a person made the following salaries over a four-week period.

Week 1	$259.70
Week 2	$263.85
Week 3	$284.40
Week 4	$271.93

What is the *average* of the salaries? First, we add the salaries:

$259.70 + $263.85 + $284.40 + $271.93 = $1079.88.

Second, we divide by the number of addends:

$$\frac{\$1079.88}{4} = \$269.97.$$

Note that

$259.70 + $263.85 + $284.40 + $271.93 = $1079.88,

and that

($269.97) + ($269.97) + ($269.97) + ($269.97) = $1079.88.

The number $269.97 is called the *average*, *arithmetic mean*, or *mean* of the set of salaries.

> To find the *average* of a set of numbers,
> a) Add them; and
> b) Then divide by the number of addends.

OBJECTIVES

After finishing Section 16.1, you should be able to:

● Determine the mean or average.
●● Determine the median.
●●● Determine the mode.

16.1 AVERAGES, MEDIANS, AND MODES

Example 1 On a five-day trip a car was driven the following number of kilometers each day: 340, 402, 380, 305, and 314. What was the average number of kilometers per day?

Solution

$$\frac{340 + 402 + 380 + 305 + 314}{5} = \frac{1741}{5} = 348.2$$

The car was driven an average of 348.2 km per day. Thus, if the car had been driven exactly 348.2 km each day, it would have gone exactly the same total distance, 1741 km.

DO EXERCISES 1–4.

Sometimes we know the sum and need only divide.

Example 2 According to EPA estimates in a recent year, a Plymouth Gran Fury was expected to travel 468 miles (highway) on 26 gallons of gasoline. What was the average number of miles per gallon?

Solution

$$\frac{468}{26} = 18$$

The average was 18 miles per gallon.

DO EXERCISE 5.

Example 3 The following are the yearly salaries of the employees of Raggs, Ltd., a clothing store. What is the average salary?

Number	Type	Salary
1	Owner	$22,000
4	Salesperson	19,000
2	Secretary	17,000
1	Custodian	16,000

Solution

a) We first find out how much is paid in salaries:

```
1 · $22,000 = $ 22,000
4 · $19,000 =   76,000
2 · $17,000 =   34,000
1 · $16,000 =   16,000
               $148,000   Total salaries paid
```

b) Then we divide by the number of people employed:

$$\frac{\$148,000}{8} = \$18,500.$$

The average salary is $18,500.

DO EXERCISE 6.

Find the average of each set of numbers.

1. 24, 185, 46

2. 85, 46.8, 105.7, 22.1

3. A student made the following scores on four tests: 78, 81, 82, and 79. What was the average score?

4. One day a car dealer sold five cars for the following amounts: $6800.94, $7680.49, $9834.88, $12,340.90, $7200.00. What was the average amount of each sale? Round to the nearest cent.

5. According to EPA estimates in a recent year, an Oldsmobile 88 was expected to travel 550 miles on 22 gallons of gasoline. What was the average number of miles per gallon?

6. The following are the salaries at the Rollo Motorcycle Shop. What is the average salary?

Number	Type	Salary
1	Owner	$22,000
2	Salesperson	18,500
2	Secretary	16,000
1	Custodian	15,500

ANSWERS ON PAGE A–39

Find the median.

7. 20, 13, 17, 14, 18

8. 18, 18, 18, 18, 18

Find the median.

9. 18, 14, 16, 13, 19, 20

10. 38, 34, 77, 33, 37, 99

11. 7, 6, 7, 5, 8, 9

Find the mode(s).

12. 88, 76, 88, 91, 91, 88, 88, 91, 112

13. 203, 201, 201, 201, 201, 202, 203, 203, 200, 203

ANSWERS ON PAGE A-39

STATISTICS AND GRAPHS

⬛⬛ MEDIANS

A student makes the following amounts selling magazines:

$79, $82, $83, $77, $85.

Listing the amounts in order, we have

$77, $79, $82, $83, $85.

The middle amount, $82, is called the *median*.

DO EXERCISES 7 AND 8.

If there are an odd number of values in the set of data, there will always be a middle value. If the set of data has an even number of values, there will be two middle values.

If there are two middle values, then the median is the number halfway between, that is, the average of the two middle values.

Example 4 Find the median: 34, 33, 35, 36.

Solution

a) Arrange the numbers in order.

33, 34, 35, 36

b) The median is the average of 34 and 35.

33, 34, 35, 36
    ↑
    —— The median is 34.5. Add 34 and 35 and divide by 2.

DO EXERCISES 9–11.

⬛⬛⬛ MODES

The *mode* of a set of numbers is that number which appears most often.

Example 5 Find the mode: 4, 13, 15, 13, 17, 17, 19, 17.

Solution

a) Arrange the numbers in order.

4, 13, 13, 15, 17, 17, 17, 19

b) The number that appears most often, the mode, is 17.

Sometimes a set of numbers has more than one mode.

Example 6 Find the mode(s): 49, 50, 50, 51, 52, 53, 53, 59.

Solution This set of numbers has two modes: 50 and 53.

DO EXERCISES 12 AND 13.

EXERCISE SET 16.1

■ ■■ ■■■ Find the average, median, and mode of each set of numbers.

1. 18, 17, 25, 25, 25, 22

2. 62, 73, 73, 78, 82

3. 5, 10, 15, 20, 25, 15, 36

4. 32, 27, 25, 13, 13, 4

5. $6.30, $7.70, $9.40, $9.40

6. $23.40, $23.40, $12.60, $42.90

7. 1, 2, 3, 4, 5

8. 9, 9, 9, 9, 9

9. The following prices per pound of hamburger were found at five supermarkets:

    $1.59, $1.49, $1.69, $1.79, $1.79.

    What was the average price per pound?

10. The following prices per pound of steak were found at five supermarkets:

    $3.99, $3.79, $3.89, $3.99, $4.09.

    What was the average price per pound?

11. According to EPA estimates in a recent year, a Ford Pinto wagon was expected to travel 627 miles (highway) on 19 gallons of gasoline. What was the average number of miles per gallon?

12. According to EPA estimates in a recent year, an AMC Matador was expected to travel 357 miles (highway) on 21 gallons of gasoline. What was the average number of miles per gallon?

13. The following are the yearly salaries of the employees of Campus Sports Shop. What is the average salary?

Number	Type	Salary
1	Owner	$24,600
5	Salesperson	19,800
3	Secretary	17,400
1	Custodian	16,500

STATISTICS AND GRAPHS

14. The following are the yearly salaries of the employees of Pizza, Unltd. What is the average salary? Round to the nearest cent.

Number	Type	Salary
1	Manager	$18,400
3	Waiters and waitresses	11,200
2	Cooks	11,400
1	Custodian	9,500

15. A student got the following scores on five tests:

76, 79, 81, 81, 93.

What was the average? the median? the mode?

16. A person made the following salaries over a four-week period:

$269.70, $273.85, $294.40, $273.85.

What was the average? the median? the mode?

Find the average, median, and mode of each set of numbers.

17. Price of IBM stock: $306\frac{1}{4}$, $298\frac{7}{8}$, $296\frac{3}{8}$, 299, $302\frac{1}{2}$, $301\frac{1}{4}$, $300\frac{5}{8}$, 295. (Round to three decimal places.)

18. Attendances at a recent world series: 56,668, 56,691, 55,992, 55,995, 55,955, 56,407. (Round to the nearest one.)

Bowling Averages. Computing a bowling average involves a special kind of rounding. In effect, we never round up. For example, suppose a bowler gets a total of 599 for 3 games. To find the average, we divide 599 by 3 and drop the amount to the right of the decimal point:

$$\frac{599}{3} \approx 199.67. \qquad \text{The bowler's average is 199.}$$

In each case find the bowling average.

19. 547 pins in 3 games

20. 4621 pins in 27 games

21. To get a B in math a student must average 80 on five tests. Scores on the first four tests were 80, 74, 81, and 75. What is the lowest score the student can get on the last test and still get a B?

22. To get an A in math a student must average 90 on five tests. Scores on the first four tests were 90, 91, 81, and 92. What is the lowest score the student can get on the last test and still get an A?

16.2 BAR GRAPHS AND FREQUENCY DISTRIBUTIONS

● BAR GRAPHS

A bar graph is shown below. Such a graph is convenient for showing comparisons.

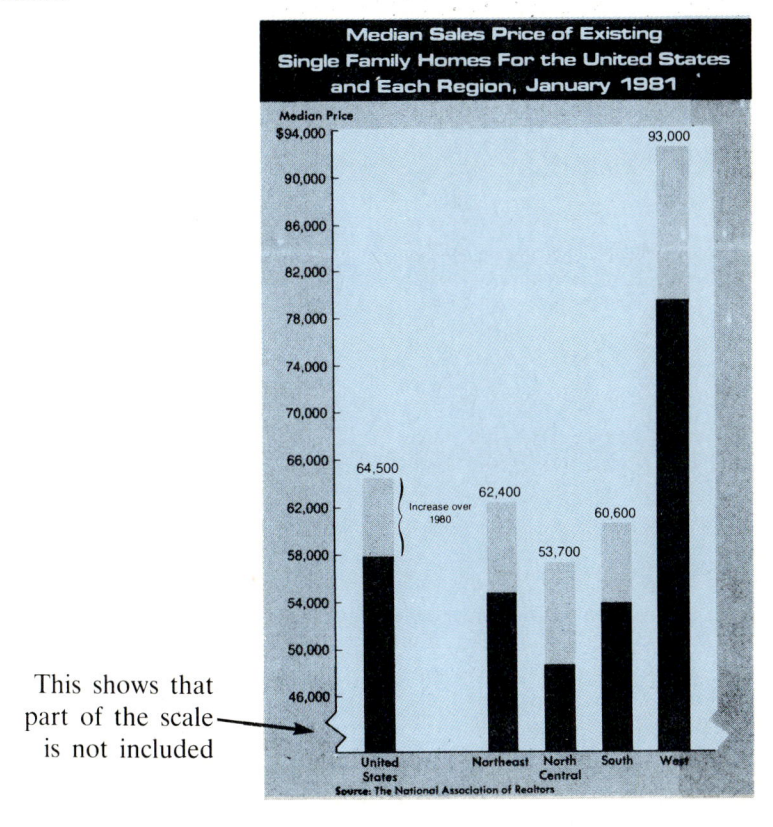

Median Sales Price of Existing Single Family Homes For the United States and Each Region, January 1981

- United States: 64,500 (Increase over 1980)
- Northeast: 62,400
- North Central: 53,700
- South: 60,600
- West: 93,000

Source: The National Association of Realtors

This shows that part of the scale is not included →

Example 1 Make a bar graph of the data in the table shown at right.

Year	Sales of XYZ Pub. Co. (in millions)
1984	$50
1985	55
1986	53
1987	57
1988	62

Solution

a) Draw and label a vertical axis. Label the axis in relation to the data.

b) Draw and label a horizontal axis.

c) Draw vertical bars to show the sales each year.

The graph is shown at right, in the margin. Note that we do not start the "Year" data at 0 since it would make the graph unduly large.

DO EXERCISE 1.

OBJECTIVES

After finishing Section 16.2, you should be able to:

● Make a bar graph for a set of data.

●● Make a bar graph of a frequency distribution.

1. Make a bar graph for the data in the table.

Year	Net Income of Anacomp, Inc. (in millions)
1978	1.5
1979	2.7
1980	4.6
1981	7.9
1982	4.6

ANSWER ON PAGE A–39

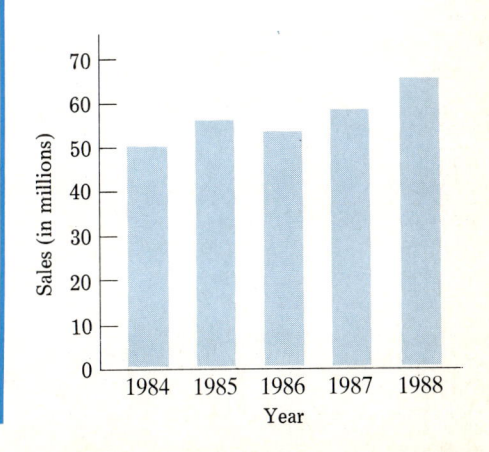

2. Make a bar graph of this frequency distribution.

Salary	Frequency
$22,000	1
$19,000	4
$17,000	2
$16,000	1

FREQUENCY DISTRIBUTIONS

When large sets of data are considered, it is sometimes convenient to group the data. For example, suppose we were analyzing the contributions of 266 people to a charity. Rather than make a graph of each of the contributions of the people, we group the data according to how many contributed, say $50–$99, then how many contributed $100–$199, and so on.

Example 2 Make a bar graph of this frequency distribution.

Contribution	Frequency
Over $2500	2
$1500–$2499	11
$1000–$1499	19
$500–$999	24
$100–$499	20
$0–$99	10

Solution

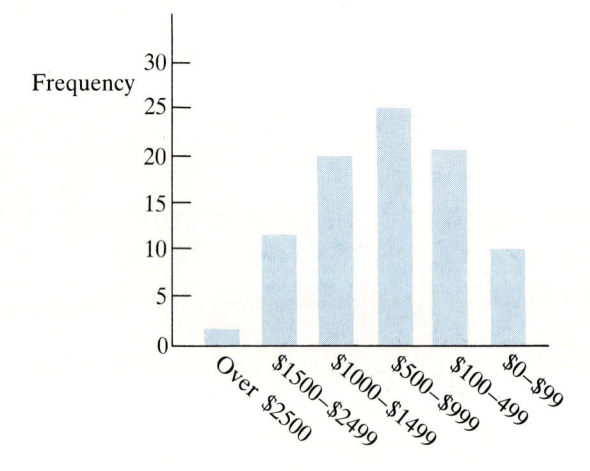

Frequencies are normally located on the vertical axis. The contributions are located on the horizontal axis. The result is six bars, one for each category.

DO EXERCISE 2.

ANSWER ON PAGE A-39

EXERCISE SET 16.2

■ Make a bar graph for each of the following.

1.

Causes of Death	Number of Deaths in U.S. in 1975 (in Thousands)
Heart	994
Cancer	366
Accidents	103
Pneumonia and influenza	56
Diabetes	35
Other	339

2.

Stock	Price Per Share
Texas Intl.	$12\frac{3}{8}$
Exxon	$53\frac{1}{4}$
Sears	21
Caesar's World	$55\frac{1}{8}$
American Motors	$7\frac{1}{2}$
General Motors	56

3.

Number of People in a Car Pool	Average Savings Per Person in a Car Pool Driving to Work
2	$427
3	553
4	617
5	654

4.

State	Average Income Per Person
Alaska	$12,081
Washington, D.C.	9,358
New Jersey	8,562
Indiana	7,218
Illinois	8,522
Ohio	7,437

STATISTICS AND GRAPHS

5.

Olympic Winners in Women's 100-Meter Dash	Time (Seconds)
Betty Cuthbert, Australia (1956)	11.5
Wilma Rudolph, United States (1960)	11.0
Wyomia Tyus, United States (1964)	11.4
Wyomia Tyus, United States (1968)	11.0
Renate Stecher, E. Germany (1972)	11.07
Annegret Richter, W. Germany (1976)	11.01

6.

Location	Annual Growth Rate
Western Sahara	10.6%
Mexico	3.5
U.S. Virgin Islands	9.6
Guam	5.0
United States	0.8
U.S.S.R.	1.0
World	1.9

■■ Make a bar graph of each frequency distribution.

7.

Letter	Frequency of Occurrence for Every 100 Letters of Writing
A	8
E	13
I	7
O	8
U	3

8.

Gasoline Sales in One Day at a Service Station	Frequency
Over $30	1
$25–$29.99	8
$20–$24.99	15
$15–$19.99	20
$10–$14.99	18
$0–$9.99	13

16.3 LINE GRAPHS AND CIRCLE GRAPHS

◼ LINE GRAPHS

An example of a line graph is shown below. Line graphs are useful for showing comparisons, especially of several sets of data.

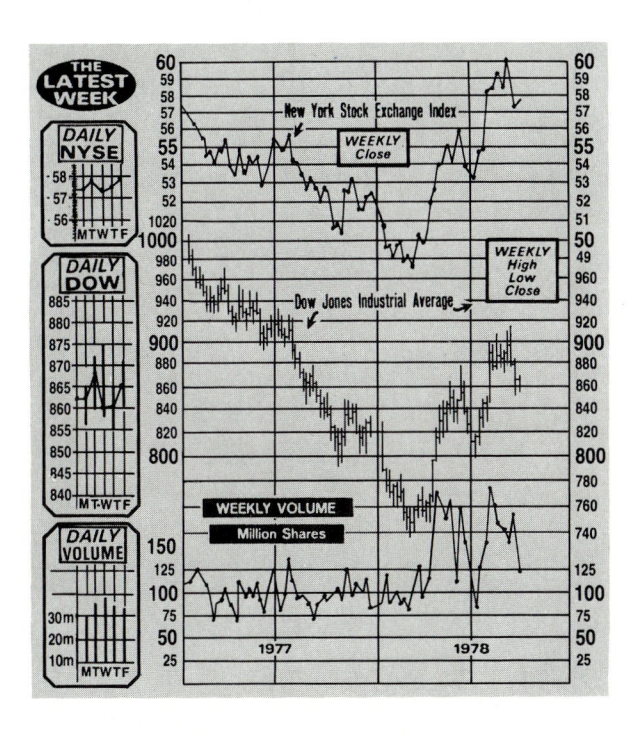

OBJECTIVES

After finishing Section 16.3, you should be able to:

◼ Make a line graph for a set of data.

◼◼ Make a circle graph for a set of data.

Example 1 Make a line graph of this set of data.

Month	Prime Rate (%)
June	10
July	13
August	20
Sept	14

Solution

a) Draw and label a vertical axis. We label it starting with some number less than or equal to all numbers in the table. In this case we start with 10, and mark units that are multiples of 5%.

b) Draw and label a horizontal axis.

c) We start at each month and move up to its corresponding percent, and mark a point.

1. Make a line graph for the data in the table below.

Year	Estimated Sales, in millions
1988	17.0
1990	19.5
1992	17.8
1994	18.1

d) Connect each pair of points with a line.

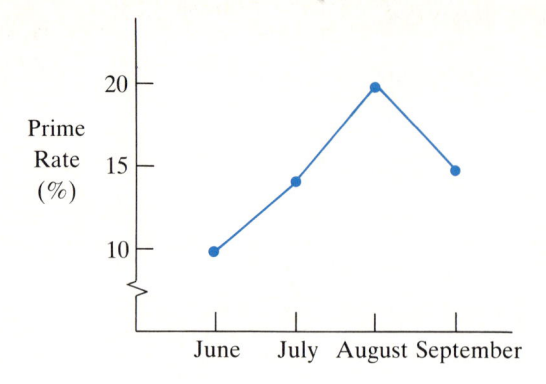

DO EXERCISE 1.

CIRCLE GRAPHS

Below is a circle graph prepared by the Indiana Gas Company for its customers. It shows how each customer's dollar is spent. Circle graphs are usually used to show percentage parts of a quantity.

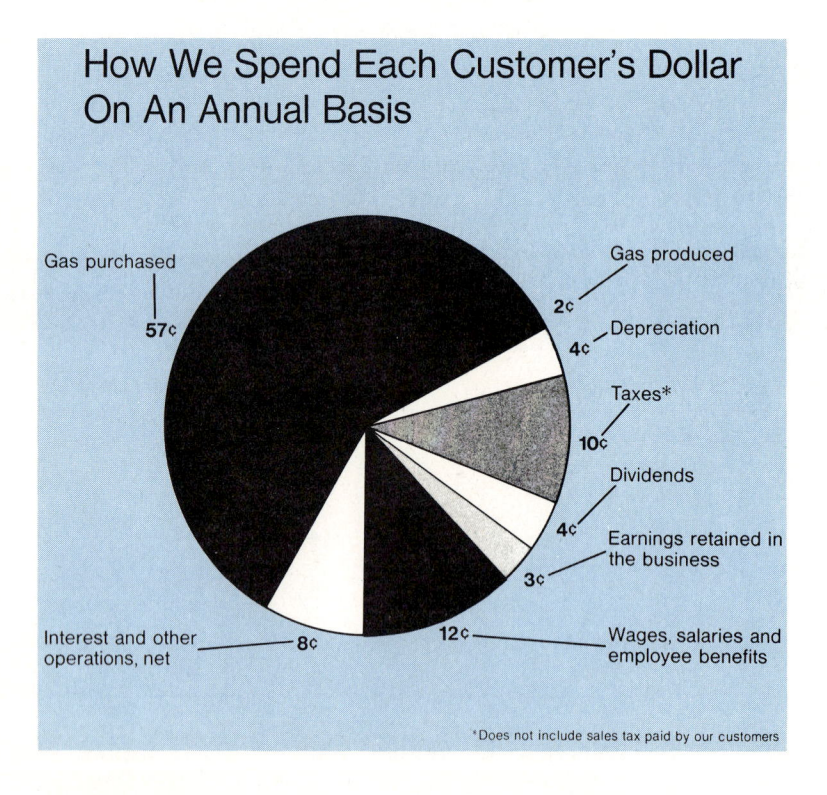

How We Spend Each Customer's Dollar On An Annual Basis

- Gas purchased 57¢
- Gas produced 2¢
- Depreciation 4¢
- Taxes* 10¢
- Dividends 4¢
- Earnings retained in the business 3¢
- Wages, salaries and employee benefits 12¢
- Interest and other operations, net 8¢

*Does not include sales tax paid by our customers

Example 1 Complete the table and make a circle graph.

ANSWER ON PAGE A-40

16.3 LINE GRAPHS AND CIRCLE GRAPHS

Item	Average Monthly Budget Costs for a Family of Four with an Intermediate Income*	Percent	Angle
Food	$ 442		
Housing	427		
Transportation	152		
Clothing	168		
Medical care	183		
Personal care	38		
Other goods and services (reading, recreation, education, etc,.)	94		
Other items such as job expenses, contributions, life insurance, etc.	81		
Total	$1585		

*According to the Bureau of Labor Statistics.

Solution

a) Find what percent each item is of the total, and multiply by 360°, the total number of degrees in a circle.

$\dfrac{442}{1585} \approx 28\%$, 28% × 360° = 0.28 × 360° ≈ 101°;

$\dfrac{427}{1585} \approx 27\%$, 27% × 360° = 0.27 × 360° ≈ 97°;

$\dfrac{152}{1585} \approx 10\%$, 10% × 360° = 0.10 × 360° ≈ 36°;

$\dfrac{168}{1585} \approx 11\%$, 11% × 360° = 0.11 × 360° ≈ 40°;

$\dfrac{183}{1585} \approx 12\%$, 12% × 360° = 0.12 × 360° ≈ 43°;

$\dfrac{38}{1585} \approx 2\%$, 2% × 360° = 0.02 × 360° ≈ 7°;

$\dfrac{94}{1585} \approx 6\%$, 6% × 360° = 0.06 × 360° ≈ 22°;

$\dfrac{81}{1585} \approx 5\%$, 5% × 360° = 0.05 × 360° ≈ 18°;

2. Complete the table and make a circle graph.

Hair color	Number of Students	Percent	Angle
Black	11		
Brown	14		
Blonde	4		
Red	3		
Total	32		

b) Draw the circle and a radius.

c) Draw angles with measures from the table.

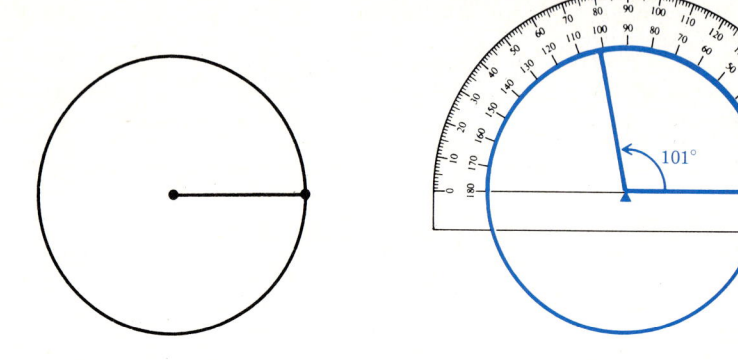

101°

d) Label each part of the circle with the corresponding item and percent.

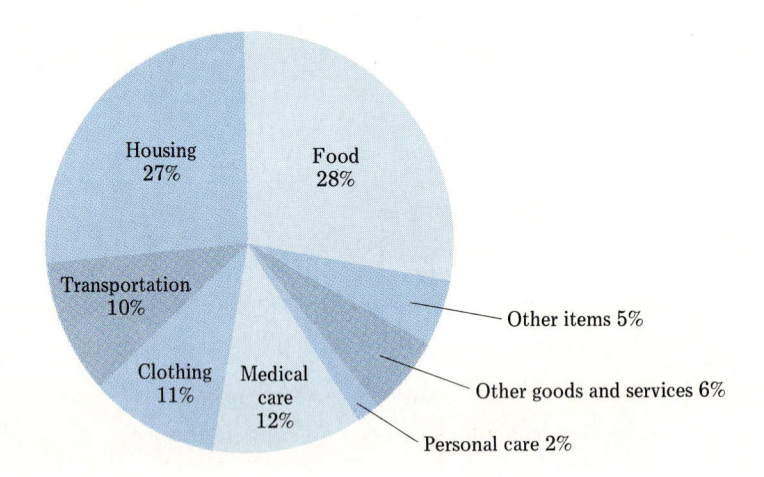

Housing 27%
Food 28%
Transportation 10%
Clothing 11%
Medical care 12%
Other items 5%
Other goods and services 6%
Personal care 2%

DO EXERCISE 2.

EXERCISE SET 16.3

■ Make a line graph for each of the following.

1.

Time of Repayment (in Months)	Total Amount Due on a Car Loan of $3000 at 11% Interest (Assuming Monthly Payments)
18	$3268
24	3356
30	3445
36	3536

2.

Year	Estimated Population of U.S. (in Millions)
1981	225
1983	228
1985	332
1987	236
1989	240
1991	244

3.

Week	Amount Spent for Recreation
1	$10.00
2	14.50
3	8.00
4	16.25
5	12.75

4.

Distance (in Miles)	Cost of 5-min Weekday Direct Dial Phone Call
50	$1.69
100	1.89
150	1.94
200	2.04
250	2.04
300	2.14

560 STATISTICS AND GRAPHS

Make two graphs together. Use a solid line (—) for men and a dashed line (---) for women.

5.

Height (in Inches)	Desirable Weight for Medium Frame Men	Women
63	133	122
64	136	126
65	139	130
66	143	135
67	147	139
68	152	143

6.

Age	Average Number of Remaining Years of Life Men	Women
50	24	30
55	20	26
60	17	22
65	14	18
70	11	14

EXERCISE SET 16.3

Complete each table and make a circle graph.

7.

Deodorant	Number Preferring	Percent	Angle
A	34		
B	26		
C	38		
D	2		
Total	100		

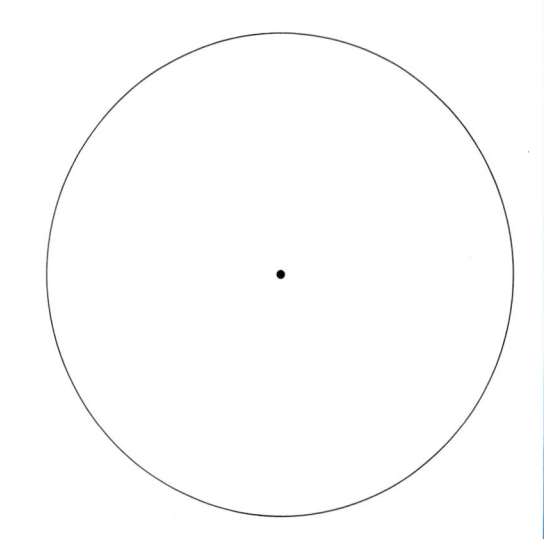

8.

Fast-food restaurant	Number Preferring	Percent	Angle
A	22		
B	30		
C	12		
D	16		
Total	80		

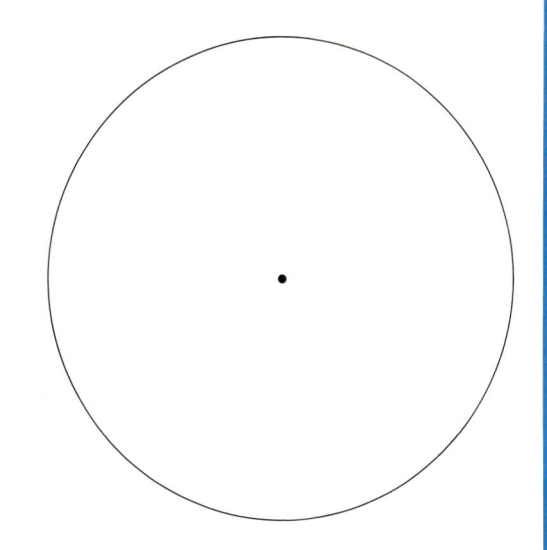

9.

Number of TV Sets in Household	Percent of Homes in U.S. in 1965	Angle
0	8	
1	72	
2 or more	20	

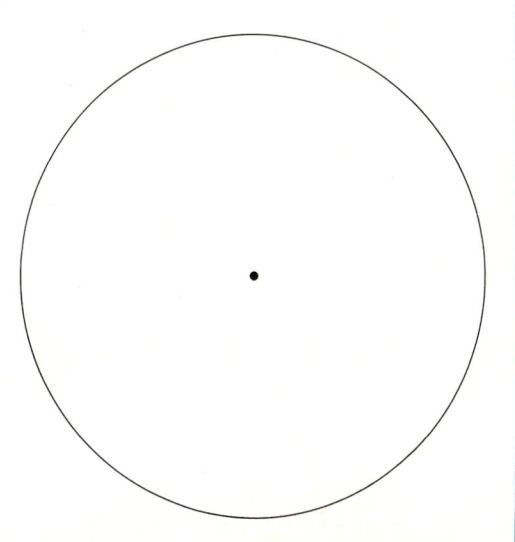

STATISTICS AND GRAPHS

10.

Number of TV Sets in Household	Percent of Homes in U.S. in 1975	Angle
0	3	
1	51	
2 or more	46	

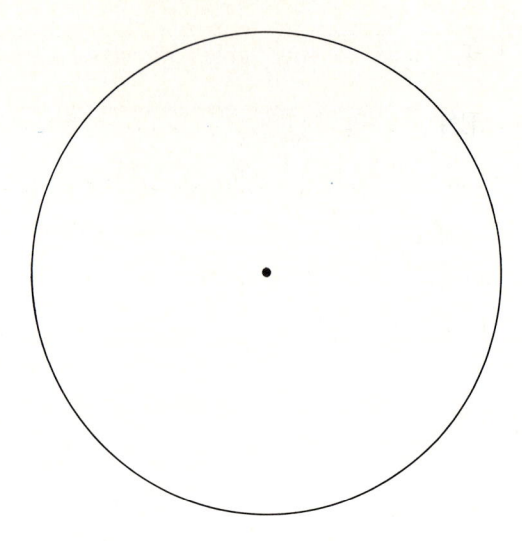

11.

Income of People in U.S. in 1981	Percent of Population	Angle
$29,000 and over	13	
$17,400–$28,999	33	
$11,600–$17,399	23	
$8100–$11,599	12	
Below $8100	19	

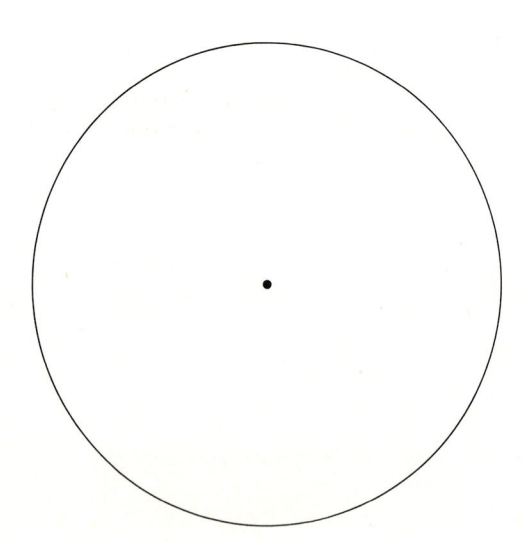

12.

Sandwich	Percent who Purchased	Angle
Hamburger	42	
Cheeseburger	38	
Fish	10	
Hot dog	10	

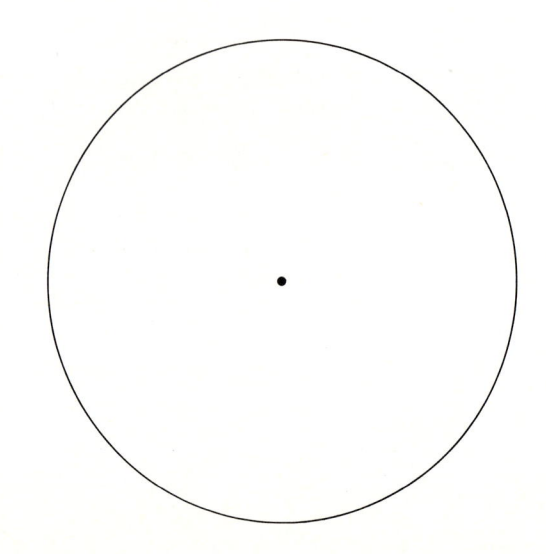

NAME _____ SCORE _____ ANSWERS

TEST OR REVIEW — CHAPTER 16

If you miss an item, review the indicated section and objective.

[16.1, •]   Find the average, median, and mode of each set of numbers.

[16.1, ••] **1.** 45, 64, 46, 45, 47, 50, 51, 68

1. _____

[16.1, •••] **2.** $1.89, $1.79, $2.49, $1.69, $1.80, $1.89

2. _____

[16.2, •]   **3.** Make a bar graph.

Sandwich	Calories
Hamburger	249
Cheeseburger	309
Fish	406
Double hamburger	350

[16.3, •]   **4.** Make a line graph.

End of Year	Average Cash Value of $10,000 Whole Life Insurance Policy
0	$ 0
5	490
10	1270
15	2000
20	2790

564   STATISTICS AND GRAPHS

[16.3, ●●]   **5.** Make a circle graph.

Brand of Denim Jeans	Number Purchased	Percent	Angle
A	5		
B	16		
C	10		
D	19		
Total	50		

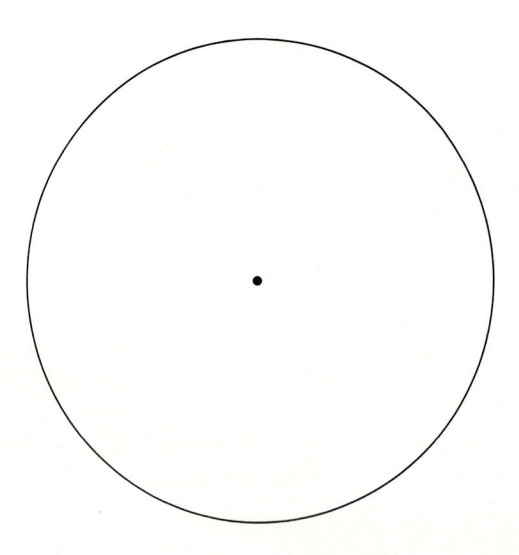

[16.2, ●●]   **6.** Make a bar graph of this frequency distribution.

Test Scores	Frequency
90–100	8
80–89	10
70–79	20
60–69	5
0–59	2

APPENDIX: THE METRIC SYSTEM

566

OBJECTIVES

After finishing this appendix, you should be able to:

- Convert between metric units of length.
- Convert between metric units of capacity.
- Convert between metric units of mass.
- Convert between metric units of temperature.

APPENDIX: THE METRIC SYSTEM

APPENDIX — THE METRIC SYSTEM

The *metric system* is used in almost every country in the world. Although there is some resistance to change, it is slowly being used more and more in the United States. Like the U. S. monetary system, the metric system is based on the number 10. Since our numbering system is also based on 10, using the metric system is advantageous.

LENGTH

The basic unit of length is the *meter*. It is just a bit longer than a yard. The other units of length are products of a meter by 10, 100, and 1000, or by fractions of a meter, $\frac{1}{10}$, $\frac{1}{100}$, and $\frac{1}{1000}$.

1 *kilo*meter (km)	= 1000 meters (m)
1 *hecto*meter (hm)	= 100 meters (m)
1 *deka*meter (dam)	= 10 meters (m)
1 *deci*meter (dm)	= $\frac{1}{10}$ meter (m)
1 *centi*meter (cm)	= $\frac{1}{100}$ meter (m)
1 *milli*meter (mm)	= $\frac{1}{1000}$ meter (m)

It will be helpful to memorize the metric prefixes shown in italics on the chart above. Think of *kilo-* for 1000; *centi-* for $\frac{1}{100}$; and so on. These prefixes are used with other metric measures as well as with length.

Converting Metric Lengths

Suppose we want to change 7.84 kilometers to meters. Note the following:

$$7.84 \text{ km} = 7.84 \times 1 \text{ km}$$
$$= 7.84 \times 1000 \text{ m} \quad 1 \text{ km} = 1000 \text{ m}$$
$$= 7840 \text{ m}.$$

The conversion amounted only to a movement of the decimal point. Think of this in terms of changing 56.9 feet to inches. A multiplication by 12 is necessary and this is much more awkward. Changing from one unit to another in the metric system amounts only to the movement of a decimal point. To see how this works look at the prefix table.

1000	100	10	1	0.1	0.01	0.001
km	hm	dam	m	dm	cm	mm

Each unit in the table is 10 times that to its right and 0.1 times that to its left. Let us see how to use the table when we wish to convert.

Example 1 Complete: 5.7 m = _____ cm.

Solution *Think:* To go from "m" to "cm" in the table is a move of 2 places to the right.

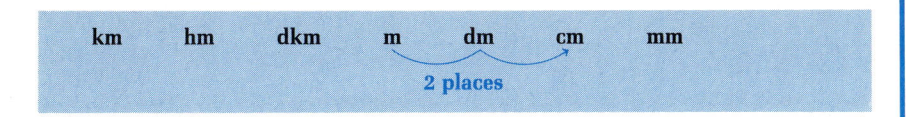

km	hm	dkm	m	dm	cm	mm

2 places

We move the decimal point 2 places to the right.

5.7   5.7 0.

Thus, 5.7 cm = 570 cm.

Example 2 Complete: 6.91 mm = _____ cm.

Solution *Think:* To go from "mm" to "cm" in the table is a move of 1 place to the left.

km	hm	dam	m	dm	cm	mm

1 place

We move the decimal point 1 place to the left.

6.9 1   0.6.9 1

Thus, 6.91 mm = 0.691 cm.

DO EXERCISES 1–4.

▰▰ CAPACITY

The metric unit of capacity (volume) is the *liter*. A liter is just a bit more than a quart. The liter is defined as follows.

> 1 liter (L) = 1000 cubic centimeters (1000 cm^3) = 1000 mL
> = 1 cubic decimeter (1 dm^3)
> 1 mL = 0.001 L = 1 cm^3

The notation "cc" is also used for cubic centimeter, particularly in medicine. The script letter ℓ is also used for liter. The milliliter (mL) is the most frequently used unit of capacity.

Changing Metric Capacities

We again use a prefix table to convert metric capacities.

1000	100	10	1	0.1	0.01	0.001
kL	hL	daL	L	dL	cL	mL

Example 3 Complete: 8.9 L = _____ mL.

Complete.

1. 7.106 mm = _____ cm

2. 2.997 km = _____ cm

3. 56.89 mm = _____ dm

4. 7.3 m = _____ cm

ANSWERS ON PAGE A–42

Complete.

5. 0.84 L = _____ mL

6. 7660 mL = _____ L

ANSWERS ON PAGE A–42

APPENDIX: THE METRIC SYSTEM

Solution *Think:* To go from "L" to "mL" in the table is a move of 3 places to the right.

| kL | hL | daL | L | dL | cL | mL |

3 places

We move the decimal point 3 places to the right.

8.9   8.9 0 0.

Thus, 8.9 L = 8900 mL.

Example 4 Complete: 314 mL = _____ L.

Solution *Think:* To go from "mL" to "L" in the table is a move of 3 places to the left.

Therefore, we move the decimal point 3 places to the left.

3 1 4.   0.3 1 4.

Thus, 314 mL = 0.314 L.

DO EXERCISES 5 AND 6.

▪▪▪ MASS

There is a difference between weight and mass even though the words are often used as though they had the same meaning. *Mass* may be measured on a balance scale and always stays the same. *Weight* is related to the gravitational pull on an object and varies with the distance that the object is from the center of the earth. The basic unit of mass is the gram (g), which is the mass of 1 cubic centimeter (1 cm^3 or 1 mL) of water at a temperature of 4°. A gram is therefore a small unit of mass.

The following table shows metric units of mass. Again, we have the same prefixes and the addition of another—the metric ton, t, which is 1000 kilograms.

1 metric ton (t)	= 1000 kilograms (kg)	1 decigram (dg)	= $\frac{1}{10}$ g
1 kilogram (kg)	= 1000 grams (g)		
1 hectogram (hg)	= 100 g	1 centigram (cg)	= $\frac{1}{100}$ g
1 dekagram (dag)	= 10 g		
		1 milligram (mg)	= $\frac{1}{1000}$ g

Changing Metric Masses

We again use a prefix table to convert metric masses.

1000	100	10	1	0.1	0.01	0.001
kg	hg	dag	g	dg	cg	mg

Example 5 Complete: 9 kg = _____ g.

Solution *Think:* To go from "kg" to "g" in the table is a move of 3 places to the right.

kg   hg   dag   g   dg   cg   mg

3 places

We move the decimal point 3 places to the right.

9.   9.0 0 0.

Thus, 9 kg = 9000 g.

Example 6 Complete: 5662 g = _____ kg.

Solution *Think:* To go from "g" to "kg" in the table is a move of 3 places to the left.

Therefore, we move the decimal point 3 places to the left.

5 6 6 2.   5.6 6 2.

Thus, 5662 g = 5.662 kg.

DO EXERCISES 7–10.

TEMPERATURE

The metric temperature scale is called *Celsius* (sometimes *centigrade*). Below we see how Celsius (C) compares with the American measure, *Fahrenheit* (F).

---

1. To convert from Celsius to Fahrenheit:

   $F = \frac{9}{5} \cdot C + 32$,   or $F = 1.8 \times C + 32$.

   Multiply by $\frac{9}{5}$, or 1.8, and then add 32.

2. To convert from Fahrenheit to Celsius:

   $C = \frac{5}{9} \cdot (F - 32)$.

   Subtract 32 and then multiply by $\frac{5}{9}$.

Example 7 Convert 37° (normal body temperature) to Fahrenheit.

Solution

$F = 1.8 \times 37° + 32°$ Substitute 37° into the equation
$ = 66.6° + 32°$
$ = 98.6°$

Complete.

7. 8.3 kg = _____ g

8. 209.4 g = _____ kg

9. 2.1 cg = _____ mg

10. 6788 mg = _____ cg

ANSWERS ON PAGE A–42

Convert to Celsius.

11. 25°F (A cold day)

Example 8 Convert 104°F to Celsius.

Solution

$$C = \frac{5}{9} \cdot (104 - 32) \quad \text{First subtract 32 from 104°.}$$

$$= \frac{5}{9} \cdot 72 \quad \text{Then multiply by } \frac{5}{9}.$$

$$= 40°$$

DO EXERCISES 11–14.

12. 32°F (Water freezes)

Convert to Fahrenheit.

13. 20°C (Room temperature)

14. −22°C (Typical temperature during the day on Mars)

ANSWERS ON PAGE A–42

EXERCISES—APPENDIX

NAME _____ CLASS _____

● **Complete.**

1. a) 1 km = _____ m
   b) 1 m = _____ km

2. a) 1 dm = _____ m
   b) 1 m = _____ dm

3. a) 1 hm = _____ m
   b) 1 m = _____ hm

4. a) 1 dam = _____ m
   b) 1 m = _____ dam

5. a) 1 mm = _____ m
   b) 1 m = _____ mm

6. a) 1 cm = _____ m
   b) 1 m = _____ cm

7. 7.8 km = _____ m

8. 10 km = _____ m

9. 87 cm = _____ m

10. 0.344 cm = _____ m

11. 7801 m = _____ km

12. 8110 m = _____ km

13. 65.55 m = _____ km

14. 7.999 m = _____ km

15. 7999 m = _____ cm

16. 546 m = _____ cm

17. 788 cm = _____ m

18. 1.08 mm = _____ m

19. 3.11 m = _____ cm

20. 4.22 m = _____ dm

21. 1 mm = _____ cm

22. 1 cm = _____ km

23. 1 km = _____ cm

24. 2 km = _____ cm

25. 4500 mm = _____ cm

26. 8,200,000 m = _____ km

27. 1.3 dam = _____ dm

28. 8 km = _____ hm

29. 0.014 mm = _____ dm

30. 672 dam = _____ km

31. 6.88 m = _____ dam

32. 1.8 m = _____ hm

●● **Complete.**

33. 1 L = _____ mL = _____ cm³

34. _____ L = 1 mL = _____ cm³

35. 96 L = _____ mL

36. 801 L = _____ mL

37. 69 mL = _____ L

38. 19 mL = _____ L

39. 0.703 mL = _____ L

40. 0.012 mL = _____ L

41. 8.012 L = _____ mL

42. 1.009 L = _____ mL

●●● **Complete.**

43. 1 kg = _____ g

44. 1 hg = _____ g

45. 1 dag = _____ g

Copyright © 1984, by Addison-Wesley Publishing Company Inc. All rights reserved.

572   APPENDIX: THE METRIC SYSTEM

46. 1 dg = _____ g   **47.** 1 cg = _____ g   **48.** 1 g = _____ mg

49. 1 g = _____ cg   **50.** 1 g = _____ dg   **51.** 25 kg = _____ g

52. 345 kg = _____ g   **53.** 789 g = _____ kg   **54.** 6300 g = _____ kg

55. 0.705 kg = _____ g   **56.** 97 kg = _____ g   **57.** 57 cg = _____ kg

58. 0.833 dg = _____ g   **59.** 7890 g = _____ kg   **60.** 6788 g = _____ kg

61. 78 mg = _____ cg   **62.** 89.2 mg = _____ cg **63.** 0.7 kg = _____ cg

64. 0.01 kg = _____ mg   **65.** 4 hg = _____ kg   **66.** 2 dag = _____ hg

67. 3.4 cg = _____ dag   **68.** 3.2 dg = _____ mg   **69.** 1 t = _____ kg

70. 2 t = _____ kg

▪▪ Convert.

Convert to Fahrenheit. Use the formula $F = \frac{9}{5} \cdot C + 32$, or $1.8 \times C + 32$.

71. 65°C   **72.** 50°C   **73.** 15°C   **74.** 90°C

75. 30.6°C (Butter melts)   **76.** 4.4°C (Ideal temperature for refrigeration of food)

Convert to Celsius. Use the formula $C = \frac{5}{9} \cdot (F - 32)$.

77. 140°F   **78.** 131°F   **79.** 59°F   **80.** 86°F

81. 1832°F (Melting point of gold)   **82.** 98.6°F (Normal body temperature)

TABLES

Table 1 Day of the Year   T–1
Table 2 Simple Interest on $100 (360-day Basis)   T–2
Table 3 Simple Interest on $100 (365-day Basis)   T–3
Table 4 Compound Interest   T–4
Table 5 Daily Compound Interest on $100 (365-day Basis)   T–6
Table 6 Daily Compound Interest on $100 (360-day Basis)   T–7
Table 7 5% Compounded Daily (360-day Basis)   T–8
Table 8 5% Compounded Continuously (360-day Basis)   T–8
Table 9 Present Value   T–9
Table 10 Amount of Annuity $S_{\overline{n}|i}$ T–11
Table 11 Present Value of Annuity $A_{\overline{n}|i}$ T–13
Table 12 Annual Percentage Rate Table for Monthly Payment Plans   T–15
Table 13 Monthly Payment Required to Amortize a Loan   T–22
Table 14 Betterment (Depreciation) Guide   T–26
Table 15 Homeowner's Insurance Rates   T–29
Table 16 Basic Premium for Automobile Insurance (Six Months)   T–33
Table 17 Rating Factors   T–34
Table 18 Life Insurance   T–34
Table 19 Table of Values   T–35
Table 20 Ordinary Life (per $1000)   T–36
Table 21 Federal Income Tax Tables   T–38
Table 22 Percentage Method Income Tax Withholding Table   T–44
Table 23 Tables for Percentage Method of Withholding   T–45
Table 24 Federal Income Tax Withholding Tables   T–46

TABLE 12
ANNUAL PERCENTAGE RATE TABLE FOR MONTHLY PAYMENT PLANS

NUMBER OF PAYMENTS	10.00%	10.25%	10.50%	10.75%	11.00%	11.25%	11.50%	11.75%	12.00%	12.25%	12.50%	12.75%	13.00%	13.25%	13.50%	13.75%
	\multicolumn{16}{c}{(FINANCE CHARGE PER $100 OF AMOUNT FINANCED)}
1	0.83	0.85	0.87	0.90	0.92	0.94	0.96	0.98	1.00	1.02	1.04	1.06	1.08	1.10	1.12	1.15
2	1.25	1.28	1.31	1.35	1.38	1.41	1.44	1.47	1.50	1.53	1.57	1.60	1.63	1.66	1.69	1.72
3	1.67	1.71	1.76	1.80	1.84	1.88	1.92	1.96	2.01	2.05	2.09	2.13	2.17	2.22	2.26	2.30
4	2.09	2.14	2.20	2.25	2.30	2.35	2.41	2.46	2.51	2.57	2.62	2.67	2.72	2.78	2.83	2.88
5	2.51	2.58	2.64	2.70	2.77	2.83	2.89	2.96	3.02	3.08	3.15	3.21	3.27	3.34	3.40	3.46
6	2.94	3.01	3.08	3.16	3.23	3.31	3.38	3.45	3.53	3.60	3.68	3.75	3.83	3.90	3.97	4.05
7	3.36	3.45	3.53	3.62	3.70	3.78	3.87	3.95	4.04	4.12	4.21	4.29	4.38	4.47	4.55	4.64
8	3.79	3.88	3.98	4.07	4.17	4.26	4.36	4.46	4.55	4.65	4.74	4.84	4.94	5.03	5.13	5.22
9	4.21	4.32	4.43	4.53	4.64	4.75	4.85	4.96	5.07	5.17	5.28	5.39	5.49	5.60	5.71	5.82
10	4.64	4.76	4.88	4.99	5.11	5.23	5.35	5.46	5.58	5.70	5.82	5.94	6.05	6.17	6.29	6.41
11	5.07	5.20	5.33	5.45	5.58	5.71	5.84	5.97	6.10	6.23	6.36	6.49	6.62	6.75	6.88	7.01
12	5.50	5.64	5.78	5.92	6.06	6.20	6.34	6.48	6.62	6.76	6.90	7.04	7.18	7.32	7.46	7.60
13	5.93	6.08	6.23	6.38	6.53	6.68	6.84	6.99	7.14	7.29	7.44	7.59	7.75	7.90	8.05	8.20
14	6.36	6.52	6.69	6.85	7.01	7.17	7.34	7.50	7.66	7.82	7.99	8.15	8.31	8.48	8.64	8.81
15	6.80	6.97	7.14	7.32	7.49	7.66	7.84	8.01	8.19	8.36	8.53	8.71	8.88	9.06	9.23	9.41
16	7.23	7.41	7.60	7.78	7.97	8.15	8.34	8.53	8.71	8.90	9.08	9.27	9.46	9.64	9.83	10.02
17	7.67	7.86	8.06	8.25	8.45	8.65	8.84	9.04	9.24	9.44	9.63	9.83	10.03	10.23	10.43	10.63
18	8.10	8.31	8.52	8.73	8.93	9.14	9.35	9.56	9.77	9.98	10.19	10.40	10.61	10.82	11.03	11.24
19	8.54	8.76	8.98	9.20	9.42	9.64	9.86	10.08	10.30	10.52	10.74	10.96	11.18	11.41	11.63	11.85
20	8.98	9.21	9.44	9.67	9.90	10.13	10.37	10.60	10.83	11.06	11.30	11.53	11.76	12.00	12.23	12.46
21	9.42	9.66	9.90	10.15	10.39	10.63	10.88	11.12	11.36	11.61	11.85	12.10	12.34	12.59	12.84	13.08
22	9.86	10.12	10.37	10.62	10.88	11.13	11.39	11.64	11.90	12.16	12.41	12.67	12.93	13.19	13.44	13.70
23	10.30	10.57	10.84	11.10	11.37	11.63	11.90	12.17	12.44	12.71	12.97	13.24	13.51	13.78	14.05	14.32
24	10.75	11.02	11.30	11.58	11.86	12.14	12.42	12.70	12.98	13.26	13.54	13.82	14.10	14.38	14.66	14.95
25	11.19	11.48	11.77	12.06	12.35	12.64	12.93	13.22	13.52	13.81	14.10	14.40	14.69	14.98	15.28	15.57
26	11.64	11.94	12.24	12.54	12.85	13.15	13.45	13.75	14.06	14.36	14.67	14.97	15.28	15.59	15.89	16.20
27	12.09	12.40	12.71	13.03	13.34	13.66	13.97	14.29	14.60	14.92	15.24	15.56	15.87	16.19	16.51	16.83
28	12.53	12.86	13.18	13.51	13.84	14.16	14.49	14.82	15.15	15.48	15.81	16.14	16.47	16.80	17.13	17.46
29	12.98	13.32	13.66	14.00	14.33	14.67	15.01	15.35	15.70	16.04	16.38	16.72	17.07	17.41	17.75	18.10
30	13.43	13.78	14.13	14.48	14.83	15.19	15.54	15.89	16.24	16.60	16.95	17.31	17.66	18.02	18.38	18.74
31	13.89	14.25	14.61	14.97	15.33	15.70	16.06	16.43	16.79	17.16	17.53	17.90	18.27	18.63	19.00	19.38
32	14.34	14.71	15.09	15.46	15.84	16.21	16.59	16.97	17.35	17.73	18.11	18.49	18.87	19.25	19.63	20.02
33	14.79	15.18	15.57	15.95	16.34	16.73	17.12	17.51	17.90	18.29	18.69	19.08	19.47	19.87	20.26	20.66
34	15.25	15.65	16.05	16.44	16.85	17.25	17.65	18.05	18.46	18.86	19.27	19.67	20.08	20.49	20.90	21.31
35	15.70	16.11	16.53	16.94	17.35	17.77	18.18	18.60	19.01	19.43	19.85	20.27	20.69	21.11	21.53	21.95
36	16.16	16.58	17.01	17.43	17.86	18.29	18.71	19.14	19.57	20.00	20.43	20.87	21.30	21.73	22.17	22.60
37	16.62	17.06	17.49	17.93	18.37	18.81	19.25	19.69	20.13	20.58	21.02	21.46	21.91	22.36	22.81	23.25
38	17.08	17.53	17.98	18.43	18.88	19.33	19.78	20.24	20.69	21.15	21.61	22.07	22.52	22.99	23.45	23.91
39	17.54	18.00	18.46	18.93	19.39	19.86	20.32	20.79	21.26	21.73	22.20	22.67	23.14	23.61	24.09	24.56
40	18.00	18.48	18.95	19.43	19.90	20.38	20.86	21.34	21.82	22.30	22.79	23.27	23.76	24.25	24.73	25.22
41	18.47	18.95	19.44	19.93	20.42	20.91	21.40	21.89	22.39	22.88	23.38	23.88	24.38	24.88	25.38	25.88
42	18.93	19.43	19.93	20.43	20.93	21.44	21.94	22.45	22.96	23.47	23.98	24.49	25.00	25.51	26.03	26.55
43	19.40	19.91	20.42	20.94	21.45	21.97	22.49	23.01	23.53	24.05	24.57	25.10	25.62	26.15	26.68	27.21
44	19.86	20.39	20.91	21.44	21.97	22.50	23.03	23.57	24.10	24.64	25.17	25.71	26.25	26.79	27.33	27.88
45	20.33	20.87	21.41	21.95	22.49	23.03	23.58	24.12	24.67	25.22	25.77	26.32	26.88	27.43	27.99	28.55
46	20.80	21.35	21.90	22.46	23.01	23.57	24.13	24.69	25.25	25.81	26.37	26.94	27.51	28.08	28.65	29.22
47	21.27	21.83	22.40	22.97	23.53	24.10	24.68	25.25	25.82	26.40	26.98	27.56	28.14	28.72	29.31	29.89
48	21.74	22.32	22.90	23.48	24.06	24.64	25.23	25.81	26.40	26.99	27.58	28.18	28.77	29.37	29.97	30.57
49	22.21	22.80	23.39	23.99	24.58	25.18	25.78	26.38	26.98	27.59	28.19	28.80	29.41	30.02	30.63	31.24
50	22.69	23.29	23.89	24.50	25.11	25.72	26.33	26.95	27.56	28.18	28.80	29.42	30.04	30.67	31.29	31.92
51	23.16	23.78	24.40	25.02	25.64	26.26	26.89	27.52	28.15	28.78	29.41	30.05	30.68	31.32	31.96	32.60
52	23.64	24.27	24.90	25.53	26.17	26.81	27.45	28.09	28.73	29.38	30.02	30.67	31.32	31.98	32.63	33.29
53	24.11	24.76	25.40	26.05	26.70	27.35	28.00	28.66	29.32	29.98	30.64	31.30	31.97	32.63	33.30	33.97
54	24.59	25.25	25.91	26.57	27.23	27.90	28.56	29.23	29.91	30.58	31.25	31.93	32.61	33.29	33.98	34.66
55	25.07	25.74	26.41	27.09	27.77	28.44	29.13	29.81	30.50	31.18	31.87	32.56	33.26	33.95	34.65	35.35
56	25.55	26.23	26.92	27.61	28.30	28.99	29.69	30.39	31.09	31.79	32.49	33.20	33.91	34.62	35.33	36.04
57	26.03	26.73	27.43	28.13	28.84	29.54	30.25	30.97	31.68	32.39	33.11	33.83	34.56	35.28	36.01	36.74
58	26.51	27.23	27.94	28.66	29.37	30.10	30.82	31.55	32.27	33.00	33.74	34.47	35.21	35.95	36.69	37.43
59	27.00	27.72	28.45	29.18	29.91	30.65	31.39	32.13	32.87	33.61	34.36	35.11	35.86	36.62	37.37	38.13
60	27.48	28.22	28.96	29.71	30.45	31.20	31.96	32.71	33.47	34.23	34.99	35.75	36.52	37.29	38.06	38.83

T-16 TABLES

TABLE 12 (cont.)

NUMBER OF PAYMENTS	\multicolumn{16}{c}{ANNUAL PERCENTAGE RATE}
	14.00%	14.25%	14.50%	14.75%	15.00%	15.25%	15.50%	15.75%	16.00%	16.25%	16.50%	16.75%	17.00%	17.25%	17.50%	17.75%
	\multicolumn{16}{c}{(FINANCE CHARGE PER $100 OF AMOUNT FINANCED)}
1	1.17	1.19	1.21	1.23	1.25	1.27	1.29	1.31	1.33	1.35	1.37	1.40	1.42	1.44	1.46	1.48
2	1.75	1.78	1.82	1.85	1.88	1.91	1.94	1.97	2.00	2.04	2.07	2.10	2.13	2.16	2.19	2.22
3	2.34	2.38	2.43	2.47	2.51	2.55	2.59	2.64	2.68	2.72	2.76	2.80	2.85	2.89	2.93	2.97
4	2.93	2.99	3.04	3.09	3.14	3.20	3.25	3.30	3.36	3.41	3.46	3.51	3.57	3.62	3.67	3.73
5	3.53	3.59	3.65	3.72	3.78	3.84	3.91	3.97	4.04	4.10	4.16	4.23	4.29	4.35	4.42	4.48
6	4.12	4.20	4.27	4.35	4.42	4.49	4.57	4.64	4.72	4.79	4.87	4.94	5.02	5.09	5.17	5.24
7	4.72	4.81	4.89	4.98	5.06	5.15	5.23	5.32	5.40	5.49	5.58	5.66	5.75	5.83	5.92	6.00
8	5.32	5.42	5.51	5.61	5.71	5.80	5.90	6.00	6.09	6.19	6.29	6.38	6.48	6.58	6.67	6.77
9	5.92	6.03	6.14	6.25	6.35	6.46	6.57	6.68	6.78	6.89	7.00	7.11	7.22	7.32	7.43	7.54
10	6.53	6.65	6.77	6.88	7.00	7.12	7.24	7.36	7.48	7.60	7.72	7.84	7.96	8.08	8.19	8.31
11	7.14	7.27	7.40	7.53	7.66	7.79	7.92	8.05	8.18	8.31	8.44	8.57	8.70	8.83	8.96	9.09
12	7.74	7.89	8.03	8.17	8.31	8.45	8.59	8.74	8.88	9.02	9.16	9.30	9.45	9.59	9.73	9.87
13	8.36	8.51	8.66	8.81	8.97	9.12	9.27	9.43	9.58	9.73	9.89	10.04	10.20	10.35	10.50	10.66
14	8.97	9.13	9.30	9.46	9.63	9.79	9.96	10.12	10.29	10.45	10.62	10.78	10.95	11.11	11.28	11.45
15	9.59	9.76	9.94	10.11	10.29	10.47	10.64	10.82	11.00	11.17	11.35	11.53	11.71	11.88	12.06	12.24
16	10.20	10.39	10.58	10.77	10.95	11.14	11.33	11.52	11.71	11.90	12.09	12.28	12.46	12.65	12.84	13.03
17	10.82	11.02	11.22	11.42	11.62	11.82	12.02	12.22	12.42	12.62	12.83	13.03	13.23	13.43	13.63	13.83
18	11.45	11.66	11.87	12.08	12.29	12.50	12.72	12.93	13.14	13.35	13.57	13.78	13.99	14.21	14.42	14.64
19	12.07	12.30	12.52	12.74	12.97	13.19	13.41	13.64	13.86	14.09	14.31	14.54	14.76	14.99	15.22	15.44
20	12.70	12.93	13.17	13.41	13.64	13.88	14.11	14.35	14.59	14.82	15.06	15.30	15.54	15.77	16.01	16.25
21	13.33	13.58	13.82	14.07	14.32	14.57	14.82	15.06	15.31	15.56	15.81	16.06	16.31	16.56	16.81	17.07
22	13.96	14.22	14.48	14.74	15.00	15.26	15.52	15.78	16.04	16.30	16.57	16.83	17.09	17.36	17.62	17.88
23	14.59	14.87	15.14	15.41	15.68	15.96	16.23	16.50	16.78	17.05	17.32	17.60	17.88	18.15	18.43	18.70
24	15.23	15.51	15.80	16.08	16.37	16.65	16.94	17.22	17.51	17.80	18.09	18.37	18.66	18.95	19.24	19.53
25	15.87	16.17	16.46	16.76	17.06	17.35	17.65	17.95	18.25	18.55	18.85	19.15	19.45	19.75	20.05	20.36
26	16.51	16.82	17.13	17.44	17.75	18.06	18.37	18.68	18.99	19.30	19.62	19.93	20.24	20.56	20.87	21.19
27	17.15	17.47	17.80	18.12	18.44	18.76	19.09	19.41	19.74	20.06	20.39	20.71	21.04	21.37	21.69	22.02
28	17.80	18.13	18.47	18.80	19.14	19.47	19.81	20.15	20.48	20.82	21.16	21.50	21.84	22.18	22.52	22.86
29	18.45	18.79	19.14	19.49	19.83	20.18	20.53	20.88	21.23	21.58	21.94	22.29	22.64	22.99	23.35	23.70
30	19.10	19.45	19.81	20.17	20.54	20.90	21.26	21.62	21.99	22.35	22.72	23.08	23.45	23.81	24.18	24.55
31	19.75	20.12	20.49	20.87	21.24	21.61	21.99	22.37	22.74	23.12	23.50	23.88	24.26	24.64	25.02	25.40
32	20.40	20.79	21.17	21.56	21.95	22.33	22.72	23.11	23.50	23.89	24.28	24.68	25.07	25.46	25.86	26.25
33	21.06	21.46	21.85	22.25	22.65	23.06	23.46	23.86	24.26	24.67	25.07	25.48	25.88	26.29	26.70	27.11
34	21.72	22.13	22.54	22.95	23.37	23.78	24.19	24.61	25.03	25.44	25.86	26.28	26.70	27.12	27.54	27.97
35	22.38	22.80	23.23	23.65	24.08	24.51	24.94	25.36	25.79	26.23	26.66	27.09	27.52	27.96	28.39	28.83
36	23.04	23.48	23.92	24.35	24.80	25.24	25.68	26.12	26.57	27.01	27.46	27.90	28.35	28.80	29.25	29.70
37	23.70	24.16	24.61	25.06	25.51	25.97	26.42	26.88	27.34	27.80	28.26	28.72	29.18	29.64	30.10	30.57
38	24.37	24.84	25.30	25.77	26.24	26.70	27.17	27.64	28.11	28.59	29.06	29.53	30.01	30.49	30.96	31.44
39	25.04	25.52	26.00	26.48	26.96	27.44	27.92	28.41	28.89	29.38	29.87	30.36	30.85	31.34	31.83	32.32
40	25.71	26.20	26.69	27.19	27.69	28.18	28.68	29.18	29.68	30.18	30.68	31.18	31.68	32.19	32.69	33.20
41	26.39	26.89	27.40	27.91	28.41	28.92	29.44	29.95	30.46	30.97	31.49	32.01	32.52	33.04	33.56	34.08
42	27.06	27.58	28.10	28.62	29.15	29.67	30.19	30.72	31.25	31.78	32.31	32.84	33.37	33.90	34.44	34.97
43	27.74	28.27	28.81	29.34	29.88	30.42	30.96	31.50	32.04	32.58	33.13	33.67	34.22	34.76	35.31	35.86
44	28.42	28.97	29.52	30.07	30.62	31.17	31.72	32.28	32.83	33.39	33.95	34.51	35.07	35.63	36.19	36.76
45	29.11	29.67	30.23	30.79	31.36	31.92	32.49	33.06	33.63	34.20	34.77	35.35	35.92	36.50	37.08	37.66
46	29.79	30.36	30.94	31.52	32.10	32.68	33.26	33.84	34.43	35.01	35.60	36.19	36.78	37.37	37.96	38.56
47	30.48	31.07	31.66	32.25	32.84	33.44	34.03	34.63	35.23	35.83	36.43	37.04	37.64	38.25	38.86	39.46
48	31.17	31.77	32.37	32.98	33.59	34.20	34.81	35.42	36.03	36.65	37.27	37.88	38.50	39.13	39.75	40.37
49	31.86	32.48	33.09	33.71	34.34	34.96	35.59	36.21	36.84	37.47	38.10	38.74	39.37	40.01	40.65	41.29
50	32.55	33.18	33.82	34.45	35.09	35.73	36.37	37.01	37.65	38.30	38.94	39.59	40.24	40.89	41.55	42.20
51	33.25	33.89	34.54	35.19	35.84	36.49	37.15	37.81	38.46	39.12	39.79	40.45	41.11	41.78	42.45	43.12
52	33.95	34.61	35.27	35.93	36.60	37.27	37.94	38.61	39.28	39.96	40.63	41.31	41.99	42.67	43.36	44.04
53	34.65	35.32	36.00	36.68	37.36	38.04	38.72	39.41	40.10	40.79	41.48	42.17	42.87	43.57	44.27	44.97
54	35.35	36.04	36.73	37.42	38.12	38.82	39.52	40.22	40.92	41.63	42.33	43.04	43.75	44.47	45.18	45.90
55	36.05	36.76	37.46	38.17	38.88	39.60	40.31	41.03	41.74	42.47	43.19	43.91	44.64	45.37	46.10	46.83
56	36.76	37.48	38.20	38.92	39.65	40.38	41.11	41.84	42.57	43.31	44.05	44.79	45.53	46.27	47.02	47.77
57	37.47	38.20	38.94	39.68	40.42	41.16	41.91	42.65	43.40	44.15	44.91	45.66	46.42	47.18	47.94	48.71
58	38.18	38.93	39.68	40.43	41.19	41.95	42.71	43.47	44.23	45.00	45.77	46.54	47.32	48.09	48.87	49.65
59	38.89	39.66	40.42	41.19	41.96	42.74	43.51	44.29	45.07	45.85	46.64	47.42	48.21	49.01	49.80	50.60
60	39.61	40.39	41.17	41.95	42.74	43.53	44.32	45.11	45.91	46.71	47.51	48.31	49.12	49.92	50.73	51.55

TABLE 12 (cont.)

NUMBER OF PAYMENTS	18.00%	18.25%	18.50%	18.75%	19.00%	19.25%	19.50%	19.75%	20.00%	20.25%	20.50%	20.75%	21.00%	21.25%	21.50%	21.75%
	\multicolumn{16}{c}{(FINANCE CHARGE PER $100 OF AMOUNT FINANCED)}
1	1.50	1.52	1.54	1.56	1.58	1.60	1.62	1.65	1.67	1.69	1.71	1.73	1.75	1.77	1.79	1.81
2	2.26	2.29	2.32	2.35	2.38	2.41	2.44	2.48	2.51	2.54	2.57	2.60	2.63	2.66	2.70	2.73
3	3.01	3.06	3.10	3.14	3.18	3.23	3.27	3.31	3.35	3.39	3.44	3.48	3.52	3.56	3.60	3.65
4	3.78	3.83	3.88	3.94	3.99	4.04	4.10	4.15	4.20	4.25	4.31	4.36	4.41	4.47	4.52	4.57
5	4.54	4.61	4.67	4.74	4.80	4.86	4.93	4.99	5.06	5.12	5.18	5.25	5.31	5.37	5.44	5.50
6	5.32	5.39	5.46	5.54	5.61	5.69	5.76	5.84	5.91	5.99	6.06	6.14	6.21	6.29	6.36	6.44
7	6.09	6.18	6.26	6.35	6.43	6.52	6.60	6.69	6.78	6.86	6.95	7.04	7.12	7.21	7.29	7.38
8	6.87	6.96	7.06	7.16	7.26	7.35	7.45	7.55	7.64	7.74	7.84	7.94	8.03	8.13	8.23	8.33
9	7.65	7.76	7.87	7.97	8.08	8.19	8.30	8.41	8.52	8.63	8.73	8.84	8.95	9.06	9.17	9.28
10	8.43	8.55	8.67	8.79	8.91	9.03	9.15	9.27	9.39	9.51	9.63	9.75	9.88	10.00	10.12	10.24
11	9.22	9.35	9.49	9.62	9.75	9.88	10.01	10.14	10.28	10.41	10.54	10.67	10.80	10.94	11.07	11.20
12	10.02	10.16	10.30	10.44	10.59	10.73	10.87	11.02	11.16	11.31	11.45	11.59	11.74	11.88	12.02	12.17
13	10.81	10.97	11.12	11.28	11.43	11.59	11.74	11.90	12.05	12.21	12.36	12.52	12.67	12.83	12.99	13.14
14	11.61	11.78	11.95	12.11	12.28	12.45	12.61	12.78	12.95	13.11	13.28	13.45	13.62	13.79	13.95	14.12
15	12.42	12.59	12.77	12.95	13.13	13.31	13.49	13.67	13.85	14.03	14.21	14.39	14.57	14.75	14.93	15.11
16	13.22	13.41	13.60	13.80	13.99	14.18	14.37	14.56	14.75	14.94	15.13	15.33	15.52	15.71	15.90	16.10
17	14.04	14.24	14.44	14.64	14.85	15.05	15.25	15.46	15.66	15.86	16.07	16.27	16.48	16.68	16.89	17.09
18	14.85	15.07	15.28	15.49	15.71	15.93	16.14	16.36	16.57	16.79	17.01	17.22	17.44	17.66	17.88	18.09
19	15.67	15.90	16.12	16.35	16.58	16.81	17.03	17.26	17.49	17.72	17.95	18.18	18.41	18.64	18.87	19.10
20	16.49	16.73	16.97	17.21	17.45	17.69	17.93	18.17	18.41	18.66	18.90	19.14	19.38	19.63	19.87	20.11
21	17.32	17.57	17.82	18.07	18.33	18.58	18.83	19.09	19.34	19.60	19.85	20.11	20.36	20.62	20.87	21.13
22	18.15	18.41	18.68	18.94	19.21	19.47	19.74	20.01	20.27	20.54	20.81	21.08	21.34	21.61	21.88	22.15
23	18.98	19.26	19.54	19.81	20.09	20.37	20.65	20.93	21.21	21.49	21.77	22.05	22.33	22.61	22.90	23.18
24	19.82	20.11	20.40	20.69	20.98	21.27	21.56	21.86	22.15	22.44	22.74	23.03	23.33	23.62	23.92	24.21
25	20.66	20.96	21.27	21.57	21.87	22.18	22.48	22.79	23.10	23.40	23.71	24.02	24.32	24.63	24.94	25.25
26	21.50	21.82	22.14	22.45	22.77	23.09	23.41	23.73	24.04	24.36	24.68	25.01	25.33	25.65	25.97	26.29
27	22.35	22.68	23.01	23.34	23.67	24.00	24.33	24.67	25.00	25.33	25.67	26.00	26.34	26.67	27.01	27.34
28	23.20	23.55	23.89	24.23	24.58	24.92	25.27	25.61	25.96	26.30	26.65	27.00	27.35	27.70	28.05	28.40
29	24.06	24.41	24.77	25.13	25.49	25.84	26.20	26.56	26.92	27.28	27.64	28.00	28.37	28.73	29.09	29.46
30	24.92	25.29	25.66	26.03	26.40	26.77	27.14	27.52	27.89	28.26	28.64	29.01	29.39	29.77	30.14	30.52
31	25.78	26.16	26.55	26.93	27.32	27.70	28.09	28.47	28.86	29.25	29.64	30.03	30.42	30.81	31.20	31.59
32	26.65	27.04	27.44	27.84	28.24	28.64	29.04	29.44	29.84	30.24	30.64	31.05	31.45	31.85	32.26	32.67
33	27.52	27.93	28.34	28.75	29.16	29.57	29.99	30.40	30.82	31.23	31.65	32.07	32.49	32.91	33.33	33.75
34	28.39	28.81	29.24	29.66	30.09	30.52	30.95	31.37	31.80	32.23	32.67	33.10	33.53	33.96	34.40	34.83
35	29.27	29.71	30.14	30.58	31.02	31.47	31.91	32.35	32.79	33.24	33.68	34.13	34.58	35.03	35.47	35.92
36	30.15	30.60	31.05	31.51	31.96	32.42	32.87	33.33	33.79	34.25	34.71	35.17	35.63	36.09	36.56	37.02
37	31.03	31.50	31.97	32.43	32.90	33.37	33.84	34.32	34.79	35.26	35.74	36.21	36.69	37.16	37.64	38.12
38	31.92	32.40	32.88	33.37	33.85	34.33	34.82	35.30	35.79	36.28	36.77	37.26	37.75	38.24	38.73	39.23
39	32.81	33.31	33.80	34.30	34.80	35.30	35.80	36.30	36.80	37.30	37.81	38.31	38.82	39.32	39.83	40.34
40	33.71	34.22	34.73	35.24	35.75	36.26	36.78	37.29	37.81	38.33	38.85	39.37	39.89	40.41	40.93	41.46
41	34.61	35.13	35.66	36.18	36.71	37.24	37.77	38.30	38.83	39.36	39.89	40.43	40.96	41.50	42.04	42.58
42	35.51	36.05	36.59	37.13	37.67	38.21	38.76	39.30	39.85	40.40	40.95	41.50	42.05	42.60	43.15	43.71
43	36.42	36.97	37.52	38.08	38.63	39.19	39.75	40.31	40.87	41.44	42.00	42.57	43.13	43.70	44.27	44.84
44	37.33	37.89	38.46	39.03	39.60	40.18	40.75	41.33	41.90	42.48	43.06	43.64	44.22	44.81	45.39	45.98
45	38.24	38.82	39.41	39.99	40.58	41.17	41.75	42.35	42.94	43.53	44.13	44.72	45.32	45.92	46.52	47.12
46	39.16	39.75	40.35	40.95	41.55	42.16	42.76	43.37	43.98	44.58	45.20	45.81	46.42	47.03	47.65	48.27
47	40.08	40.69	41.30	41.92	42.54	43.15	43.77	44.40	45.02	45.64	46.27	46.90	47.53	48.16	48.79	49.42
48	41.00	41.63	42.26	42.89	43.52	44.15	44.79	45.43	46.07	46.71	47.35	47.99	48.64	49.28	49.93	50.58
49	41.93	42.57	43.22	43.86	44.51	45.16	45.81	46.46	47.12	47.77	48.43	49.09	49.75	50.41	51.08	51.74
50	42.86	43.52	44.18	44.84	45.50	46.17	46.83	47.50	48.17	48.84	49.52	50.19	50.87	51.55	52.23	52.91
51	43.79	44.47	45.14	45.82	46.50	47.18	47.86	48.55	49.23	49.92	50.61	51.30	51.99	52.69	53.38	54.08
52	44.73	45.42	46.11	46.80	47.50	48.20	48.89	49.59	50.30	51.00	51.71	52.41	53.12	53.83	54.55	55.26
53	45.67	46.38	47.08	47.79	48.50	49.22	49.93	50.65	51.37	52.09	52.81	53.53	54.26	54.98	55.71	56.44
54	46.62	47.34	48.06	48.79	49.51	50.24	50.97	51.70	52.44	53.17	53.91	54.65	55.39	56.14	56.88	57.63
55	47.57	48.30	49.04	49.78	50.52	51.27	52.02	52.76	53.52	54.27	55.02	55.78	56.54	57.30	58.06	58.82
56	48.52	49.27	50.03	50.78	51.54	52.30	53.06	53.83	54.60	55.37	56.14	56.91	57.68	58.46	59.24	60.02
57	49.47	50.24	51.01	51.79	52.56	53.34	54.12	54.90	55.68	56.47	57.25	58.04	58.84	59.63	60.43	61.22
58	50.43	51.22	52.00	52.79	53.58	54.38	55.17	55.97	56.77	57.57	58.38	59.18	59.99	60.80	61.62	62.43
59	51.39	52.20	53.00	53.80	54.61	55.42	56.23	57.05	57.87	58.68	59.51	60.33	61.15	61.98	62.81	63.64
60	52.36	53.18	54.00	54.82	55.64	56.47	57.30	58.13	58.96	59.80	60.64	61.48	62.32	63.17	64.01	64.86

TABLE 12 (cont.)

NUMBER OF PAYMENTS	22.00%	22.25%	22.50%	22.75%	23.00%	23.25%	23.50%	23.75%	24.00%	24.25%	24.50%	24.75%	25.00%	25.25%	25.50%	25.75%
	\multicolumn{16}{c}{(FINANCE CHARGE PER \$100 OF AMOUNT FINANCED)}
1	1.83	1.85	1.87	1.90	1.92	1.94	1.96	1.98	2.00	2.02	2.04	2.06	2.08	2.10	2.12	2.15
2	2.76	2.79	2.82	2.85	2.88	2.92	2.95	2.98	3.01	3.04	3.07	3.10	3.14	3.17	3.20	3.23
3	3.69	3.73	3.77	3.82	3.86	3.90	3.94	3.98	4.03	4.07	4.11	4.15	4.20	4.24	4.28	4.32
4	4.62	4.68	4.73	4.78	4.84	4.89	4.94	5.00	5.05	5.10	5.16	5.21	5.26	5.32	5.37	5.42
5	5.57	5.63	5.69	5.76	5.82	5.89	5.95	6.02	6.08	6.14	6.21	6.27	6.34	6.40	6.46	6.53
6	6.51	6.59	6.66	6.74	6.81	6.89	6.96	7.04	7.12	7.19	7.27	7.34	7.42	7.49	7.57	7.64
7	7.47	7.55	7.64	7.73	7.81	7.90	7.99	8.07	8.16	8.24	8.33	8.42	8.51	8.59	8.68	8.77
8	8.42	8.52	8.62	8.72	8.82	8.91	9.01	9.11	9.21	9.31	9.40	9.50	9.60	9.70	9.80	9.90
9	9.39	9.50	9.61	9.72	9.83	9.94	10.04	10.15	10.26	10.37	10.48	10.59	10.70	10.81	10.92	11.03
10	10.36	10.48	10.60	10.72	10.84	10.96	11.08	11.21	11.33	11.45	11.57	11.69	11.81	11.93	12.06	12.18
11	11.33	11.47	11.60	11.73	11.86	12.00	12.13	12.26	12.40	12.53	12.66	12.80	12.93	13.06	13.20	13.33
12	12.31	12.46	12.60	12.75	12.89	13.04	13.18	13.33	13.47	13.62	13.76	13.91	14.05	14.20	14.34	14.49
13	13.30	13.46	13.61	13.77	13.93	14.08	14.24	14.40	14.55	14.71	14.87	15.03	15.18	15.34	15.50	15.66
14	14.29	14.46	14.63	14.80	14.97	15.13	15.30	15.47	15.64	15.81	15.98	16.15	16.32	16.49	16.66	16.83
15	15.29	15.47	15.65	15.83	16.01	16.19	16.37	16.56	16.74	16.92	17.10	17.28	17.47	17.65	17.83	18.02
16	16.29	16.48	16.68	16.87	17.06	17.26	17.45	17.65	17.84	18.03	18.23	18.42	18.62	18.81	19.01	19.21
17	17.30	17.50	17.71	17.92	18.12	18.33	18.53	18.74	18.95	19.16	19.36	19.57	19.78	19.99	20.20	20.40
18	18.31	18.53	18.75	18.97	19.19	19.41	19.62	19.84	20.06	20.28	20.50	20.72	20.95	21.17	21.39	21.61
19	19.33	19.56	19.79	20.02	20.26	20.49	20.72	20.95	21.19	21.42	21.65	21.89	22.12	22.35	22.59	22.82
20	20.35	20.60	20.84	21.09	21.33	21.58	21.82	22.07	22.31	22.56	22.81	23.05	23.30	23.55	23.79	24.04
21	21.38	21.64	21.90	22.16	22.41	22.67	22.93	23.19	23.45	23.71	23.97	24.23	24.49	24.75	25.01	25.27
22	22.42	22.69	22.96	23.23	23.50	23.77	24.04	24.32	24.59	24.86	25.13	25.41	25.68	25.96	26.23	26.50
23	23.46	23.74	24.03	24.31	24.60	24.88	25.17	25.45	25.74	26.02	26.31	26.60	26.88	27.17	27.46	27.75
24	24.51	24.80	25.10	25.40	25.70	25.99	26.29	26.59	26.89	27.19	27.49	27.79	28.09	28.39	28.69	29.00
25	25.56	25.87	26.18	26.49	26.80	27.11	27.43	27.74	28.05	28.36	28.68	28.99	29.31	29.62	29.94	30.25
26	26.62	26.94	27.26	27.59	27.91	28.24	28.56	28.89	29.22	29.55	29.87	30.20	30.53	30.86	31.19	31.52
27	27.68	28.02	28.35	28.69	29.03	29.37	29.71	30.05	30.39	30.73	31.07	31.42	31.76	32.10	32.45	32.79
28	28.75	29.10	29.45	29.80	30.15	30.51	30.86	31.22	31.57	31.93	32.28	32.64	33.00	33.35	33.71	34.07
29	29.82	30.19	30.55	30.92	31.28	31.65	32.02	32.39	32.76	33.13	33.50	33.87	34.24	34.61	34.98	35.36
30	30.90	31.28	31.66	32.04	32.42	32.80	33.18	33.57	33.95	34.33	34.72	35.10	35.49	35.88	36.26	36.65
31	31.98	32.38	32.77	33.17	33.56	33.96	34.35	34.75	35.15	35.55	35.95	36.35	36.75	37.15	37.55	37.95
32	33.07	33.48	33.89	34.30	34.71	35.12	35.53	35.94	36.35	36.77	37.18	37.60	38.01	38.43	38.84	39.26
33	34.17	34.59	35.01	35.44	35.86	36.29	36.71	37.14	37.57	37.99	38.42	38.85	39.28	39.71	40.14	40.58
34	35.27	35.71	36.14	36.58	37.02	37.46	37.90	38.34	38.78	39.23	39.67	40.11	40.56	41.01	41.45	41.90
35	36.37	36.83	37.28	37.73	38.18	38.64	39.09	39.55	40.01	40.47	40.92	41.38	41.84	42.31	42.77	43.23
36	37.49	37.95	38.42	38.89	39.35	39.82	40.29	40.77	41.24	41.71	42.19	42.66	43.14	43.61	44.09	44.57
37	38.60	39.08	39.56	40.05	40.53	41.02	41.50	41.99	42.48	42.96	43.45	43.94	44.43	44.93	45.42	45.91
38	39.72	40.22	40.72	41.21	41.71	42.21	42.71	43.22	43.72	44.22	44.73	45.23	45.74	46.25	46.75	47.26
39	40.85	41.36	41.87	42.39	42.90	43.42	43.93	44.45	44.97	45.49	46.01	46.53	47.05	47.57	48.10	48.62
40	41.98	42.51	43.04	43.56	44.09	44.62	45.16	45.69	46.22	46.76	47.29	47.83	48.37	48.91	49.45	49.99
41	43.12	43.66	44.20	44.75	45.29	45.84	46.39	46.94	47.48	48.04	48.59	49.14	49.69	50.25	50.80	51.36
42	44.26	44.82	45.38	45.94	46.50	47.06	47.62	48.19	48.75	49.32	49.89	50.46	51.03	51.60	52.17	52.74
43	45.41	45.98	46.56	47.13	47.71	48.29	48.87	49.45	50.03	50.61	51.19	51.78	52.36	52.95	53.54	54.13
44	46.56	47.15	47.74	48.33	48.93	49.52	50.11	50.71	51.31	51.91	52.51	53.11	53.71	54.31	54.92	55.52
45	47.72	48.33	48.93	49.54	50.15	50.76	51.37	51.98	52.59	53.21	53.82	54.44	55.06	55.68	56.30	56.92
46	48.89	49.51	50.13	50.75	51.37	52.00	52.63	53.26	53.89	54.52	55.15	55.78	56.42	57.05	57.69	58.33
47	50.06	50.69	51.33	51.97	52.61	53.25	53.89	54.54	55.18	55.83	56.48	57.13	57.78	58.44	59.09	59.75
48	51.23	51.88	52.54	53.19	53.85	54.51	55.16	55.83	56.49	57.15	57.82	58.49	59.15	59.82	60.50	61.17
49	52.41	53.08	53.75	54.42	55.09	55.77	56.44	57.12	57.80	58.48	59.16	59.85	60.53	61.22	61.91	62.60
50	53.59	54.28	54.96	55.65	56.34	57.03	57.73	58.42	59.12	59.81	60.51	61.21	61.92	62.62	63.33	64.03
51	54.78	55.48	56.19	56.89	57.60	58.30	59.01	59.73	60.44	61.15	61.87	62.59	63.31	64.03	64.75	65.47
52	55.98	56.69	57.41	58.13	58.86	59.58	60.31	61.04	61.77	62.50	63.23	63.97	64.70	65.44	66.18	66.92
53	57.18	57.91	58.65	59.38	60.12	60.87	61.61	62.35	63.10	63.85	64.60	65.35	66.11	66.86	67.62	68.38
54	58.38	59.13	59.88	60.64	61.40	62.16	62.92	63.68	64.44	65.21	65.98	66.75	67.52	68.29	69.07	69.84
55	59.59	60.36	61.13	61.90	62.67	63.45	64.23	65.01	65.79	66.57	67.36	68.14	68.93	69.72	70.52	71.31
56	60.80	61.59	62.38	63.17	63.96	64.75	65.54	66.34	67.14	67.94	68.74	69.55	70.36	71.16	71.97	72.79
57	62.02	62.83	63.63	64.44	65.25	66.06	66.87	67.68	68.50	69.32	70.14	70.96	71.78	72.61	73.44	74.27
58	63.25	64.07	64.89	65.71	66.54	67.37	68.20	69.03	69.86	70.70	71.54	72.38	73.22	74.06	74.91	75.76
59	64.48	65.32	66.15	67.00	67.84	68.68	69.53	70.38	71.23	72.09	72.94	73.80	74.66	75.52	76.39	77.25
60	65.71	66.57	67.42	68.28	69.14	70.01	70.87	71.74	72.61	73.48	74.35	75.23	76.11	76.99	77.87	78.76

TABLE 12 (cont.)

NUMBER OF PAYMENTS	26.00%	26.25%	26.50%	26.75%	27.00%	27.25%	27.50%	27.75%	28.00%	28.25%	28.50%	28.75%	29.00%	29.25%	29.50%	29.75%
	\multicolumn{16}{c}{ANNUAL PERCENTAGE RATE — (FINANCE CHARGE PER $100 OF AMOUNT FINANCED)}
1	2.17	2.19	2.21	2.23	2.25	2.27	2.29	2.31	2.33	2.35	2.37	2.40	2.42	2.44	2.46	2.48
2	3.26	3.29	3.32	3.36	3.39	3.42	3.45	3.48	3.51	3.54	3.58	3.61	3.64	3.67	3.70	3.73
3	4.36	4.41	4.45	4.49	4.53	4.58	4.62	4.66	4.70	4.74	4.79	4.83	4.87	4.91	4.96	5.00
4	5.47	5.53	5.58	5.63	5.69	5.74	5.79	5.85	5.90	5.95	6.01	6.06	6.11	6.17	6.22	6.27
5	6.59	6.66	6.72	6.79	6.85	6.91	6.98	7.04	7.11	7.17	7.24	7.30	7.37	7.43	7.49	7.56
6	7.72	7.79	7.87	7.95	8.02	8.10	8.17	8.25	8.32	8.40	8.48	8.55	8.63	8.70	8.78	8.85
7	8.85	8.94	9.03	9.11	9.20	9.29	9.37	9.46	9.55	9.64	9.72	9.81	9.90	9.98	10.07	10.16
8	9.99	10.09	10.19	10.29	10.39	10.49	10.58	10.68	10.78	10.88	10.98	11.08	11.18	11.28	11.38	11.47
9	11.14	11.25	11.36	11.47	11.58	11.69	11.80	11.91	12.03	12.14	12.25	12.36	12.47	12.58	12.69	12.80
10	12.30	12.42	12.54	12.67	12.79	12.91	13.03	13.15	13.28	13.40	13.52	13.64	13.77	13.89	14.01	14.14
11	13.46	13.60	13.73	13.87	14.00	14.13	14.27	14.40	14.54	14.67	14.81	14.94	15.08	15.21	15.35	15.48
12	14.64	14.78	14.93	15.07	15.22	15.37	15.51	15.66	15.81	15.95	16.10	16.25	16.40	16.54	16.69	16.84
13	15.82	15.97	16.13	16.29	16.45	16.61	16.77	16.93	17.09	17.24	17.40	17.56	17.72	17.88	18.04	18.20
14	17.00	17.17	17.35	17.52	17.69	17.86	18.03	18.20	18.37	18.54	18.72	18.89	19.06	19.23	19.41	19.58
15	18.20	18.38	18.57	18.75	18.93	19.12	19.30	19.48	19.67	19.85	20.04	20.22	20.41	20.59	20.78	20.96
16	19.40	19.60	19.79	19.99	20.19	20.38	20.58	20.78	20.97	21.17	21.37	21.57	21.76	21.96	22.16	22.36
17	20.61	20.82	21.03	21.24	21.45	21.66	21.87	22.08	22.29	22.50	22.71	22.92	23.13	23.34	23.55	23.77
18	21.83	22.05	22.27	22.50	22.72	22.94	23.16	23.39	23.61	23.83	24.06	24.28	24.51	24.73	24.96	25.18
19	23.06	23.29	23.53	23.76	24.00	24.23	24.47	24.71	24.94	25.18	25.42	25.65	25.89	26.13	26.37	26.61
20	24.29	24.54	24.79	25.04	25.28	25.53	25.78	26.03	26.28	26.53	26.78	27.04	27.29	27.54	27.79	28.04
21	25.53	25.79	26.05	26.32	26.58	26.84	27.11	27.37	27.63	27.90	28.16	28.43	28.69	28.96	29.22	29.49
22	26.78	27.05	27.33	27.61	27.88	28.16	28.44	28.71	28.99	29.27	29.55	29.82	30.10	30.38	30.66	30.94
23	28.04	28.32	28.61	28.90	29.19	29.48	29.77	30.07	30.36	30.65	30.94	31.23	31.53	31.82	32.11	32.41
24	29.30	29.60	29.90	30.21	30.51	30.82	31.12	31.43	31.73	32.04	32.34	32.65	32.96	33.27	33.57	33.88
25	30.57	30.89	31.20	31.52	31.84	32.16	32.48	32.80	33.12	33.44	33.76	34.08	34.40	34.72	35.04	35.37
26	31.85	32.18	32.51	32.84	33.18	33.51	33.84	34.18	34.51	34.84	35.18	35.51	35.85	36.19	36.52	36.86
27	33.14	33.48	33.83	34.17	34.52	34.87	35.21	35.56	35.91	36.26	36.61	36.96	37.31	37.66	38.01	38.36
28	34.43	34.79	35.15	35.51	35.87	36.23	36.59	36.96	37.32	37.68	38.05	38.41	38.78	39.15	39.51	39.88
29	35.73	36.10	36.48	36.85	37.23	37.61	37.98	38.36	38.74	39.12	39.50	39.88	40.26	40.64	41.02	41.40
30	37.04	37.43	37.82	38.21	38.60	38.99	39.38	39.77	40.17	40.56	40.95	41.35	41.75	42.14	42.54	42.94
31	38.35	38.76	39.16	39.57	39.97	40.38	40.79	41.19	41.60	42.01	42.42	42.83	43.24	43.65	44.06	44.48
32	39.68	40.10	40.52	40.94	41.36	41.78	42.20	42.62	43.05	43.47	43.90	44.32	44.75	45.17	45.60	46.03
33	41.01	41.44	41.88	42.31	42.75	43.19	43.62	44.06	44.50	44.94	45.38	45.82	46.26	46.70	47.15	47.59
34	42.35	42.80	43.25	43.70	44.15	44.60	45.05	45.51	45.96	46.42	46.87	47.33	47.79	48.24	48.70	49.16
35	43.69	44.16	44.62	45.09	45.56	46.02	46.49	46.96	47.43	47.90	48.37	48.85	49.32	49.79	50.27	50.74
36	45.05	45.53	46.01	46.49	46.97	47.45	47.94	48.42	48.91	49.40	49.88	50.37	50.86	51.35	51.84	52.33
37	46.41	46.90	47.40	47.90	48.39	48.89	49.39	49.89	50.40	50.90	51.40	51.91	52.41	52.92	53.42	53.93
38	47.77	48.29	48.80	49.31	49.82	50.34	50.85	51.37	51.89	52.41	52.93	53.45	53.97	54.49	55.02	55.54
39	49.15	49.68	50.20	50.73	51.26	51.79	52.33	52.86	53.39	53.93	54.46	55.00	55.54	56.08	56.62	57.16
40	50.53	51.07	51.62	52.16	52.71	53.26	53.81	54.35	54.90	55.46	56.01	56.56	57.12	57.67	58.23	58.79
41	51.92	52.48	53.04	53.60	54.16	54.73	55.29	55.86	56.42	56.99	57.56	58.13	58.70	59.28	59.85	60.42
42	53.32	53.89	54.47	55.05	55.63	56.21	56.79	57.37	57.95	58.54	59.12	59.71	60.30	60.89	61.48	62.07
43	54.72	55.31	55.90	56.50	57.09	57.69	58.29	58.89	59.49	60.09	60.69	61.30	61.90	62.51	63.11	63.72
44	56.13	56.74	57.35	57.96	58.57	59.19	59.80	60.42	61.03	61.65	62.27	62.89	63.51	64.14	64.76	65.39
45	57.55	58.17	58.80	59.43	60.06	60.69	61.32	61.95	62.59	63.22	63.86	64.50	65.13	65.77	66.42	67.06
46	58.97	59.61	60.26	60.90	61.55	62.20	62.84	63.49	64.15	64.80	65.45	66.11	66.76	67.42	68.08	68.74
47	60.40	61.06	61.72	62.38	63.05	63.71	64.38	65.05	65.71	66.38	67.06	67.73	68.40	69.08	69.75	70.43
48	61.84	62.52	63.20	63.87	64.56	65.24	65.92	66.60	67.29	67.98	68.67	69.36	70.05	70.74	71.44	72.13
49	63.29	63.98	64.68	65.37	66.07	66.77	67.47	68.17	68.87	69.58	70.29	70.99	71.70	72.41	73.13	73.84
50	64.74	65.45	66.16	66.88	67.59	68.31	69.03	69.75	70.47	71.19	71.91	72.64	73.37	74.10	74.83	75.56
51	66.20	66.93	67.66	68.39	69.12	69.86	70.59	71.33	72.07	72.81	73.55	74.29	75.04	75.78	76.53	77.28
52	67.67	68.41	69.16	69.91	70.66	71.41	72.16	72.92	73.67	74.43	75.19	75.95	76.72	77.48	78.25	79.02
53	69.14	69.90	70.67	71.43	72.20	72.97	73.74	74.52	75.29	76.07	76.85	77.62	78.41	79.19	79.97	80.76
54	70.62	71.40	72.18	72.97	73.75	74.54	75.33	76.12	76.91	77.71	78.50	79.30	80.10	80.90	81.71	82.51
55	72.11	72.91	73.71	74.51	75.31	76.12	76.92	77.73	78.55	79.36	80.17	80.99	81.81	82.63	83.45	84.27
56	73.60	74.42	75.24	76.06	76.88	77.70	78.53	79.35	80.18	81.02	81.85	82.68	83.52	84.36	85.20	86.04
57	75.10	75.94	76.77	77.61	78.45	79.29	80.14	80.98	81.83	82.68	83.53	84.39	85.24	86.10	86.96	87.82
58	76.61	77.46	78.32	79.17	80.03	80.89	81.75	82.62	83.48	84.35	85.22	86.10	86.97	87.85	88.72	89.60
59	78.12	78.99	79.87	80.74	81.62	82.50	83.38	84.26	85.15	86.03	86.92	87.81	88.71	89.60	90.50	91.40
60	79.64	80.53	81.42	82.32	83.21	84.11	85.01	85.91	86.81	87.72	88.63	89.54	90.45	91.37	92.28	93.20

TABLES T-19

TABLE 12 (cont.)

NUMBER OF PAYMENTS	6.00%	6.25%	6.50%	6.75%	7.00%	7.25%	7.50%	7.75%	8.00%	8.25%	8.50%	8.75%	9.00%	9.25%	9.50%	9.75%
\multicolumn{17}{c}{(FINANCE CHARGE PER $100 OF AMOUNT FINANCED)}
301	93.66	98.29	102.97	107.70	112.48	117.31	122.18	127.11	132.07	137.09	142.14	147.24	152.37	157.55	162.77	168.02
302	94.02	98.67	103.37	108.13	112.93	117.78	122.67	127.62	132.60	137.64	142.71	147.83	152.99	158.19	163.43	168.71
303	94.39	99.06	103.78	108.55	113.37	118.24	123.16	128.12	133.13	138.19	143.29	148.43	153.61	158.83	164.09	169.39
304	94.76	99.45	104.19	108.98	113.82	118.71	123.65	128.63	133.67	138.74	143.86	149.02	154.23	159.47	164.75	170.07
305	95.12	99.83	104.59	109.41	114.27	119.18	124.14	129.14	134.20	139.29	144.43	149.62	154.84	160.11	165.41	170.76
306	95.49	100.22	105.00	109.83	114.72	119.65	124.63	129.66	134.73	139.85	145.01	150.21	155.46	160.75	166.08	171.44
307	95.86	100.61	105.41	110.26	115.16	120.12	125.12	130.17	135.26	140.40	145.59	150.81	156.08	161.39	166.74	172.13
308	96.23	101.00	105.82	110.69	115.61	120.59	125.61	130.68	135.79	140.96	146.16	151.41	156.70	162.03	167.40	172.81
309	96.60	101.39	106.23	111.12	116.06	121.06	126.10	131.19	136.33	141.51	146.74	152.01	157.32	162.68	168.07	173.50
310	96.97	101.77	106.64	111.55	116.51	121.53	126.59	131.70	136.86	142.07	147.31	152.61	157.94	163.32	168.73	174.19
311	97.34	102.16	107.04	111.98	116.96	122.00	127.08	132.22	137.40	142.62	147.89	153.21	158.56	163.96	169.40	174.88
312	97.71	102.55	107.45	112.41	117.41	122.47	127.57	132.73	137.93	143.18	148.47	153.81	159.19	164.61	170.07	175.57
313	98.08	102.94	107.86	112.84	117.86	122.94	128.07	133.24	138.47	143.73	149.05	154.41	159.81	165.25	170.73	176.26
314	98.45	103.33	108.27	113.27	118.32	123.41	128.56	133.76	139.00	144.29	149.63	155.01	160.43	165.90	171.40	176.95
315	98.82	103.72	108.69	113.70	118.77	123.89	129.05	134.27	139.54	144.85	150.21	155.61	161.05	166.54	172.07	177.64
316	99.19	104.12	109.10	114.13	119.22	124.36	129.55	134.79	140.07	145.41	150.79	156.21	161.68	167.19	172.74	178.33
317	99.56	104.51	109.51	114.56	119.67	124.83	130.04	135.30	140.61	145.97	151.37	156.81	162.30	167.84	173.41	179.02
318	99.93	104.90	109.92	115.00	120.13	125.31	130.54	135.82	141.15	146.53	151.95	157.42	162.93	168.48	174.08	179.71
319	100.31	105.29	110.33	115.43	120.58	125.78	131.03	136.34	141.69	147.09	152.53	158.02	163.56	169.13	174.75	180.40
320	100.68	105.68	110.75	115.86	121.03	126.26	131.53	136.85	142.23	147.65	153.11	158.63	164.18	169.78	175.42	181.10
321	101.05	106.08	111.16	116.30	121.49	126.73	132.03	137.37	142.77	148.21	153.70	159.23	164.81	170.43	176.09	181.79
322	101.42	106.47	111.57	116.73	121.94	127.21	132.52	137.89	143.31	148.77	154.28	159.84	165.44	171.08	176.76	182.49
323	101.80	106.86	111.99	117.16	122.40	127.68	133.02	138.41	143.85	149.33	154.86	160.44	166.06	171.73	177.44	183.18
324	102.17	107.26	112.40	117.60	122.85	128.16	133.52	138.93	144.39	149.89	155.45	161.05	166.69	172.38	178.11	183.88
325	102.55	107.65	112.81	118.03	123.31	128.64	134.02	139.45	144.93	150.46	156.03	161.66	167.32	173.03	178.78	184.57
326	102.92	108.05	113.23	118.47	123.76	129.11	134.51	139.97	145.47	151.02	156.62	162.26	167.95	173.68	179.46	185.27
327	103.29	108.44	113.64	118.90	124.22	129.59	135.01	140.49	146.01	151.58	157.20	162.87	168.58	174.34	180.13	185.97
328	103.67	108.84	114.06	119.34	124.68	130.07	135.51	141.01	146.55	152.15	157.79	163.48	169.21	174.99	180.81	186.67
329	104.04	109.23	114.48	119.78	125.14	130.55	136.01	141.53	147.10	152.71	158.38	164.09	169.84	175.64	181.48	187.37
330	104.42	109.63	114.89	120.21	125.59	131.03	136.51	142.05	147.64	153.28	158.96	164.70	170.48	176.30	182.16	188.07
331	104.80	110.02	115.31	120.65	126.05	131.51	137.01	142.57	148.18	153.84	159.55	165.31	171.11	176.95	182.84	188.77
332	105.17	110.42	115.73	121.09	126.51	131.99	137.51	143.10	148.73	154.41	160.14	165.92	171.74	177.61	183.52	189.47
333	105.55	110.82	116.15	121.53	126.97	132.47	138.02	143.62	149.27	154.98	160.73	166.53	172.37	178.26	184.19	190.17
334	105.93	111.21	116.56	121.97	127.43	132.95	138.52	144.14	149.82	155.54	161.32	167.14	173.01	178.92	184.87	190.87
335	106.30	111.61	116.98	122.40	127.89	133.43	139.02	144.67	150.36	156.11	161.91	167.75	173.64	179.58	185.55	191.57
336	106.68	112.01	117.40	122.84	128.35	133.91	139.52	145.19	150.91	156.68	162.50	168.36	174.28	180.23	186.23	192.27
337	107.06	112.41	117.82	123.28	128.81	134.39	140.03	145.72	151.46	157.25	163.09	168.98	174.91	180.89	186.91	192.98
338	107.44	112.81	118.24	123.72	129.27	134.87	140.53	146.24	152.00	157.82	163.68	169.59	175.55	181.55	187.59	193.68
339	107.82	113.20	118.65	124.16	129.73	135.36	141.03	146.77	152.55	158.39	164.27	170.21	176.18	182.21	188.28	194.38
340	108.20	113.60	119.07	124.60	130.19	135.84	141.54	147.29	153.10	158.96	164.86	170.82	176.82	182.87	188.96	195.09
341	108.57	114.00	119.49	125.05	130.66	136.32	142.04	147.82	153.65	159.53	165.46	171.43	177.46	183.53	189.64	195.79
342	108.95	114.40	119.92	125.49	131.12	136.81	142.55	148.35	154.20	160.10	166.05	172.05	178.10	184.19	190.32	196.50
343	109.33	114.80	120.34	125.93	131.58	137.29	143.06	148.87	154.75	160.67	166.64	172.67	178.73	184.85	191.01	197.21
344	109.71	115.20	120.76	126.37	132.04	137.77	143.56	149.40	155.30	161.24	167.24	173.28	179.37	185.51	191.69	197.91
345	110.09	115.61	121.18	126.81	132.51	138.26	144.07	149.93	155.85	161.82	167.83	173.90	180.01	186.17	192.38	198.62
346	110.48	116.01	121.60	127.26	132.97	138.75	144.58	150.46	156.40	162.39	168.43	174.52	180.65	186.83	193.06	199.33
347	110.86	116.41	122.02	127.70	133.44	139.23	145.08	150.99	156.95	162.96	169.02	175.14	181.29	187.50	193.75	200.04
348	111.24	116.81	122.45	128.14	133.90	139.72	145.59	151.52	157.50	163.54	169.62	175.75	181.93	188.16	194.43	200.75
349	111.62	117.21	122.87	128.59	134.37	140.20	146.10	152.05	158.05	164.11	170.22	176.37	182.58	188.83	195.12	201.46
350	112.00	117.61	123.29	129.03	134.83	140.69	146.61	152.58	158.61	164.68	170.81	176.99	183.22	189.49	195.81	202.17
351	112.38	118.02	123.72	129.48	135.30	141.18	147.12	153.11	159.16	165.26	171.41	177.61	183.86	190.16	196.49	202.88
352	112.77	118.42	124.14	129.92	135.76	141.67	147.63	153.64	159.71	165.83	172.01	178.23	184.50	190.82	197.18	203.59
353	113.15	118.82	124.56	130.37	136.23	142.15	148.14	154.17	160.27	166.41	172.61	178.85	185.15	191.49	197.87	204.30
354	113.53	119.23	124.99	130.81	136.70	142.64	148.65	154.71	160.82	166.99	173.21	179.47	185.79	192.15	198.56	205.01
355	113.92	119.63	125.41	131.26	137.17	143.13	149.16	155.24	161.37	167.56	173.81	180.10	186.43	192.82	199.25	205.72
356	114.30	120.04	125.84	131.71	137.63	143.62	149.67	155.77	161.93	168.14	174.41	180.72	187.08	193.49	199.94	206.44
357	114.68	120.44	126.27	132.15	138.10	144.11	150.18	156.31	162.49	168.72	175.01	181.34	187.73	194.16	200.63	207.15
358	115.07	120.85	126.69	132.60	138.57	144.60	150.69	156.84	163.04	169.30	175.61	181.96	188.37	194.82	201.32	207.87
359	115.45	121.25	127.12	133.05	139.04	145.09	151.20	157.37	163.60	169.88	176.21	182.59	189.02	195.49	202.01	208.58
360	115.84	121.66	127.54	133.50	139.51	145.58	151.72	157.91	164.16	170.46	176.81	183.21	189.66	196.16	202.71	209.30

TABLE 12 (cont.)

NUMBER OF PAYMENTS	10.00%	10.25%	10.50%	10.75%	11.00%	11.25%	11.50%	11.75%	12.00%	12.25%	12.50%	12.75%	13.00%	13.25%	13.50%	13.75%
	(FINANCE CHARGE PER $100 OF AMOUNT FINANCED)															
301	173.31	178.64	184.00	189.40	194.83	200.29	205.78	211.30	216.85	222.43	228.04	233.67	239.33	245.01	250.72	256.45
302	174.02	179.37	184.75	190.17	195.62	201.11	206.62	212.17	217.74	223.34	228.97	234.63	240.31	246.01	251.74	257.50
303	174.73	180.10	185.50	190.95	196.42	201.93	207.46	213.03	218.63	224.25	229.91	235.58	241.29	247.02	252.77	258.55
304	175.43	180.83	186.26	191.72	197.22	202.75	208.31	213.90	219.52	225.16	230.84	236.54	242.27	248.02	253.80	259.60
305	176.14	181.56	187.01	192.49	198.01	203.57	209.15	214.76	220.41	226.08	231.77	237.50	243.25	249.03	254.82	260.65
306	176.85	182.29	187.76	193.27	198.81	204.39	209.99	215.63	221.30	226.99	232.71	238.46	244.23	250.03	255.85	261.70
307	177.55	183.02	188.51	194.05	199.61	205.21	210.84	216.50	222.19	227.90	233.65	239.42	245.21	251.04	256.88	262.75
308	178.26	183.75	189.27	194.82	200.41	206.03	211.68	217.37	223.08	228.82	234.58	240.38	246.20	252.04	257.91	263.80
309	178.97	184.48	190.02	195.60	201.21	206.85	212.53	218.23	223.97	229.73	235.52	241.34	247.18	253.05	258.94	264.86
310	179.68	185.21	190.78	196.38	202.01	207.68	213.38	219.10	224.86	230.65	236.46	242.30	248.17	254.06	259.97	265.91
311	180.39	185.95	191.53	197.16	202.81	208.50	214.22	219.97	225.75	231.56	237.40	243.26	249.15	255.07	261.01	266.97
312	181.10	186.68	192.29	197.94	203.62	209.33	215.07	220.85	226.65	232.48	238.34	244.23	250.14	256.08	262.04	268.02
313	181.82	187.41	193.05	198.72	204.42	210.15	215.92	221.72	227.54	233.40	239.28	245.19	251.13	257.09	263.07	269.08
314	182.53	188.15	193.81	199.50	205.22	210.98	216.77	222.59	228.44	234.32	240.22	246.16	252.11	258.10	264.11	270.14
315	183.24	188.89	194.56	200.28	206.03	211.81	217.62	223.46	229.33	235.24	241.17	247.12	253.10	259.11	265.14	271.19
316	183.96	189.62	195.32	201.06	206.83	212.63	218.47	224.34	230.23	236.16	242.11	248.09	254.09	260.12	266.18	272.25
317	184.67	190.36	196.08	201.84	207.64	213.46	219.32	225.21	231.13	237.08	243.05	249.05	255.08	261.13	267.21	273.31
318	185.39	191.10	196.84	202.63	208.44	214.29	220.17	226.09	232.03	238.00	244.00	250.02	256.07	262.15	268.25	274.37
319	186.10	191.83	197.60	203.41	209.25	215.12	221.03	226.96	232.93	238.92	244.94	250.99	257.06	263.16	269.29	275.43
320	186.82	192.57	198.37	204.19	210.06	215.95	221.88	227.84	233.83	239.84	245.89	251.96	258.06	264.18	270.32	276.49
321	187.53	193.31	199.13	204.98	210.86	216.78	222.73	228.71	234.73	240.77	246.83	252.93	259.05	265.19	271.36	277.55
322	188.25	194.05	199.89	205.76	211.67	217.61	223.59	229.59	235.63	241.69	247.78	253.90	260.04	266.21	272.40	278.62
323	188.97	194.79	200.65	206.55	212.48	218.45	224.44	230.47	236.53	242.61	248.73	254.87	261.04	267.23	273.44	279.68
324	189.69	195.53	201.42	207.34	213.29	219.28	225.30	231.35	237.43	243.54	249.68	255.84	262.03	268.24	274.48	280.74
325	190.41	196.28	202.18	208.13	214.10	220.11	226.15	232.23	238.33	244.46	250.62	256.81	263.02	269.26	275.52	281.81
326	191.13	197.02	202.95	208.91	214.91	220.95	227.01	233.11	239.23	245.39	251.57	257.78	264.02	270.28	276.57	282.87
327	191.85	197.76	203.71	209.70	215.72	221.78	227.87	233.99	240.14	246.32	252.52	258.76	265.02	271.30	277.61	283.94
328	192.57	198.51	204.48	210.49	216.54	222.62	228.73	234.87	241.04	247.25	253.47	259.73	266.01	272.32	278.65	285.01
329	193.29	199.25	205.25	211.28	217.35	223.45	229.59	235.75	241.95	248.17	254.43	260.71	267.01	273.34	279.70	286.07
330	194.01	199.99	206.01	212.07	218.16	224.29	230.45	236.64	242.85	249.10	255.38	261.68	268.01	274.36	280.74	287.14
331	194.73	200.74	206.78	212.86	218.98	225.13	231.31	237.52	243.76	250.03	256.33	262.66	269.01	275.39	281.79	288.21
332	195.46	201.49	207.55	213.65	219.79	225.96	232.17	238.40	244.67	250.96	257.28	263.63	270.01	276.41	282.83	289.28
333	196.18	202.23	208.32	214.45	220.61	226.80	233.03	239.29	245.58	251.89	258.24	264.61	271.01	277.43	283.88	290.35
334	196.90	202.98	209.09	215.24	221.42	227.64	233.89	240.17	246.48	252.82	259.19	265.59	272.01	278.46	284.93	291.42
335	197.63	203.73	209.86	216.03	222.24	228.48	234.75	241.06	247.39	253.76	260.15	266.57	273.01	279.48	285.97	292.49
336	198.35	204.47	210.63	216.83	223.06	229.32	235.62	241.94	248.30	254.69	261.10	267.54	274.01	280.50	287.02	293.56
337	199.08	205.22	211.40	217.62	223.87	230.16	236.48	242.83	249.21	255.62	262.06	268.52	275.02	281.53	288.07	294.63
338	199.81	205.97	212.18	218.42	224.69	231.00	237.34	243.72	250.12	256.56	263.02	269.50	276.02	282.56	289.12	295.71
339	200.53	206.72	212.95	219.21	225.51	231.84	238.21	244.61	251.03	257.49	263.97	270.49	277.02	283.58	290.17	296.78
340	201.26	207.47	213.72	220.01	226.33	232.69	239.08	245.50	251.95	258.42	264.93	271.47	278.03	284.61	291.22	297.85
341	201.99	208.22	214.50	220.81	227.15	233.53	239.94	246.38	252.86	259.36	265.89	272.45	279.03	285.64	292.27	298.93
342	202.72	208.98	215.27	221.60	227.97	234.37	240.81	247.27	253.77	260.30	266.85	273.43	280.04	286.67	293.32	300.00
343	203.45	209.73	216.05	222.40	228.79	235.22	241.68	248.16	254.68	261.23	267.81	274.41	281.04	287.70	294.37	301.00
344	204.18	210.48	216.82	223.20	229.61	236.06	242.54	249.06	255.60	262.17	268.77	275.40	282.05	288.73	295.43	302.15
345	204.91	211.23	217.60	224.00	230.44	236.91	243.41	249.95	256.51	263.11	269.73	276.38	283.06	289.76	296.48	303.23
346	205.64	211.99	218.38	224.80	231.26	237.75	244.28	250.84	257.43	264.05	270.69	277.37	284.06	290.79	297.54	304.31
347	206.37	212.74	219.15	225.60	232.08	238.60	245.15	251.73	258.34	264.99	271.65	278.35	285.07	291.82	298.59	305.39
348	207.10	213.50	219.93	226.40	232.91	239.45	246.02	252.63	259.26	265.93	272.62	279.34	286.08	292.85	299.64	306.46
349	207.83	214.25	220.71	227.20	233.73	240.29	246.89	253.52	260.18	266.87	273.58	280.32	287.09	293.88	300.70	307.54
350	208.57	215.01	221.49	228.00	234.56	241.14	247.76	254.41	261.10	267.81	274.54	281.31	288.10	294.92	301.76	308.62
351	209.30	215.76	222.27	228.81	235.38	241.99	248.63	255.31	262.01	268.75	275.51	282.30	289.11	295.95	302.81	309.70
352	210.03	216.52	223.05	229.61	236.21	242.84	249.51	256.20	262.93	269.69	276.47	283.29	290.12	296.99	303.87	310.78
353	210.77	217.28	223.83	230.41	237.03	243.69	250.38	257.10	263.85	270.63	277.44	284.27	291.13	298.02	304.93	311.87
354	211.50	218.04	224.61	231.22	237.86	244.54	251.25	258.00	264.77	271.57	278.41	285.26	292.15	299.06	305.99	312.95
355	212.24	218.80	225.39	232.02	238.69	245.39	252.13	258.89	265.69	272.52	279.37	286.25	293.16	300.09	307.05	314.03
356	212.98	219.55	226.17	232.83	239.52	246.24	253.00	259.79	266.61	273.46	280.34	287.24	294.17	301.13	308.11	315.11
357	213.71	220.31	226.95	233.63	240.35	247.09	253.88	260.69	267.53	274.41	281.31	288.23	295.19	302.16	309.17	316.19
358	214.45	221.07	227.74	234.44	241.18	247.95	254.75	261.59	268.45	275.35	282.27	289.23	296.20	303.20	310.23	317.28
359	215.19	221.84	228.52	235.25	242.01	248.80	255.63	262.49	269.38	276.30	283.24	290.22	297.22	304.24	311.29	318.36
360	215.93	222.60	229.31	236.05	242.84	249.65	256.50	263.39	270.30	277.24	284.21	291.21	298.23	305.28	312.35	319.45

TABLE 13
MONTHLY PAYMENT REQUIRED TO
AMORTIZE A LOAN

10.750%

TERM	15 Years	16 Years	17 Years	18 Years	19 Years	20 Years	21 Years	22 Years	23 Years	24 Years	25 Years	30 Years	35 Years	40 Years
AMOUNT														
5	.06	.06	.06	.06	.06	.06	.06	.05	.05	.05	.05	.05	.05	.05
10	.12	.11	.11	.11	.11	.11	.11	.10	.10	.10	.10	.10	.10	.10
15	.17	.17	.17	.16	.16	.16	.16	.15	.15	.15	.15	.15	.14	.14
25	.29	.28	.27	.27	.26	.26	.26	.25	.25	.25	.25	.24	.23	.23
50	.57	.55	.54	.53	.52	.51	.51	.50	.49	.49	.49	.47	.46	.46
75	.85	.82	.81	.79	.78	.77	.76	.75	.74	.73	.73	.71	.69	.69
100	1.13	1.10	1.07	1.05	1.04	1.02	1.01	.99	.98	.98	.97	.94	.92	.91
200	2.25	2.19	2.14	2.10	2.07	2.04	2.01	1.98	1.96	1.95	1.93	1.87	1.84	1.82
300	3.37	3.28	3.21	3.15	3.10	3.05	3.01	2.97	2.94	2.92	2.89	2.81	2.76	2.73
400	4.49	4.38	4.28	4.20	4.13	4.07	4.01	3.96	3.92	3.89	3.85	3.74	3.68	3.64
500	5.61	5.47	5.35	5.25	5.16	5.08	5.01	4.95	4.90	4.86	4.82	4.67	4.59	4.55
600	6.73	6.56	6.42	6.30	6.19	6.10	6.02	5.94	5.88	5.83	5.78	5.61	5.51	5.46
700	7.85	7.66	7.49	7.35	7.22	7.11	7.02	6.93	6.86	6.80	6.74	6.54	6.43	6.36
800	8.97	8.75	8.56	8.39	8.25	8.13	8.02	7.92	7.84	7.77	7.70	7.47	7.35	7.27
900	10.09	9.84	9.63	9.44	9.28	9.14	9.02	8.91	8.82	8.74	8.66	8.41	8.26	8.18
1000	11.21	10.94	10.70	10.49	10.31	10.16	10.02	9.90	9.80	9.71	9.63	9.34	9.18	9.09
2000	22.42	21.87	21.39	20.98	20.62	20.31	20.04	19.80	19.59	19.41	19.25	18.67	18.36	18.17
3000	33.63	32.80	32.08	31.46	30.93	30.46	30.06	29.70	29.39	29.11	28.87	28.01	27.53	27.26
4000	44.84	43.73	42.77	41.95	41.23	40.61	40.07	39.60	39.18	38.81	38.49	37.34	36.71	36.34
5000	56.05	54.66	53.46	52.43	51.54	50.77	50.09	49.50	48.97	48.51	48.11	46.68	45.88	45.42
6000	67.26	65.59	64.16	62.92	61.85	60.92	60.11	59.39	58.77	58.22	57.73	56.01	55.06	54.51
7000	78.47	76.52	74.85	73.41	72.16	71.07	70.12	69.29	68.56	67.92	67.35	65.35	64.23	63.59
8000	89.68	87.45	85.54	83.89	82.46	81.22	80.14	79.19	78.36	77.62	76.97	74.68	73.41	72.68
9000	100.89	98.38	96.23	94.38	92.77	91.38	90.16	89.09	88.15	87.32	86.59	84.02	82.58	81.76
10000	112.10	109.31	106.92	104.86	103.08	101.53	100.17	98.99	97.94	97.02	96.21	93.35	91.76	90.84
11000	123.31	120.24	117.61	115.35	113.39	111.68	110.19	108.88	107.74	106.73	105.84	102.69	100.93	99.93
12000	134.52	131.17	128.31	125.84	123.69	121.83	120.21	118.78	117.53	116.43	115.46	112.02	110.11	109.01
13000	145.73	142.10	139.00	136.32	134.00	131.98	130.22	128.68	127.32	126.13	125.08	121.36	119.28	118.10
14000	156.94	153.03	149.69	146.81	144.31	142.14	140.24	138.58	137.12	135.83	134.70	130.69	128.46	127.18
15000	168.15	163.97	160.38	157.29	154.62	152.29	150.26	148.48	146.91	145.53	144.32	140.03	137.63	136.26
16000	179.36	174.90	171.07	167.78	164.92	162.44	160.27	158.37	156.71	155.24	153.94	149.36	146.81	145.35
17000	190.57	185.83	181.77	178.26	175.23	172.59	170.29	168.27	166.50	164.94	163.56	158.70	155.98	154.43
18000	201.78	196.76	192.46	188.75	185.54	182.75	180.31	178.17	176.29	174.64	173.18	168.03	165.16	163.52
19000	212.99	207.69	203.15	199.24	195.85	192.90	190.32	188.07	186.09	184.34	182.80	177.37	174.33	172.60
20000	224.19	218.62	213.84	209.72	206.15	203.05	200.34	197.97	195.88	194.04	192.42	186.70	183.51	181.68
21000	235.40	229.55	224.53	220.21	216.46	213.20	210.36	207.87	205.68	203.75	202.04	196.04	192.68	190.77
22000	246.61	240.48	235.22	230.69	226.77	223.36	220.37	217.76	215.47	213.45	211.67	205.37	201.86	199.85
23000	257.82	251.41	245.92	241.18	237.08	233.51	230.39	227.66	225.26	223.15	221.29	214.71	211.03	208.94
24000	269.03	262.34	256.61	251.67	247.38	243.66	240.41	237.56	235.06	232.85	230.91	224.04	220.21	218.02
25000	280.24	273.27	267.30	262.15	257.69	253.81	250.42	247.46	244.85	242.55	240.53	233.38	229.38	227.10
26000	291.45	284.20	277.99	272.64	268.00	263.96	260.44	257.36	254.66	252.26	250.15	242.71	238.56	236.19
27000	302.66	295.13	288.68	283.12	278.31	274.12	270.46	267.25	264.44	261.96	259.77	252.04	247.73	245.27
28000	313.87	306.06	299.37	293.61	288.61	284.27	280.48	277.15	274.23	271.66	269.39	261.38	256.91	254.36
29000	325.08	317.00	310.07	304.09	298.92	294.42	290.49	287.05	284.03	281.36	279.01	270.71	266.08	263.44
30000	336.29	327.93	320.76	314.58	309.23	304.57	300.51	296.95	293.82	291.06	288.63	280.05	275.26	272.52
31000	347.50	338.86	331.45	325.07	319.54	314.73	310.53	306.85	303.61	300.77	298.25	289.38	284.43	281.61
32000	358.71	349.79	342.14	335.55	329.84	324.88	320.54	316.74	313.41	310.47	307.87	298.72	293.61	290.69
33000	369.92	360.72	352.83	346.04	340.15	335.03	330.56	326.64	323.20	320.17	317.50	308.05	302.78	299.78
34000	381.13	371.65	363.53	356.52	350.46	345.18	340.58	336.54	332.99	329.87	327.12	317.39	311.96	308.86
35000	392.34	382.58	374.22	367.01	360.77	355.34	350.59	346.44	342.79	339.57	336.74	326.72	321.13	317.94
36000	403.55	393.51	384.91	377.50	371.07	365.49	360.61	356.34	352.58	349.28	346.36	336.06	330.31	327.03
37000	414.76	404.44	395.60	387.98	381.38	375.64	370.63	366.23	362.38	358.98	355.98	345.39	339.48	336.11
38000	425.97	415.37	406.29	398.47	391.69	385.79	380.64	376.13	372.17	368.68	365.60	354.73	348.66	345.20
39000	437.17	426.30	416.98	408.95	402.00	395.94	390.66	386.03	381.96	378.38	375.22	364.06	357.83	354.28
40000	448.38	437.23	427.68	419.44	412.30	406.10	400.68	395.93	391.76	388.08	384.84	373.40	367.01	363.36
41000	459.59	448.16	438.37	429.92	422.61	416.25	410.69	405.83	401.55	397.79	394.46	382.73	376.18	372.45
42000	470.80	459.09	449.06	440.41	432.92	426.40	420.71	415.73	411.35	407.49	404.08	392.07	385.36	381.53
43000	482.01	470.03	459.75	450.90	443.23	436.55	430.73	425.62	421.14	417.19	413.70	401.40	394.53	390.62
44000	493.22	480.96	470.44	461.38	453.53	446.71	440.74	435.52	430.93	426.89	423.33	410.74	403.71	399.70
45000	504.43	491.89	481.14	471.87	463.84	456.86	450.76	445.42	440.73	436.59	432.95	420.07	412.88	408.78
46000	515.64	502.82	491.83	482.35	474.15	467.01	460.78	455.32	450.52	446.30	442.57	429.41	422.06	417.87
47000	526.85	513.75	502.52	492.84	484.46	477.16	470.79	465.22	460.31	456.00	452.19	438.74	431.23	426.95
48000	538.06	524.68	513.21	503.33	494.76	487.31	480.81	475.11	470.11	465.70	461.81	448.08	440.41	436.04
49000	549.27	535.61	523.90	513.81	505.07	497.47	490.83	485.01	479.90	475.40	471.43	457.41	449.58	445.12
50000	560.48	546.54	534.59	524.30	515.38	507.62	500.84	494.91	489.70	485.10	481.05	466.75	458.76	454.20
55000	616.53	601.19	588.05	576.73	566.92	558.38	550.93	544.40	538.67	533.61	529.16	513.42	504.63	499.62
60000	672.57	655.85	641.51	629.16	618.45	609.14	601.01	593.89	587.63	582.12	577.26	560.09	550.51	545.04
65000	728.62	710.50	694.97	681.59	669.99	659.90	651.10	643.38	636.60	630.63	625.37	606.77	596.38	590.46
70000	784.67	765.15	748.43	734.01	721.53	710.67	701.18	692.87	685.57	679.14	673.47	653.44	642.26	635.88
75000	840.72	819.81	801.89	786.44	773.07	761.43	751.26	742.36	734.54	727.65	721.57	700.12	688.13	681.30
80000	896.76	874.46	855.35	838.87	824.60	812.19	801.35	791.85	783.51	776.16	769.68	746.79	734.01	726.72
85000	952.81	929.11	908.81	891.30	876.14	862.95	851.43	841.34	832.48	824.67	817.78	793.46	779.88	772.14
90000	1008.86	983.77	962.27	943.73	927.68	913.71	901.52	890.83	881.45	873.18	865.89	840.14	825.76	817.56
95000	1064.91	1038.42	1015.72	996.16	979.21	964.47	951.60	940.32	930.42	921.69	913.99	886.81	871.63	862.98
100000	1120.95	1093.07	1069.18	1048.59	1030.75	1015.23	1001.68	989.81	979.39	970.20	962.10	933.49	917.51	908.40

TABLE 13 (cont.)

11.000%

TERM AMOUNT	15 Years	16 Years	17 Years	18 Years	19 Years	20 Years	21 Years	22 Years	23 Years	24 Years	25 Years	30 Years	35 Years	40 Years
5	.06	.06	.06	.06	.06	.06	.06	.06	.05	.05	.05	.05	.05	.05
10	.12	.12	.11	.11	.11	.11	.11	.11	.10	.10	.10	.10	.10	.10
15	.18	.17	.17	.16	.16	.16	.16	.16	.15	.15	.15	.15	.15	.14
25	.29	.28	.28	.27	.27	.26	.26	.26	.25	.25	.25	.24	.24	.24
50	.57	.56	.55	.54	.53	.52	.51	.51	.50	.50	.50	.48	.47	.47
75	.86	.84	.82	.80	.79	.78	.77	.76	.75	.75	.74	.72	.71	.70
100	1.14	1.11	1.09	1.07	1.05	1.04	1.02	1.01	1.00	.99	.99	.96	.94	.93
200	2.28	2.22	2.18	2.14	2.10	2.07	2.04	2.02	2.00	1.98	1.97	1.91	1.88	1.86
300	3.41	3.33	3.26	3.20	3.15	3.10	3.06	3.03	3.00	2.97	2.95	2.86	2.82	2.79
400	4.55	4.44	4.35	4.27	4.19	4.13	4.08	4.03	3.99	3.96	3.93	3.81	3.75	3.72
500	5.69	5.55	5.43	5.33	5.24	5.17	5.10	5.04	4.99	4.95	4.91	4.77	4.69	4.65
600	6.82	6.66	6.52	6.40	6.29	6.20	6.12	6.05	5.99	5.93	5.89	5.72	5.63	5.57
700	7.96	7.77	7.60	7.46	7.34	7.23	7.14	7.06	6.98	6.92	6.87	6.67	6.56	6.50
800	9.10	8.88	8.69	8.53	8.38	8.26	8.16	8.06	7.98	7.91	7.85	7.62	7.50	7.43
900	10.23	9.99	9.77	9.59	9.43	9.29	9.17	9.07	8.98	8.90	8.83	8.58	8.44	8.36
1000	11.37	11.10	10.86	10.66	10.48	10.33	10.19	10.08	9.98	9.89	9.81	9.53	9.37	9.29
2000	22.74	22.19	21.71	21.31	20.95	20.65	20.38	20.15	19.95	19.77	19.61	19.05	18.74	18.57
3000	34.10	33.28	32.57	31.96	31.43	30.97	30.57	30.22	29.92	29.65	29.41	28.57	28.11	27.85
4000	45.47	44.37	43.42	42.61	41.90	41.29	40.76	40.29	39.89	39.53	39.21	38.10	37.48	37.14
5000	56.83	55.46	54.27	53.26	52.38	51.61	50.95	50.37	49.86	49.41	49.01	47.62	46.85	46.42
6000	68.20	66.55	65.13	63.91	62.85	61.94	61.14	60.44	59.83	59.29	58.81	57.14	56.22	55.70
7000	79.57	77.64	75.98	74.56	73.33	72.26	71.33	70.51	69.80	69.17	68.61	66.67	65.59	64.99
8000	90.93	88.73	86.84	85.21	83.80	82.58	81.51	80.58	79.77	79.05	78.41	76.19	74.96	74.27
9000	102.30	99.82	97.69	95.86	94.28	92.90	91.70	90.66	89.74	88.93	88.22	85.71	84.33	83.55
10000	113.66	110.91	108.54	106.51	104.75	103.22	101.89	100.73	99.71	98.81	98.02	95.24	93.70	92.83
11000	125.03	122.00	119.40	117.16	115.23	113.55	112.08	110.80	109.68	108.69	107.82	104.76	103.07	102.12
12000	136.40	133.09	130.25	127.81	125.70	123.87	122.27	120.87	119.65	118.57	117.62	114.28	112.44	111.40
13000	147.76	144.18	141.10	138.46	136.18	134.19	132.46	130.94	129.62	128.45	127.42	123.81	121.81	120.68
14000	159.13	155.27	151.96	149.11	146.65	144.51	142.65	141.02	139.59	138.33	137.22	133.33	131.18	129.97
15000	170.49	166.36	162.81	159.76	157.12	154.83	152.84	151.09	149.56	148.21	147.02	142.85	140.55	139.25
16000	181.86	177.45	173.67	170.41	167.60	165.16	163.02	161.16	159.53	158.09	156.82	152.38	149.92	148.53
17000	193.23	188.54	184.52	181.06	178.07	175.48	173.21	171.23	169.50	167.97	166.62	161.90	159.29	157.82
18000	204.59	199.63	195.37	191.71	188.55	185.80	183.40	181.31	179.47	177.85	176.43	171.42	168.66	167.10
19000	215.96	210.72	206.23	202.36	199.02	196.12	193.59	191.38	189.44	187.73	186.23	180.95	178.03	176.38
20000	227.32	221.81	217.08	213.01	209.50	206.44	203.78	201.45	199.41	197.61	196.03	190.47	187.40	185.66
21000	238.69	232.90	227.93	223.67	219.97	216.76	213.97	211.52	209.38	207.49	205.83	199.99	196.77	194.95
22000	250.06	243.99	238.79	234.32	230.45	227.09	224.16	221.59	219.35	217.37	215.63	209.52	206.14	204.23
23000	261.42	255.08	249.64	244.97	240.92	237.41	234.35	231.67	229.32	227.25	225.43	219.04	215.51	213.51
24000	272.79	266.17	260.50	255.62	251.40	247.73	244.53	241.74	239.29	237.13	235.23	228.56	224.87	222.80
25000	284.15	277.26	271.35	266.27	261.87	258.05	254.72	251.81	249.26	247.01	245.03	238.09	234.24	232.08
26000	295.52	288.35	282.20	276.92	272.35	268.37	264.91	261.88	259.23	256.89	254.83	247.61	243.61	241.36
27000	306.89	299.44	293.06	287.57	282.82	278.70	275.10	271.96	269.20	266.77	264.64	257.13	252.98	250.64
28000	318.25	310.53	303.91	298.22	293.29	289.02	285.29	282.03	279.17	276.65	274.44	266.66	262.35	259.93
29000	329.62	321.62	314.77	308.87	303.77	299.34	295.48	292.10	289.14	286.53	284.24	276.18	271.72	269.21
30000	340.98	332.71	325.62	319.52	314.24	309.66	305.67	302.17	299.11	296.41	294.04	285.70	281.09	278.49
31000	352.35	343.80	336.47	330.17	324.72	319.98	315.85	312.24	309.08	306.29	303.84	295.23	290.46	287.78
32000	363.72	354.89	347.33	340.82	335.19	330.31	326.04	322.32	319.05	316.17	313.64	304.75	299.83	297.06
33000	375.08	365.98	358.18	351.47	345.67	340.63	336.23	332.39	329.02	326.05	323.44	314.27	309.20	306.34
34000	386.45	377.07	369.03	362.12	356.14	350.95	346.42	342.46	338.99	335.93	333.24	323.79	318.57	315.63
35000	397.81	388.16	379.89	372.77	366.62	361.27	356.61	352.53	348.96	345.81	343.04	333.32	327.94	324.91
36000	409.18	399.25	390.74	383.42	377.09	371.59	366.80	362.61	358.93	355.69	352.85	342.84	337.31	334.19
37000	420.55	410.34	401.60	394.07	387.57	381.91	376.99	372.68	368.90	365.57	362.65	352.36	346.68	343.47
38000	431.91	421.43	412.45	404.72	398.04	392.24	387.18	382.75	378.87	375.46	372.45	361.89	356.05	352.76
39000	443.28	432.52	423.30	415.37	408.52	402.56	397.36	392.82	388.84	385.34	382.25	371.41	365.42	362.04
40000	454.64	443.61	434.16	426.02	418.99	412.88	407.55	402.89	398.81	395.22	392.05	380.93	374.79	371.32
41000	466.01	454.70	445.01	436.68	429.47	423.20	417.74	412.97	408.78	405.10	401.85	390.46	384.16	380.61
42000	477.38	465.79	455.86	447.33	439.94	433.52	427.93	423.04	418.75	414.98	411.65	399.98	393.53	389.89
43000	488.74	476.88	466.72	457.98	450.41	443.85	438.12	433.11	428.72	424.86	421.45	409.50	402.90	399.17
44000	500.11	487.97	477.57	468.63	460.89	454.17	448.31	443.18	438.69	434.74	431.25	419.03	412.27	408.45
45000	511.47	499.06	488.43	479.28	471.36	464.49	458.50	453.26	448.66	444.62	441.06	428.55	421.64	417.74
46000	522.84	510.15	499.28	489.93	481.84	474.81	468.69	463.33	458.63	454.50	450.86	438.07	431.01	427.02
47000	534.21	521.24	510.13	500.58	492.31	485.13	478.87	473.40	468.60	464.38	460.66	447.60	440.38	436.30
48000	545.57	532.33	520.99	511.23	502.79	495.46	489.06	483.47	478.57	474.26	470.46	457.12	449.74	445.59
49000	556.94	543.42	531.84	521.88	513.26	505.78	499.25	493.54	488.54	484.14	480.26	466.64	459.11	454.87
50000	568.30	554.51	542.70	532.53	523.74	516.10	509.44	503.62	498.51	494.02	490.06	476.17	468.48	464.15
55000	625.13	609.96	596.96	585.78	576.11	567.71	560.38	553.98	548.36	543.42	539.07	523.78	515.33	510.57
60000	681.96	665.41	651.23	639.03	628.48	619.32	611.33	604.34	598.21	592.82	588.07	571.40	562.18	556.98
65000	738.79	720.86	705.50	692.29	680.86	670.93	662.27	654.70	648.06	642.22	637.08	619.02	609.03	603.40
70000	795.62	776.31	759.77	745.54	733.23	722.54	713.21	705.06	697.91	691.62	686.08	666.63	655.88	649.81
75000	852.45	831.76	814.04	798.79	785.60	774.15	764.16	755.42	747.76	741.02	735.09	714.25	702.72	696.23
80000	909.28	887.21	868.31	852.04	837.98	825.76	815.10	805.78	797.61	790.43	784.10	761.86	749.57	742.64
85000	966.11	942.66	922.58	905.30	890.35	877.37	866.05	856.14	847.46	839.83	833.10	809.48	796.42	789.06
90000	1022.94	998.11	976.85	958.55	942.72	928.97	916.99	906.51	897.31	889.23	882.11	857.10	843.27	835.47
95000	1079.77	1053.56	1031.12	1011.80	995.10	980.58	967.93	956.87	947.16	938.63	931.11	904.71	890.11	881.88
100000	1136.60	1109.01	1085.39	1065.05	1047.47	1032.19	1018.88	1007.23	997.01	988.03	980.12	952.33	936.96	928.30

TABLE 13 (cont.)

11.250%

TERM AMOUNT	15 Years	16 Years	17 Years	18 Years	19 Years	20 Years	21 Years	22 Years	23 Years	24 Years	25 Years	30 Years	35 Years	40 Years
5	.06	.06	.06	.06	.06	.06	.06	.06	.06	.06	.06	.05	.05	.05
10	.12	.12	.12	.11	.11	.11	.11	.11	.11	.11	.11	.10	.10	.10
15	.18	.17	.17	.17	.16	.16	.16	.16	.16	.16	.15	.15	.15	.15
25	.29	.29	.28	.28	.27	.27	.26	.26	.26	.26	.25	.25	.24	.24
50	.58	.57	.56	.55	.54	.53	.52	.52	.51	.51	.50	.49	.48	.48
75	.87	.85	.83	.82	.80	.79	.78	.77	.77	.76	.75	.73	.72	.72
100	1.16	1.13	1.11	1.09	1.07	1.05	1.04	1.03	1.02	1.01	1.00	.98	.96	.95
200	2.31	2.26	2.21	2.17	2.13	2.10	2.08	2.05	2.03	2.02	2.00	1.95	1.92	1.90
300	3.46	3.38	3.31	3.25	3.20	3.15	3.11	3.08	3.05	3.02	3.00	2.92	2.87	2.85
400	4.61	4.51	4.41	4.33	4.26	4.20	4.15	4.10	4.06	4.03	4.00	3.89	3.83	3.80
500	5.77	5.63	5.51	5.41	5.33	5.25	5.19	5.13	5.08	5.03	5.00	4.86	4.79	4.75
600	6.92	6.76	6.62	6.49	6.39	6.30	6.22	6.15	6.09	6.04	5.99	5.83	5.74	5.69
700	8.07	7.88	7.72	7.58	7.46	7.35	7.26	7.18	7.11	7.05	6.99	6.80	6.70	6.64
800	9.22	9.01	8.82	8.66	8.52	8.40	8.29	8.20	8.12	8.05	7.99	7.78	7.66	7.59
900	10.38	10.13	9.92	9.74	9.58	9.45	9.33	9.23	9.14	9.06	8.99	8.75	8.61	8.54
1000	11.53	11.26	11.02	10.82	10.65	10.50	10.37	10.25	10.15	10.06	9.99	9.72	9.57	9.49
2000	23.05	22.51	22.04	21.64	21.29	20.99	20.73	20.50	20.30	20.12	19.97	19.43	19.13	18.97
3000	34.58	33.76	33.06	32.45	31.93	31.48	31.09	30.75	30.45	30.18	29.95	29.14	28.70	28.45
4000	46.10	45.01	44.07	43.27	42.58	41.98	41.45	40.99	40.59	40.24	39.93	38.86	38.26	37.94
5000	57.62	56.26	55.09	54.09	53.22	52.47	51.81	51.24	50.74	50.30	49.92	48.57	47.83	47.42
6000	69.15	67.51	66.11	64.90	63.86	62.96	62.18	61.49	60.89	60.36	59.90	58.28	57.39	56.90
7000	80.67	78.76	77.12	75.72	74.51	73.45	72.54	71.74	71.04	70.42	69.88	67.99	66.96	66.38
8000	92.19	90.01	88.14	86.53	85.15	83.95	82.90	81.98	81.18	80.48	79.86	77.71	76.52	75.87
9000	103.72	101.26	99.16	97.35	95.79	94.44	93.26	92.23	91.33	90.54	89.85	87.42	86.09	85.35
10000	115.24	112.51	110.17	108.17	106.43	104.93	103.62	102.48	101.48	100.60	99.83	97.13	95.65	94.83
11000	126.76	123.76	121.19	118.98	117.08	115.42	113.98	112.73	111.63	110.66	109.81	106.84	105.22	104.31
12000	138.29	135.01	132.21	129.80	127.72	125.92	124.35	122.97	121.77	120.72	119.79	116.56	114.78	113.80
13000	149.81	146.26	143.22	140.62	138.36	136.41	134.71	133.22	131.92	130.78	129.78	126.27	124.35	123.28
14000	161.33	157.51	154.24	151.43	149.01	146.90	145.07	143.47	142.07	140.84	139.76	135.98	133.91	132.76
15000	172.86	168.76	165.26	162.25	159.65	157.39	155.43	153.72	152.22	150.90	149.74	145.69	143.48	142.24
16000	184.38	180.01	176.27	173.06	170.29	167.89	165.79	163.96	162.36	160.96	159.72	155.41	153.04	151.73
17000	195.90	191.26	187.29	183.88	180.93	178.38	176.15	174.21	172.51	171.02	169.71	165.12	162.61	161.21
18000	207.43	202.51	198.31	194.70	191.58	188.87	186.52	184.46	182.66	181.08	179.69	174.83	172.17	170.69
19000	218.95	213.76	209.33	205.51	202.22	199.36	196.88	194.71	192.81	191.14	189.67	184.54	181.74	180.17
20000	230.47	225.01	220.34	216.33	212.86	209.86	207.24	204.95	202.95	201.20	199.65	194.26	191.30	189.66
21000	242.00	236.26	231.36	227.15	223.51	220.35	217.60	215.20	213.10	211.26	209.64	203.97	200.87	199.14
22000	253.52	247.51	242.38	237.96	234.15	230.84	227.96	225.45	223.25	221.32	219.62	213.68	210.43	208.62
23000	265.04	258.76	253.39	248.78	244.79	241.33	238.32	235.70	233.40	231.38	229.60	223.40	220.00	218.10
24000	276.57	270.01	264.41	259.59	255.43	251.83	248.69	245.94	243.54	241.44	239.58	233.11	229.56	227.59
25000	288.09	281.26	275.43	270.41	266.08	262.32	259.05	256.19	253.69	251.50	249.56	242.82	239.13	237.07
26000	299.61	292.51	286.44	281.23	276.72	272.81	269.41	266.44	263.84	261.56	259.55	252.53	248.69	246.55
27000	311.14	303.76	297.46	292.04	287.36	283.30	279.77	276.69	273.99	271.61	269.53	262.25	258.26	256.03
28000	322.66	315.01	308.48	302.86	298.01	293.80	290.13	286.93	284.13	281.67	279.51	271.96	267.82	265.52
29000	334.18	326.26	319.49	313.67	308.65	304.29	300.49	297.18	294.28	291.73	289.49	281.67	277.39	275.00
30000	345.71	337.51	330.51	324.49	319.29	314.78	310.86	307.43	304.43	301.79	299.48	291.38	286.95	284.48
31000	357.23	348.77	341.53	335.31	329.93	325.27	321.22	317.68	314.58	311.85	309.46	301.10	296.52	293.96
32000	368.76	360.02	352.54	346.12	340.58	335.77	331.58	327.92	324.72	321.91	319.44	310.81	306.08	303.45
33000	380.28	371.27	363.56	356.94	351.22	346.26	341.94	338.17	334.87	331.97	329.42	320.52	315.65	312.93
34000	391.80	382.52	374.58	367.76	361.86	356.75	352.30	348.42	345.02	342.03	339.41	330.23	325.21	322.41
35000	403.33	393.77	385.60	378.57	372.51	367.24	362.66	358.67	355.16	352.09	349.39	339.95	334.78	331.90
36000	414.85	405.02	396.61	389.39	383.15	377.74	373.03	368.91	365.31	362.15	359.37	349.66	344.34	341.38
37000	426.37	416.27	407.63	400.20	393.79	388.23	383.39	379.16	375.46	372.21	369.35	359.37	353.91	350.86
38000	437.90	427.52	418.65	411.02	404.43	398.72	393.75	389.41	385.61	382.27	379.34	369.08	363.47	360.34
39000	449.42	438.77	429.66	421.84	415.08	409.21	404.11	399.66	395.75	392.33	389.32	378.80	373.04	369.83
40000	460.94	450.02	440.68	432.65	425.72	419.71	414.47	409.90	405.90	402.39	399.30	388.51	382.60	379.31
41000	472.47	461.27	451.70	443.47	436.36	430.20	424.84	420.15	416.05	412.45	409.28	398.22	392.17	388.79
42000	483.99	472.52	462.71	454.29	447.01	440.69	435.20	430.40	426.20	422.51	419.27	407.93	401.73	398.27
43000	495.51	483.77	473.73	465.10	457.65	451.19	445.56	440.65	436.34	432.57	429.25	417.65	411.30	407.76
44000	507.04	495.02	484.75	475.92	468.29	461.68	455.92	450.89	446.49	442.63	439.23	427.36	420.86	417.24
45000	518.56	506.27	495.76	486.73	478.93	472.17	466.28	461.14	456.64	452.69	449.21	437.07	430.43	426.72
46000	530.08	517.52	506.78	497.55	489.58	482.66	476.64	471.39	466.79	462.75	459.20	446.79	439.99	436.20
47000	541.61	528.77	517.80	508.37	500.22	493.16	487.01	481.64	476.93	472.81	469.18	456.50	449.56	445.69
48000	553.13	540.02	528.81	519.18	510.86	503.65	497.37	491.88	487.08	482.87	479.16	466.21	459.12	455.17
49000	564.65	551.27	539.83	530.00	521.51	514.14	507.73	502.13	497.23	492.93	489.14	475.92	468.69	464.65
50000	576.18	562.52	550.85	540.82	532.15	524.63	518.09	512.38	507.38	502.99	499.12	485.64	478.25	474.13
55000	633.79	618.77	605.93	594.90	585.36	577.10	569.90	563.62	558.11	553.28	549.04	534.20	526.08	521.55
60000	691.41	675.02	661.02	648.98	638.58	629.56	621.71	614.85	608.85	603.58	598.95	582.76	573.90	568.96
65000	749.03	731.28	716.10	703.06	691.79	682.02	673.52	666.09	659.59	653.88	648.86	631.32	621.73	616.37
70000	806.65	787.53	771.19	757.14	745.01	734.48	725.32	717.33	710.32	704.18	698.77	679.89	669.55	663.79
75000	864.26	843.78	826.27	811.22	798.22	786.95	777.13	768.56	761.06	754.48	748.68	728.45	717.38	711.20
80000	921.88	900.03	881.35	865.30	851.44	839.41	828.94	819.80	811.80	804.77	798.60	777.01	765.20	758.61
85000	979.50	956.28	936.44	919.38	904.65	891.87	880.75	871.04	862.54	855.07	848.51	825.58	813.02	806.02
90000	1037.12	1012.53	991.52	973.46	957.86	944.34	932.56	922.28	913.27	905.37	898.42	874.14	860.85	853.44
95000	1094.73	1068.79	1046.61	1027.54	1011.08	996.80	984.37	973.51	964.01	955.67	948.33	922.70	908.67	900.85
100000	1152.35	1125.04	1101.69	1081.63	1064.29	1049.26	1036.18	1024.75	1014.75	1005.97	998.24	971.27	956.50	948.26

TABLE 13 (cont.)

11.500%

TERM AMOUNT	15 Years	16 Years	17 Years	18 Years	19 Years	20 Years	21 Years	22 Years	23 Years	24 Years	25 Years	30 Years	35 Years	40 Years
5	.06	.06	.06	.06	.06	.06	.06	.06	.06	.06	.06	.05	.05	.05
10	.12	.12	.12	.11	.11	.11	.11	.11	.11	.11	.11	.10	.10	.10
15	.18	.18	.17	.17	.17	.16	.16	.16	.16	.16	.16	.15	.15	.15
25	.30	.29	.28	.28	.28	.27	.27	.27	.26	.26	.26	.25	.25	.25
50	.59	.58	.56	.55	.55	.54	.53	.53	.52	.52	.51	.50	.49	.49
75	.88	.86	.84	.83	.82	.80	.80	.79	.78	.77	.77	.75	.74	.73
100	1.17	1.15	1.12	1.10	1.09	1.07	1.06	1.05	1.04	1.03	1.02	1.00	.98	.97
200	2.34	2.29	2.24	2.20	2.17	2.14	2.11	2.09	2.07	2.05	2.04	1.99	1.96	1.94
300	3.51	3.43	3.36	3.30	3.25	3.20	3.17	3.13	3.10	3.08	3.05	2.98	2.93	2.91
400	4.68	4.57	4.48	4.40	4.33	4.27	4.22	4.17	4.14	4.10	4.07	3.97	3.91	3.88
500	5.85	5.71	5.60	5.50	5.41	5.34	5.27	5.22	5.17	5.13	5.09	4.96	4.89	4.85
600	7.01	6.85	6.71	6.59	6.49	6.40	6.33	6.26	6.20	6.15	6.10	5.95	5.86	5.81
700	8.18	7.99	7.83	7.69	7.57	7.47	7.38	7.30	7.23	7.17	7.12	6.94	6.84	6.78
800	9.35	9.13	8.95	8.79	8.65	8.54	8.43	8.34	8.27	8.20	8.14	7.93	7.81	7.75
900	10.52	10.28	10.07	9.89	9.74	9.60	9.49	9.39	9.30	9.22	9.15	8.92	8.79	8.72
1000	11.69	11.42	11.19	10.99	10.82	10.67	10.54	10.43	10.33	10.25	10.17	9.91	9.77	9.69
2000	23.37	22.83	22.37	21.97	21.63	21.33	21.08	20.85	20.66	20.49	20.33	19.81	19.53	19.37
3000	35.05	34.24	33.55	32.95	32.44	32.00	31.61	31.28	30.98	30.73	30.50	29.71	29.29	29.05
4000	46.73	45.65	44.73	43.94	43.25	42.66	42.15	41.70	41.31	40.97	40.66	39.62	39.05	38.74
5000	58.41	57.06	55.91	54.92	54.07	53.33	52.68	52.12	51.63	51.21	50.83	49.52	48.81	48.42
6000	70.10	68.47	67.09	65.90	64.88	63.99	63.22	62.55	61.96	61.45	60.99	59.42	58.57	58.10
7000	81.78	79.89	78.27	76.89	75.69	74.66	73.76	72.97	72.29	71.69	71.16	69.33	68.33	67.78
8000	93.46	91.30	89.45	87.87	86.50	85.32	84.29	83.39	82.61	81.93	81.32	79.23	78.09	77.47
9000	105.14	102.71	100.63	98.85	97.31	95.98	94.83	93.82	92.94	92.17	91.49	89.13	87.85	87.15
10000	116.82	114.12	111.81	109.83	108.13	106.65	105.36	104.24	103.26	102.41	101.65	99.03	97.62	96.83
11000	128.51	125.53	123.00	120.82	118.94	117.31	115.90	114.67	113.59	112.65	111.82	108.94	107.38	106.52
12000	140.19	136.94	134.18	131.80	129.75	127.98	126.43	125.09	123.91	122.89	121.98	118.84	117.14	116.20
13000	151.87	148.36	145.36	142.78	140.56	138.64	136.97	135.51	134.24	133.13	132.15	128.74	126.90	125.88
14000	163.55	159.77	156.54	153.77	151.38	149.31	147.51	145.94	144.57	143.37	142.31	138.65	136.66	135.56
15000	175.23	171.18	167.72	164.75	162.19	159.97	158.04	156.36	154.89	153.61	152.48	148.55	146.42	145.25
16000	186.92	182.59	178.90	175.73	173.00	170.63	168.58	166.78	165.22	163.85	162.64	158.45	156.18	154.93
17000	198.60	194.00	190.08	186.72	183.81	181.30	179.11	177.21	175.54	174.09	172.80	168.35	165.94	164.61
18000	210.28	205.41	201.26	197.70	194.62	191.96	189.65	187.63	185.87	184.33	182.97	178.26	175.70	174.30
19000	221.96	216.83	212.44	208.68	205.44	202.63	200.18	198.06	196.20	194.57	193.13	188.16	185.47	183.98
20000	233.64	228.24	223.62	219.66	216.25	213.29	210.72	208.48	206.52	204.81	203.30	198.06	195.23	193.66
21000	245.32	239.65	234.81	230.65	227.06	223.96	221.26	218.90	216.85	215.05	213.46	207.97	204.99	203.34
22000	257.01	251.06	245.99	241.63	237.87	234.62	231.79	229.33	227.17	225.29	223.63	217.87	214.75	213.03
23000	268.69	262.47	257.17	252.61	248.69	245.28	242.33	239.75	237.50	235.53	233.79	227.77	224.51	222.71
24000	280.37	273.88	268.35	263.60	259.50	255.95	252.86	250.17	247.82	245.77	243.96	237.67	234.27	232.39
25000	292.05	285.30	279.53	274.58	270.31	266.61	263.40	260.60	258.15	256.01	254.12	247.58	244.03	242.08
26000	303.73	296.71	290.71	285.56	281.12	277.28	273.94	271.02	268.48	266.25	264.29	257.48	253.79	251.76
27000	315.42	308.12	301.89	296.54	291.93	287.94	284.47	281.45	278.80	276.49	274.45	267.38	263.55	261.44
28000	327.10	319.53	313.07	307.53	302.75	298.61	295.01	291.87	289.13	286.73	284.62	277.29	273.32	271.12
29000	338.78	330.94	324.25	318.51	313.56	309.27	305.54	302.29	299.45	296.97	294.78	287.19	283.08	280.81
30000	350.46	342.35	335.43	329.49	324.37	319.93	316.08	312.72	309.78	307.21	304.95	297.09	292.84	290.49
31000	362.14	353.77	346.61	340.48	335.18	330.60	326.61	323.14	320.11	317.45	315.11	307.00	302.60	300.17
32000	373.83	365.18	357.80	351.46	345.99	341.26	337.15	333.56	330.43	327.69	325.28	316.90	312.36	309.86
33000	385.51	376.59	368.98	362.44	356.81	351.93	347.69	343.99	340.76	337.93	335.44	326.80	322.12	319.54
34000	397.19	388.00	380.16	373.43	367.62	362.59	358.22	354.41	351.08	348.17	345.60	336.70	331.88	329.22
35000	408.87	399.41	391.34	384.41	378.43	373.26	368.76	364.84	361.41	358.41	355.77	346.61	341.64	338.90
36000	420.55	410.82	402.52	395.39	389.24	383.92	379.29	375.26	371.73	368.65	365.93	356.51	351.40	348.59
37000	432.24	422.24	413.70	406.37	400.06	394.58	389.83	385.68	382.06	378.89	376.10	366.41	361.16	358.27
38000	443.92	433.65	424.88	417.36	410.87	405.25	400.36	396.11	392.39	389.13	386.26	376.32	370.93	367.95
39000	455.60	445.06	436.06	428.34	421.68	415.91	410.90	406.53	402.71	399.37	396.43	386.22	380.69	377.63
40000	467.28	456.47	447.24	439.32	432.49	426.58	421.44	416.95	413.04	409.61	406.59	396.12	390.45	387.32
41000	478.96	467.88	458.42	450.31	443.30	437.24	431.97	427.38	423.36	419.85	416.76	406.02	400.21	397.00
42000	490.64	479.29	469.61	461.29	454.12	447.91	442.51	437.80	433.69	430.09	426.92	415.93	409.97	406.68
43000	502.33	490.71	480.79	472.27	464.93	458.57	453.04	448.23	444.01	440.33	437.09	425.83	419.73	416.37
44000	514.01	502.12	491.97	483.25	475.74	469.23	463.58	458.65	454.34	450.57	447.25	435.73	429.49	426.05
45000	525.69	513.53	503.15	494.24	486.55	479.90	474.11	469.07	464.67	460.81	457.42	445.64	439.25	435.73
46000	537.37	524.94	514.33	505.22	497.37	490.56	484.65	479.50	474.99	471.05	467.58	455.54	449.01	445.41
47000	549.05	536.35	525.51	516.20	508.18	501.23	495.19	489.92	485.32	481.29	477.75	465.44	458.78	455.10
48000	560.74	547.76	536.69	527.19	518.99	511.89	505.72	500.34	495.64	491.53	487.91	475.34	468.54	464.78
49000	572.42	559.18	547.87	538.17	529.80	522.56	516.26	510.77	505.97	501.77	498.07	485.25	478.30	474.46
50000	584.10	570.59	559.05	549.15	540.61	533.22	526.79	521.19	516.30	512.01	508.24	495.15	488.06	484.15
55000	642.51	627.65	614.96	604.07	594.67	586.54	579.47	573.31	567.92	563.21	559.06	544.67	536.86	532.56
60000	700.92	684.70	670.86	658.98	648.74	639.86	632.15	625.43	619.55	614.41	609.89	594.18	585.67	580.97
65000	759.33	741.76	726.77	713.90	702.80	693.18	684.83	677.55	671.18	665.61	660.71	643.69	634.47	629.39
70000	817.74	798.82	782.67	768.81	756.86	746.51	737.51	729.67	722.81	716.81	711.53	693.21	683.28	677.80
75000	876.15	855.88	838.58	823.73	810.92	799.83	790.19	781.79	774.44	768.01	762.36	742.72	732.09	726.22
80000	934.56	912.94	894.48	878.64	864.98	853.15	842.87	833.90	826.07	819.21	813.18	792.24	780.89	774.63
85000	992.97	970.00	950.39	933.56	919.04	906.47	895.55	886.02	877.70	870.41	864.00	841.75	829.70	823.04
90000	1051.38	1027.05	1006.29	988.47	973.10	959.79	948.23	938.14	929.33	921.61	914.83	891.27	878.50	871.46
95000	1109.79	1084.11	1062.20	1043.39	1027.16	1013.11	1000.90	990.26	980.96	972.81	965.65	940.78	927.31	919.87
100000	1168.19	1141.17	1118.10	1098.30	1081.22	1066.43	1053.58	1042.38	1032.59	1024.01	1016.47	990.30	976.11	968.29

TABLE 14
BETTERMENT (DEPRECIATION) GUIDE

Dwelling — Personal Property

Dwelling Items

Item	Years Average Life	Item	Years Average Life
Roofing		Cloth Awnings	4-5
Flat surface	10	Furnaces (including compressors	
Built-up (3 layers of roll roofing)	10	or motors)	
Asphalt Composition Shingles	20	(Coal, Gas, Oil)	20
Wood Shingles	30	Equipment Pertaining to a Dwelling	
Metal	20	Water Heater (Gas or Electric)	5-10
Painting and Decorating	3-5	Well Pumps	5-10
Exterior Painting	3-5	Sump Pumps	7-10
Interior Painting	3-5		

Personal Property

NOTE: Consideration should be given to the quality, use and maintenance when estimating the average life of personal property items.

Item	Years Average Life	Item	Years Average Life
Major Appliances		Rugs	
Stoves (Gas or Electric)	10-15	$5.95 per yard or less	7
Freezers	10-15	Over $5.95 to $9.95 per yard	10
Sewing Machines	10-20	Over $9.95 to $12.95 per yard	12
Refrigerators	10-15	Over $12.95 to $20.95 per yard	15
Window Air Conditioners		Draperies	5-10
(including compressors or motors)	7-10	Clothing (See Guide for Wearing Apparel	
Portable Dishwashers	7-10	and Household Furnishings)	
Automatic Washers	7-10	Outdoor Equipment	
Automatic Dryers	7-10	Push Mower	10
Small Appliances		Power Mower	5-10
Electric Toasters	5-10	Riding Mower	5-7
Electric Mixers	5-10	Electric Edgers, Hedge Clippers,	
Electric Can Openers, Knife		Trimmers, etc.	7-10
Sharpeners, Meat Slicers	5-10	Tools	
Electric Toothbrushes	5	Power & Hand Tools	7-10
TV Sets	8-10	Sports Equipment	
Picture Tubes	2-5	Golf Clubs	10
TV & Radio Antennas	6-10	Tennis Rackets	5
Radios		Tricycles	3
Portable or Transistor	5	Guns, Hand & Rifle	20
Console & Table Model	7-10	Baseball, Basketball, Football	
Stereos & Hi-Fi	7-10	and Similar Equipment	3
Vacuum Cleaners	7-10	Bicycles	5-10
Electric Irons	5-7		

TABLE 14 (cont.)

Personal Property (cont.)

Item	Years Average Life	Item	Years Average Life
Kitchen Utensils & Everyday Dishware	5-10	Children's Toys	1
Fine Silver & China	25	Furniture	
Lawn Furniture	3-5	Hard-Finished	10-20
Swing Sets & Other Playground Equipment	3-5	Upholstered	5-10
		Upholstered Material	5

Wearing Apparel and Household Furnishings
Women's & Girl's Wear

Item	Years Average Life	Item	Years Average Life
Aprons		Negligee	2
Regular	1		
Fancy	4	Nightwear	2
Blouses		Raincoats	
Sports	2	Fabric	3
Dress	3	Plastic	2
Coats		Robes — See Housecoats	
Cloth	3		
Leather	5	Scarves	
Plastic	2	Sheer	2
Fur	10	Heavy	3
Dresses		Shoes	
House	1	Walking	2
Afternoon	3	Work	1
Street	2	Dress	2
Evening or Cocktail		Evening, Formal	5
High Fashion	3	Slacks	
Basic	5	Lounging	2
Gloves		Sport	2
Leather	2	Dress	3
Fabric	1	Slips	2
Hats			
Straw	1	Slippers	2
Felt	2		
Fur	5	Sportswear	2
Housecoats		Suits	
Lightweight	1	Basic	4
Quilted	3	High Fashion	3
Heavy	3		

TABLE 14 (cont.)

Men's & Boy's Wear

Item	Years Average Life	Item	Years Average Life
Bathing Suits	2	Shirts	
Coats		Dress	2
Overcoats	4	Sports	
Topcoats	3	Woven Cotton and Synthetic	2
Leather	5	Knit-All Types	2
Formal Wear	5	Woven Woolen	3
Gloves	2	Slacks	
Hats		Wool & Blends	4
Straw	1	Cotton & Synthetic	2
Felt	2	Socks	1
Fur	5	Sports Coats	
Leather Jackets & Coats	5	Wool & Wool Blends	4
Neckties	1	Cotton & Synthetic	2
Nightwear	2	Sportswear — Other Than Shirts	2
Raincoats		Suits — Summer Weight	
Plastic Film	2	Wool & Wool Blends	3
Fabric & Rubber	3	Synthetic & Cotton	2
Robes		Suits — Winter Weight	4
Silk	3	Sweaters	3
Other Fabric	2	Underwear	2
Beach Robes	2	Vests — Fancy	2
Shoes		Work Clothing	2
Men's	3		
Boy's	1		

TABLE 15
HOMEOWNER'S INSURANCE RATES

ZONE I
PROTECTION CLASS: 1-4

ANNUAL PREMIUMS

	\$50 ALL-PERIL DEDUCTIBLE						\$100 ALL-PERIL DEDUCTIBLE					
	MASONRY OR MAS. VENEER			FRAME			MASONRY OR MAS. VENEER			FRAME		
	FORM			FORM			FORM			FORM		
AMOUNT	1	2	3	1	2	3	1	2	3	1	2	3
\$ 5,000*	41	47	48	41	48	49	37	43	44	37	44	45
7,000*	43	49	50	43	49	51	39	45	46	39	45	46
8,000	44	50	51	44	50	52	40	45	46	40	45	47
10,000	45	51	53	45	52	54	41	46	48	41	47	49
12,000	46	53	54	46	54	55	42	48	49	42	49	50
14,000	49	56	57	49	56	58	45	51	52	45	51	53
15,000	50	57	58	50	58	59	45	52	53	45	53	54
16,000	52	59	61	52	60	62	47	54	55	47	55	56
17,000	54	61	62	54	62	63	49	55	56	49	56	57
18,000	55	63	64	55	64	65	50	57	58	50	58	59
19,000	58	65	66	58	65	66	53	59	60	53	59	60
20,000	59	66	68	59	67	69	54	60	62	54	61	63
21,000	61	69	70	61	70	71	55	63	64	55	64	65
22,000	63	71	72	63	71	73	57	65	66	57	65	66
23,000	65	73	74	65	74	75	59	66	67	59	67	68
24,000	68	76	78	68	78	79	62	69	71	62	71	72
25,000	72	80	82	72	81	83	65	73	75	65	74	75
26,000	75	84	85	75	85	86	68	76	77	68	77	78
27,000	78	87	89	78	89	90	71	79	81	71	81	82
28,000	81	91	92	81	93	94	74	83	84	74	85	86
29,000	84	93	95	84	95	96	76	85	86	76	86	87
30,000	86	97	98	86	99	100	78	88	89	78	90	91
31,000	90	101	103	90	103	104	82	92	94	82	94	95
32,000	94	105	107	94	107	108	85	95	97	85	97	98
33,000	97	109	111	97	111	112	88	99	101	88	101	102
34,000	101	113	115	101	115	117	92	103	105	92	105	106
35,000	104	116	118	104	118	119	95	105	107	95	107	108
36,000	107	120	122	107	122	123	97	109	111	97	111	112
37,000	111	124	126	111	126	128	101	113	115	101	115	116
38,000	114	128	130	114	130	131	104	116	118	104	118	119
39,000	118	132	134	118	134	136	107	120	122	107	122	124
40,000	122	136	138	122	138	140	111	124	125	111	125	127
42,000	129	144	146	129	146	148	117	131	133	117	133	135
44,000	136	152	154	136	154	156	124	138	140	124	140	142
46,000	143	160	163	143	163	165	130	145	148	130	148	150
48,000	150	168	171	150	171	173	136	153	155	136	155	157
50,000	158	177	179	158	179	182	144	161	163	144	163	165
60,000	194	217	220	194	221	223	176	197	200	176	201	203
70,000	230	257	261	230	262	264	209	234	237	209	238	240
80,000	266	297	301	266	304	305	242	270	274	242	276	277
90,000	302	337	342	302	346	347	275	306	311	275	315	316

TABLE 15 (cont.)

	\$50 ALL-PERIL DEDUCTIBLE						\$100 ALL-PERIL DEDUCTIBLE					
	MASONRY OR MAS. VENEER			FRAME			MASONRY OR MAS. VENEER			FRAME		
	FORM			FORM			FORM			FORM		
AMOUNT	1	2	3	1	2	3	1	2	3	1	2	3
$100,000	338	377	383	338	387	388	307	343	348	307	352	353
150,000	535	634	684	535	655	688	486	576	622	486	595	625
200,000	744	932	1042	744	964	1045	676	847	947	676	876	950
@10,000	39	48	54	39	50	54	35	44	49	35	45	49

PROTECTION CLASS: 9

AMOUNT	1	2	3	1	2	3	1	2	3	1	2	3
$ 5,000*	58	65	66	64	72	73	53	59	60	58	65	66
7,000*	61	68	69	67	76	77	55	62	63	61	69	70
8,000	62	70	71	70	78	79	56	64	65	64	71	72
10,000	64	72	73	71	79	80	58	65	66	65	72	73
12,000	66	73	74	73	81	82	60	66	67	66	74	75
14,000	70	77	78	78	86	87	64	70	71	71	78	79
15,000	71	79	80	79	87	88	65	72	73	72	79	80
16,000	74	82	83	82	91	92	67	75	76	75	83	84
17,000	76	85	86	85	94	95	69	77	78	77	85	86
18,000	79	87	88	87	97	98	72	79	80	79	88	89
19,000	81	90	91	90	99	100	74	82	83	82	90	91
20,000	84	93	94	93	102	103	76	85	86	85	93	94
21,000	86	96	97	97	106	107	78	87	88	88	96	97
22,000	89	99	100	100	109	110	81	90	91	91	99	100
23,000	92	102	103	102	112	113	84	93	94	93	102	103
24,000	97	107	108	108	118	119	88	97	98	98	107	108
25,000	101	112	113	112	123	124	92	102	103	102	112	113
26,000	106	117	118	118	129	130	96	106	107	107	117	118
27,000	110	122	123	123	134	135	100	111	112	112	122	123
28,000	115	127	128	128	140	141	105	115	116	116	127	128
29,000	118	130	131	132	144	145	107	118	119	120	131	132
30,000	123	135	136	137	149	150	112	123	124	125	135	136
31,000	128	141	142	142	156	157	116	128	129	129	142	143
32,000	133	147	148	148	162	163	121	134	135	135	147	148
33,000	138	152	153	154	168	169	125	138	139	140	153	154
34,000	144	158	159	159	174	175	131	144	145	145	158	159
35,000	147	162	163	164	178	179	134	147	148	149	162	163
36,000	152	167	168	169	185	186	138	152	153	154	168	169
37,000	158	173	174	175	191	192	144	157	158	159	174	175
38,000	162	179	180	181	197	198	147	163	164	165	179	180
39,000	167	185	186	186	203	204	152	168	169	169	185	186
40,000	173	190	191	192	210	211	157	173	174	175	191	192
42,000	183	202	203	203	222	223	166	184	185	185	202	203
44,000	193	213	214	215	234	235	175	194	195	195	213	214
46,000	203	224	225	226	246	247	185	204	205	205	224	225
48,000	213	235	236	238	259	260	194	214	215	216	235	236
50,000	224	246	247	249	272	273	204	224	225	226	247	248

TABLE 15 (cont.)

	\$50 ALL-PERIL DEDUCTIBLE						\$100 ALL-PERIL DEDUCTIBLE					
	MASONRY OR MAS. VENEER			FRAME			MASONRY OR MAS. VENEER			FRAME		
	FORM			FORM			FORM			FORM		
AMOUNT	1	2	3	1	2	3	1	2	3	1	2	3
$ 60,000	275	302	303	307	334	335	250	275	276	279	304	305
70,000	325	358	359	365	397	398	295	325	326	332	361	362
80,000	375	414	415	422	459	460	341	376	377	384	417	418
90,000	426	470	471	480	522	523	387	427	428	436	475	476
100,000	476	526	527	537	584	585	433	478	479	488	531	532
150,000	752	887	932	853	986	1023	684	806	847	775	896	930
200,000	1045	1304	1417	1188	1450	1559	950	1185	1288	1080	1318	1417
@10,000	54	67	73	61	75	81	49	61	66	55	68	74

PROTECTION CLASS: 10-11

AMOUNT	1	2	3	1	2	3	1	2	3	1	2	3
$ 5,000*	64	72	73	68	76	77	58	65	66	62	69	70
7,000*	67	76	77	72	80	81	61	69	70	65	73	74
8,000	70	78	79	74	81	82	64	71	72	67	74	75
10,000	71	79	80	76	84	85	65	72	73	69	76	77
12,000	73	81	82	78	86	87	66	74	75	71	78	79
14,000	78	86	87	82	90	91	71	78	79	75	82	83
15,000	79	87	88	84	92	93	72	79	80	76	84	85
16,000	82	91	92	87	95	96	75	83	84	79	86	87
17,000	85	94	95	90	99	100	77	85	86	82	90	91
18,000	87	97	98	93	101	102	79	88	89	85	92	93
19,000	90	99	100	96	104	105	82	90	91	87	95	96
20,000	93	102	103	99	107	108	85	93	94	90	97	98
21,000	97	106	107	102	112	113	88	96	97	93	102	103
22,000	100	109	110	105	115	116	91	99	100	95	105	106
23,000	102	112	113	109	118	119	93	102	103	99	107	108
24,000	108	118	119	114	124	125	98	107	108	104	113	114
25,000	112	123	124	120	130	131	102	112	113	109	118	119
26,000	118	129	130	125	135	136	107	117	118	114	123	124
27,000	123	134	135	131	141	142	112	122	123	119	128	129
28,000	128	140	141	136	148	149	116	127	128	124	135	136
29,000	132	144	145	140	151	152	120	131	132	127	137	138
30,000	137	149	150	146	157	158	125	135	136	133	143	144
31,000	142	156	157	151	164	165	129	142	143	137	149	150
32,000	148	162	163	157	170	171	135	147	148	143	155	156
33,000	154	168	169	164	177	178	140	153	154	149	161	162
34,000	159	174	175	169	183	184	145	158	159	154	166	167
35,000	164	178	179	174	188	189	149	162	163	158	171	172
36,000	169	185	186	180	194	195	154	168	169	164	176	177
37,000	175	191	192	186	201	202	159	174	175	169	183	184
38,000	181	197	198	192	207	208	165	179	180	175	188	189
39,000	186	203	204	198	214	215	169	185	186	180	195	196
40,000	192	210	211	204	220	221	175	191	192	185	200	201

TABLE 15 (cont.)

	\$50 ALL-PERIL DEDUCTIBLE							\$100 ALL-PERIL DEDUCTIBLE						
	MASONRY OR MAS. VENEER			FRAME			MASONRY OR MAS. VENEER			FRAME		
	FORM			FORM			FORM			FORM		
AMOUNT	1	2	3	1	2	3	1	2	3	1	2	3
$ 42,000	203	222	223	216	234	235	185	202	203	196	213	214
44,000	215	234	235	229	246	247	195	213	214	208	224	225
46,000	226	246	247	240	259	260	205	224	225	218	235	236
48,000	238	259	260	253	273	274	216	235	236	230	248	249
50,000	249	272	273	265	286	287	226	247	248	241	260	261
60,000	307	334	335	326	351	352	279	304	305	296	319	320
70,000	365	397	398	387	417	418	332	361	362	352	379	380
80,000	422	459	460	448	482	483	384	417	418	407	438	439
90,000	480	522	523	509	548	549	436	475	476	463	498	499
100,000	537	584	585	571	614	615	488	531	532	519	558	559
150,000	853	986	1023	906	1036	1075	775	896	930	824	942	977
200,000	1188	1450	1559	1261	1524	1637	1080	1318	1417	1146	1385	1488
@10,000	61	75	81	65	79	84	55	68	74	59	72	76

PROTECTION CLASS: 7-8

AMOUNT	1	2	3	1	2	3	1	2	3	1	2	3
$ 5,000*	46	50	52	49	52	54	42	45	47	45	47	49
7,000*	48	52	55	51	55	57	44	47	50	46	50	52
8,000	49	54	56	52	56	59	45	49	51	47	51	54
10,000	50	55	57	55	58	60	45	50	52	50	53	55
12,000	52	57	58	56	60	61	47	52	53	51	55	56
14,000	55	60	62	59	63	65	50	55	56	54	57	59
15,000	56	61	63	60	64	66	51	55	57	55	58	60
16,000	58	63	66	62	67	68	53	57	60	56	61	62
17,000	61	66	68	65	69	70	55	60	62	59	63	64
18,000	62	68	70	66	70	72	56	62	64	60	64	65
19,000	64	70	71	68	72	74	58	64	65	62	65	67
20,000	66	71	73	70	75	76	60	65	66	64	68	69
21,000	69	74	76	73	77	79	63	67	69	66	70	72
22,000	71	76	78	75	80	81	65	69	71	68	73	74
23,000	73	79	80	78	82	83	66	72	73	71	75	76
24,000	76	83	84	82	86	88	69	75	76	75	78	80
25,000	80	86	89	86	90	92	73	78	81	78	82	84
26,000	84	90	92	89	94	96	76	82	84	81	85	87
27,000	87	94	96	93	98	101	79	85	87	85	89	92
28,000	91	98	101	98	103	104	83	89	92	89	94	95
29,000	93	100	103	100	105	107	85	91	94	91	95	97
30,000	96	104	107	104	109	111	87	95	97	95	99	101
31,000	101	109	111	108	114	115	92	99	101	98	104	105
32,000	105	113	116	113	118	121	95	103	105	103	107	110
33,000	109	118	121	116	123	125	99	107	110	105	112	114
34,000	113	122	125	121	128	130	103	111	114	110	116	118
35,000	116	125	128	124	130	133	105	114	116	113	118	121
36,000	120	130	132	129	135	137	109	118	120	117	123	125

TABLE 15 (cont.)

	\$50 ALL-PERIL DEDUCTIBLE						\$100 ALL-PERIL DEDUCTIBLE					
	MASONRY OR MAS. VENEER			FRAME			MASONRY OR MAS. VENEER			FRAME		
	FORM			FORM			FORM			FORM		
AMOUNT	1	2	3	1	2	3	1	2	3	1	2	3
$ 37,000	124	134	137	133	140	142	113	122	125	121	127	129
38,000	128	138	141	137	144	147	116	125	128	125	131	134
39,000	132	142	145	141	149	151	120	129	132	128	135	137
40,000	136	147	150	146	154	155	124	134	136	133	140	141
42,000	144	155	158	155	162	165	131	141	144	141	147	150
44,000	152	164	168	163	171	174	138	149	153	148	155	158
46,000	160	173	177	172	181	183	145	157	161	156	165	166
48,000	168	182	185	180	190	193	153	165	168	164	173	175
50,000	176	190	194	189	199	202	160	173	176	172	181	184
60,000	216	234	238	232	244	249	196	213	216	211	222	226
70,000	256	277	282	275	289	296	233	252	256	250	263	269
80,000	295	320	326	319	334	342	268	291	296	290	304	311
90,000	335	363	369	362	378	389	305	330	335	329	344	354
100,000	374	406	413	405	423	436	340	369	375	368	385	396
150,000	591	685	736	642	712	779	537	623	669	584	647	708
200,000	822	1006	1119	893	1045	1188	747	915	1017	812	950	1080
@10,000	42	52	58	46	54	61	38	47	53	42	49	55

*SECONDARY LOCATIONS ONLY

TABLE 16
BASIC PREMIUM FOR AUTOMOBILE INSURANCE (Six Months)

Liability	Cost	Liability	Cost
10/ 20/10	$21.80	Collision (Medium-size car, $100 deductible)	
25/ 50/10	$24.40	1984 model	$46.80
50/100/10	$25.40	1983 and 1982	$39.80
100/300/50	$28.80	1981 and 1980	$35.20
Medical		1979 and older	$28.00
5,000	$ 3.40	Uninsured Motorist Coverage	
25,000	$ 6.60	10/ 20	$ 1.00
Comprehensive (Medium-size car, actual cash value)		25/ 50	$ 2.30
1984 model	$27.40	100/300	$ 4.80
1983 and 1982	$23.20		
1981 and 1980	$20.60		
1979 and older	$17.80		

TABLE 17
RATING FACTORS

Classification	Factor
Over age 25 married male or female less than 30 miles/week/work	1.10
Over age 25 married male or female more than 30 less than 100 miles/week/work	1.20
Over age 25 married male or female more than 100 miles/week/work	1.35
Under 21 married male less than 30 miles/week/work	1.90
Under 21 married male over 30 miles/week/work	2.10
21 or 22 married male less than 30 miles/week/work	1.50
21 or 22 married male more than 30 miles/week/work	1.70
23 or 24 married male less than 30 miles/week/work	1.25
23 or 24 married male over 30 miles/week/work	1.45
Single female under age 21	1.95
Single female under age 21 over 30 miles/week/work	2.15
Single female 21 to 24	1.60
Single female 21 to 24 over 30 miles/week/work	1.85
Single male under age 21	3.65
Single male under age 21 over 30 miles/week/work	3.95
Single male 21 to 25	2.90
Single male 21 to 25 over 30 miles/week/work	3.65
Single male over age 25	1.65
Single male over age 25 over 30 miles/week/work	1.90

TABLE 18
LIFE INSURANCE

Schedule of Insurance

The Amount payable per $1000 of Initial Face Amount will be determined at the corresponding Policy Year at death. Policy Year 1 begins on the Date of Issue, Policy Year 2 begins one year after the Date of Issue, etc.

Policy Year	Amount per $1000 of Initial Face Amount	Policy Year	Amount per $1000 of Initial Face Amount	Policy Year	Amount per $1000 of Initial Face Amount
1	$1000	6	$761	11	$438
2	958	7	704	12	361
3	913	8	643	13	278
4	865	9	579	14	191
5	815	10	511	15	99

TABLE 19
TABLE OF VALUES

Guaranteed Cash or Loan Value, Reduced Paid-up Insurance, Extended Term Insurance
Applicable to a Policy without Either Paid-up Additions or Dividend Accumulations and without Indebtedness
Values at end of years other than those shown will be quoted on request.

Years In Force with all Due Premiums Paid	Age 20 Guar. Cash/Loan (per $1,000)	Age 20 Reduced Paid-up	Age 20 Ext. Term Yrs.	Age 20 Ext. Term Days	Age 21 Guar. Cash/Loan	Age 21 Reduced Paid-up	Age 21 Ext. Term Yrs.	Age 21 Ext. Term Days	Age 22 Guar. Cash/Loan	Age 22 Reduced Paid-up	Age 22 Ext. Term Yrs.	Age 22 Ext. Term Days	Age 23 Guar. Cash/Loan	Age 23 Reduced Paid-up	Age 23 Ext. Term Yrs.	Age 23 Ext. Term Days	Age 24 Guar. Cash/Loan	Age 24 Reduced Paid-up	Age 24 Ext. Term Yrs.	Age 24 Ext. Term Days	Years In Force
1/2	-	-	0	60	-	-	0	60	-	-	0	60	-	-	0	60	-	-	0	60	1/2
1	-	-	0	60	-	-	0	60	-	-	0	60	-	-	0	60	-	-	0	60	1
2	$1	$3	0	141	$1	$3	0	136	$1	$3	0	131	$1	$3	0	126	$1	$3	0	122	2
3	12	33	4	139	13	35	4	205	13	34	4	140	14	36	4	189	15	38	4	228	3
4	25	67	8	180	26	68	8	166	27	70	8	143	29	73	8	209	30	74	8	166	4
5	39	102	12	60	40	103	11	336	42	106	11	330	44	109	11	309	45	109	11	195	5
6	53	136	15	41	55	138	14	335	56	138	14	176	59	143	14	164	61	145	14	66	6
7	67	169	17	164	69	170	17	36	71	172	16	266	74	175	16	188	76	177	16	40	7
8	81	200	19	113	84	203	19	2	87	206	18	243	90	209	18	113	92	209	17	287	8
9	96	232	20	344	99	234	20	186	102	237	20	23	105	239	19	217	109	243	19	90	9
10	111	263	22	86	114	265	21	258	118	269	21	107	122	272	20	314	125	274	20	107	10
11	125	290	23	49	129	294	22	238	133	297	22	57	137	300	21	235	141	303	21	44	11
12	139	316	23	305	143	319	23	104	148	324	22	303	152	326	22	93	157	330	21	280	12
13	154	344	24	175	158	346	23	318	163	350	23	127	168	353	22	297	173	357	22	98	13
14	169	370	24	356	173	371	24	114	178	374	23	269	184	380	23	87	189	383	22	234	14
15	184	395	25	124	189	398	24	264	194	400	24	37	200	405	23	201	205	407	22	333	15
16	198	417	25	187	203	419	24	313	209	423	24	101	215	427	23	251	221	431	23	33	16
17	212	437	25	219	218	441	24	363	224	445	24	137	230	448	23	274	236	451	23	44	17
18	226	457	25	226	232	461	24	358	238	464	24	121	245	469	23	273	252	473	23	57	18
19	240	477	25	209	247	481	24	357	254	486	24	135	260	488	23	251	267	492	23	26	19
20	255	497	25	198	262	501	24	335	269	505	24	103	276	509	23	234	283	512	23	0	20
to Age 60	566	788	19	131	562	783	19	67	557	776	18	352	552	769	18	278	546	761	18	188	to Age 60
to Age 65	642	837	17	78	638	831	17	14	634	826	16	320	629	820	16	248	625	815	16	191	to Age 65

NONFORFEITURE FACTOR FOR EACH $1,000 OF FACE AMOUNT (See "Basis of Values" on page 7)

	First 10 Years	11th Through 15th Year	First 10 Years	11th Through 15th Year	First 10 Years	11th Through 15th Year	First 10 Years	11th Through 15th Year	First 10 Years	11th Through 15th Year
	$15.36	$14.19	$15.80	$14.58	$16.26	$15.00	$16.73	$15.43	$17.23	$15.89

Years In Force with all Due Premiums Paid	Age 25 Guar. Cash/Loan	Age 25 Reduced Paid-up	Age 25 Ext. Term Yrs.	Age 25 Ext. Term Days	Age 26 Guar. Cash/Loan	Age 26 Reduced Paid-up	Age 26 Ext. Term Yrs.	Age 26 Ext. Term Days	Age 27 Guar. Cash/Loan	Age 27 Reduced Paid-up	Age 27 Ext. Term Yrs.	Age 27 Ext. Term Days	Age 28 Guar. Cash/Loan	Age 28 Reduced Paid-up	Age 28 Ext. Term Yrs.	Age 28 Ext. Term Days	Age 29 Guar. Cash/Loan	Age 29 Reduced Paid-up	Age 29 Ext. Term Yrs.	Age 29 Ext. Term Days	Years In Force
1/2	-	-	0	60	-	-	0	60	-	-	0	60	-	-	0	60	-	-	0	60	1/2
1	-	-	0	60	-	-	0	60	$1	$3	0	112	$1	$3	0	107	$1	$3	0	102	1
2	$1	$3	0	117	$1	$3	0	112	2	5	0	213	2	5	0	203	3	7	0	290	2
3	16	40	4	258	17	41	4	278	18	43	4	291	19	45	4	295	20	46	4	293	3
4	31	75	8	115	33	78	8	143	34	79	8	78	35	80	8	8	37	83	8	4	4
5	47	112	11	155	49	114	11	104	50	114	10	342	52	116	10	276	54	118	10	203	5
6	63	146	13	325	65	148	13	213	67	150	13	95	70	153	13	29	72	155	12	264	6
7	79	180	15	308	82	183	15	202	84	184	15	39	87	187	14	285	90	190	14	160	7
8	95	212	17	144	98	215	16	363	102	219	16	253	105	221	16	94	108	223	15	296	8
9	112	245	18	274	116	249	18	133	119	251	17	310	123	254	17	157	127	257	17	2	9
10	129	277	19	303	133	280	19	129	137	283	18	317	141	286	18	135	146	290	17	349	10
11	145	305	20	213	149	308	20	16	154	312	19	213	158	314	19	10	163	318	18	199	11
12	161	332	21	64	166	336	20	242	171	340	20	53	176	343	19	224	181	346	19	29	12
13	178	360	21	259	183	364	21	53	188	366	20	209	193	369	19	364	199	374	19	177	13
14	194	385	22	15	200	390	21	185	205	392	20	326	211	396	20	126	217	400	19	289	14
15	211	411	22	125	217	415	21	280	223	419	21	68	229	422	20	218	235	425	20	3	15
16	227	434	22	176	233	437	21	319	239	441	21	94	246	445	20	257	252	448	20	31	16
17	242	454	22	177	249	459	21	333	256	463	21	121	262	466	20	251	269	470	20	37	17
18	258	475	22	180	265	480	21	326	272	483	21	104	279	487	20	247	287	492	20	44	18
19	274	496	22	163	282	501	21	321	289	504	21	91	297	509	20	245	304	512	20	14	19
20	291	517	22	150	298	520	21	278	306	525	21	60	314	529	20	207	322	533	19	353	20
to Age 60	540	752	18	98	535	745	18	23	528	735	17	288	522	727	17	203	515	717	17	105	to Age 60
to Age 65	620	808	16	119	615	801	16	48	610	795	15	343	605	788	15	278	599	781	15	200	to Age 65

NONFORFEITURE FACTOR FOR EACH $1,000 OF FACE AMOUNT (See "Basis of Values" on page 7)

	First 10 Years	11th Through 15th Year	First 10 Years	11th Through 15th Year	First 10 Years	11th Through 15th Year	First 10 Years	11th Through 15th Year	First 10 Years	11th Through 15th Year
	$17.75	$16.36	$18.29	$16.86	$18.85	$17.38	$19.44	$17.92	$20.06	$18.49

After the year for which a value is first shown, values as of any time during a policy year will be determined by the Company with allowance for the time elapsed in such year, and for any period in such year for which due premiums have been paid. However, if payment is made prior to the end of the period for which due premiums have been paid, the amount of such payment will be the Guaranteed Cash Value as of the end of that period less interest (at the effective rate of 5% per year) from the date of payment to the end of the period.

TABLE 20
ORDINARY LIFE (per $1000)

Age At Issue	Life-M	Life-F	Non-Smokers	W.P.	A.D.B.	Years To Pay Up W/Divs.	Total Mo. Inc. At 65 Male	Total Mo. Inc. At 65 Female	Interest Adj. Cost Index* 10 Yrs.	Interest Adj. Cost Index* 20 Yrs.
0	$ 7.77	$ 7.58		$ .20	$ .64	24	$15.24	$14.04	$ 3.46	$ 2.01
1	7.77	7.58		.20	.66	24	14.96	13.77	2.88	1.72
2	7.89	7.69		.21	.69	24	14.64	13.48	2.82	1.67
3	8.03	7.82		.21	.72	24	14.34	13.20	2.77	1.65
4	8.17	7.95		.22	.75	24	14.04	12.92	2.73	1.66
5	8.32	8.09		.22	.78	24	13.72	12.63	2.70	1.64
6	8.49	8.25		.23	.79	24	13.41	12.35	2.69	1.65
7	8.66	8.42		.23	.81	24	13.10	12.06	2.68	1.63
8	8.84	8.59		.24	.82	24	12.79	11.78	2.76	1.65
9	9.03	8.78		.24	.84	24	12.49	11.50	2.77	1.68
10	9.23	8.97		.25	.86	24	12.19	11.22	2.79	1.69
11	9.44	9.17		.25	.87	24	11.89	10.95	2.83	1.72
12	9.65	9.37		.26	.89	24	11.60	10.66	2.87	1.75
13	9.88	9.59		.26	.91	25	11.31	10.41	2.93	1.80
14	10.12	9.82		.27	.92	25	11.02	10.15	3.00	1.83
15	10.36	10.05		.28	.94	25	10.75	9.90	3.07	1.89
16	10.61	10.29		.28	.94	25	10.50	9.66	3.07	1.89
17	10.87	10.53		.29	.94	25	10.23	9.42	3.16	1.89
18	11.15	10.79		.30	.94	25	10.00	9.21	3.19	1.92
19	11.43	11.04		.31	.93	25	9.75	8.98	3.22	1.95
20	11.72	11.29	$ 11.42	.32	.91	25	9.51	8.76	3.25	1.96
21	12.04	11.58	11.71	.33	.90	25	9.31	8.57	3.23	2.00
22	12.37	11.88	12.02	.34	.89	25	9.09	8.37	3.30	2.02
23	12.72	12.20	12.35	.35	.88	25	8.88	8.17	3.31	2.06
24	13.08	12.53	12.68	.37	.87	25	8.67	7.98	3.41	2.11
25	13.46	12.87	13.03	.38	.88	25	8.46	7.79	3.45	2.18
26	13.91	13.28	13.46	.40	.88	25	8.29	7.63	3.54	2.25
27	14.38	13.70	13.92	.41	.88	25	8.11	7.46	3.56	2.38
28	14.88	14.15	14.40	.43	.89	25	7.93	7.30	3.70	2.47
29	15.39	14.61	14.89	.45	.90	25	7.75	7.13	3.85	2.64
30	15.93	15.10	15.42	.48	.91	25	7.57	6.97	3.95	2.77
31	16.50	15.61	15.97	.50	.92	24	7.39	6.81	4.06	2.95
32	17.09	16.13	16.53	.53	.93	24	7.23	6.66	4.26	3.14
33	17.72	16.69	17.14	.56	.94	24	7.05	6.49	4.43	3.37
34	18.37	17.26	17.77	.59	.96	24	6.87	6.32	4.62	3.59
35	19.06	17.86	18.43	.63	.97	24	6.69	6.16	4.84	3.89
36	19.79	18.50	19.13	.67	.98	24	6.50	5.99	5.13	4.23
37	20.57	19.19	19.89	.72	1.00	24	6.31	5.81	5.46	4.58
38	21.38	19.90	20.67	.77	1.01	24	6.12	5.64	5.82	5.00
39	22.22	20.64	21.48	.82	1.02	24	5.93	5.46	6.14	5.42
40	23.12	21.44	22.34	.88	1.04	24	5.72	5.27	6.59	5.93
41	24.05	22.26	23.24	.95	1.06	24	5.54	5.10	6.97	6.40
42	25.03	23.12	24.18	1.02	1.07	23	5.35	4.93	7.48	6.96
43	26.06	24.02	25.17	1.11	1.09	23	5.15	4.74	7.96	7.54
44	27.15	24.99	26.20	1.20	1.11	23	4.95	4.56	8.50	8.20
45	28.29	26.01	27.29	1.30	1.13	23	4.74	4.36	9.10	8.89
46	29.47	27.06	28.42	1.42	1.14	23	4.56	4.20	9.55	9.44
47	30.71	28.17	29.60	1.55	1.16	23	4.37	4.02	10.06	10.09
48	32.02	29.35	30.85	1.69	1.18	22	4.18	3.85	10.64	10.77
49	33.40	30.60	32.18	1.85	1.20	22	3.97	3.66	11.21	11.55
50	34.86	31.93	33.58	2.04	1.22	22	3.76	3.46	11.95	12.42
51	36.40	33.34	35.06	2.24	1.25	22	3.50	3.22	12.69	13.33
52	38.03	34.84	36.63	2.46	1.27	21	3.30	3.04	13.45	14.29
53	39.74	36.41	38.28	2.71	1.29	21	3.10	2.86	14.36	15.38
54	41.56	38.09	40.04	2.98	1.32	21	2.89	2.66	15.31	16.53
55	43.83	39.87	41.91	3.27	1.35	21	2.68	2.46	16.35	17.82
56	45.53	41.79	43.87	3.58	1.38	20	2.44	2.24	17.47	19.12
57	47.71	43.84	45.97	3.87	1.41	20	2.18	2.00	18.72	20.57
58	50.01	46.01	48.18	4.16	1.45	20	1.91	1.75	20.00	22.12

TABLE 20 (cont.)

Age At Issue	ANNUAL PREMIUMS Life-M	Life-F	Non-Smokers	W.P.	A.D.B.	Years To Pay Up W/Divs.	Total Mo. Inc. At 65 Male	Female	Interest Adj. Cost Index* 10 Yrs.	20 Yrs.
59	52.45	48.33	50.51	4.42	1.48	19	1.63	1.50	21.51	23.84
60	55.03	50.79	53.03		1.52	19	1.35	1.24	23.23	25.69
61	57.79	53.37	55.79		1.56	19	1.06	.97	24.93	27.64
62	60.71	56.08	58.71		1.59	19	.75	.69	26.87	29.74
63	63.81	58.96	61.81		1.64	18	.44	.40	28.99	32.02
64	67.09	62.04	65.09		1.68	18	.10	.10	31.29	34.52
65	70.57	65.30	68.57		1.72	18			33.71	37.18
66	74.35	68.86	72.35			18	10 Yrs and		36.45	40.10
67	78.34	72.62	76.34			17	Life Alt		39.33	43.23
68	82.55	76.59	80.55			17	Larger Inc		42.42	46.54
69	86.99	80.78	84.99			17	Incl Guar CV		45.75	50.08
70	91.66	85.20	89.66			17	+ Term Div +		49.30	53.82
71	96.80	90.08	94.80			16	CV of Pd Up		53.06	
72	102.22	95.24	100.22			16	Addns		57.17	
73	107.95	100.70	105.95			16			61.59	
74	114.05	106.52	112.05			15			66.38	
75	120.57	112.76	118.57			15			71.67	

*Figures are for basic male rates. Adjust as necessary for policy fee, non-smoker discount, female discount

Minimum Policy Ages 0-14 $1,500. Ages 15-75 $2,000. Non-Smokers $10,000.

TERMINAL DIVIDENDS, IF ANY, ARE INCLUDED IN THE LAST FOUR COLUMNS ABOVE

TABLE 21
FEDERAL INCOME TAX TABLES

Example: Mr. and Mrs. Green are filing a joint return. Their taxable income on line 16 of Form 1040A is $23,270. First, they find the $23,250-$23,300 income line. Next, they find the column for married filing jointly and read down the column. The amount shown where the income line and filing status column meet is $3,706. This is the tax amount they must write on line 19a of Form 1040A.

At least	But less than	Single	Married filing jointly	Married filing separately	Head of a household
			Your tax is—		
23,250	23,300	4,767	3,706	5,894	4,379
23,300	23,350	4,783	3,718	5,916	4,393
23,350	23,400	4,798	3,731	5,938	4,407

| If 1040A, line 16, OR 1040EZ, line 7 is— || And you are— |||| If 1040A, line 16, OR 1040EZ, line 7 is— || And you are— |||| If 1040A, line 16, OR 1040EZ, line 7 is— || And you are— ||||
At least	But less than	Single	Married filing jointly	Married filing separately	Head of a household	At least	But less than	Single	Married filing jointly	Married filing separately	Head of a household	At least	But less than	Single	Married filing jointly	Married filing separately	Head of a household
			Your tax is—						Your tax is—						Your tax is—		
0	1,700	0	0	0	0	**3,000**						5,500	5,550	452	256	549	410
1,700	1,725	0	0	a2	0	3,000	3,050	87	0	165	87	5,550	5,600	460	263	557	417
1,725	1,750	0	0	5	0	3,050	3,100	93	0	172	93	5,600	5,650	468	270	565	424
1,750	1,775	0	0	8	0	3,100	3,150	99	0	179	99	5,650	5,700	476	277	573	431
1,775	1,800	0	0	11	0	3,150	3,200	105	0	186	105	5,700	5,750	484	284	581	438
1,800	1,825	0	0	14	0	3,200	3,250	111	0	193	111						
1,825	1,850	0	0	17	0	3,250	3,300	117	0	200	117	5,750	5,800	492	291	589	445
1,850	1,875	0	0	20	0	3,300	3,350	123	0	207	123	5,800	5,850	500	298	597	452
1,875	1,900	0	0	23	0	3,350	3,400	129	0	214	129	5,850	5,900	508	305	605	459
1,900	1,925	0	0	26	0	3,400	3,450	136	c3	221	135	5,900	5,950	516	312	613	466
1,925	1,950	0	0	29	0	3,450	3,500	143	9	228	141	5,950	6,000	524	319	622	473
1,950	1,975	0	0	32	0	3,500	3,550	150	15	235	147	**6,000**					
1,975	2,000	0	0	35	0	3,550	3,600	157	21	242	153	6,000	6,050	532	326	631	480
2,000						3,600	3,650	164	27	249	159	6,050	6,100	540	333	641	487
2,000	2,025	0	0	38	0	3,650	3,700	171	33	256	165	6,100	6,150	548	340	650	494
2,025	2,050	0	0	41	0	3,700	3,750	178	39	263	171	6,150	6,200	556	347	660	501
2,050	2,075	0	0	44	0							6,200	6,250	564	354	669	508
2,075	2,100	0	0	47	0	3,750	3,800	185	45	270	177						
2,100	2,125	0	0	50	0	3,800	3,850	192	51	277	183	6,250	6,300	572	361	679	515
						3,850	3,900	199	57	285	189	6,300	6,350	580	368	688	522
2,125	2,150	0	0	53	0	3,900	3,950	206	63	293	195	6,350	6,400	588	375	698	529
2,150	2,175	0	0	56	0	3,950	4,000	213	69	301	201	6,400	6,450	596	382	707	536
2,175	2,200	0	0	59	0	**4,000**						6,450	6,500	604	389	717	543
2,200	2,225	0	0	62	0	4,000	4,050	220	75	309	207						
2,225	2,250	0	0	65	0	4,050	4,100	227	81	317	213	6,500	6,550	612	396	726	550
						4,100	4,150	234	87	325	219	6,550	6,600	621	403	736	558
2,250	2,275	0	0	68	0	4,150	4,200	241	93	333	225	6,600	6,650	629	410	745	566
2,275	2,300	0	0	71	0	4,200	4,250	248	99	341	231	6,650	6,700	638	417	755	574
2,300	2,325	b2	0	74	b2							6,700	6,750	646	424	764	582
2,325	2,350	5	0	77	5	4,250	4,300	255	105	349	237						
2,350	2,375	8	0	80	8	4,300	4,350	262	111	357	243	6,750	6,800	655	431	774	590
						4,350	4,400	269	117	365	249	6,800	6,850	663	438	783	598
2,375	2,400	11	0	83	11	4,400	4,450	276	123	373	256	6,850	6,900	672	445	793	606
2,400	2,425	14	0	86	14	4,450	4,500	284	129	381	263	6,900	6,950	680	452	802	614
2,425	2,450	17	0	89	17							6,950	7,000	689	459	812	622
2,450	2,475	20	0	92	20	4,500	4,550	292	135	389	270	**7,000**					
2,475	2,500	23	0	95	23	4,550	4,600	300	141	397	277	7,000	7,050	697	466	821	630
						4,600	4,650	308	147	405	284	7,050	7,100	706	473	831	638
2,500	2,525	26	0	98	26	4,650	4,700	316	153	413	291	7,100	7,150	714	480	840	646
2,525	2,550	29	0	101	29	4,700	4,750	324	159	421	298	7,150	7,200	723	487	850	654
2,550	2,575	32	0	104	32							7,200	7,250	731	494	859	662
2,575	2,600	35	0	107	35	4,750	4,800	332	165	429	305						
2,600	2,625	38	0	110	38	4,800	4,850	340	171	437	312	7,250	7,300	740	501	869	670
						4,850	4,900	348	177	445	319	7,300	7,350	748	508	878	678
2,625	2,650	41	0	113	41	4,900	4,950	356	183	453	326	7,350	7,400	757	515	888	686
2,650	2,675	44	0	116	44	4,950	5,000	364	189	461	333	7,400	7,450	765	522	897	694
2,675	2,700	47	0	119	47	**5,000**						7,450	7,500	774	529	907	702
2,700	2,725	50	0	122	50	5,000	5,050	372	195	469	340						
2,725	2,750	53	0	125	53	5,050	5,100	380	201	477	347	7,500	7,550	782	536	916	710
						5,100	5,150	388	207	485	354	7,550	7,600	791	543	926	718
2,750	2,775	56	0	128	56	5,150	5,200	396	213	493	361	7,600	7,650	799	550	935	726
2,775	2,800	59	0	131	59	5,200	5,250	404	219	501	368	7,650	7,700	808	558	945	734
2,800	2,825	62	0	135	62							7,700	7,750	816	566	954	742
2,825	2,850	65	0	138	65	5,250	5,300	412	225	509	375						
2,850	2,875	68	0	142	68	5,300	5,350	420	231	517	382	7,750	7,800	825	574	964	750
						5,350	5,400	428	237	525	389	7,800	7,850	833	582	973	758
2,875	2,900	71	0	145	71	5,400	5,450	436	243	533	396	7,850	7,900	842	590	983	766
2,900	2,925	74	0	149	74	5,450	5,500	444	249	541	403	7,900	7,950	850	598	992	774
2,925	2,950	77	0	152	77							7,950	8,000	859	606	1,002	782
2,950	2,975	80	0	156	80												
2,975	3,000	83	0	159	83												

Continued on next page

a If your taxable income is exactly $1,700, your tax is zero.
b If your taxable income is exactly $2,300, your tax is zero.
c If your taxable income is exactly $3,400, your tax is zero.

TABLE 21 (cont.)

| If 1040A, line 16, OR 1040EZ, line 7 is— || And you are— ||||If 1040A, line 16, OR 1040EZ, line 7 is— || And you are— ||||If 1040A, line 16, OR 1040EZ, line 7 is— || And you are— ||||
At least	But less than	Single	Married filing jointly	Married filing separately	Head of a household	At least	But less than	Single	Married filing jointly	Married filing separately	Head of a household	At least	But less than	Single	Married filing jointly	Married filing separately	Head of a household
			Your tax is—						Your tax is—						Your tax is—		
8,000						10,750	10,800	1,380	1,054	1,637	1,313	13,500	13,550	1,991	1,543	2,374	1,898
						10,800	10,850	1,391	1,062	1,650	1,323	13,550	13,600	2,002	1,552	2,388	1,909
8,000	8,050	867	614	1,012	790	10,850	10,900	1,402	1,070	1,662	1,333	13,600	13,650	2,014	1,562	2,403	1,920
8,050	8,100	876	622	1,023	798	10,900	10,950	1,413	1,078	1,675	1,343	13,650	13,700	2,025	1,571	2,417	1,931
8,100	8,150	884	630	1,034	806	10,950	11,000	1,424	1,086	1,687	1,353	13,700	13,750	2,037	1,581	2,432	1,942
8,150	8,200	893	638	1,045	814	**11,000**						13,750	13,800	2,048	1,590	2,446	1,953
8,200	8,250	901	646	1,056	822	11,000	11,050	1,435	1,094	1,700	1,363	13,800	13,850	2,060	1,600	2,461	1,964
8,250	8,300	910	654	1,067	830	11,050	11,100	1,446	1,102	1,712	1,373	13,850	13,900	2,071	1,609	2,475	1,975
8,300	8,350	918	662	1,078	838	11,100	11,150	1,457	1,110	1,725	1,383	13,900	13,950	2,083	1,619	2,490	1,986
8,350	8,400	927	670	1,089	846	11,150	11,200	1,468	1,118	1,737	1,393	13,950	14,000	2,094	1,628	2,504	1,997
8,400	8,450	935	678	1,100	854	11,200	11,250	1,479	1,126	1,750	1,403	**14,000**					
8,450	8,500	944	686	1,111	862	11,250	11,300	1,490	1,134	1,762	1,413	14,000	14,050	2,106	1,638	2,519	2,008
8,500	8,550	953	694	1,122	870	11,300	11,350	1,501	1,142	1,775	1,423	14,050	14,100	2,117	1,647	2,533	2,019
8,550	8,600	962	702	1,133	878	11,350	11,400	1,512	1,150	1,787	1,433	14,100	14,150	2,129	1,657	2,548	2,030
8,600	8,650	972	710	1,144	886	11,400	11,450	1,523	1,158	1,800	1,443	14,150	14,200	2,140	1,666	2,562	2,041
8,650	8,700	981	718	1,155	894	11,450	11,500	1,534	1,166	1,812	1,453	14,200	14,250	2,152	1,676	2,577	2,052
8,700	8,750	991	726	1,166	903	11,500	11,550	1,545	1,174	1,825	1,463	14,250	14,300	2,163	1,685	2,591	2,063
8,750	8,800	1,000	734	1,177	913	11,550	11,600	1,556	1,182	1,837	1,473	14,300	14,350	2,175	1,695	2,606	2,074
8,800	8,850	1,010	742	1,188	923	11,600	11,650	1,567	1,190	1,850	1,483	14,350	14,400	2,186	1,704	2,620	2,085
8,850	8,900	1,019	750	1,199	933	11,650	11,700	1,578	1,198	1,862	1,493	14,400	14,450	2,198	1,714	2,635	2,096
8,900	8,950	1,029	758	1,210	943	11,700	11,750	1,589	1,206	1,875	1,503	14,450	14,500	2,209	1,723	2,649	2,107
8,950	9,000	1,038	766	1,221	953	11,750	11,800	1,600	1,214	1,887	1,513	14,500	14,550	2,221	1,733	2,664	2,118
9,000						11,800	11,850	1,611	1,222	1,900	1,524	14,550	14,600	2,232	1,742	2,678	2,129
9,000	9,050	1,048	774	1,232	963	11,850	11,900	1,622	1,230	1,912	1,535	14,600	14,650	2,244	1,752	2,693	2,140
9,050	9,100	1,057	782	1,243	973	11,900	11,950	1,633	1,239	1,925	1,546	14,650	14,700	2,255	1,761	2,707	2,151
9,100	9,150	1,067	790	1,254	983	11,950	12,000	1,644	1,248	1,937	1,557	14,700	14,750	2,267	1,771	2,722	2,162
9,150	9,200	1,076	798	1,265	993	**12,000**						14,750	14,800	2,278	1,780	2,736	2,173
9,200	9,250	1,086	806	1,276	1,003	12,000	12,050	1,655	1,258	1,950	1,568	14,800	14,850	2,290	1,790	2,751	2,184
9,250	9,300	1,095	814	1,287	1,013	12,050	12,100	1,666	1,267	1,962	1,579	14,850	14,900	2,301	1,799	2,765	2,195
9,300	9,350	1,105	822	1,298	1,023	12,100	12,150	1,677	1,277	1,975	1,590	14,900	14,950	2,313	1,809	2,780	2,206
9,350	9,400	1,114	830	1,309	1,033	12,150	12,200	1,688	1,286	1,987	1,601	14,950	15,000	2,324	1,818	2,795	2,217
9,400	9,450	1,124	838	1,320	1,043	12,200	12,250	1,699	1,296	2,000	1,612	**15,000**					
9,450	9,500	1,133	846	1,331	1,053	12,250	12,300	1,710	1,305	2,012	1,623	15,000	15,050	2,337	1,828	2,812	2,228
9,500	9,550	1,143	854	1,342	1,063	12,300	12,350	1,721	1,315	2,026	1,634	15,050	15,100	2,350	1,837	2,828	2,239
9,550	9,600	1,152	862	1,353	1,073	12,350	12,400	1,732	1,324	2,040	1,645	15,100	15,150	2,364	1,847	2,845	2,251
9,600	9,650	1,162	870	1,364	1,083	12,400	12,450	1,743	1,334	2,055	1,656	15,150	15,200	2,377	1,856	2,861	2,262
9,650	9,700	1,171	878	1,375	1,093	12,450	12,500	1,754	1,343	2,069	1,667	15,200	15,250	2,391	1,866	2,878	2,274
9,700	9,750	1,181	886	1,386	1,103	12,500	12,550	1,765	1,353	2,084	1,678	15,250	15,300	2,404	1,875	2,894	2,285
9,750	9,800	1,190	894	1,397	1,113	12,550	12,600	1,776	1,362	2,098	1,689	15,300	15,350	2,418	1,885	2,911	2,297
9,800	9,850	1,200	902	1,408	1,123	12,600	12,650	1,787	1,372	2,113	1,700	15,350	15,400	2,431	1,894	2,927	2,308
9,850	9,900	1,209	910	1,419	1,133	12,650	12,700	1,798	1,381	2,127	1,711	15,400	15,450	2,445	1,904	2,944	2,320
9,900	9,950	1,219	918	1,430	1,143	12,700	12,750	1,809	1,391	2,142	1,722	15,450	15,500	2,458	1,913	2,960	2,331
9,950	10,000	1,228	926	1,441	1,153	12,750	12,800	1,820	1,400	2,156	1,733	15,500	15,550	2,472	1,923	2,977	2,343
10,000						12,800	12,850	1,831	1,410	2,171	1,744	15,550	15,600	2,485	1,932	2,993	2,354
10,000	10,050	1,238	934	1,452	1,163	12,850	12,900	1,842	1,419	2,185	1,755	15,600	15,650	2,499	1,942	3,010	2,366
10,050	10,100	1,247	942	1,463	1,173	12,900	12,950	1,853	1,429	2,200	1,766	15,650	15,700	2,512	1,951	3,026	2,377
10,100	10,150	1,257	950	1,475	1,183	12,950	13,000	1,864	1,438	2,214	1,777	15,700	15,750	2,526	1,961	3,043	2,389
10,150	10,200	1,266	958	1,487	1,193	**13,000**						15,750	15,800	2,539	1,970	3,059	2,400
10,200	10,250	1,276	966	1,500	1,203	13,000	13,050	1,876	1,448	2,229	1,788	15,800	15,850	2,553	1,980	3,076	2,412
10,250	10,300	1,285	974	1,512	1,213	13,050	13,100	1,887	1,457	2,243	1,799	15,850	15,900	2,566	1,989	3,092	2,423
10,300	10,350	1,295	982	1,525	1,223	13,100	13,150	1,899	1,467	2,258	1,810	15,900	15,950	2,580	1,999	3,109	2,435
10,350	10,400	1,304	990	1,537	1,233	13,150	13,200	1,910	1,476	2,272	1,821	15,950	16,000	2,593	2,008	3,125	2,446
10,400	10,450	1,314	998	1,550	1,243	13,200	13,250	1,922	1,486	2,287	1,832	**16,000**					
10,450	10,500	1,323	1,006	1,562	1,253	13,250	13,300	1,933	1,495	2,301	1,843	16,000	16,050	2,607	2,019	3,142	2,458
10,500	10,550	1,333	1,014	1,575	1,263	13,300	13,350	1,945	1,505	2,316	1,854	16,050	16,100	2,620	2,030	3,158	2,469
10,550	10,600	1,342	1,022	1,587	1,273	13,350	13,400	1,956	1,514	2,330	1,865	16,100	16,150	2,634	2,041	3,175	2,481
10,600	10,650	1,352	1,030	1,600	1,283	13,400	13,450	1,968	1,524	2,345	1,876	16,150	16,200	2,647	2,052	3,191	2,492
10,650	10,700	1,361	1,038	1,612	1,293	13,450	13,500	1,979	1,533	2,359	1,887	16,200	16,250	2,661	2,063	3,208	2,504
10,700	10,750	1,371	1,046	1,625	1,303												

Continued on next page

TABLE 21 (cont.)

If 1040A, line 16, OR 1040EZ, line 7 is—		And you are—				If 1040A, line 16, OR 1040EZ, line 7 is—		And you are—				If 1040A, line 16, OR 1040EZ, line 7 is—		And you are—			
At least	But less than	Single	Married filing jointly	Married filing separately	Head of a household	At least	But less than	Single	Married filing jointly	Married filing separately	Head of a household	At least	But less than	Single	Married filing jointly	Married filing separately	Head of a household
		Your tax is—						Your tax is—						Your tax is—			
16,250	16,300	2,674	2,074	3,224	2,515	**19,000**						21,750	21,800	4,302	3,331	5,290	3,959
16,300	16,350	2,688	2,085	3,241	2,527							21,800	21,850	4,318	3,343	5,309	3,973
16,350	16,400	2,701	2,096	3,257	2,538	19,000	19,050	3,450	2,679	4,217	3,189	21,850	21,900	4,333	3,356	5,329	3,987
16,400	16,450	2,715	2,107	3,274	2,550	19,050	19,100	3,465	2,690	4,237	3,203	21,900	21,950	4,349	3,368	5,348	4,001
16,450	16,500	2,728	2,118	3,290	2,561	19,100	19,150	3,481	2,701	4,256	3,217	21,950	22,000	4,364	3,381	5,368	4,015
						19,150	19,200	3,496	2,712	4,276	3,231	**22,000**					
16,500	16,550	2,742	2,129	3,307	2,573	19,200	19,250	3,512	2,723	4,295	3,245						
16,550	16,600	2,755	2,140	3,323	2,584							22,000	22,050	4,380	3,393	5,387	4,029
16,600	16,650	2,769	2,151	3,340	2,596	19,250	19,300	3,527	2,734	4,315	3,259	22,050	22,100	4,395	3,406	5,407	4,043
16,650	16,700	2,782	2,162	3,356	2,607	19,300	19,350	3,543	2,745	4,334	3,273	22,100	22,150	4,411	3,418	5,426	4,057
16,700	16,750	2,796	2,173	3,373	2,619	19,350	19,400	3,558	2,756	4,354	3,287	22,150	22,200	4,426	3,431	5,446	4,071
						19,400	19,450	3,574	2,767	4,373	3,301	22,200	22,250	4,442	3,443	5,465	4,085
16,750	16,800	2,809	2,184	3,389	2,630	19,450	19,500	3,589	2,778	4,393	3,315						
16,800	16,850	2,823	2,195	3,406	2,642							22,250	22,300	4,457	3,456	5,485	4,099
16,850	16,900	2,836	2,206	3,422	2,653	19,500	19,550	3,605	2,789	4,412	3,329	22,300	22,350	4,473	3,468	5,504	4,113
16,900	16,950	2,850	2,217	3,439	2,665	19,550	19,600	3,620	2,800	4,432	3,343	22,350	22,400	4,488	3,481	5,524	4,127
16,950	17,000	2,863	2,228	3,455	2,676	19,600	19,650	3,636	2,811	4,451	3,357	22,400	22,450	4,504	3,493	5,543	4,141
17,000						19,650	19,700	3,651	2,822	4,471	3,371	22,450	22,500	4,519	3,506	5,563	4,155
						19,700	19,750	3,667	2,833	4,490	3,385						
17,000	17,050	2,877	2,239	3,472	2,688							22,500	22,550	4,535	3,518	5,582	4,169
17,050	17,100	2,890	2,250	3,488	2,699	19,750	19,800	3,682	2,844	4,510	3,399	22,550	22,600	4,550	3,531	5,602	4,183
17,100	17,150	2,904	2,261	3,505	2,711	19,800	19,850	3,698	2,855	4,529	3,413	22,600	22,650	4,566	3,543	5,621	4,197
17,150	17,200	2,917	2,272	3,521	2,722	19,850	19,900	3,713	2,866	4,549	3,427	22,650	22,700	4,581	3,556	5,641	4,211
17,200	17,250	2,931	2,283	3,538	2,734	19,900	19,950	3,729	2,877	4,568	3,441	22,700	22,750	4,597	3,568	5,660	4,225
						19,950	20,000	3,744	2,888	4,588	3,455						
17,250	17,300	2,944	2,294	3,554	2,745	**20,000**						22,750	22,800	4,612	3,581	5,680	4,239
17,300	17,350	2,958	2,305	3,571	2,757							22,800	22,850	4,628	3,593	5,699	4,253
17,350	17,400	2,971	2,316	3,587	2,768	20,000	20,050	3,760	2,899	4,607	3,469	22,850	22,900	4,643	3,606	5,719	4,267
17,400	17,450	2,985	2,327	3,604	2,780	20,050	20,100	3,775	2,910	4,627	3,483	22,900	22,950	4,659	3,618	5,740	4,281
17,450	17,500	2,998	2,338	3,620	2,791	20,100	20,150	3,791	2,921	4,646	3,497	22,950	23,000	4,674	3,631	5,762	4,295
						20,150	20,200	3,806	2,932	4,666	3,511	**23,000**					
17,500	17,550	3,012	2,349	3,637	2,803	20,200	20,250	3,822	2,943	4,685	3,525						
17,550	17,600	3,025	2,360	3,653	2,814							23,000	23,050	4,690	3,643	5,784	4,309
17,600	17,650	3,039	2,371	3,671	2,826	20,250	20,300	3,837	2,956	4,705	3,539	23,050	23,100	4,705	3,656	5,806	4,323
17,650	17,700	3,052	2,382	3,691	2,837	20,300	20,350	3,853	2,968	4,724	3,553	23,100	23,150	4,721	3,668	5,828	4,337
17,700	17,750	3,066	2,393	3,710	2,849	20,350	20,400	3,868	2,981	4,744	3,567	23,150	23,200	4,736	3,681	5,850	4,351
						20,400	20,450	3,884	2,993	4,763	3,581	23,200	23,250	4,752	3,693	5,872	4,365
17,750	17,800	3,079	2,404	3,730	2,860	20,450	20,500	3,899	3,006	4,783	3,595						
17,800	17,850	3,093	2,415	3,749	2,872							23,250	23,300	4,767	3,706	5,894	4,379
17,850	17,900	3,106	2,426	3,769	2,883	20,500	20,550	3,915	3,018	4,802	3,609	23,300	23,350	4,783	3,718	5,916	4,393
17,900	17,950	3,120	2,437	3,788	2,895	20,550	20,600	3,930	3,031	4,822	3,623	23,350	23,400	4,798	3,731	5,938	4,407
17,950	18,000	3,133	2,448	3,808	2,906	20,600	20,650	3,946	3,043	4,841	3,637	23,400	23,450	4,814	3,743	5,960	4,421
18,000						20,650	20,700	3,961	3,056	4,861	3,651	23,450	23,500	4,829	3,756	5,982	4,435
						20,700	20,750	3,977	3,068	4,880	3,665						
18,000	18,050	3,147	2,459	3,827	2,918							23,500	23,550	4,846	3,768	6,004	4,450
18,050	18,100	3,160	2,470	3,847	2,929	20,750	20,800	3,992	3,081	4,900	3,679	23,550	23,600	4,863	3,781	6,026	4,466
18,100	18,150	3,174	2,481	3,866	2,941	20,800	20,850	4,008	3,093	4,919	3,693	23,600	23,650	4,881	3,793	6,048	4,482
18,150	18,200	3,187	2,492	3,886	2,952	20,850	20,900	4,023	3,106	4,939	3,707	23,650	23,700	4,898	3,806	6,070	4,498
18,200	18,250	3,202	2,503	3,905	2,965	20,900	20,950	4,039	3,118	4,958	3,721	23,700	23,750	4,916	3,818	6,092	4,514
						20,950	21,000	4,054	3,131	4,978	3,735						
18,250	18,300	3,217	2,514	3,925	2,979	**21,000**						23,750	23,800	4,933	3,831	6,114	4,530
18,300	18,350	3,233	2,525	3,944	2,993							23,800	23,850	4,951	3,843	6,136	4,546
18,350	18,400	3,248	2,536	3,964	3,007	21,000	21,050	4,070	3,143	4,997	3,749	23,850	23,900	4,968	3,856	6,158	4,562
18,400	18,450	3,264	2,547	3,983	3,021	21,050	21,100	4,085	3,156	5,017	3,763	23,900	23,950	4,986	3,868	6,180	4,578
18,450	18,500	3,279	2,558	4,003	3,035	21,100	21,150	4,101	3,168	5,036	3,777	23,950	24,000	5,003	3,881	6,202	4,594
						21,150	21,200	4,116	3,181	5,056	3,791	**24,000**					
18,500	18,550	3,295	2,569	4,022	3,049	21,200	21,250	4,132	3,193	5,075	3,805						
18,550	18,600	3,310	2,580	4,042	3,063							24,000	24,050	5,021	3,893	6,224	4,610
18,600	18,650	3,326	2,591	4,061	3,077	21,250	21,300	4,147	3,206	5,095	3,819	24,050	24,100	5,038	3,906	6,246	4,626
18,650	18,700	3,341	2,602	4,081	3,091	21,300	21,350	4,163	3,218	5,114	3,833	24,100	24,150	5,056	3,918	6,268	4,642
18,700	18,750	3,357	2,613	4,100	3,105	21,350	21,400	4,178	3,231	5,134	3,847	24,150	24,200	5,073	3,931	6,290	4,658
						21,400	21,450	4,194	3,243	5,153	3,861	24,200	24,250	5,091	3,943	6,312	4,674
18,750	18,800	3,372	2,624	4,120	3,119	21,450	21,500	4,209	3,256	5,173	3,875						
18,800	18,850	3,388	2,635	4,139	3,133							24,250	24,300	5,108	3,956	6,334	4,690
18,850	18,900	3,403	2,646	4,159	3,147	21,500	21,550	4,225	3,268	5,192	3,889	24,300	24,350	5,126	3,968	6,356	4,706
18,900	18,950	3,419	2,657	4,178	3,161	21,550	21,600	4,240	3,281	5,212	3,903	24,350	24,400	5,143	3,981	6,378	4,722
18,950	19,000	3,434	2,668	4,198	3,175	21,600	21,650	4,256	3,293	5,231	3,917	24,400	24,450	5,161	3,993	6,400	4,738
						21,650	21,700	4,271	3,306	5,251	3,931	24,450	24,500	5,178	4,006	6,422	4,754
						21,700	21,750	4,287	3,318	5,270	3,945						

Continued on next page

TABLE 21 (cont.)

If 1040A, line 16, OR 1040EZ, line 7 is—		And you are—				If 1040A, line 16, OR 1040EZ, line 7 is—		And you are—				If 1040A, line 16, OR 1040EZ, line 7 is—		And you are—			
At least	But less than	Single	Married filing jointly	Married filing separately	Head of a house-hold	At least	But less than	Single	Married filing jointly	Married filing separately	Head of a house-hold	At least	But less than	Single	Married filing jointly	Married filing separately	Head of a house-hold
		Your tax is—						Your tax is—						Your tax is—			
24,500	24,550	5,196	4,018	6,444	4,770	27,250	27,300	6,158	4,813	7,654	5,650	**30,000**					
24,550	24,600	5,213	4,031	6,466	4,786	27,300	27,350	6,176	4,827	7,676	5,666						
24,600	24,650	5,231	4,044	6,488	4,802	27,350	27,400	6,193	4,842	7,698	5,682	30,000	30,050	7,182	5,615	8,865	6,604
24,650	24,700	5,248	4,059	6,510	4,818	27,400	27,450	6,211	4,856	7,720	5,698	30,050	30,100	7,202	5,632	8,889	6,623
24,700	24,750	5,266	4,073	6,532	4,834	27,450	27,500	6,228	4,871	7,742	5,714	30,100	30,150	7,222	5,648	8,914	6,642
												30,150	30,200	7,242	5,665	8,938	6,661
24,750	24,800	5,283	4,088	6,554	4,850	27,500	27,550	6,246	4,885	7,764	5,730	30,200	30,250	7,262	5,681	8,963	6,680
24,800	24,850	5,301	4,102	6,576	4,866	27,550	27,600	6,263	4,900	7,786	5,746						
24,850	24,900	5,318	4,117	6,598	4,882	27,600	27,650	6,281	4,914	7,808	5,762	30,250	30,300	7,282	5,698	8,987	6,699
24,900	24,950	5,336	4,131	6,620	4,898	27,650	27,700	6,298	4,929	7,830	5,778	30,300	30,350	7,302	5,714	9,012	6,718
24,950	25,000	5,353	4,146	6,642	4,914	27,700	27,750	6,316	4,943	7,852	5,794	30,350	30,400	7,322	5,731	9,036	6,737
25,000												30,400	30,450	7,342	5,747	9,061	6,756
25,000	25,050	5,371	4,160	6,664	4,930	27,750	27,800	6,333	4,958	7,874	5,810	30,450	30,500	7,362	5,764	9,085	6,775
25,050	25,100	5,388	4,175	6,686	4,946	27,800	27,850	6,351	4,972	7,896	5,826						
25,100	25,150	5,406	4,189	6,708	4,962	27,850	27,900	6,368	4,987	7,918	5,842	30,500	30,550	7,382	5,780	9,110	6,794
25,150	25,200	5,423	4,204	6,730	4,978	27,900	27,950	6,386	5,001	7,940	5,858	30,550	30,600	7,402	5,797	9,134	6,813
25,200	25,250	5,441	4,218	6,752	4,994	27,950	28,000	6,403	5,016	7,962	5,874	30,600	30,650	7,422	5,813	9,159	6,832
						28,000						30,650	30,700	7,442	5,830	9,183	6,851
25,250	25,300	5,458	4,233	6,774	5,010	28,000	28,050	6,421	5,030	7,984	5,890	30,700	30,750	7,462	5,846	9,208	6,870
25,300	25,350	5,476	4,247	6,796	5,026	28,050	28,100	6,438	5,045	8,006	5,906						
25,350	25,400	5,493	4,262	6,818	5,042	28,100	28,150	6,456	5,059	8,028	5,922	30,750	30,800	7,482	5,863	9,232	6,889
25,400	25,450	5,511	4,276	6,840	5,058	28,150	28,200	6,473	5,074	8,050	5,938	30,800	30,850	7,502	5,879	9,257	6,908
25,450	25,500	5,528	4,291	6,862	5,074	28,200	28,250	6,491	5,088	8,072	5,954	30,850	30,900	7,522	5,896	9,281	6,927
												30,900	30,950	7,542	5,912	9,306	6,946
25,500	25,550	5,546	4,305	6,884	5,090	28,250	28,300	6,508	5,103	8,094	5,970	30,950	31,000	7,562	5,929	9,330	6,965
25,550	25,600	5,563	4,320	6,906	5,106	28,300	28,350	6,526	5,117	8,116	5,986	**31,000**					
25,600	25,650	5,581	4,334	6,928	5,122	28,350	28,400	6,543	5,132	8,138	6,002	31,000	31,050	7,582	5,945	9,355	6,984
25,650	25,700	5,598	4,349	6,950	5,138	28,400	28,450	6,561	5,146	8,160	6,018	31,050	31,100	7,602	5,962	9,379	7,003
25,700	25,750	5,616	4,363	6,972	5,154	28,450	28,500	6,578	5,161	8,182	6,034	31,100	31,150	7,622	5,978	9,404	7,022
												31,150	31,200	7,642	5,995	9,428	7,041
25,750	25,800	5,633	4,378	6,994	5,170	28,500	28,550	6,596	5,175	8,204	6,050	31,200	31,250	7,662	6,011	9,453	7,060
25,800	25,850	5,651	4,392	7,016	5,186	28,550	28,600	6,613	5,190	8,226	6,066						
25,850	25,900	5,668	4,407	7,038	5,202	28,600	28,650	6,631	5,204	8,248	6,082	31,250	31,300	7,682	6,028	9,477	7,079
25,900	25,950	5,686	4,421	7,060	5,218	28,650	28,700	6,648	5,219	8,270	6,098	31,300	31,350	7,702	6,044	9,502	7,098
25,950	26,000	5,703	4,436	7,082	5,234	28,700	28,750	6,666	5,233	8,292	6,114	31,350	31,400	7,722	6,061	9,526	7,117
26,000													31,400	31,450	7,742	6,077	9,551	7,136
26,000	26,050	5,721	4,450	7,104	5,250	28,750	28,800	6,683	5,248	8,314	6,130	31,450	31,500	7,762	6,094	9,575	7,155
26,050	26,100	5,738	4,465	7,126	5,266	28,800	28,850	6,702	5,262	8,336	6,148						
26,100	26,150	5,756	4,479	7,148	5,282	28,850	28,900	6,722	5,277	8,358	6,167	31,500	31,550	7,782	6,110	9,600	7,174
26,150	26,200	5,773	4,494	7,170	5,298	28,900	28,950	6,742	5,291	8,380	6,186	31,550	31,600	7,802	6,127	9,624	7,193
26,200	26,250	5,791	4,508	7,192	5,314	28,950	29,000	6,762	5,306	8,402	6,205	31,600	31,650	7,822	6,143	9,649	7,212
						29,000						31,650	31,700	7,842	6,160	9,673	7,231
26,250	26,300	5,808	4,523	7,214	5,330	29,000	29,050	6,782	5,320	8,424	6,224	31,700	31,750	7,862	6,176	9,698	7,250
26,300	26,350	5,826	4,537	7,236	5,346	29,050	29,100	6,802	5,335	8,446	6,243						
26,350	26,400	5,843	4,552	7,258	5,362	29,100	29,150	6,822	5,349	8,468	6,262	31,750	31,800	7,882	6,193	9,722	7,269
26,400	26,450	5,861	4,566	7,280	5,378	29,150	29,200	6,842	5,364	8,490	6,281	31,800	31,850	7,902	6,209	9,747	7,288
26,450	26,500	5,878	4,581	7,302	5,394	29,200	29,250	6,862	5,378	8,512	6,300	31,850	31,900	7,922	6,226	9,771	7,307
												31,900	31,950	7,942	6,242	9,796	7,326
26,500	26,550	5,896	4,595	7,324	5,410	29,250	29,300	6,882	5,393	8,534	6,319	31,950	32,000	7,962	6,259	9,820	7,345
26,550	26,600	5,913	4,610	7,346	5,426	29,300	29,350	6,902	5,407	8,556	6,338	**32,000**					
26,600	26,650	5,931	4,624	7,368	5,442	29,350	29,400	6,922	5,422	8,578	6,357	32,000	32,050	7,982	6,275	9,845	7,364
26,650	26,700	5,948	4,639	7,390	5,458	29,400	29,450	6,942	5,436	8,600	6,376	32,050	32,100	8,002	6,292	9,869	7,383
26,700	26,750	5,966	4,653	7,412	5,474	29,450	29,500	6,962	5,451	8,622	6,395	32,100	32,150	8,022	6,308	9,894	7,402
												32,150	32,200	8,042	6,325	9,918	7,421
26,750	26,800	5,983	4,668	7,434	5,490							32,200	32,250	8,062	6,341	9,943	7,440
26,800	26,850	6,001	4,682	7,456	5,506	29,500	29,550	6,982	5,465	8,644	6,414						
26,850	26,900	6,018	4,697	7,478	5,522	29,550	29,600	7,002	5,480	8,666	6,433	32,250	32,300	8,082	6,358	9,967	7,459
26,900	26,950	6,036	4,711	7,500	5,538	29,600	29,650	7,022	5,494	8,688	6,452	32,300	32,350	8,102	6,374	9,992	7,478
26,950	27,000	6,053	4,726	7,522	5,554	29,650	29,700	7,042	5,509	8,710	6,471	32,350	32,400	8,122	6,391	10,016	7,497
27,000							29,700	29,750	7,062	5,523	8,732	6,490	32,400	32,450	8,142	6,407	10,041	7,516
												32,450	32,500	8,162	6,424	10,065	7,535
27,000	27,050	6,071	4,740	7,544	5,570	29,750	29,800	7,082	5,538	8,754	6,509	32,500	32,550	8,182	6,440	10,090	7,554
27,050	27,100	6,088	4,755	7,566	5,586	29,800	29,850	7,102	5,552	8,776	6,528	32,550	32,600	8,202	6,457	10,114	7,573
27,100	27,150	6,106	4,769	7,588	5,602	29,850	29,900	7,122	5,567	8,798	6,547	32,600	32,650	8,222	6,473	10,139	7,592
27,150	27,200	6,123	4,784	7,610	5,618	29,900	29,950	7,142	5,582	8,820	6,566	32,650	32,700	8,242	6,490	10,163	7,611
27,200	27,250	6,141	4,798	7,632	5,634	29,950	30,000	7,162	5,599	8,842	6,585	32,700	32,750	8,262	6,506	10,188	7,630

Continued on next page

TABLE 21 (cont.)

If 1040A, line 16, OR 1040EZ, line 7 is—		And you are—				If 1040A, line 16, OR 1040EZ, line 7 is—		And you are—				If 1040A, line 16, OR 1040EZ, line 7 is—		And you are—			
At least	But less than	Single	Married filing jointly	Married filing separately	Head of a household	At least	But less than	Single	Married filing jointly	Married filing separately	Head of a household	At least	But less than	Single	Married filing jointly	Married filing separately	Head of a household
			Your tax is—						Your tax is—						Your tax is—		
32,750	32,800	8,282	6,523	10,212	7,649	35,500	35,550	9,439	7,450	11,560	8,736	38,250	38,300	10,649	8,522	12,907	9,864
32,800	32,850	8,302	6,539	10,237	7,668	35,550	35,600	9,461	7,469	11,584	8,757	38,300	38,350	10,671	8,542	12,932	9,884
32,850	32,900	8,322	6,556	10,261	7,687	35,600	35,650	9,483	7,489	11,609	8,777	38,350	38,400	10,693	8,561	12,956	9,905
32,900	32,950	8,342	6,572	10,286	7,706	35,650	35,700	9,505	7,508	11,633	8,798	38,400	38,450	10,715	8,581	12,981	9,925
32,950	33,000	8,362	6,589	10,310	7,725	35,700	35,750	9,527	7,528	11,658	8,818	38,450	38,500	10,737	8,600	13,005	9,946
33,000																	
33,000	33,050	8,382	6,605	10,335	7,744	35,750	35,800	9,549	7,547	11,682	8,839	38,500	38,550	10,759	8,620	13,030	9,966
33,050	33,100	8,402	6,622	10,359	7,763	35,800	35,850	9,571	7,567	11,707	8,859	38,550	38,600	10,781	8,639	13,054	9,987
33,100	33,150	8,422	6,638	10,384	7,782	35,850	35,900	9,593	7,586	11,731	8,880	38,600	38,650	10,803	8,659	13,079	10,007
33,150	33,200	8,442	6,655	10,408	7,801	35,900	35,950	9,615	7,606	11,756	8,900	38,650	38,700	10,825	8,678	13,103	10,028
33,200	33,250	8,462	6,671	10,433	7,820	35,950	36,000	9,637	7,625	11,780	8,921	38,700	38,750	10,847	8,698	13,128	10,048
						36,000											
33,250	33,300	8,482	6,688	10,457	7,839	36,000	36,050	9,659	7,645	11,805	8,941	38,750	38,800	10,869	8,717	13,152	10,069
33,300	33,350	8,502	6,704	10,482	7,858	36,050	36,100	9,681	7,664	11,829	8,962	38,800	38,850	10,891	8,737	13,177	10,089
33,350	33,400	8,522	6,721	10,506	7,877	36,100	36,150	9,703	7,684	11,854	8,982	38,850	38,900	10,913	8,756	13,201	10,110
33,400	33,450	8,542	6,737	10,531	7,896	36,150	36,200	9,725	7,703	11,878	9,003	38,900	38,950	10,935	8,776	13,226	10,130
33,450	33,500	8,562	6,754	10,555	7,915	36,200	36,250	9,747	7,723	11,903	9,023	38,950	39,000	10,957	8,795	13,250	10,151
														39,000			
33,500	33,550	8,582	6,770	10,580	7,934	36,250	36,300	9,769	7,742	11,927	9,044	39,000	39,050	10,979	8,815	13,275	10,171
33,550	33,600	8,602	6,787	10,604	7,953	36,300	36,350	9,791	7,762	11,952	9,064	39,050	39,100	11,001	8,834	13,299	10,192
33,600	33,650	8,622	6,803	10,629	7,972	36,350	36,400	9,813	7,781	11,976	9,085	39,100	39,150	11,023	8,854	13,324	10,212
33,650	33,700	8,642	6,820	10,653	7,991	36,400	36,450	9,835	7,801	12,001	9,105	39,150	39,200	11,045	8,873	13,348	10,233
33,700	33,750	8,662	6,836	10,678	8,010	36,450	36,500	9,857	7,820	12,025	9,126	39,200	39,250	11,067	8,893	13,373	10,253
33,750	33,800	8,682	6,853	10,702	8,029	36,500	36,550	9,879	7,840	12,050	9,146	39,250	39,300	11,089	8,912	13,397	10,274
33,800	33,850	8,702	6,869	10,727	8,048	36,550	36,600	9,901	7,859	12,074	9,167	39,300	39,350	11,111	8,932	13,422	10,294
33,850	33,900	8,722	6,886	10,751	8,067	36,600	36,650	9,923	7,879	12,099	9,187	39,350	39,400	11,133	8,951	13,446	10,315
33,900	33,950	8,742	6,902	10,776	8,086	36,650	36,700	9,945	7,898	12,123	9,208	39,400	39,450	11,155	8,971	13,471	10,335
33,950	34,000	8,762	6,919	10,800	8,105	36,700	36,750	9,967	7,918	12,148	9,228	39,450	39,500	11,177	8,990	13,495	10,356
34,000																	
34,000	34,050	8,782	6,935	10,825	8,124	36,750	36,800	9,989	7,937	12,172	9,249	39,500	39,550	11,199	9,010	13,520	10,376
34,050	34,100	8,802	6,952	10,849	8,143	36,800	36,850	10,011	7,957	12,197	9,269	39,550	39,600	11,221	9,029	13,544	10,397
34,100	34,150	8,823	6,968	10,874	8,162	36,850	36,900	10,033	7,976	12,221	9,290	39,600	39,650	11,243	9,049	13,569	10,417
34,150	34,200	8,845	6,985	10,898	8,183	36,900	36,950	10,055	7,996	12,246	9,310	39,650	39,700	11,265	9,068	13,593	10,438
34,200	34,250	8,867	7,001	10,923	8,203	36,950	37,000	10,077	8,015	12,270	9,331	39,700	39,750	11,287	9,088	13,618	10,458
						37,000											
34,250	34,300	8,889	7,018	10,947	8,224	37,000	37,050	10,099	8,035	12,295	9,351	39,750	39,800	11,309	9,107	13,642	10,479
34,300	34,350	8,911	7,034	10,972	8,244	37,050	37,100	10,121	8,054	12,319	9,372	39,800	39,850	11,331	9,127	13,667	10,499
34,350	34,400	8,933	7,051	10,996	8,265	37,100	37,150	10,143	8,074	12,344	9,392	39,850	39,900	11,353	9,146	13,691	10,520
34,400	34,450	8,955	7,067	11,021	8,285	37,150	37,200	10,165	8,093	12,368	9,413	39,900	39,950	11,375	9,166	13,716	10,540
34,450	34,500	8,977	7,084	11,045	8,306	37,200	37,250	10,187	8,113	12,393	9,433	39,950	40,000	11,397	9,185	13,740	10,561
														40,000			
34,500	34,550	8,999	7,100	11,070	8,326	37,250	37,300	10,209	8,132	12,417	9,454	40,000	40,050	11,419	9,205	13,765	10,581
34,550	34,600	9,021	7,117	11,094	8,347	37,300	37,350	10,231	8,152	12,442	9,474	40,050	40,100	11,441	9,224	13,789	10,602
34,600	34,650	9,043	7,133	11,119	8,367	37,350	37,400	10,253	8,171	12,466	9,495	40,100	40,150	11,463	9,244	13,814	10,622
34,650	34,700	9,065	7,150	11,143	8,388	37,400	37,450	10,275	8,191	12,491	9,515	40,150	40,200	11,485	9,263	13,838	10,643
34,700	34,750	9,087	7,166	11,168	8,408	37,450	37,500	10,297	8,210	12,515	9,536	40,200	40,250	11,507	9,283	13,863	10,663
34,750	34,800	9,109	7,183	11,192	8,429	37,500	37,550	10,319	8,230	12,540	9,556	40,250	40,300	11,529	9,302	13,887	10,684
34,800	34,850	9,131	7,199	11,217	8,449	37,550	37,600	10,341	8,249	12,564	9,577	40,300	40,350	11,551	9,322	13,912	10,704
34,850	34,900	9,153	7,216	11,241	8,470	37,600	37,650	10,363	8,269	12,589	9,597	40,350	40,400	11,573	9,341	13,936	10,725
34,900	34,950	9,175	7,232	11,266	8,490	37,650	37,700	10,385	8,288	12,613	9,618	40,400	40,450	11,595	9,361	13,961	10,745
34,950	35,000	9,197	7,249	11,290	8,511	37,700	37,750	10,407	8,308	12,638	9,638	40,450	40,500	11,617	9,380	13,985	10,766
35,000																	
35,000	35,050	9,219	7,265	11,315	8,531	37,750	37,800	10,429	8,327	12,662	9,659	40,500	40,550	11,639	9,400	14,010	10,786
35,050	35,100	9,241	7,282	11,339	8,552	37,800	37,850	10,451	8,347	12,687	9,679	40,550	40,600	11,661	9,419	14,034	10,807
35,100	35,150	9,263	7,298	11,364	8,572	37,850	37,900	10,473	8,366	12,711	9,700	40,600	40,650	11,683	9,439	14,059	10,827
35,150	35,200	9,285	7,315	11,388	8,593	37,900	37,950	10,495	8,386	12,736	9,720	40,650	40,700	11,705	9,458	14,083	10,848
35,200	35,250	9,307	7,333	11,413	8,613	37,950	38,000	10,517	8,405	12,760	9,741	40,700	40,750	11,727	9,478	14,108	10,868
						38,000											
35,250	35,300	9,329	7,352	11,437	8,634	38,000	38,050	10,539	8,425	12,785	9,761	40,750	40,800	11,749	9,497	14,132	10,889
35,300	35,350	9,351	7,372	11,462	8,654	38,050	38,100	10,561	8,444	12,809	9,782	40,800	40,850	11,771	9,517	14,157	10,909
35,350	35,400	9,373	7,391	11,486	8,675	38,100	38,150	10,583	8,464	12,834	9,802	40,850	40,900	11,793	9,536	14,181	10,930
35,400	35,450	9,395	7,411	11,511	8,695	38,150	38,200	10,605	8,483	12,858	9,823	40,900	40,950	11,815	9,556	14,206	10,950
35,450	35,500	9,417	7,430	11,535	8,716	38,200	38,250	10,627	8,503	12,883	9,843	40,950	41,000	11,837	9,575	14,230	10,971

Continued on next page

TABLE 21 (cont.)

If 1040A, line 16, OR 1040EZ, line 7 is—		And you are—				If 1040A, line 16, OR 1040EZ, line 7 is—		And you are—				If 1040A, line 16, OR 1040EZ, line 7 is—		And you are—			
At least	But less than	Single	Married filing jointly	Married filing separately	Head of a household	At least	But less than	Single	Married filing jointly	Married filing separately	Head of a household	At least	But less than	Single	Married filing jointly	Married filing separately	Head of a household
		Your tax is—						Your tax is—						Your tax is—			

41,000 | 44,000 | 47,000

41,000	41,050	11,859	9,595	14,255	10,991	44,000	44,050	13,331	10,765	15,737	12,221	47,000	47,050	14,831	11,996	17,237	13,637
41,050	41,100	11,881	9,614	14,279	11,012	44,050	44,100	13,356	10,784	15,762	12,242	47,050	47,100	14,856	12,018	17,262	13,662
41,100	41,150	11,903	9,634	14,304	11,032	44,100	44,150	13,381	10,804	15,787	12,262	47,100	47,150	14,881	12,040	17,287	13,686
41,150	41,200	11,925	9,653	14,328	11,053	44,150	44,200	13,406	10,823	15,812	12,283	47,150	47,200	14,906	12,062	17,312	13,711
41,200	41,250	11,947	9,673	14,353	11,073	44,200	44,250	13,431	10,843	15,837	12,303	47,200	47,250	14,931	12,084	17,337	13,735
41,250	41,300	11,969	9,692	14,377	11,094	44,250	44,300	13,456	10,862	15,862	12,324	47,250	47,300	14,956	12,106	17,362	13,760
41,300	41,350	11,991	9,712	14,402	11,114	44,300	44,350	13,481	10,882	15,887	12,344	47,300	47,350	14,981	12,128	17,387	13,784
41,350	41,400	12,013	9,731	14,426	11,135	44,350	44,400	13,506	10,901	15,912	12,365	47,350	47,400	15,006	12,150	17,412	13,809
41,400	41,450	12,035	9,751	14,451	11,155	44,400	44,450	13,531	10,921	15,937	12,385	47,400	47,450	15,031	12,172	17,437	13,833
41,450	41,500	12,057	9,770	14,475	11,176	44,450	44,500	13,556	10,940	15,962	12,406	47,450	47,500	15,056	12,194	17,462	13,858
41,500	41,550	12,081	9,790	14,500	11,196	44,500	44,550	13,581	10,960	15,987	12,426	47,500	47,550	15,081	12,216	17,487	13,882
41,550	41,600	12,106	9,809	14,524	11,217	44,550	44,600	13,606	10,979	16,012	12,447	47,550	47,600	15,106	12,238	17,512	13,907
41,600	41,650	12,131	9,829	14,549	11,237	44,600	44,650	13,631	10,999	16,037	12,467	47,600	47,650	15,131	12,260	17,537	13,931
41,650	41,700	12,156	9,848	14,573	11,258	44,650	44,700	13,656	11,018	16,062	12,488	47,650	47,700	15,156	12,282	17,562	13,956
41,700	41,750	12,181	9,868	14,598	11,278	44,700	44,750	13,681	11,038	16,087	12,510	47,700	47,750	15,181	12,304	17,587	13,980
41,750	41,800	12,206	9,887	14,622	11,299	44,750	44,800	13,706	11,057	16,112	12,535	47,750	47,800	15,206	12,326	17,612	14,005
41,800	41,850	12,231	9,907	14,647	11,319	44,800	44,850	13,731	11,077	16,137	12,559	47,800	47,850	15,231	12,348	17,637	14,029
41,850	41,900	12,256	9,926	14,671	11,340	44,850	44,900	13,756	11,096	16,162	12,584	47,850	47,900	15,256	12,370	17,662	14,054
41,900	41,950	12,281	9,946	14,696	11,360	44,900	44,950	13,781	11,116	16,187	12,608	47,900	47,950	15,281	12,392	17,687	14,078
41,950	42,000	12,306	9,965	14,720	11,381	44,950	45,000	13,806	11,135	16,212	12,633	47,950	48,000	15,306	12,414	17,712	14,103

42,000 | 45,000 | 48,000

42,000	42,050	12,331	9,985	14,745	11,401	45,000	45,050	13,831	11,155	16,237	12,657	48,000	48,050	15,331	12,436	17,737	14,127
42,050	42,100	12,356	10,004	14,769	11,422	45,050	45,100	13,856	11,174	16,262	12,682	48,050	48,100	15,356	12,458	17,762	14,152
42,100	42,150	12,381	10,024	14,794	11,442	45,100	45,150	13,881	11,194	16,287	12,706	48,100	48,150	15,381	12,480	17,787	14,176
42,150	42,200	12,406	10,043	14,818	11,463	45,150	45,200	13,906	11,213	16,312	12,731	48,150	48,200	15,406	12,502	17,812	14,201
42,200	42,250	12,431	10,063	14,843	11,483	45,200	45,250	13,931	11,233	16,337	12,755	48,200	48,250	15,431	12,524	17,837	14,225
42,250	42,300	12,456	10,082	14,867	11,504	45,250	45,300	13,956	11,252	16,362	12,780	48,250	48,300	15,456	12,546	17,862	14,250
42,300	42,350	12,481	10,102	14,892	11,524	45,300	45,350	13,981	11,272	16,387	12,804	48,300	48,350	15,481	12,568	17,887	14,274
42,350	42,400	12,506	10,121	14,916	11,545	45,350	45,400	14,006	11,291	16,412	12,829	48,350	48,400	15,506	12,590	17,912	14,299
42,400	42,450	12,531	10,141	14,941	11,565	45,400	45,450	14,031	11,311	16,437	12,853	48,400	48,450	15,531	12,612	17,937	14,323
42,450	42,500	12,556	10,160	14,965	11,586	45,450	45,500	14,056	11,330	16,462	12,878	48,450	48,500	15,556	12,634	17,962	14,348
42,500	42,550	12,581	10,180	14,990	11,606	45,500	45,550	14,081	11,350	16,487	12,902	48,500	48,550	15,581	12,656	17,987	14,372
42,550	42,600	12,606	10,199	15,014	11,627	45,550	45,600	14,106	11,369	16,512	12,927	48,550	48,600	15,606	12,678	18,012	14,397
42,600	42,650	12,631	10,219	15,039	11,647	45,600	45,650	14,131	11,389	16,537	12,951	48,600	48,650	15,631	12,700	18,037	14,421
42,650	42,700	12,656	10,238	15,063	11,668	45,650	45,700	14,156	11,408	16,562	12,976	48,650	48,700	15,656	12,722	18,062	14,446
42,700	42,750	12,681	10,258	15,088	11,688	45,700	45,750	14,181	11,428	16,587	13,000	48,700	48,750	15,681	12,744	18,087	14,470
42,750	42,800	12,706	10,277	15,112	11,709	45,750	45,800	14,206	11,447	16,612	13,025	48,750	48,800	15,706	12,766	18,112	14,495
42,800	42,850	12,731	10,297	15,137	11,729	45,800	45,850	14,231	11,468	16,637	13,049	48,800	48,850	15,731	12,788	18,137	14,519
42,850	42,900	12,756	10,316	15,162	11,750	45,850	45,900	14,256	11,490	16,662	13,074	48,850	48,900	15,756	12,810	18,162	14,544
42,900	42,950	12,781	10,336	15,187	11,770	45,900	45,950	14,281	11,512	16,687	13,098	48,900	48,950	15,781	12,832	18,187	14,568
42,950	43,000	12,806	10,355	15,212	11,791	45,950	46,000	14,306	11,534	16,712	13,123	48,950	49,000	15,806	12,854	18,212	14,593

43,000 | 46,000 | 49,000

43,000	43,050	12,831	10,375	15,237	11,811	46,000	46,050	14,331	11,556	16,737	13,147	49,000	49,050	15,831	12,876	18,237	14,617
43,050	43,100	12,856	10,394	15,262	11,832	46,050	46,100	14,356	11,578	16,762	13,172	49,050	49,100	15,856	12,898	18,262	14,642
43,100	43,150	12,881	10,414	15,287	11,852	46,100	46,150	14,381	11,600	16,787	13,196	49,100	49,150	15,881	12,920	18,287	14,666
43,150	43,200	12,906	10,433	15,312	11,873	46,150	46,200	14,406	11,622	16,812	13,221	49,150	49,200	15,906	12,942	18,312	14,691
43,200	43,250	12,931	10,453	15,337	11,893	46,200	46,250	14,431	11,644	16,837	13,245	49,200	49,250	15,931	12,964	18,337	14,715
43,250	43,300	12,956	10,472	15,362	11,914	46,250	46,300	14,456	11,666	16,862	13,270	49,250	49,300	15,956	12,986	18,362	14,740
43,300	43,350	12,981	10,492	15,387	11,934	46,300	46,350	14,481	11,688	16,887	13,294	49,300	49,350	15,981	13,008	18,387	14,764
43,350	43,400	13,006	10,511	15,412	11,955	46,350	46,400	14,506	11,710	16,912	13,319	49,350	49,400	16,006	13,030	18,412	14,789
43,400	43,450	13,031	10,531	15,437	11,975	46,400	46,450	14,531	11,732	16,937	13,343	49,400	49,450	16,031	13,052	18,437	14,813
43,450	43,500	13,056	10,550	15,462	11,996	46,450	46,500	14,556	11,754	16,962	13,368	49,450	49,500	16,056	13,074	18,462	14,838
43,500	43,550	13,081	10,570	15,487	12,016	46,500	46,550	14,581	11,776	16,987	13,392	49,500	49,550	16,081	13,096	18,487	14,862
43,550	43,600	13,106	10,589	15,512	12,037	46,550	46,600	14,606	11,798	17,012	13,417	49,550	49,600	16,106	13,118	18,512	14,887
43,600	43,650	13,131	10,609	15,537	12,057	46,600	46,650	14,631	11,820	17,037	13,441	49,600	49,650	16,131	13,140	18,537	14,911
43,650	43,700	13,156	10,628	15,562	12,078	46,650	46,700	14,656	11,842	17,062	13,466	49,650	49,700	16,156	13,162	18,562	14,936
43,700	43,750	13,181	10,648	15,587	12,098	46,700	46,750	14,681	11,864	17,087	13,490	49,700	49,750	16,181	13,184	18,587	14,960
43,750	43,800	13,206	10,667	15,612	12,119	46,750	46,800	14,706	11,886	17,112	13,515	49,750	49,800	16,206	13,206	18,612	14,985
43,800	43,850	13,231	10,687	15,637	12,139	46,800	46,850	14,731	11,908	17,137	13,539	49,800	49,850	16,231	13,228	18,637	15,009
43,850	43,900	13,256	10,706	15,662	12,160	46,850	46,900	14,756	11,930	17,162	13,564	49,850	49,900	16,256	13,250	18,662	15,034
43,900	43,950	13,281	10,726	15,687	12,180	46,900	46,950	14,781	11,952	17,187	13,588	49,900	49,950	16,281	13,272	18,687	15,058
43,950	44,000	13,306	10,745	15,712	12,201	46,950	47,000	14,806	11,974	17,212	13,613	49,950	50,000	16,306	13,294	18,712	15,083

TABLE 22
PERCENTAGE METHOD INCOME TAX WITHHOLDING TABLE

Payroll Period	One withholding allowance
Weekly	$19.23
Biweekly	38.46
Semimonthly	41.66
Monthly	83.33
Quarterly	250.00
Semiannually	500.00
Annually	1,000.00
Daily or miscellaneous (each day of the payroll period) .	3.85

TABLE 23
TABLES FOR PERCENTAGE METHOD OF WITHHOLDING

If the Payroll Period with Respect to an Employee is Weekly

(a) SINGLE person—including head of household:

If the amount of wages is:	The amount of income tax to be withheld shall be:
Not over $27	0

Over—	But not over—		of excess over—
$27	—$62	12%	—$27
$62	—$171	$4.20 plus 16%	—$62
$171	—$240	$21.64 plus 20%	—$171
$240	—$325	$35.44 plus 24%	—$240
$325	—$433	$55.84 plus 30%	—$325
$433	—$535	$88.24 plus 34%	—$433
$535		$122.92 plus 37%	—$535

(b) MARRIED person—

If the amount of wages is:	The amount of income tax to be withheld shall be:
Not over $46	0

Over—	But not over—		of excess over—
$46	—$117	12%	—$46
$117	—$230	$8.52 plus 16%	—$117
$230	—$356	$26.60 plus 19%	—$230
$356	—$454	$50.54 plus 24%	—$356
$454	—$556	$74.06 plus 27%	—$454
$556	—$658	$101.60 plus 32%	—$556
$658		$134.24 plus 37%	—$658

If the Payroll Period With Respect to an Employee is Biweekly

(a) SINGLE person—including head of household:

If the amount of wages is:	The amount of income tax to be withheld shall be:
Not over $54	0

Over—	But not over—		of excess over—
$54	—$123	12%	—$54
$123	—$342	$8.28 plus 16%	—$123
$342	—$481	$43.32 plus 20%	—$342
$481	—$650	$71.12 plus 24%	—$481
$650	—$865	$111.68 plus 30%	—$650
$865	—$1,069	$176.18 plus 34%	—$865
$1,069		$245.54 plus 37%	—$1,069

(b) MARRIED person—

If the amount of wages is:	The amount of income tax to be withheld shall be:
Not over $92	0

Over—	But not over—		of excess over—
$92	—$234	12%	—$92
$234	—$461	$17.04 plus 16%	—$234
$461	—$713	$53.36 plus 19%	—$461
$713	—$908	$101.24 plus 24%	—$713
$908	—$1,112	$148.04 plus 27%	—$908
$1,112	—$1,315	$203.12 plus 32%	—$1,112
$1,315		$268.08 plus 37%	—$1,315

If the Payroll Period With Respect to an Employee is Semimonthly

(a) SINGLE person—including head of household:

If the amount of wages is:	The amount of income tax to be withheld shall be:
Not over $58	0

Over—	But not over—		of excess over—
$58	—$133	12%	—$58
$133	—$371	$9.00 plus 16%	—$133
$371	—$521	$47.08 plus 20%	—$371
$521	—$704	$77.08 plus 24%	—$521
$704	—$938	$121.00 plus 30%	—$704
$938	—$1,158	$191.20 plus 34%	—$938
$1,158		$266.00 plus 37%	—$1,158

(b) MARRIED person—

If the amount of wages is:	The amount of income tax to be withheld shall be:
Not over $100	0

Over—	But not over—		of excess over—
$100	—$253	12%	—$100
$253	—$499	$18.36 plus 16%	—$253
$499	—$772	$57.72 plus 19%	—$499
$772	—$983	$109.59 plus 24%	—$772
$983	—$1,204	$160.23 plus 27%	—$983
$1,204	—$1,425	$219.90 plus 32%	—$1,204
$1,425		$290.62 plus 37%	—$1,425

If the Payroll Period With Respect to an Employee is Monthly

(a) SINGLE person—including head of household:

If the amount of wages is:	The amount of income tax to be withheld shall be:
Not over $117	0

Over—	But not over—		of excess over—
$117	—$267	12%	—$117
$267	—$742	$18.00 plus 16%	—$267
$742	—$1,042	$94.00 plus 20%	—$742
$1,042	—$1,408	$154.00 plus 24%	—$1,042
$1,408	—$1,875	$241.84 plus 30%	—$1,408
$1,875	—$2,317	$381.94 plus 34%	—$1,875
$2,317		$532.22 plus 37%	—$2,317

(b) MARRIED person—

If the amount of wages is:	The amount of income tax to be withheld shall be:
Not over $200	0

Over—	But not over—		of excess over—
$200	—$506	12%	—$200
$506	—$998	$36.72 plus 16%	—$506
$998	—$1,545	$115.44 plus 19%	—$998
$1,545	—$1,967	$219.37 plus 24%	—$1,545
$1,967	—$2,408	$320.65 plus 27%	—$1,967
$2,408	—$2,850	$439.72 plus 32%	—$2,408
$2,850		$581.16 plus 37%	—$2,850

TABLE 24
FEDERAL INCOME TAX WITHHOLDING TABLES

SINGLE PERSONS—WEEKLY PAYROLL PERIOD

And the wages are—		And the number of withholding allowances claimed is—										
At least	But less than	0	1	2	3	4	5	6	7	8	9	10 or more
			The amount of income tax to be withheld shall be—								
$0	$27	$0	$0	$0	$0	$0	$0	$0	$0	$0	$0	$0
27	28	.10	0	0	0	0	0	0	0	0	0	0
28	29	.20	0	0	0	0	0	0	0	0	0	0
29	30	.30	0	0	0	0	0	0	0	0	0	0
30	31	.40	0	0	0	0	0	0	0	0	0	0
31	32	.50	0	0	0	0	0	0	0	0	0	0
32	33	.70	0	0	0	0	0	0	0	0	0	0
33	34	.80	0	0	0	0	0	0	0	0	0	0
34	35	.90	0	0	0	0	0	0	0	0	0	0
35	36	1.00	0	0	0	0	0	0	0	0	0	0
36	37	1.10	0	0	0	0	0	0	0	0	0	0
37	38	1.30	0	0	0	0	0	0	0	0	0	0
38	39	1.40	0	0	0	0	0	0	0	0	0	0
39	40	1.50	0	0	0	0	0	0	0	0	0	0
40	41	1.60	0	0	0	0	0	0	0	0	0	0
41	42	1.70	0	0	0	0	0	0	0	0	0	0
42	43	1.90	0	0	0	0	0	0	0	0	0	0
43	44	2.00	0	0	0	0	0	0	0	0	0	0
44	45	2.10	0	0	0	0	0	0	0	0	0	0
45	46	2.20	0	0	0	0	0	0	0	0	0	0
46	47	2.30	0	0	0	0	0	0	0	0	0	0
47	48	2.50	.20	0	0	0	0	0	0	0	0	0
48	49	2.60	.30	0	0	0	0	0	0	0	0	0
49	50	2.70	.40	0	0	0	0	0	0	0	0	0
50	51	2.80	.50	0	0	0	0	0	0	0	0	0
51	52	2.90	.60	0	0	0	0	0	0	0	0	0
52	53	3.10	.80	0	0	0	0	0	0	0	0	0
53	54	3.20	.90	0	0	0	0	0	0	0	0	0
54	55	3.30	1.00	0	0	0	0	0	0	0	0	0
55	56	3.40	1.10	0	0	0	0	0	0	0	0	0
56	57	3.50	1.20	0	0	0	0	0	0	0	0	0
57	58	3.70	1.40	0	0	0	0	0	0	0	0	0
58	59	3.80	1.50	0	0	0	0	0	0	0	0	0
59	60	3.90	1.60	0	0	0	0	0	0	0	0	0
60	62	4.10	1.80	0	0	0	0	0	0	0	0	0
62	64	4.40	2.00	0	0	0	0	0	0	0	0	0
64	66	4.70	2.30	0	0	0	0	0	0	0	0	0
66	68	5.00	2.50	.20	0	0	0	0	0	0	0	0
68	70	5.30	2.70	.40	0	0	0	0	0	0	0	0
70	72	5.70	3.00	.70	0	0	0	0	0	0	0	0
72	74	6.00	3.20	.90	0	0	0	0	0	0	0	0
74	76	6.30	3.50	1.20	0	0	0	0	0	0	0	0
76	78	6.60	3.70	1.40	0	0	0	0	0	0	0	0
78	80	6.90	3.90	1.60	0	0	0	0	0	0	0	0
80	82	7.30	4.20	1.90	0	0	0	0	0	0	0	0
82	84	7.60	4.50	2.10	0	0	0	0	0	0	0	0
84	86	7.90	4.80	2.40	0	0	0	0	0	0	0	0
86	88	8.20	5.20	2.60	.30	0	0	0	0	0	0	0
88	90	8.50	5.50	2.80	.50	0	0	0	0	0	0	0
90	92	8.90	5.80	3.10	.80	0	0	0	0	0	0	0
92	94	9.20	6.10	3.30	1.00	0	0	0	0	0	0	0
94	96	9.50	6.40	3.60	1.20	0	0	0	0	0	0	0
96	98	9.80	6.80	3.80	1.50	0	0	0	0	0	0	0
98	100	10.10	7.10	4.00	1.70	0	0	0	0	0	0	0
100	105	10.70	7.60	4.60	2.10	0	0	0	0	0	0	0
105	110	11.50	8.40	5.40	2.70	.40	0	0	0	0	0	0
110	115	12.30	9.20	6.20	3.30	1.00	0	0	0	0	0	0
115	120	13.10	10.00	7.00	3.90	1.60	0	0	0	0	0	0
120	125	13.90	10.80	7.80	4.70	2.20	0	0	0	0	0	0
125	130	14.70	11.60	8.60	5.50	2.80	.50	0	0	0	0	0
130	135	15.50	12.40	9.40	6.30	3.40	1.10	0	0	0	0	0
135	140	16.30	13.20	10.20	7.10	4.00	1.70	0	0	0	0	0
140	145	17.10	14.00	11.00	7.90	4.80	2.30	0	0	0	0	0
145	150	17.90	14.80	11.80	8.70	5.60	2.90	.60	0	0	0	0
150	160	19.10	16.00	13.00	9.90	6.80	3.80	1.50	0	0	0	0

TABLES T-47

TABLE 24 (cont.)

SINGLE PERSONS—WEEKLY PAYROLL PERIOD

And the wages are—		And the number of withholding allowances claimed is—										
At least	But less than	0	1	2	3	4	5	6	7	8	9	10 or more
			The amount of income tax to be withheld shall be—										
$160	$170	$20.70	$17.60	$14.60	$11.50	$8.40	$5.30	$2.70	$.40	$0	$0	$0
170	180	22.50	19.20	16.20	13.10	10.00	6.90	3.90	1.60	0	0	0
180	190	24.50	20.80	17.80	14.70	11.60	8.50	5.40	2.80	.50	0	0
190	200	26.50	22.60	19.40	16.30	13.20	10.10	7.00	4.00	1.70	0	0
200	210	28.50	24.60	21.00	17.90	14.80	11.70	8.60	5.60	2.90	.60	0
210	220	30.50	26.60	22.80	19.50	16.40	13.30	10.20	7.20	4.10	1.80	0
220	230	32.50	28.60	24.80	21.10	18.00	14.90	11.80	8.80	5.70	3.00	.70
230	240	34.50	30.60	26.80	22.90	19.60	16.50	13.40	10.40	7.30	4.20	1.90
240	250	36.60	32.60	28.80	24.90	21.20	18.10	15.00	12.00	8.90	5.80	3.10
250	260	39.00	34.60	30.80	26.90	23.10	19.70	16.60	13.60	10.50	7.40	4.30
260	270	41.40	36.80	32.80	28.90	25.10	21.30	18.20	15.20	12.10	9.00	5.90
270	280	43.80	39.20	34.80	30.90	27.10	23.20	19.80	16.80	13.70	10.60	7.50
280	290	46.20	41.60	37.00	32.90	29.10	25.20	21.40	18.40	15.30	12.20	9.10
290	300	48.60	44.00	39.40	34.90	31.10	27.20	23.40	20.00	16.90	13.80	10.70
300	310	51.00	46.40	41.80	37.20	33.10	29.20	25.40	21.60	18.50	15.40	12.30
310	320	53.40	48.80	44.20	39.60	35.10	31.20	27.40	23.50	20.10	17.00	13.90
320	330	55.80	51.20	46.60	42.00	37.40	33.20	29.40	25.50	21.70	18.60	15.50
330	340	58.80	53.60	49.00	44.40	39.80	35.20	31.40	27.50	23.70	20.20	17.10
340	350	61.80	56.10	51.40	46.80	42.20	37.60	33.40	29.50	25.70	21.80	18.70
350	360	64.80	59.10	53.80	49.20	44.60	40.00	35.40	31.50	27.70	23.80	20.30
360	370	67.80	62.10	56.30	51.60	47.00	42.40	37.80	33.50	29.70	25.80	22.00
370	380	70.80	65.10	59.30	54.00	49.40	44.80	40.20	35.50	31.70	27.80	24.00
380	390	73.80	68.10	62.30	56.50	51.80	47.20	42.60	37.90	33.70	29.80	26.00
390	400	76.80	71.10	65.30	59.50	54.20	49.60	45.00	40.30	35.70	31.80	28.00
400	410	79.80	74.10	68.30	62.50	56.80	52.00	47.40	42.70	38.10	33.80	30.00
410	420	82.80	77.10	71.30	65.50	59.80	54.40	49.80	45.10	40.50	35.90	32.00
420	430	85.80	80.10	74.30	68.50	62.80	57.00	52.20	47.50	42.90	38.30	34.00
430	440	88.90	83.10	77.30	71.50	65.80	60.00	54.60	49.90	45.30	40.70	36.10
440	450	92.30	86.10	80.30	74.50	68.80	63.00	57.20	52.30	47.70	43.10	38.50
450	460	95.70	89.20	83.30	77.50	71.80	66.00	60.20	54.70	50.10	45.50	40.90
460	470	99.10	92.60	86.30	80.50	74.80	69.00	63.20	57.50	52.50	47.90	43.30
470	480	102.50	96.00	89.50	83.50	77.80	72.00	66.20	60.50	54.90	50.30	45.70
480	490	105.90	99.40	92.90	86.50	80.80	75.00	69.20	63.50	57.70	52.70	48.10
490	500	109.30	102.80	96.30	89.70	83.80	78.00	72.20	66.50	60.70	55.10	50.50
500	510	112.70	106.20	99.70	93.10	86.80	81.00	75.20	69.50	63.70	57.90	52.90
510	520	116.10	109.60	103.10	96.50	90.00	84.00	78.20	72.50	66.70	60.90	55.30
520	530	119.50	113.00	106.50	99.90	93.40	87.00	81.20	75.50	69.70	63.90	58.20
530	540	123.00	116.40	109.90	103.30	96.80	90.20	84.20	78.50	72.70	66.90	61.20
540	550	126.70	119.80	113.30	106.70	100.20	93.60	87.20	81.50	75.70	69.90	64.20
550	560	130.40	123.20	116.70	110.10	103.60	97.00	90.50	84.50	78.70	72.90	67.20
560	570	134.10	126.90	120.10	113.50	107.00	100.40	93.90	87.50	81.70	75.90	70.20
570	580	137.80	130.60	123.50	116.90	110.40	103.80	97.30	90.80	84.70	78.90	73.20
580	590	141.50	134.30	127.20	120.30	113.80	107.20	100.70	94.20	87.70	81.90	76.20
590	600	145.20	138.00	130.90	123.80	117.20	110.60	104.10	97.60	91.00	84.90	79.20
600	610	148.90	141.70	134.60	127.50	120.60	114.00	107.50	101.00	94.40	87.90	82.20
610	620	152.60	145.40	138.30	131.20	124.10	117.40	110.90	104.40	97.80	91.30	85.20
620	630	156.30	149.10	142.00	134.90	127.80	120.80	114.30	107.80	101.20	94.70	88.20
630	640	160.00	152.80	145.70	138.60	131.50	124.40	117.70	111.20	104.60	98.10	91.60
640	650	163.70	156.50	149.40	142.30	135.20	128.10	121.10	114.60	108.00	101.50	95.00
650	660	167.40	160.20	153.10	146.00	138.90	131.80	124.70	118.00	111.40	104.90	98.40
660	670	171.10	163.90	156.80	149.70	142.60	135.50	128.40	121.40	114.80	108.30	101.80
670	680	174.80	167.60	160.50	153.40	146.30	139.20	132.10	124.90	118.20	111.70	105.20
680	690	178.50	171.30	164.20	157.10	150.00	142.90	135.80	128.60	121.60	115.10	108.60
690	700	182.20	175.00	167.90	160.80	153.70	146.60	139.50	132.30	125.20	118.50	112.00
700	710	185.90	178.70	171.60	164.50	157.40	150.30	143.20	136.00	128.90	121.90	115.40
710	720	189.60	182.40	175.30	168.20	161.10	154.00	146.90	139.70	132.60	125.50	118.80
720	730	193.30	186.10	179.00	171.90	164.80	157.70	150.60	143.40	136.30	129.20	122.20
730	740	197.00	189.80	182.70	175.60	168.50	161.40	154.30	147.10	140.00	132.90	125.80
			37 percent of the excess over $740 plus—										
$740 and over		198.80	191.70	184.60	177.50	170.30	163.20	156.10	149.00	141.90	134.80	127.60

TABLE 24 (cont.)

SINGLE PERSONS—MONTHLY PAYROLL PERIOD

And the wages are—		And the number of withholding allowances claimed is—										
At least	But less than	0	1	2	3	4	5	6	7	8	9	10 or more
		The amount of income tax to be withheld shall be—										
$0	$116	$0	$0	$0	$0	$0	$0	$0	$0	$0	$0	$0
116	120	.20	0	0	0	0	0	0	0	0	0	0
120	124	.60	0	0	0	0	0	0	0	0	0	0
124	128	1.10	0	0	0	0	0	0	0	0	0	0
128	132	1.60	0	0	0	0	0	0	0	0	0	0
132	136	2.10	0	0	0	0	0	0	0	0	0	0
136	140	2.60	0	0	0	0	0	0	0	0	0	0
140	144	3.00	0	0	0	0	0	0	0	0	0	0
144	148	3.50	0	0	0	0	0	0	0	0	0	0
148	152	4.00	0	0	0	0	0	0	0	0	0	0
152	156	4.50	0	0	0	0	0	0	0	0	0	0
156	160	5.00	0	0	0	0	0	0	0	0	0	0
160	164	5.40	0	0	0	0	0	0	0	0	0	0
164	168	5.90	0	0	0	0	0	0	0	0	0	0
168	172	6.40	0	0	0	0	0	0	0	0	0	0
172	176	6.90	0	0	0	0	0	0	0	0	0	0
176	180	7.40	0	0	0	0	0	0	0	0	0	0
180	184	7.80	0	0	0	0	0	0	0	0	0	0
184	188	8.30	0	0	0	0	0	0	0	0	0	0
188	192	8.80	0	0	0	0	0	0	0	0	0	0
192	196	9.30	0	0	0	0	0	0	0	0	0	0
196	200	9.80	0	0	0	0	0	0	0	0	0	0
200	204	10.20	.20	0	0	0	0	0	0	0	0	0
204	208	10.70	.70	0	0	0	0	0	0	0	0	0
208	212	11.20	1.20	0	0	0	0	0	0	0	0	0
212	216	11.70	1.70	0	0	0	0	0	0	0	0	0
216	220	12.20	2.20	0	0	0	0	0	0	0	0	0
220	224	12.60	2.60	0	0	0	0	0	0	0	0	0
224	228	13.10	3.10	0	0	0	0	0	0	0	0	0
228	232	13.60	3.60	0	0	0	0	0	0	0	0	0
232	236	14.10	4.10	0	0	0	0	0	0	0	0	0
236	240	14.60	4.60	0	0	0	0	0	0	0	0	0
240	248	15.30	5.30	0	0	0	0	0	0	0	0	0
248	256	16.20	6.20	0	0	0	0	0	0	0	0	0
256	264	17.20	7.20	0	0	0	0	0	0	0	0	0
264	272	18.20	8.20	0	0	0	0	0	0	0	0	0
272	280	19.50	9.10	0	0	0	0	0	0	0	0	0
280	288	20.80	10.10	.10	0	0	0	0	0	0	0	0
288	296	22.10	11.00	1.00	0	0	0	0	0	0	0	0
296	304	23.30	12.00	2.00	0	0	0	0	0	0	0	0
304	312	24.60	13.00	3.00	0	0	0	0	0	0	0	0
312	320	25.90	13.90	3.90	0	0	0	0	0	0	0	0
320	328	27.20	14.90	4.90	0	0	0	0	0	0	0	0
328	336	28.50	15.80	5.80	0	0	0	0	0	0	0	0
336	344	29.70	16.80	6.80	0	0	0	0	0	0	0	0
344	352	31.00	17.80	7.80	0	0	0	0	0	0	0	0
352	360	32.30	19.00	8.70	0	0	0	0	0	0	0	0
360	368	33.60	20.20	9.70	0	0	0	0	0	0	0	0
368	376	34.90	21.50	10.60	.60	0	0	0	0	0	0	0
376	384	36.10	22.80	11.60	1.60	0	0	0	0	0	0	0
384	392	37.40	24.10	12.60	2.60	0	0	0	0	0	0	0
392	400	38.70	25.40	13.50	3.50	0	0	0	0	0	0	0
400	420	40.90	27.60	15.20	5.20	0	0	0	0	0	0	0
420	440	44.10	30.80	17.60	7.60	0	0	0	0	0	0	0
440	460	47.30	34.00	20.70	10.00	0	0	0	0	0	0	0
460	480	50.50	37.20	23.90	12.40	2.40	0	0	0	0	0	0
480	500	53.70	40.40	27.10	14.80	4.80	0	0	0	0	0	0
500	520	56.90	43.60	30.30	17.20	7.20	0	0	0	0	0	0
520	540	60.10	46.80	33.50	20.10	9.60	0	0	0	0	0	0
540	560	63.30	50.00	36.70	23.30	12.00	2.00	0	0	0	0	0
560	580	66.50	53.20	39.90	26.50	14.40	4.40	0	0	0	0	0
580	600	69.70	56.40	43.10	29.70	16.80	6.80	0	0	0	0	0
600	640	74.50	61.20	47.90	34.50	21.20	10.40	.40	0	0	0	0
640	680	80.90	67.60	54.30	40.90	27.60	15.20	5.20	0	0	0	0
680	720	87.30	74.00	60.70	47.30	34.00	20.70	10.00	0	0	0	0
720	760	93.70	80.40	67.10	53.70	40.40	27.10	14.80	4.80	0	0	0
760	800	101.70	86.80	73.50	60.10	46.80	33.50	20.10	9.60	0	0	0
800	840	109.70	93.20	79.90	66.50	53.20	39.90	26.50	14.40	4.40	0	0
840	880	117.70	101.00	86.30	72.90	59.60	46.30	32.90	19.60	9.20	0	0
880	920	125.70	109.00	92.70	79.30	66.00	52.70	39.30	26.00	14.00	4.00	0

TABLES **T-49**

TABLE 24 (cont.)

SINGLE PERSONS—MONTHLY PAYROLL PERIOD

And the wages are—		And the number of withholding allowances claimed is—									
At least	But less than	0	1	2	3	4	5	6	7	8	9	10 or more
		The amount of income tax to be withheld shall be—									
$920	$960	$133.70	$117.00	$100.30	$85.70	$72.40	$59.10	$45.70	$32.40	$19.10	$8.80	$0
960	1,000	141.70	125.00	108.30	92.10	78.80	65.50	52.10	38.80	25.50	13.60	3.60
1,000	1,040	149.70	133.00	116.30	99.70	85.20	71.90	58.50	45.20	31.90	18.50	8.40
1,040	1,080	158.40	141.00	124.30	107.70	91.60	78.30	64.90	51.60	38.30	24.90	13.20
1,080	1,120	168.00	149.00	132.30	115.70	99.00	84.70	71.30	58.00	44.70	31.30	18.00
1,120	1,160	177.60	157.60	140.30	123.70	107.00	91.10	77.70	64.40	51.10	37.70	24.40
1,160	1,200	187.20	167.20	148.30	131.70	115.00	98.30	84.10	70.80	57.50	44.10	30.80
1,200	1,240	196.80	176.80	156.80	139.70	123.00	106.30	90.50	77.20	63.90	50.50	37.20
1,240	1,280	206.40	186.40	166.40	147.70	131.00	114.30	97.70	83.60	70.30	56.90	43.60
1,280	1,320	216.00	196.00	176.00	156.00	139.00	122.30	105.70	90.00	76.70	63.30	50.00
1,320	1,360	225.60	205.60	185.60	165.60	147.00	130.30	113.70	97.00	83.10	69.70	56.40
1,360	1,400	235.20	215.20	195.20	175.20	155.20	138.30	121.70	105.00	89.50	76.10	62.80
1,400	1,440	245.50	224.80	204.80	184.80	164.80	146.30	129.70	113.00	96.30	82.50	69.20
1,440	1,480	257.50	234.40	214.40	194.40	174.40	154.40	137.70	121.00	104.30	88.90	75.60
1,480	1,520	269.50	244.50	224.00	204.00	184.00	164.00	145.70	129.00	112.30	95.70	82.00
1,520	1,560	281.50	256.50	233.60	213.60	193.60	173.60	153.70	137.00	120.30	103.70	88.40
1,560	1,600	293.50	268.50	243.50	223.20	203.20	183.20	163.20	145.00	128.30	111.70	95.00
1,600	1,640	305.50	280.50	255.50	232.80	212.80	192.80	172.80	153.00	136.30	119.70	103.00
1,640	1,680	317.50	292.50	267.50	242.50	222.40	202.40	182.40	162.40	144.30	127.70	111.00
1,680	1,720	329.50	304.50	279.50	254.50	232.00	212.00	192.00	172.00	152.30	135.70	119.00
1,720	1,760	341.50	316.50	291.50	266.50	241.60	221.60	201.60	181.60	161.60	143.70	127.00
1,760	1,800	353.50	328.50	303.50	278.50	253.50	231.20	211.20	191.20	171.20	151.70	135.00
1,800	1,840	365.50	340.50	315.50	290.50	265.50	240.80	220.80	200.80	180.80	160.80	143.00
1,840	1,880	377.50	352.50	327.50	302.50	277.50	252.50	230.40	210.40	190.40	170.40	151.00
1,880	1,920	390.50	364.50	339.50	314.50	289.50	264.50	240.00	220.00	200.00	180.00	160.00
1,920	1,960	404.10	376.50	351.50	326.50	301.50	276.50	251.50	229.60	209.60	189.60	169.60
1,960	2,000	417.70	389.40	363.50	338.50	313.50	288.50	263.50	239.20	219.20	199.20	179.20
2,000	2,040	431.30	403.00	375.50	350.50	325.50	300.50	275.50	250.50	228.80	208.80	188.80
2,040	2,080	444.90	416.60	388.20	362.50	337.50	312.50	287.50	262.50	238.40	218.40	198.40
2,080	2,120	458.50	430.20	401.80	374.50	349.50	324.50	299.50	274.50	249.50	228.00	208.00
2,120	2,160	472.10	443.80	415.40	387.10	361.50	336.50	311.50	286.50	261.50	237.60	217.60
2,160	2,200	485.70	457.40	429.00	400.70	373.50	348.50	323.50	298.50	273.50	248.50	227.20
2,200	2,240	499.30	471.00	442.60	414.30	386.00	360.50	335.50	310.50	285.50	260.50	236.80
2,240	2,280	512.90	484.60	456.20	427.90	399.60	372.50	347.50	322.50	297.50	272.50	247.50
2,280	2,320	526.50	498.20	469.80	441.50	413.20	384.80	359.50	334.50	309.50	284.50	259.50
2,320	2,360	540.80	511.80	483.40	455.10	426.80	398.40	371.50	346.50	321.50	296.50	271.50
2,360	2,400	555.60	525.40	497.00	468.70	440.40	412.00	383.70	358.50	333.50	308.50	283.50
2,400	2,440	570.40	539.60	510.60	482.30	454.00	425.60	397.30	370.50	345.50	320.50	295.50
2,440	2,480	585.20	554.40	524.20	495.90	467.60	439.20	410.90	382.60	357.50	332.50	307.50
2,480	2,520	600.00	569.20	538.30	509.50	481.20	452.80	424.50	396.20	369.50	344.50	319.50
2,520	2,560	614.80	584.00	553.10	523.10	494.80	466.40	438.10	409.80	381.50	356.50	331.50
2,560	2,600	629.60	598.80	567.90	537.10	508.40	480.00	451.70	423.40	395.00	368.50	343.50
2,600	2,640	644.40	613.60	582.70	551.90	522.00	493.60	465.30	437.00	408.60	380.50	355.50
2,640	2,680	659.20	628.40	597.50	566.70	535.90	507.20	478.90	450.60	422.20	393.90	367.50
2,680	2,720	674.00	643.20	612.30	581.50	550.70	520.80	492.50	464.20	435.80	407.50	379.50
2,720	2,760	688.80	658.00	627.10	596.30	565.50	534.60	506.10	477.80	449.40	421.10	392.80
2,760	2,800	703.60	672.80	641.90	611.10	580.30	549.40	519.70	491.40	463.00	434.70	406.40
2,800	2,840	718.40	687.60	656.70	625.90	595.10	564.20	533.40	505.00	476.60	448.30	420.00
2,840	2,880	733.20	702.40	671.50	640.70	609.90	579.00	548.20	518.60	490.20	461.90	433.60
2,880	2,920	748.00	717.20	686.30	655.50	624.70	593.80	563.00	532.20	503.80	475.50	447.20
2,920	2,960	762.80	732.00	701.10	670.30	639.50	608.60	577.80	547.00	517.40	489.10	460.80
2,960	3,000	777.60	746.80	715.90	685.10	654.30	623.40	592.60	561.80	531.00	502.70	474.40
3,000	3,040	792.40	761.60	730.70	699.90	669.10	638.20	607.40	576.60	545.70	516.30	488.00
3,040	3,080	807.20	776.40	745.50	714.70	683.90	653.00	622.20	591.40	560.50	529.90	501.60
3,080	3,120	822.00	791.20	760.30	729.50	698.70	667.80	637.00	606.20	575.30	544.50	515.20
3,120	3,160	836.80	806.00	775.10	744.30	713.50	682.60	651.80	621.00	590.10	559.30	528.80
3,160	3,200	851.60	820.80	789.90	759.10	728.30	697.40	666.60	635.80	604.90	574.10	543.30
		37 percent of the excess over $3,200 plus—									
$3,200 and over		859.00	828.20	797.30	766.50	735.70	704.80	674.00	643.20	612.30	581.50	550.70

TABLE 24 (cont.)

MARRIED PERSONS—WEEKLY PAYROLL PERIOD

And the wages are—		And the number of withholding allowances claimed is—										
At least	But less than	0	1	2	3	4	5	6	7	8	9	10 or more
		The amount of income tax to be withheld shall be—										
$0	$47	$0	$0	$0	$0	$0	$0	$0	$0	$0	$0	$0
47	48	.20	0	0	0	0	0	0	0	0	0	0
48	49	.30	0	0	0	0	0	0	0	0	0	0
49	50	.40	0	0	0	0	0	0	0	0	0	0
50	51	.50	0	0	0	0	0	0	0	0	0	0
51	52	.60	0	0	0	0	0	0	0	0	0	0
52	53	.80	0	0	0	0	0	0	0	0	0	0
53	54	.90	0	0	0	0	0	0	0	0	0	0
54	55	1.00	0	0	0	0	0	0	0	0	0	0
55	56	1.10	0	0	0	0	0	0	0	0	0	0
56	57	1.20	0	0	0	0	0	0	0	0	0	0
57	58	1.40	0	0	0	0	0	0	0	0	0	0
58	59	1.50	0	0	0	0	0	0	0	0	0	0
59	60	1.60	0	0	0	0	0	0	0	0	0	0
60	62	1.80	0	0	0	0	0	0	0	0	0	0
62	64	2.00	0	0	0	0	0	0	0	0	0	0
64	66	2.30	0	0	0	0	0	0	0	0	0	0
66	68	2.50	.20	0	0	0	0	0	0	0	0	0
68	70	2.70	.40	0	0	0	0	0	0	0	0	0
70	72	3.00	.70	0	0	0	0	0	0	0	0	0
72	74	3.20	.90	0	0	0	0	0	0	0	0	0
74	76	3.50	1.20	0	0	0	0	0	0	0	0	0
76	78	3.70	1.40	0	0	0	0	0	0	0	0	0
78	80	3.90	1.60	0	0	0	0	0	0	0	0	0
80	82	4.20	1.90	0	0	0	0	0	0	0	0	0
82	84	4.40	2.10	0	0	0	0	0	0	0	0	0
84	86	4.70	2.40	0	0	0	0	0	0	0	0	0
86	88	4.90	2.60	.30	0	0	0	0	0	0	0	0
88	90	5.10	2.80	.50	0	0	0	0	0	0	0	0
90	92	5.40	3.10	.80	0	0	0	0	0	0	0	0
92	94	5.60	3.30	1.00	0	0	0	0	0	0	0	0
94	96	5.90	3.60	1.20	0	0	0	0	0	0	0	0
96	98	6.10	3.80	1.50	0	0	0	0	0	0	0	0
98	100	6.30	4.00	1.70	0	0	0	0	0	0	0	0
100	105	6.80	4.50	2.10	0	0	0	0	0	0	0	0
105	110	7.40	5.10	2.70	.40	0	0	0	0	0	0	0
110	115	8.00	5.70	3.30	1.00	0	0	0	0	0	0	0
115	120	8.60	6.30	3.90	1.60	0	0	0	0	0	0	0
120	125	9.40	6.90	4.50	2.20	0	0	0	0	0	0	0
125	130	10.20	7.50	5.10	2.80	.50	0	0	0	0	0	0
130	135	11.00	8.10	5.70	3.40	1.10	0	0	0	0	0	0
135	140	11.80	8.70	6.30	4.00	1.70	0	0	0	0	0	0
140	145	12.60	9.50	6.90	4.60	2.30	0	0	0	0	0	0
145	150	13.40	10.30	7.50	5.20	2.90	.60	0	0	0	0	0
150	160	14.60	11.50	8.40	6.10	3.80	1.50	0	0	0	0	0
160	170	16.20	13.10	10.00	7.30	5.00	2.70	.40	0	0	0	0
170	180	17.80	14.70	11.60	8.60	6.20	3.90	1.60	0	0	0	0
180	190	19.40	16.30	13.20	10.20	7.40	5.10	2.80	.50	0	0	0
190	200	21.00	17.90	14.80	11.80	8.70	6.30	4.00	1.70	0	0	0
200	210	22.60	19.50	16.40	13.40	10.30	7.50	5.20	2.90	.60	0	0
210	220	24.20	21.10	18.00	15.00	11.90	8.80	6.40	4.10	1.80	0	0
220	230	25.80	22.70	19.60	16.60	13.50	10.40	7.60	5.30	3.00	.70	0
230	240	27.50	24.30	21.20	18.20	15.10	12.00	8.90	6.50	4.20	1.90	0
240	250	29.40	25.90	22.80	19.80	16.70	13.60	10.50	7.70	5.40	3.10	.80
250	260	31.30	27.70	24.40	21.40	18.30	15.20	12.10	9.10	6.60	4.30	2.00
260	270	33.20	29.60	26.00	23.00	19.90	16.80	13.70	10.70	7.80	5.50	3.20
270	280	35.10	31.50	27.80	24.60	21.50	18.40	15.30	12.30	9.20	6.70	4.40
280	290	37.00	33.40	29.70	26.20	23.10	20.00	16.90	13.90	10.80	7.90	5.60
290	300	38.90	35.30	31.60	28.00	24.70	21.60	18.50	15.50	12.40	9.30	6.80
300	310	40.80	37.20	33.50	29.90	26.30	23.20	20.10	17.10	14.00	10.90	8.00

TABLE 24 (cont.)

MARRIED PERSONS—WEEKLY PAYROLL PERIOD

And the wages are—		And the number of withholding allowances claimed is—										
At least	But less than	0	1	2	3	4	5	6	7	8	9	10 or more
		The amount of income tax to be withheld shall be—										
$310	$320	$42.70	$39.10	$35.40	$31.80	$28.10	$24.80	$21.70	$18.70	$15.60	$12.50	$9.40
320	330	44.60	41.00	37.30	33.70	30.00	26.40	23.30	20.30	17.20	14.10	11.00
330	340	46.50	42.90	39.20	35.60	31.90	28.30	24.90	21.90	18.80	15.70	12.60
340	350	48.40	44.80	41.10	37.50	33.80	30.20	26.50	23.50	20.40	17.30	14.20
350	360	50.30	46.70	43.00	39.40	35.70	32.10	28.40	25.10	22.00	18.90	15.80
360	370	52.70	48.60	44.90	41.30	37.60	34.00	30.30	26.70	23.60	20.50	17.40
370	380	55.10	50.50	46.80	43.20	39.50	35.90	32.20	28.60	25.20	22.10	19.00
380	390	57.50	52.80	48.70	45.10	41.40	37.80	34.10	30.50	26.80	23.70	20.60
390	400	59.90	55.20	50.60	47.00	43.30	39.70	36.00	32.40	28.70	25.30	22.20
400	410	62.30	57.60	53.00	48.90	45.20	41.60	37.90	34.30	30.60	26.90	23.80
410	420	64.70	60.00	55.40	50.80	47.10	43.50	39.80	36.20	32.50	28.80	25.40
420	430	67.10	62.40	57.80	53.20	49.00	45.40	41.70	38.10	34.40	30.70	27.10
430	440	69.50	64.80	60.20	55.60	51.00	47.30	43.60	40.00	36.30	32.60	29.00
440	450	71.90	67.20	62.60	58.00	53.40	49.20	45.50	41.90	38.20	34.50	30.90
450	460	74.30	69.60	65.00	60.40	55.80	51.20	47.40	43.80	40.10	36.40	32.80
460	470	77.00	72.00	67.40	62.80	58.20	53.60	49.30	45.70	42.00	38.30	34.70
470	480	79.70	74.50	69.80	65.20	60.60	56.00	51.40	47.60	43.90	40.20	36.60
480	490	82.40	77.20	72.20	67.60	63.00	58.40	53.80	49.50	45.80	42.10	38.50
490	500	85.10	79.90	74.70	70.00	65.40	60.80	56.20	51.60	47.70	44.00	40.40
500	510	87.80	82.60	77.40	72.40	67.80	63.20	58.60	54.00	49.60	45.90	42.30
510	520	90.50	85.30	80.10	74.90	70.20	65.60	61.00	56.40	51.70	47.80	44.20
520	530	93.20	88.00	82.80	77.60	72.60	68.00	63.40	58.80	54.10	49.70	46.10
530	540	95.90	90.70	85.50	80.30	75.10	70.40	65.80	61.20	56.50	51.90	48.00
540	550	98.60	93.40	88.20	83.00	77.80	72.80	68.20	63.60	58.90	54.30	49.90
550	560	101.30	96.10	90.90	85.70	80.50	75.30	70.60	66.00	61.30	56.70	52.10
560	570	104.50	98.80	93.60	88.40	83.20	78.00	73.00	68.40	63.70	59.10	54.50
570	580	107.70	101.50	96.30	91.10	85.90	80.70	75.50	70.80	66.10	61.50	56.90
580	590	110.90	104.70	99.00	93.80	88.60	83.40	78.20	73.20	68.50	63.90	59.30
590	600	114.10	107.90	101.70	96.50	91.30	86.10	80.90	75.70	70.90	66.30	61.70
600	610	117.30	111.10	104.90	99.20	94.00	88.80	83.60	78.40	73.30	68.70	64.10
610	620	120.50	114.30	108.10	102.00	96.70	91.50	86.30	81.10	76.00	71.10	66.50
620	630	123.70	117.50	111.30	105.20	99.40	94.20	89.00	83.80	78.70	73.50	68.90
630	640	126.90	120.70	114.50	108.40	102.20	96.90	91.70	86.50	81.40	76.20	71.30
640	650	130.10	123.90	117.70	111.60	105.40	99.60	94.40	89.20	84.10	78.90	73.70
650	660	133.30	127.10	120.90	114.80	108.60	102.50	97.10	91.90	86.80	81.60	76.40
660	670	136.80	130.30	124.10	118.00	111.80	105.70	99.80	94.60	89.50	84.30	79.10
670	680	140.50	133.50	127.30	121.20	115.00	108.90	102.70	97.30	92.20	87.00	81.80
680	690	144.20	137.10	130.50	124.40	118.20	112.10	105.90	100.00	94.90	89.70	84.50
690	700	147.90	140.80	133.70	127.60	121.40	115.30	109.10	103.00	97.60	92.40	87.20
700	710	151.60	144.50	137.40	130.80	124.60	118.50	112.30	106.20	100.30	95.10	89.90
710	720	155.30	148.20	141.10	134.00	127.80	121.70	115.50	109.40	103.20	97.80	92.60
720	730	159.00	151.90	144.80	137.70	131.00	124.90	118.70	112.60	106.40	100.50	95.30
730	740	162.70	155.60	148.50	141.40	134.30	128.10	121.90	115.80	109.60	103.50	98.00
740	750	166.40	159.30	152.20	145.10	138.00	131.30	125.10	119.00	112.80	106.70	100.70
750	760	170.10	163.00	155.90	148.80	141.70	134.50	128.30	122.20	116.00	109.90	103.70
760	770	173.80	166.70	159.60	152.50	145.40	138.20	131.50	125.40	119.20	113.10	106.90
770	780	177.50	170.40	163.30	156.20	149.10	141.90	134.80	128.60	122.40	116.30	110.10
780	790	181.20	174.10	167.00	159.90	152.80	145.60	138.50	131.80	125.60	119.50	113.30
790	800	184.90	177.80	170.70	163.60	156.50	149.30	142.20	135.10	128.80	122.70	116.50
800	810	188.60	181.50	174.40	167.30	160.20	153.00	145.90	138.80	132.00	125.90	119.70
810	820	192.30	185.20	178.10	171.00	163.90	156.70	149.60	142.50	135.40	129.10	122.90
820	830	196.00	188.90	181.80	174.70	167.60	160.40	153.30	146.20	139.10	132.30	126.10
830	840	199.70	192.60	185.50	178.40	171.30	164.10	157.00	149.90	142.80	135.70	129.30
840	850	203.40	196.30	189.20	182.10	175.00	167.80	160.70	153.60	146.50	139.40	132.50
850	860	207.10	200.00	192.90	185.80	178.70	171.50	164.40	157.30	150.20	143.10	136.00
		37 percent of the excess over $860 plus—										
$860 and over		209.00	201.90	194.70	187.60	180.50	173.40	166.30	159.20	152.00	144.90	137.80

T-52 TABLES

TABLE 24 (cont.)

MARRIED PERSONS—MONTHLY PAYROLL PERIOD

And the wages are—		And the number of withholding allowances claimed is—										
At least	But less than	0	1	2	3	4	5	6	7	8	9	10 or more
			The amount of income tax to be withheld shall be—										
$0	$200	$0	$0	$0	$0	$0	$0	$0	$0	$0	$0	$0
200	204	.20	0	0	0	0	0	0	0	0	0	0
204	208	.70	0	0	0	0	0	0	0	0	0	0
208	212	1.20	0	0	0	0	0	0	0	0	0	0
212	216	1.70	0	0	0	0	0	0	0	0	0	0
216	220	2.20	0	0	0	0	0	0	0	0	0	0
220	224	2.60	0	0	0	0	0	0	0	0	0	0
224	228	3.10	0	0	0	0	0	0	0	0	0	0
228	232	3.60	0	0	0	0	0	0	0	0	0	0
232	236	4.10	0	0	0	0	0	0	0	0	0	0
236	240	4.60	0	0	0	0	0	0	0	0	0	0
240	248	5.30	0	0	0	0	0	0	0	0	0	0
248	256	6.20	0	0	0	0	0	0	0	0	0	0
256	264	7.20	0	0	0	0	0	0	0	0	0	0
264	272	8.20	0	0	0	0	0	0	0	0	0	0
272	280	9.10	0	0	0	0	0	0	0	0	0	0
280	288	10.10	.10	0	0	0	0	0	0	0	0	0
288	296	11.00	1.00	0	0	0	0	0	0	0	0	0
296	304	12.00	2.00	0	0	0	0	0	0	0	0	0
304	312	13.00	3.00	0	0	0	0	0	0	0	0	0
312	320	13.90	3.90	0	0	0	0	0	0	0	0	0
320	328	14.90	4.90	0	0	0	0	0	0	0	0	0
328	336	15.80	5.80	0	0	0	0	0	0	0	0	0
336	344	16.80	6.80	0	0	0	0	0	0	0	0	0
344	352	17.80	7.80	0	0	0	0	0	0	0	0	0
352	360	18.70	8.70	0	0	0	0	0	0	0	0	0
360	368	19.70	9.70	0	0	0	0	0	0	0	0	0
368	376	20.60	10.60	.60	0	0	0	0	0	0	0	0
376	384	21.60	11.60	1.60	0	0	0	0	0	0	0	0
384	392	22.60	12.60	2.60	0	0	0	0	0	0	0	0
392	400	23.50	13.50	3.50	0	0	0	0	0	0	0	0
400	420	25.20	15.20	5.20	0	0	0	0	0	0	0	0
420	440	27.60	17.60	7.60	0	0	0	0	0	0	0	0
440	460	30.00	20.00	10.00	0	0	0	0	0	0	0	0
460	480	32.40	22.40	12.40	2.40	0	0	0	0	0	0	0
480	500	34.80	24.80	14.80	4.80	0	0	0	0	0	0	0
500	520	37.40	27.20	17.20	7.20	0	0	0	0	0	0	0
520	540	40.60	29.60	19.60	9.60	0	0	0	0	0	0	0
540	560	43.80	32.00	22.00	12.00	2.00	0	0	0	0	0	0
560	580	47.00	34.40	24.40	14.40	4.40	0	0	0	0	0	0
580	600	50.20	36.80	26.80	16.80	6.80	0	0	0	0	0	0
600	640	55.00	41.60	30.40	20.40	10.40	.40	0	0	0	0	0
640	680	61.40	48.00	35.20	25.20	15.20	5.20	0	0	0	0	0
680	720	67.80	54.40	41.10	30.00	20.00	10.00	0	0	0	0	0
720	760	74.20	60.80	47.50	34.80	24.80	14.80	4.80	0	0	0	0
760	800	80.60	67.20	53.90	40.60	29.60	19.60	9.60	0	0	0	0
800	840	87.00	73.60	60.30	47.00	34.40	24.40	14.40	4.40	0	0	0
840	880	93.40	80.00	66.70	53.40	40.00	29.20	19.20	9.20	0	0	0
880	920	99.80	86.40	73.10	59.80	46.40	34.00	24.00	14.00	4.00	0	0
920	960	106.20	92.80	79.50	66.20	52.80	39.50	28.80	18.80	8.80	0	0
960	1,000	112.60	99.20	85.90	72.60	59.20	45.90	33.60	23.60	13.60	3.60	0
1,000	1,040	119.60	105.60	92.30	79.00	65.60	52.30	39.00	28.40	18.40	8.40	0
1,040	1,080	127.20	112.00	98.70	85.40	72.00	58.70	45.40	33.20	23.20	13.20	3.20
1,080	1,120	134.80	119.00	105.10	91.80	78.40	65.10	51.80	38.40	28.00	18.00	8.00
1,120	1,160	142.40	126.60	111.50	98.20	84.80	71.50	58.20	44.80	32.80	22.80	12.80
1,160	1,200	150.00	134.20	118.30	104.60	91.20	77.90	64.60	51.20	37.90	27.60	17.60
1,200	1,240	157.60	141.80	125.90	111.00	97.60	84.30	71.00	57.60	44.30	32.40	22.40
1,240	1,280	165.20	149.40	133.50	117.70	104.00	90.70	77.40	64.00	50.70	37.40	27.20
1,280	1,320	172.80	157.00	141.10	125.30	110.40	97.10	83.80	70.40	57.10	43.80	32.00
1,320	1,360	180.40	164.60	148.70	132.90	117.10	103.50	90.20	76.80	63.50	50.20	36.80
1,360	1,400	188.00	172.20	156.30	140.50	124.70	109.90	96.60	83.20	69.90	56.60	43.20
1,400	1,440	195.60	179.80	163.90	148.10	132.30	116.40	103.00	89.60	76.30	63.00	49.60
1,440	1,480	203.20	187.40	171.50	155.70	139.90	124.00	109.40	96.00	82.70	69.40	56.00
1,480	1,520	210.80	195.00	179.10	163.30	147.50	131.60	115.80	102.40	89.10	75.80	62.40
1,520	1,560	218.40	202.60	186.70	170.90	155.10	139.20	123.40	108.80	95.50	82.20	68.80

TABLE 24 (cont.)

MARRIED PERSONS—MONTHLY PAYROLL PERIOD

And the wages are—		And the number of withholding allowances claimed is—										
At least	But less than	0	1	2	3	4	5	6	7	8	9	10 or more
		The amount of income tax to be withheld shall be—										
$1,560	$1,600	$227.80	$210.20	$194.30	$178.50	$162.70	$146.80	$131.00	$115.20	$101.90	$88.60	$75.20
1,600	1,640	237.40	217.80	201.90	186.10	170.30	154.40	138.60	122.80	108.30	95.00	81.60
1,640	1,680	247.00	227.00	209.50	193.70	177.90	162.00	146.20	130.40	114.70	101.40	88.00
1,680	1,720	256.60	236.60	217.10	201.30	185.50	169.60	153.80	138.00	122.10	107.80	94.40
1,720	1,760	266.20	246.20	226.20	208.90	193.10	177.20	161.40	145.60	129.70	114.20	100.80
1,760	1,800	275.80	255.80	235.80	216.50	200.70	184.80	169.00	153.20	137.30	121.50	107.20
1,800	1,840	285.40	265.40	245.40	225.40	208.30	192.40	176.60	160.80	144.90	129.10	113.60
1,840	1,880	295.00	275.00	255.00	235.00	215.90	200.00	184.20	168.40	152.50	136.70	120.90
1,880	1,920	304.60	284.60	264.60	244.60	224.60	207.60	191.80	176.00	160.10	144.30	128.50
1,920	1,960	314.20	294.20	274.20	254.20	234.20	215.20	199.40	183.60	167.70	151.90	136.10
1,960	2,000	324.20	303.80	283.80	263.80	243.80	223.80	207.00	191.20	175.30	159.50	143.70
2,000	2,040	335.00	313.40	293.40	273.40	253.40	233.40	214.60	198.80	182.90	167.10	151.30
2,040	2,080	345.80	323.30	303.00	283.00	263.00	243.00	223.00	206.40	190.50	174.70	158.90
2,080	2,120	356.60	334.10	312.60	292.60	272.60	252.60	232.60	214.00	198.10	182.30	166.50
2,120	2,160	367.40	344.90	322.40	302.20	282.20	262.20	242.20	222.20	205.70	189.90	174.10
2,160	2,200	378.20	355.70	333.20	311.80	291.80	271.80	251.80	231.80	213.30	197.50	181.70
2,200	2,240	389.00	366.50	344.00	321.50	301.40	281.40	261.40	241.40	221.40	205.10	189.30
2,240	2,280	399.80	377.30	354.80	332.30	311.00	291.00	271.00	251.00	231.00	212.70	196.90
2,280	2,320	410.60	388.10	365.60	343.10	320.60	300.60	280.60	260.60	240.60	220.60	204.50
2,320	2,360	421.40	398.90	376.40	353.90	331.40	310.20	290.20	270.20	250.20	230.20	212.10
2,360	2,400	432.20	409.70	387.20	364.70	342.20	319.80	299.80	279.80	259.80	239.80	219.80
2,400	2,440	443.60	420.50	398.00	375.50	353.00	330.50	309.40	289.40	269.40	249.40	229.40
2,440	2,480	456.40	431.30	408.80	386.30	363.80	341.30	319.00	299.00	279.00	259.00	239.00
2,480	2,520	469.20	442.50	419.60	397.10	374.60	352.10	329.60	308.60	288.60	268.60	248.60
2,520	2,560	482.00	455.30	430.40	407.90	385.40	362.90	340.40	318.20	298.20	278.20	258.20
2,560	2,600	494.80	468.10	441.40	418.70	396.20	373.70	351.20	328.70	307.80	287.80	267.80
2,600	2,640	507.60	480.90	454.20	429.50	407.00	384.50	362.00	339.50	317.40	297.40	277.40
2,640	2,680	520.40	493.70	467.00	440.40	417.80	395.30	372.80	350.30	327.80	307.00	287.00
2,680	2,720	533.20	506.50	479.80	453.20	428.60	406.10	383.60	361.10	338.60	316.60	296.60
2,720	2,760	546.00	519.30	492.60	466.00	439.40	416.90	394.40	371.90	349.40	326.90	306.20
2,760	2,800	558.80	532.10	505.40	478.80	452.10	427.70	405.20	382.70	360.20	337.70	315.80
2,800	2,840	571.60	544.90	518.20	491.60	464.90	438.50	416.00	393.50	371.00	348.50	326.00
2,840	2,880	584.90	557.70	531.00	504.40	477.70	451.00	426.80	404.30	381.80	359.30	336.80
2,880	2,920	599.70	570.50	543.80	517.20	490.50	463.80	437.60	415.10	392.60	370.10	347.60
2,920	2,960	614.50	583.60	556.60	530.00	503.30	476.60	450.00	425.90	403.40	380.90	358.40
2,960	3,000	629.30	598.40	569.40	542.80	516.10	489.40	462.80	436.70	414.20	391.70	369.20
3,000	3,040	644.10	613.20	582.40	555.60	528.90	502.20	475.60	448.90	425.00	402.50	380.00
3,040	3,080	658.90	628.00	597.20	568.40	541.70	515.00	488.40	461.70	435.80	413.30	390.80
3,080	3,120	673.70	642.80	612.00	581.20	554.50	527.80	501.20	474.50	447.80	424.10	401.60
3,120	3,160	688.50	657.60	626.80	596.00	567.30	540.60	514.00	487.30	460.60	434.90	412.40
3,160	3,200	703.30	672.40	641.60	610.80	580.10	553.40	526.80	500.10	473.40	446.80	423.20
3,200	3,240	718.10	687.20	656.40	625.60	594.70	566.20	539.60	512.90	486.20	459.60	434.00
3,240	3,280	732.90	702.00	671.20	640.40	609.50	579.00	552.40	525.70	499.00	472.40	445.70
3,280	3,320	747.70	716.80	686.00	655.20	624.30	593.50	565.20	538.50	511.80	485.20	458.50
3,320	3,360	762.50	731.60	700.80	670.00	639.10	608.30	578.00	551.30	524.60	498.00	471.30
3,360	3,400	777.30	746.40	715.60	684.80	653.90	623.10	592.30	564.10	537.40	510.80	484.10
3,400	3,440	792.10	761.20	730.40	699.60	668.70	637.90	607.10	576.90	550.20	523.60	496.90
3,440	3,480	806.90	776.00	745.20	714.40	683.50	652.70	621.90	591.00	563.00	536.40	509.70
3,480	3,520	821.70	790.80	760.00	729.20	698.30	667.50	636.70	605.80	575.80	549.20	522.50
3,520	3,560	836.50	805.60	774.80	744.00	713.10	682.30	651.50	620.60	589.80	562.00	535.30
3,560	3,600	851.30	820.40	789.60	758.80	727.90	697.10	666.30	635.40	604.60	574.80	548.10
3,600	3,640	866.10	835.20	804.40	773.60	742.70	711.90	681.10	650.20	619.40	588.60	560.90
3,640	3,680	880.90	850.00	819.20	788.40	757.50	726.70	695.90	665.00	634.20	603.40	573.70
3,680	3,720	895.70	864.80	834.00	803.20	772.30	741.50	710.70	679.80	649.00	618.20	587.30
		37 percent of the excess over $3,720 plus—										
$3,720 and over		903.10	872.20	841.40	810.60	779.70	748.90	718.10	687.20	656.40	625.60	594.70

ANSWERS

CHAPTER 1

MARGIN EXERCISES, SECTION 1.1, pp. 2–4

1. Twenty-four **2.** Thirty-seven **3.** Eighty-eight **4.** 5 billion, 674 million, 316 thousand, 997 **5.** 220 million, 456 thousand, 203
6. Five billion, six hundred seventy-four million, three hundred sixteen thousand, nine hundred ninety-seven
7. Two hundred twenty million, four hundred fifty-six thousand, two hundred three **8.** 69 **9.** 1159 **10.** 10,787 **11.** 14,944
12. 8258 **13.** 5315 kWh **14.** $749

EXERCISE SET 1.1, pp. 5–6

1. Thirty-eight **3.** Seventy-six **5.** 56 thousand, 789 **7.** 7 billion, 894 million, 556 thousand, 745
9. Fifty-six thousand, seven hundred eighty-nine
11. Seven billion, eight hundred ninety-four million, five hundred fifty-six thousand, seven hundred forty-five **13.** 23
15. 108 **17.** 876 **19.** $84,211 **21.** 1034 **23.** 1257 **25.** 9309 **27.** 15,511 **29.** 78,666 **31.** 166,572 **33.** 2204 **35.** 6385
37. 446 kWh **39.** $6888 **41.** 182 **43.** $2527 **45.** $16,266 **47.** $191,690

MARGIN EXERCISES, SECTION 1.2, pp. 7–10

1. 6 **2.** 7 **3.** 8 **4.** 174 **5.** 43 **6.** 5811 **7.** 478 **8.** 90 **9.** 4742 **10.** 381 **11.** 779 **12.** 1236 **13.** 3387 **14.** 4585
15. $1375 **16.** $741

EXERCISE SET 1.2, pp. 11–12

1. 11 **3.** 16 **5.** 23 **7.** 16 **9.** 572 **11.** 26 **13.** 408 **15.** 185 **17.** 4011 **19.** 3486 **21.** 7732 **23.** 36 **25.** 301
27. 5674 **29.** 38,379 **31.** 22,555 **33.** $1655 **35.** $857 **37.** 5508 **39.** $10,994 **41.** $2615 **43.** $28,789,088
45. 58 is incorrect. It should be 59.

MARGIN EXERCISES, SECTION 1.3, pp. 13–16

1. 28 **2.** 40 **3.** 63 **4.** 3055 **5.** 6188 **6.** 33,423 **7.** 425,034 **8.** 263,948 **9.** 50,122,408 **10.** 697,680 **11.** 3,606,400
12. 1035 mi **13.** $4742

EXERCISE SET 1.3, pp. 17–18

1. 240 **3.** 12,840 **5.** 540,000 **7.** 204 **9.** 7456 **11.** 1316 **13.** 61,632 **15.** 78,144 **17.** 184,832 **19.** 94,554 **21.** 675,360
23. 8,042,027 **25.** 109,989 **27.** 23,050,584 **29.** 1008 mi **31.** $10,368 **33.** $702 **35.** $384 **37.** $11,900 **39.** $28,477,128
41.
```
    4367
  × 2158
  ───────
 9,423,986
```

MARGIN EXERCISES, SECTION 1.4, pp. 19–22

1. 5 **2.** 6 **3.** 9 **4.** 789 **5.** 314 **6.** 708 r 2 **7.** 560 **8.** 217; 3 **9.** 45 **10.** $1088

EXERCISE SET 1.4, pp. 23–24

1. 99 r 3 **3.** 116 **5.** 609 r 6 **7.** 3217 **9.** 24 r 15 **11.** 32 r 16 **13.** 46 **15.** 116 r 9 **17.** 504 **19.** 550 r 2 **21.** 900
23. 25 r 7 **25.** 7 **27.** 185 r 129 **29.** 86; 13 **31.** 863 **33.** 33 **35.** $156 **37.** $47,500 **39.** 61 **41.** 7896

MARGIN EXERCISES, SECTION 1.5, pp. 25–28

1. $\frac{1}{6}$ ← Numerator ← Denominator **2.** $\frac{5}{7}$ ← Numerator ← Denominator **3.** $\frac{22}{3}$ ← Numerator ← Denominator **4.** $\frac{5}{8}$ **5.** $\frac{2}{3}$ **6.** $\frac{3}{4}$ **7.** $\frac{4}{6}$ **8.** $\frac{1}{6}$ **9.** $\frac{3}{19}$; $\frac{4}{19}$ **10.** 1, 1, 1
11. 0, 0, 0 **12.** 6, 10, 277 **13.** $6\frac{7}{8}$ **14.** $15\frac{9}{10}$ **15.** $8\frac{1}{8}$ **16.** $4\frac{3}{4}$ **17.** $5\frac{9}{16}$ **18.** $\frac{7}{3}$ **19.** $\frac{31}{8}$ **20.** $\frac{164}{15}$ **21.** 2 **22.** Impossible
23. Impossible **24.** 10 **25.** Impossible **26.** 0

A–1

EXERCISE SET 1.5, pp. 29-30

1. 5; 6   3. 51; 13   5. $\frac{2}{3}, \frac{1}{3}$ 7. $\frac{2200}{8760}$ 9. 1   11. 0   13. 19   15. 1   17. $18\frac{8}{9}$ 19. $59\frac{11}{12}$ 21. $1\frac{4}{5}$ 23. $2\frac{3}{8}$ 25. $4\frac{7}{10}$ 27. $9\frac{1}{6}$
29. $57\frac{5}{6}$ 31. $8\frac{79}{100}$ 33. $\frac{4}{3}$ 35. $\frac{37}{5}$ 37. $\frac{93}{10}$ 39. $\frac{9944}{100}$ 41. $\frac{134}{9}$ 43. $\frac{373}{15}$ 45. $\frac{40{,}693{,}237}{8910}$ 47. Impossible   49. 0

MARGIN EXERCISES, SECTION 1.6, pp. 31-34

1. $\frac{1}{12}$ 2. $\frac{3}{40}$ 3. $\frac{55}{72}$ 4. $\frac{12}{18}$ 5. $\frac{2}{3}$ 6. $\frac{5}{8}$ 7. $\frac{3}{4}$ 8. $\frac{1}{2}$ 9. $\frac{1}{4}$ 10. 9   11. 8   12. $\frac{2}{3}$ 13. 12   14. 6   15. $25\frac{1}{2}$ 16. $33\frac{1}{3}$ lb
17. $192\frac{1}{2}$ min

EXERCISE SET 1.6, pp. 35-36

1. $\frac{1}{5}$ 3. $\frac{3}{4}$ 5. 3   7. $\frac{7}{12}$ 9. $\frac{3}{8}$ 11. 8   13. 6   15. $\frac{5}{17}$ 17. $\frac{1}{3}$ 19. $\frac{10}{27}$ 21. 15   23. 90   25. 6   27. 12   29. $4\frac{1}{4}$
31. $35\frac{91}{100}$ 33. 147   35. $1\frac{1}{12}$ 37. $\$13\frac{3}{5}$ 39. $\$1962\frac{1}{2}$ 41. 96 mi   43. $247\frac{1}{2}$ mi
45. $2\frac{1}{2}$ lb of rattlesnake meat, $\frac{5}{8}$ cup flour, $\frac{1}{3}$ teaspoon pepper, $1\frac{1}{4}$ cups vinegar, 3 cups cooking oil

MARGIN EXERCISES, SECTION 1.7, pp. 37-40

1. $\frac{4}{3}$ 2. $\frac{5}{6}$ 3. 6   4. 24   5. $\frac{1}{18}$ 6. $\frac{1}{54}$ 7. $\frac{8}{15}$ 8. $2\frac{5}{8}$ 9. $\frac{1}{64}$ 10. 12   11. $1\frac{1}{3}$ 12. 800   13. 20

EXERCISE SET 1.7, pp. 41-42

1. $\frac{6}{5}$ 3. $\frac{1}{6}$ 5. 18   7. $\frac{12}{13}$ 9. $\frac{4}{5}$ 11. $3\frac{3}{8}$ 13. $\frac{3}{7}$ 15. 35   17. 1   19. $\frac{2}{3}$ 21. $2\frac{1}{4}$ 23. 10   25. $\frac{1}{6}$ 27. 2   29. $1\frac{37}{68}$
31. $1\frac{14}{59}$ 33. $\frac{7}{30}$ 35. $4\frac{1}{2}$ 37. 30   39. 400   41. 25   43. $85\frac{1}{3}$ 45. 27

MARGIN EXERCISES, SECTION 1.8, pp. 43-44

1. (a) 12, 24, 36, 48, 60, 72, 84, 96, 108, ...; (b) 18, 36, 54, 72, 90, 108, 126, ...; (c) 36, 72, 108, ...; (d) 36   2. 60   3. 42   4. 15

EXERCISE SET 1.8, pp. 45-46

1. 30   3. 10   5. 63   7. 15   9. 72   11. 315   13. 12   15. 12   17. 100   19. 20   21. 48   23. 24   25. 16   27. 24
29. 8   31. 40   33. 7560   35. 960

MARGIN EXERCISES, SECTION 1.9, pp. 47-50

1. $\frac{5}{8}$ 2. $\frac{2}{3}$ 3. $26\frac{1}{3}$ 4. $1\frac{1}{6}$ 5. $\frac{17}{21}$ 6. $\frac{23}{24}$ 7. $22\frac{5}{8}$ 8. $20\frac{17}{24}$ 9. $\$48\frac{1}{8}$ 10. $17\frac{1}{12}$ yd

EXERCISE SET 1.9, pp. 51-52

1. $\frac{5}{6}$ 3. $\frac{7}{9}$ 5. $\frac{5}{18}$ 7. $1\frac{1}{2}$ 9. $1\frac{5}{24}$ 11. $\frac{43}{60}$ 13. $1\frac{3}{20}$ 15. $1\frac{1}{100}$ 17. 8   19. $14\frac{1}{3}$ 21. $5\frac{3}{20}$ 23. $8\frac{2}{3}$ 25. $10\frac{19}{24}$ 27. $14\frac{9}{10}$
29. $29\frac{9}{16}$ 31. $14\frac{7}{8}$ 33. $17\frac{7}{8}$ 35. $51\frac{11}{20}$ 37. $\$51\frac{3}{8}$ 39. $84\frac{4}{5}$ cm, $441\frac{3}{100}$ sq cm   41. $21\frac{7}{12}$ yd   43. $23\frac{7}{15}$ lb   45. 438

MARGIN EXERCISES, SECTION 1.10, pp. 53-56

1. $\frac{2}{3}$ 2. $\frac{2}{3}$ 3. $8\frac{2}{3}$ 4. $\frac{1}{4}$ 5. $\frac{1}{30}$ 6. $\frac{11}{63}$ 7. $6\frac{17}{24}$ 8. $2\frac{3}{8}$ 9. $\$18\frac{7}{8}$ 10. $23\frac{1}{4}$

EXERCISE SET 1.10, pp. 57–58

1. $\frac{2}{5}$ **3.** $\frac{5}{8}$ **5.** $\frac{1}{3}$ **7.** $\frac{1}{18}$ **9.** $\frac{1}{24}$ **11.** $\frac{3}{5}$ **13.** $\frac{83}{100}$ **15.** $\frac{17}{60}$ **17.** $6\frac{2}{3}$ **19.** $4\frac{1}{15}$ **21.** $4\frac{1}{2}$ **23.** $13\frac{7}{12}$ **25.** $8\frac{4}{5}$ **27.** $31\frac{17}{24}$
29. $5\frac{3}{4}$ **31.** $14\frac{3}{8}$ **33.** $17\frac{1}{8}$ **35.** $16\frac{15}{16}$ **37.** $\$27\frac{5}{8}$ **39.** $14\frac{9}{10}$ ft **41.** $\frac{1}{8}$ **43.** $94\frac{1}{2}$ mi **45.** $3\frac{7}{12}$ hr

TEST OR REVIEW, CHAPTER 1, pp. 59–60

1. 12,974 **2.** 21,615 **3.** $6609 **4.** 4111 **5.** 4259 **6.** $76 **7.** 3648 **8.** 151,636 **9.** $13,625 **10.** 46 r 7 **11.** 209
12. $485 **13.** $\frac{3}{17}$ **14.** $\frac{17}{3}$ **15.** $4\frac{5}{12}$ **16.** $\frac{1}{8}$ **17.** $22\frac{3}{4}$ **18.** $\$5512\frac{1}{2}$ **19.** $6\frac{2}{3}$ **20.** 4 **21.** 160 **22.** 48 **23.** $1\frac{1}{2}$ **24.** $14\frac{7}{12}$
25. 39 in. **26.** $\frac{1}{12}$ **27.** $3\frac{3}{8}$ **28.** $2\frac{1}{2}$ in.

CHAPTER 2

READINESS CHECK, p. 62

1. [1.1, ■] 38 **2.** [1.1, ■] 830 **3.** [1.9, ■] $\frac{38}{100}$ **4.** [1.9, ■] $\frac{830}{1000}$ **5.** [1.2, ■] 182 **6.** [1.10, ■] $\frac{182}{100}$
7. [1.3, ■] 175 **8.** [1.6, ■] $\frac{1}{100}$ **9.** [1.6, ■] $\frac{1}{1000}$ **10.** [1.6, ■], [1.6, ■] $3\frac{4}{5}$ **11.** [1.6, ■], [1.6, ■] $\frac{9}{20}$
12. [1.6, ■], [1.6, ■] $\frac{7}{20}$ **13.** [1.4, ■] 9 **14.** [1.4, ■] 342 **15.** [1.4, ■] 16 **16.** [1.4, ■] 87

MARGIN EXERCISES, SECTION 2.1, pp. 63–66

1. Eighteen and forty-nine hundredths **2.** Six hundred forty-five thousandths **3.** Twelve and five ten-thousandths
4. Eighteen and $\frac{49}{100}$ dollars **5.** Two thousand, three hundred forty-six and $\frac{76}{100}$ dollars **6.** $\frac{568}{1000}$ **7.** $\frac{23}{10}$ **8.** $\frac{8904}{100}$ **9.** $18\frac{3}{10}$
10. $7\frac{3019}{10,000}$ **11.** 4.131 **12.** 0.4131 **13.** 5.73 **14.** 14.57 **15.** 22.07 **16.** 3.019 **17.** 7.6783 **18.** 7695¢ **19.** 14¢
20. $0.95 **21.** $7.95

EXERCISE SET 2.1, pp. 67–68

1. Thirty-four and eight hundred ninety-one thousandths **3.** Nine hundred three ten-thousandths
5. Three hundred twenty-six and $\frac{48}{100}$ dollars **7.** $\frac{67}{100}$ dollars **9.** $\frac{1}{1000}$ **11.** $\frac{1}{100}$ **13.** $\frac{49}{10}$ **15.** $\frac{59}{100}$ **17.** $\frac{309}{100}$ **19.** $\frac{9075}{10}$
21. $\frac{9999}{1000}$ **23.** $\frac{7843}{100}$ **25.** $\frac{20,007}{10,000}$ **27.** $\frac{78,898}{10}$ **29.** $\frac{121,456}{10,000}$ **31.** $\frac{617,499}{1000}$ **33.** $18\frac{46}{100}$ **35.** $4\frac{13}{1000}$ **37.** $234\frac{5}{10}$ **39.** $5\frac{4111}{10,000}$
41. 0.1 **43.** 0.0001 **45.** 0.7 **47.** 0.07 **49.** 8.9 **51.** 7.74 **53.** 307.9 **55.** 9.999 **57.** 0.0039 **59.** 0.00001 **61.** 9.3
63. 17.95 **65.** 6.014 **67.** 126.8 **69.** 8995¢ **71.** 45¢ **73.** 109¢ **75.** 12,895¢ **77.** $0.95 **79.** $1.79 **81.** $12.95 **83.** $0.42

MARGIN EXERCISES, SECTION 2.2, pp. 69–72

1. 284.455 **2.** 268.63 **3.** 27.676 **4.** 64.683 **5.** 99.59 **6.** 239.883 **7.** $2388.18 **8.** $1931.55

EXERCISE SET 2.2, pp. 73–74

1. 444.94 **3.** 390.617 **5.** 155.724 **7.** 2.145 **9.** 1107.9 **11.** 63.79 **13.** 33.1961 **15.** 32.234 **17.** 26.835 **19.** 0.6
21. 47.91 **23.** 0.996 **25.** 1.9193 **27.** 99.21 **29.** 0.981 **31.** 75.001 **33.** 0.1112 **35.** $1394.58 **37.** $3843.22 **39.** $3.21
41. $6.34 **43.** 39,595.3 **45.** 1022.6 **47.** 6.4° **49.** $205,860.85

MARGIN EXERCISES, SECTION 2.3, pp. 75–80

1. 5.868 **2.** 0.5868 **3.** 6404.9 **4.** 51.53808 **5.** 2681 **6.** 26,810 **7.** 268,100 **8.** 26.81 **9.** 2.681 **10.** 0.2681 **11.** 48.9 **12.** 15.82 **13.** 1.28 **14.** 17.95 **15.** 856 **16.** 0.85 **17.** 218.75 **18.** $117.75 **19.** 32 miles per gallon

EXERCISE SET 2.3, pp. 81–82

1. 9.968 **3.** 386.104 **5.** 179.5 **7.** 0.1894 **9.** 15.288 **11.** 527.28 **13.** 1.40756 **15.** 3.60558 **17.** 1.25 **19.** 0.41 **21.** 8.5 **23.** 9.3 **25.** 0.95 **27.** 5.689 **29.** 18.75 **31.** 660 **33.** $145.15 **35.** $81.26 **37.** 26 miles per gallon **39.** $18,123.78 **41.** $190.49 **43.** $650,556 **45.** $10

MARGIN EXERCISES, SECTION 2.4, pp. 83–86

1. 2.8 **2.** 13.9 **3.** 7.0 **4.** 7.8 **5.** 34.7 **6.** 0.03 **7.** 7890 **8.** 7900 **9.** 0.943 **10.** 8.004 **11.** 43.112 **12.** 37.401 **13.** 7459.355 **14.** 7459.35 **15.** 7459.4 **16.** 7459 **17.** 7460 **18.** 7500 **19.** 7000 **20.** $0.02 **21.** $17.97 **22.** $1267.89 **23.** 0.625 **24.** 1.75 **25.** $0.1\overline{6}$ **26.** $0.\overline{6}$ **27.** $7.\overline{63}$ **28.** $0.\overline{09}$ **29.** 17.5 miles per gallon

EXERCISE SET 2.4, pp. 87–88

1. 745.07; 745.1; 745; 750; 700 **3.** 6780.51; 6780.5; 6781; 6780; 6800 **5.** $17.99; $18.00 **7.** $346.08; $346 **9.** $17.00 **11.** $190.00 **13.** 0.375 **15.** 0.6 **17.** 0.8125 **19.** 0.725 **21.** $1.\overline{6}$ **23.** $0.\overline{83}$ **25.** $0.\overline{4}$ **27.** $1.\overline{18}$ **29.** $4.08\overline{3}$ **31.** 0.85 **33.** 31.9 miles per gallon **35.** $2.44 **37.** $6.08 **39.** $11,786 **41.** $0.\overline{1}; 0.\overline{01}; 0.\overline{001}; 0.\overline{0001}$

MARGIN EXERCISES, SECTION 2.5, pp. 89–90

1. 5^3 **2.** 5^5 **3.** $(1.08)^2$ **4.** 10^4 **5.** 10,000 **6.** 512 **7.** 1.331 **8.** 1.02515625 **9.** 5 **10.** 43 **11.** 5.8 **12.** 1 **13.** 1 **14.** 1

EXERCISE SET 2.5, pp. 91–92

1. 3^4 **3.** 5^2 **5.** 7^5 **7.** 10^5 **9.** 1^8 **11.** 25 **13.** 59,049 **15.** 100 **17.** 6561 **19.** 512 **21.** 1 **23.** 3.24 **25.** 0.001 **27.** 219.04 **29.** $\frac{16}{25}$ **31.** 1 **33.** 28.3 **35.** 5 **37.** 27 **39.** 1 **41.** 1 **43.** 1 **45.** 1 **47.** 677.12 **49.** 1259.712

MARGIN EXERCISES, SECTION 2.6, pp. 93–94

1. 1843 **2.** 83 **3.** 584 **4.** 84 **5.** 1568 **6.** 1880 **7.** 305 **8.** 34,279.2

EXERCISE SET 2.6, pp. 95–96

1. 434 **3.** 160 **5.** 1400 **7.** 125 **9.** 14 **11.** 27 **13.** 1856 **15.** 47 **17.** 2136 **19.** 12,544

MARGIN EXERCISES, SECTION 2.7, pp. 97–100

1. 9 **2.** 9 **3.** No **4.** Yes **5.** 5 **6.** 10 **7.** 32 **8.** 32 **9.** 45 **10.** 76.5 **11.** 3311 **12.** 16 **13.** 644 **14.** 8.6 **15.** 156 **16.** 70.18 **17.** 412,896 **18.** 12,003.6 **19.** 2000 **20.** 6.396

EXERCISE SET 2.7, pp. 101–102

1. 7 **3.** 8 **5.** 5 **7.** 18 **9.** 15 **11.** 9 **13.** 7 **15.** 0 **17.** 79 **19.** 45 **21.** 131 **23.** 222 **25.** 603 **27.** 1470.1 **29.** 4056 **31.** 8 **33.** 14 **35.** 32 **37.** 143 **39.** 1166.4 **41.** 1857.5 **43.** 15 **45.** 480 **47.** 124 **49.** 45 **51.** 89,280 **53.** 159,744 **55.** 205 **57.** 95 **59.** No solution

MARGIN EXERCISES, SECTION 2.8, pp. 103–104

1. 240 **2.** $711.60 **3.** $2599.20 **4.** $2320 **5.** $\dfrac{I}{P \cdot R}$ **6.** $Q + b$

CHAPTER 3

EXERCISE SET 2.8, pp. 105–106

1. $12,497.50   **3.** $336   **5.** 50.24 yd   **7.** $12,544   **9.** $\dfrac{A}{W}$ **11.** $\dfrac{I}{R \cdot T}$ **13.** $A - I$ **15.** $A - 2x$ **17.** $\dfrac{A - y}{3}$ **19.** $\dfrac{A}{(1 + i)^n}$

MARGIN EXERCISES, SECTION 2.9, pp. 107–108

1. $n + 37 = 73$; 36   **2.** $x - 256.4 = 377.9$; 634.3   **3.** $0.7 \times n = 49$; 70   **4.** $145{,}000{,}000 = p + 132{,}000{,}000$; 13,000,000
5. $14{,}500 = 1.16P$; $12,500

EXERCISE SET 2.9, pp. 109–110

1. $0.64 \times n = 48$; 75   **3.** $n + 5 = 22$; 17   **5.** $n = 5 + 4$; 9   **7.** $78{,}114 = 4 \times A$; 19,528.5 km²
9. $35 = \dfrac{2}{5} \times s$; 87.5 words per minute   **11.** $78.3 = m + 13.5$; 64.8°C   **13.** $640 = 1.6 \times s$; 400 kWh   **15.** $1175 = 1.8 \times C$; $652.78

TEST OR REVIEW, CHAPTER 2, pp. 111–112

1. $\dfrac{678}{100}$ **2.** 18.95   **3.** $13.99   **4.** 139¢   **5.** 86.0298   **6.** 9.342   **7.** $3010.65   **8.** 430.8   **9.** 55.6   **10.** $55.92   **11.** 34.1
12. $124.00   **13.** 1.1875   **14.** $2.91\overline{6}$ **15.** 15.2 miles per gallon   **16.** 1.1236   **17.** 929   **18.** 358.22   **19.** 4000   **20.** $\dfrac{B}{R}$
21. $20,000

CHAPTER 3

READINESS CHECK, p. 114

1. [1.8, ●●] =   **2.** [1.8, ●●] ≠   **3.** [2.3, ●●] 0.09   **4.** [2.3, ●●] 9.5   **5.** [2.3, ●●] 0.47   **6.** [2.3, ●●] 152
7. [2.3, ●] 43   **8.** [2.3, ●] 0.08   **9.** [2.3, ●] 0.867   **10.** [2.3, ●] 7   **11.** [1.5, ●●●] $33\dfrac{1}{3}$ **12.** [1.5, ●●●] $37\dfrac{1}{2}$
13. [2.4, ●●] $0.\overline{6}$ **14.** [2.4, ●●] 0.875

MARGIN EXERCISES, SECTION 3.1, pp. 114–118

1. 6 and 3, 40 and 20, 100 and 50   **2.** 9 and 6, 15 and 10, 60 and 40   **3.** $\dfrac{3}{2}$ **4.** $\dfrac{7}{11}$ **5.** $\dfrac{0.189}{3.4}$ **6.** $\dfrac{9}{3}$ **7.** $\dfrac{9}{6}$ **8.** $\dfrac{6}{9}$
9. $\dfrac{5928}{22{,}800}$ **10.** $\dfrac{4}{7\frac{2}{3}}$ **11.** Yes   **12.** No   **13.** No   **14.** 14   **15.** $11\dfrac{1}{4}$ **16.** 10.5   **17.** 9   **18.** 10.8   **19.** 5   **20.** 12   **21.** $\dfrac{3}{10}$
22. 1100   **23.** 4   **24.** 14.5

EXERCISE SET 3.1, pp. 119–120

1. $\dfrac{4}{5}$ **3.** $\dfrac{0.4}{12}$ **5.** $\dfrac{2}{12}$ **7.** No   **9.** Yes   **11.** 45   **13.** 12   **15.** 10   **17.** 20   **19.** 5   **21.** 18   **23.** 22   **25.** 28   **27.** $9\dfrac{1}{3}$
29. $2\dfrac{8}{9}$ **31.** 0.06   **33.** 5   **35.** 1   **37.** 1   **39.** 14   **41.** 40 $\dfrac{\text{km}}{\text{hr}}$ **43.** 11 $\dfrac{\text{m}}{\text{sec}}$ **45.** 152 $\dfrac{\text{yd}}{\text{day}}$ **47.** 25; $\dfrac{1}{25}$ **49.** $\dfrac{623}{1000}$ **51.** $2\dfrac{1}{2}$

MARGIN EXERCISES, SECTION 3.2, pp. 121–122

1. 3360 km   **2.** $148.50   **3.** 4000 mi   **4.** 140 oz

EXERCISE SET 3.2, pp. 123–124

1. $1.32   **3.** $133\dfrac{1}{3}$ mi   **5.** $25\dfrac{1}{5}$ **7.** $4680   **9.** $11\dfrac{1}{4}$ **11.** 322   **12.** 7500   **15.** $1\dfrac{1}{4}$ m   **17.** 650 mi   **19.** 780,000

A-6 CHAPTER 3 ANSWERS — SECTION 3.3 TO SECTION 3.5

MARGIN EXERCISES, SECTION 3.3, pp. 125–130

1. $\frac{90}{100}$; $90 \times \frac{1}{100}$; 90×0.01 2. $\frac{3.4}{100}$; $3.4 \times \frac{1}{100}$; 3.4×0.01 3. $\frac{100}{100}$; $100 \times \frac{1}{100}$; 100×0.01 4. 0.34 5. 0.789 6. 0.1208

7. 0.021 8. 24% 9. 347% 10. 100% 11. 40% 12. 25% 13. 87.5% 14. $66.\overline{6}\%$ or $66\frac{2}{3}\%$ 15. $83.\overline{3}\%$ or $83\frac{1}{3}\%$

16. 57% 17. 76% 18. $\frac{3}{5}$ 19. $\frac{13}{400}$ 20. $\frac{2}{3}$ 21.

$\frac{1}{5}$	$\frac{5}{6}$	$\frac{3}{8}$
0.2	$0.83\overline{3}$	0.375
20%	$83.\overline{3}\%$ or $83\frac{1}{3}\%$	$37\frac{1}{2}\%$

EXERCISE SET 3.3, pp. 131–132

1. $\frac{80}{100}$; $80 \times \frac{1}{100}$; 80×0.01 3. $\frac{12.5}{100}$; $12.5 \times \frac{1}{100}$; 12.5×0.01 5. 0.18 7. 0.789 9. 0.01 11. 4.25 13. 0.0118

15. 0.6711 17. 78% 19. 8% 21. 56.2% 23. 80% 25. 100% 27. 101.5% 29. 79% 31. 6% 33. 90% 35. 150%

37. 12.5% 39. 60% 41. $16.\overline{6}\%$ or $16\frac{2}{3}\%$ 43. $166.\overline{6}\%$ or $166\frac{2}{3}\%$ 45. 105% 47. 57.5% 49. $\frac{3}{5}$ 51. $\frac{1}{8}$ 53. $\frac{2}{3}$ 55. $\frac{5}{6}$

57. $\frac{7}{80}$ 59. $\frac{34}{25}$ 61. $\frac{7}{20}$

63.

$\frac{1}{8}$	$\frac{1}{6}$	$\frac{1}{5}$	$\frac{1}{4}$	$\frac{1}{3}$	$\frac{3}{8}$	$\frac{2}{5}$	$\frac{1}{2}$	$\frac{3}{5}$	$\frac{5}{8}$	$\frac{2}{3}$	$\frac{3}{4}$	$\frac{4}{5}$	$\frac{5}{6}$	$\frac{7}{8}$	1
0.125	$0.1\overline{6}$	0.2	0.25	$0.\overline{3}$	0.375	0.4	0.5	0.6	0.625	$0.\overline{6}$	0.75	8.0	$0.8\overline{3}$	0.875	1.0
$12\frac{1}{2}\%$ or 12.5%	$16\frac{2}{3}\%$ or $16.\overline{6}\%$	20%	25%	$33\frac{1}{3}\%$ or $33.\overline{3}\%$	$37\frac{1}{2}\%$ or 37.5%	40%	50%	60%	$62\frac{1}{2}\%$ or 62.5%	$66\frac{2}{3}\%$ or $66.\overline{6}\%$	75%	80%	$83\frac{1}{3}\%$ or $83.\overline{3}\%$	$87\frac{1}{2}\%$ or 87.5%	100%

65. 6.3% 67. 6.8% 69. 116.1%

MARGIN EXERCISES, SECTION 3.4A, pp. 133–136

1. $12\% \times 50 = n$ 2. $w = 40\% \times \$60$ 3. $\$45 = 20\% \times n$ 4. $120\% \times m = 60$ 5. $16 = n\% \times 40$

6. $\$7104 = a\% \times \$9600$ 7. 74 8. $35.20 9. 225 10. $50 11. 40% 12. 12.5%

MARGIN EXERCISES, SECTION 3.4A, pp. 137–138

1. $y = 41\% \times 89$; 36.49 3. $89 = n\% \times 100$; 89 5. $13 = 25\% \times b$; 52 7. 90 9. 45 11. 15 13. 1.05 15. 24%

17. 200% 19. 50% 21. 125% 23. 40 25. $40 27. 88 29. 20 31. $880; $843.20

MARGIN EXERCISES, SECTION 3.4B, pp. 139–142

1. $\frac{a}{50} = \frac{12}{100}$ 2. $\frac{a}{60} = \frac{40}{100}$ 3. $\frac{45}{b} = \frac{20}{100}$ 4. $\frac{60}{b} = \frac{120}{100}$ 5. $\frac{16}{40} = \frac{n}{100}$ 6. $\frac{10.5}{84} = \frac{n}{100}$ 7. 6 8. 35.2 9. $225 10. 50

11. 40% 12. 12.5%

EXERCISE SET 3.4B, pp. 143–144

1. $\frac{a}{74} = \frac{82}{100}$ 3. $\frac{4.3}{5.9} = \frac{n}{100}$ 5. $\frac{14}{b} = \frac{25}{100}$ 7. $42 9. 440 11. 80 13. 2.88 15. 25% 17. 102% 19. 25%

21. 93.75% 23. $72 25. 90 27. 88 29. 20 31. $1200; $1118.64

MARGIN EXERCISES, SECTION 3.5, pp. 145–148

1. $1890 2. $1890 3. $88 4. $88 5. 14% 6. 14%

CHAPTER 4 SECTION 3.5 TO SECTION 4.3 A–7

EXERCISE SET 3.5, pp. 149–150

1. $4800   **3.** $490   **5.** 87.5%   **7.** 8%; 92%; 600   **9.** 888   **11.** 9.1%   **13.** 25%   **15.** 239.76   **17.** $5784.96

MARGIN EXERCISES, SECTION 3.6, pp. 152–156

1. 9%   **2.** 3.5%   **3.** $10,682   **4.** $13.41

EXERCISE SET 3.6, pp. 157–158

1. $20,455.20   **3.** 25%   **5.** 9%   **7.** $3920   **11.** 7.5%   **13.** 13.4%
15. No. In Exercise 13 we are asking "$20 is what percent of $500?" In Exercise 14 we are asking "$20 is what percent of $520?"
17. 5%   **19.** 12%   **21.** 35,100   **23.** 4.084 billion   **25.** 4836.21

TEST OR REVIEW, CHAPTER 3, pp. 159–160

1. 2.24   **2.** $5.61   **3.** 0.874   **4.** 31%   **5.** 95%   **6.** $\frac{19}{200}$ **7.** 15.52   **8.** $1500   **9.** 78.4%   **10.** $132   **11.** $737
12. $13,001.10   **13.** 8%   **14.** 7.4%   **15.** $1.00

CHAPTER 4

READINESS CHECK, p. 162

1. [2.2, ●●] 10.06   **2.** [2.2, ●●] 209.27   **3.** [2.3, ●] 4.451811   **4.** [2.3, ●] 5480.175   **5.** [2.4, ●] 4.45
6. [2.4, ●] 5480.18   **7.** [2.5, ●●] 16   **8.** [2.5, ●●] 1.0404

MARGIN EXERCISES, SECTION 4.1, pp. 163–166

1. $240   **2.** 247.50   **3.** $1.00   **4.** 15%   **5.** $180   **6.** 75.11   **7.** $665

EXERCISE SET 4.1, pp. 167–168

1. $65.00   **3.** $510.00   **5.** $225.00   **7.** $6.75   **9.** 17%   **11.** 15%   **13.** 11%   **15.** $7000   **17.** $1900   **19.** $6576.92
21. $1500   **23.** $168.02   **25.** $322.43   **27.** $128.78   **29.** $1610   **31.** $852   **33.** $1775   **35.** 9%, $46,852.50
37. $372.08, 9.5%

MARGIN EXERCISES, SECTION 4.2, pp. 169–171

1. $18.26   **2.** $15.45   **3.** $9.33   **4.** $1250.01

MARGIN EXERCISES, SOMETHING EXTRA, p. 172

1. $8.00   **2.** $36.00   **3.** $32.00   **4.** $30.00

EXERCISE SET 4.2, pp. 173–174

1. $5.83   **3.** $6.00   **5.** $72.00   **7.** $172.50   **9.** $106.67   **11.** $0.90   **13.** $19.07   **15.** $16.13   **17.** $15.60   **19.** $1374.32
21. $820.40   **23.** $778.75   **25.** $740.18

MARGIN EXERCISES, SECTION 4.3, pp. 175–176

1. $9.59   **2.** $312.46

EXERCISE SET 4.3, pp. 177–178

1. $20.71   **3.** $4.68   **5.** $24.72   **7.** $89.35   **9.** $459.12   **11.** $66.78   **13.** $113.27   **15.** $16.44   **17.** $10.38   **19.** $456.04
21. $812.48   **23.** $748.33

MARGIN EXERCISES, SECTION 4.4, pp. 179–180

1. $20.97 **2.** $28.11

EXERCISE SET 4.4, pp. 181–182

1. $51.92 **2.** $190.49 **5.** $143.56 **7.** $18.33 **9.** $172.90 **11.** $25.73 **13.** $221.43 **15.** $33.48 **17.** $17.44 **19.** $90.78 **21.** $158.09 **23.** $23,300.69 **25.** $15,002.05

MARGIN EXERCISES, SECTION 4.5, pp. 183–188

1. $42.61 **2.** $13.22 **3.** $9.84 **4.** $84.41

EXERCISE SET 4.5, pp. 189–190

1. $800.00 **3.** $416.50 **5.** $704.00 **7.** $683.13 **9.** $154.52 **11.** $56.52 **13.** $21.63 **15.** $789.04 **17.** $410.79 **19.** $694.36 **21.** $673.77 **23.** $152.40 **25.** $6.75 **27.** $14.06

MARGIN EXERCISES, SECTION 4.6, pp. 191–192

1. $24.18 **2.** $24.18 **3.** $1449

EXERCISE SET 4.6, pp. 193–194

1. $60.90 **3.** $30.38 **5.** $98.00 **7.** $199.68 **9.** $120.00 **11.** $231.84 **13.** $60.90 **15.** $42.63 **17.** $249.73 **19.** $90.00 **21.** $51.01 **23.** $1061.21; $61.21 **25.** $2756.25; $256.25 **27.** $609.54

MARGIN EXERCISES, SECTION 4.7, pp. 195–196

1. $327.60 **2.** $429.55 **3.** $1175.46

EXERCISE SET 4.7, pp. 197–198

1. $20.20 **3.** $53.82 **5.** $194.05 **7.** $56.00 **9.** $155.83 **11.** $125.38 **13.** $143.39 **15.** $400 **17.** $1105.71 **19.** $6097.88 **21.** $102.41 **23.** $704.25 **25.** $3046.01 **27.** $1125.55 **29.** $2633.27 **31.** $3250.11 **33.** $16,010.32 **35.** $6312.39

MARGIN EXERCISES, SECTION 4.8, pp. 199–200

1. $27.09 **2.** $36.66 **3.** $973.52 **4.** $973.60

EXERCISE SET 4.8, pp. 201–202

1. $1.90 **3.** $2.60 **5.** $1.73 **7.** $0.91 **9.** $7.44 **11.** $2.63 **13.** $1.77 **15.** $2.18 **17.** $4.22 **19.** $5.57

MARGIN EXERCISES, SECTION 4.9, pp. 203–204

1. 8.77% **2.** 13.37%, 13.42%: 13% compounded semiannually earns more

EXERCISE SET 4.9, pp. 205–206

1. 5.09% **3.** 8.24% **5.** 12.55% **7.** 5.06% **9.** 8.16% **11.** 12.36% **13.** 6.92% **15.** 9.38%, 9.57%: $9\frac{1}{4}$% compounded quarterly earns more **17.** 10.75%, 10.92%: $10\frac{1}{2}$% compounded quarterly earns more **19.** 14.93%, 15.02%: $14\frac{1}{2}$% compounded semiannually earns more **21.** 9.38%, 9.72%: $9\frac{1}{2}$% compounded semiannually earns more **23.** 7.79% **25.** 9.96%

MARGIN EXERCISES, SECTION 4.10, pp. 207–208

1. $4701.15 **2.** $7323.24

EXERCISE SET 4.10, pp. 209–210

1. $4909.65 **3.** $7435.55 **5.** $12,548.24 **7.** $2192.07 **9.** $4891.53 **11.** $2308.33 **13.** $915.41 **15.** $2313.60 **17.** $3069.57

CHAPTER 5

TEST OR REVIEW, CHAPTER 4, pp. 211–212

1. $900 **2.** $60,000 **3.** $1100 **4.** $37.40 **5.** $19.93 **6.** $24.84 **7.** $287.96 **8.** $28.28 **9.** $262.48 **10.** $3276.99 **11.** $17,091.37 **12.** $2.52 **13.** $1.59 **14.** 8.24% **15.** 10.51%, 10.38%: $10\frac{1}{4}$% compounded semiannually earns more **16.** $20,102.60

CHAPTER 5

READINESS CHECK, p. 214

1. [2.2, ●] $602.79 **2.** [2.2, ●] $1170.57 **3.** [2.2, ●] $2712.92 **4.** [2.2, ●] $2445.42 **5.** [2.2, ●] $272.99 **6.** [2.2, ●] $737.04

MARGIN EXERCISES, SECTION 5.1, pp. 215–221

1. [check #6854 to Chuck's Records for $17.95, Seventeen and 95/100]

2. (a) Your Name (b) For deposit only Your Name (c) Pay to the order of Joe Banks Your Name

3. 43 51334, $43.10 **4.** Solo's Concrete, $2.89 **5.** $728.17 **6.** $276.00 **7.** $3101.03

EXERCISES SET 5.1, pp. 223–228

1. [check #6855 to Ferber's for $29.99, Twenty nine and 99/100]

3.

Check #6857
Pay to the order of: Jay Haus
$19.25
Nineteen and 25/100 DOLLARS
UBT University Bank and Trust
Your Name

5. Your Name

7. Pay to the order of Jim Felbo
Your Name

9. 40 041 8, $7.50   11. Jo Pyle, $14.87

13. $530.76   15. $950.23   17. $925.08   19. $941.83   21. $2654.15   23. $634.99   25. $113.47   27. $213.00   29. $3206.52

MARGIN EXERCISES, SECTION 5.2, pp. 229–232

1. New balance = $583.88 + $459.69 − $10 = $1033.57   2. $514.48

3. ①

CHECK NUMBER	PAYEE	AMOUNT
		$62.17
		45.82

TOTAL CHECKS OUTSTANDING (ENTER ON LINE 4) $107.99

②
1. STATEMENT BALANCE $456.85
2. ADD DEPOSITS NOT CREDITED ON THIS STATEMENT $167.98
3. SUB TOTAL $624.83
4. SUBTRACT CHECKS OUTSTANDING $107.99
5. BALANCE $516.84

③
CHECKBOOK BALANCE $516.84
LESS BANK CHARGES $—
CHECK BOOK BALANCE $516.84

4. Adjusted statement balance = $635.98 + $78.19 − $176.32 = $537.85; adjusted check balance = $539.53 − $1.68 = $537.85

CHAPTER 5 SECTION 5.2 A-11

EXERCISE SET 5.2, pp. 233–234

1. $572.54 **3.** $339.69 **5.** $61.40 **7.** $215.53

9.

List your outstanding checks below:

CHECK NUMBER	PAYEE	AMOUNT
		$125.63
		462.13
TOTAL CHECKS OUTSTANDING (ENTER ON LINE 4)		$587.76

Balance your account below:

1. STATEMENT BALANCE	$403.09	
2. ADD DEPOSITS NOT CREDITED ON THIS STATEMENT	$525.48	
3. SUB TOTAL		
4. SUBTRACT CHECKS OUTSTANDING	$587.76	
5. BALANCE	$340.81	

CHECKBOOK BALANCE	$340.81	
LESS BANK CHARGES	$—	
CHECK BOOK BALANCE	$340.81	

11.

List your outstanding checks below:

CHECK NUMBER	PAYEE	AMOUNT
		$51.23
		79.96
TOTAL CHECKS OUTSTANDING (ENTER ON LINE 4)		$131.19

Balance your account below:

1. STATEMENT BALANCE	$737.22	
2. ADD DEPOSITS NOT CREDITED ON THIS STATEMENT	$159.17	
3. SUB TOTAL		
4. SUBTRACT CHECKS OUTSTANDING	$131.19	
5. BALANCE	$765.20	

CHECKBOOK BALANCE	$765.92	
LESS BANK CHARGES	$0.72	
CHECK BOOK BALANCE	$765.20	

13.

① Outstanding checks: $42.63, $115.95; Total checks outstanding: $158.58

② Balance your account:
1. Statement Balance: $823.41
2. Add Deposits not credited: $426.83
3. Sub Total: $1250.24
4. Subtract Checks Outstanding: $158.58
5. Balance: $1091.66

③ Checkbook Balance: $1091.66; Less Bank Charges: —; Check Book Balance: $1091.66

15.

① Outstanding checks: $321.90; Total checks outstanding: $321.90

② Balance your account:
1. Statement Balance: $986.57
2. Add Deposits not credited: $527.80
3. Sub Total: $1514.37
4. Subtract Checks Outstanding: $321.90
5. Balance: $1192.47

③ Checkbook Balance: $1194.22; Less Bank Charges: $1.75; Check Book Balance: $1192.47

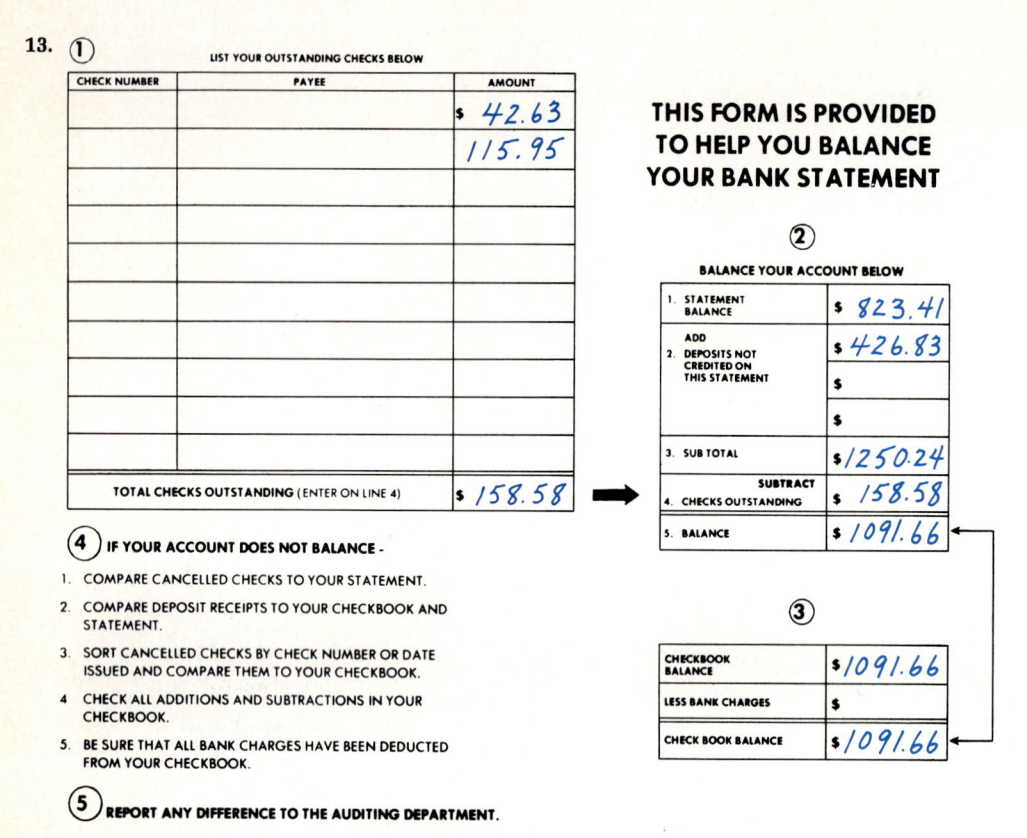

17. $20.00   **19.** $19.85

MARGIN EXERCISES, SECTION 5.3, pp. 235–238

1. $458.48   **2.** $299.29   **3.** 9.98%   **4.** 8.26%   **5.** 10.16%   **6.** $10,019.14

CHAPTER 5 SECTION 5.3 TO TEST OR REVIEW **A–13**

EXERCISE SET 5.3, pp. 239–240

1. $618.00 **3.** $513.00 **5.** $300.68 **7.** 9.22% **9.** 9.08% **11.** $15,032.56 **13.** $15,031.47 **15.** $15,030.35

TEST OR REVIEW, CHAPTER 5, pp. 241–243

1. Check made out to Foster's for $87.65, eighty seven and 65/100 dollars, signed Your Name.

2. (a) Your name (b) For deposit only / Your name (c) Pay to the order of Kleeber's / Your name

3. 037 614 0; $14.27 **4.** Everhoff's $4.75 **5.** $433.53 **6.** $685.86 **7.** $109.62 **8.** $1422.08 **9.** $1214.02

11. $516.33 **12.** $5010.98

10. Outstanding checks: $56.28, $14.96; Total checks outstanding $71.24. Statement balance $413.17; Deposits not credited $418.32; Sub total $831.49; Checks outstanding $71.24; Balance $760.25. Checkbook balance $760.25; Check book balance $760.25.

CHAPTER 6

READINESS CHECK, p. 246

1. [4.2, ●] September 2   2. [4.2, ●] December 22   3. [4.2, ●] $44.38   4. [4.2, ●] $75.00   5. [2.2, ●●] 1605.9
6. [2.2, ●●] 1708.34

MARGIN EXERCISES, SECTION 6.1, pp. 247–250

1. $75.00   2. September 27   3. $1980, $4020   4. $10.65, $589.35   5. $714.28   6. $8116.88

EXERCISE SET 6.1, pp. 251–252

1. $33.00   3. $214.50   5. $540.00   7. October 3   9. February 10   11. November 29   13. $770; $2730   15. $15, $435
17. $15.53, $734.47   19. $4.40, $888.10   21. $4545.45   23. $4736.84   25. $2577.32   27. $6463.29   29. $40.41
31. $18.10, $800.21   33. $4803.36

MARGIN EXERCISES, SECTION 6.2, pp. 253–256

1. $816.18   2. $1143.61   3. $1619.34

EXERCISE SET 6.2, pp. 257–258

1. 93, $113.67, $186.33, $3813.67   3. 66, $69.65, $1930.35, $1523.15   5. 152, $295.56, $154.44, $4845.56
7. 99, $186.55, $433.06, $4412.50   9. $2355.26   11. $3813.56   13. 93, $112.11, 0, $4000   15. 66, $68.76, 0, $3456.77
17. $3579.49   19. $4101.35   21. 95, $95.78, $354.22, $2845.78   23. 397, $331.67, $1668.33, $983.25

MARGIN EXERCISES, SECTION 6.3, pp. 260–261

1. $804.07   2. $1530.28

EXERCISE SET 6.3, pp. 263–264

1. New Balance = $4440   3. 152, $23.22, $523.22, $3591.85   5. Amount = $1539.29, New Balance = 0
7. 578, $99.76, $549.76, $5850.24   9. 171, $62.97, $1022.97, $4562.42   11. $2318.46   13. New Balance = $4440
15. 152, $32.07, $732.07, $3599.73   17. Amount = $3548.43, New Balance = 0   19. $1302.96   21. $3842.65
23. 635, $90.03, $540.03, $3395.97   25. 120, $75.62, $2075.62, $971.48

MARGIN EXERCISES, SECTION 6.4, pp. 266–267

1. $6.35   2. $8.12   3. $14.78   4. $73, 368.19   5. $7.12   6. $9.09   7. $16.55   8. $32,865.85

SOMETHING EXTRA—ERROR PATTERN, p. 268

1. This is an annuity-due situation. $S_{\overline{25}|12}$ should be $S_{\overline{26}|12}$. The correct amount is $298,667.86
2. The interest rate is 3% quarterly, $S_{\overline{20}|12}$ should be $S_{\overline{20}|3}$. The correct amount is $10,748.15

EXERCISE SET 6.4, pp. 269–270

1. $19.34   3. $4099.55   5. $3867.46   7. $3061.13   9. $4348.11   11. $6204.15   13. $28,507.26   15. $18,059.97
17. $7346.71   19. $4386.52   21. $4408.90   23. $4391.59   25. $6374.76   27. $29,291.21   29. $49,618.74

MARGIN EXERCISES, SECTION 6.5, pp. 271–274

1. $600   2. $1000   3. $940   4. $30,000   5. $22,500   6. $27,500   7. $540,585.20   8. $20,000   9. $15,000   10. $30,000
11. $5760   12. $6000   13. $3600   14. $796,083.48

CHAPTER 7   SECTION 6.5 TO SECTION 7.3   A–15

EXERCISE SET 6.5, pp. 275–276

1. $39,309   **3.** $540,585   **5.** $767,042   **7.** $1,532,183   **9.** $2,421,625   **11.** $528,758.10   **13.** $463,822.89   **15.** $879,598
17. $386,390   **19.** $71,268   **21.** $21,428   **23.** $99,151.56   **25.** $22,557.75

MARGIN EXERCISES, SECTION 6.6, pp. 278–280

1. $3.60   **2.** $4.56   **3.** $5.65   **4.** $10,814.33   **5.** $4.04   **6.** $5.11   **7.** $6.33   **8.** $2614.55

EXERCISE SET 6.6, pp. 281–282

1. $75,967.41   **3.** $113,004.46   **5.** $24,031.57   **7.** $1938.88   **9.** $21,888   **11.** $1164.20   **13.** $32,298.80   **15.** $34,006.79
17. $23,469.00   **19.** $20,445.50   **21.** $16,608.16   **23.** $13,447.92   **25.** $1233.96   **27.** $7670.74

TEST OR REVIEW, CHAPTER 6, pp. 283–284

1. $78.75   **2.** September 4   **3.** $231, $3969   **4.** $1235.00   **5.** $1234.14   **6.** $9183.39   **7.** $2435.61   **8.** $1,291,653.80
9. $109,606.03   **10.** $10,630.72   **11.** $2957   **12.** $31,795.77

CHAPTER 7

READINESS CHECK, p. 286

1. [3.1, ●●●] 11.024   **2.** [3.1, ●●●] .148   **3.** [2.3, ●●●] $84.74   **4.** [2.3, ●●●] $495.14   **5.** [1.6, ●●●] $4.62   **6.** [1.6, ●●●] $16.96

MARGIN EXERCISES, SECTION 7.1, pp. 286–292

1. $663.08   **2.** 10.25%   **3.** 12.75%   **4.** 12.36%   **5.** 10.79%

EXERCISE SET 7.1, pp. 293–294

1. $4075.36   **3.** $18,600.00   **5.** 16%   **7.** $15\frac{1}{4}$ **9.** 13%   **11.** 17%   **13.** 21.46%   **15.** 10.92%   **17.** 33.80%   **19.** 14.98%
21. 14.52%   **23.** $1455.83

MARGIN EXERCISES, SECTION 7.2, pp. 295–300

1. $249.10   **2.** $644.44   **3.** $637.08   **4.** $503.68, $98,754   **5.** $674.00, $13,25, $59,898.05   **6.** $523.50, $25.35, $59,803.25

EXERCISE SET 7.2, pp. 301–302

1. $42.14   **3.** $42.24   **5.** $126.40   **7.** $122.10   **9.** $839.41   **11.** $524.86   **13.** $666.53, $20.72, $59,225.98
15. $500.97, $47.88, $57,205.57

MARGIN EXERCISES, SECTION 7.3, pp. 303–306

1. $109.89   **2.** $12.30   **3.** 19.50%   **4.** $80   **5.** $12.19   **6.** $26.70

EXERCISE SET 7.3, pp. 307–308

1. $840   **3.** $360   **5.** $120.56   **7.** $363.33   **9.** $14\frac{1}{2}$%   **11.** $16\frac{1}{4}$%   **13.** $65, $23.54, 12%   **15.** $8\frac{1}{2}$%, $33.12, $15\frac{1}{2}$%
17. 9%, $432, 16%   **19.** $450, $21.19, 12%   **21.** $600, 8%, $14\frac{3}{4}$%   **23.** $32.00   **25.** $19.00   **27.** $47.60   **29.** $51.66
31. $58.23

MARGIN EXERCISES, SECTION 7.4, pp. 309–312

1. $5.00 **2.** $\frac{15}{78}$ **3.** $9.23, $350.77 **4.** $29.19, $1320.81

EXERCISE SET 7.4, pp. 313–314

1. $20.77 **3.** $1.40 **5.** $3.40 **7.** $12.44 **9.** $8.60 **11.** $13.85 **13.** $459.23 **15.** $23.60 **17.** $206.60 **19.** $167.56
21. $151.40 **23.** $966.15 **25.** $14.44, $438.31 **27.** $48.77, $1580.65

MARGIN EXERCISES, SECTION 7.5, pp. 315–320

1. $6.54 **2.** $9.98 **3.** $258.94 **4.** $30.00 **5.** $400 **6.** $489.23 **7.** $6.23

EXERCISE SET 7.5, pp. 321–324

1.

3. $424.35

[Sears Charge statement for Francis T. Hoyt, 321 Edge Rd., Sumner, IA 50103; Account 3 47601 57893 4; Billing Date Nov 21, 1984; Previous Balance $376.28; New Balance $378.72; Minimum Payment $16.00. Transactions: Finance Charge on avg daily bal of $346.85 — $5.20; 11/03 Payment $50.00; 11/08 Housewares $10.28; 11/15 Automotive Accessories $36.96.]

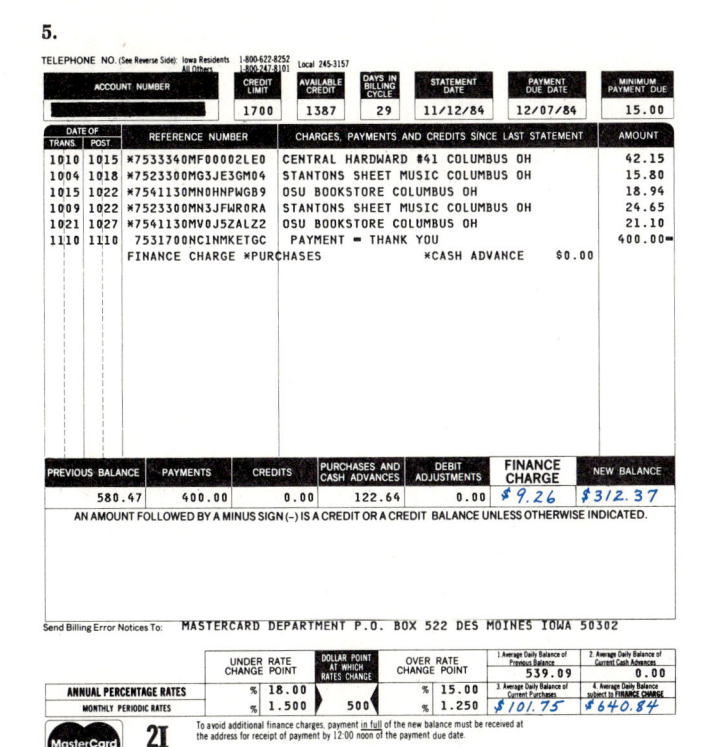

5.

ACCOUNT NUMBER	CREDIT LIMIT	AVAILABLE CREDIT	DAYS IN BILLING CYCLE	STATEMENT DATE	PAYMENT DUE DATE	MINIMUM PAYMENT DUE
	1700	1387	29	11/12/84	12/07/84	15.00

DATE OF TRANS	POST	REFERENCE NUMBER	CHARGES, PAYMENTS AND CREDITS SINCE LAST STATEMENT	AMOUNT
1010	1015	*7533340MF00002LE0	CENTRAL HARDWARD #41 COLUMBUS OH	42.15
1004	1018	*7523300MG3JE3GM04	STANTONS SHEET MUSIC COLUMBUS OH	15.80
1015	1022	*7541130MN0HNPWGB9	OSU BOOKSTORE COLUMBUS OH	18.94
1009	1022	*7523300MN3JFWR0RA	STANTONS SHEET MUSIC COLUMBUS OH	24.65
1021	1027	*7541130MV0J5ZALZ2	OSU BOOKSTORE COLUMBUS OH	21.10
1110	1110	7531700NC1NMKETGC	PAYMENT - THANK YOU	400.00−
		FINANCE CHARGE *PURCHASES *CASH ADVANCE $0.00		

PREVIOUS BALANCE	PAYMENTS	CREDITS	PURCHASES AND CASH ADVANCES	DEBIT ADJUSTMENTS	FINANCE CHARGE	NEW BALANCE
580.47	400.00	0.00	122.64	0.00	$9.26	$312.37

Under Rate Change Point: 18.00% / 1.500
Dollar Point At Which Rates Change: 500
Over Rate Change Point: 15.00% / 1.250

1. Average Daily Balance of Previous Balance: 539.09
2. Average Daily Balance of Current Cash Advances: 0.00
3. Average Daily Balance of Current Purchases: $101.75
4. Average Daily Balance subject to FINANCE CHARGE: $640.84

7.

ACCOUNT NUMBER	CREDIT LIMIT	AVAILABLE CREDIT	DAYS IN BILLING CYCLE	STATEMENT DATE	PAYMENT DUE DATE	MINIMUM PAYMENT DUE
	600	74	30	11/10/84	12/05/84	26.00

DATE OF TRANS	POST	REFERENCE NUMBER	CHARGES, PAYMENTS AND CREDITS SINCE LAST STATEMENT	AMOUNT
1019	1020	*7531700MM1EP7MGDV	TARGET #171 BILLINGS BILLINGS MT	33.24
1025	1025	7531700MV1N3M9P53	PAYMENT - THANK YOU	52.00−
		FINANCE CHARGE *PURCHASES *CASH ADVANCE $0.00		

PREVIOUS BALANCE	PAYMENTS	CREDITS	PURCHASES AND CASH ADVANCES	DEBIT ADJUSTMENTS	FINANCE CHARGE	NEW BALANCE
536.24	52.00	0.00	33.24	0.00	7.81	525.29

Under Rate Change Point: 18.00% / 1.500
Dollar Point At Which Rates Change: 500
Over Rate Change Point: 15.00% / 1.250

1. Average Daily Balance of Previous Balance: 500.28
2. Average Daily Balance of Current Cash Advances: 0.00
3. Average Daily Balance of Current Purchases: 24.38
4. Average Daily Balance subject to FINANCE CHARGE: 524.66

TEST OR REVIEW, CHAPTER 7, pp. 325–326

1. $946.00   2. 13%   3. 12.30%   4. $145.41   5. $653.72, $33.53, $58,075.12   6. $1144.00   7. 13%   8. $46.00   9. $5.23
10. $374.77   11. $10.81

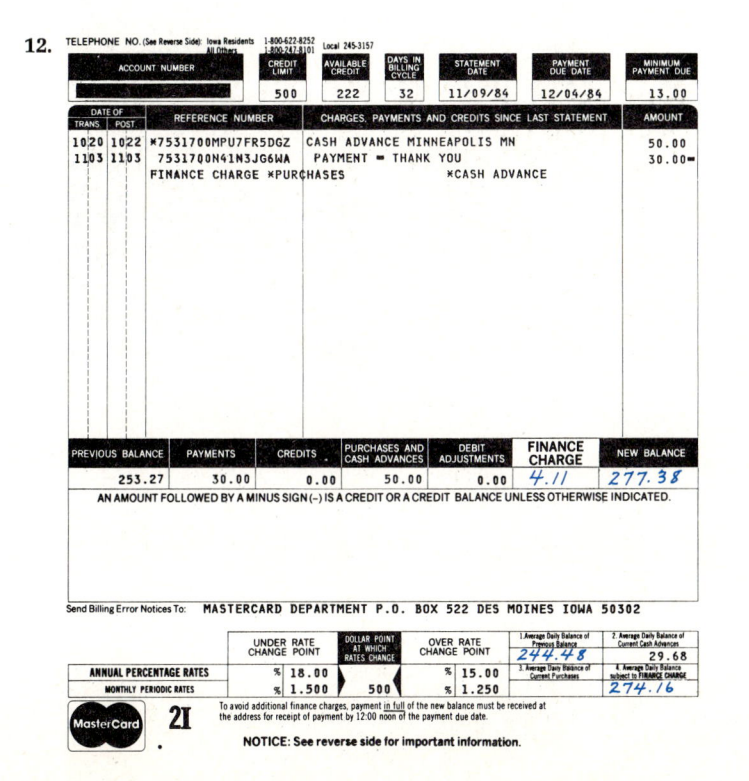

12.

ACCOUNT NUMBER	CREDIT LIMIT	AVAILABLE CREDIT	DAYS IN BILLING CYCLE	STATEMENT DATE	PAYMENT DUE DATE	MINIMUM PAYMENT DUE
	500	222	32	11/09/84	12/04/84	13.00

DATE OF TRANS	POST	REFERENCE NUMBER	CHARGES, PAYMENTS AND CREDITS SINCE LAST STATEMENT	AMOUNT
1020	1022	*7531700MPU7FR5DGZ	CASH ADVANCE MINNEAPOLIS MN	50.00
1103	1103	7531700N41N3JG6WA	PAYMENT - THANK YOU	30.00−
		FINANCE CHARGE *PURCHASES *CASH ADVANCE		

PREVIOUS BALANCE	PAYMENTS	CREDITS	PURCHASES AND CASH ADVANCES	DEBIT ADJUSTMENTS	FINANCE CHARGE	NEW BALANCE
253.27	30.00	0.00	50.00	0.00	4.11	277.38

Under Rate Change Point: 18.00% / 1.500
Dollar Point At Which Rates Change: 500
Over Rate Change Point: 15.00% / 1.250

1. Average Daily Balance of Previous Balance: 244.48
2. Average Daily Balance of Current Cash Advances: 29.68
3. Average Daily Balance of Current Purchases:
4. Average Daily Balance subject to FINANCE CHARGE: 274.16

CHAPTER 8

READINESS CHECK, p. 328

1. [2.3, ■] $59,500 **2.** [2.3, ■] $15,281.25 **3.** [3.4A, ■][3.4B, ■] $33.75 **4.** [2.2, ■] $1721.25
5. [2.2, ■] $1619.75 **6.** [2.3, ■][2.4, ■] 0.08 **7.** [2.3, ■][2.4, ■] 16.0

MARGIN EXERCISES, SECTION 8.1, pp. 330–332

1. $2919.75 **2.** $33.030 **3.** $2805.25 **4.** $32,520

EXERCISE SET 8.1, pp. 333–334

1. $6660 **3.** 1874.25 **5.** $11,870 **7.** $26,395 **9.** $1102.50 **11.** $4715 **13.** $11,576.25 **15.** $41,012.50 **17.** $382,350

MARGIN EXERCISES, SECTION 8.2, pp. 335–336

1. 7.8% **2.** 11.0% **3.** 11.6 **4.** 6.4

EXERCISE SET 8.2, pp. 337–338

1. 7.6% **3.** 4.5% **5.** 1.8% **7.** 15.0 **9.** 7.0 **11.** 10.0 **13.** 9.0%

MARGIN EXERCISES, SECTION 8.3, pp. 339–342

1. $2080 **2.** $18,157.50 **3.** 8.5% **4.** 9.2%

EXERCISE SET 8.3, pp. 343–344

1. $2017.50 **3.** $2150 **5.** $9775 **7.** $14,687.50 **9.** $9250 **11.** 8.7% **13.** 10.2% **15.** 9.2% **17.** 5.4% **19.** 8.6%
21. $353,010; 9.5%

TEST OR REVIEW, CHAPTER 8, pp. 345–346

1. $4296.75 **2.** $5710 **3.** $4128.25 **4.** $5540 **5.** 3.1% **6.** 13.0 **7.** $2961.25 **8.** $17,115 **9.** 6.3% **10.** 8.6%

CHAPTER 9

READINESS CHECK, p. 348

1. [1.1, ■] 750 **2.** [1.1, ■] 200 **3.** [1.1, ■] 1,341 **4.** [1.1, ■] 67 **5.** [3.4A, ■] $11,200 **6.** [1.3, ■] $20,375
7. [2.3, ■] 56.16 **8.** [2.3, ■] 91.26 **9.** [1.6, ■] 37,500 **10.** [1.6, ■] 48,000 **11.** [1.2, ■] 420 **12.** [1.2, ■] 1150

MARGIN EXERCISES, SECTION 9.1, pp. 349–356

1. $45.00 **2.** $464 **3.** $65,000 **4.** $10,000 **5.** $6617.65 **6.** up to $24,000 for contents, up to $9600 for living expenses
7. $187.50 **8.** $240.00 **9.** $446.00 **10.** $1011.00

EXERCISE SET 9.1, pp. 357–358

1. $850.00 **3.** $150.00 **5.** $612.00 **7.** $45,000 **9.** $5,000 **11.** $4090.91
13. up to $18,500 for contents, up to $7400 for living expenses **15.** $840.00 **17.** $475 **19.** $78 **21.** $125 **23.** $325
25. $349 **27.** $1045

CHAPTER 10 — SECTION 9.2 TO SECTION 10.2

MARGIN EXERCISES, SECTION 9.2, pp. 359–363

1. $100,000 **2.** $2435 **3.** $3632 **4.** $3250 **5.** $600 **6.** $21 **7.** $1868 **8.** $402.34

EXERCISES SET 9.2, pp. 365–366

1. (a) $6,250, (b) $100,000 **3.** (a) 0, (b) $238 **5.** (a) $3679, (b) $5000 **7.** (a) 0, (b) $5675 **9.** (a) $100, (b) $3446 **11.** (a) 0, (b) $275,000 **13.** (a) $2000, (b) $50,000 **15.** (a) 0, (b) $4200 **17.** (a) 0, (b) $317 **19.** (a) $500, (b) $280 **21.** $176.72 **23.** $193.50 **25.** $287.66 **27.** $306.14 **29.** $148.17 **31.** $875,876.50

MARGIN EXERCISES, SECTION 9.3, pp. 368–374

1. $20,265 **2.** $5330 **3.** The extended term insurance option is 23 years, 251 days. **4.** $12,930 **5.** $302.00 **6.** $504.75 **7.** $669.60 **8.** (a) $26.54, (b) $318.48

EXERCISE SET 9.3, pp. 375–376

1. $28,880 **3.** $20,440 **5.** $10,600 **7.** $2380 **9.** 23 years **11.** 20 years, 247 days **13.** $30,760 **15.** $27,825 **17.** $405.30 **19.** $402.00 **21.** $313.75 **23.** $119.26, $477.04 **25.** $84,835 **27.** $80.27

TEST OR REVIEW, CHAPTER 9, pp. 377–378

1. $4687.50 **2.** $1800 **3.** $220 **4.** $3500 **5.** $100,000 **6.** $2450 **7.** $389.36 **8.** $36,675 **9.** $6440 **10.** $30,000 for 19 years, 213 days **11.** $40,050 **12.** $187.95 **13.** $510.80 **14.** $415.20

CHAPTER 10

READINESS CHECK, p. 380

1. [3.4A, ●●] 2¢ **2.** [3.4A, ●●] $17,550 **3.** [2.2, ●] $30.11 **4.** [2.2, ●] $24,020.00 **5.** [2.3, ●●] 4191.26 **6.** [1.4, ●] .015

MARGIN EXERCISES, SECTION 10.1, pp. 380–382

1. 4¢ **2.** 3¢ **3.** $28.36 **4.** $4790.10 **5.** $7393.27

EXERCISE SET 10.1, pp. 383–384

1. 3¢ **3.** 5¢ **5.** 3¢ **7.** $7.50 **9.** $1954.16 **11.** $49.50 **13.** $252.00 **15.** $6465.71 **17.** $9425.00 **19.** $145.38 **21.** $11.60, $301.55 **23.** $229.99, 3%

MARGIN EXERCISES, SECTION 10.2, pp. 385–386

1. $22,360 **2.** 12,457 mills **3.** $111.11

EXERCISE SET 10.2, pp. 387–388

1. $31,247.50 **3.** $37,125 **5.** $37,440 **7.** 4.15 mills **9.** 1.22% **11.** $689.51 **13.** $252.97 **15.** $307.35 **17.** 15.09 mills

A–20 CHAPTER 10 ANSWERS SECTION 10.3

MARGIN EXERCISES, SECTION 10.3, pp. 393, 396

1.

Department of the Treasury — Internal Revenue Service

Form 1040EZ Income Tax Return for Single filers with no dependents (0)

OMB No. 1545-0675

Instructions are on the back of this form.
Tax Table is in the 1040EZ and 1040A Tax Package.

Name and address

Use the IRS mailing label. If you don't have a label, print or type:

Name (first, initial, last): Jerry K. Reid
Social security number: 356 13 2684
Present home address: 17 Northwestern Ave.
City, town or post office, State, and ZIP code: Burlingame, CA 94010

Presidential Election Campaign Fund
Check this box ☑ if you want $1 of your tax to go to this fund.

Figure your tax

Attach Copy B of Forms W-2 here

1 Wages, salaries, and tips. Attach your W-2 form(s). ... 1 20,225.00

2 Interest income of $400 or less. If more than $400, you cannot use Form 1040EZ. ... 2 250.00

3 Add line 1 and line 2. This is your **adjusted gross income**. ... 3 20,475.00

4 Allowable part of your charitable contributions. Complete the worksheet on page 18. Do not write more than $25. ... 4 15.00

5 Subtract line 4 from line 3. ... 5 20,460.00

6 Amount of your personal exemption. ... 6 1,000.00

7 Subtract line 6 from line 5. This is your **taxable income**. ... 7 19,460.00

8 Enter your Federal income tax withheld. This is shown on your W-2 form(s). ... 8 4,010.00

9 Use the tax table on pages 26-31 to find the **tax** on your taxable income on line 7. ... 9 3,589.00

Refund or amount you owe

Attach tax payment here

10 If line 8 is larger than line 9, subtract line 9 from line 8. Enter the amount of your **refund**. ... 10 421.00

11 If line 9 is larger than line 8, subtract line 8 from line 9. Enter the **amount you owe**. Attach check or money order for the full amount payable to "Internal Revenue Service." ... 11

Sign your return

I have read this return. Under penalties of perjury, I declare that to the best of my knowledge and belief, the return is correct and complete.

Your signature: X Jerry K. Reid
Date: April 5, 1984

For Privacy Act and Paperwork Reduction Act Notice, see page 34.

2.

Department of the Treasury—Internal Revenue Service

Form 1040A US Individual Income Tax Return (0)

OMB No. 1545-0085

Step 1
Name and address
Use the IRS mailing label. Otherwise, print or type.

Your first name and initial (if joint return, also give spouse's name and initial) | Last name | Your social security no.

Present home address | Spouse's social security no.

City, town or post office, State, and ZIP code | Your occupation | Spouse's occupation

Presidential Election Campaign Fund
Do you want $1 to go to this fund?...... ☐ Yes ☐ No
If joint return, does your spouse want $1 to go to this fund? ☐ Yes ☐ No

Step 2
Filing status
(Check only one)
and Exemptions

1 ☐ Single (See if you can use Form 1040EZ.)
2 ☑ Married filing joint return (even if only one had income)
3 ☐ Married filing separate return. Enter spouse's social security no. above and full name here. _____
4 ☐ Head of household (with qualifying person). If the qualifying person is your unmarried child but not your dependent, write this child's name here. _____

Always check the exemption box labeled Yourself. Check other boxes if they apply.

5a ☑ Yourself ☐ 65 or over ☐ Blind
 b ☑ Spouse   ☐ 65 or over ☐ Blind

Write number of boxes checked on 5a and b **2**

c First names of your dependent children who lived with you _____

Write number of children listed on 5c ☐

Attach Copy B of Forms W-2 here

d Other dependents:
(1) Name | (2) Relationship | (3) Number of months lived in your home. | (4) Did dependent have income of $1,000 or more? | (5) Did you provide more than one-half of dependent's support?

Write number of other dependents listed on 5d ☐

e Total number of exemptions claimed.......

Add numbers entered in boxes above **2**

Step 3
Adjusted gross income

6 Wages, salaries, tips, etc. (Attach Forms W-2)........... 6 **37020 —**
7 Interest income (Complete page 2 if over $400 or you have any All-Savers interest)... 7 **110 —**
8a Dividends _____ (Complete page 2 if over $400) 8b Exclusion _____ Subtract line 8b from 8a 8c
9a Unemployment compensation (insurance). Total from Form(s) 1099-UC _____
 b Taxable amount, if any, from worksheet on page 16 of Instructions......... 9b
10 Add lines 6, 7, 8c, and 9b. This is your total income......... 10 **37,130 —**
11 Deduction for a married couple when both work. Complete the worksheet on page 17.... 11 **75 —**
12 Subtract line 11 from line 10. This is your adjusted gross income......... 12 **37,055 —**

Step 4
Taxable income

13 Allowable part of your charitable contributions. Complete the worksheet on page 18..... 13 **15 —**
14 Subtract line 13 from line 12....... 14 **37,040 —**
15 Multiply $1,000 by the total number of exemptions claimed in box 5e....... 15 **2,000 —**
16 Subtract line 15 from line 14. This is your taxable income........ 16 **35,040 —**

Step 5
Tax, credits, and payments

Attach check or money order here

17a Partial credit for political contributions. See page 19....... ■ 17a
 b Total Federal income tax withheld, from W-2 form(s). (If line 6 is more than $32,400, see page 19.)........ 17b **8300 —**

Stop Here and Sign Below if You Want IRS to Figure Your Tax

 c Earned income credit, from worksheet on page 21...... 17c
18 Add lines 17a, b, and c. These are your total credits and payments........ 18 **8300 —**
19a Find tax on amount on line 16. Use tax table, pages 26-31..... 19a **7265 —**
 b Advance EIC payment (from W-2 form(s))........ 19b
20 Add lines 19a and 19b. This is your total tax....... 20 **7265 —**

Step 6
Refund or amount you owe

21 If line 18 is larger than line 20, subtract line 20 from line 18. Enter the amount to be **refunded to you**....... 21 **1035 —**
22 If line 20 is larger than line 18, subtract line 18 from line 20. Enter the **amount you owe**. Attach payment for full amount payable to "Internal Revenue Service."........ 22

Step 7
Sign your return

I have read this return and any attachments filed with it. Under penalties of perjury, I declare that to the best of my knowledge and belief, the return and attachments are correct and complete.

▶ Your signature | Date | ▶ Spouse's signature (If filing jointly, BOTH must sign)

Paid preparer's signature | Date | Check if self-employed ☐ | Preparer's social security no.

Firm's name (or yours, if self-employed) _____ E.I. no.
Address and Zip code _____

For **Privacy Act and Paperwork Reduction Act Notice**, see page 34.

A-22 CHAPTER 10 ANSWERS   SECTION 10.3

EXERCISE SET 10.3, pp. 397–400

1.

Department of the Treasury — Internal Revenue Service

Form 1040EZ Income Tax Return for Single filers with no dependents (0)

OMB No. 1545-0675

Instructions are on the back of this form.
Tax Table is in the 1040EZ and 1040A Tax Package.

Name and address

Use the IRS mailing label. If you don't have a label, print or type:

Name (first, initial, last)   Social security number

Present home address

City, town or post office, State, and ZIP code

Presidential Election Campaign Fund
Check this box ☐ if you want $1 of your tax to go to this fund.

Figure your tax

Attach Copy B of Forms W-2 here

1	Wages, salaries, and tips. Attach your W-2 form(s).	1	14780.—
2	Interest income of $400 or less. If more than $400, you cannot use Form 1040EZ.	2	70.—
3	Add line 1 and line 2. This is your **adjusted gross income**.	3	14850.—
4	Allowable part of your charitable contributions. Complete the worksheet on page 18. Do not write more than $25.	4	15.—
5	Subtract line 4 from line 3.	5	14835.—
6	Amount of your personal exemption.	6	1,000.00
7	Subtract line 6 from line 5. This is your **taxable income**.	7	13835.—
8	Enter your Federal income tax withheld. This is shown on your W-2 form(s).	8	2340.—
9	Use the tax table on pages 26-31 to find the **tax** on your taxable income on line 7.	9	2060.—

Refund or amount you owe

Attach tax payment here

10 If line 8 is larger than line 9, subtract line 9 from line 8. Enter the amount of your **refund**. 10 280.

11 If line 9 is larger than line 8, subtract line 8 from line 9. Enter the **amount you owe**. Attach check or money order for the full amount payable to "Internal Revenue Service." 11 .

Sign your return

I have read this return. Under penalties of perjury, I declare that to the best of my knowledge and belief, the return is correct and complete.

Your signature   Date

X

For **Privacy Act and Paperwork Reduction Act Notice, see page 34.**

CHAPTER 10 SECTION 10.3 **A–23**

3.

Department of the Treasury—Internal Revenue Service

Form 1040A US Individual Income Tax Return (0)

OMB No. 1545-0085

Step 1
Name and address
Use the IRS mailing label. Otherwise, print or type.

Your first name and initial (if joint return, also give spouse's name and initial) | Last name | Your social security no.

Present home address | Spouse's social security no.

City, town or post office, State, and ZIP code | Your occupation
| Spouse's occupation

Presidential Election Campaign Fund
Do you want $1 to go to this fund?........ ☐ Yes ☐ No
If joint return, does your spouse want $1 to go to this fund? ☐ Yes ☐ No

Step 2
Filing status
(Check only one)
and Exemptions

1 ☐ Single (See if you can use Form 1040EZ.)
2 ☑ Married filing joint return (even if only one had income)
3 ☐ Married filing separate return. Enter spouse's social security no. above and full name here. _____
4 ☐ Head of household (with qualifying person). If the qualifying person is your unmarried child but not your dependent, write this child's name here. _____

Always check the exemption box labeled Yourself. Check other boxes if they apply.

5a ☑ Yourself ☐ 65 or over ☐ Blind
 b ☑ Spouse ☐ 65 or over ☐ Blind

Write number of boxes checked on 5a and b **2**

c First names of your dependent children who lived with you _JEFF, Jill_

Write number of children listed on 5c **2**

Attach Copy B of Forms W-2 here

d Other dependents: (1) Name (2) Relationship (3) Number of months lived in your home. (4) Did dependent have income of $1,000 or more? (5) Did you provide more than one-half of dependent's support?

Write number of other dependents listed on 5d ☐

e Total number of exemptions claimed........

Add numbers entered in boxes above **4**

Step 3
Adjusted gross income

6 Wages, salaries, tips, etc. (Attach Forms W-2)........ 6 **48260.—**
7 Interest income (Complete page 2 if over $400 or you have any All-Savers interest)....... 7 **140.—**
8a Dividends _____ (Complete page 2 if over $400) 8b Exclusion _____ Subtract line 8b from 8a 8c
9a Unemployment compensation (insurance). Total from Form(s) 1099-UC _____
 b Taxable amount, if any, from worksheet on page 16 of Instructions........ 9b
10 Add lines 6, 7, 8c, and 9b. This is your total income........ 10 **48400.—**
11 Deduction for a married couple when both work. Complete the worksheet on page 17..... 11 **170.—**
12 Subtract line 11 from line 10. This is your adjusted gross income........ 12 **48230.—**

Step 4
Taxable income

13 Allowable part of your charitable contributions. Complete the worksheet on page 18..... 13 **20.—**
14 Subtract line 13 from line 12........ 14 **48210.—**
15 Multiply $1,000 by the total number of exemptions claimed in box 5e........ 15 **4000.—**
16 Subtract line 15 from line 14. This is your taxable income........ 16 **44210.—**

Step 5
Tax, credits, and payments

17a Partial credit for political contributions. See page 19...... ■ 17a
 b Total Federal income tax withheld, from W-2 form(s). (If line 6 is more than $32,400, see page 19.)....... 17b **8271.—**

Stop Here and Sign Below if You Want IRS to Figure Your Tax

Attach check or money order here

 c Earned income credit, from worksheet on page 21.......... 17c
18 Add lines 17a, b, and c. These are your total credits and payments........ 18 **8271.—**
19a Find tax on amount on line 16. Use tax table, pages 26-31...... 19a **10843.—**
 b Advance EIC payment (from W-2 form(s))........ 19b
20 Add lines 19a and 19b. This is your total tax........ 20 **10843.—**

Step 6
Refund or amount you owe

21 If line 18 is larger than line 20, subtract line 20 from line 18. Enter the amount to be **refunded to you**........ 21
22 If line 20 is larger than line 18, subtract line 18 from line 20. Enter the **amount you owe**. Attach payment for full amount payable to "Internal Revenue Service."........ 22 **2572.—**

Step 7
Sign your return

I have read this return and any attachments filed with it. Under penalties of perjury, I declare that to the best of my knowledge and belief, the return and attachments are correct and complete.

▶ Your signature | Date | ▶ Spouse's signature (If filing jointly, BOTH must sign)

Paid preparer's signature | Date | Check if self-employed ☐ | Preparer's social security no.

Firm's name (or yours, if self-employed) | E.I. no.
Address and Zip code

For **Privacy Act and Paperwork Reduction Act Notice,** see page 34.

A-24 CHAPTER 10 ANSWERS — TEST OR REVIEW

TEST OR REVIEW, CHAPTER 10, pp. 401–404

1. $1.49   2. $9482.69   3. $16,740   4. 10.579 mills   5. $673.23

6.

Department of the Treasury — Internal Revenue Service

Form 1040EZ Income Tax Return for Single filers with no dependents (0)

OMB No. 1545-0675

Instructions are on the back of this form.
Tax Table is in the 1040EZ and 1040A Tax Package.

Name and address

Use the IRS mailing label. If you don't have a label, print or type:

Name (first, initial, last)   Social security number

Present home address

City, town or post office, State, and ZIP code

Presidential Election Campaign Fund
Check this box ☐ if you want $1 of your tax to go to this fund.

Figure your tax

1 Wages, salaries, and tips. Attach your W-2 form(s).   1   24820.—

2 Interest income of $400 or less. If more than $400, you cannot use Form 1040EZ.   2   70.—

Attach Copy B of Forms W-2 here

3 Add line 1 and line 2. This is your **adjusted gross income**.   3   24890.—

4 Allowable part of your charitable contributions. Complete the worksheet on page 18. Do not write more than $25.   4   25.—

5 Subtract line 4 from line 3.   5   24865.—

6 Amount of your personal exemption.   6   1,000.00

7 Subtract line 6 from line 5. This is your **taxable income**.   7   23865.—

8 Enter your Federal income tax withheld. This is shown on your W-2 form(s).   8   5200.—

9 Use the tax table on pages 26-31 to find the **tax** on your taxable income on line 7.   9   4968.—

Refund or amount you owe

10 If line 8 is larger than line 9, subtract line 9 from line 8. Enter the amount of your **refund**.   10   232.—

Attach tax payment here

11 If line 9 is larger than line 8, subtract line 8 from line 9. Enter the **amount you owe**. Attach check or money order for the full amount payable to "Internal Revenue Service."   11   .

Sign your return

I have read this return. Under penalties of perjury, I declare that to the best of my knowledge and belief, the return is correct and complete.

Your signature   Date

X

For **Privacy Act and Paperwork Reduction Act Notice**, see page 34.

CHAPTER 10   TEST OR REVIEW   A-25

7.

Department of the Treasury—Internal Revenue Service

Form 1040A US Individual Income Tax Return (0)

OMB No. 1545-0085

Step 1
Name and address

Use the IRS mailing label. Otherwise, print or type.

Your first name and initial (if joint return, also give spouse's name and initial)   Last name   Your social security no.

Present home address   Spouse's social security no.

City, town or post office, State, and ZIP code   Your occupation

Spouse's occupation

Presidential Election Campaign Fund

Do you want $1 to go to this fund? ☐ Yes ☐ No
If joint return, does your spouse want $1 to go to this fund? ☐ Yes ☐ No

Step 2
Filing status
(Check only one)
and Exemptions

1. ☐ Single (See if you can use Form 1040EZ.)
2. ☑ Married filing joint return (even if only one had income)
3. ☐ Married filing separate return. Enter spouse's social security no. above and full name here.
4. ☐ Head of household (with qualifying person). If the qualifying person is your unmarried child but not your dependent, write this child's name here.

Always check the exemption box labeled Yourself. Check other boxes if they apply.

5a ☑ Yourself   ☐ 65 or over   ☐ Blind   Write number of boxes checked on 5a and b **2**
   b ☑ Spouse   ☐ 65 or over   ☐ Blind

c First names of your dependent children who lived with you
     SARA   Write number of children listed on 5c **1**

Attach Copy B of Forms W-2 here

d Other dependents: (1) Name   (2) Relationship   (3) Number of months lived in your home.   (4) Did dependent have income of $1,000 or more?   (5) Did you provide more than one-half of dependent's support?   Write number of other dependents listed on 5d ☐

e Total number of exemptions claimed . . . . Add numbers entered in boxes above **3**

Step 3
Adjusted gross income

6. Wages, salaries, tips, etc. (Attach Forms W-2) 6   **27460.—**
7. Interest income (Complete page 2 if over $400 or you have any All-Savers interest) . . . 7   **210.—**
8a Dividends _____ (Complete page 2 if over $400)   8b Exclusion _____ Subtract line 8b from 8a   8c
9a Unemployment compensation (insurance). Total from Form(s) 1099-UC _____
   b Taxable amount, if any, from worksheet on page 16 of Instructions 9b
10. Add lines 6, 7, 8c, and 9b. This is your total income 10   **27670.—**
11. Deduction for a married couple when both work. Complete the worksheet on page 17. 11   **112.—**
12. Subtract line 11 from line 10. This is your adjusted gross income 12   **27558.**

Step 4
Taxable income

13. Allowable part of your charitable contributions. Complete the worksheet on page 18. 13   **20.—**
14. Subtract line 13 from line 12 14   **27538.—**
15. Multiply $1,000 by the total number of exemptions claimed in box 5e 15   **3000.—**
16. Subtract line 15 from line 14. This is your taxable income 16   **24538.**

Step 5
Tax, credits, and payments

Attach check or money order here

17a Partial credit for political contributions. See page 19 . . . . . 17a
   b Total Federal income tax withheld, from W-2 form(s). (If line 6 is more than $32,400, see page 19.) . . . . 17b   **3540.—**

Stop Here and Sign Below if You Want IRS to Figure Your Tax

   c Earned income credit, from worksheet on page 21 . . . . . 17c
18. Add lines 17a, b, and c. These are your total credits and payments 18   **3540.—**
19a Find tax on amount on line 16. Use tax table, pages 26-31 . . . 19a   **4018.**
   b Advance EIC payment (from W-2 form(s)) 19b
20. Add lines 19a and 19b. This is your total tax 20   **4018.—**

Step 6
Refund or amount you owe

21. If line 18 is larger than line 20, subtract line 20 from line 18. Enter the amount to be **refunded to you** 21
22. If line 20 is larger than line 18, subtract line 18 from line 20. Enter the **amount you owe**. Attach payment for full amount payable to "Internal Revenue Service." 22   **478.—**

Step 7
Sign your return

I have read this return and any attachments filed with it. Under penalties of perjury, I declare that to the best of my knowledge and belief, the return and attachments are correct and complete.

Your signature   Date   Spouse's signature (If filing jointly, BOTH must sign)

Paid preparer's signature   Date   Check if self-employed ☐   Preparer's social security no.

Firm's name (or yours, if self-employed)   E.I. no.
Address and Zip code

For **Privacy Act and Paperwork Reduction Act Notice,** see page 34.

A-26 CHAPTER 10 ANSWERS — TEST OR REVIEW

8.

Department of the Treasury—Internal Revenue Service

Form 1040A US Individual Income Tax Return (0)

OMB No. 1545-0085

Step 1 — Name and address
(Use the IRS mailing label. Otherwise, print or type.)

Your first name and initial (if joint return, also give spouse's name and initial) — Last name — Your social security no.

Present home address — Spouse's social security no.

City, town or post office, State, and ZIP code — Your occupation — Spouse's occupation

Presidential Election Campaign Fund
Do you want $1 to go to this fund? ☐ Yes ☐ No
If joint return, does your spouse want $1 to go to this fund? ☐ Yes ☐ No

Step 2 — Filing status (Check only one) **and Exemptions**

1. ☐ Single (See if you can use Form 1040EZ.)
2. ☐ Married filing joint return (even if only one had income)
3. ☐ Married filing separate return. Enter spouse's social security no. above and full name here.
4. ☑ Head of household (with qualifying person). If the qualifying person is your unmarried child but not your dependent, write this child's name here.

Always check the exemption box labeled Yourself. Check other boxes if they apply.

5a. ☑ Yourself ☐ 65 or over ☐ Blind
 b. ☐ Spouse ☐ 65 or over ☐ Blind — Write number of boxes checked on 5a and b: **1**
 c. First names of your dependent children who lived with you: **LORA** — Write number of children listed on 5c: **1**
 d. Other dependents: (1) Name (2) Relationship (3) Number of months lived in your home (4) Did dependent have income of $1,000 or more? (5) Did you provide more than one-half of dependent's support? — Write number of other dependents listed on 5d: ☐
 e. Total number of exemptions claimed — Add numbers entered in boxes above: **2**

(Attach Copy B of Forms W-2 here)

Step 3 — Adjusted gross income

6. Wages, salaries, tips, etc. (Attach Forms W-2) ... 6 **15280 —**
7. Interest income (Complete page 2 if over $400 or you have any All-Savers interest) ... 7 **40 —**
8a. Dividends _____ (Complete page 2 if over $400) 8b Exclusion _____ Subtract line 8b from 8a ... 8c
9a. Unemployment compensation (insurance). Total from Form(s) 1099-UC _____
 b. Taxable amount, if any, from worksheet on page 16 of Instructions ... 9b
10. Add lines 6, 7, 8c, and 9b. This is your total income ... 10 **15320 —**
11. Deduction for a married couple when both work. Complete the worksheet on page 17 ... 11
12. Subtract line 11 from line 10. This is your adjusted gross income ... 12 **15320 —**

Step 4 — Taxable income

13. Allowable part of your charitable contributions. Complete the worksheet on page 18 ... 13 **10 —**
14. Subtract line 13 from line 12 ... 14 **15310 —**
15. Multiply $1,000 by the total number of exemptions claimed in box 5e ... 15 **2000 —**
16. Subtract line 15 from line 14. This is your taxable income ... 16 **13310 —**

Step 5 — Tax, credits, and payments

17a. Partial credit for political contributions. See page 19 ... ■ 17a
 b. Total Federal income tax withheld, from W-2 form(s). (If line 6 is more than $32,400, see page 19.) ... 17b **1590 —**
 Stop Here and Sign Below if You Want IRS to Figure Your Tax
 c. Earned income credit, from worksheet on page 21 ... 17c
18. Add lines 17a, b, and c. These are your total credits and payments ... 18 **1590 —**
19a. Find tax on amount on line 16. Use tax table, pages 26-31 ... 19a **1854 —**
 b. Advance EIC payment (from W-2 form(s)) ... 19b
20. Add lines 19a and 19b. This is your total tax ... 20 **1854 —**

(Attach check or money order here)

Step 6 — Refund or amount you owe

21. If line 18 is larger than line 20, subtract line 20 from line 18. Enter the amount to be refunded to you ... 21
22. If line 20 is larger than line 18, subtract line 18 from line 20. Enter the amount you owe. Attach payment for full amount payable to "Internal Revenue Service." ... 22 **264 —**

Step 7 — Sign your return

I have read this return and any attachments filed with it. Under penalties of perjury, I declare that to the best of my knowledge and belief, the return and attachments are correct and complete.

Your signature — Date — Spouse's signature (If filing jointly, BOTH must sign)
Paid preparer's signature — Date — Check if self-employed ☐ — Preparer's social security no.
Firm's name (or yours, if self-employed) — E.I. no.
Address and Zip code

For **Privacy Act and Paperwork Reduction Act Notice**, see page 34.

CHAPTER 11

READINESS CHECK, p. 406

1. [1.2, ◉] $2840   **2.** [1.2, ◉] $360   **3.** [1.1, ◉◉] 89,000   **4.** [1.1, ◉◉] 78,000   **5.** [3.3, ▣▣] 6.4%   **6.** [3.3, ▣▣] 3.8%

MARGIN EXERCISES, SECTION 11.1, pp. 406–408

1. $3880   **2.** $2103   **3.** $5367   **4.** $2092   **5.** The loss was $346.

EXERCISE SET 11.1, pp. 409–410

1. $1233   **3.** $669   **5.** $2204   **7.** $2417   **9.** $957   **11.** $8613   **13.** $2252   **15.** $1855

17. Gross profit = $5245.81: The loss was $454.06.

MARGIN EXERCISES, SECTION 11.2, pp. 411–414

1. $105,000 − ($80,000 + $2000 + $19,000) = $4000   **2.** $140,000 − ($102,000 + $5,000 + $24,000) = $9000

3. $4,000 + $1,500 = $5,500   **4.** $9,000 + $4,000 = $13,000   **5.** $5,500 − $3,500 = $2,000   **6.** $13,000 − $3,500 = $9,500

7. (0.15)($2,000) = $300   **8.** $2,000 − $300 = $1,700   **9.** $9,500 − $1,400 = $8,100   **10.** 1.6%   **11.** 1%   **12.** 26.3%

EXERCISE SET 11.2, pp. 415–416

1.

TRAUX COMPANY
MARBLEBORO, MASSACHUSETTS

Income Statement	1986	1985
Net sales	250,000	210,000
Cost of sales and operating expenses		
Cost of goods sold	187,000	163,000
Depreciation	9,000	6,000
Selling and administrating expenses	43,000	38,000
Operating profit	11,000	3,000
Other income		
Dividends and interest	12,000	8,000
Total income	23,000	11,000
Less bond interest	6,000	6,000
Income before federal tax	17,000	5,000
Federal tax	2,550	750
Net profit for year	14,450	4,250

3.

HUSKY TOOLS
PORTSMOUTH, MAINE

Income Statement	Percent Change	1986	1985
Net sales	17.5	370,000	315,000
Cost of sales and operating expenses			
Cost of goods sold		230,000	160,000
Depreciation		10,000	10,000
Selling and administrating expenses	11.1	50,000	45,000
Operating profit	−20	80,000	100,000

(continued)

Income Statement	Percent Change	1986	1985
Other income			
Dividends and interest		30,000	5,000
Total income	4.8	110,000	105,000
Less bond interest		20,000	20,000
Income before federal tax		90,000	85,000
Federal tax		16,000	14,000
Net profit for year	4.2	74,000	71,000

5.

	1986	1985
Traux Company	5.7%	2.0%
Microelectronics	22.3%	no
Husky Tools	20%	22.5%

MARGIN EXERCISES, SECTION 11.3, pp. 417–424

1. $5,200 + $9,800 + $20,000 + $43,000 = $78,000   2. $7,000 + $13,000 + $28,000 + $41,000 = $89,000
3. $6,000 + $45,000 + $11,000 + $1,500 = $63,500   4. $6,000 + $48,000 + $14,000 + $2,000 = $70,000
5. $63,500 − $11,500 = $52,000   6. $70,000 − $14,000 = $56,000   7. $78,000 + $52,000 + $1,000 + $1,000 = $132,000
8. $89,000 + $56,000 + $2,000 + $1,000 = $148,000   9. $21,000 + $9,000 + $2,000 + $1,000 = $33,000
10. $25,000 + $8,000 + $6,700 + $1,300 = $41,000   11. $33,000 + $35,000 = $68,000
12. $41,000 + $35,000 = $76,000   13. $33,000 + $9,000 + $22,000 = $64,000
14. $33,000 + $9,000 + $30,000 = $72,000   15. $68,000 + $64,000 = $132,000
16. $76,000 + $72,000 = $148,000   17. 2.4 to 1   18. 1.7 to 1

EXERCISE SET 11.3, pp. 425–426

1.

MARLAX INDUSTRIES
McALLEN, TEXAS

Balance Sheet-December 31, 1985

Assets	1985
Current Assets	
Cash	25,000
Marketable securities at cost ($19,000)	15,000
Accounts receivable ($1500)	32,000
Inventories	48,000
Total current assets	120,000

(continued)

Assets	1985
Fixed Assets	
Land	12,000
Buildings	80,000
Machinery	42,000
Office equipment	8,000
	142,000
Less accumulated depreciation	16,000
Net fixed assets	126,000
Prepayments and deferred charges	3,000
Intangibles	2,000
Total assets	251,000

3. $77,000   **5.** 1.7 to 1

TEST OR REVIEW, CHAPTER 11, pp. 427–430

1. $4813   **2.** $4461

3.

HARBISON WALKER
PITTSBURGH, PENNSYLVANIA

Income Statement	1986	Percent of Net Sales
Net sales	205,000	
Cost of sales and operating expenses		
Cost of goods sold	110,000	
Depreciation	18,000	
Selling and administrating expenses	37,000	
Operating profit	40,000	19.5
Other income		
Dividends and interest	5,000	
Total income	45,000	22.0
Less bond interest	15,000	
Income before federal tax	30,000	
Federal tax	4,600	
Net profit for year	25,400	12.4

4.

TELEX INDUSTRIES
TULSA, OK

Income Statement	Percent Change	1986	1985
Net sales	16.7	315,000	270,000
Cost of sales and operating expenses			
Cost of goods sold		170,000	145,000
Depreciation		30,000	25,000
Selling and administrating expenses		80,000	70,000
Operating profit	16.7	35,000	30,000
Other income			
Dividends and interest	25.0	15,000	12,000
Total income		50,000	42,000
Less bond interest		10,000	10,000
Income before federal tax		40,000	32,000
Federal tax		6,400	5,000
Net profit for year	24.4	33,600	27,000

5. 11.1%   6. 10.7%

7.

ARMSTRONG COMPANY
ELY, NEVADA

Balance Sheet-December 31, 1985

Assets	1985
Current Assets	
Cash	12,000
Marketable securities at cost ($35,000)	26,000
Accounts receivable ($3200)	51,000
Inventories	63,000
Total current assets	152,000
Fixed Assets	
Land	21,000
Buildings	93,000
Machinery	49,000
Office equipment	8,000
	171,000
Less accumulated depreciation	18,000
Net fixed assets	153,000
Prepayments and deferred charges	27,000
Intangibles	4,000
Total assets	336,000

8.

ARMSTRONG COMPANY	
Liabilities	**1985**
Current liabilities	
Accounts payable	34,000
Notes payable	13,000
Accrued expenses payable	46,000
Federal income tax payable	11,000
Total current liabilities	104,000
Long term liabilities	
Bonds: 11% interest due 2005	60,000
Total liabilities	164,000
Stockholders Equity	
Capital stock	
Common stock, $5 par value each, 25,000 shares	125,000
Capital surplus	28,000
Accumulated retained earnings	19,000
Total stockholders equity	172,000
Total liabilities and stockholders equity	336,000

9. $48,000 **10.** 1.5 to 1 **11.** .86 to 1

CHAPTER 12

READINESS CHECK, p. 432

1. [3.4A, ●●] 60 × .25 = 15 **2.** [3.4A, ●●] 56.63 × .83 = 47 **3.** [3.4A, ●●] $7.50 **4.** [3.4A, ●●] $24.84
5. [3.3, ●●] 40% **6.** [3.3, ●●] 60% **7.** [3.3, ●●●] 63% **8.** [3.3, ●●●] 43.2%

MARGIN EXERCISES, SECTION 12.1, pp. 432–434

1. $413 **2.** $122.49 **3.** $516 **4.** 20% **5.** $75.06

EXERCISE SET 12.1, pp. 435–436

1. $34.49 **3.** $1569.40 **5.** $35.00 **7.** $31.48 **9.** $629.99 **11.** $13.83 **13.** 20% **15.** 40% **17.** $410.64 **19.** $585.29
21. $137.22, $361.77 **23.** $34\frac{2}{3}$%, $5.20

MARGIN EXERCISES, SECTION 12.2, pp. 437–438

1. $39.52 **2.** $39.52 **3.** $38.12 **4.** $96.22

EXERCISE SET 12.2, pp. 439–440

1. $223.40 **3.** $18.99 **5.** $10.56 **7.** $33.72 **9.** $32.15 **11.** $20.79 **13.** $88.71, $27.28 **15.** $78.89, $20.10

A-32 CHAPTER 13 ANSWERS

SECTION 12.3 TO SECTION 13.1

MARGIN EXERCISES, SECTION 12.3, pp. 441–442

1. 28%   **2.** 29.6%, $2923.00   **3.** The second single discount (19.2%) is a better buy than the first (19.0%).

EXERCISE SET 12.3, pp. 443–444

1. 33%   **3.** 18%   **5.** 21%   **7.** 33%   **9.** 24%   **11.** 27.3%   **13.** 17.9%   **15.** $47.71   **17.** $1017.50
19. The second single discount (23.2%) is a better buy than the first (22.6%).
21. The second single discount (26.5%) is a better buy than the first (25.6%).   **23.** 36.7%, $146.79

MARGIN EXERCISES, SECTION 12.4, pp. 445–446

1. $136.36   **2.** $787.12

EXERCISE SET 12.4, pp. 447–448

1. $1428.28   **3.** $3926.75   **5.** $1013.13   **7.** $2696.28   **9.** $8812.76

MARGIN EXERCISES, SECTION 12.5, pp. 449–450

1. $1250.00   **2.** $27,595   **3.** $11,900

EXERCISE SET 12.5, pp. 451–452

1. $420.00   **3.** $11,000.00   **5.** $598.75   **7.** $584.10   **9.** $1968.00   **11.** $873.00   **13.** $354.00   **15.** $460.00   **17.** $18,009.10
19. $7500   **21.** $11,681   **23.** $40,936   **25.** $53,573

MARGIN EXERCISES, SECTION 12.6, pp. 453–454

1. $15,041.15 (FIFO); $12,978.40 (LIFO); $14,015.92 (weighted average)
2. $12,232.80 (FIFO); $10,170.05 (LIFO); $11,231.41 (weighted average)

EXERCISE SET 12.6, pp. 455–456

1. $15,745.10   **3.** $14,977.76   **5.** $2321.60   **7.** $1792.00   **9.** $1742.16   **11.** $871.90   **13.** $4009.05   **15.** $3824.53
17. $1806.64   **19.** $383.65   **21.** $440.25   **23.** $409.31

TEST OR REVIEW, CHAPTER 12, pp. 457–458

1. $33   **2.** 25%   **3.** $39.96   **4.** 23.5%   **5.** The first single discount ($19\frac{1}{4}$%) is a better buy than the second (19%).
6. $1562.29   **7.** $1978.00   **8.** $23,134   **9.** $776.55   **10.** $374.75

CHAPTER 13

READINESS CHECK, p. 460

1. [2.2, ■] $2391.66   **2.** [2.2, ■] $4175.00   **3.** [2.3, ■] $409.50   **4.** [2.3, ■], [2.4, ■] $548.44
5. [3.4A, ■], [3.4B, ■] $660

MARGIN EXERCISES, SECTION 13.1, pp. 461–462

1. $7100; $1420; 20%

2.

Year	Rate of depreciation	Annual depreciation	Value	Total depreciation
0			$8700	
1	$\frac{1}{5}$ or 20%	$1420	7280	$1420
2	20%	1420	5860	2840
3	20%	1420	4440	4260
4	20%	1420	3020	5680
5	20%	1420	1600	7100

CHAPTER 13

EXERCISE SET 13.1, pp. 465–466

1. (a) $6000; (b) $1500   **3.** (a) 450; (b) $56.25   **5.** (a) $50,000; (b) $1500

7.

Year	Rate of depreciation	Annual depreciation	Value	Total depreciation
0			$8000	
1	$\frac{1}{4}$ or 25%	$1500	6500	$1500
2	25%	1500	5000	3000
3	25%	1500	3500	4500
4	25%	1500	2000	6000

9.

Year	Rate of depreciation	Annual depreciation	Value	Total depreciation
0			$450	
1	$\frac{1}{8}$ or 12.5%	$56.25	393.75	$ 56.25
2	12.5%	56.25	337.50	112.50
3	12.5%	56.25	281.25	168.75
4	12.5%	56.25	225.00	225.00
5	12.5%	56.25	168.75	281.25
6	12.5%	56.25	112.50	337.50
7	12.5%	56.25	56.25	393.75
8	12.5%	56.25	0	450.00

11. $1500, $1500, $48,500; $3000, $1500, $47,000

MARGIN EXERCISES, SECTION 13.2, pp. 467–468

1.

Year	Rate of depreciation	Annual depreciation	Value	Total depreciation
0			$8700	
1	$\frac{2}{5}$ or 40%	$3480	5220	$3480
2	40%	2088	3132	5568
3	40%	1252.80	1879.20	6820.80
4		279.20	1600	7100
5		0	1600	7100

EXERCISE SET 13.2, pp. 469–470

1.

Year	Rate of depreciation	Annual depreciation	Value	Total depreciation
0			$8000	
1	$\frac{2}{4}$ or 50%	$4000	4000	$4000
2	50%	2000	2000	6000
3		0	2000	6000
4		0	2000	6000

3.

Year	Rate of depreciation	Annual depreciation	Value	Total depreciation
*0			$2500	
1	$\frac{2}{6}$ or $33\frac{1}{3}$%	$833.33	1666.67	$ 833.33
2	$33\frac{1}{3}$%	555.56	1111.11	1388.89
3	$33\frac{1}{3}$%	370.37	740.74	1759.26
4	$33\frac{1}{3}$%	246.91	493.83	2006.17
5	$33\frac{1}{3}$%	164.61	329.22	2170.78
6	$33\frac{1}{3}$%	109.74	219.48	2280.52

CHAPTER 13 ANSWERS — SECTION 13.3

5.

Year	Rate of depreciation	Annual depreciation	Value	Total depreciation
0			$5400	
1	$\frac{2}{5}$ or 40%	$2160	3240	$2160
2	40%	1296	1944	3456
3	40%	777.60	1166.40	4233.60
4		166.40	1000.00	4400.00
5		0	1000.00	4400.00

7. $3750, $\frac{3}{80}$ or 3.75%, $96.250;

$3609.38, $\frac{3}{80}$ or 3.75%, $92.640.62

MARGIN EXERCISES, SECTION 13.3, pp. 471–472

1. (a) $\frac{5}{15}, \frac{4}{15}, \frac{3}{15}, \frac{2}{15}, \frac{1}{15}$; (b) $2366.67, $6333.33; $1893.33, $4440.00; $1420.00, $3020.00

2.

Year	Rate of depreciation	Annual depreciation	Value	Total depreciation
0			$8700	
1	$\frac{5}{15}$	$2366.67	6333.33	$2366.67
2	$\frac{4}{15}$	1893.33	4440.00	4260.00
3	$\frac{3}{15}$	1420.00	3020.00	5680.00
4	$\frac{2}{15}$	946.67	2073.33	6626.67
5	$\frac{1}{15}$	473.33	1600.00	7100.00

EXERCISE SET 13.3, pp. 473–474

1. $\frac{4}{10}, \frac{3}{10}, \frac{2}{10}, \frac{1}{10}$ **3.** $\frac{8}{36}, \frac{7}{36}, \frac{6}{36}, \frac{5}{36}, \frac{4}{36}, \frac{3}{36}, \frac{2}{36}, \frac{1}{36}$

5.

Year	Rate of depreciation	Annual depreciation	Value	Total depreciation
0			$8000	
1	$\frac{4}{10}$	$2400	5600	$2400
2	$\frac{3}{10}$	1800	3800	4200
3	$\frac{2}{10}$	1200	2600	5400
4	$\frac{1}{10}$	600	2000	6000

7.

Year	Rate of depreciation	Annual depreciation	Value	Total depreciation
0			$450	
1	$\frac{8}{36}$	$100	350	$100.00
2	$\frac{7}{36}$	87.50	262.50	187.50
3	$\frac{6}{36}$	75.00	187.50	262.50
4	$\frac{5}{36}$	62.50	125.00	325.00
5	$\frac{4}{36}$	50.00	75.00	375.00
6	$\frac{3}{36}$	37.50	37.50	412.50
7	$\frac{2}{36}$	25.00	12.50	437.50
8	$\frac{1}{36}$	12.50	0	450.00

9. $\frac{25}{325}$, $6153.85, $73,846.15;

$\frac{24}{325}$, $5907.69, $67,938.46

CHAPTER 13 — SECTION 13.4 TO TEST OR REVIEW — A-35

MARGIN EXERCISES, SECTION 13.4, pp. 476–477

1.

Year	Rate of depreciation	Annual depreciation	Value	Total depreciation
0			$300,000	
1	25%	$ 75,000	225,000	$ 75,000
2	38%	114,000	111,000	189,000
3	37%	111,000	0	300,000

2.

Year	Rate of depreciation	Annual depreciation	Value	Total depreciation
0			$200,000	
1	15%	$30,000	170,000	$ 30,000
2	22%	44,000	126,000	74,000
3	21%	42,000	84,000	116,000
4	21%	42,000	42,000	158,000
5	21%	42,000	0	200,000

EXERCISE SET 13.4, pp. 479–480

1.

Year	Rate of depreciation	Annual depreciation	Value	Total depreciation
0			$15,000	
1	25%	$3,750	11,250	$ 3,750
2	38%	5,700	5,550	9,450
3	37%	5,550	0	15,000

3.

Year	Rate of depreciation	Annual depreciation	Value	Total depreciation
0			$210,000	
1	15%	$31,500	178,500	$ 31,500
2	22%	46,200	132,300	77,700
3	21%	44,100	88,200	121,800
4	21%	44,100	44,100	165,900
5	21%	44,100	0	210,000

5.

Year	Rate of depreciation	Annual depreciation	Value	Total depreciation
0			$130,000	
1	8%	$10,400	119,600	$ 10,400
2	14%	18,200	101,400	28,600
3	12%	15,600	85,800	44,200
4	10%	13,000	72,800	57,200
5	10%	13,000	59,800	70,200
6	10%	13,000	46,800	83,200
7	9%	11,700	35,100	94,900
8	9%	11,700	23,400	106,600
9	9%	11,700	11,700	118,300
10	9%	11,700	0	130,000

TEST OR REVIEW, CHAPTER 13, pp. 481–482

1.

Year	Rate of depreciation	Annual depreciation	Value	Total depreciation
0			$8500	
1	$\frac{1}{5}$ or 20%	$1700	6800	$1700
2	20%	1700	5100	3400
3	20%	1700	3400	5100
4	20%	1700	1700	6800
5	20%	1700	0	8500

2.

Year	Rate of depreciation	Annual depreciation	Value	Total depreciation
0			$8500	
1	$\frac{2}{5}$ or 40%	$3400	5100	$3400
2	40%	2040	3060	5440
3	40%	1224	1836	6664
4	40%	734.40	1101.60	7398.40
5	40%	440.64	660.96	7839.04

3. $\frac{5}{15}, \frac{4}{15}, \frac{3}{15}, \frac{2}{15}, \frac{1}{15}$

4.

Year	Rate of depreciation	Annual depreciation	Value	Total depreciation
0			$8500	
1	$\frac{5}{15}$	$2833.33	5666.67	$2833.33
2	$\frac{4}{15}$	2266.67	3400	5100
3	$\frac{3}{15}$	1700	1700	6800
4	$\frac{2}{15}$	1133.33	566.67	7933.33
5	$\frac{1}{15}$	566.67	0	8500

5.

Year	Rate of depreciation	Annual depreciation	Value	Total depreciation
0			$8500	
1	15%	$1275	7225	$1275
2	22%	1870	5355	3145
3	21%	1785	3570	4930
4	21%	1785	1785	6715
5	21%	1785	0	8500

CHAPTER 14

READINESS CHECK p. 484

1. [2.2, ●●] $13.34 **2.** [2.2, ●●] $70.00 **3.** [2.3, ●●] $22.00 **4.** [2.3, ●●] $4.80 **5.** [2.3, ●●] $8.57
6. [2.3, ●●] $381.67 **7.** [3.4A, ●●] 37.7% **8.** [3.4A, ●●] $144.75

MARGIN EXERCISES, SECTION 14.1, pp. 484–486

1. $23.55 **2.** $23.05 **3.** 52% **4.** $45.15 **5.** $3.70

EXERCISE SET 14.1, pp. 487–489

1. $1899 **3.** $79.00 **5.** $20.07 **7.** $302 **9.** $39.19 **11.** $6750 **13.** 37% **15.** 48% **17.** 61% **19.** $8203.80 **21.** $7788
23. $159.08 **25.** $81.44 **27.** $375.00 **29.** $75.59 **31.** $155.70 **33.** $5.93 **35.** $1.05, 49% **37.** $14.70, 72%

MARGIN EXERCISES, SECTION 14.2, pp. 492–493

1. 34% **2.** $174 **3.** $86.94 **4.** $3.25

EXERCISE SET 14.2, pp. 495–496

1. 21% **3.** 40% **5.** 40% **7.** 38% **9.** $49.00 **11.** $22.38 **13.** $42.31 **15.** $587.65 **17.** $22.86 **19.** $181.97
21. $27.47 **23.** $3.75 **25.** 75, $.75

MARGIN EXERCISES, SECTION 14.3, pp. 497–500

1. $6.00 **2.** $4.60 **3.** $5591.30 **4.** 29% **5.** 57%

EXERCISE SET 14.3, pp. 501–502

1. $41.50 **3.** $191.50 **5.** $136.80 **7.** $96.75 **9.** $7.00 **11.** $210.00 **13.** $299.00 **15.** $103.53 **17.** 19% **19.** 25%
21. 11% **23.** 25%

TEST OR REVIEW, CHAPTER 14, pp. 503–504

1. $17.95 **2.** 35% **3.** $120.40 **4.** $25.00 **5.** 31% **6.** $199.92 **7.** $11.21 **8.** $544.62 **9.** $1347.50 **10.** $178.50 **11.** 17% **12.** 50%

CHAPTER 15

READINESS CHECK, p. 506

1. [2.2, ●●] $54.08 **2.** [2.2, ●●] $282.63 **3.** [2.2, ●●] $27.20 **4.** [2.2, ●●] $247.20 **5.** [3.4A, ●●] $2278.00 **6.** [3.4A, ●●] $3291.20 **7.** [1.4, ●●] $1400 **8.** [1.4, ●●] $346.15

MARGIN EXERCISES, SECTION 15.1, pp. 506–508

1. $86.42 **2.** $407.68 **3.** $426.79

EXERCISE SET 15.1, pp. 509–510

1. $338.00 **3.** $348.75 **5.** $524.52 **7.** $461.76 **9.** $414.40 **11.** $240.00 **13.** $200.00 **15.** $250.00 **17.** $242.00 **19.** $562.65 **21.** $363.00 **23.** $425.89

MARGIN EXERCISES, SECTION 15.2, pp. 511–512

1. $60.00 **2.** $28.99 **3.** $433.88

EXERCISE SET 15.2, pp. 513–514

1. $235.20 **3.** $220.00 **5.** $441.60 **7.** $396.18 **9.** $535.00 **11.** $396.00 **13.** $255.00 **15.** $581.25 **17.** $530.58 **19.** $525.72 **21.** $32.97, $30.62 **23.** $30.66, $28.47

MARGIN EXERCISES, SECTION 15.3, pp. 515–516

1. $150.00 **2.** $295.38 **3.** $1250.00 **4.** $1416.67

EXERCISE SET 15.3, pp. 517–518

1. $2426.67, $29,120 **3.** $650, $7800 **5.** $1300, $15,600 **7.** $319.85, $693.00 **9.** $769.23, $1666.67 **11.** $269.23, $538.46, $583.33, $1166.67 **13.** $207.69, $415.38, $450.00, $10,800 **15.** $325, $704.17, $1408.33, $16,900 **17.** $288.46, $576.92, $1250, $15,000 **19.** $450, $487.50, $975.00, $11,700 **21.** $280.11, $560.21, $606.90, $1213.79 **23.** $414.15, $828.30, $897.33, $1794.65

MARGIN EXERCISES, SECTION 15.4, pp. 519–522

1. $70,000 **2.** $410 **3.** $3980 **4.** $232 **5.** $1110 **6.** $61 above draw **7.** $663.07

EXERCISE SET 15.4, pp. 523–524

1. $4760 **3.** $500 **5.** $1600 **7.** $192 **9.** $347 **11.** $325 **13.** $671 **15.** $632.10

MARGIN EXERCISES, SECTION 15.5, pp. 525–528

1. $171.62 **2.** $19.93 **3.** $132.30 **4.** $19.50

EXERCISE SET 15.5, pp. 529–530

1. $333.52 **3.** $402.68 **5.** $49.80 **7.** $331.40 **9.** $400.70 **11.** $49

CHAPTER 15 ANSWERS

MARGIN EXERCISES, SECTION 15.6, pp. 531–532

1. $1574.50   **2.** $2412   **3.** $150.66   **4.** $2737.60

EXERCISE SET 15.6, pp. 533–534

1. $1676.49   **3.** $2256   **5.** $2874.30   **7.** $1656.05   **9.** $1547.98   **11.** $1250.89   **13.** $1825.95   **15.** $1917.60   **17.** $4495.80
19. $4495.80   **21.** $4944.60   **23.** $3032.60   **25.** $2927.40   **27.** $3044.25   **29.** $3643.26

MARGIN EXERCISES, SECTION 15.7, pp. 535–540

1. $161.71   **2.** $1403, $1111.27   **3.** 1:24 p.m., $39   **4.** $351.12, $52.26, $8.83, $21.24   **5.** $312.03

EXERCISE SET 15.7, pp. 541–542

1.

WEEKLY TIME TICKET

Employee's Name: DANA GARNER
Week Ending: JULY 24, 1984

JOB NAME OR NO.	KIND OF WORK DONE	S	M	T	W	T	F	S	HRS.	RATE	AMOUNT
36824	ASSEMBLY		3	4	1.7	2	5		15.7	6.50	102.05
47895	MAINTENANCE		2.4	1.8	5.4	3.3	0.6		13.5	6.50	87.75
18462	TROUBLESHOOTING		0.9	1.1		1.8	1.8		5.6	6.50	36.40
49183	PRESS WORK		1.7	1.1	0.9	0.9	0.6		5.2	6.50	33.80

Total Regular Time: 8 8 8 8 8   40   260.00
Approved: apt
Withhold: 16.80   F.I.C.A.: 17.42   Savings: 18.75
Total Earnings: 260.00   Total Deductions: 52.97
Date Paid: 7/27/84   Check No. 2395   NET PAY: 207.03

3.

WEEKLY TIME TICKET

Employee's Name: STANLEE OTT
Week Ending: JULY 24, 1984

JOB NAME OR NO.	KIND OF WORK DONE	S	M	T	W	T	F	S	HRS.	RATE	AMOUNT
47895	MAINTENANCE		0.5	1.5	2.2	3	2.5		9.7	5.75	55.78
18263	WELDING		1.2	3.2	5.1	0.6	3.1		13.2	5.75	75.90
18462	TROUBLESHOOTING		5.1	1.7	0.2	0.7	1.6		9.3	5.75	53.47
49183	PRESS WORK			1.6	0.4	0.5	0.4		2.9	5.75	16.68
62171	GLAZING		1.2		0.1	3.2	0.4		4.9	5.75	28.17

Total Regular Time: 8 8 8 8 8   40   230.00
Approved: apt
Withhold: 21.20   F.I.C.A.: 15.41   INS.: 20.50
Total Earnings: 230.00   Total Deductions: 57.11
Date Paid: 7/27/84   Check No. 2397   NET PAY: 172.89

CHAPTER 16 TEST OR REVIEW TO SECTION 16.2 **A-39**

5.

	PAYROLL JOURNAL				SHEET NO. ____

WORK WEEK, BEGINS—DAY _Monday_   TIME OF DAY _____   DATE OF PAYMENT _July 27, 1984_

EMPLOYEE'S NAME	EXEMPTIONS	HOURS OF WORK								REGULAR RATE OF PAY	EARNINGS			DEDUCTIONS							NET CASH WAGES PAID
	FED.	STATE	S	M	T	W	T	F	S	TOTAL HOURS		AT REGULAR RATE	EXTRA FOR OVERTIME	OTHER WAGES	TOTAL WAGES	F.O.A.B. TAX	FED. WITH-HOLDING TAX	STATE WITH-HOLDING TAX	SAV	CONT	INS	TOTAL DEDUCTIONS	
Dana Garner (M)				8	8	8	8	8		40	6.50/hr.	260 00			260 00	17 42	16 80		18 75			52 97	207 03
Dale Farrar (S)				8	8	8	8	8		40	6.75/hr.	270 00			270 00	18 09	34 80			5 50		58 39	211 61
Stanlee Ott (M)				8	8	8	8	8		40	5.75/hr.	230 00			230 00	15 41	21 20				20 50	57 11	172 89
Tracey Stoltz (S)				8	8	8	8	8		40	6.25/hr.	250 00			250 00	16 75	34 60					51 35	198 65

7. $21.90, $11.48   **9.** $15.57, $8.81   **11.** $1044.93, $174.02

TEST OR REVIEW, CHAPTER 15, pp. 543–544

1. $157.50   **2.** $37.20   **3.** $454.58   **4.** $600   **5.** $340.38   **6.** $5940   **7.** $478.59   **8.** $43.19   **9.** $147.50   **10.** $2686.05
11. $4495.80   **12.** $218.08   **13.** $405.60   **14.** $24.54

CHAPTER 16

READINESS CHECK, p. 546

1. [2.3, ● ●] 285.5   **2.** [2.3, ● ●] 50.4   **3.** [2.3, ● ●][2.4, ● ●] 5.013

MARGIN EXERCISES, SECTION 16.1, pp. 547–548

1. 85   **2.** 64.9   **3.** 80   **4.** $8771.44   **5.** 25   **6.** $17,750   **7.** 17   **8.** 18   **9.** 17   **10.** 37.5   **11.** 7   **12.** 88   **13.** 201, 203

EXERCISE SET 16.1, pp. 549–550

1. 22; 23.5; 25   **3.** 18; 15; 15   **5.** $8.20; $8.55; $9.40   **7.** 3; 3; 1, 2, 3, 4, 5   **9.** $1.67   **11.** 33   **13.** $19,230   **15.** 82; 81; 81
17. $299.984; $299.813; All   **19.** 182   **21.** 90

MARGIN EXERCISE, SECTION 16.2, pp. 551–552

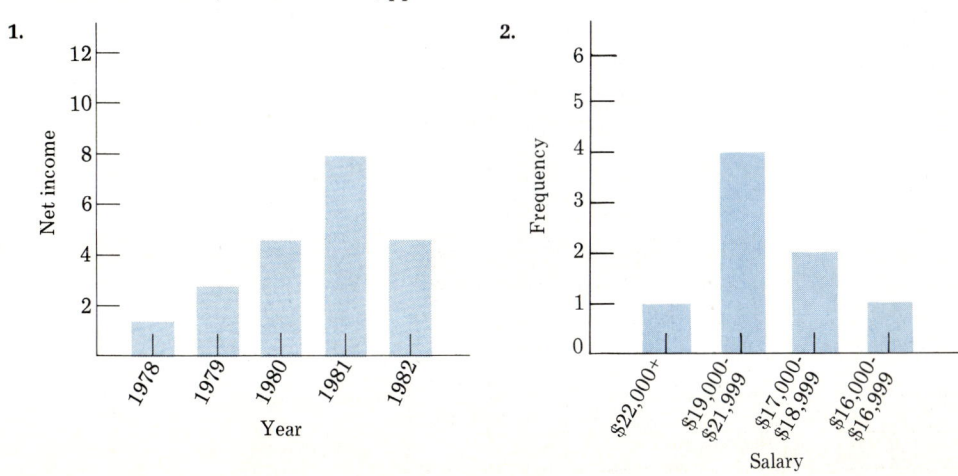

EXERCISE SET 16.2, pp. 553–554

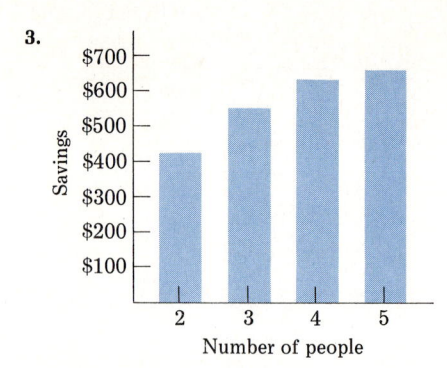

1. [Bar graph: Number of deaths (in thousands) by cause — Heart ~990, Cancer ~360, Accidents ~105, Pneumonia/influenza ~60, Diabetes ~45, Other ~330]

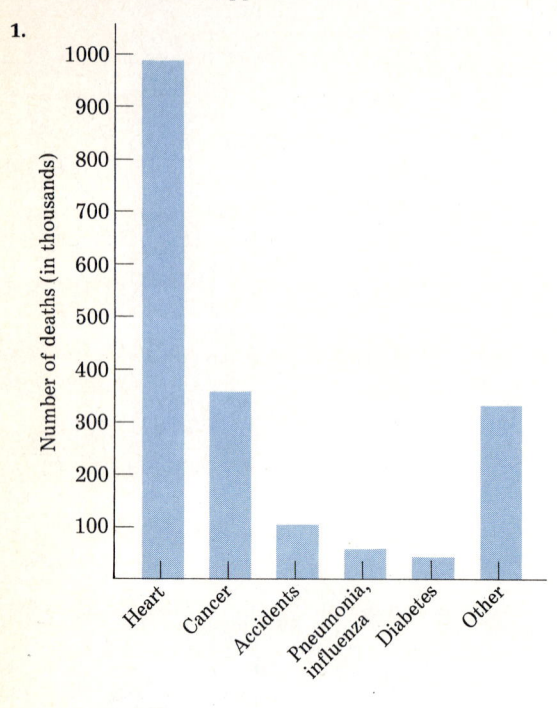

3. [Bar graph: Savings vs. Number of people — 2: $425, 3: $550, 4: $630, 5: $660]

5. [Bar graph: Time (in seconds) by Winners — Cuthbert 11.50, Rudolph 11.00, Tyus (1964) 11.40, Tyus (1968) 11.00, Stecher 11.05, Richter 11.01]

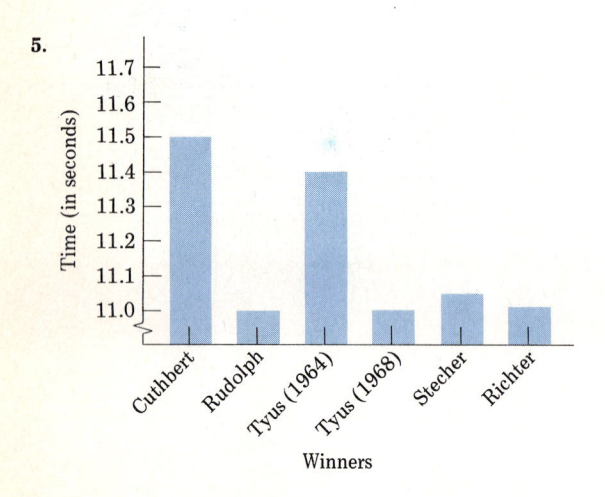

7. [Bar graph: Frequency of letters — A: 8, E: 13, I: 6, O: 8, U: 3]

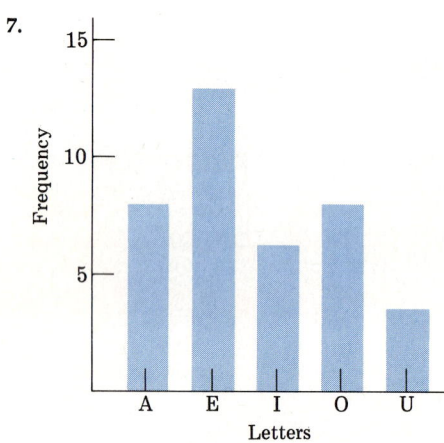

MARGIN EXERCISES, SECTION 16.3, pp. 555–558

1. [Line graph: Estimated sales (in millions) by Year — 1988: 17.0, 1990: 19.5, 1992: 17.8, 1994: 18.15]

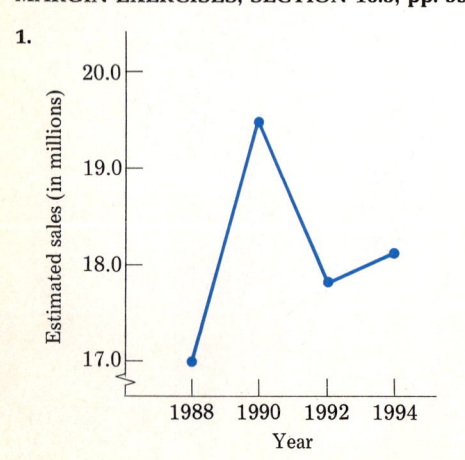

2. [Pie chart: Black 34%, Brown 44%, Red 9%, Blonde 13%]

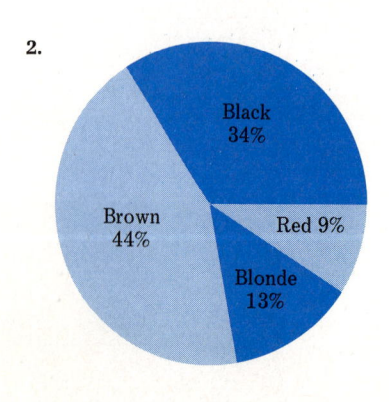

EXERCISE SET 16.3, pp. 559–562

1.

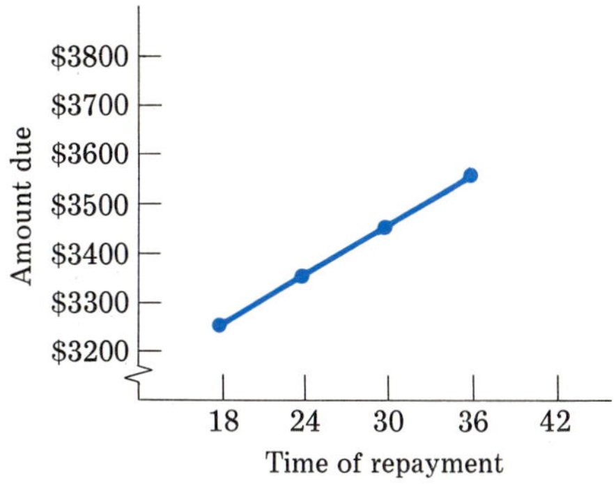
Amount due
$3800
$3700
$3600
$3500
$3400
$3300
$3200
18 24 30 36 42
Time of repayment

3.

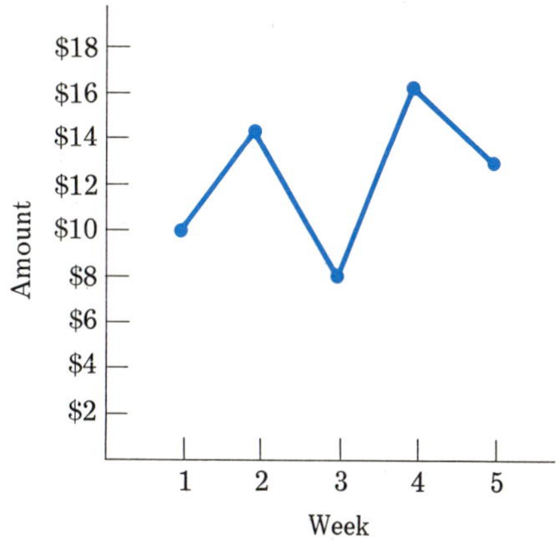
Amount
$18
$16
$14
$12
$10
$8
$6
$4
$2
1 2 3 4 5
Week

5.

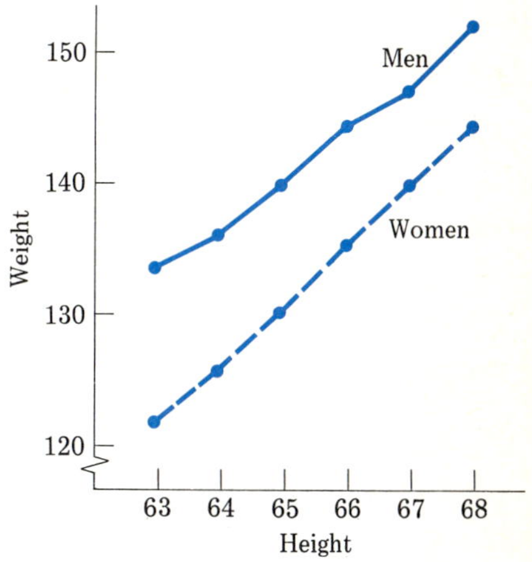
Weight
150
140
130
120
Men
Women
63 64 65 66 67 68
Height

7.

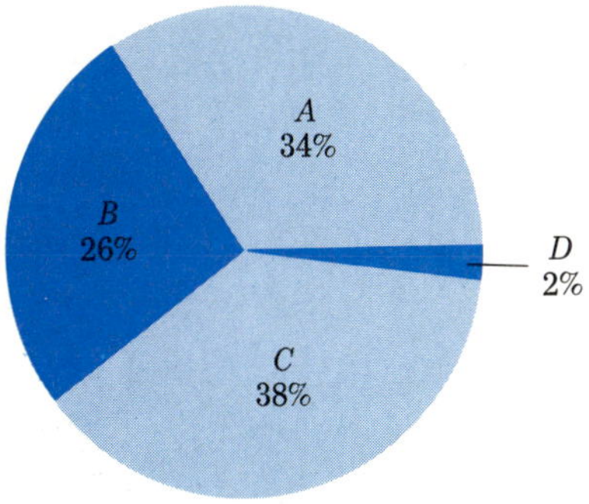
A 34%
B 26%
C 38%
D 2%

9.

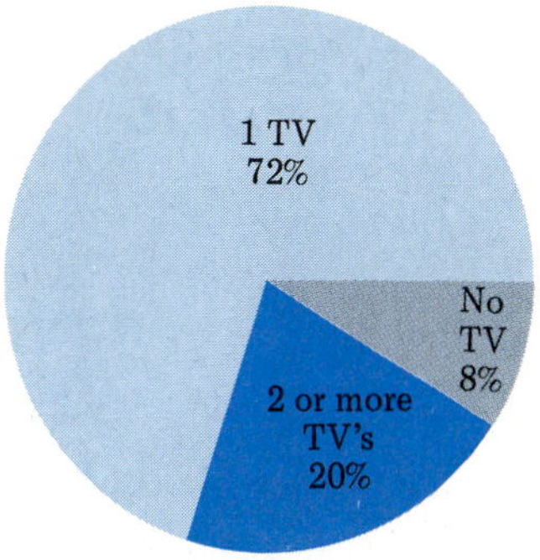
1 TV 72%
No TV 8%
2 or more TV's 20%

11.

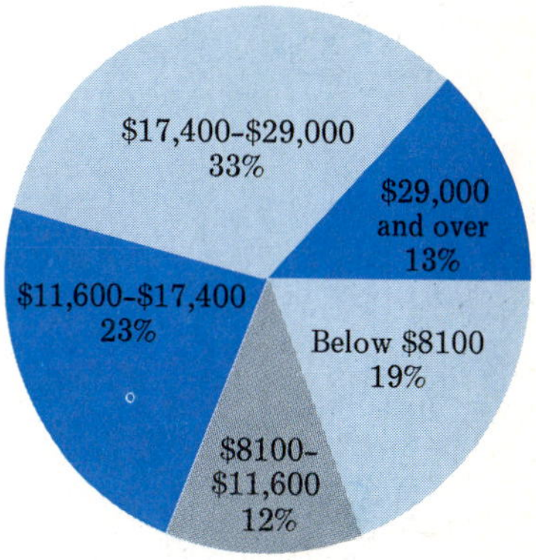
$17,400–$29,000 33%
$29,000 and over 13%
$11,600–$17,400 23%
Below $8100 19%
$8100–$11,600 12%

TEST OR REVIEW, CHAPTER 16, pp. 563–564

1. 52; 48.5; 45 **2.** $1.925; $1.845; $1.89

3.

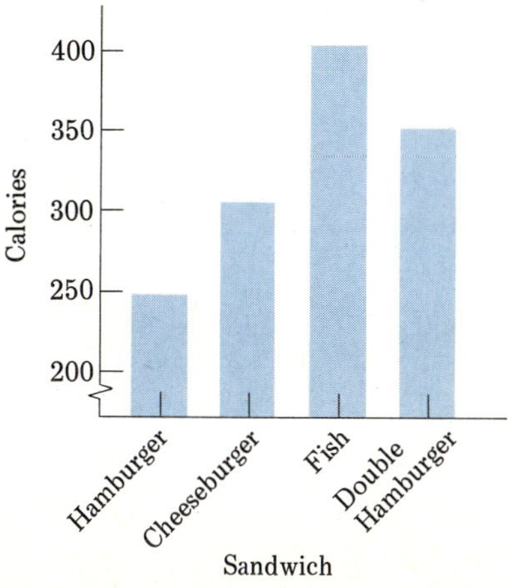
Calories
400
350
300
250
200
Hamburger
Cheeseburger
Fish
Double Hamburger
Sandwich

4.

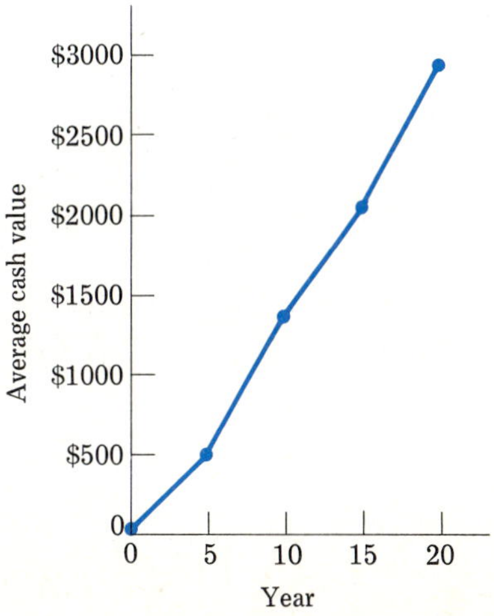
Average cash value
$3000
$2500
$2000
$1500
$1000
$500
0
0 5 10 15 20
Year

5.

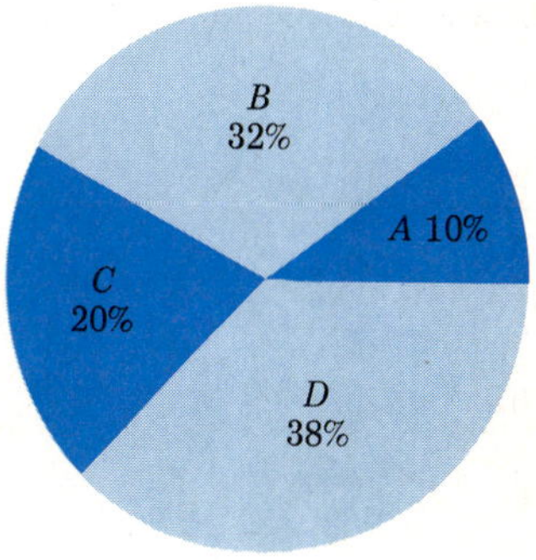
B 32%
A 10%
C 20%
D 38%

6.

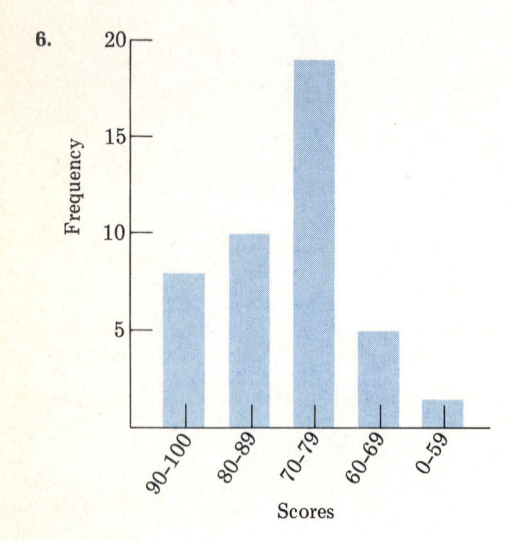

[Histogram: Frequency vs Scores. 90-100: 8, 80-89: 10, 70-79: 19, 60-69: 5, 0-59: 1]

APPENDIX: THE METRIC SYSTEM

MARGIN EXERCISES, pp. 567–570

1. 0.7106   **2.** 299,700   **3.** 0.5689   **4.** 730   **5.** 840   **6.** 7.66   **7.** 8300   **8.** 0.2094   **9.** 21   **10.** 678.8   **11.** $-4°C$
12. $0°C$ **13.** $68°F$ **14.** $-8°F$

EXERCISE SET, pp. 571–572

1. (a) 1000; (b) 0.001   **3.** (a) 100; (b) 0.01   **5.** (a) 0.001; (b) 1000   **7.** 7800   **9.** 0.87   **11.** 7.801   **13.** 0.06555   **15.** 799,900
17. 7.88   **19.** 311   **21.** 0.1   **23.** 100,000   **25.** 450   **27.** 130   **29.** 0.00014   **31.** 0.688   **33.** 1000; 1000   **35.** 96,000
37. 0.069   **39.** 0.000703   **41.** 8012   **43.** 1000   **45.** 10   **47.** 0.01   **49.** 100   **51.** 25,000   **53.** 0.789   **55.** 705   **57.** 0.57
59. 7.89   **61.** 7.8   **63.** 70,000   **65.** 0.4   **67.** 0.0034   **69.** 1000   **71.** $149°F$ **73.** $59°F$ **75.** $87.08°F$ **77.** $60°C$
79. $15°C$ **81.** $1000°C$

INDEX

INDEX

Accelerated Cost Recovery System (ACRS)
    and depreciation, 475–480
Accountants, 459
Accounts payable, 420
Accounts receivable, 418
Accrued expenses payable, 421
Accumulated retained earnings, 422–423
ACRS; see Accelerated Cost Recovery System
Add-on interest, 303
    APR for, 304–305
Addition
    of decimals, 69
    of fractions, 47–52
    problems involving, 4–6
    of whole numbers, 2–6
Administration
    business, 405
    expenses of, 412
    personal trust, 379
Advertising, 113
Annual percentage rate (APR), 286–294
    for add-on interest, 304–305
Annuities, 265–270
    ordinary, 265–266, 277–278
    present value of, 277–282
Approximate time interest
    360-day, 179
    365-day, 179–180
APR; see Annual percentage rate
Assets
    current, 417
    fixed, 418–419
Automobile insurance, 359–366
    cost of, 362–363
Averages, 546–547

Balance
    checking account, 219–220, 229–234
    declining, 467–470
Balance sheets, 417–426
    analysis of, 423–424
Bank cards, 317–320
Bank statement reconciliation, 219–220, 229–234
Banker's method of interest computation, 169–174, 179
Bar graphs, 551
Base finding, 134–135
Bayless, James R., 245
Bonds, 421–422
    buying of, 340–341
    and commissions, 339–344
    current yield on, 341–342
    interest on, 412–413
Bookkeeping, 213
Borczon, Roxanne, 1
Brokers, 327
Business administration, 405
Business consultants, 285
Business owner's fire insurance, 348–349
Butters, Mary Anne, 113
Buying
    of bonds, 340–341
    of stocks, 329–330, 332

Capacity measurement, 567–568
Capital stock, 422
Capital surplus, 422
Car insurance, 359–366
    cost of, 362–363
Carucci, Ray, 405
Cash, 417
Cash discounts, 445–448
Cash value of life insurance, 368–369
Certified public accountants (CPA), 459
Charge cards, 315–324
Charges
    deferred, 419
    finance, 286
Checking accounts, 214–234
    balancing of, 219–220, 229–234
Checks
    endorsing of, 215–216
    information on, 216–218
    payment by, 214–228
    writing of, 214–215
Circle graphs, 556–558
Commissions, 519–524
    and bonds, 339–344
    and stocks, 328–334
Common stock, 422
Compound interest, 191–194
    continuous, 200
    daily, 199–200
    tables for, 195–198
Computerized payroll, 537–539
Consultants
    business, 285
    financial, 327
Consumer credit, 285–326
Continuous compound interest, 200
Conversion, 83–88
    decimals to fractions, 63–64
    decimals to percent, 126–127
    fractions to decimals, 64–65, 84–86
    fractions to percent, 127–128
    metric length, 566–567
    percent to decimals, 126
    percent to fractions, 128–129
Cost-price basis of pricing, 484–489
Costs
    accelerated recovery system for, 475–480
    automobile insurance, 362–363
    dealer, 493
    of goods sold, 411–412, 449, 450
    of homeowner's insurance, 353–356
    of life insurance, 371–374
    operating expenses, 411
    retailer, 445–446, 484–485, 486
    of sales, 411
    see also Expenses
CPA; see Certified public accountants
Credit
    consumer, 285–326
    installment, 285–326
    revolving, 315–317
Credit cards, 315–324
Current assets, 417
Current liabilities, 420

Current yield on bonds, 341–342

Daily compound interest, 199–200
Daryanani, Michael, 483
Data processing, 213
    jobs in, 545
Dealer cost, 493
Decimal equivalents, 129
Decimals, 62–68
    addition with, 69
    applications of, 65–66
    conversion from fractions to, 64–65, 84–86
    conversion to fractions from, 63–64
    conversion from percent to, 126
    conversion to percent from, 126–127
    division using, 76–82
    division of by whole numbers, 76–77
    multiplication using, 75–82
    subtraction with, 70
    and word names, 63
Declining-balance method of depreciation, 467–470, 475
Deferred charges, 419
Deposit slips, 221
Depreciation, 412, 419, 459–482
    and Accelerated Cost Recovery System, 475–480
    declining-balance method of, 467–470, 475
    and federal taxes, 475–480
    straight-line method of, 460–466, 475
    sum-of-the-years'-digits method of, 471–474, 475
    tax, 475–477
    units-of-production method of, 475
Dickerson, Barbara, 213
Differential piecework earnings, 511
Discount rates, 433–434
    changing several to single rate, 441–444
    comparison of, 442
Discounts, 246–252, 432–436
    cash, 445–448
    trade, 432–440
Distribution of frequency, 552
Division, 38–39
    of decimals, 76–82
    of fractions, 37–42
    problems involving, 21–24
    of whole numbers, 19–24
    by zero, 28
Dow-Jones Industrial Average, 332
Dreyfus IRA, 272

Early payment of loans, 309–314
Earnings
    accumulated retained, 422–423
    gross, 506–508
    piecework, 511–514
    ratio of price to, 335–338
    see also Income
Effective interest rates, 203–208
Employees
    salaried, 515–518
    wages of; see Payroll

Endorsement of checks, 215–216
Equation solving, 97–102
Equivalents, 129
Error patterns, 268
Estimating, 83–88
Exact interest method, 175–178
Expenses
   accrued, 421
   administrating, 412
   operating, 411
   selling, 412
   see also Costs
Exponential expression evaluation, 89–90
Exponential notation, 89
Exponents, 89–92
Extended term coverage, 369

Federal taxes, 389–400, 413
   and depreciation, 475–480
   payable, 421
   withholding of, 525–530
Finance charges, 286
Financial consultants, 327
Financial institution management, 161
Financial statements, 405–430
Financial transactions, 235–240
Fire insurance, 348–349
Fixed assets, 418–419
Formulas, 103–106
Fractional equivalents, 129
Fractions, 25–30
   addition using, 47–52
   conversion from decimals to, 63–64
   conversion to decimals from, 64–65, 84–86
   conversion from percent to, 128–129
   conversion to percent from, 127–128
   division using, 37–42
   multiplication using, 31, 33
   simplification using, 31–32, 33
   subtraction using, 53–58
   for whole numbers, 26–27
Frequency distributions, 552

Goods sold cost, 411–412, 449, 450
Graphs
   bar, 551
   circle, 556–558
   line, 555–556
Gross earnings, 506–508
Gross profit, 406–407, 454

Homeowner's insurance, 349–353
   cost of, 353–356
Hsia, Ho Ming, 61

Income, 412
   net, 407–408
   see also Earnings
Income statements, 411–416
   analysis of, 413–414
Income tax; see Federal taxes
Individual Retirement Accounts (IRA), 271–273
Installment credit, 285–326

interest in, 305–306
Insurance, 347–378
   automobile; see Automobile insurance
   business owner's fire, 348–349
   extended term, 369
   fire, 348–349
   homeowner's; see Homeowner's insurance
   life; see Life insurance
   reduced paid up, 369–376
Intangibles, 419–420
Interest, 161–212, 303–308
   add-on, 303, 304–305
   banker's method of computation of, 169–174, 179
   bond, 412–413
   comparing of rate of, 204
   compound; see Compound interest
   continuous compound, 200
   daily compound, 199–200
   effective rate of, 203–208
   exact, 175–178
   finding of rate of, 164
   installment plan, 305–306
   nominal rate of, 203–208
   on notes, 246–247
   payments of, 165, 298–300
   rate of, 164, 167–168, 203–208
   rebates on, 309–310
   simple; see Simple interest
   360-day, 169–174, 179, 183–185
   365-day, 179–180, 185–188
Inventory, 418, 449–452
   special methods of, 453–456
   valuation of, 453–454
IRA; See Individual Retirement Accounts

Journal of payroll, 536–537

Kaufman, Barton L., 347
Keogh plans, 273–274

LCD; see Least common denominator
LCM; see Least common multiple
Least common denominator (LCD), 43–44
Least common multiple (LCM), 43–46
Legal secretaries, 1
Length measurement and conversion, 566–567
Liabilities
   current, 420
   long-term, 421
Life insurance, 367–376
   agents for, 347
   cash value of, 368–369
   cost of, 371–374
Line graphs, 555–556
Loan officers, 245
Loans, 246–264
   early payment of, 309–314
   see also Notes
Long-term liabilities, 421
Loss, 406–410

Management, 431

financial institution, 161
   restaurant, 61
Markdown, 497–502
Marketable securities, 418
Marketing, 113
Markup, 484, 491–492
Mass, 568–569
McCord, Elizabeth, 379
Measurements, 566–572
   of capacity, 567–568
   of length, 566–567
Medians, 548
Merchandising, 483
Merchant's Rule, 259–264
Metric system, 566–572
Mixed numbers, 25–30
Modes, 548
Money market mutual funds, 236–238
Monthly payments, 295–298
Multiplication
   of decimals, 75–82
   of fractions, 31, 33
   problems involving, 15–18
   of whole numbers, 13–18
Mutual funds, 236–238

Net income, 407–408
Net pay, 535–536
Net profit, 413
Net sales, 411
Nominal interest rates, 203–208
Non-whole number divisors, 77–80
Notes, 246–252
   interest on, 246–247
   payable, 421
   see also Loans
Numbers
   mixed, 25–30
   whole; see Whole numbers
   word names for, 2

One as exponent, 89–90
Operating expenses, 411
Order of operations, 93–96
Ordinary annuities, 265–266
   present value of, 277–278
Overtime
   commission, 522
   piecework earnings, 512

Paid up coverage, 369–376
Pay, 506–510, 535–536
Payables, 420
Payments
   by check, 214–228
   early, 309–314
   interest, 165, 298–300
   monthly, 295–298
   principal, 298–300
Payroll, 505–544
   computerized, 537–539
   journal of, 536–537
Percent, 125
   application of, 145–150
   conversion from decimals to, 126–127

Percent (cont.)
  conversion to decimals from, 126
  conversion from fractions to, 127–128
  conversion to fractions from, 128–129
  finding of, 133–134
  increase and decrease in, 151–160
  problems in, 133–138, 139–144
  and proportions, 139–144
  of regular price, 498–499
  of selling price, 491–492, 499–500
  translating problems in, 133
Percentage method of tax withholding, 525–526
Personal trust administrator, 379
Piecework plans, 511–514
Place value, 2
Prepayments, 419
Present value, 207–210
  of annuities, 277–282
Price-earnings ratio of stocks, 335–338
Prices, 432–436, 483–504
  and cost, 484–489
  selling; see Selling price
Principal, 168
  finding of, 164–165
  payments of, 298–300
Profit
  gross, 406–407, 454
  and loss, 406–410
  net, 413
Property taxes, 385–388
Proportions, 115–116
  problems in, 121–124
  solving of, 116–118
  solving percent problems using, 139–144
  translating to, 139–140
Purchasing, 431–458

Rates, 118
  annual percentage; see Annual percentage rate
  discount, 433–434, 441–444
  finding of, 135–136
  interest; see Interest, rate of
Ratio, 114–115
Realtors, 505
Rebates on interest, 309–310
Receivables, 418
Reciprocals, 37
Reconciliation of bank statements, 229–234
Reduced paid up coverage, 369–376
Regular price, 498–499
Resler, Gerald E., 161
Restaurant management, 61
Retailer costs, 445–446, 484–485, 486

Retained earnings, 422–423
Retirement accounts, 271–274
Revolving credit, 315–317
Rounding, 83–84

Salaried employees, 515–518
Sales
  cost of, 411
  net, 411
  taxes on, 380–384
  see also Selling
Savings accounts, 235–236
  vs. stocks, 332
Schnicke, Clarence, W., 327
Securities, 418
Self-employed persons tax, 532
Selling
  expenses of, 412
  of stocks, 331–332
Selling price, 491–496, 498
  percent of, 491–492, 499–500
  and pricing, 491–496
Several trade discounts, 437–440
Simple interest, 162–166, 167
  tables for, 183–190
Simplification using fractional notation, 31–32, 33
Single rate equivalent of several discount rates, 441
Social security taxes, 531–534
Special inventory methods, 453–456
Statements from bank, 229–234
Statistics, 545–564
Stock brokers, 327
Stocks
  buying of, 329–330, 332
  capital, 422
  and commissions, 328–334
  common, 422
  price-earnings ratio of, 335–338
  vs. savings accounts, 332
  selling of, 331–332
  yield of, 335–338
Straight-line method of depreciation, 460–466, 475
Straight piecework earnings, 511
Substitution in formulas, 103–104
Subtraction
  of decimals, 70
  of fractions, 53–58
  problems involving, 9–12
  of whole numbers, 7–12
Sum-of-the-years'-digits method of depreciation, 471–474, 475
  tables for, 183–185

Tax depreciation, 475–477
Taxes, 379–404
  federal; see Federal taxes
  income; see Federal taxes
  percentage method of withholding, 525–526
  property, 385–388
  sales, 380–384
  self-employed persons, 532
  social security, 531–534
  wage bracket method of withholding, 527–528
  withholding of, 525–530
Taylor, Henry M., 285
Teletype operators, 545
Temperature, 569–570
Term coverage, 369
Theodorou, Dixie Chavis, 431
360-day interest method, 169–174, 179, 183–185
365-day interest method, 179–180, 185–188
Trade discounts, 432–433
  several, 437–440
Trust administrators, 379

United States Rule, 253–258
Units of production method of depreciation, 475

Venezia, Toni, 545

Wage bracket method of tax withholding, 527–528
Wages; see Payroll
Whole numbers
  addition of, 2–6
  division of, 19–24
  division of decimals by, 76–77
  fractional notation for, 26–27
  multiplication of, 13–18
  subtraction of, 7–12
Wignall, Patty Sanchez, 505
Withholding of federal income tax, 525–530
Word names
  and decimal notation, 63
  for numbers, 2

Yield
  on bonds, 341–342
  on stocks, 335–338

Zero
  as an exponent, 90
  division by, 28